Soccer Science

Tony Strudwick

Editor

Human Kinetics

Library of Congress Cataloging-in-Publication Data

Names: Strudwick, Tony, editor.
Title: Soccer science / Tony Strudwick, editor.
Description: Champaign, IL : Human Kinetics, [2016] | Includes
    bibliographical references and index.
Identifiers: LCCN 2015042253
Subjects: LCSH: Soccer. | Sports sciences.
Classification: LCC GV943 .S66 2016 | DDC 796.334--dc23 LC record available at http://lccn.loc.gov/2015042253

ISBN: 978-1-4504-9679-7 (print)

Acquisitions Editor: Chris Wright; **Developmental Editor:** Cynthia McEntire; **Managing Editor:** Nicole Moore; **Copyeditor:** Bob Replinger; **Proofreader:** Anne Rumery; **Indexer:** Nancy Ball; **Permissions Manager:** Martha Gullo; **Graphic Designer:** Dawn Sills; **Cover Typography:** Keith Blomberg; **Cover Image:** Jonathan Kay; **Photo Asset Manager:** Laura Fitch; **Visual Production Assistant:** Joyce Brumfield; **Photo Production Manager:** Jason Allen; **Art Manager:** Kelly Hendren; **Illustrations:** © Human Kinetics unless otherwise noted; **Printer:** Sheridan Books

Human Kinetics books are available at special discounts for bulk purchase. Special editions or book excerpts can also be created to specification. For details, contact the Special Sales Manager at Human Kinetics.

Printed in the United States of America   10 9 8 7 6 5 4 3 2 1

The paper in this book is certified under a sustainable forestry program.

Human Kinetics
Website: www.HumanKinetics.com

United States: Human Kinetics
P.O. Box 5076
Champaign, IL 61825-5076
800-747-4457
e-mail: info@hkusa.com

Canada: Human Kinetics
475 Devonshire Road Unit 100
Windsor, ON N8Y 2L5
800-465-7301 (in Canada only)
e-mail: info@hkcanada.com

Europe: Human Kinetics
107 Bradford Road
Stanningley
Leeds LS28 6AT, United Kingdom
+44 (0) 113 255 5665
e-mail: hk@hkeurope.com

Australia: Human Kinetics
57A Price Avenue
Lower Mitcham, South Australia 5062
08 8372 0999
e-mail: info@hkaustralia.com

New Zealand: Human Kinetics
P.O. Box 80
Mitcham Shopping Centre, South Australia 5062
0800 222 062
e-mail: info@hknewzealand.com

E6313

This book is dedicated to my family:
Susanne, Olivia and Thomas. Always by my side.
Special thanks also to Mum and Dad
and all the many staff, players and coaches
who have been part of this incredible journey.

Contents

Foreword

I played for Manchester United my entire career. I was fortunate to be part of a great youth team and won the European Cup in 1999 with my best friends. I played through the most successful period in the club's history and shared a dressing room with legends of the game such as Robson, Cantona, Giggs, Keane and Ronaldo. Focus and intensity were always at the core of our success. At Manchester United, it was always about working hard enough so they would let us stay. As a player in a big team, I had to know I could rely on teammates to produce big moments. That breeds confidence and ensures that, as a player, I embrace all the ideas of modern preparation to maximize performance.

Looking back to my early career, I would go to extreme lengths to improve my performance. Much of this was self-managed and self-driven, but even then, I was totally committed to maximizing what talent I had. If I thought my left foot needed work, I would go out on my own and kick a ball against a wall for an hour. I remember one day after weights, I stayed on the pitch at the Cliff and started passing the ball against a brick wall. Left foot, right foot hundreds of times. This is what Geir Jordet in chapter 16 refers to as passionately playing the game and relentlessly pursuing performance.

Over the course of my playing career, preparation for individual players and teams changed significantly. Sport science, fitness, video analysis, recognition of how players learn, and the science behind the boots, kit and ball have all moved to another level. Generally, technology, society and soccer have all changed. What has not changed, however, is the desire to gain a competitive advantage. There are many ways to win a soccer match by outrunning your opponents, outpassing your opponents and outfighting your opponents.

At Manchester United there was always a plan across the entire season. This plan was rigorously developed over years of intuition and coach education. There was always a consideration for physical development and intense training methods. This is why the team could grind out last-minute wins and late-season charges towards Premiership titles. Winning does not happen by chance, and meticulous planning and a desire to drive performance year after year were critical for sustained success under Sir Alex Ferguson.

The English Premier League is one of the most physically demanding leagues in the world. We were often expected to play three games in a week, travelling in Europe and then playing against physically resilient teams like Stoke, Blackburn and Everton. There were never any easy games in the EPL, so it was important to train hard off the field in the gym so that we had the physical resources to cope. The science of soccer training was not well developed in my early days as a player, but towards the later stages of my playing career I enjoyed the benefit of sport scientists, medical interventions, performance laboratories and recovery monitoring.

The game itself has also changed in the last 20 years. Each generation has seen a modification in terms of tactical variation and physical evolution: the Arsenal 'Invincibles' of 2004, Jose Mourinho's Chelsea team of the mid-2000s, Pep Guardiola's Barcelona, Jurgen Klopp's Borussia Dortmund. In general, players, coaches and teams that have embraced a contemporary approach have gained a competitive advantage. Tactical trends in soccer have also evolved. At the highest level of participation, successful teams are constantly striving for competitive advantage through increased tactical variations, dynamic interchanges and systems of play that are flexible and adaptable. To understand these changes, you have to have an appreciation of all the significant changes that have occurred in the game. That is why I particularly enjoyed reading *Soccer Science*. It helps formulate ideas and strategies that are beneficial to both players and coaches.

With the use of the modern video-based match analysis systems, much detailed information on players' fitness and performance is now available. Indeed, modern players now have a wealth of data from analytics and designated staff to ensure performance is maintained at the highest level. *Soccer Science* provides an in-depth look into the critical areas of contemporary preparation. These will certainly give you a clearer understanding of the requirements for high-performance soccer.

Modern coaches may operate without the benefit of soccer scientists, performance analysts and physiologists. In these conditions, it is imperative to embrace scientific principles to assist in team preparation. Coaches need to be familiar with new ideas for preparing teams and players. These processes will ultimately determine competitive advantage. *Soccer Science* is an excellent guide for coaches and players at all levels.

Good luck.
Gary Neville

Introduction

Application of Soccer Science

—Tony Strudwick

Soccer is played by 250 million people in more than 200 countries, making it the world's most popular sport. The worldwide influence and daily interest attract ever-increasing attention and intelligent focus into the sport. Many academic institutions around the world now offer programmes of study specifically related to soccer. In an applied setting, a major shift has occurred towards scientific methods of preparing soccer players for competition. Many soccer teams now routinely employ practitioners from the various subdisciplines of sport science with the aim of improving sporting performance.

In general, the coaches and teams that have adopted a scientific approach have been rewarded with success by gaining an advantage over competitors. It has taken some time for the accumulation of scientific-based knowledge to be translated into a form usable by practitioners. Efforts are being made to compile scientific information and make it accessible to the soccer world. This book is a step in that direction.

The discipline of soccer science is multifaceted and multidisciplinary, so it requires input from a variety of areas and from a range of specialists. Soccer science studies the application of scientific principles and techniques with the aim of improving soccer performance. The study of soccer science traditionally incorporates areas of *physiology*, *psychology* and *biomechanics*, but it also includes topics such as skill acquisition, performance analysis, technology and coaching science. Soccer science also helps practitioners understand the physical and psychological effects of soccer participation thereby providing the best techniques for soccer and the most appropriate methods of preventing injuries to an athlete involved in the performance of the sport.

Throughout the past few decades, the demand for soccer scientists and performance consultants has been growing because of the ever-increasing focus in the soccer world on achieving the best results possible. Researchers have developed a greater understanding on how the human body reacts to exercise, training, different environments and many other stimuli. The application of soccer science has a self-evident part to play in improving soccer performance. Important features of the performance model, such as devising training programmes, monitoring performance and establishing preparation for competition, are informed by such knowledge. You will learn how to use scientific principles to maximize individual soccer performance and athlete preparation across all levels and standards of the game.

A wealth of information has now been accumulated in soccer. Experiential and science-based knowledge abounds concerning the sport. Yet the full breadth and depth of scientific information have not always been suitably or sufficiently disseminated to those who would benefit most from it. *Soccer Science* fills this void with the most current research in the sport. An international expert in a specific facet of the game addresses each topic. Every chapter is filled with facts, findings and insights for optimizing individual and team soccer performance. The author panel features the world's foremost authorities from the English Premier League, Major League Soccer, European and Champions League soccer teams, senior international teams, the Hyundai A-League, FIFA medical staff, international soccer consultants and leading academic institutions. They offer unique insights across soccer history, biomechanics, physiology, psychology, skill acquisition, coaching and tactical approaches and performance analysis. Their detailed coverage of these topics is one of the most significant and comprehensive published works on the sport.

The book will appeal to serious soccer coaches, strength and conditioning specialists responsible for training soccer teams and players, sport scientists, academic researchers, practitioners, students with a great interest in the sport, support staff affiliated with advanced-level soccer programmes and committed soccer players. The book offers the right balance of sophistication and accessibility, as seen in the chapter titles, text and visual elements augmenting the content. Topics throughout the work are significant to those with more knowledge and experience and provoke interest in those still learning the finer points of the sport. The book is accessible as a cover-to-cover resource or as individual parts or chapters as deemed necessary.

Tried-and-true methods gained through extensive on-field experience are given their due, but prevailing myths are exposed and dispelled for your benefit. Pertinent team, player and coach examples demonstrate that many existing approaches have scientific principles underlying their effectiveness, though people are often unaware of them. Sidebars and other special elements throughout the book feature unique topics that add colour to the sport.

The content of the book remains multidisciplinary in scope, although the overall focus is narrowed to concentrate on how soccer science can support practitioners in improving soccer performance. The book is subdivided into individual parts collating the themes of each chapter under separate subsections:

Part I Foundations of Soccer Science

Part II Talent Identification and Player Development

Part III Biomechanical and Technological Applications

Part IV Physiological Demands in Training and Competition

Part V Psychological and Mental Demands

Part VI Tactics and Strategies

Part VII Match Performance and Analysis

Part I focuses on foundations of soccer and science. Carter outlines the evolution of soccer preparation within the context of changing paradigms. In chapter 2, Duncan and Strudwick provide an overview on how sport science and soccer were introduced to one another and how they have subsequently developed and mutually benefited one another. Developments are explored along a timeline of key events, which feature the transitions that soccer science has gone through and is benefitting from. These developments are discussed within the context of national and cultural frameworks.

In part II, the focus shifts to player identification and player development. In chapter 3, Mujika and Castagna explore the key areas to building a performance plan for young soccer players, based on their experiences at Athletic Club Bilbao. This chapter provides practical examples of how sport science departments and coaching staff can help clubs and academies optimize their player development system. In chapter 4, Unnithan and Iga provide an overview of the factors that influence the development of young soccer players. In chapter 5, Ford explores the concept of skill acquisition and the role of skill performance in sport. Evidence-based principles derived from contemporary research examining skill acquisition are explained in relation to the soccer activities that players engage in throughout their lives.

In part III, biomechanics and technological applications are explored. In a quest for optimal performance, the physical demands on soccer players are greater than ever before as they compete at local, regional, national and international levels. In chapter 6, Blazevich and Nimphius explore the biomechanical principles of soccer performance. They illustrate how biomechanical measurement techniques are used for assessing, intervening in and subsequently improving performance. In chapter 7, Smith outlines the role of biomechanical analysis in soccer, providing an overview of methods available for analysing skills such as running, heading, executing the throw-in, kicking and goalkeeping. Haines and Cohen in chapter 8 address specific biomechanical and neuromuscular issues that must be incorporated into conditioning programmes outside the generic team training sessions. The information details how such activities should form an integral part of the holistic performance plan for soccer players. In chapter 9, Sterzing illustrates the practical considerations, testing efforts and scientific research applied to the soccer shoe. He provides an overview of the general principles of soccer shoe and soccer surface behaviour, the influence of soccer shoes and surfaces on performance and injury prevention, and guidelines for choosing a shoe. In chapter 10, Harland and Hanson review the evolution of the soccer ball, focussing on materials and constructions, evaluations and developments, dynamics of an impact and flight characteristics. The authors conclude with suggestions on exploiting these effects for competitive advantage in soccer performance.

Part IV contains five chapters on physiological demands of training and competition. In chapter 11, Dupont and McCall consider the activity profile and various conditioning methods to improve the physical qualities required by soccer players. In chapter 12, Strudwick and Walker focus on translating into practice the requirements of soccer, offering special insight into planning, training methods and sessions relevant to real working practices in soccer. The role of strength and conditioning in the athletic development of soccer players is also covered. Special reference is given to designing programmes for specific age groups. In chapter 13, Kirkendall reviews the influence of the environment on exercise, providing an account of the strategies—some behavioural, some physiological—that can prepare soccer players for training and competition at environmental extremes. Ranchordas in chapter 14 provides an overview of the nutritional practices that can enhance athletic performance and recovery in soccer players. He details requirements for special populations and the importance of nutrition for illness and injury. More important, the author provides practical recommendations on implementing some of the evidence in a professional setting along with some suggested menu plans. In chapter 15, Bizzini and Junge outline the most relevant literature on injuries and provide an update on preventive interventions, with a special focus on the FIFA 11+ injury prevention programme for soccer players.

In part V, the focus shifts towards psychology and the mental demands of competitive soccer. In chapter 16, Jordet highlights the key psychological behaviours that are hypothesized to develop, facilitate or support elite soccer performance. An 11-point model constitutes a functional checklist of behaviours that can help both coaches and players become more aware of the directions that their daily work on psychological dimensions can take. In chapter 17, Pain provides an account of the applied interventions that a sport psychologist or coach can implement to facilitate psychological development in soccer players. The author outlines the five Cs of mental toughness, which is the framework adopted by the Football Association (FA) in England when working with teams and, increasingly, professional academies and grassroots clubs. Based on his applied work inside the senior squad at several English Premier League teams, chapter 18 by Nesti explores the type of psychological issues that sport psychologists and coaches have to address in elite soccer. He highlights the most important issues that players face and suggests how these can be understood in relation to research and theory in psychology and sport psychology.

A coaching emphasis is adopted in part VI, which provides an overview of tactics and strategies. Soccer science is informed by or serves to inform a coaching philosophy from training field to competitive match play. Examples from individual players, teams and coaches illustrate this topic and give exposure to behind-the-scenes preparation that can guide practice. Chapter 19 by Bangsbo and Peitersen focusses on systems of play. The authors describe the most popular systems that national and top club teams have used in recent years and how some well-known managers and their teams have developed successful team tactics using various systems and strategies. In chapter 20, Erith and Curneen demonstrate how science contributes to the training and preparation of defensive players. They examine the role of the modern fullback and central defender, identify the specific demands for each of these positions and illustrate the principles of defending. In chapter 21, noting their applied experience at Seattle Sounders FC, Tenney and Schmid provide an overview of the physiological aspects of midfield players and illustrate appropriate principles of performance planning in coaching practice. The authors describe how a coaching staff and sport science department interact in an applied setting to make real interventions in training methodology, fatigue management and player selection for midfield players. In chapter 22, Hawkins and Robinson illustrate the key physical training components for attacking players. They address the various options available to coaches and provide examples of drills incorporated into training at an elite level. Consideration is also given to both the physical and tactical requirements of teams and individuals to enhance the efficiency and effectiveness of attacking play.

Part VII illustrates how match analysis and subsequent evaluation of performance have gained acceptance across the professional soccer community. In chapter 23, Mackenzie and Cushion draw on their experiences working at an elite end of soccer to provide an overview of the role of the performance analyst. They explore the role of performance analysis and provide working examples of how principles of good practice can be adapted by those working at other levels. In chapter 24, Carling provides an overview on the analysis techniques used to collect and evaluate information on match performance. He highlights a range of methods from simple manual techniques to the latest state-of-the-art computer and video technologies and discusses the relative strengths and shortcomings of each method. In chapter 25, Smith provides a detailed study on the events that precede goal scoring. He draws on his extensive research to provide detailed information on how goals are scored. His analysis is performed from the viewpoint of technique and tactics and provides valuable information that can be translated into successful match strategy.

The integration of soccer science should be a normative activity in the coaching process. Soccer science is underpinned by concrete scientific principles that have been recognized as key ingredients in assisting those with talent, commitment and interest in reaching their potential. In these circumstances, the objectives of soccer science have to be unambiguous and linked to an overall coaching strategy. Moreover, all involved—coaches, administrators, support personnel and athletes—need to understand and accept soccer science. Finally, it must be communicated well enough to establish performance indicators that can be used to monitor progress.

Soccer science will continue to evolve and refine its practices as new research and evidence become known. The information in this book offers a solid foundation for improving athletic performance and ensuring success.

Key to Diagrams

X	Attacker
O	Defender
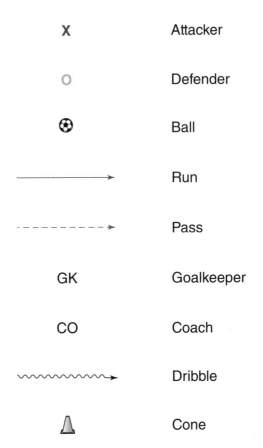	Ball
⟶	Run
- - - - - - ⟶	Pass
GK	Goalkeeper
CO	Coach
∿∿∿∿∿⟶	Dribble
◣	Cone

PART

I

Foundations
of Soccer Science

CHAPTER 1

Evolution of Soccer Science

—Neil Carter

In 1887 William Sudell, the chairman of Preston North End, proclaimed the following:

> *I consider football is played more scientifically now than ever it was and that is solely due to the fact that in a professional team the men are under the control of the management and are constantly playing together.*
>
> *(Carter 2006, 18)*

Of course, the word *scientifically* was used here in broad terms rather than in any strict definitional sense, but only two years after professionalism had been legalized, his thinking highlighted the new soccer climate. Sudell was the de facto manager of Preston North End and a pioneering figure in developing a more rational and systematic approach to improving performance on the soccer pitch. He bought the players, selected the team and decided the tactics. Under his stewardship, Preston North End won the double of Football League and FA Cup in 1888–89.

This chapter outlines the historical background regarding the preparation of soccer players up to 1990. It focuses on three key areas: training, coaching and sports medicine. This relationship was conditioned by four main agencies: the nature of the commercialization process of soccer, the changing role of the manager, medical and scientific developments during this period and the cultural traditions of soccer.

A Brief History of Early Soccer

First, an outline of the early years of association football will aid in understanding the historical trajectory of the preparation of players (see Mason 1980; Collins 1998; Taylor 2008).

Contrary to popular perception, association football did not begin in 1863 with the formation of the Football Association. The FA was initially a socially exclusive forum, consisting of former public schoolboys and Oxbridge graduates, who met to clarify the rules of football played in their individual institutions; they did not aim to become a national governing body. Football instead needs to be understood in a generic sense during this period. The game was played throughout Britain under a variety of local rules, although Sheffield was the centre of Britain's first football culture in the 1860s. By 1867 the FA was a weak organization of only 10 clubs, and there was discussion that it should fold (Taylor 2008).

The process of bifurcation of football into two distinct codes—association and rugby—began in the 1870s, especially with the formation of the Rugby Football Union in 1871 and the establishment that same year of the FA Cup. Unlike football, rugby did not have a national competition, and this factor would prove crucial in the growing popularity of football because of its association with civic pride and local rivalry. Because of the Yorkshire Cup, rugby was the dominant code in West Yorkshire, but elsewhere, including Lancashire, there were no rugby cup competitions. Football filled this gap.

In 1883 Blackburn Olympic became the first northern team to win the FA Cup by defeating Old Etonians. It was the last occasion when an Old Boys' club representing social elites from the South would appear in the final. Clubs from the North and the Midlands now dominated association football at the elite level, and the demand and pressure for success increased as well. Clubs began to recruit the best players available and to pay them, contravening FA rules. The issue was resolved in 1885 when the FA legalized the practice, albeit with certain conditions.

For a brief period football descended into a free market, causing several clubs to fold because of their inability to pay the wages of players. The formation of the Football League in 1888 provided some financial stability for its original 12 members because it guaranteed a set of fixtures, assuaging a dependency on attractive friendly fixtures and a good run in the FA Cup. The foundations of modern soccer had been established.

Commercialization of Soccer

With the establishment of soccer as an industry, clubs began to take on the characteristics of businesses. Players were now employees who had to be paid. Gate money was the main source of income, and clubs gradually began to move into purpose-built soccer grounds. Greater imperative was placed on success because of the demands of the local crowd and newspapers. Virtually all those playing at the game's upper echelons converted from clubs based on a membership or subscriber democracy model to limited liability companies with directors and shareholders (Carter 2006).

But the FA restricted commercialism from the outset, and these rules were in place deep into the 20th century. This limitation shaped the demand and nature of soccer's relationship with coaching, medicine and science. Directors were not allowed to draw a salary, a ruling that was not revoked until 1981, when Manchester United's Martin Edwards became the first to do so. Share dividends were initially pegged to 5 per cent and only rose intermittently over the 20th century. In 1983 Tottenham Hotspur was the first club to float itself on the stock market, ushering in a more free-market direction as other clubs followed. Until then the motivations of directors were largely nonfinancial, curbing the incentive to invest in or experiment with new management techniques.

In economic terms the Football League was a cartel, but in a cultural sense the strong helped the weak, a relationship that was bolstered through the implementation of equalization measures. From 1914 until 1983 the away team received a share of the gate money, for example. Importantly, interventions in the labour market stymied the competition for players. The Football League introduced a retain-and-transfer system in 1893, and in 1901 the FA imposed a maximum wage. Initially, the maximum wage was set at £4 per week, although the league did not prevent clubs from breaching it, and was £20 when it was abolished in 1961. In 1963 the retain-and-transfer system was modified, and in 1978 freedom of contract was established. The Bosman ruling in 1995 further liberalized the labour market.

Starting in the 1960s the big-city clubs gradually began to dominate, partly because of these changes in the labour market. Professional soccer players had always been assets, but as their value increased, clubs invested more resources in ensuring they were better prepared through more sophisticated training methods, better coaching and more modern sports medicine facilities.

Role of the Manager

At the centre of these changes in the relationship of soccer with science has been the manager. In the 21st century, soccer managers are perceived as charismatic, all-powerful figures with big personalities. Yet the development of their role has never been straightforward. Instead, it differed from club to club and was shaped by the wider social and soccer context, especially commercial factors (Carter 2006).

The management of early professional clubs reflected broader class relations within Victorian society. Initially, the directors, who were mainly members of the local middle classes, selected the team and decided which players to buy and sell. The secretary was largely a deferential figure who handled the club's administration. The players were from working-class backgrounds, and a trainer, from a similar social background, looked after them on a day-to-day basis. The legacy of these social relations continued to persist throughout the 20th century.

But several managerial figures were pioneers during this period. As we have seen, William Sudell was an early innovator. In 1886 Aston Villa advertised for a manager 'who will be required to devote his whole time under direction of Committee' (quoted in Carter 2006, 31). George Ramsay, a former player and the then current honorary secretary, was offered the job, but up until his retirement in 1924 he was known as a secretary. As the soccer competition intensified, the role of the secretary (later secretary-manager) expanded to include more responsibilities for team recruitment and selection. Tom Watson was perhaps the first proto soccer manager. After winning the Football League on three occasions with Sunderland in the 1890s, he was headhunted by Liverpool and won two titles with them. In the process he became the first managerial figure to win the league with two different clubs. His role is difficult to determine, but through sheer personality he likely gained influence and responsibilities at his clubs over time.

The man who modernized the role and image of the soccer manager more than anyone else was Herbert Chapman. Uniquely, he won both the league and FA Cup with Huddersfield Town and Arsenal, still the only manager to do so. But it was during his time at Arsenal (1925–34) when he defined the job of the soccer manager. Chapman was in sole charge of team affairs, picking and buying players. He also bought players like David Jack and Alex James for large transfer fees. Chapman decided the tactics and was responsible for the team's adjustment to the new offside law in 1925–26. He also understood the need for a psychological approach to managing the players. Chapman's profile and standing in the press helped to reinforce the image of the manager as a powerful, all-important figure. This image became the template for future managers.

During the early postwar period men like Matt Busby and Stan Cullis further illustrated the manager's importance through their success at Manchester United and Wolverhampton Wanderers, respectively. At many clubs, however, the directors still held much influence over matters on the field. The abolition of the maximum wage proved to be an important turning point in the history of soccer management. The greater financial risks now involved made directors realize that they needed a soccer expert to run the team. The manager's role was gradually redefined, especially at the top clubs, to concentrate more on team affairs. Following the departure of Bill Shankly at Liverpool in 1974, for example, the secretary Peter Robinson was given sole responsibility for the club's administration, and Bob Paisley was in charge of the team.

Moreover, with the growing coverage of soccer on television the image of the manager as a big personality was further fortified through men like Malcolm Allison and Ron Atkinson, who became media celebrities in their own right. The assumption that the managerial hand alone guided team performance, therefore, had become more deeply woven in the popular soccer consciousness. This sensibility gained acceptance not only on the terraces but also among directors and managers themselves.

Early Soccer Trainers and Training

Performance on the pitch has been the chief area of concern for all soccer clubs throughout the professional era. The methods employed, however, need to be understood in their wider historical context.

From the late 1880s the players were mostly left in the charge of the trainer. Trainers were responsible for maintaining both discipline and physical fitness. Here we will concentrate on fitness.

The recognition of the importance of preparation and training of athletes was not new. Ideas on what constituted the athletic body had begun to take shape in the late 18th century. Instead of scientists, the coaches and trainers (the terms were interchangeable) of prizefighters, pedestrians and rowers from the late 1700s were the first practitioners of bodily instruction. Their training theories were empirically based, derived from observation, experience and an oral tradition from which coaches and trainers formed their own communities of practices within tight social networks, especially families (Day 2012; Carter 2012).

Initially, ideas on what constituted training for soccer players were limited, and the first generation of soccer trainers was largely made up of former professional athletes and athletics and rowing trainers. At least this group had some experience of fitness training and treating injuries (see next section). Jack Concannon, a well-known distance runner from Widnes, was hired by Preston in the 1880s. He put the players through a physical preparation similar to that of professional boxers, runners and rowers. Bill Dawson had been a professional sprinter, and in 1890–91 he was recruited as the trainer of Stoke City FC, replacing another professional runner, Charlie Wright. Dawson admitted that he did not know anything about soccer but 'I knew how to get a man fit' (quoted in Carter 2007, 61). James McPherson, another former athlete of Victorian Britain, was trainer of Newcastle United FC from 1903 to 1928. His son, James Jr, an example of keeping specialized knowledge in the family, succeeded him. Some, such as Hubert Dillon, had military experience; in 1910 Dillon was appointed trainer of Birmingham City FC. He had also worked as a chief physical instructor in an education college teaching Swedish drill (Carter 2007).

Therefore, little emphasis was placed on practicing technique or ball skills, which later drew criticism. Moreover, training could be intermittent—two days a week—because not all early professionals were full time. Instead, the emphasis was on fitness.

Training could vary, and some clubs incorporated elements of contemporary physical culture. This included everything from the use of Indian clubs and dumbbells to 20 minutes of skipping, ball punching, sprinting and walking up to 9 miles (14 km). At Tottenham in 1904 training started at 10 a.m. with an hour of sprinting and ball practice and then some skipping. A bath and a rub-down followed, and after dinner some of the players went for a walk.

The tradition of lapping the pitch continued well into the 1900s. Despite growing criticisms, coaching was almost nonexistent. One recurring mantra was that if players were denied practicing with the ball during the week, they would be hungry for it on Saturday. Nat Lofthouse commented that when they got the ball on Saturday they didn't know what to do with it (Carter 2006).

Soccer and Sports Medicine

Because professional soccer players were assets of clubs and injuries were an occupational hazard, the players' welfare and medical provision took on greater importance.

Initially, besides having fitness duties, the trainer provided day-to-day medical care and treated and managed player injuries. Although the image of the soccer trainer with a bucket and magic sponge has been both mythologized and derided, the role needs to be seen in context. In particular, it provides insight into the history of the relationship between sport and medicine, especially with regard to physiotherapy, as well as ongoing tensions between orthodox medicine and alternative practices (Carter 2010).

The only organization that offered training that would have been any use to a soccer trainer was the female-only Society of Trained Masseuses, formed in 1894. Massage was a popular medical practice in Victorian Britain and among athletics coaches. Soccer trainers gained a reputation as 'rubbers', and a prematch rub-down was a ritual that continued well into the 20th century. Highlighting the huge trade in quack remedies during this period, a niche market for massage liniments, herbal potions, patent pills and tonics became available to the sporting world.

Soccer clubs also appointed doctors. At first many acted in honorary roles; some doctors were even directors of the club. In other cases the role was passed down among partners in a practice. Not until 1963 did the FA appoint the first England team doctor, Alan Bass from Arsenal, again in an honorary position. The sports medicine market for doctors was—and continues to be—a narrow one. Many doctors developed an interest in sport, but few had specialist knowledge of sports injuries. Instead, they learned on the job. Others just enjoyed being part of a soccer club and having the opportunity to share in their success and mix in various social circles. The informal nature of the doctor's role continued until the end of the 20th century (Carter 2009).

Medical facilities for professional soccer players, however, were far from primitive. Instead, players enjoyed medical care better than the vast majority of the working population. In the 1890s John Allison's Footballers Hospital opened in Manchester, probably the earliest example of a sports injuries clinic. The hospital performed surgery on athletes and offered rehabilitation services following injury. The bigger clubs were unsurprisingly able to offer the best medical facilities. In 1914 Aston Villa outlined proposals for building a special room for the doctor to be fitted up with X-rays, radium and other modern appliances (Carter 2007).

During the interwar years the trainer began to take on a more physiotherapeutic role. Although massage was still part of the job, this shift owed something to the legacy of physiotherapy from the First World War, which had been a treatment used for the rehabilitation of disabled soldiers. Moreover, a larger body of medical expertise on the treatment of injuries emerged, including Charles Heald's pioneering book *Injuries and Sport*, published in 1931.

Most trainers now came from the first generation of former players, and some had gained medical experience during the war. By 1938 it was claimed that the medical knowledge of a growing number of trainers was supported with diplomas in massage and physical instruction. Arsenal's Tom Whittaker was the most famous trainer during this period. After he retired from playing in 1925, the club sent him to study physiotherapeutic methods under the tutelage of pioneering orthopaedic surgeon Sir Robert Jones. Whittaker was later the regular trainer of the England team and the trainer for the British Davis Cup team, and he ran an informal sports injury clinic at Highbury.

Demand was growing for electro-medical apparatus as well as hydrotherapy, exercise machines and the use of ultraviolet light treatment. But this shift to modernity continued to complement traditional applications. One treatment for pulled muscles was for players to sit all afternoon with towels over their legs and pour boiling and then cold water over them.

Following the Second World War the trainer's role gradually became more professional. Some clubs began to hire trained physiotherapists, and some trainers had backgrounds in remedial gymnastics from Pinderfields Hospital in Wakefield. Treatments began to shift away from a dependency on machines to manual techniques (Carter 2010).

In 1958 the FA instituted courses for trainers on treatment of injury, although they were never compulsory. Even up to the 21st century, clubs were reluctant to surrender control over whom they could employ and appointments were made through soccer's old boy network.

From the 1960s soccer players were becoming increasingly critical of the medical treatment they received. This attitude echoed a greater scepticism of medicine generally, and players began to seek second opinions outside the soccer club without permission. Some visited osteopaths, for example.

Development of Coaching and Tactics

Coaching has a long history in British sport, especially in athletics, cricket and rowing, stretching to the early 19th century (Day 2012). Soccer, however, was not part of this tradition.

Various reasons may have accounted for this. First, the game's amateur ethos generally precluded an instinct for coaching within the game's hierarchy. Ironically, the Corinthians, the most famous and socially exclusive amateur soccer club, who occasionally provided the bulk of the England team, was formed in 1882 with the intention of giving more opportunities to practise together to defeat Scotland. The ideology of amateurism, however, generally emphasized being the best on the day. Second, early trainers knew little about soccer, whereas working-class players considered soccer a craft, one in which they honed their skills through individual practice, and they were resistant to any instruction. Third, as the inventors of the game, Britons had little incentive for improvement because of a lack of international competition—at first, anyway.

Nevertheless, some early developments occurred. In 1893 Aston Villa recruited Joe Grierson from Middlesbrough, who was renowned for his specialist goalkeeping and weight-training regimes. Moreover, tactics were part of soccer from the outset. In its infancy as a professional sport, association football had been a vigorous game, characterized by rushes and an emphasis on physical contact. Heavy shoulder charges were part of the play, and goalkeepers received no protection. Yet tactics and distinctive styles of play were not absent, highlighting that teams thought about the game. During the 1870s both the Royal Engineers and Queen's Park were noted for their combination play, that is, passing. In one game in 1885 it was said that Preston North End was 'machine like . . . in working the ball along the ground'. The opponents by contrast 'did their work in rushes' (Carter 2006, 44). Preston had been the first team to play consistently with two fullbacks, three halfbacks and only five forwards. Known as the attacking centre-half formation, it endured until 1925 when the offside law was changed (Carter 2006).

Tactics were usually the preserve of the on-field captain, and managers had little coaching input. Early examples of tracksuit managers were Herbert Chapman and Frank Buckley, another early innovator. When he was manager of Wolves, Buckley introduced mechanical inventions to supplement training sessions, including a purpose-built machine that fired out soccer balls at various angles for players to control. A space under the Molineux stand was fitted with rubber walls at which players kicked a ball that would then return at unpredictable angles, again to improve ball control. Buckley's most famous innovation was to inject his players with monkey gland extracts, part of the treatment for rejuvenation. The whole episode was later sensationalized in the newspapers, although he claimed that its purpose was to increase players' resistance to colds (Carter 2006).

Yet coaching was generally patchy. In 1934, on the initiative of its secretary Stanley Rous, the FA began coaching courses in schools. As a referee who had travelled the world, Rous recognised that standards abroad were improving and that the British game was falling behind. Coaching schemes were expanded after World War II. Supervised by Walter Winterbottom, these plans were attempts by the FA to modernize and were the beginning of the English game's shift towards a technocracy and away from its amateur values.

The appointment of Winterbottom as England team manager as well as director of coaching was part of this process. But development still lagged behind methods used in Europe, where coaching, perhaps because of a greater tradition of bodily instruction in activities such as gymnastics, was more firmly part of the game. The management culture in other European countries differed from the British experience, and by the early 1960s most European clubs and national teams employed only qualified coaches. In Italy, for example, the first soccer management course was introduced in 1946, and a diploma was initiated two years later.

In Britain, however, resistance towards coaching persisted. Many working-class players mistrusted anything theoretical, and coaching challenged firmly held beliefs that English soccer was based on individual skill and masculine toughness. Stan Cullis regarded most coaching as too theoretical and academic, and he worried that some of his players would come back from England games with new-fangled ideas.

Yet as attitudes towards education in society began to change, others were increasingly embracing these new technocratic developments in soccer. One of the first managers to do so was Don Revie, who became renowned for his dossiers on the opposition to highlight their strengths and weaknesses. By the 1960s more people consciously thought about the game, planned set pieces and in general tried not to leave things to chance.

It was not until the 21st century that English soccer introduced mandatory qualifications for managers. The directors of soccer clubs, reflecting wider tensions within the game, had been reluctant to cede control over whom they could appoint. But by the 1970s a coaching qualification was almost a de facto requirement for aspiring managers (Carter 2006).

Coaching developments in this period mirrored those in tactics. Although Hungary had exposed its limitations in 1953 and 1954, English soccer was not moribund as new tactical ideas emerged. Tottenham Hotspur's manager Arthur Rowe instituted a continental-style push-and-run method that helped Spurs win the league in 1951. Stan Cullis, on the other hand, had a different philosophy. Derided as kick and rush, the tactics of the Wolves team in the 1950s was actually more sophisticated. He emphasized playing the game in the opponent's half by employing a pressing game with a smothering defence. Wolves would then look to play long passes to their wingers. Cullis had adapted the tactics of Frank Buckley and was supported by Charles Reep, a statistician who had advocated direct play. Of course, tactical formations were only as good as the players available, and during games they were always fluid. But through greater contact with European teams, tactics became more flexible (Carter 2006).

At the same time European coaches explored other tactical approaches. From the mid-'50s to the mid-'60s, Spanish, Portuguese and Italian clubs dominated the European Cup. In Italy the *catenaccio* defensive system stifled attacking play. Following Celtic's victory in 1967, however, power shifted to northern Europe because teams from this region placed greater emphasis on pace and fitness. A pressing game emerged; it has been claimed that the pressing game originated in its scientific form under Viktor Maslov at Dynamo Kiev. Latin European teams were not allowed as much time on the ball, negating their technical advantage over the teams from the north. The total soccer of Ajax and Holland was the most famous development of this period and was perhaps the last major tactical innovation, until Barcelona's recent but brief reign through the monopolization of possession with tiki-taka. Because of the increasing globalization of soccer, a greater harmonization of playing styles has since emerged due to the greater contact between coaches and players at club and international levels (Wilson 2008).

Through Charles Hughes, director of coaching from 1982 through 1997, the FA continued to advocate the benefits of direct play. Hughes built on the work of Reep and the notion of performance analysis, which emphasized getting the ball forward as quickly as possible. As a result, a generation of coaches were proselytized with this philosophy based on a percentages game. But tactics across the English game were not uniform. Liverpool's domination of European soccer was built on the team's ability to keep possession of the ball as well as any team on the continent.

Conclusion

In 1992 the establishment of the Premier League signalled a change in the relationship between soccer and science. Greater intensity emerged as the commercialization of soccer increased. The value of players increased exponentially, as did the financial rewards for staying in the Premier League. As a result, these developments necessitated a greater investment in medical and scientific facilities and resources. In many ways, however, little had changed from the dawn of professional soccer in the 1880s. Clubs had always invested in the welfare of their players, but the nature of this process was shaped by the prevailing context—commercial, soccer and social.

Since the establishment of the Premier League, a shift has occurred towards more systematic methods of preparing elite players for match play.

Contemporary coaches have been exposed to scientific approaches in preparing teams for competition. Certainly, examples of good practice can be seen in elite English soccer. Indeed, coaching practice that for many years was based largely on tradition, emulation and intuition is now giving way to an approach based on scientific evidence. This shift has resulted in better informed practitioners working with teams, stronger links with scientific institutes and more coaches being willing to accept the changing role of sports science in elite soccer.

The evolution of soccer science will be further explored in chapter 2 with particular reference to the English Premier League. Moreover, chapter 2 discusses how the principles of sport science have led to establishing innovation and personalization within modern soccer, including an examination of cross-cultural analysis from continental and subcontinental perspectives.

CHAPTER 2

National and Cultural Influences

—Craig Duncan and Tony Strudwick

Played by 250 million players in more than 200 countries, soccer is the world's most popular sport. The worldwide influence and public interest on a daily basis attract ever-increasing sponsorship and investment into the sport. Professional soccer clubs now appear to operate as service enterprises engaged in the business of performance, entertainment and financial profit (Bourke 2003). This movement towards the business end of sport has been significantly influenced by the financial rewards associated with sponsorship, media and the new competition structures that reward successful teams with big-money prizes. Clearly, with professional soccer clubs working as business enterprises, a shift has occurred towards advanced sport science support structures to assist in talent development and player management.

This chapter provides a comprehensive account of how soccer science was introduced and where and how it varies on a national and cultural level. In addition, the chapter explains how principles from research have led to establishing innovation and personalization within modern soccer. Cross-cultural analysis from continental and subcontinental perspectives will be explored with particular references to English and Australian and North American models of evolution. In addition, the influence of Scandinavian physiologists and Italian fitness coaches on soccer preparation will be examined.

Cultural Systems

Soccer in many countries cannot be appreciated and quantified aside from the nation's culture, traditions, environment and values. Soccer reflects national culture because it permeates all levels of society. These cultural systems influence styles of play, methods of preparation and patterns of behaviour that form a durable template by which ideas are transferred from one generation to the other. Climatic reasons probably explain why South

Americans in their warm climate play at a different pace to their European counterparts. Brazilian soccer, well documented in *Soccer Madness* (Lever 1983), is 'alegre', soccer to a Samba beat—joyous, flamboyant, skilful, free flowing and spontaneous. Just as soccer has permeated other cultures, it holds the potential of affecting Brazilian society at all levels of participation and spectatorship, with deeply ingrained expectations. Following Brazil's failure at the 2010 FIFA World Cup, the Brazilian national coach Dunga was heavily criticized and later fired because of his pragmatic, mechanistic and fundamentally defensive-minded style of play, a style of play that is clearly misaligned to the creative style associated with Brazilian culture.

In seeking to ascertain how the culture of a society may affect the development of methods of soccer preparation, we need to recognize that culture itself is an extremely complex phenomenon. Culture is typically referred to as a pattern of behaviours and basic assumptions that are invented, discovered or developed by a given group as it learns to cope with its problems of external adaptation and internal integration (Schein 1991). At a more visible level, culture describes ideas and images that are transferred from one generation or group to another. On a soccer level, we can assume that methods of preparation and styles of play have become so deeply entrenched in organizational structure that any attempt to challenge traditional practice is often received with caution and resistance. Nonetheless, the increasing concern with financial profit in professional soccer will inevitably lead to evolving methods of player preparation and a move away from overreliance on traditional methods.

Sport Science

Sport science is a discipline that studies the application of scientific principles and techniques and has the aim of improving sporting performance. The study of sport science traditionally incorporates areas of *psychology* and *biomechanics* but also includes other topics such as sport nutrition. Sport science also helps practitioners understand the physical and psychological effects of a sport, thereby providing the best techniques for a sport and the most appropriate methods of preventing injuries to an athlete involved in the performance of the sport. Key areas of research in soccer include the effect of nutrition and training on performance and recovery from participation, the effect of training volume on the immune system, the biomechanics and motor control of elite sporting performance, talent identification and development, cognition and muscle function, and motivation and mental toughness.

Sport scientists and performance consultants are increasingly in demand because of the ever-increasing focus within the soccer world on achieving the best results possible. Through the study of science and sport, researchers have developed greater understanding on how the human body reacts to exercise, training, various environments and many other stimuli.

The application of sport science has a self-evident part to play in improving soccer performance. Important features of a model, such as devising training programmes, monitoring performance and establishing preparation for competition are informed by such knowledge. The primary role of sport science in soccer is to use scientific principles to maximize individual performance and player preparation. Practitioners therefore need to manipulate the training process effectively to achieve those objectives.

Evolution of Soccer Science

Historically, soccer has been viewed as being inappropriate for scientific investigations. Three decades ago, the soccer environment was one in which the scientist was likely to be greeted 'at worst with suspicion and hostility and at best with muted scepticism' (Reilly 1979). The first World Congress of Science and Football in 1987 represented a major shift forward in effecting a link between theory and football practice, being the first occasion when representatives of all the football codes came together for a common purpose. Since then the event championed by the late Professor Tom Reilly has been held every four years. Subsequent meetings have been organized in Eindhoven (1991), Cardiff (1995), Sydney (1999), Lisbon (2003), Antalya (2007) and Nagoya (2011). The aims of the movement in science and football were to

- bring together scientists whose work is directly related to football and practitioners keen to obtain current information about its scientific aspects,
- bridge the gap between research and practice so that scientific knowledge about football can be communicated and applied, and
- debate the common threads among the football codes, in both research and practice.

The material communicated at the World Congress of Science and Football is published as proceedings and contributes to the scientific knowledge base. All manuscripts are subject to peer review, so strict quality control is applied to the findings reported in the public domain. The steering group is also pivotal in supporting satellite meetings and facilitating links with relevant governing and professional bodies. This connection has led to various workshops and provided the platform for special issues devoted to topics such as talent identification in the *Journal of Sports Sciences* (see Williams and Reilly 2000). Clearly, this movement has facilitated a growing acceptance of sport science support models across all football codes.

Given the popularity of soccer and the need to identify best practices to support soccer development, the World Conference on Science and Soccer was introduced in Liverpool (2008) and has been subsequently held in Port

Elizabeth (2010) and Ghent (2012). The World Conference on Science and Soccer was an initiative from the International Steering Group on Science and Football and under the auspices of the World Commission of Science and Sports. This conference sought to develop the already successful thematic content included in congresses such as the World Congress of Science and Football by focusing the subject matter on soccer.

The conference is now aimed at all people who have a particular interest in the scientific study or the practical performance of soccer players from the grassroots level to the elite professional level. These include academics and sport scientists, full- and part-time (youth) coaches, strength and conditioning specialists, sports medics and physiotherapists, exercise physiologists, club administrators, teachers and students.

Origins of Soccer Science: Professor Tom Reilly

Professor Tom Reilly was instrumental in applying scientific analysis in professional soccer. Moreover, much of the subsequent movement towards scientific applications to the football codes and progressive professionalization of the codes can be attributed to Professor Reilly's early applied work. In the study of English First Division players, Reilly and Thomas (1976) used video recordings in conjunction with pitch markings to assess work rates. Observations were made from a seat in the stand overlooking the halfway line, and a coded commentary of events was registered on a tape recorder. Distance was estimated in 1-mile (1.6 km) units by using cues on the pitch and on its boundaries. The percentages of activity for the total distance covered during match play consisted of 37 per cent jogging, 25 per cent walking, 20 per cent cruising, 11 per cent sprinting and 7 per cent utility movements. High-intensity activities were the least frequently performed actions; sprinting and cruising accounted for 62 plus or minus 15 and 114 plus or minus 16 discrete bouts, respectively. Although these data were derived in the 1970s, Reilly (1994) reported that observations made on World Cup players performing in the English League in 1990 indicate that these profiles were still representative of elite club soccer at that time.

The application of motion analysis to soccer has enabled the objective recording and interpretation of match events by describing the characteristic patterns of activity in soccer. In 1979 Professor Reilly wrote *What Research Tells the Coach About Soccer*. Aware that soccer coaches in England had no interest in scientific applications, he published it in the United States instead.

> *There was not much point in putting it out in the UK. It would have only sold half-a-dozen copies. The Americans were much more interested in sport science in general and it did quite well over there.*
>
> (Reilly 1994; Bent et al. 1999, 92)

The critical message from Reilly's findings was that soccer is an intermittent type of activity in which periods of short, high-intensity exercise are randomly interspersed with longer periods of either active rest or passive recovery. Training of soccer players should therefore be tailored accordingly. In addition, soccer players can be described as lean and muscular and having a reasonably high level in all areas of physical performance. That is, players need to be aerobically fit to run for long distances and anaerobically fit to produce bursts of power during the most intense phases of the game, especially during the later stages of the game when fatigue becomes more apparent.

These findings were largely ignored by the English soccer establishment, where for generations of coaches, fitness was equated with the ability to run long distances, a belief largely motivated by the increasing number of military PT instructors freelancing their services to prepare soccer players, particularly during the preseason period of conditioning. Many of the coaches in English soccer appear not to have recognized that preparing a soldier to trek long distances over varied terrain was different from preparing an elite soccer player. Nonetheless, during the 1980s there was a growing wave of interest from universities and research institutes of sport into the scientific applications of training principles. Towards the late 1980s many universities and institutes of higher education in England began to fund research into sport science and offer it as an undergraduate course. Leading institutions such as Loughborough University provided a breeding ground for coaches, technical directors and physiologists to study scientific principles and techniques with the aim of improving sporting performance. Figure 2.1 shows some of the significant milestones in the development of soccer science in England.

Scandinavian Influence on Sport Science

Around the same period of the late 1980s, several Scandinavian universities were applying validated scientific protocols in search of methods to improve fitness training of soccer players. Physiologists at Stockholm's Karolinska Institute and the University of Copenhagen's August Krogh Institute began establishing formal links with professional soccer clubs, thus providing motivation to apply the most effective and cutting-edge methods of player preparation. Applied physiologists such as Bjorn Ekblom, Jens Bangsbo and Paul Balsom, inspired by the early work of Tom Reilly, started to produce a series of works on applied science in soccer. The message was clear:

Soccer is not a science, but science can improve the level of soccer.

(Bangsbo 7)

In 1994 Jens Bangsbo published a series of scientific papers in a user-friendly book titled *Fitness Training in Football: A Scientific Approach*. The work explored the physiological principles of soccer with coaching guidelines for

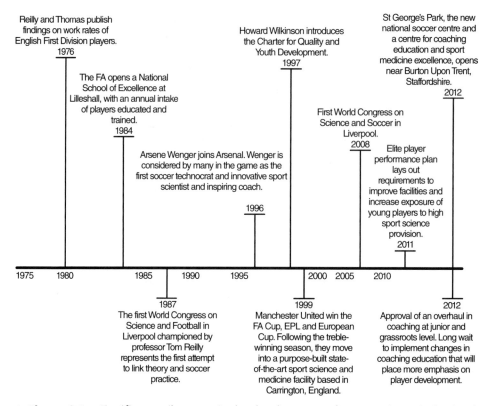

Reilly and Thomas publish findings on work rates of English First Division players. 1976

The FA opens a National School of Excellence at Lilleshall, with an annual intake of players educated and trained. 1984

Arsene Wenger joins Arsenal. Wenger is considered by many in the game as the first soccer technocrat and innovative sport scientist and inspiring coach. 1996

Howard Wilkinson introduces the Charter for Quality and Youth Development. 1997

First World Congress on Science and Soccer in Liverpool. 2008

Elite player performance plan lays out requirements to improve facilities and increase exposure of young players to high sport science provision. 2011

St George's Park, the new national soccer centre and a centre for coaching education and sport medicine excellence, opens near Burton Upon Trent, Staffordshire. 2012

1975   1980   1985   1990   1995   2000   2005   2010

1987 The first World Congress on Science and Football in Liverpool championed by professor Tom Reilly represents the first attempt to link theory and soccer practice.

1999 Manchester United win the FA Cup, EPL and European Cup. Following the treble-winning season, they move into a purpose-built state-of-the-art sport science and medicine facility based in Carrington, England.

2012 Approval of an overhaul in coaching at junior and grassroots level. Long wait to implement changes in coaching education that will place more emphasis on player development.

▶ **Figure 2.1** Significant milestones in the development of soccer science in England.

the application of those principles. The Danish Football Association was so impressed with the message that it immediately dispatched the work to every club in the country. It was especially appropriate to Scandinavia, where the season is shorter than in many other European countries. Moreover, soccer players in Scandinavia had limited time for training, so they needed to make the best use of it. Because of the Danish Football Association's endorsement, the work spread quickly throughout Scandinavia and became popular with coaches and players alike.

Jens Bangsbo has had a profound effect on the accumulation of scientifically based knowledge to soccer. A former professional soccer player in Denmark, Bangsbo has written many important research papers on the physiology of movement patterns in soccer as well as more recent works exploring the physical capacity of high-level soccer players in relation to playing position (Bangsbo, Krustrup and Mohr 2003) and the benefits of high-intensity training (Iaia and Bangsbo 2010). In addition, Bangsbo has occupied a position of assistant manager of the Italian professional soccer team Juventus FC and works as a fitness coach for the Danish national soccer team. More recently, Bangsbo developed the Yo-Yo Intermittent Endurance Test as an assessment specifically targeted at games players (Bangsbo 1996).

The test incorporates exercise patterns found in soccer and consists of 40 bouts of 15-second high-intensity running interspersed with 10-second recovery periods. Many elite soccer teams now incorporate the Yo-Yo tests as a field-based assessment of a player's soccer-specific intermittent endurance capacity.

According to Bangsbo (2008), fitness training for soccer players can be divided into aerobic, anaerobic and specific muscle training. Each type of training has subcategories, which allow a precise execution of the training when the aim of the training is known. A critical factor when training soccer players is scheduling when to do what (i.e., planning the training), and Bangsbo has managed to provide concrete training plans for the practitioner to assimilate when working with players. In line with this, Bangsbo and colleagues (2006) were instrumental in providing evidence that soccer performance can be maintained and improved by reducing the amount of low-intensity training and keeping a sufficient amount of high-intensity training. This idea is fundamental to the concept of tapering in sport (Mujika 2010), and coaches and sport scientists alike should understand it in the seasonal preparation of soccer players. See more on this topic in chapter 12.

In 1992 Bangsbo used his scientific approach to help the Danish team win the European Championship. This success was achieved in spite of an unusual preparation period. As a result many coaches reconsidered how to optimize training regimens for elite international soccer tournaments.

Because of the late exclusion of Yugoslavia, the Danish team was selected only 10 days before the start of the European Championship. At that time, about half of the players playing in teams outside Denmark had holidays for 3 to 5 weeks because the season had ended for most of the European tournaments. The other players were taking part in the Danish League, which was still ongoing at the time of selection. The players who had played abroad trained together, whereas the remaining players continued their training in their clubs to finish the Danish League. Therefore, the team was together for only 6 days before the start of the tournament.

The preparation was definitely not optimal; the players who had played abroad did not have sufficient fitness at the start of the tournament. Nevertheless, the situation was advantageous in that the players did not become mentally exhausted, which usually happens for some players during a long-lasting tournament after a long preparation period. Bangsbo and the coaches decided on a strategy for the team, taking into account many factors, such as the need for tactical development, optimizing the fitness of the players and psychology.

Bangsbo continued to develop the key features of his physiological preparation model and subsequently published his ideas in *Journal of Exercise Science and Fitness* (Bangsbo et al. 2006). The critical areas of the model remain today; emphasis is placed on how to reduce training load without lowering the performance level of the players. In addition, the suggested aerobic and anaerobic training regimens are performed mainly with the ball, which has several advantages. First, it ensures that the muscles used during the game are trained. Second, the players develop technical and tactical skills under conditions similar to those encountered during a match. Third, the training usually provides greater motivation for the players compared with training without the ball.

Although much of the early work of Tom Reilly and the Scandinavian physiologists was largely ignored within the coaching circles of the English Football Association, an influx of foreign coaches, the appearance of foreign players and a growing number of returning exiles from abroad facilitated a cultural shift within the Premier League. Many of the more successful teams such as Sir Alex Ferguson's Manchester United began sending their coaches to visit European clubs to study training and coaching techniques first hand. Indeed, Ferguson was constantly searching for innovative ways to gain a competitive advantage, and this effort led to changes in player dietary practices, the development of new training routines and the exponential growth in advanced player support staff such as sport and vision scientists. Such cutting-edge enthusiasm and thinking led to the development of state-of-the-art facilities at their training base in Carrington and innovative training methods more aligned to European philosophy than to a culture based on wisdom and tradition. The product of innovative coaching and first-class player recruitment and talent management led to Manchester United winning the FA Cup, Premier League and European Cup in 1999.

In 1996 Arsene Wenger was named manager of Arsenal Football Club, and two years later the club completed a Premier League and FA Cup double. At a time when England as a sporting nation was considered blinkered and backwards, Arsene Wenger revolutionized the way that the Arsenal players viewed the game of soccer. Wenger was considered the first soccer technocrat, an innovative sport scientist, a consummate psychologist and an inspiring coach. Almost immediately, the players became more professional in the way they trained, paid more attention to their diet and adopted a more scientific and structured approach to preparation. The following passage gives a clear insight into how Wenger viewed Latin and English culture:

> *Of the two, Latin culture is easily more rational. It is more open to analysis and self-examination than English culture. And there is a good reason for this. If you think about it, the culture of a country is dictated by what they learn in school. We in France have Descartes. His rationalism is the basis for all of French thought and culture. In Italy you have Machiavelli, who is also about being rational and calculating. Here in England, maybe because they are an island, they are more warlike, more passionate. They view it like an old-style duel, a fight to the death, come what may. When an Englishman goes into war, that's it, he either comes back triumphant or he comes back dead. But the Italian or the Frenchman is not like that.*

He will calculate, he will think about things, he will do what he needs to do to protect his own interests.

(Arsene Wenger in Vialli and Marcotti 2007, 120)

Clearly, evidence in the Premier League indicated that English clubs were finally adopting a more scientific approach to soccer fitness. At Arsenal Football Club, players such as Tony Adams, Martin Keown, Lee Dixon and David Seaman frequently commented on the benefits of stretching, diet and innovative training routines in prolonging and maximizing playing careers.

The Italian Model for Soccer Preparation

In Italy, soccer is considered primarily a sport discipline, constantly discussed and analysed from both a technical–tactical and physiological perspective. In addition, any worthwhile technical movement is not successfully achieved without being supported by specific biochemical, biophysical and physiological research. An excellent passage from *The Italian Job* (Vialli and Marcotti 2006) accurately depicts the Italian model of philosophical inquiry in soccer:

In Italy, our minds work rather differently. We always believe there is a better way and we spend most of our time criticizing the status quo. Our brains are livelier, more capable of critical thinking. And that's why we're more progressive, more open to change, to dialogue. If we see something isn't working, we'll try something different. And this applies to everything, from the players to the managers to the tactics.

(Marcello Lippi in Vialli and Marcotti 2007, 117)

The reality of this philosophy was first developed and refined in professional circles of Italian soccer coaches and then gradually spread to influence the whole of the soccer world, particularly within the English Premier League. This diffusion has led to the development of various technical and scientific soccer doctrines and clearly demonstrates that Italian soccer is constantly searching for something new.

The origins of Italian training methods for soccer players can be traced back to the early 1970s. These approaches were influenced by young track and field coaches who applied the principles of training theory. Before this movement, people generally believed that the training methods used in one particular sport could not be applied to other sport disciplines. Although it was accepted that soccer has its own peculiar features, it was also suggested that various training methods produce highly specific changes in the athlete's body and that laws govern such important changes. This theory of training, which was originally developed by Soviet scientists, led to the development of physiologically based knowledge that was translated into a form usable for Italian soccer coaches.

The formative work of Enrico Arcelli (who has been credited with having a major influence on developing the profession of the fitness coach) paved the way for Italian fitness coaches to be officially acknowledged by the Italian Soccer Association and the development of the Italian Association of Fitness Coaches in Soccer (AIPAC). This movement elevated the status of the fitness coach within the soccer coaching structure, thus solidifying the important relationship between head coach and fitness practitioner. Moreover, many Italian fitness coaches consequently built strong, long-lasting relationships with coaches and ex-players alike. The migration of fitness coaches into the English Premier League with Italian coaches is a testament to these long-lasting relationships and has had a huge influence on English soccer conditioning. Indeed, Italian fitness coaches such as Roberto Sassi, Antonio Pintus, Ivan Carminati and Valter Di Salvo have occupied roles at Chelsea, Manchester City and Manchester United in recent years.

Clearly, the advancement of conditioning programmes in the Italian domestic game led to advancements of individual soccer athletes and the evolution of the great AC Milan team of the late 1980s, in which Arrigho Sacchi and fitness coach Vincenzo Pincolini developed highly athletic players such as Marco Van Basten, Ruud Gullit, Frank Rijkaard, Franco Baresi, Roberto Donadoni and Paolo Maldini. To illustrate the influence that these fitness coaches had on the preparation of English Premier League conditioning programmes, table 2.1 provides an example of an Italian preseason programme for English Premier League players. At that particular moment in British soccer, the classic preseason programme delivered by English-based coaches was typically based on long-distances runs, high-volume work and a distinct lack of direction in terms of strength work and technical–tactical integration. The influence of a more scientific approach had a profound effect on conditioning programmes for English-based practitioners. Although some of the concepts are now somewhat dated, they nevertheless created a pathway to execute training plans based on testing, monitoring and sound scientific principles. The conditioning programme was accumulated through personal communication.

MilanLab:
The Search for Excellence and Innovation

Professional soccer clubs spend huge amounts of money on player wages and transfer fees. If players are unavailable because of injury, they can be seen as ineffective products. Every match missed through injury can potentially be a wasted weekly wage. Using this reality to focus on prevention, cure and development of the scientific approach to elite professional soccer, AC Milan set up the MilanLab at the Milanello Training Centre to combat this problem.

A dominating vision of MilanLab is understanding health as a total state of physical, mental and social well-being that depends on balancing three

Table 2.1 Preseason Training Schedule for a Six-Day Period of an English Premier League Team (2000)—Italian-Based Coaching Staff

Day	a.m.	p.m.
1	Mognoni test Optojump test Real power test 10 m sprint test Half-squat leg strength (4 × 10 at 60%) 2 × 1,000 m at 4 min., 10 sec. (3 min. recovery)	Free
2	10 min. jogging and stretching 10 min. abdominal exercises 10 min. upper-body conditioning 20 min. leg strength and plyometric training 10 min. technical ball work 3 × 25 m sprints 3 × 1,000 m runs at 5% anaerobic threshold (4 min. recovery)	Free
3	10 min. stretching 10 min. abdominal work 10 min. plyometric training 4 × 1,000 m runs at 5% anaerobic threshold (4 min. recovery)	60 min. technical and tactical training (not all players)
4	10 min. jogging and stretching 10 min. proprioception training 10 min. abdominal work 3 × 25 m sprints 20 min. leg strength 20 min. technical ball work 5 × 1,000 m runs at 5% anaerobic threshold (4 min. recovery)	Free
5	10 min. abdominals 20 min. leg strength and plyometric training 6 × 1,000 m runs at 5% anaerobic threshold (4 min. recovery)	60 min. technical session with coaches (not all players)
6	10 min. jogging and stretching 10 min. proprioception training 10 min. abdominal work 3 × 25 m sprints 60 min. technical and tactical work	Free

principal functional levels. These include the structural, biochemical and mental components:

- *Structural area*: A chiropractic approach emphasizes the intrinsic ability of the body to recover without drugs or surgical intervention.
- *Biochemical area*: The body is considered a physical, chemical and biological entity. The focus is on the biochemical changes occurring in the body during exercise.
- *Mental area*: The study and monitoring of the psychological state of the athlete takes advantage of the Mind Room, a glassed-in facility that helps players relax and relieve stress. Mental state is also monitored through various psychometric tests.

MilanLab is a high-tech scientific research centre set up by AC Milan and based inside the Milanello Training Centre. Its purpose is to optimize the psychophysical management of the athletes. This task is entrusted to MilanLab, which represents the ideal combination of science, technology, IT, cybernetics and psychology.

MilanLab takes advantage of the latest advanced and sophisticated software technologies available to collect and process information. The system of artificial intelligence collects and processes the information, a self-taught mechanism with the ability to learn through the process of memorized data that can determine which factors will cause a player to suffer an injury. The psychophysical information regarding every player is gathered through a sophisticated system of wiring connected to the Unysis output point and supported by hardware installation supplied by AMD. At this point, a sophisticated software programme developed by computer associates performs neural analysis and uses artificial intelligence to transform vast amounts of numeric medical statistics into meaningful predictions through the PAS (predictive analysis server) technology, a system that works to predict the possible risks to the players.

MilanLab is a multidisciplinary research and development project that looks to the future, by taking advantage of data gained from experience. Within this, MilanLab has developed research partnerships with the most prestigious international research centres: SENSEable City Lab of the Massachusetts Institute of Technology (MIT) in Boston (United States), the department of bioengineering of the University of Louvain-la-Neuve (Belgium) and the Centre of Research in Epistemology Knowledge and Application (CRESA) of the University Vita-Salute San Raffaele Italy.

The underlying philosophy behind MilanLab is that the more people involved in working towards the same goal, the better the service is to the players and subsequently the better the individual results are. During its height, the club's nontechnical performance team included two medical doctors (one an expert in performance nutrition), one head sport scientist, four sport scientists or conditioners, one chiropractor, two sport psychologists (one full time), six physiotherapists, two masseurs, one Pilates teacher (part time), two match analysts (one full time) and one computer analyst.

MilanLab prides itself on the fact that the individual service to the players is better than most. In addition, it attributed a 92 per cent reduction in injury rates to the scientific support system. The best students from local universities are recruited to assist and increase staffing numbers (no salaries paid, offering work experience only). The students are able to follow strategies and programmes set by the department head to ensure that development occurs. On joining AC Milan, each player must watch a presentation shown by MilanLab staff members to learn the training structure at the club as well as how each player benefits from it. The huge backing and emphasis placed on MilanLab from the technical staff also adds to the importance and implementation of the project.

The staff was not only highly satisfied with the minimal injury rates of the first-team squad at AC Milan but also took pride in the fact that they have helped prolong the careers of a number of elite international players through good training and recovery methods: Costacurta 41, Maldini 39, Serginho 37, Fiori 38, Cafu 38, Favalli 36, Kalac 35, Dida 34, Inzaghi 34, Ba 34, Simic 32, Oddo 31, Ronaldo 31, Brocci 31, Emerson 31, Nesta 31. Ten to 12 years ago AC Milan believed they needed approximately 35 players in the first-team squad. Following 2007–2008, they have since recognized that they could get through the season with fewer than 22 players, an improvement they attributed to the work performed at MilanLab.

Elite Player Performance Plan

The introduction of the Elite Player Performance Plan (EPPP) in 2011 has contributed to enhanced understanding of how sport science can be integrated into the coaching process within elite youth development.

Considered the first major overhaul of England's youth development system in over 13 years, the EPPP was created out of a desire by the game's key stakeholders to produce more and better home-grown players for the English professional leagues. Its aim is to deliver an environment that promotes excellence, nurtures talent and systematically supports the development of young players capable of playing first-team soccer.

The EPPP sets out specific processes and criteria that support the implementation of core themes considered necessary to the development of elite young players between the ages of 9 and 21. Among others, these themes include enhanced access to age-specific soccer coaching and physical and mental development programmes that specialist age-group coaches and support staff deliver.

Recognition of the sport science disciplines within the EPPP is evident in the mandatory requirements within the audit process that awards a tiered categorization grade. The level of categorization determines the number of qualified sport science staff an academy is required to employ. For example, a category one academy requires a head of sport science and medicine as well as a lead sport scientist, a strength and conditioning coach and two performance analysts. In addition to levels of staffing, age-specific sport science protocols such as physical screening, performance testing, psychological profiling and the integrated use of GPS and match analysis need to be in use to attain a category status.

A vehicle within the EPPP that enables sport science to work effectively within the academy environment is the mandatory operation of a multi-disciplinary team. Providing a platform to support the player development process, the age-group coach works with the sport scientists and medical and education teams in the assessment, planning, delivery and review of team and individual programmes.

Involvement of the sport science team in the development process facilitates an opportunity to support and advise the coach, support staff and ultimately the player. Besides having a strong knowledge base and practical understanding of how sport science theory can be applied to the developing player, practitioners need to have the skills to communicate with others and work effectively as part of the support team. Sport science staff will be involved in a variety of situations from individual player performance review meetings to educational workshops for staff, players and parents. They need to understand both cultural and contextual factors, as well as be able to translate and interpret complex issues such as testing results or training data into clear, relevant and applicable advice and guidance.

As a structured, long-term player development model, the EPPP provides sport science with an opportunity to generate valuable insights into the components associated with the progression of elite young players. The application of research methods by sport science staff can provide a robust and evidence-based mechanism to monitor, evaluate and provide feedback on all aspects of the academy programme such as performance testing, growth and maturation screening, training load and intensity, and educational attainment. The findings generated can provide accurate insights for all stakeholders within the game on how the youth development system as a whole and the players within it are progressing.

The need within the EPPP staffing structure for a head of sport science and medicine may lead to a sport scientist taking on departmental management and leadership responsibilities. Here the development of new skills in areas such as long-term strategy planning, budget management and performance reviews will be necessary.

The EPPP has provided guidelines and a framework for sport science to support the coaching process within the elite academy structure. The challenge for sport scientists is to continue working as part of a multidisciplinary team to create a long-term development programme that meets the holistic needs of elite young soccer players.

The Australian Journey Through Sport Science

In 1976 Australia had its worst-ever performance at an Olympic games. The Australian team of 180 competitors departed Montreal with no gold, one silver and four bronze medals. This result was viewed as calamitous for a country that prides itself on sporting achievements. But a major positive from this failure was the establishment of the Australian Institute of Sport (AIS). This centre of athletic excellence, developed on strong foundations of sport science, sports medicine and research, has established an international reputation for Australia as a leader in sport science.

Although the AIS has been the catalyst for Australia's outstanding reputation in sport science in recent times, Australians have been at the forefront of sport science since the 1940s. Pioneers such as Frank Cotton, a Sydney University physiology professor, and his student and former Australian swimming coach Forbes Carlile were revolutionizing training for many years before the AIS was established. This history and the use of sport science in other team sports have had a major influence on soccer in Australia.

Based in Canberra, the AIS offers scholarships to athletes from targeted sports; soccer is one of these sports. Athletes live at the AIS and complete their schooling in the local area. The soccer programme has evolved over the years. When it first began, players were inducted at age 16 and stayed for two years on average; this squad would become the basis for the national U20 World Cup team. But in more recent times the players are inducted at an earlier age and form the foundations of the national U17 World Cup team.

The scholarship holders train extensively and live as full-time professional soccer players. They have the resources of the AIS to use, as the coach desires. A sport scientist and strength and conditioning coach are assigned to the programme, and the players have an extensive programme that maximizes their potential not only as athletes but also as players. The players are extensively tested and monitored to ensure they are meeting targets set by the coaching and sport science staff.

This work at the AIS has developed soccer players who were outstanding from a physiological perspective. Many FIFA game reports from World Cup competitions have identified the physiological strength of Australian teams. The information from the AIS filtered down into the Australian National League, which was in existence from 1977 through 2004, and the A League, which has operated from 2005 to the present. These leagues have been identified as physiologically demanding; the total distance covered during matches has been comparable with that in top European competitions (Wehbe, Hartwig and Duncan 2014).

For a competitive edge, soccer coaches also look to other Australian sports, such as Australian Rules (AFL), Rugby League and Rugby Union. Furthermore, some teams have enlisted expertise from individual sports such as triathlon and athletics to maximize the physiological condition of their players. AFL probably leads the world in applied sport science in relationship to team sports, and much of what has been done in soccer is a reflection of the processes in AFL.

A driving force behind sport science in AFL is the salary cap. A salary cap permits only a designated amount of money to be spent on player salaries. A salary cap is also used for soccer in Australia, and the arrangement is also common in sports in the United States. The salary cap ensures that great attention must be given to the well-being of the playing staff because player resources are limited. This situation is in contrast to major European soccer competitions where unlimited spending is common for a number of clubs.

At present the professional soccer competition in Australia (A-League) has a salary cap of A$2.5 million. Although one Australian and one international marquee are permitted outside the salary cap, player resources are obviously limited. Therefore, as in the other team sport codes in Australia, much attention is given to maximizing the performance of a player whilst reducing the risk of injury. Furthermore, because the salary cap allows no team to gain an advantage, teams must focus on getting small advantages from other areas, such as sport science.

The first important step in gaining an advantage through sport science is to ensure that the structure and staffing is efficient. Traditionally, a soccer team has a manager and coaching staff, fitness or strength and conditioning coach, physiotherapist and medical doctor. All too often, this structure is disjointed and has too many avenues of coordination. As figure 2.2 demonstrates, the head coach can be bombarded from all angles with information referring to a player's status, and this information is often clouded by personal and occupational bias.

The model shown in figure 2.2 is not the most effective method of structuring a sport science and sports medicine (SMSM) department. AFL clubs over the years have developed a more positive structure that many clubs throughout Australia and the world are now adopting in soccer. This structure, represented in figure 2.3, works effectively because communication channels are streamlined and the head coach is not overwhelmed with information. The structure is based on that used at national and statewide institutes. The human performance or sport science and sports medicine (SSSM) unit structure gives the best possible chance for players to receive appropriate management.

The model shown in figure 2.3 has been common in AFL for a number of years. The director of SSSM or human performance may come from a sport science, physiotherapy or strength and conditioning background and reports directly to the head coach. In contrast, soccer clubs in Europe have

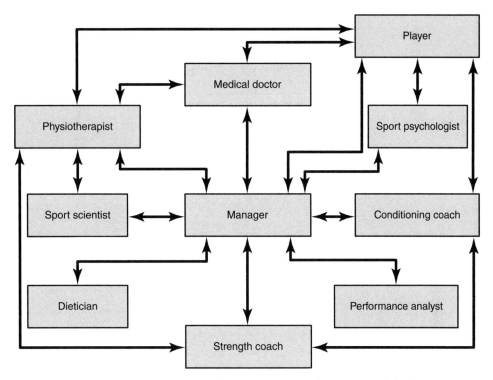

▶ **Figure 2.2** Common structure of sport science and sports medicine in soccer.

A great example of the progressive nature of sport science in Australia has been the introduction of global positioning systems (GPS) to team sports. Over 15 years ago the concept and development of these systems was begun at the AIS, and these systems are now used internationally.

a medically trained person as the director. This structure can and in most instances does have a research component, and most clubs in Australia have relationships with universities, which ensure the continued progression of applied sport science.

GPS and other methods of monitoring training have been used extensively in all Australian team sports. They have become increasingly common in soccer. Furthermore, soccer has also benefited in respect to performance analysis, which plays a major role in other soccer codes. The development of software to enhance game analysis has been driven by the requirements of AFL and Rugby League to get an added advantage, and this is now commonplace in Australian soccer.

The focus on the management of fatigue and recovery has developed out of necessity. The A-League is a nationwide competition. Travel is extensive;

Human performance unit

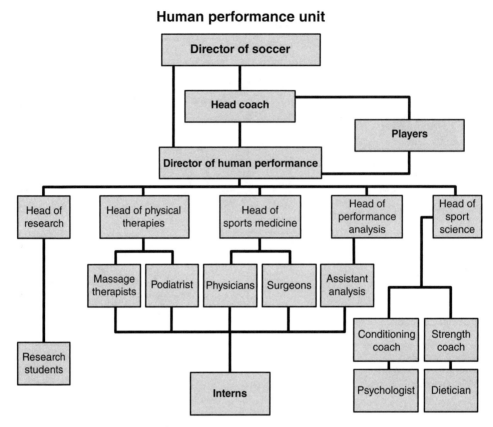

▶ **Figure 2.3** Human performance or SSSM model.

teams have to travel for up to five hours by air for a domestic competition game. Australian teams are also involved in the Asian Champions League, which can mean that a team has a midweek game that involves up to nine hours of air travel. Furthermore, the competition is played in the summer months, so training and playing temperatures are often greater than 30 degrees Celsius. Therefore, sport science must be applied.

The use of sport science in soccer in Australia has been questioned in recent years. A number of critics have suggested that sport science has had too much influence on Australian soccer. The influence from other sports has been rejected as not being suitable for the world game. Australia has been known for having physically outstanding players as identified by numerous FIFA analyses at international tournaments, but the issues related to technique and tactics have led to a major revolution in Australian soccer in recent years.

After not qualifying for a World Cup since 1974, Australia qualified in 2006 with Dutch coach Guus Hiddink at the helm. Evidently, sport science played a major role in this success with respect to recovery procedures and management of fatigue in the final qualifying matches against Uruguay. Australia had a successful World Cup, reaching the round of 16 before being eliminated by eventual champions Italy in the final minute of the match.

Guus Hiddink departed after the World Cup, but Football Federation Australia (FFA) determined that Australian soccer should be based on the Dutch model. Therefore, the technical direction took a Dutch focus. The programme quickly identified that Australian players from young to old were deficient in technical ability. It also identified that too much time in training was spent on physical conditioning, so a curriculum with a specific soccer conditioning section was produced.

This model developed with no input from Australian practitioners, and little sport science was included in Australian coaching courses. In effect, the model dismissed the influence of Australian sport science as problematic and focused more on the technical and tactical aspects of soccer. Although this initiative should have been applauded, it was difficult to understand that a nation that is a world leader in sport science should not use its resources to enhance the physiological ability of players.

In addition, the soccer conditioning strategy employed was not validated, and it quickly became evident that the strategy had numerous issues. The model was essentially a one-size-fits-all conditioning approach, which ignored the individuality of players and the basic scientific concept of individual differences. The model was based on a variety of small-sided games (SSG) that put no emphasis on monitoring external or internal load, injury prevention or most other aspects of a well-balanced training programme. Furthermore, in a unique situation in world soccer, the national federation attempted to make this conditioning model the standard for all professional teams in Australia and to require all conditioning coaches to be certified in this style of conditioning.

Australian soccer science was at a crossroads. Obviously, a balance was needed between sport science and the requirements to be a successful soccer player. The advanced state of sport science in Australia had identified an imbalance with the coaching of technique and tactics, but completely shutting the door on sport science was not the answer. It was suggested that coach education must improve, but not at the detriment of sport science.

More recently, a change in national team management has led to the reintegration of sport science in Australian soccer. The FFA has reintroduced the role of head of sport science, and each national team has a sport scientist on staff. Furthermore, all players identified by national coaches are monitored daily, and these physiological data enhance team performance. A balance has finally been reached, and sport science will continue to play a role in the development of Australian soccer players into the future.

North American Soccer and Science

The last two decades in Major League Soccer (MLS) have witnessed a changing environment. Sport science is now being taken seriously, and traditional methods of managing, planning, decision making and player preparation have been abandoned for a more structured approach. Elite soccer players in MLS now have access to scientific support systems, high-quality coaching and innovative training facilities. This shift in thinking has been the result of an influx of coaches and managers from overseas and a dissemination of ideas from England, Europe and Australia.

MLS is similar to many other leagues in the world in length and number of games. The regular season runs from March until October, and the playoff runs through the first week of December. Many MLS teams currently employ advanced monitoring systems to ensure that the correct decisions are made with regard to individual player requirements. During the 2012 MLS All-Star Game, Adidas debuted the miCoach system, which allowed coaches (and fans) to track players in real time. GPS monitors, heat maps and other location-based data-collection devices are available to clubs. The league has also partnered with Opta, a company that collects and displays additional facts about performance. The net effect has been an increase in data analytics, more performance profiling and an increasingly prominent role of sport science in athletic preparation.

Traditionally, athletic development in North America has been based on strength and conditioning models of preparation. Moreover, in the preparation of elite soccer players, strength and conditioning practitioners were typically responsible for delivering training programmes that concentrated on gym-based activities. The ultimate objective of these programmes is to develop the ability of the athlete to apply force. Recently, however, a more holistic approach to athletic development that uses sport science principles has been applied. An increase has occurred in the number of sport science practitioners, such as Dave Tenney (Seattle Sounders FC), Tony Jouax (Chicago Fire), Mateus Manoel (Sporting Kansas City), Skylar Richards (FC Dallas) and Paolo Pacione (Montreal Impact).

The rise in sport science in MLS has the capacity to provide the following:

- Analytical research on the Adidas miCoach system and GPS data from training and games
- Optimal planning and travel scheduling for key fixtures
- Sport science solutions for dealing with environmental challenges such as playing in hot environments, playing at altitude and competing on synthetic playing surfaces

- Key educational messages on recovery, nutrition and lifestyle-based management that are supported by sound scientific research
- Key planning of match and training schedules

In addition, the rise in advanced sport science networks has seen the following changing landscape in the last few years within MLS:

- Increase in number of staff supporting athletic development and performance
- Changing role of the fitness coach to support field-based integration of sport science planning
- Rise in analytical systems and models supporting performance
- Increase in scientific research in field-based environments

The Fourth World Conference on Science and Soccer (WCSS) was held in the United States for the first time in 2014. Given the popularity of soccer and the need to identify best practices to support soccer development, the scientific community in the United States is now poised to collaborate with leading scientists worldwide to conduct research on all aspects of soccer.

The WCSS was aimed at people who are interested in the study or practical performance of soccer players, including sport scientists, coaches, strength and conditioning specialists, sports physiotherapists, exercise physiologists, professors and students. Although leading scientists and practitioners addressed the emerging new challenges in the various domains of the soccer-related world, the conference also showed that sport science is now being taken seriously in North America.

Conclusion

The aim of this chapter was to provide a comprehensive account of how soccer science has evolved over the past three decades. In particular, it has demonstrated that preparation and sport science cannot be quantified without an appreciation of traditions, environment and values at a cultural level. Clearly, modern developments in scientific research and integration have led to establishing innovation and personalization within modern soccer. The remainder of the book explores the current research within science and soccer and disseminates the accumulated information to those who would most benefit from it.

Talent Identification and Player Development

CHAPTER 3

Practical Aspects of Player Selection and Development

—Iñigo Mujika and Carlo Castagna

Selecting and developing soccer players is not an easy task. Many professional clubs invest a lot of time, effort and financial resources trying to develop some or most of their first-team players through their own academy system rather than hiring players in the ever more expensive player transfer market.

To select and develop home-grown soccer players, club academies need to create a clear path for their youth players. Based on our experience in this area at Athletic Club Bilbao and other high-level soccer clubs, we argue that several points are helpful to building a performance plan for young soccer players:

- Clubs and staff need to understand the evolution of soccer players over time.
- Clubs and staff need to identify and understand the evolving demands of the game from grassroots to the professional ranks.
- Clubs and staff need to identify and understand the multiple factors that determine performance in a complex sport such as soccer.
- The training load supported by each player over time needs to be precisely quantified to ensure progression.
- Training time, often limited by school, commuting and other demands placed on youth players, needs to be optimized. Relative individualisation of training is key, even within the framework of a team sport such as soccer.

- Keeping the players free of injury is another key to maximizing training time and ensuring a long and successful soccer career.
- Clubs and staff need to consider players' social development, favouring education and relationships with family, peers and the community.

This chapter provides some practical examples of how sport science departments and coaching staffs can help clubs and soccer academies optimize their player development systems using this performance plan.

Understanding Player Evolution Over Time

As indicated by Mujika (2008), the sport science literature dealing with the issue of developing athletes to achieve elite performance has been dominated by the classical dichotomy between an athlete's genetic endowment (i.e., nature) and environmental influences (i.e., nurture). Research has clearly established that various physiological characteristics associated with success in specific sports and athletic events have a strong genetic influence. In addition, research has shown that the response to a given training programme is, to a large extent, genetically determined.

In view of such evidence, it would be naive to assume a blank-slate thesis in the context of developing expertise in soccer. Environmental factors clearly play a major role in the development of the elite player.

For instance, a grounded theory of psychosocial competencies and environmental conditions associated with success in adolescent soccer indicates that discipline, resilience, commitment and social support are necessary to succeed in a highly competitive sport such as professional soccer (Holt and Dunn 2004). But the most important of all environmental factors associated with athletic expertise is undoubtedly training and practice. In this respect, two considerably disparate approaches to talent development are favoured by different groups of researchers: the deliberate practice framework, characterized by early specialization and repeated and extended exposure to the task domain to develop the skills necessary for successful performance, and the developmental model of sport participation, which supports the notion that early diversification in sport participation and large amounts of deliberate play (as opposed to deliberate practice) are good predictors of elite sport achievement.

Although late specialization associated with the developmental model of sport participation can lead to athletic excellence in some instances, early specialization and deliberate practice in a sport like soccer are in general the preferred path to elite performance (Mujika 2008). Indeed, the relationship between engagement in deliberate practice over extended periods and elite performance is now well established by sport scientists. Helsen et al. (2000) reviewed the results of studies that assessed the progress of international, national and provincial players based on accumulated practice, amount of

Increasing players' availability to train at the time of their growth spurt could be a good strategy to ensure progress. If this schedule is organized in a coordinated effort with the school authorities, increased training demands should not negatively affect players' academic performance.

practice per week and relative importance and demands of various practice and everyday activities. A positive linear relationship was found between accumulated individual practice plus team practice and skill. These authors reported major differences in the accumulated amount of training hours between international, national and regional level players.

A simple analysis of the amount of accumulated hours of team practice in the youth academy of a professional club made by the authors of this chapter revealed that a player who moved through the under-age categories of the academy between the ages of 10 and 20 years completely injury free accumulated less than 6,000 hours (unpublished observations). This was considered far from ideal, especially keeping in mind that in today's Western societies children have limited possibilities to engage in unstructured individual practice or play. A solution to increase the total amount of training time came from offering the players and their parents or tutors the possibility of transferring the youth players to a school linked with the club from the age of 15 years. This school organized its courses in such a way that players were available for training in the morning and the afternoon. Although players did not necessarily always train twice a day, they did have the possibility to do so within the plan designed by the coaching staff. This move allowed the club to increase the total amount of team practice significantly over the ages of 15 to 18 years without a negative effect on the players' academic performance.

Extensive exposure to practice induces adaptations to the specific physical, physiological and psychological demands of the sport. In addition, players also develop perceptual and cognitive skills that discriminate between elite and nonelite players, such as advanced cue utilization, pattern recognition, visual search behaviours, assessment of situational probabilities and strategic decision making. On the other hand, some experts argue that early specialization may have costly consequences in terms of injuries, dropout rate and lifelong participation in sport as a recreational and health-promoting activity.

Elite sport programmes and youth soccer academies often have elaborate protocols intended to detect talented players early and select those who show certain physical and psychological traits that are thought to contribute to success in the sport. Experienced coaches and scouts take for granted that differences in talent determine the fate of players (Helsen et al. 2000), and although they often believe that they select players based on their eye for talent, what they seem to be identifying is early maturation and physical

In sports in which body size, power and strength are advantageous, early maturing children within an age cohort presumably have an advantage over peers who are late maturing. The former are thus more frequently represented among athletes during adolescence.

precocity. Indeed, it is widely recognized that the rate of maturation affects performance characteristics such as aerobic power, muscular strength, power, endurance and speed, in addition to body size and fat-free mass.

Early maturing children are also more likely to be identified as talented and transferred to top teams, benefiting from more and higher-quality coaching and experience at more advanced competitive levels. These effects may then in turn lead to a higher perception of competence and self-efficacy.

This phenomenon has been labelled the relative age effect. The occurrence of the relative age effect has been attributed to the large biological variability within chronological age groupings during childhood and adolescence. The relative age effect is present in most soccer clubs and national teams. We undertook a study to determine whether a relative age effect is already noticeable before players reach the ranks of professional clubs to analyse the influence of age, skill and competition level on the incidence of the relative age effect in soccer players, and assess the influence of player selection systems used in soccer. Because the existence of a relative age effect may be particularly problematic for soccer clubs that rely heavily on players developed in their own youth academies and for clubs that select their players from relatively small population groups, we analysed the case of Athletic Club Bilbao, which selects its senior players from a limited pool of players either born or developed in the Basque Country, which has a population of less than three million. The presence of a relative age effect would add another significant limitation to the club's recruitment philosophy. To this end, we analysed the birth date distribution of five separate pools of subjects: the general male population of the Basque Country, players involved in school soccer (i.e., the lowest level of formal participation in organized soccer), youth players registered in the soccer federation from which Athletic Bilbao selects its academy players, Athletic Club Bilbao's academy players, and Athletic Club Bilbao's first-team players.

Our results revealed that although the birth date distribution was perfectly balanced throughout the year in the general population of the Basque Country, the birth date distribution of all studied soccer groups was different from that of the population from which the players were extracted; players born in the first and second quarters of the selection year were clearly overrepresented. This relative age effect was already present at the lowest levels of participation in organized soccer, increased along with the competitive level of the players in the developmental stages and remained patent at the

Clubs and academies are encouraged to revise their selection policies to ensure that talented players who could eventually make the professional ranks are not left behind simply because they were not born in the early days of the selection year.

professional ranks. This bias represents a significant loss of potential youth soccer talent. Solutions should be sought by all those involved in the soccer talent selection and development process (Mujika et al. 2009c).

These results imply that the relatively older players enjoy early recognition from talent scouts, presumably because of their likely physical superiority. This observation is in line with previous findings that showed that players born early in the selection year were more likely to be recognized as talented, to be transferred to higher-level teams and consequently to receive higher-quality coaching. Similarly, from the age of 12 years a higher dropout rate occurs among youth soccer players born late in the selection year. These findings are in keeping with the observed cascade effect or residual bias in our study. Because many of the physiological and physical components used to determine sport performance change with growth, biological maturity should be considered in the evaluation of performance capacity more than chronological age.

Understanding the Demands of the Game

Soccer is played by a variable number of players and pitch dimensions across the academy ages. The aim is to develop game understanding progressively and make the game as enjoyable as possible. Soccer associations all over the world usually organize tournaments and youth championships using modified small-sided versions of adult soccer, usually with at least four outfield players on a side. These small-sided versions of association soccer allow players to perform more ball contacts during the game, thus training their individual and team skills under match-play conditions. Modified versions of adult soccer, which enable progressive development of individual and team skills, should be considered general learning activities. Expertise in the 11-a-side version is the final goal. The coaching staff has to identify and decide the most suitable time to introduce the youth player to a standard soccer context. At present no evidence addresses the most successful pedagogical procedure to obtain stable and satisfying results in this regard. Successful match play comes from thorough game understanding, adequate physical fitness and proper technical and tactical skill. A useful venture could be to develop a communicative code among players to prompt the effective application of game strategies. Guidelines in developing this communicative tool may be of great interest in the development of game understanding.

Although game tactics and match strategies are often designed and set by the coach, allowing youth players the freedom to participate or decide on these may be the best way to develop a thorough understanding of the tactical demands of the game.

The physiological demands of youth soccer are generally similar to those reported for adult soccer. Differences are mainly observed in the domain of match activities. In general, when the 11-a-side game is considered, young soccer players cover proportionally less distance in the selected arbitrary match activities. The most remarkable differences are observed in the high-intensity categories. But differences in the energy cost of performing each activity and in absolute performance make the relative demands (i.e., percentage of the individual maximum) quite similar. Despite the popularity of youth soccer, the interest shown by researchers in the physiological and motion demands of the youth game is proportionally limited, and further research is certainly required.

Technological advancements in the last decade enabled the development of reasonably valid and precise match-analysis systems that can be implemented during competitive and training games. We examined the precision of four popular match-analysis systems in a population of young elite-level soccer players. The results of this research showed that a multi-camera semiautomated, individual player video-camera tracking and GPS (one and five cycles per second) systems were able to profile match activities during a competitive game. But large differences between systems were present in the determination of the absolute distances covered, meaning that any comparisons of results between different match-analysis systems should be done with caution (Randers et al. 2010). Match activities described in terms of space coverage in arbitrary speed categories is often related to individual fitness in players of different competitive levels, irrespective of age or sex. Descriptive and experimental evidence strongly supports the use of match-analysis systems to track the external load imposed on players during weekly training sessions. These systems may be particularly interesting when proposing ball drills, because player involvement may significantly vary among players.

The use of GPS systems of suitable sampling frequency (five cycles per second or higher), which are becoming more affordable and now allow the viewing of player movement patterns in real time, may be a suitable option for soccer academies interested in providing scientific coaching to their developing players.

In this regard, the variable to be considered to profile the external load of the players is of utmost importance. Distance covered in selected speed categories is often used as a cue of the external load imposed on players during training and matches. Although this approach provides meaningful information relating to fatigue development, it does not provide a detailed figure of match-play kinematic performance because accelerations and decelerations are not considered. Using triaxial accelerometers at an operational frequency of 100 cycles per second, often coupled with portable GPS systems, attempts have been made to provide quantitative information on the external load experienced by players. But reporting the acceleration-profile analysis misses the velocity aspect of playing that contributes to the external load when acceleration is low.

An approach accounting for the instantaneous variations in acceleration and speed has been suggested. The proposed method estimated the energy expenditure of playing activities, identified as a player's metabolic power, from the product of instantaneous speed and the magnitude of accelerations. The latter are converted into estimated energy cost assuming acceleration as corresponding to running uphill at constant speed. The metabolic power approach enables a logically valid estimation of a player's individual energy expenditure during the game, equating the external load of activities to the interplay between instantaneous acceleration and deceleration (Osgnach et al. 2010). Despite the interest of this novel approach, the energy cost assumptions (i.e., constant uphill running), the population used for developing the estimation equation and the noise of acceleration in real-life activities (i.e., actual match play) suggest that further investigation is needed to establish method validity. Furthermore, the outcome variable expressed as relative power (watt per kilogram) does not provide a clear measure of the internal load, given the lack of a gold standard test to set the individual maximal power and the global nature of the measurement. Therefore, this metabolic power approach makes identification of the underpinning energetic pathway difficult, because a given power output may be potentially determined by different metabolic pathways. Additionally, the individual responses to similar energetic production may have a distinct effect on a player's physiological system (internal load).

The total distance covered during a competitive youth soccer game (11v11, age 12 to 15 years) ranges between 6 and 6.5 kilometres for an average duration of 30 minutes per half. As in adult soccer, total distance covered in the second half decreases significantly (by 3.8 per cent) in U15 international-level youth soccer players. A conservation of activities performed at high intensity (speed greater than 13 kilometres per hour) is observed irrespective of player age group. The influence of intermittent high-intensity endurance on match performance has been reported in youth soccer, suggesting that aerobic training is important even at the youth level. Studying elite-level youth soccer players (U13 to U18), Mendez-Villanueva et al. (2013) reported age and playing-role dependent demands of actual match play. This study showed that except for strikers, superior aerobic fitness was unlikely to affect distance covered during a match, but this quality was associated with reduced individual running demand during the game. These authors suggested that aerobic fitness was related to a reduction in individual demands during the game. Note that these results may be affected by differences in training status, age of the players and competitive level of the opponents.

A study of highly trained young soccer players examined whether substantial changes in either maximal sprinting speed or maximal aerobic speed (as inferred from peak incremental test speed) can affect repeated high-intensity running during games. Using a GPS for time-motion analysis during international club games, the authors found that changes in repeated sprint activity during games do not necessarily match changes in physical fitness. Game tactical and strategic requirements were likely to modulate players' on-field activity patterns independently (at least partially) of their physical capacities (Buchheit et al. 2013). Another study assessed the effect of maximal sprinting speed on the peak speed attained during friendly international club-level matches, using the same global positioning technology. The authors found that faster players reached higher absolute peak running speeds in games than did their slower counterparts regardless of playing position. None of the players reached their maximal sprinting speed during the matches, and the fastest players attained a lower percentage of their maximal sprinting speed. Using these preliminary results, the authors suggested that maximal sprinting speed can affect what a player can do in actual playing conditions and that playing position influences the expression of sprinting speed during match play (Mendez-Villanueva et al. 2011). These results, however, may have been severely influenced by the competitive level of the matches considered (i.e., player motivation and level of the opposition).

Despite the financial and practical difficulties associated with match performance and time-motion analysis, this method is certainly a critical aspect for the development of youth players into elite-level adult players. In this regard, ball drill training load should be accurately monitored with state-of-the-art technology or any other means within reach of club staff to track the individual training profiles of youth players. For example, affordable video analysis systems coupled with interactive software packages developed to this aim can be an alternative option to the more expensive GPS. Appointing a training load analyst may be required to overcome the usual practical problems encountered in providing prompt feedback to the coaching staff to guide the daily training process based on the training load variables monitored.

Understanding Performance-Determining Factors

Understanding the factors that contribute to or limit performance in soccer is not an easy task. A possible reason for the apparent paucity of soccer-related research is that this type of research is difficult to conduct. The first difficulty that sport scientists face is that the physiological determinants of soccer performance are not clearly understood in comparison with most individual sports involving various types of locomotion, such as running, swimming, cycling, rowing or various modes of jumping, throwing and lifting. Nonetheless, identifying physiological qualities is a sine qua non among other attributes needed by athletes to be competitive in the soccer field.

Second, performance itself is a difficult concept to define in the world of soccer. What is performance in a sport like soccer? Scoring more goals? Maintaining a higher playing tempo than the opposition for the duration of a match? Being able to execute skills and display qualities under the intense pressures of competition? Sport scientists are used to dealing with precise, quantifiable, numerical data, and although these can be indicators of an athlete's potential to perform, actual performance within a soccer framework is a relatively abstract concept.

Tracking performance attributes in selected fitness tests relevant to soccer and comparing results within and across competitive levels may be a viable method to categorize the physical requirements of the game. This cross-sectional approach, when applied with specific cohorts of players, could provide useful information to guide talent selection and development. We used such a cross-sectional approach to assess the fitness determinants of success in men's and women's soccer by comparing performances of players of different competitive levels and sexes in a battery of tests assessing soccer-specific intermittent endurance, sprint ability, jumping, ability to quickly change direction and ball dribbling. Our results showed that in postadolescent soccer, players' intermittent high-intensity endurance (i.e., Yo-Yo Intermittent Recovery Test) and ability to change direction (i.e., agility) were able to discriminate between competitive levels in both male and female players (Mujika et al. 2009a). These results are in line with those reported by Vaeyens et al. (2006) in a semilongitudinal study performed across the 12- to 16-year-old span in elite and subelite male soccer players. This study showed that aerobic fitness discriminated between competitive levels only in U15 and U16 players, whereas neuromuscular performance (i.e., sprinting, jumping performance) was a differentiating factor at the U13 and U14 stage. At any time young elite-level soccer players were superior in strength,

Agility and soccer-specific intermittent endurance are major factors that stress sex and age differences among soccer players. Training and talent identification should focus on these fitness traits in postadolescent players of both sexes.

flexibility, speed, aerobic endurance, anaerobic capacity and technical skills. These findings support the dynamic nature of talent development in soccer, suggesting the need to change performance-determining parameters and criteria in a long-term context.

Soccer is a multisprint sport, and the ability to repeat sprints with minimal recovery time and performance decrement is relevant for soccer match play. Repeated sprint ability has been shown to discriminate between competitive levels in young soccer players and to be related to their maturation status. We investigated the age-related differences in repeated sprint ability and blood lactate responses in 134 youth soccer players (Mujika et al. 2009b). Players from the development programme of Athletic Club Bilbao were grouped according to their respective under-age team (U11 to U18). The players performed a repeated sprint ability test consisting of six 30-metre sprints with 30 seconds total for each sprint and remaining recover time. The test variables were total time, per cent sprint decrement and posttest peak lactate concentration. Total time to perform the six sprints improved from the U11 to U15 age groups, whereas no further significant improvements were evident from U15 to U18. No significant differences in per cent sprint decrement were reported among groups. Posttest peak blood lactate increased from one age group to the next but remained constant when adjusted for age-related difference in body mass. Peak lactate concentration was moderately correlated with sprint time. These results suggest that performance in repeated sprint ability improves during maturation of highly trained youth soccer players, although a plateau occurs from 15 years of age. These age-related differences correlate strongly with differences in physical characteristics and glycolytic potential of the players. In contrast to expectations based on previous suggestions, per cent sprint decrement during repeated sprints did not deteriorate with age, and peak blood lactate relative to body mass was similar among age groups, indicating that well-trained preadolescent and adolescent soccer players possess well-developed fatigue resistance and glycolytic potential.

The sport science literature on repeated sprint ability specific to field-based team sports has increased considerably in recent years. This attention has come from researchers, trainers and practitioners interested in quantifying this aspect of fitness for team sports. We now know that repeated sprint ability improves substantially with age from U11 to U15 age groups and that a plateau occurs from the U15 to U18 age groups. We also assessed the relationships between repeated sprint ability and other fundamental

Because of these findings, we recommend that coaches in junior soccer pre-scribe physical training that accounts for variations in short-term disruptions or impairment of physical performance during this developmental period. Soccer academies should consistently carry out testing to assess player evolution over time and identify factors that could determine individual player performance at various stages of development.

fitness qualities of agility, explosive leg power and aerobic conditioning in a cohort of highly trained youth soccer players in U11 to U18 (Spencer et al. 2011). Our findings showed that repeated sprint ability associates differently with other fundamental fitness tests throughout the teenage years in highly trained soccer players, although stabilization of these relationships occurs by the age of 18 years. Indeed, the relationships of repeated sprint ability with the assorted fitness tests varied considerably between the age groups, especially for agility and explosive leg power, whereas the relationships of repeated sprint ability with acceleration and aerobic conditioning were less variable with age.

Quantifying Training Loads to Ensure Progression

A major difficulty associated with player development and soccer research is quantification of training. This aspect of training ensures progression in the development process. It is also key for high-quality sport science research, particularly to assess the influence of training loads on physiological responses, adaptations and the relationships between these measures and performance capabilities. Generally, soccer training is characterized by a diverse range of training activities, often under highly variable environmental conditions. Coaching staff and sport scientists also need to consider the degree of individual variability in responses and adaptations to training. All these issues complicate the integration of training variables into quantifiable units.

Several methods have been used to assess the physiological load imposed on soccer players during training activities and match play, such as heart rate, blood lactate concentration, muscle metabolites and rating of perceived exertion. The effect of various training methods and manipulation of training variables such as type of exercise, pitch dimension and coach encouragement have also been addressed. Although all these methods have their pros and cons, clubs and academies somehow need to address the issue of training quantification. Without proper quantification of the training load, relating the work done by the players to the performance outcome is not possible.

Quantification of training is key not only for the evaluation of training effects but also for training systematization and prescription.

The principle of training progression requires a unified training plan for the entire career of a developing soccer player. Academies should control the training load imposed on their players from season to season to ensure progression. In this respect, getting input from an expert in training design to guide the coaches could be advised. This approach should ensure that the training content in terms of fitness development, technical skill acquisition and tactical awareness of a U16 player are never less demanding than they were when the same player was in the U14 category simply because of the different level of demand of different coaches within the academy structure.

Optimising Training Time Through Relative Individualization

The principle of training individualization dictates that training benefits are more likely to be optimized when training programmes reflect individual athlete's needs and capacities, but this principle is often neglected in team sport settings. Individualized training in a youth elite soccer setting might be an effective strategy to enhance individual player performance, as we showed in a case study investigation of a 16-year old striker from Athletic Club Bilbao's youth development academy. His coach pointed out that for several months the player's performance during training and matches had dropped below expected levels (insufficient high-intensity activity and lack of goal scoring), and he often cramped during matches. Medical, nutritional and psychological assessments ruled out illness and nutritional, psychological and social-behaviour disorders. Retrospective analysis of the player's growth and fitness testing data indicated that power and speed had a positive evolution, but a clear involution was identified in markers of aerobic power. Performance on the Yo-Yo Intermittent Recovery Test Level 1 was also well below expectations. A seven-week individual training programme targeting aerobic power and high lactate production was prescribed for the player. Specific sessions were performed twice a week for the first three weeks and once a week thereafter during the initial 30 to 35 minutes of team training time. On completion of each individual session, the player joined his teammates for the remainder of the training time. Each session was directly supervised by a coach. The intervention represented just 9.5 per cent of the player's total training time.

The programme contributed to a 32 per cent improvement in match fitness, assessed by means of the Yo-Yo Intermittent Recovery Test Level 1. The conclusion was that individualized training adapted to the specific needs of each player could contribute to optimizing player development and performance in an elite youth soccer academy setting.

Although this type of one-on-one training approach is impossible to implement for all players of a club's academy, alternatives can be explored. Based on this preliminary investigation, it was decided that all players U15 and older could benefit from an individualized aerobic power training programme. Using the data obtained from sprint and intermittent endurance tests carried out on all academy players, we determined individual training speeds for weekly 30-minute aerobic power training sessions. Players were grouped by similar running speeds to facilitate implementation. Despite its modest time requirement, this intervention contributed to spectacular improvements in all players' Yo-Yo Intermittent Recovery Test performance and it translated directly to match performance in the form of reduced fatigue towards the end of the game. This observation was in agreement with the relationship identified between performance in the Yo-Yo Intermittent Recovery Test and high-intensity running distance during the final 15 minutes of match play (Mohr et al. 2010).

Keeping Players Free of Injury

Elite professional soccer is characterized by its long competitive periods within and between national and international competitions. For instance, a player from any of the major European soccer clubs usually competes domestically (league and cup) and internationally (Champions League or Europa League) from mid-August to mid-May or June. Every other year club competition is immediately followed by national team competition—continental championship or World Cup. This scheduling results in some elite-level players taking part in more than 60 matches during the season. A similar trend for frequent competition (age group league, local, national and international tournaments, and so on) is becoming the norm in the youth ranks. The relatively high risk of injury associated with soccer training and competition is a factor adding to the difficulties of accumulating sufficient practice time to develop the natural talent that players may have. Players who are injured may be more prone to drop out, and the rate of improvement of injured players stops because of a lack of training and a lessened opportunity to move on through the academy ranks.

Preventing injury is critical for youth players because minor injuries increase the risk of more severe injuries and because the best predictor of an injury is a history of having a particular injury. In recent years, injury prevention programmes have been developed, and many of them have been proved to reduce the incidence of soccer-related noncontact injuries significantly.

Injury prevention should not be an option in youth soccer, but an integral part of every training session in every training programme.

A few years ago, FIFA's Medical and Research Centre (F-MARC) developed a 10-exercise warm-up programme intended to prevent injuries and focus on core stabilization, eccentric training of thigh muscles, proprioceptive training, dynamic stabilization and plyometrics. As soon as the programme became available, we did a preliminary study at Athletic Club Bilbao, where we applied it for four months to the U13 and U14 teams. We then retrospectively compared the number of injuries and their severity (in terms of days of training and competition missed by the players) during that period with the injury records of the same period of the previous three seasons in players of those two age groups. Although it was just a preliminary retrospective study, the results were impressive. We observed a 47 per cent reduction in the number of injuries and a 73 per cent reduction in the number of missed days of training and competition. Of course, these results led us to implement the programme on all the teams at the academy. Subsequent prospective studies carried out by other investigators on large cohorts of players have confirmed the effectiveness of this and other injury prevention programmes (Soligard et al. 2008).

Implementing injury prevention programmes should be a priority for soccer academies and player development programmes. A healthy player is a player who can train and develop, as well as contribute to his or her own tactical development and that of teammates. The time dedicated to injury prevention should be considered an integral part of training time, not time taken away from training.

Conclusion

In soccer, identifying, developing and nurturing talented players have become increasingly important. The spiralling cost of purchasing players on the transfer market has reinforced the need for professional soccer clubs to put appropriate talent identification and development structures into place. Identifying soccer potential at an early age ensures that players receive specialist coaching to accelerate the talent development process. With the need to develop young talented players, soccer scientists need to identify the key physiological, biomechanical and psychological characteristics that are required for elite performance.

The following key take-home messages should be considered for soccer science practitioners involved in the talent identification process:

- The focus of talent identification is to identify players with long-term potential.
- The role of maturation will have a significant influence on current performance, but not necessarily long-term potential.
- Players should not be deselected because of their current size.

- Physical, physiological, psychological and sociological attributes as well as technical abilities, either alone or in combination, should be considered.
- Education of practitioners, players and parents concerning the objectives of talent identification is critical.
- The process of talent identification is driven by science and years of accumulated knowledge.

Talent identification in soccer should not be formulaic. A fundamental oversight of many practitioners is to view formulaic frameworks as paths to success. Success in soccer is multifactorial and too complex to follow any single formula. Therefore, soccer science practitioners should not be too prescriptive. Talent, innate abilities and chance are recognized as significant elements to sporting achievement. The role of talent identification and development is critical in optimizing these elements.

CHAPTER 4

Development of the Young Soccer Player

—Viswanath B. Unnithan and John Iga

Soccer clubs, whether they are at the elite end of the spectrum or are community-based programmes, want to develop a team identity. Perhaps the best way to do this is to have a core of young players who have emerged from the club's own youth-development initiatives. These players tend to have greater affinity with the club and understand the club ethos from an early age. To achieve this goal, monitoring the development of the young soccer player is important from a physical, technical and tactical perspective.

At an elite level, only a limited time is available for youth players to demonstrate their playing potential before decisions are made to retain or release them. Identifying the key physiological components for success in soccer becomes important for coaches and practitioners. Also, only a finite number of training sessions are available for the elite youth soccer player in any given training cycle. Therefore, quantifying the rhythm and tempo of every training session is important to ensure that the training intensity is synchronous with that of the match-play intensity and that the quality of each training session is optimized.

Elite-level youth soccer players constitute a minuscule proportion of children and adolescents engaged in soccer. Consequently, for players who engage in soccer at lower levels, the aim is to create an environment that maximizes the enjoyment for the participants. Gaining an understanding of the factors that influence the development of young soccer players benefits coaches at both the elite and nonelite levels.

Three major areas are reviewed in this chapter. Although most of the research information is drawn from evidence relating to the elite youth soccer player, the potential applications for other levels of youth soccer is stated. Three areas are covered:

- Growth and maturation of the youth soccer player
- Movement patterns and physiological demands of match play in elite youth soccer
- Physiological components of success for the youth soccer player

Glossary of Key Terms

Growth is the measurable change in size, physique, body composition and various body systems.

Maturation is the progress towards a mature state. Maturation itself can vary in the timing and the rate of progress towards the mature state.

Chronological age is the age of the child with respect to his or her birth date (years).

Biological age is a person's maturation status.

Growth and Maturation of the Elite Youth Soccer Player

Young soccer players who are performing training practices or playing in competitive matches can appear, at times, limited in their physical and technical performance. The question for every coach is whether the performance is a result of fundamental limitations in the soccer-specific skill set of the player or whether the person is a late-maturing player, performing well for his or her current stage of development. Understanding the basic concepts of growth and maturation and the way in which those measurements can be applied in soccer settings can help address this question.

It is worth considering the effect that biological maturation can have on motor performance when evaluating the ability of a player to execute the high level of technical skill required in elite youth soccer. Limited evidence suggests that delays or regressions in sensorimotor function relative to the adolescent growth spurt could potentially contribute to athletic awkwardness, which is sometimes noted at this crucial developmental stage for the elite youth soccer player (Quatman-Yates et al. 2012). Current evidence suggests that neurocognitive processing capacity, neuromuscular control and coordination and regulation of postural control are not fully developed at the initiation of the growth spurt (Largo, Fischer and Rousson 2003). Simple motor control (controlling the ball, passing and shooting) tasks therefore can be more challenging during the adolescent growth spurt.

Also, measuring growth and maturation may help in identifying the optimal time to train soccer-specific attributes in youth soccer players. Understanding the process of growth is also essential for understanding the developmental changes that occur in the physiology of the young athlete, because developmental changes in body systems can both inhibit and enhance the changes that occur with training. Being able to separate one from the other is important in determining the efficacy of training interventions in young athletes.

The growth and maturation of the young soccer player is separated into three main age ranges:

- 6 through 11 years (considered the foundation phase in soccer)
- 12 through 15 years (development phase)
- 16 through 19 years (performance phase)

The foundation phase is characterized by some maturity-related size differences but little physiological differentiation in performance capacity. The development phase is associated with large, maturity-related variations in body size that are commensurate with individual differences in the specific physiological attributes required for successful soccer performance. The catch-up growth of late-maturing individuals occurs during the performance phase and reduces the amount of maturity-associated variation in size and physical performance. Individualized training programmes can be initiated at this time to enhance particular physiological determinants of soccer performance. As is discussed later, various methods can be used to assess maturity, but when using skeletal age as the main criterion, male soccer players through childhood (up to 12 years) tend to be on time in terms of their biological development. From 13 to 15 years of age, more early maturing and fewer late-maturing boys tend to predominate in any group of young soccer players (Malina 2011).

Methods of Estimating Biological Maturity

Maturation is a process, and maturity is a state (Malina, Bouchard and Bar-Or 2004). Individuals vary in their level of maturity (maturity status) at any given chronological age, in timing (when the maturation process occurs) and in tempo (rate of maturation). As previously stated, the tempo of biological maturation does not proceed in time with a child's chronological age. Some are biologically advanced for their chronological age (early maturers), some are on time, and some lag behind their chronological age (late maturers).

The differences in the rate of maturation can influence motor performance (Rowland 2011) and ultimately soccer performance. The most commonly used indicators of maturity are

- maturation of the skeleton,
- somatic maturation and
- sexual maturation.

The evaluation of skeletal maturation has the highest level of precision but is also the most expensive to conduct. Evaluating somatic maturation is relatively inexpensive and has a reasonable level of precision associated with its usage. Because assessments of sexual maturity have limited utility outside the realms of research and clinical settings and because the procedures involved with these methods are quite invasive in nature, only indicators of skeletal and somatic maturity will be discussed.

Skeletal Maturity

The evaluation of skeletal maturity is recognized as the best method for assessing biological maturity states. It is an ideal marker of maturity because its maturation spans the entire growth period.

A single skeletal age (SA) measurement in isolation has limited usefulness, but used in conjunction with a chronological age measurement, it has value in identifying early versus late biological maturity states.

The maturation of the skeleton can be tracked relatively easily through radiographs or X-rays. The bones of the left hand and wrist provide the primary basis for assessing skeletal maturity in the growing child and adolescent. The rationale for selecting this part of the body is that the skeletal maturational processes that occur in this location are reflective of the rest of the skeleton. Exposure to radiation is minimal, less than natural background radiation. Changes in each bone in the hand and wrist area with growth are uniform, and these form the basis for assessing skeletal maturity (Malina 2011).

Other methods can be used for estimating skeletal age, but their validity and utility can be challenged. For example, ultrasound assessment has been demonstrated to overestimate SA in late-maturing individuals and underestimate SA in early-maturing individuals, leading to the conclusion that ultrasound should not be considered a valid alternative to radiographic images (Malina et al. 2010). Overall, however, SA is a sound marker of biological maturity. These techniques can be applied throughout the maturation period, the estimates are both reliable and precise, and SA reflects the maturation of an important biological system. The disadvantages are exposure to low-level radiation and the need for specific training and quality control checks to evaluate the reliability of the techniques (Malina 2011).

Somatic Maturity

Directly assessing maturity status by body (somatic) measurement is not possible because body size is not an indicator of maturity. Indirectly, however, maturity indicators can be identified from body dimensions, particularly stature. If longitudinal stature data are available, then the point at which an inflection occurs in the growth curve marks the adolescent growth spurt. This information can also be used to derive indicators of maturity such as the age at the onset of the growth spurt and the age at the maximal rate of growth during the spurt (age at peak height velocity, or PHV). Furthermore, if adult stature is estimated, then percentage of adult size at different ages can be used as a maturity indicator. In males, acceleration of growth begins at 10 to 11 years, peaks at 14 years and stops at 18 years of age. In females, acceleration of growth begins at 9.5 years, peaks at 12 years, and stops at 15 years of age.

Consequently, with an understanding of the tempo of growth, plotting a graph of stature versus chronological age provides further markers of somatic maturity. The take-off point (initiation of the growth spurt) and the PHV (maximum rate of growth during the spurt) both give an indicator of somatic maturity (Malina, Bouchard and Bar-Or 2004). As previously stated, age at peak height velocity reflects the timing of a maturation event, and the velocity in growth provides an indication of tempo. Age at PHV is a useful somatic maturity indicator, but the problem is that it requires longitudinal data that span adolescence.

For the data to be meaningful, the values should really span from 8 to 10 years of age up to 16 to 18 years of age. Peak height velocity can also be used as a reference point against which changes in physiological measurements such as strength and power can be compared. Further information on this issue can be found in the section 'Physical Preparation of Youth Soccer Players'.

Another measure of somatic maturity is the calculation of per cent of adult height. To use per cent adult stature as a surrogate of somatic maturity, an estimate of final adult height is required. One method that was used to obtain this measurement was developed by Sherar et al. (2005). Adolescents who are closer to their adult height compared with individuals of similar chronological age are likely to be more advanced in their maturity status. Per cent of adult stature needs further validation work, but it could be valuable as part of an array of maturity measures.

Within elite youth soccer, predicting adult stature from somatic measures that do not require a measure of skeletal age could be valuable for the coach and sport scientist from a talent identification perspective. Beunen et al. (1997) developed a height prediction formula for boys between 12.5 and 16.5 years old that did not need an estimate of skeletal age. This method uses chronological age, stature, sitting height, and subscapular and triceps skinfold measurements to predict adult height. The standard error associated with this technique is 3.0 to 4.2 centimetres. Other prediction equations have also been developed to address this question. Mirwald et al. (2002) investi-gated the changing relationship between leg length and sitting height with growth as an indicator of maturity states. Through this relationship, these researchers developed a noninvasive, practical method of predicting years from the peak height velocity (maturity-offset value) for boys aged 8 to 16 years. This approach used a combination of anthropometric variables (height, sitting height and leg length), chronological age and the interaction terms.

The researchers were confident that years from PHV could be estimated within one year in 95 per cent of all predictions. These researchers did cau-tion that more validation work was required for this prediction equation and that care must be taken when obtaining the sitting height, because this variable was used throughout the formula. Consequently, any error in this measurement would magnify the error in the maturity-offset value.

An alternative approach was developed by Sherar et al. (2005), who extended the work of Mirwald et al. (2002). These researchers also used simple markers such as chronological age, height, weight, leg length and sitting height and a combination of interaction terms to determine a maturity-offset value. But they also derived an estimate of final adult height. This prediction of final adult height was derived from a series of maturity and sex-specific height velocity curves. These curves were derived for early, average and late maturers, and the area under the curve was used to develop reference values to predict adult height. Either technique (Sherar et al. 2005; Mirwald et al. 2002) could be used in a soccer setting to estimate maturity-offset values, but the Sherar et al. (2005) technique has the advantage of providing an accurate (within 5.35 centimetres 95 per cent of the time) estimate of final adult height.

Application of Growth and Maturation Measurements Within Youth Soccer

Differences in maturity may have important implications on the performance and training of youth soccer players. Children and adolescents advanced in maturity tend to be taller and heavier and perform better in strength- and power-related tasks compared with their later maturing counterparts (Malina, Bouchard and Bar-Or 2004).

These attributes may influence success in soccer and may sway the views of adults who make decisions on the fates of young players. Moreover, evidence suggests that the relative trainability of many of the physical fitness aspects associated with success in soccer is influenced by the maturity of the player. These concerns emphasize the importance of assessing the maturity of youth soccer players. Information on a player's maturity status may help ensure that appropriate conclusions are drawn about a person's current performance level and his or her potential to become an elite player and enable the correct matching of training to a player's biological development to optimize his or her long-term physiological development. The following sections outline the application of measurements of growth and maturity within youth soccer.

As previously described, individual variations occur in the timing and tempo of adolescent growth and development. These differences are usually most apparent at around midadolescence, typically between the ages of 12 to 15 years of age, where marked differences in biological development will occur within a group of boys of the same chronological age. This point is illustrated in figure 4.1 in which the hand and wrist radiographs of three boys selected to train in the talent development programme of a club in the English professional soccer league are shown. As can be seen, although

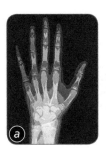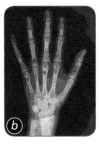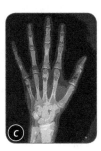

▶ **Figure 4.1** Hand and wrist radiographs of three boys affiliated with the talent development programme of a club in the English Premier League. The X-rays in this example have been interpreted according to the TW3 method.

Viswanath B. Unnithan and John Iga

the three boys are identical in chronological age, they differ markedly in biological maturity.

Despite their similar chronological ages, the boys differ markedly in biological maturity as indicated by their skeletal age and percentage of attained predicted adult stature. Player B appears to be developing on time because his skeletal age appears to approximate his chronological age. Player A may be classified as being delayed because his skeletal age is lower than his chronological age by more than one year, and player C may be said to be advanced in skeletal maturity because his skeletal age is greater than his chronological age by more than one year. Differences in skeletal age are also reflected in the attained percentage of adult stature; player C has attained a higher proportion of his estimated adult stature than his counterparts have.

To derive meaning, skeletal age should be considered in relation to an individual's chronological age; this can be achieved by comparing skeletal age with chronological age either as a division of skeletal age by chronological age or, as depicted in figure 4.1, as the difference between skeletal age and chronological age. This latter option is perhaps the most widely used method by researcher and practitioners. When relative skeletal age is determined as the difference between skeletal age and chronological age, a positive score is taken as indicating that skeletal age is in advance of chronological age, whereas a negative score indicates that skeletal age lags behind chronological age. Additionally, with this approach, individuals can be classified into contrasting maturity categories (on time, late or early) on the basis of the magnitude of the difference between skeletal age and chronological age (see figure 4.1).

The skeletal age determined by any of the three commonly used methods to interpret hand and wrist radiographs can also be used in equations to estimate, with a reasonable degree of certainty, a person's adult stature (Bayley and Pinneau 1952; Roche, Wainer and Thissen 1975; Tanner et al.

2001). In the presence of a valid estimate of final adult stature, the relative proportion of this value that a person has attained may be used as an indicator of somatic maturity, and the validity of this approach has been confirmed (Malina et al. 2005). In figure 4.1, the percentage of attained adult stature of three youth soccer player is shown; it can be seen that player C is closer to his predicted adult stature and is therefore advanced in somatic maturity compared with players A and B. Percentage of attained adult stature may be used to distinguish youngsters who are tall at a given chronological age because of genetic endowment from those who may be tall because they are advanced in maturity. Its application, however, in grouping soccer players for training or competition remains to be demonstrated. In figure 4.1, differences in skeletal age are also mirrored in the relative amount of estimated adult stature that the boys have already attained, highlighting how somatic and skeletal markers of maturation may be used to provide a more comprehensive appraisal of a young player's maturity.

If funding and technology are not available to make assessments of skeletal maturity, but longitudinal recordings of height (stature) are available, then the rate of growth can still be calculated. From these calculations, the onset and the magnitude of the adolescent growth spurt may be identified and used to indicate the somatic maturity of an individual. To allow the identification of these biological landmarks, recordings of stature should ideally be made at least four times per year over several years. Standard measuring procedures, such as those endorsed by the International Society for the Advancement of Kinanthropometry (ISAK) should be followed when making these recordings (Marfell-Jones et al. 2006). Ideally, assessments should be made by the same person and at an identical time of the day (preferably early in the morning) to control for errors attributable to individual differences in the measurement technique and time of day effects on the recordings. Table 4.1 shows a youth soccer player's stature measurements, determined quarterly, over a two-and-half-year period. As can be seen, although the player in this example has grown 15.4 centimetres over this period, his rate of growth indicates that he is in fact growing at a progressively slower rate. Although these data may be taken as providing evidence that the player has gone through his rapid growth spurt, this conclusion cannot be stated with certainty because sufficient longitudinal data are not available. This example serves to confirm the need for serial data, perhaps over a period of 8 to 10 years, with measurements commencing during late childhood so that the inflection and the peak in the growth curve can be identified and used to describe the onset and the extent of the growth spurt.

In an attempt to equate the competition environment and allow boys of different maturity status equal opportunities to demonstrate their potential, there is evidence that some tournament organizers have attempted to match boys of the same chronological age on the basis of their body size (Simmons and Paull 2001). Although individuals advanced in biological age tend to be

Table 4.1 Stature Recorded for a Youth Soccer Player (Player C) Quarterly Over a Two-and-a-Half-Year Period

	Chronological age (years)	Stature (cm)	Rate of growth (cm/quarter)
August	11.7	154.4	–
November	12.0	157.2	2.8
February	12.2	159.9	2.7
May	12.4	162.4	2.5
August	12.7	164.2	1.8
November	13.0	165.9	1.7
February	13.2	167.6	1.7
May	13.4	169.1	1.5
August	13.7	169.5	0.4
November	14.0	169.8	0.3
February	14.2	170.0	0.2

taller than their later maturing counterparts (Malina, Bouchard and Bar-Or 2004), this approach does not allow for individual variations in the timing and tempo of adolescent growth and development and is therefore limited in application. Moreover, differences in stature, in particular, at a given chronological age during adolescence may reflect genetic endowment as well as a range of socioeconomic factors such as ready access to health care and appropriate nutrition. Consequently, the use of measures of stature as a means of correcting against differences in maturity is not without question.

In situations in which the determination of skeletal age is not possible and sufficient longitudinal data are not available to allow the determination of the adolescent growth spurt, as may be the case if a player joins the talent development programme of a club during his early to midteens, predictive equations may be applied to estimate final adult stature. As previously discussed, if an estimate of adult stature is available, then the percentage of adult size attained may be used as an indicator of maturity. Although several equations have been proposed that do not require skeletal age to estimate final adult height (Beunen et al. 1997; Roche, Tyleshevski and Rogers 1983; Khamis and Roche 1994), the formulae described by Sherar et al. (2005) seems to be gaining popularity. Note that the formulae were derived from the growth data of nonathletic and predominantly white boys and girls living in North America and Belgium. Moreover, data suggest that during adolescence, boys of African and Asian ancestry, on average, tend to be in advance of youths of European descent in indicators of skeletal maturity (Ontell et al. 1996). Consequently, the application of these predictive equations generated from samples of nonathletic boys to youth soccer player from diverse ethnic backgrounds, who during mid- to late adolescence are typically characterized as being advanced in maturity, remains to be confirmed. Future research efforts may be directed towards validating these equations within youth soccer, particularly within boys and girls of various ethnicities.

A final important consideration, and one often neglected by practitioners, when applying predictive equations relates to the error associated with the predictive formulae. Note that all predictive equations carry a certain amount of error. These errors should be considered when drawing conclusions on the estimated adult stature of an individual. For example, the estimate of adult stature obtained from the formula published by Sherar and co-workers (2005) includes a margin of error of plus or minus 5.35 centimetres. Consequently, if a boy's adult stature was estimated to be 186.0 centimetres, when the errors associated with this equation are considered, he may be as tall as 191.4 centimetres or as short as 180.7 centimetres when he has finished growing.

Movement and Physiological Characteristics of Youth Soccer: An Evaluation of Match Play

Understanding the movement patterns and the physiological strain of youth soccer players during competitive match play is important because training sessions can then be tailored to meet the actual demands of match play (Buchheit et al. 2010b). Consequently, the following sections highlight the movement characteristics of competitive match play in youth soccer with respect to general movement patterns and position-specific characteristics and describe the physiological load associated with competitive match play in youth soccer. An in-depth discussion of the technology used to obtain time-motion data is beyond the scope of this section, but evidence shows that video-based coding underestimates both total distance covered and high-intensity running compared with global positioning systems (Randers et al. 2010).

When comparing the total distance covered in matches, there appears to be some agreement that elite youth soccer players at the U12 level can cover approximately 6,000 metres in two 30-minute halves (Castagna, D'Ottavio and Abt 2003; Harley et al. 2010). Also, unsurprisingly, with increasing age, the total distance covered (metres) increases (Buchheit et al. 2010b); when, these distances are adjusted by playing time (minutes), few differences are noted between age groups (table 4.2).

Total distance covered represents just one aspect of the movement pattern of the elite youth soccer player. During competitive match play, players cover ground at high (HID) and very-high intensities (VHID). When looking at the total absolute distance (metres) covered at these two intensities, U16 players cover a greater amount of territory compared to their U12 peers, but when adjusting the distances covered by the minutes played, few differences exist (table 4.2).

Table 4.2 Selected Time-Motion Characteristics of Youth Soccer Matches

Reference	Number of subjects	Age (years)	Format
Capranica et al. 2001	6	11	11 a side
Castagna, D'Ottavio and Abt 2003	12	11.8	11 a side
Harley et al. 2010	112	U12 up to U16	11 a side for all age groups

Time-motion data

Continuous running of less than 10 sec. occupied 64% of all running activities.
Total distance: 6,175 ± 318 m
U12 total distance: 5,967 ± 1,227 m
U16 total distance: 7,672 ± 2,578 m
U12 HID: 1,713 ± 371 m
U16 HID: 2,481 ± 1,044 m
U12 VHID: 662 ± 180 m
U16 VHID: 951 ± 479 m
U12 sprint distance: 174 ± 64 m
U16 sprint distance: 302 ± 184 m
When expressed related to match exposure (minutes played), many of the differences between age groups disappeared.

All values are mean ± SD. HID: high-intensity distance covered; VHID: very high-intensity distance covered.

A similar pattern emerged for sprint distances covered when comparing the U12 with the U16 cohorts (table 4.2). The implications of these findings are twofold. First, the greater absolute (metres) total distance covered by U16 compared with U12 cohorts could be a product of the greater match time that the older boys are exposed to. But it could be a result of the greater aerobic fitness of the older age group, resulting from a combination of maturation and training (Harley et al. 2010). The information regarding the total distance covered in metres can be obtained relatively easily using GPS systems that are widely available and used in soccer. This information is important when comparing individuals within the same squad. But if comparisons between age groups are needed, simply dividing the total distance covered by the number of minutes played by the player will make for a more realistic comparison between age groups.

Within current training regimens, repeated sprint activities are set at the high end of physiological demands. Evidence from match-play analysis seems to suggest that it may be better to focus on high-intensity repeated sprint work and speed agility drills rather than high-intensity and duration repeated sprint drills. Evidence from research that investigated repeated sprint sequences in U13 to U18 match play demonstrated that older players performed more repeated sprint sequences than younger players did; when age-specific, relative speed thresholds were calculated, the opposite was noted. Other interesting findings from this research were that the number of repeated sprints per sequence was low (2.7 plus or minus 0.3), the sprint duration was less than three seconds, and the percentage of repeated sprint sequences across all age cohorts was low (5 to 30 per cent). These data challenge the importance of repeated sprint activity as a physical component of age-group youth soccer. The limitations associated with these findings, however, were that it was not clear how elite the boys used in this study were and whether the tempo of match play that these boys played at was equivalent to that seen in European soccer leagues (Buchheit et al. 2010c).

Also, the various speed zones that the players operate in (high intensity, very high intensity) should be determined relative to the maximal age-specific velocity (Harley et al. 2010). This information can be obtained relatively easily by measuring the maximum sprint speed over a designated distance and using this information to create more age-appropriate speed zones. Valuable research studies (Capranica et al. 2001; Castagna et al. 2009) that have previously been conducted in the area of time-motion analyses in youth soccer have used fixed-speed categories. The potential limitation of this approach is the uncertainty of when players cross certain movement thresholds. Creating age-specific speed thresholds allows the speed of movement during a match to be expressed relative to the maximum running speed of the player.

Among elite youth soccer players, specialized match running patterns appear to suggest that these players have good tactical awareness of position-specific movements, even at a young age. Position-specific time-motion analyses within youth soccer research are limited because at younger age groups, less emphasis is placed on developing position specificity; this aspect gains greater significance within older age groups. The limited work in this area (Buchheit et al. 2010b) confirmed that a movement pattern seen in adult soccer is also seen in youth soccer. Irrespective of age and playing time, centre backs cover the lowest total distance and cover the least distance when conducting very high-intensity activities, and wide midfielders and strikers cover the largest distance when performing very high-intensity activities. A fitness consequence of these positional differences in running patterns may be seen in youth soccer players.

A coach who wants to improve the individual fitness level of a player could possibly alter the playing position of the youth player during training to change the physiological load on the player and enhance his or her fitness level.

Evidence is limited with regard to the role that maturity status may have on the movement patterns within youth soccer (Stroyer, Hansen and Klausen 2004). The evidence from this single study, which grouped players based on their pubertal status, found that elite players who were at the start of puberty performed more jumps within the 11-a-side, 30-minutes-per-half game format that was used in the study compared with their nonelite peers. This result could suggest that training or self-selection may have a key effect on developing jumping skills and power at the early pubertal stage. No other differences were found in movement characteristics (expressed as a percentage of total playing time) when comparing elite youth players who were at the beginning or end of puberty. Despite this lack of differences, more position-specific movement patterns emerged at the late pubertal stage. This finding suggests that by late puberty, the player has acquired a more mature tactical understanding of the role that he or she plays in the team and the demands of the various roles within the team start to diversify.

The evidence from studies performed in this area highlights the importance of being able to sustain a high level of cardiorespiratory endurance during youth soccer match play and suggests that training drills that mimic this type of physiological load would be valuable in the development of the young soccer player. But data are limited with regard to the physiological loading during competitive 11-a-side match play in youth soccer (Capranica et al. 2001). At the U12 level, well-trained young soccer players were found to have heart rates greater than 170 beats per minute for 88 per cent of the first half and 80 per cent of the second half. Similar heart rate findings were noted at the U15 level during 11-a-side match play, and a relative exercise intensity of approximately 86 per cent was seen during both the first and second half of matches (Castagna et al. 2009; Billows, Reilly and George 2005). Blood lactate levels also ranged from 3.1 to 8.1 millimoles per litre during an 11-a-side game in a group of 11-year-old soccer players (Castagna et al. 2009). No significant differences were noted in blood lactate levels between the first and second half of soccer matches in this same group of players.

The wide variation in lactate data is hard to interpret because only a small number of subjects participated in the study. The evidence is still unclear about whether children and adolescents generate low levels of lactate during exercise or they are particularly efficient in dealing with the buildup of this waste product during exercise. One training technique for the coach that could provide a way to combine tactical, technical and aerobic fitness gains is the use of small-sided games. A detailed review of this training modality is beyond the scope of this chapter, but a recent, excellent review paper by Hill-Haas et al. 2011 offers further information on this topic.

To summarize, these are the key training implications based on the demands of the game:

- Evidence from the literature suggests that elite U12 soccer players can cover 6,000 metres in two 30-minute halves. This distance increases with increasing age during match play. Consequently, the development of aerobic endurance appears to be an important component of any training programme for the youth soccer player.

- During competitive match play, youth soccer players of all ages perform significant bouts of high- and very high-intensity running. Therefore, developing this area through training will improve the capacity to sustain these high-intensity bouts.

- With increasing age, the youth soccer player has to perform more repeated sprint activities. Consequently, training should develop the components that can assist sprinting, such as strength; power is developed through gains in strength. Furthermore, agility training and flexibility training can also improve sprinting speed.

- With increasing age, position specificity becomes a key issue; consequently, training has to reflect this. With older age groups, individualized training needs to be considered to satisfy the physiological demands of the playing position and rectify any deficits in the physiological profile of the player.

Physical Preparation of Youth Soccer Players

The preceding sections have outlined the effect of growth and maturation on the youth soccer player and described the demands of match play for the child and adolescent soccer player. This final section provides specific evidence from the research with regard to the type of training that could be used to enhance soccer-specific fitness attributes for the youth soccer player.

The evidence suggests that, as in the adult game, the physical demands of youth soccer are multifaceted. Players need to have reasonably good endurance levels so that they can sustain work rates for a relatively long time and reproduce bouts of intense sprinting actions. Many activities in soccer are forceful and explosive (e.g., tackling, jumping, kicking, turning and accelerating); therefore, good levels of muscle strength and power are critical. Figure 4.2 illustrates the range of fitness aspects important for soccer. To train these fitness aspects so that a player is sufficiently conditioned to meet the demands of the game, a range of training techniques should be employed.

When designing training programmes for youths, recognize that there may be optimal periods during a young player's development when certain types of training may be more appropriate than others, making the training more complicated than the training of adults.

These so-called windows of opportunity seem to coincide with the onset of puberty in most children, but may occur earlier in others. Training adaptations before this transition point may be minimal.

This section is concerned with the physiological training of elite youth soccer players. Considerations of aerobic and speed endurance training are followed by a specific focus on speed and agility training. Strength and power training are reviewed before a brief review of training to improve flexibility is offered.

Soccer is essentially an endurance-based sport that includes random, sporadic episodes of intense physical activity. No research has considered the effects of soccer-specific training on the aerobic endurance of preadoles-

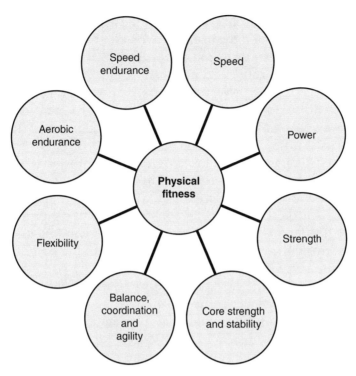

▶ **Figure 4.2**   Schematic that depicts the range of physical fitness attributes for soccer.

cent youths, but evidence from the extant literature has indicated a blunted response to training in preadolescent boys (Rowland 2004). In well-controlled experimental studies, researchers have typically reported gains of 0 to 10 per cent following aerobic endurance training with preadolescents (Rowland 2004). Although maturational factors can probably explain most of these attenuated responses, the lack of appropriate intensity and duration of training might have contributed to the blunted training response. The energy demands of exercise at a given speed of locomotion have been shown to increase when dribbling a ball (Reilly and Ball 1984). Consequently, exercising with a ball may be used to provide a more potent training stimulus for preadolescent boys. In older youth players, aerobic endurance training has resulted in a trend for improved physical performance during preseason matches (Impellizzeri et al. 2006). A variety of training methods including high-intensity interval training (McMillian et al. 2004), repeated sprint training (Bravo et al. 2008) and small-sided games (Impellizzeri et al. 2006; Hill-Haas et al. 2009) have been shown to improve the aerobic endurance in older youth soccer players. The use of small-sided games as a training modality is particularly noteworthy. This training method is highly efficient because in one exercise session, multiple objectives including physical conditioning and tactical and technical training may be realized (Hill-Haas et al. 2011).

Unpublished findings from the doctoral thesis of Dr Juan Luis Martinez Garcia (2004) demonstrated the usefulness of small-sided games as a way to improve the cardiorespiratory fitness of young (10 years old) Spanish soccer players. Three groups of children, matched for chronological and biological age, were selected for the project. One group performed ball work only in the form of small-sided game training. The second group trained in a more traditional way, with a combination of small-sided games and running. The third group was simply a group of recreationally active children. Heart rate (HR) measured during the 20-metre progressive shuttle test (PST) was used as the outcome measure to assess changes in cardiorespiratory fitness. All the boys were tested at the start of preseason, six weeks into the season and at the end of the season. The results demonstrated that the group that trained using small-sided games only had a significantly lower HR at a given running speed during the 20-metre PST compared with the other two groups. These preliminary findings suggest that small-sided game training was effective in improving the cardiorespiratory fitness of these young soccer players. Similar findings were noted in an older age group (13 years old).

Despite the importance attributed to repeated sprint-type actions in soccer, no research has considered the effects of repeated sprint training in preadolescent and adolescent youth soccer players, and the evidence from the broad literature is inconclusive (Rowland 2004). Nonetheless, the potential for development of the anaerobic energy system in preadolescent boys may be especially limited (Reilly, Bangsbo and Franks 2000). Postadolescent soccer players have demonstrated gains in repeat sprint performance tests following appropriate training. Buchheit et al. (2010a) examined the effects of two different training approaches on repeated sprint performance in adolescent boys (14.5 plus or minus 0.5 years). Participants performed repeated sprint training or explosive strength training once a week over a 10-week training period. Changes in explosive strength and repeated sprint ability were specific to the exercise modality. These data highlight the importance of matching the exercise stimulus to the desired outcome of training. Note that the participants in this study had no experience of explosive power or repeated sprint training. Although the frequency and intensity of exercise used in this study were sufficient to improve explosive power and repeated sprint performance in novice players, progressively higher exercise demands would have to be placed on those players to elicit further gains in performance.

Preadolescent, adolescent and postadolescent boys have all been shown to increase their sprinting performance with training. Venturelli, Bishop and Pettene (2008) demonstrated that coordination training consisting of a variety of ladder and skipping exercises was more effective in increasing sprint speed and ball-dribbling performance than linear speed training alone in preadolescent boys. These authors reasoned that the coordination training performed in their study may therefore provide a greater neural stimulus than liner sprint training does, resulting in better intramuscular and intermuscular coordination. In adolescent and postadolescent soccer players, explosive power (Buchheit et al. 2010a; Mujika, Santisteban and Castagna 2009), repeated sprint training and plyometric training (Meylan and Malatesta 2009) have all been demonstrated to improve sprinting performance.

The ability to change direction when running at pace (agility) has been shown to be the most discriminating physical attribute between elite and subelite youth soccer players (Reilly et al. 2000). Despite this acceptance, information concerning the optimal training of this fitness aspect in youths is limited (Meylan and Malatesta 2009). In adults, agility has been related to strength, power and running technique; straight sprint training has been shown to have no effect on agility performance (Sheppard and Young 2006). These findings provide insight about the trainable physical qualities that might result in improved ability to change direction when running at pace. Given the importance of this fitness attribute to successful performance, further research may consider the optimal training methods for the development of agility in youth soccer players. Note that in some boys awkwardness seems to occur at around adolescence, which is thought to be linked to disproportionate increases in leg length relative to trunk length. Only 10 to 30 per cent of adolescent boys appear to be affected, and the effects are transient (Beunen and Malina 1988).

As previously stated, explosive actions such as jumping, sprinting and changes of direction are essential to optimal performance not only in adults but also in youth soccer players. The power output during such activities is related to the strength of the muscles involved in the movements (Reilly, Bangsbo and Franks 2000). Increasing the magnitude of forces that these muscles can generate may improve performance in such activities. In the context of resistance training, the terms *strength* and *power* are often used synonymously, but the two terms relate to two different physiological properties of skeletal muscle; strength relates to the maximum amount of force that a muscle can generate when activated by voluntary command, whereas power refers to the ability to generate force quickly. Historically, children and youths have been discouraged from participating in resistance-training programmes because of fear over safety and concern regarding its effectiveness (Vrijen 1978). Research evidence suggests that when following a carefully planned and well-supervised resistance-training programme, children and youths can train safely and effectively to improve their muscular strength (Stratton et al. 2004). Indeed, prepubertal children have been demonstrated to experience comparable relative strength gains compared with postadolescent youths following resistance training (Pfeiffer and Francis 1986). Prepubertal strength gains are probably mediated by neural factors (increased activation of the muscle); postpuberty, with an appropriate training stimulus, youths can develop muscle hypertrophy while gaining strength with resistance training. In some situations, some players may need to build muscle mass (hypertrophy training). For example, players making the transition from youth to senior soccer may benefit from increasing muscle mass to cope with the greater physical demands of open-age soccer. Safety should always remain the major issue in resistance training in adolescent populations. Appropriate teaching, planning, supervision and equipment are fundamental to a safe and positive framework for the implementation of a resistance-training programme.

Good range of motion about the joints may help reduce the risk of injury and contribute to physical and technical performance. The rapid growth experienced during midadolescence may result in a transient loss in flexibility (Micheli 1983). Despite the intuitive appeal of this hypothesis, substantive evidence is lacking. Nonetheless, youth soccer players might be advised to undertake regular stretching exercises to facilitate good joint range of motion.

Practical Recommendations for Coaches

The schematic shown in figure 4.3 provides indicative examples of the type of fitness training for the foundation phase (prepuberty, 6 to 11 years), development phase (pubertal, U12–U13), development phase (pubertal, U14–U15), performance phase (postpubertal, U16–U17) and the transitional phase (postpubertal, U18–U19) of the youth soccer player.

In U12 and U13, the power, strength and speed development takes the form of developing the fundamentals in those areas (e.g., working on the mechanics of running). For U14 and U15, the caveat is that the more biologically mature individuals can have enhanced, individualized training in speed, power and strength. At the U16 and U17 stage, programmes for

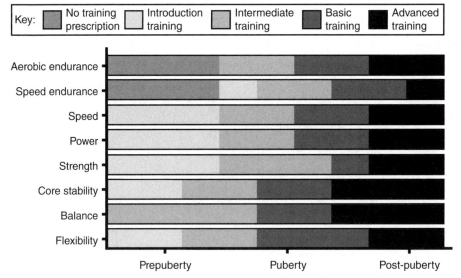

▶ **Figure 4.3** Physiological development strategy for youth soccer players.

Adapted from J. Iga, B. Durst, W. Gregson, M. Portas, and T. Reilly, 2006, Physiological development strategy for youth football players, UEFA, http://coach.xnet.uefa.com.

the development of strength, power and speed can be initiated based on the individual needs of each player. At U18 and U19, individualized programmes can be developed for strength, power, speed, core strength and flexibility to enhance soccer-specific physiological attributes. Agility and speed training can be integrated into soccer-specific drills.

Conclusion

The large individual variation in growth and maturation has a significant effect on both performance (time-motion characteristics) and training. Consequently, accurately measuring the maturity status and the predicted, final adult stature of the youth soccer player can provide information that will help to optimize the training and playing environment for the young player. But practitioners must be aware that caution must still be used when using these predictive formulae of final adult stature.

Time-motion analyses and evaluations of physiological loading during competitive match play in youth soccer are labour intensive but worth doing because they will provide a template on which age-specific training can be developed.

Growth and maturation influence all aspects of soccer-specific fitness and the capacity of these physical characteristics to respond to training.

CHAPTER 5

Skill Acquisition and Learning Through Practice and Other Activities

—Paul R. Ford

The development of expert performance in youth players and the further improvement of it in adult players are the primary goals of coaches, support staff and administrators. Many factors contribute to the development and improvement of expert performance in players, most of which are detailed in this book. One of the key factors is the acquisition of skill in players and the role of skill during performance in the sport. Soccer activities, such as practice, lead to skill acquisition, and through soccer activities, such as match play, expert performance in the sport is observed. Most youth and adult players experience soccer mainly through formal, structured, coach-led activities. Those activities are *practice*, in which the intention is to improve performance, and *competition*, in which the intention is to win. In a few countries, such as Brazil, child soccer players experience the sport mainly through informal and participant-led *play* activity, in which the intention is to have fun and enjoyment (Ford et al. 2012).

In this chapter, evidence-based principles derived from contemporary research examining expert performance and skill acquisition are explained in relation to the soccer activities that players engage in across their lives. Practical examples are given throughout the chapter to show how the principles apply. Readers interested in the finer details of the scientific studies and hypotheses that these principles are derived from are directed to the reference section for further information. In the first section of the chapter, expert performance by outfield players during the primary soccer activity of competition or match play is reviewed. In the second section, practice activity is addressed, and the effects of different types of practice on skill acquisition for match play are discussed. In the third section, the coaching behaviours of instruction and feedback are reviewed to show how they affect skill acquisition for match play. In the fourth section, a review of the intentions underlying the various soccer activities is provided, along with discussion of how they can be manipulated to create optimal soccer activity for players across their life spans. In the final section, some of the other activities that youth players engage in are reviewed, including warming up and watching the game. For the purposes of this chapter, children are defined as being aged 5 to 12 years, adolescents are defined as being aged 13 to 18 years, and adults are 18 years of age and older.

Formal Soccer Activities

Players acquire skill and demonstrate performance through engagement in soccer activities, such as practice and match play. In this section, skill acquisition and performance in formal soccer activities are explained using evidence-based principles derived from modern research. In the first subsection, expert performance by outfield players during competition or match play is reviewed. Expert performance by players in match play involves effective decision making to select and execute successful technical and movement skills in any given situation. The underlying mechanisms of effective decision making include visual search or scanning, recognition, tactical knowledge and neurological processes. In the second subsection, various types of practice activities are reviewed to show their effect on skill acquisition for match play. Practice led by coaches usually involves drills and game-based activities, which have a differential effect on skill acquisition. The final subsection reviews various instructional methods and their effect on skill acquisition.

Match Play

Most observers of the game have an opinion about what constitutes expert performance by players in soccer match play. Even casual observers of the game recognize that expert performance during a soccer match consists of players successfully executing technical skills with the ball, such as passing, dribbling, controlling, heading and shooting. Players execute other successful movements with and without the ball, such as running, walking, jumping and changing direction. Scientists use the term *motor skills* to describe these technical and movement skills. Many observers know that expert performance in soccer consists of more than just the successful execution of motor skills. They may be aware that it consists of players executing an appropriate and successful motor skill at the correct moment in any given situation that the players find themselves in. The term *decision making* is used to describe this process of selecting and executing appropriate motor skills in a situation. Colloquial terms are used in soccer to describe the processes that lead to successful decision making, including players having the ability to 'read the game', having 'vision', or having 'insight'. Scientists use the term *perceptual-cognitive skills* to describe decision making and the processes that lead to it. The following paragraphs contain a brief review of this science, which will provide a clear and evidence-based definition of expert performance by players during match play.

Perceptual-cognitive skills are involved in what is colloquially called "reading the game", or what scientists may term *situation assessment* (Williams & Ford 2013). These skills include visual search strategy, recognition, assessing options, and anticipation. Researchers (e.g., Roca et al. 2013) have shown that expert players during a match use their visual systems in a quantitatively different manner in comparison with lesser-skilled players. During a match, the visual search strategy of expert players usually involves a greater frequency of fixations to key locations around the pitch when compared with lesser-skilled players. The locations they fixate vision on include other key players and their movements, the ball and spaces around the pitch. When in possession of the ball, they are able to conduct this visual search of the match environment whilst executing their motor skills, using proprioception along with vision to maintain control of the ball. Those researchers have shown that expert players temporarily switch their visual search strategy during situations in a match that occur very close to them, such as a 1v1. In those situations, their strategy involves longer fixations on the player in possession of the ball or a player of interest, along with brief switches of fixation or the use of peripheral vision to various locations, such as other players of interest. In contrast, regardless of the situation during a match, the visual search strategy of lesser-skilled players usually involves longer fixations on the ball and the player in possession of it. Moreover, when in possession of the ball, lesser-skilled players tend to fixate their vision upon it to maintain control.

Information from the match situation enters the visual system through the light-sensitive sensory receptors in the retina of the eye through the optic nerve to visual processing areas of the brain. Information about movement and body orientation in that environment is also derived through proprioception and its kinaesthetic sensory receptors located in muscles, tendons, joints and skin. Proprioceptive information flows through the afferent neurons to the motor areas of the brain, such as the somatosensory area (Yang 2015). A key perceptual-cognitive process that probably occurs in visual regions of the brain is termed *recognition*. Researchers (e.g., Roca et al. 2013) have shown that expert players are better able to recognize the incoming information from the match environment compared with lesser-skilled players. The three types of recognition skills are the ability to recognize advanced postural cues and clues emanating from the movements of other players, patterns and structure in play and current location on the pitch.

An ability to use advanced postural cues enables players to recognize very early in the movement of other players what motor skills they will execute. For example, an expert defender will recognize early in the movement of an opposing striker that he or she will shoot the ball at goal by recognizing advanced cues emanating from the striker's movements, such as an early head or eye movement or the start of the kicking-leg swing. During a match, all players emit these advanced postural cues from their movements, and expert players are able to recognize these cues as they emerge. In a similar manner, expert players are able to recognize patterns and structures that repeat during match play, such as a 2v1 situation, an overlap run, or a flat back four line, and they consistently recognize these structures early in their reoccurrence in the game. Moreover, at any moment in the game, they are able to recognize or are aware of where they are on the pitch, such as on the edge of the penalty area or close to the touchline. The ability of expert players to recognize advanced postural cues from the movements of other players, to recognize patterns and structure in play and to be aware of their current location enables them to anticipate and predict the motor skills that other players will execute. In addition, players may assess options and probabilities of potential outcomes for the current situation when it affords them enough time to do so, whereas in time-limited situations, their perception of the situation is directly coupled to their actions to affect it.

Other perceptual-cognitive skills are involved in what is colloquially known as "affecting the game", or what scientists may term *intervention*. These skills include decision making in terms of action selection, planning and execution, which are also linked to the tactical and contextual knowledge of the player. For expert players, the skills involved in the decisions that affect the game run in parallel and interact with those involved in the just-described assessment or "reading of the game" (Williams & Ford 2013). Expert players probably combine the incoming visual information from the current situation in the match with their tactical and contextual knowledge about it. Motor areas of the brain, such as the posterior parietal cortex within the motor cortex, are involved in action selection, planning, programming, initiating, execution and control, and some movement is also controlled by the spinal cord. Nerve impulses are sent from these brain areas through efferent neurons to the skeletal muscle fibres for action to be executed (Yang 2015). Casual observers of the match see those action selections executed by the player as technical and movement skills in the situation she or he is currently engaging in, such as a pass, change of direction or head movement to shift visual search. Those movements and actions appear to the observer to be extremely fluid, almost automatic, perhaps controlled by the intuitive, fast, implicit and automatic mode of thought termed System 1 by Kahneman (2003).

Decision making in terms of action selection and execution is not only driven by current events in the match situation but also guided by the tactical and contextual knowledge of the player. The tactical knowledge of players appears to manifest itself during the match in a fluid, almost automatic manner, again perhaps controlled by the fast, implicit and intuitive mode of thought termed System *1* by Kahneman (2003). In the future, scientists will provide neurophysiological accounts of the brain areas where players store and access tactical and contextual knowledge during performance. Currently, scientists have provided only conceptual accounts of those processes. For example, McPherson and Kernodle (2003) use research evidence to conceptualize two acquired memory adaptations that guide the interpretation of sensory input and the selection of actions during expert decision making. Action plan profiles match the current conditions in the situation with appropriate perceptual or motor actions. Current conditions are other player positions or movements, ball placement and patterns or structure in play. Current event profiles are contextual or tactical information in regards to current, past and future factors. These contextual factors can be situational (e.g., score in the match), player's own characteristics (e.g., size and skill level), phase of play (e.g., team out of possession), tactical (e.g., instruction from the coach), teammate and opponent characteristics (e.g., in possession tendencies) and environmental characteristics (e.g., weather). These two conceptual memory structures are thought to function through rule-based procedures that link external conditions to goals, actions and their regulation.

For example, during a match, a winger might find him- or herself in possession of the ball in a 1v1 situation out wide in the attacking third with teammates and defenders moving into the penalty area. In this situation, the player's decision may be to select and execute an early cross of the ball to his or her teammates as they enter the penalty area, which would involve an action plan profile guiding this process. However, every situation in a match contains contextual and tactical factors that influence the decision that players select. For example, when the winger's team is winning with limited time left, the player might retain possession by turning back towards his or her own goal rather than play a cross into the penalty area that may lead to loss of possession. Additionally, if the coach has instructed the winger to do this, then he or she may turn back and retain possession. In these cases, McPherson and Kernodle (2003) hold that the player's decision and action would be guided by a current event profile that contains this tactical and contextual information.

Coach-Led Practice

Nearly all soccer players experience the game through formal, structured, coach-led practice activities or coaching sessions. The intention underlying this activity is to improve the performance of the players and team for the main activity of match play. Therefore, the transfer of skill acquisition and learning from the practice activity to match play should be the key consideration when designing practice. One of the difficulties faced in designing practice activity is recreating the conditions of match play to facilitate transfer of learning.

The activities that coaches have players engage in during practice can be placed into two categories. The first category is drill-type activities that focus on technique or skills with the ball but without opponents or with limited opposition. These activities contain no or limited match-like decision-making activity. The coach instructs the players about the action selection decisions before the drill so that each decision for the athlete involves only one degree of freedom. The second category is game-based activities that replicate match play by including a ball, teammates and opponents. These games include small-sided games, unidirectional games, possession games, phases of play and full matches. These activities contain match-like decision-making because players select and execute decisions themselves based on the positioning of the ball, teammates, opponents and space. Action selection decisions in these games usually involve two or more degrees of freedom. These two practice activity categories have different effects on the transfer of learning and skill acquisition to match play, which are detailed in the following sections. Practical examples are provided throughout to support the science underpinning the effects of these activities.

Drill Activities

This section describes the effects of drill-type activities on the transfer of learning and skill acquisition to match play. These drill activities can focus on technique, skills or fitness with the ball, usually with no or limited opposition. Figure 5.1 shows a typical drill activity used by coaches during practice. Drill activities have limitations in terms of their effects on the skill acquisition of players. First, drill activities provide less opportunity for players to acquire the perceptual, cognitive and motor skills required for expert performance in soccer match play, such as anticipation and decision making. These drill activities contain no or limited match-like decision making for the players. The coach has predetermined the action selection decisions for them, so they are not active decision makers during the activity.

Second, the specificity of drill activities is relatively low when compared with the transfer environment of match play. Specificity in this instance

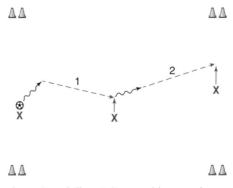

▶ **Figure 5.1** A typical passing drill activity used by coaches.

refers to how similar player performances are during the practice in terms of movement, actions and decisions compared with those they perform in match play. In drill activities, specificity is relatively low because the movements, actions and decisions of players look and are somewhat different from those they use during match play. For example, the drill activity shown in figure 5.1 involves players executing skills whilst standing still, which they would rarely do during a match. Third, the underlying structure of drill activities may not be conducive to players' acquisition of skill. Some definitions of the different types of underlying practice structures are shown in table 5.1. Drill activities usually contain blocked, constant and massed attempts of a skill, which has generally been shown to be less effective for learning motor skills compared with random, variable and distributed attempts (for a review, see Schmidt & Lee 2011).

Overall, drill activities contain a lack of active decision making for players, a lack of specificity and an underlying structure that leads to less learning compared with other structures, which are all factors likely to reduce skill acquisition for match play.

Drills can be adapted to improve the transfer of learning to match play by including match-like decision-making activity so that players become active decision makers. Players must make groups of match-like decisions themselves based on the positioning of teammates, opponents and space. One method for adapting drill activity to contain match-like decision making

Table 5.1 Definitions of Some of the Underlying Structures of Practice Activities, Particularly Practice of Motor Skills

BLOCKED VERSUS RANDOM	
Blocked	Attempts at one skill occur multiple times in succession without interruption from another skill before moving on to multiple attempts at the next skill and so on.
Random	Attempts at multiple skills occur in a random order so that one skill is usually followed by an attempt at another skill and so on.
CONSTANT VERSUS VARIABLE	
Constant	Each attempt at a skill contains many factors that are the same, such as distance, speed, angle and so on.
Variable	Each attempt at a skill contains factors that are different, such as distance, speed, angle and so on.
MASSED VERSUS DISTRIBUTED	
Massed	Attempts at a skill occur multiple times in succession with a short time interval or no time interval between attempts.
Distributed	Attempts at a skill occur with a large time interval between them, possibly with attempts at other skills occurring during that interval.
ACTIVE DECISION MAKING VERSUS NONACTIVE DECISION MAKING	
Active	Activity in which the main action execution decisions for the player in possession have at least two or more degrees of freedom or options, mostly involving moving opposition.
Nonactive	Activity in which the main action execution decisions for the player in possession of the ball have only one degree of freedom or option.

is to add opposition players and teammates. Opposition players have an advantage in drills because limits are set on what their opponents can do, which makes it easier for them to predict and counter those actions than during normal match play. Therefore, constraints and limits must be placed on the defending opponents in these adapted drills. For example, opposition players could be banned from tackling or blocking passes and are allowed only to pressure the opponent. The typical drill activity shown in figure 5.1 can be adapted to contain active match-like decision making for the players, as shown in figure 5.2.

The specificity of the drill activities shown in figures 5.1 and 5.2 is relatively low because the movements, actions and decisions of the players involved all look and are somewhat different from those they use during match play. The specificity of drill activities can be increased using various methods, including ensuring that play is directional, having players perform in positions from the match, ensuring that distances are similar to those in the match, having pitch conditions similar to those of the match and ensuring that the players are making decisions themselves as they would in a match. Figure 5.3 shows how the drills in figures 5.1 and 5.2 might be adapted to contain a higher level of specificity to the match. These adapted drills contain match-like decision making for players. Moreover, the underlying structure of the practice changes to contain a more random, variable and distributed order of skill attempts, which has generally been shown to be better for learning motor skills compared with blocked, constant and massed orders (for a review, see Schmidt & Lee 2011).

Games Activities

This section describes the transfer of learning and skill acquisition from games activities to match play. These games include small-sided games, unidirectional games, possession games, phases of play and full matches. The players are active decision makers in these games because they must

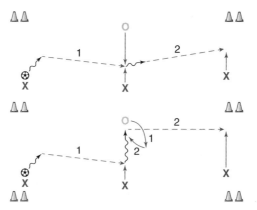

▶ **Figure 5.2** The passing drill activity from figure 5.1 has been adapted to contain some active match-like decision making for the players.

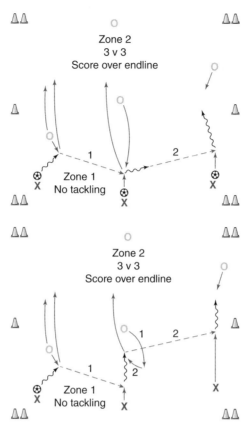

▶ **Figure 5.3**   The passing drill activity from figures 5.1 and 5.2 adapted to contain a higher level of specificity.

make groups of match-like decisions themselves based on the positioning of teammates, opponents and space. Moreover, games activities usually contain a higher level of specificity to match play when compared with drill-based activity. The movements, actions and decisions of the players in games activities are similar to those they use during match play. Furthermore, games activities have an underlying structure that contains a random, variable and distributed order of skill attempts, which has generally been shown to be better for learning motor skills compared with a blocked, constant and massed order (for a review, see Schmidt & Lee 2011).

Games are an excellent activity to bring about skill acquisition that transfers well to the main activity of match play. Games activities have minor limitations in terms of their effect on the skill acquisition of players. These problems are the level of difficulty of games activity for novice and young players, the potential lack of repetitive attempts at key skills and tactics in these games and some issues around the specificity of these games. These problems and some solutions to them are outlined in the next paragraphs.

First, games activities can be challenging for novice and young players because of the ability of opponents to limit their time and space on the ball

Challenge Point Hypothesis

The challenge point hypothesis forwarded by Guadagnoli and Lee (2004) outlines the effect on learning of the interaction between the difficulty of a practice task and the ability of a performer. In this framework, task difficulty consists of two categories: nominal task difficulty and functional task difficulty. Nominal task difficulty is the constant difficulty of the task regardless of who is performing it or the conditions it is being performed under. Functional task difficulty is how challenging the task is for the person performing it and the conditions in which it is being performed. Learning is related to the information arising from performance. The optimal challenge point occurs at the point of functional task difficulty containing the ideal amount of potential interpretable information for the learner. As learners become more skilled, the challenge point must rise so that functional task difficulty becomes greater, enabling the learner to obtain increased information.

and to regain possession. Usually, coaches reduce the challenge of soccer for novices or younger players by having them engage in drill activities. Players engaging in drill activities limits skill acquisition as detailed in the previous section. Instead, coaches can adapt games so that they are less challenging for novice players. The games can be made progressively more challenging as the players become more skilled. Coaches can use methods to adapt the challenge point (see the sidebar 'Challenge Point Hypothesis') of small-sided games so that they are appropriate for the skill level of their players. These methods are to make the pitch size larger, reduce the number of players on each team, have players or the coaches act as 'floaters' who play for whichever team is in possession, ban slide tackling or tackling from the floor, and ban tackling completely allowing pressure on the player in possession and the blocking of passes as options for defenders with limits placed on ball touches for attackers (Ford & Williams 2013).

Second, games may lack the repetition of attempts at key skills or situations required for skill acquisition and learning to occur. Coaches can adapt games to bring about greater repetition of attempts at key skills, situations and tactics by players. To do this, the rules of the game can be changed to have players engage in more repetitive attempts than normal (see the sidebar 'Constraints-Led Approach'). To some degree, coaches already do change the rules in games activities towards this goal. One method to increase the number of attempts is to change the rules about how the players score goals in the game. Some examples of small-sided games in which the rules for scoring have been changed to cause a relatively higher frequency of attempts at specific skills and tactics than normal are presented in figure 5.4.

Third, some aspects of games activities lack specificity because players make movements, actions and decisions that look and are different from those they make during match play. For example, players in small-sided

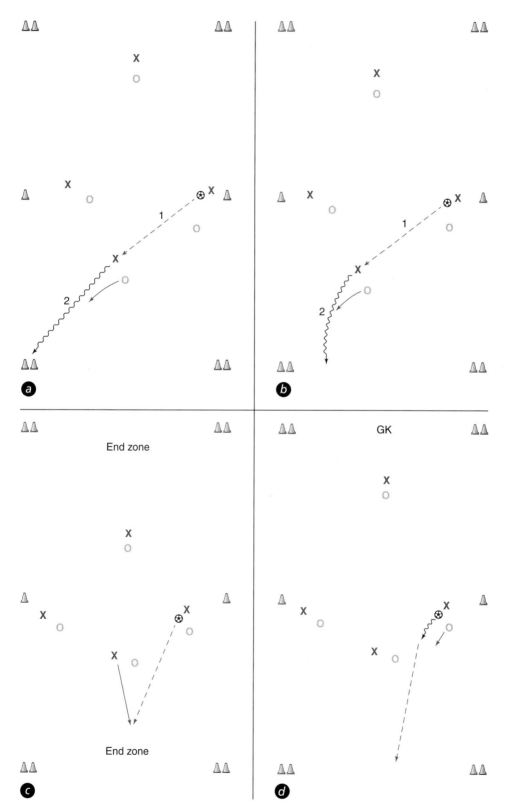

▶ **Figure 5.4** Small-sided games in which rules for scoring changed to increase frequency of (*a*) switching play and turning, (*b*) dribbling, (*c*) forward passing and forward running and (*d*) shooting.

Constraints-Led Approach

The constraints-led approach is outlined in detail by Davids, Button and Bennett (2008). It views the task, environment and individual as having parts, components or constraints. Those constraints can be manipulated to bring about skill acquisition and learning. Task constraints are probably the easiest for a coach to manipulate, and many coaches already do this during practice to some degree. To manipulate task constraints in soccer, coaches can change the way goals are scored, the ball, the pitch size and shape, and the number of players and what they can do. Davids et al. have usefully termed the manipulation of task constraints as *bending the rules*. Individual constraints are those related to the characteristics of the players themselves, such as genes, fatigue, psychological state or amount of experience. Environmental constraints are external and physical in nature, such as weather, pitch surface and temperature. During goal-directed action, these three interacting constraints influence the human system and shape the emergence of coordinated action. Coaches can manipulate all three constraints for their players so that during performance the desired coordinated action will emerge and the players will acquire them.

games do not often head the ball or play long passes, and teams in these games do not play in formations used during match play. Coaches can change the rules of small-sided games, possession games and unidirectional games to increase the specificity of the activity and the frequency of skills, such as heading and long passing (for some examples, see figure 5.5). Coaches can increase specificity by positioning players in formations during small-sided games and unidirectional games that are similar to those found during match play, such as the diamond formation used in 4v4 games that often repeats in microform during 11v11 games.

Recreating the conditions found in match play during practice is a difficult, if not impossible, task for coaches. Therefore, repeated full matches and phases of play on grass pitches are ideal conditions for skill acquisition, particularly for adolescent players. In these activities, opposition tactics and strategies should vary between bouts and the activities should be used as learning experiences.

Instructional Strategies

During formal, structured, coach-led practice activity or coaching sessions, players usually experience relatively high amounts of augmented instruction, feedback and demonstrations from a coach or coaches (Ford, Yates & Williams 2010). Some of these coaching behaviours also occur in the changing room, meeting room, pitch side during match play or in other soccer-related activities. The intention underpinning these coaching behaviours is to improve the performance of the players and team for the main activity of match play. The aspects of performance that coaches seek to improve

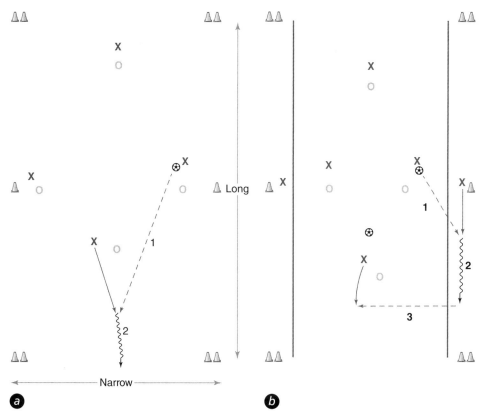

▶ **Figure 5.5** Small-sided games in which rules have been changed to increase frequency of (a) long forward passes and (b) crossing and heading.

using these behaviours are mainly technical or movement skills and tactical knowledge, as well as other aspects, such as concentration, effort and motivation. In this section, evidence-based principles are briefly discussed regarding the effects of augmented verbal instruction and feedback on the skill acquisition of players as they develop from childhood through adolescence into adulthood.

Instruction and feedback from coaches and significant others helps the learning of complex tasks. Explicit verbal instruction and feedback of the type provided by coaches, however, can lead to performance and learning decrements for players in the early stages of learning when they are placed under stress, such as when a young player is performing in match play (Masters & Poolton 2013) (see the sidebar 'Motor Skill and the Reinvestment Hypothesis'). Moreover, instructions and feedback focusing on movements have been shown to lead to performance and learning decrements regardless of the skill level of the players, presumably because those instructions interrupt the fluid, automatic movement processes involved in expert performance (Wulf 2007).

Therefore, researchers have suggested that coaches of people in the earlier stages of learning should use an instructional strategy known as the

Motor Skill and the Reinvestment Hypothesis

Penalty kick shootouts provide a good example of how stress causes the motor skill execution of players to break down when normally it would not. Youth players likely experience stress in many other situations during match play. Masters and Poolton (2013) have shown that motor skill execution does not break down under stress when people have no or few rules about how to execute it, which is evidence that those people have implicit knowledge about the skill. In contrast, motor skill execution does break down under stress when people have multiple rules about how to execute it, which is known as explicit knowledge. Masters and Poolton (2013) forwarded the reinvestment hypothesis to explain how explicit rules and knowledge about the mechanics of a skill lead to performance decrement. In stressful situations, performers with this explicit knowledge base pay too much attention to these rules, thereby interrupting motor processes that would normally run automatically. In contrast, those with no rules about the mechanics of a skill cannot do this and therefore do not interrupt those processes. Motor skill, and at least some decision making, should probably be underpinned by an implicit knowledge base. Some methods to have youth players acquire this implicit knowledge base are errorless learning, analogy learning and guided discovery.

hands-off approach (Ford & Williams 2013). The hands-off instructional strategy involves relatively low amounts of augmented instruction, feedback and demonstrations from the coach. The role of the coach in this case is to design, implement and adapt the practice so that players are acquiring skill from engaging in the activity without the need for extensive augmented verbal instruction and feedback. For novice players, researchers have shown that the accumulation of explicit knowledge and rules by learners through their intrinsic feedback mechanisms when they make errors should also be discouraged. Errorless learning involves practice with a reduced amount of learning errors, rather than no errors, thereby inhibiting the accumulation by learners of explicit rules through the hypothesis testing that occurs when errors are made (Masters & Poolton 2013). Coaches can encourage the acquisition of an implicit knowledge base in novice players by lowering the challenge point of the practice activity to the appropriate level whilst ensuring that during it the players are active decision makers. Some examples of errorless learning activities containing active decision making for novice players are shown in figure 5.6. As child players become more skilled, the challenge point of the practice activities can be progressively raised to levels appropriate for their current skill level, with a focus on engagement in games activities.

Skilled adolescent players need to continue improving their performance beyond its current level. Engagement in well-designed games-based activities

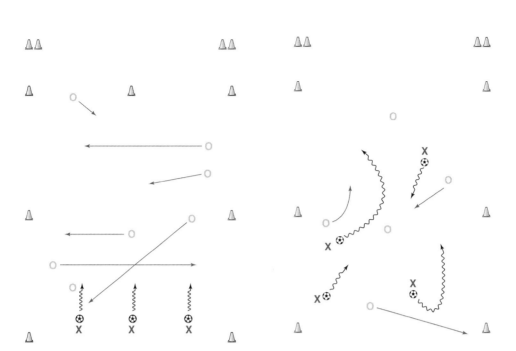

▶ **Figure 5.6** Two dribbling errorless learning activities containing active decision making on the ball for novice players.

during practice will still likely lead to skill acquisition for these players. A key aspect of match-play performance that requires improvement for these players is their tactical and contextual knowledge. Games activities can be set up to have players acquire this tactical and contextual knowledge. Some examples of how coaches can do this are as follows:

- Limit time to a five-minute countdown and start with team A up 1-0 on team B. Set goals for team A to maintain the score and for team B to score.
- Start with one team that contains one player less than the other, similar to a game situation in which a team has a player sent off or temporarily injured.
- Have one team play with all their players in a deep-lying defence, possibly with fast counterattacks when they regain possession of the ball.
- Have one team play a fast pressing game all over the pitch.
- Have the teams set up in different team formations that govern their starting positions and roles.
- Have one team play a direct style of soccer in which they move the ball forward quickly.

Moreover, researchers have shown that tactical and contextual knowledge can be enhanced in skilled players by being explicitly thought out, planned, instructed and discussed with coaches and other players (see the sidebar 'Fast Versus Slow Thinking'). Some examples of this knowledge are how the team should play in or out of possession of the ball, how the team should play when winning a match close to its end and how players should perform in specific positions. Augmented verbal instruction and feedback on these and other tactical and contextual factors may be appropriate for skilled adoles-

Fast Versus Slow Thinking

Kahneman (2003) describes a two-system view of human thought in which intuition is distinguished from reasoning. System 1 is the intuitive, implicit, fast and automatic mode of thought. Its contents are precepts, as well as concepts, but it can be evoked by language. It deals with intuitive judgements. In contrast, System 2 is the reasoned, explicit, slow, controlled, conscious, deliberate and effortful mode of thought. It involves reasoned judgements, self-monitoring and analysing. The two-system view of thought described by Kahneman (2003) may explain some contradictory findings in sport research. On the one hand, findings show that the performance of expert players is seemingly effortless, automatic and intuitive, whereas on the other hand they deliberately prepare, plan, discuss and reflect on performance. For example, the System 1 mode of thought outlined by Kahneman (2003) appears to be at work in flow state. Jackson and Csikszentmihalyi (1999) define flow as a psychological state in which a person is fully absorbed in the activity at hand so that she or he performs optimally without effort or self-consciousness but with a sense of control, transformation of time and feeling of intrinsic reward. In contrast, the System 2 mode of thought appears to be at work in a study by Richards, Collins and Mascarenhas (2012). They showed that expert team players who engaged in deliberate planning, team meetings, debriefs, performance analysis, reflection and discussion on tactics improved their rapid, on-court performance. In the Richards et al. study, the deliberate off-court learning was followed by a period of on-court physical practice. These contradictory findings suggest that when outside match play, expert players may deliberately plan, prepare, analyse and reflect on performance, which appears to be the System 2 mode of thought in action. In contrast, before and during match play they appear to "get in the zone" and experience flow state, which may be System 1 in action. Ericsson and Towne (2010) hold that even before and during performance, experts can monitor, access, use and update any part of the knowledge underpinning their performance, suggesting that they have the ability to switch rapidly between the two modes of thought during domain-specific tasks. The reason for this is that many of their performance processes are automated, freeing up attentional capacity to engage in controlled processing about any aspect of performance, if required.

cent players, although coaches should still ensure that they do not overload players with information and that they involve players in this process. Other researchers have shown that instructions and feedback that direct the attention of skilled players to their movements will still likely lead to performance and learning decrements (Wulf 2007). Alternative instructional strategies are available to coaches when skilled players require movement or technical changes, such as using instructions and feedback that focus their attention on external aspects of performance, using metaphors and analogies, or using short cues (Masters & Poolton 2013; Wulf 2007).

Late adolescent and adult players are required to win soccer matches and improve their performance beyond its current level. The instructional strategies outlined for younger adolescent players also likely apply to these older players. In addition, the tactical and contextual knowledge they require relates not only to their own performance but also to the performance of their opponents so that they can counter any problems that opponents may pose in match play. Scouting and video recording of recent opponent performance is a key part of this process. Performance and video analysis plays an important instructional role in ensuring that players acquire knowledge about their own and their opponents' performance. It can be used in the preparation for and reflection on performance in match play. Such information is thought to develop complex memory representations in expert players used in the monitoring, control and evaluation of their performance during match play (Ericsson 2003; McPherson & Kernodle 2003). These memory representations of match-play performance can probably be enhanced in players by other processes, including observation, performance, reflection, imagery, discussion, instruction, and the slow, deliberate, conscious and effortful mode of thought called System 2 by Kahneman (2003). Between matches, some expert players may be deliberately, explicitly and cognitively involved in enhancing these mental representations that also serve to monitor their performance and help improve it beyond its current level. In contrast, during match play, they may experience total absorption in the task or the flow state described by Jackson and Csikszentmihalyi (1999).

Intentions and Motivations Underpinning Activities

The underlying intentions of the coaches, players and significant others involved in the soccer activities of match play, practice or play influences their behaviour during it and skill acquisition in players. This section outlines the intentions and motivations underlying these three activities and their effect on skill acquisition and the development of expert performance.

The intention of practice is to improve the performance of players and the team beyond its current level. Well-designed practice activity is underpinned by goal setting that seeks to improve specific aspects of current performance.

Those aspects of performance should be highly relevant to the development and improvement of the player, unit or team at that current time. They can be any of the physical, psychological, tactical or skill attributes that construct performance in the sport. The term *deliberate practice* has been used to describe this type of activity (see the sidebar 'Power Law of Practice'). Deliberate practice requires a prior objective analysis of competition performance to identify the aspect of performance that will lead to the greatest amount of improvement. Deliberate practice is engaged in to improve the identified key aspect of performance. It is effortful for those engaging in it, it contains repetition and interpretable feedback for the performer, and because it is effortful it requires adequate rest and recovery periods before more of it can be engaged in. The motivation to engage in it is to improve future performance, not necessarily because the activity is enjoyable. The amount of deliberate practice engaged in by performers is highly correlated to their attained level of performance (Ericsson 2003).

In soccer, however, practice activity does not often contain the characteristics of deliberate practice (Ford & Williams 2013). A lot of practice activity in soccer is characterized by players practicing aspects of performance that they can already perform successfully. The term *maintenance practice* can be used to describe this type of activity. Soccer coaches should seek to increase the amount of deliberate practice that adolescent and adult players engage in because this activity improves the performance of players and teams beyond its current level. Coaches can have their players engage in deliberate practice by using methods including objectively analysing performance to identify aspects of it that are limiting greater success, setting goals for players and the team aimed at improving those aspects of their performance, scheduling practice activity designed to improve those specific aspects of

Power Law of Practice

The power law of practice holds that in the early stages of learning a new task or domain, performance improvement is rapid, whereas later in the process the rate begins to slow or plateau (Newell & Rosenbloom 1981). For many performers, the plateau occurs because they are competent at the task and are satisfied to remain at that level of performance. But Ericsson (2003) used the term *arrested development* to describe this plateau in performance that occurs later in learning. It represents a level of competent performance that many people are satisfied with. He holds that expert performers are not satisfied with being merely competent; consequently, they engage in an activity termed *deliberate practice*. Engagement in this activity is how they continually improve their performance beyond its current level. The amount of engagement in deliberate practice activity is highly related to the person's current level of performance with greater amounts being associated with better performance.

performance, evaluating performance and its progression in players and the team, motivating players to engage in deliberate practice activity and creating an environment within a club or team that consistently seeks to improve all aspects of performance.

The intention underlying match play is to win, and a further intention is for the players and team to perform well. In situations in which match play does not affect league positions, tournament progression or winning trophies, such as during early adolescence, then the intention of match play can also be to improve the future performance of the players. In this case, goal setting can focus the attention of players and coaches onto task-specific goals, such as maintaining possession, and their subgoals, such as creating space, rather than on the result of the match. Generally, adolescent and adult players are mature enough and sufficiently developed to engage in activity in which the primary intention is to win or to improve performance beyond its current level. Child players may not be ready to engage in these activities because they are at a lower level of growth, maturity and development compared with adolescent and adult players. Therefore, activities in which the primary intention is to win or improve performance might not be appropriate for child players or, as the sidebar 'The Power Law of Practice' demonstrates, required.

For child players, play activity in which the primary intention is for participants to have fun and enjoyment may be more appropriate. The participants themselves usually lead play activity using small-sided games with rules adapted from adult norms. Play activity is predicted to enhance the long-term intrinsic motivation of players to participate further in the sport (Côté, Baker & Abernethy 2007). Intrinsic motivation enhancement is thought to be caused by the primary intention of play activity being fun and enjoyment, as well as by its fulfilment of the basic needs of participants for autonomy, relatedness and competence (Deci & Ryan 2000). The small-sided games that form most play activity can also lead to the acquisition of decision-making ability (e.g., Roca, Williams & Ford 2012) and possibly an implicit knowledge base underpinning player performance, which is probably superior to an explicit knowledge for children. Therefore, play is an ideal activity for child players to engage in.

Play activity in soccer is often thought of as being unstructured, informal and led by the participants themselves. Examples of this type of activity are street soccer, beach soccer, playground soccer and park soccer. Elite soccer players in Brazil have been shown to experience the sport during childhood mainly through large amounts of this informal and participant-led play activity (Ford et al. 2012). In most countries, however, child players do not engage in this informal soccer-specific play activity or engage in it only in small amounts. Adults can use several methods to increase the amount of soccer-specific play activity that child players engage in. These approaches include changing formal coaching sessions and adapting the formal match-play programme so that the child players are engaging in soccer-specific play activity (for an example, see the sidebar 'Manchester United 4v4 Scheme for U9s'). Other methods include creating school playgrounds and areas in parks where children can safely engage in soccer-specific play activity and encouraging child players to engage in more safe, unstructured, informal soccer-specific play activity (Ford & Williams 2013).

Adults need to adapt the structured, formal, coach-led soccer activities that child players engage in to become more like play activity. An advantage of formal, structured soccer-specific play activity compared with informal, unstructured play activity is that coaches can cleverly design formal activity to ensure that optimal skill acquisition occurs for the child players. The games activities described earlier are ideal as soccer-specific play activity for child players. More specifically, small-sided games (e.g., 4v4) and unidirectional games (e.g., 2v1) are ideal activities when they are adapted to the appropriate challenge point for the skill level of the players (see the sidebar 'Challenge Point Hypothesis') and to bring about greater frequency of repetitive attempts at specific skills, situations and tactics (see figure 5.5). Players can engage in these games as play activities for fun and enjoyment

Manchester United 4v4 Scheme for U9s

In England, the Premier League granted permission for the Manchester United Youth Academy U9 squad to play a game format different from that normally used in this age group. Rather than play the normal single 8v8 match used by these teams, the Manchester United players and their visiting opponents engage in a series of 4v4 matches. Squads are divided into teams of four who rotate through four different conditioned games. The club provide enough appropriately sized pitches for these games so that all players in both squads can play at the same time. No player sits out at any time unless injured. Games last for eight minutes, and the players referee themselves. No scores from the games are held or recorded. They play a minimum of six games, but often more as time allows. A two-minute break is given between games for rest, rehydration and organization. The coaches and significant others, such as parents, create a vibrant, playful and fun atmosphere, and no instruction or pressure is exerted on players. Parents view the games from a gallery that is relatively far from the pitches compared with normal. The four conditioned games have been cleverly designed to bring about greater frequency of repetitive attempts at key skills, situations and tactics by players through changing the way goals are scored. For example, the line ball game has a scoring line instead of goals; players must dribble over the line to score, thereby increasing the amount of this skill from normal. The rationale for this scheme is to recreate the playful learning environment that professional players engaged in at that age and to create highly skilled players (Fenoglio 2003).

without being aware that the games will also lead to skill acquisition and performance improvement. This learning environment must be manipulated so that players regularly encounter the whole range of tasks, skills and tactics that constitute soccer performance. Coaches and significant others can use a hands-off instructional strategy during this activity, but they should ensure that the environment they create is relaxed, fun and enjoyable for the players. A method that coaches can use to enhance this learning environment for child players during coaching sessions is to incorporate fun analogies, such as those from popular child culture. For example, the challenge point of a 4v4 game can be lowered by having the team out of possession move around the pitch as 'zombies' with stiff limbs!

Other Activities

Youth players often engage in activities other than soccer during their development, including warm-ups, speed and agility activities, other sports and soccer observation. During formal soccer coaching sessions, players often engage in warm-ups and speed and agility activities. The warm-up at the start of the session prepares the players for the forthcoming soccer activities. Players engage in speed and agility activities to improve those aspects of performance. Adolescent players can engage in these activities with the explicit intention of performance improvement. Child players, however, may not be ready to engage in the same activities as adolescents because of their lack of growth, maturity and development. Therefore, coaches of child players must ensure that warm-up activities are fun and enjoyable, are appropriate for child players and contain the conditions that are optimal for skill acquisition. Tag games, such as freeze tag, infection tag or Band-Aid tag are ideal playful activities that contain optimal conditions for child players as part of a warm-up. These games are fun, and they contain perceptual-motor processes that are similar to those that occur in match play. Tag games are also an excellent activity to improve the speed and agility of players without them being aware that the activity is designed to improve those aspects of performance. Coaches can progress tag games to include soccer balls. Some examples of this activity are having players dribble the ball around a square avoiding each other or having half without soccer balls harassing but not tackling players in possession who have to dribble to escape their attention.

Youth players spend much time observing expert professional players through attending live matches and observing film of live or recorded matches. Scientists have shown that observation is a key method of skill acquisition for learners in many tasks and domains (for a review, see Schmidt & Lee 2011). In soccer, youth players should regularly observe the expert performance of older expert players and teams so that they can mimic those players. Coaches, support staff and significant others should encourage and support young players to observe these expert players and teams. Performance analysts can create edited video of expert players and teams performing in match play for young players to watch. Young players must encounter and observe the whole range of tasks, skills and tactics that constitute soccer performance, including those special and novel moments of skill execution by expert players or teams that are colloquially known as creative play.

Youth players often engage in other sports besides soccer. Engagement in other sports during childhood is hypothesized to benefit the development of expertise through transfer of attributes developed in a different sport to the primary sport. Transfer of attributes between sports is more likely to happen when the two sports are similar (e.g., soccer and futsal by elite players in Brazil; Ford et al. 2012), contain similar elements (e.g., soccer and athletics) or cause adaptations that counter those negatively developed in the primary sport that may lead to injury (e.g., strong quadriceps muscles and weak hamstring muscles in soccer players) (Schmidt & Lee 2011). Engagement in other sports during childhood might benefit the development of expertise by providing some protection against the negative consequences of too much engagement in the primary sport, such as burnout and overuse injuries. For this purpose at least, child players should engage in other sport activity outside their engagement in soccer, whereas adolescent players should engage in one or two other sports beyond soccer during this period of their lives (Côté, Baker and Abernethy 2007).

Conclusion

Youth soccer players rely on coaches, support staff and significant others to help them fulfil their dreams of becoming expert players in adulthood, as well as to ensure that their current engagement is rewarding. Moreover, expert professional players rely on coaches, support staff and significant others to fulfil their goals of winning matches and trophies. Coaches, support staff, and significant others can use evidence-based principles derived from contemporary research to optimize and develop expert performance in soccer players. Expert performance by outfield players during the primary soccer activity of competition or match play involves players successfully executing appropriate perceptual, cognitive and motor skills, such as decision making and technical actions. The transfer of skill acquisition and learning from soccer practice activity to match play can be optimized by using games-based activities, as well as drill activities in which players are active decision makers, as opposed to drill activities in which they are not. Methods can be used to increase the transfer of learning from these practice activities. These approaches include having players select and execute decisions based on the positioning of the ball, other players and space; increasing the specificity of the activity; ensuring that the players are executing somewhat repetitive attempts at a skill or tactic and ensuring that the difficulty is appropriate for the skill and age of the players. Moreover, the intentions underlying soccer activity can be manipulated to provide appropriate and optimal soccer activity for players across their lifespans. For child players, the optimal activity is likely soccer-specific play in which the intention is to have fun. Games-based activities may be best for this purpose, and coaches can adapt them so that players are optimally acquiring skill without knowing that this is the case. For adolescent players, and particularly for adult players, practice should be engaged in with the intention to improve aspects of performance that can lead to the greatest increase in success, whereas match play should be engaged in with the intention to win. For adolescents, match play can be engaged in with the intention of improving future performance by focusing attention on task-specific goals, such as maintaining possession. The amount and type of coaching instruction and feedback should be appropriate to the age of the players. For child players, coaches should use a hands-off instructional approach involving limited amounts of instruction and feedback, whereas with older players the augmented information should probably mainly focus on tactics and motivation. Coaches, support staff and significant others should ensure that their players engage in meaningful amounts per week of the soccer activity described in this chapter, although not so much that the activity leads to negative consequences, such as overtraining, overuse injury or burnout.

Biomechanical and Technological Applications

CHAPTER 6

Biomechanical Principles of Soccer

—Anthony Blazevich and Sophia Nimphius

Biomechanics is an area of science devoted to the study of the mechanics (i.e., the physical laws) of biological systems at the cellular, tissue and whole organism levels. In sports biomechanics, the description of movement (kinematics) and the forces that produce movement (kinetics) are studied in pursuit of optimizing physical performance whilst minimizing injury risk. An understanding of sports biomechanics is particularly important in soccer because physical laws govern players' abilities to move rapidly to catch or evade an opponent, jump to head a ball, apply forces to the ball to pass with high accuracy or velocity, or create swerve on a kicked or headed ball. Therefore, an understanding of biomechanical principles is required to improve performance, from beginners to advanced players.

Although a comprehensive understanding of sports biomechanics requires the gathering of a significant knowledge base, this chapter introduces the basic biomechanical principles that underpin factors related to soccer performance. The possession of biomechanics knowledge allows us to have theoretical understanding of which biomechanical factors underpin performance in soccer and why knowledge of biomechanics can enhance the ability to improve soccer performance. Further, understanding how biomechanical principles are used to assess, intervene in and subsequently improve performance is important. For example, sporting teams are now using equipment that can measure biomechanical variables such as the magnitude of forces during tackles or when heading a ball, assess running movement patterns using accelerometers and inertial motion sensors (IMUs), or quantify distances and speeds of travel using global positioning systems (GPS) or, more recently, global navigation satellite systems (GNSS) for enhancement of performance. Therefore, knowledge associated with the following biomechanical principles will provide insight into the underpinning determinants of performance:

- Description of movement (kinematics)
- Force production for movement (kinetics)
- Biomechanics of producing movement, from a cellular to a whole-body level
- Principles of work, power and energy
- Integrated principles of kinetics and kinematics

Description of Movement (Kinematics)

The description of the movement pattern of a task (i.e., kinematics) involves an account of the shape, form, pattern and sequencing of the movements with respect to how long it takes to move. Kinematics can be split into linear and angular components, and they can be described using either only the magnitude of a descriptor (termed a *scalar* quantity; e.g., 10-degree range of motion, lift 50 centimetres, run 5 metres) or by both a magnitude and direction of movement (a vector quantity; e.g., run 10 metres straight ahead, rotate 5 degrees clockwise). Furthermore, considering that most movements are actually angular (i.e., circular; limbs tend to rotate about the joints), understand that angular motions can result in linear movements. For example, angular motions about the hip, knee and ankle joints during a soccer kick cause the ball to travel in a linear manner after the foot strikes it.

Linear Motion

The most basic linear kinematic quantities are the measures of distance and displacement. Distance, a scalar quantity, describes how far an object has cumulatively travelled. In comparison, displacement is a vector quantity (i.e., it has a magnitude and direction) that defines the straight-line distance from an initial position to a final position. Therefore, if two players run the

Practical Applications

The ability to clear the ball away from the goal is a critical skill for goalkeepers. Video analysis is a useful tool from the biomechanics toolbox that allows us to watch the movement of the player in replay at a slower-than-normal speed and to identify potential technique faults that might reduce kicking performance. For example, if in video analysis a coach notices that the goalkeeper's support leg during the kick is collapsing, current biomechanics theories support that this would prevent an effective transfer of the linear momentum of the body to the angular momentum of the kicking limb and ultimately affect the distance that the ball will be kicked.

length of the field but one player weaves while dribbling the ball, the weaving player will run a greater distance although both players will have the same displacement. The variable measured depends on the purpose of the measurement. For example, to quantify the work a player has done during a training session, we should calculate the total distance run in that session because the displacement might be zero if the player starts and ends the session in the same spot. But to measure the effectiveness of a run within a phase of play in the game, we might measure how much distance was run for a required displacement to occur (e.g., to get from halfway to the six-yard box; a large distance might suggest an inefficient movement strategy). In essence, effectiveness (whether the task required is completed) is different from efficiency (completing the task within the shortest distance or with the least energy expenditure). Clearly, both have implications for performance.

When either a distance is travelled or a displacement occurs within a given period, the speed or velocity of the movement can be described. Speed describes the change in distance over a given period; this is a scalar quantity. In comparison, velocity describes the displacement over a given period; this is a vector quantity. The standard unit for both is metres per second (m/s or m·s^{-1}), but its use is specific to the description needed. For example, we might want to know the velocity of a player within a single play in a game (i.e., the speed and direction), but we might also want to know the average speed of a player during a soccer game (again, the velocity might be zero if the player finishes in the same place that he or she started!).

Finally, acceleration describes the rate of change in velocity, calculated as the velocity divided by the change in time (measured in units of m/s^2 or m·s^{-2}). Many of us are familiar with the concept of acceleration, but its description can be complicated. For example, we typically describe the direction of acceleration as positive or negative (e.g., we might say that acceleration from left to right is positive). If a player accelerates (increases velocity) to the right, then this is positive acceleration, a vector quantity. If the player subsequently slows down (decreases velocity) whilst running to the right, then he or she has undergone negative acceleration. This is sometimes simply called deceleration, but the term *deceleration* can cause some confusion when considering travel in the negative direction. If the player then increases velocity when moving to the left, he or she is accelerating (increasing velocity) in the negative direction, which is therefore a negative acceleration because of the direction of travel. Finally, when the player then slows down (decreases velocity) whilst running left, he or she has a positive acceleration even though he or she is decelerating because velocity is decreasing in the negative direction. Of course, if the player maintains a constant velocity, including standing still, then acceleration is zero. Note that acceleration is always a vector quantity and is subsequently affected by both magnitude and direction.

Practical Applications

A commonly used piece of technology in sport today is the global positioning system (GPS) or global navigation satellite system (GNSS) unit, which uses satellite information as well as built-in inertial motion units (IMUs) within a device placed on the athlete to estimate the distance travelled during training or games. Additionally, using these units, the speed and acceleration of an athlete can be examined by coaches and sport scientists to understand the number and intensity of efforts performed by the athlete on the field. Understanding the difference between speed and velocity allows the coach or sport scientist to know that when the athlete changes direction, the distance travelled is included in the calculation rather than just the starting and finishing position. The use of speed zones allows coaches to classify the distance travelled at each relative intensity, providing critical information about the amount of physical conditioning provided and allowing training load monitoring.

Angular Motion

The measurement of angular movement begins with the basic measurement of angular position. It is commonly measured in degrees, but the standard international unit of measurement is radians (which is equivalent to 57.3 degrees). Joint angles are a commonly measured angular position quantity. As shown in figure 6.1, the measurement of a joint angle can be described as the angle formed by the longitudinal axes of the segments (i.e., a relative angle) or as an absolute joint angle (i.e., the angle between the body segments with respect to a fixed reference, such as the vertical plane, as is common for describing trunk angles shown in figure 6.1). Angular displacement can then be calculated as the change in angular position (difference between final and initial position), and angular distance is used to quantify the cumulative movement range (i.e., sum of all rotations between final and initial position). Other angular variables are calculated just as their linear equivalents were: Angular speed is defined as the change in angular distance per change in time (measured in degrees per second; $°\cdot s^{-1}$), angular velocity is the angular displacement per change in time ($°\cdot s^{-1}$), and angular acceleration the change in angular velocity per change in time ($°\cdot s^{-2}$).

Again, remember that angular motions can result in a linear movement. In fact, the linear velocity of the end point of a limb is equal to the radius of the limb segments multiplied by the angular velocity of the segments (velocity = radius × angular velocity; $v = r\omega$). This shows, for example, that the speed of the foot before kicking a ball is dictated by the angular speed at the joints in the lower limb as well as the distance of the foot from the hip; the longer the leg, the faster the foot speed. So the angular velocities of the joints dictate the linear velocities of the hands and feet, and ultimately the speed of a run or kick.

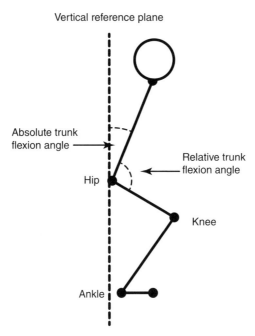

Vertical reference plane

Absolute trunk flexion angle

Relative trunk flexion angle

Hip

Knee

Ankle

▶ **Figure 6.1**   Comparison of the measurement of an absolute joint angle versus a relative joint angle.

Force Production for Movement (Kinetics)

A force is defined as either a push or pull whereby one object applies a force to another. A force causes the linear (straight-line) motion of an object when the force is applied through the centre of mass, but it results in rotation when the force is applied at a distance from the centre of mass.

The forces within the human body (i.e., internal forces) are generated by muscles and then transferred to the skeleton by elastic tendons. This arrangement results in the force being applied at a distance away from a point of rotation (joint), causing joint rotation; it is therefore called a joint torque. The magnitude of a torque is a function of the force magnitude and the moment arm of the force (measured as the perpendicular distance from the pivot point to the line of action of the force). Therefore, joints in the body that have larger moment arms, that is, large distances between the joint centre and the line of action of the muscle, are more suited to high torque production.

When standing still, the centre of mass remains directly above and within the boundary of what is called the base of support; this is the area defined by the edges of the feet. When the centre of mass is within the base of support, the player has stability. But the centre of mass moves outside the base of support when the player produces joint torques that are sufficient to allow her or him to run, resulting in mobility. This interaction between internal and external torques to provide stability and mobility at appropriate times is crucial during play in soccer. An understanding of movement, therefore, requires an understanding of muscle force and torque production as well as the tendon force transfer that results in coordinated joint movement, which is described later. Through this understanding, we can move the theoretical knowledge into application for maximizing force and torque production during sporting specific movements most pertinent to performance.

Newton's three laws of motion govern these forces, which result in either linear or angular motion. These three laws are important because they describe the interrelationships between forces and the resulting motion. The laws and their practical implications for understanding or improving performance are described in the following sections.

Law of Inertia

Newton's first law, the law of inertia, states that a body will remain in a state of rest or at constant velocity unless acted on by an external force. For that reason, a ball continues to travel at a constant velocity unless a player places a force on that ball (by kicking, catching or heading it) or an external force such as air resistance or friction slows it. Of course, the law of inertia also explains why a ball at rest remains motionless unless a player applies a force on it.

Practical implications revolve around the fact that without external forces such as gravity, a ball kicked would not have the traditionally parabolic (curved) path that players rely on for predicting ball movement. But understanding that an external force provided by air pressure differences around the ball as it spins (see the section on the Magnus effect later in this chapter) allows a player to vary the path of a ball to enhance the probability of goal scoring.

Law of Acceleration

Newton's second law, the law of acceleration, states that a force applied to an object results in an acceleration of the object that is proportional to the force applied, in the direction of the force and inversely proportional to the object's mass (Force = mass × acceleration; $F = ma$). This law is one of the most fundamental laws of mechanics, and it explains angular motion because it indicates that a torque is equal to the mass multiplied by the angular acceleration.

This law forms the basis of all human motion, including running speed and changing direction as well as coming out on top during a collision. From a coaching perspective, the law teaches that applying a greater magnitude of force is the key to accelerating faster, changing direction more acutely or kicking a ball farther. In combination with the third law, the effectiveness of movement is determined.

Law of Action and Reaction

Newton's third law, the law of action and reaction, states that for every action there is an equal and opposite reaction. Practically, it states that when one object applies a force to another, the second object applies a force back on the first that is equal in magnitude and opposite in direction. This law gives rise to the term *ground reaction force*, which describes the reaction (opposite) force exerted by the ground when a player pushes against it, which propels the player during running or jumping.

Applying a force gives rise to acceleration, but the direction in which that force is produced determines whether the player effectively moves the object (e.g., a ball or him- or herself). The direction of force application dictates the direction of the opposite and equal reaction that pushes the player forward during running or upward during jumping to head a ball; this equal and opposite force that moves the player is called the ground reaction force. Of course, when a player heads a ball, the ball applies a force to the head just as she or he applies a force to the ball.

These laws lay the foundation for understanding other principles, such as conservation of momentum, that have application to soccer and are discussed later in this chapter.

Biomechanics of Producing Movement

To move (e.g., to accelerate a limb, ourselves or the ball), forces must be applied. This force production process is complex, but by understanding it we can discover ways to improve our movement success (e.g., speed, efficiency, accuracy). Understanding the process will also allow us to develop strategies to improve a player's physical parameters, such as strength, speed and power.

Force Production at the Cellular Level: Muscle Fibres

Muscles are molecular motors that, when activated by the nervous system, produce force. These forces result from interactions at the microscopic level between two protein filaments: actin and myosin. Activity within rotating heads of the myosin filament actively engages and then pulls on the actin filament (see figure 6.2). The pull-detach-reattach-pull cycle of myosin on actin causes shortening of the sarcomere, which is the smallest functional unit of muscle. Serially arranged lines of thousands of sarcomeres lie beside others within a muscle fibre. The muscle fibre is a body cell that has the unique ability to produce force. These muscle fibres collectively form muscles, and the length and number of muscle fibres largely dictate the ability of a muscle to produce forces at different shortening and lengthening speeds and through specific ranges of length change.

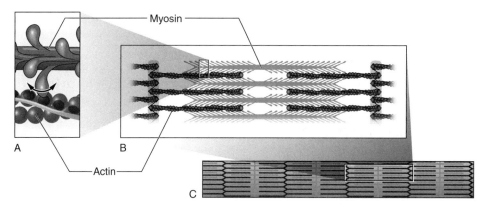

▶ **Figure 6.2** (a) Muscle force production results from active movement of the head of the myosin molecule, which pulls on the actin molecule. (b) These molecules are part of a complex protein structure called a sarcomere, which is the functional unit of muscle. (c) Sarcomeres are arranged in series as well as in parallel within muscle fibres (i.e., muscle cells). A muscle is composed of hundreds or thousands of muscle fibres.

Force Production at the Tissue Level: Muscles and Tendons

Muscles are designed with unique structures, and their fibre arrangements vary considerably. For example, some muscles are designed with relatively short fibres arranged at an angle to the tendon (pennate muscles). Such muscles can produce large forces because the pennate arrangement of the fibres allows more contractile tissue to attach to the tendon. The short fibres ensure that the muscle is relatively stiff, even when inactive, which allows an efficient stretch and shortening of the tendon during movement (examples are the gastrocnemius and soleus muscles in the calf; this phenomenon is described in more detail later). Other muscles have longer fibres, which are considered ideal for fast muscle shortening speeds (e.g., the hamstring muscles can shorten rapidly). The fibres of such muscles typically attach almost parallel to the tendon, that is, with a small pennation angle, so that the overall muscle size is minimized and the force production is in line with the tendon and thus efficient. Ultimately, the fibre arrangement of the muscle, often referred to as its architecture, is the most significant anatomical factor in its force production characteristics.

The force transmitted by muscles to the skeleton depends not only on the capacity of the muscles but also on the elasticity of the tendons, which connect the muscles to the skeleton. The dry mass of tendons is largely composed of elastic collagen fibres, which are grouped into fascicles within the tendon. Collagen is stretched when force is applied, but it then recoils with high efficiency (i.e., with small energy loss, or hysteresis) when force decreases, so the same behaviour is seen in tendons.

In fact, the recoil speed of tendons is far greater than the maximum shortening speed of muscles, so it is useful to apply a muscle force to stretch a tendon and then allow the tendon recoil to produce a rapid shortening of the whole muscle–tendon unit. Such an interaction between muscles and tendons results in high movement speeds because the power output of the muscles is amplified by the fast-shortening tendons. This characteristic is especially important in soccer when a player needs to kick a ball, run at high speeds or jump to head the ball (see figure 6.3).

In the example shown in figure 6.3, the muscle is only slightly active immediately before the knee is flexed (prelanding) during a countermovement jump performed from a run (e.g., to head a ball), and the tendon does not stretch much. During the knee flexion phase at midjump, the muscle force is high but the body's velocity is low because it is in transition between descending and ascending phases. Here the tendon is significantly stretched and energy is stored; notice that the muscle is shortened as the tendon is stretched. Before takeoff the tendon recoils at a high speed, so power output is high; at this point, the muscle tends to have almost completed its shortening and its force output is submaximum.

When two springs are arranged in series, such as in a muscle–tendon unit, more energy will be stored in the most compliant (least stiff) spring. Because tendons have lesser hysteresis than muscle (i.e., tendons lose possibly 15 per cent of their energy during lengthening and shortening, whereas muscles may lose approximately 50 per cent), it is preferable to increase the stiffness

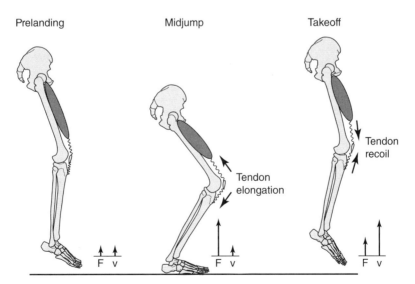

▶ **Figure 6.3** Tendons act to amplify the power output of the muscles. The bones of the upper (femur) and lower (tibia and fibula) limbs interact during contraction of the thigh (quadriceps) muscle, which provides force through the patellar tendon during jumping. F = force applied to the ground; v = velocity of movement.

Practical Applications

The interaction between muscles and tendons results in high movement velocities because the fast-shortening tendons amplify muscular force. Therefore, understanding how to train the muscles and tendons, as well as understanding how to make best use of the tendons is vital (see the section on the kinetic chain later in this chapter).

of muscles so that the tendon is, by comparison, relatively compliant. Muscles with shorter fibres or greater force capacity will be highly stiff; in fact, long tendons in the forearm and lower leg often attach to muscles with relatively short fibres. Thus, some muscle–tendon units (e.g., the Achilles tendon–calf muscle complex) are uniquely designed to allow optimum storage and release of elastic energy, which contributes to running, jumping and kicking ability.

Force Production at the System Level: Muscles and Bones as Lever Systems

When the muscles produce force through a tendon to a bone to create movement, the muscle and bone function as a lever system. The muscle provides the force, the bone acts as a rigid bar, and the joint is the pivot point (or fulcrum).

Classes of Lever Systems

There are three types of lever systems (see figure 6.4). In a first-class lever system, forces are applied to the pivot point on the side opposite the load. This type is often referred to as the seesaw lever system because of its likeness. An example in the human body of the action of this lever is a force-generating agonist muscle (e.g., the calf muscles at the ankle) being counteracted by an antagonist muscle (e.g., the tibialis anterior muscle at the front of the shin).

In a second-class lever system, forces are applied to the same side as the load but farther from the pivot point and in the opposite direction. The human body has no broadly accepted examples of such a lever system during concentric muscle actions, but if the arm is flexed to 90 degrees at the elbow and a load is placed on the hand that overcomes the upward force produced by the biceps muscle (i.e., the muscle lengthens eccentrically), this would be considered a second-class lever system.

In a third-class lever system, forces are again applied to the same side as the load but closer to the pivot point and in the opposite direction. Most joints in the human body are designed as third-class lever systems, the best example being the biceps brachii applying an upward (flexion) force at the elbow to overcome the resistance of a load in the hand that applies a down-

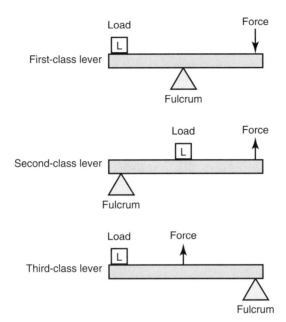

▶ **Figure 6.4**   Bones (rigid bar), joints (fulcrum) and muscles (force) form lever systems within the body. Most joints are third-class lever systems, which are ideal for large joint excursions or high joint angular velocities.

ward (extension) force. Understanding lever systems becomes important when we try to understand how torques are produced about the joints and, in particular, how to achieve high-speed joint rotations during explosive movements such as running, jumping and kicking.

Joint Torque Production

A torque (also called the moment of force) is the rotary effect of a force when applied at a distance from the centre of rotation of a joint (pivot point). In third-class lever systems, for example, muscle forces are applied against the bone at small distances from the joint, which causes a rotary force, or torque, to be developed (see figure 6.5). Ultimately, the purpose of forces generated by active muscles and recoiling tendons is to create joint torque, which results in skeletal movements involved in running, jumping and kicking.

The torque magnitude is affected by two main parameters: (1) the muscle force (F_m) applied and (2) the distance of force application from the joint centre, which is also called the moment arm (MA) of the force. Because most lever systems in the human body are third-class systems and the moment arm is relatively small, large muscle forces are required to develop the torques necessary for fast running and jumping activities. This can be beneficial because the large muscle forces stretch the elastic tendons, which then also recoil to improve movement power. Although the small moment

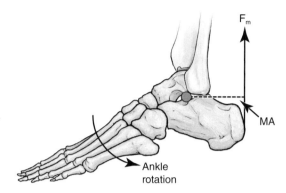

▶ **Figure 6.5** Joint torque production. Muscles produce forces (F_m) through tendons that are attached to bone. The distance between a joint centre (silver disc) and the line of action of a tendon is the moment arm (MA). Generation of a muscle force creates a joint torque with the magnitude $F_m \times$ MA.

arms are not ideal for the development of large joint torques, they ensure that small length changes in the muscle–tendon unit result in relatively large joint excursions (i.e., large changes in joint angle). Thus, the human musculoskeletal system seems to be designed to produce forces over large ranges of motion, and thus at high movement speeds. We can thus perform skills such as kicking balls at high speeds, as long as the necessary muscle force can be produced.

The development of a torque about a joint as a result of muscle force is a great example of an internal torque. However, a force can be applied external to a body and may thus produce an external torque. For example, a player applies an external force when kicking a ball. If the force is slightly off centre, that is, if the line of force application is not in the centre of the ball, the ball will rotate, or spin. The importance of ball spin will become clear later in the chapter, as will the importance of understanding the relationship between internal and external torques for improving soccer performance.

Practical Applications

Our musculoskeletal system is arranged to allow high speeds of movement using third-class levers. Second-class levers, on the other hand, are known for being beneficial in force generation (think of a wheelbarrow). To form a second-class lever arrangement, we must use multijoint configurations (total body position), such as when we perform a push-up and put force through our hands with the axis at our feet against the force of our centre of mass. Knowing how the body position we adopt can affect our ability to produce force or velocity through leverage is important for optimizing performance.

Work, Power and Energy

Work, or more specifically mechanical work, is the product of force and displacement (W = F × s; measured in joules), and the total work done on an object is the sum of all the forces acting and all the displacements that have occurred. As shown in figure 6.6, the foot remains in contact with the ball during a kick for a displacement of between 0.15 and 0.4 metres. Therefore, the work done on the ball is calculated as the displacement multiplied by the force during that displacement. Work is a vector quantity (it has direction), and therefore positive work is done if the force applied and the displacement are in the same direction, whereas negative work is done when the direction is opposite to the force (think of the eccentric, or lowering, phase of a bench press exercise). Note that the amount of work done is independent of the time needed to complete that work, although our next variable, power, is a direct function of the time in which the work is completed.

What is often thought to be more important in running, jumping and kicking is that this work is done rapidly. The rate of doing work (W/t, where t = time) is called power, which is measured in watts. Because mechanical work is the product of force and displacement (F × s), and total work is the product of force and distance (W = F × d; i.e., sum of all displacements), force applied over a measured displacement in a short time results in high power output (P = F × s/t). Remember also that velocity is equal to the displacement achieved in a given time (v = s/t), so power (P) is equal to force times velocity (F × v). Therefore, work can be defined either as the rate of doing

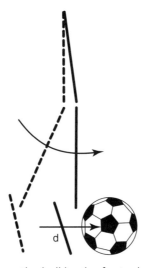

▶ **Figure 6.6** Work is done on the ball by the foot when it is kicked because a force, F, is applied over distance, d (dashed leg = start of ball contact; solid leg = end of ball contact). If the rate of work is high, the ball will gain significant kinetic energy (1/2mv², where m is the ball's mass and v is its velocity) and will therefore travel at a fast velocity.

work or as the product of force and velocity. Either way, if more joint power is developed and properly coordinated, a player can kick a ball faster, run faster or jump higher. In this regard, improvements in power output can be considered important for soccer performance.

An object such as a soccer ball gains energy when a force is applied to it. The increase in energy can be seen as an increase in the velocity of the ball. This form of energy is called kinetic energy (KE), which is the energy of movement and is a function of the mass and velocity of an object (KE = $\frac{1}{2}mv^2$, where m is the mass of the object and v is its velocity). Any object that moves has kinetic energy, and a goal of running, jumping and kicking is to increase the kinetic energy of the body or ball.

Energy, however, can be neither created nor destroyed, so the kinetic energy must come from some other source. One way to get this energy is to find it externally. For example, a ball will gain kinetic energy (i.e., its velocity will change) if work is done on it. In fact, the change in kinetic energy of the ball ($\frac{1}{2}mv^2$) is exactly equal to the work done on it (F × s), so F × s = $\frac{1}{2}mv^2$. This relationship between work and energy is called the work–energy relationship. Because these two quantities are equal to one another, they are measured in the same unit: joules (J).

Kinetic energy can also come from the conversion of other forms of energy. For example, a ball has potential energy (PE) if it is held above the ground; it has the potential to gain velocity because it will fall if it is dropped and will transfer this potential energy (because of the height) into kinetic energy that will result in increasing velocity as it falls to the ground. This potential to move results from the fact that the force of gravity will accelerate the ball if it is left to fall, so this form of energy is called gravitational potential energy (PE_{grav}). In fact, the heavier the ball is or the higher above the ground it is, the greater the potential energy it has because PE_{grav} = mgh, where m is the ball's mass, g is acceleration because of gravity, and h is the height of the ball above the ground. A player who jumps to head a ball gains potential energy as he or she gets higher during the jump and simultaneously loses kinetic energy at the top of the jump as he or she briefly stops before falling back down; the player has zero kinetic energy because his or her velocity is zero. When a player falls after heading the ball, he or she loses potential energy (in the form of height) but gains kinetic energy (in the form of velocity) while accelerating towards the ground.

To jump or kick a ball, however, the body or leg needs to gain kinetic energy. Because gravitational potential energy cannot be used to do this, the player needs to find energy from somewhere else. In this case, it comes from both muscle work and the elastic potential energy stored in the tendons. In fact, muscles can also store and release elastic energy, but this ability is compromised when the muscles shorten whilst doing work. Muscles produce forces that stretch the tendons, storing elastic potential energy ($PE_{elastic}$). The amount of stored energy is related to the stiffness (k) of the tendon and the

Practical Applications

A constant interplay occurs between mechanical work and the energy of a system. Practically, it is important to understand how energy can be transferred between objects, such as the foot or head and the ball during kicking or heading, or the foot and ground during running, to optimize soccer performance.

amount of stretch (elongation) that is imposed (x), such that $PE_{elastic} = \frac{1}{2}kx^2$. This stored elastic energy is then released at high speeds as the leg swings to kick a ball or as the player leaves the ground in a jump, so power production is high (i.e., the rate of energy release is high). In fact, when a player kicks the ball (i.e., does work on the ball), the ball compresses and elastic energy is stored in it. Just before the ball leaves the foot, it begins to expand at high speed so that the stored elastic potential energy is released and contributes to the kinetic energy of the ball. Changes in ball properties can change its ability to store and release energy. For example, when the ball is either cold or inflated to very high pressure, it will compress less for a given force, so its energy storage capacity will be reduced and it will be harder to kick (or head) at high speeds.

Integrated Principles of Kinetics and Kinematics

The movements performed in soccer result from a complex interplay between the forces produced and the environment. By understanding this complexity, we can then understand the best ways to produce forces to optimize movement and thus soccer performance.

Impulse–Momentum Relationship

More force is required, or that force has to be applied for longer, to move a larger mass or accelerate that mass to a faster velocity. For example, more force must be produced for longer to push a car than to kick a ball. The magnitude and time of force application is described by the impulse (J), which is the product of force (F) and time (t): $J = F \times t$ (measured in newton-seconds, Ns). A mass (m) that has a velocity (v) has a momentum (p), so $p = m \times v$ (measured in kg·m·s^{-1}); that is, a big object that is moving quickly has a large momentum. Because the change in momentum of an object is directly proportional to the impulse applied to it, we can say that $Ft = mv$, which is referred to as the impulse–momentum relationship. So when two opponents come together to try to win the ball, the victor will be the one who can apply sufficient force for an appropriate time to change the momentum of the opponent away from the ball.

Practical Applications

Improving running technique to apply forces more effectively during turning, or improving force-generating capacity to apply larger forces, is necessary to improve the ability to change direction during running.

The direction of force application is also important when considering the application of an impulse. For example, to accelerate the body while running in a straight line, the horizontal impulse needs to be directed backwards against the ground (think of extending the leg backwards from the point of foot contact with the ground) to provide forward momentum whilst at the same time having a vertical impulse to overcome gravity, allowing that forward momentum to result in significant displacement during the flight phase of a run. The impulse applied into the ground is then applied equally and in the opposite direction back to the runner by the ground, allowing the runner to overcome gravity for flight time during running whilst also increasing horizontal impulse for forward momentum. But when a player runs in an arc (i.e., curvilinearly), she or he needs to produce laterally directed forces continually to accelerate towards the centre of the arc. The need to produce this force is caused by another force that continually acts to force the player to move in a straight line: the centripetal force (F_c). This force depends on mass (m), running velocity (v) and the radius of the arc being run (r), such that $F_c = m \times (v^2/r)$. Therefore, greater impulses are required to run faster or in a tighter arc. Another way to conceptualize this is to remember that a change in velocity occurs when a player changes either speed or direction, so the player is in a continual state of acceleration when running an arc, even if the speed is constant. If the player does not apply a force to accelerate continually into the turn, she or he would end up running in a straight line.

Angular Impulse–Angular Momentum Relationship

Of course, a player often needs to rotate body segments or the whole body during kicking, throwing and running movements (see the next section on the kinetic chain). Impulses that cause (or stop) rotations are called angular impulses (calculated as torque multiplied by time), and they result in a change in the angular momentum (H) of a limb or the body. So the impulse–momentum relationship can be set in the context of angular motion too.

The angular momentum of an object (or the body) is a function of its moment of inertia (I), which describes the distance of a mass (m) from the point about which it rotates (k, otherwise known as the radius of gyration; see figure 6.7). So an object whose mass is located farther from a pivot point has a greater moment of inertia, which usually makes it harder to move or to stop moving.

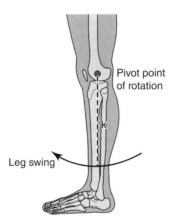

Pivot point
of rotation

k

Leg swing

▶ **Figure 6.7** A mass is considered to rotate about a joint at a distance k (radius of gyration); the greater the mass (m) or the distance is, the greater the moment of inertia is. The angular velocity (ω) of a swinging limb is influenced by the angular impulse, which creates an angular momentum (H) such that $H = mk^2\omega$; reducing m or k will cause an increase in ω if H is constant.

Angular momentum is also a function of the angular velocity of the object (ω). Therefore, just as linear momentum is determined by the mass and velocity of an object, angular momentum is determined by the moment of inertia of an object (mass × distance) and angular velocity. The formula is $H = mk^2\omega$, which shows that increasing the mass or angular velocity of an object will increase its angular momentum proportionally, but increasing the distance of the mass from the pivot point (point of rotation) will have a more significant effect (i.e., to the square of the distance). This point is important because it shows that keeping a mass closer to the point of rotation is vital to obtain high angular velocities for a given angular momentum. Of course, because the angular momentum is determined by the angular impulse, keeping the mass closer to the point of rotation is important to obtain a high angular velocity for a given angular impulse. We can use this information to improve running speeds or reduce the time for changes of direction. For example, the knee is flexed during the recovery phase of running (i.e., when it is brought towards the front of the body) to reduce the moment of inertia and thus increase angular velocity, and the limbs are often brought closer to the body when the player swivels, turns or changes direction.

Kinetic Chain

Complex multijoint movements, such as those used in running, jumping, kicking and throwing, require coordinated and precise timing of movements at individual joints. Therefore, the body moves as if it were a system of segments linked at the joints and driven in motion by the muscles and tendons. This moving chain of segments is referred to as the kinetic chain.

Kinetic chain movements can be classified as either open, when at least one end of the chain (e.g., the hand during a throw) is completely free to move, or closed, when both ends of the chain are not able to move freely (e.g., during a leg press exercise in the gym; see figure 6.8). In soccer most movements are considered open, although the arms in a throw-in are not completely free to move because they are attached to the ball and therefore

▶ **Figure 6.8** Kinetic chain movements: (*a*) A leg press exercise is an example of a closed kinetic chain movement because both ends of the chain (lower limb) are fixed. Simultaneous joint extensions create a push-like movement that allows large forces to be developed in the leg press. (*b*) A soccer kick is an open kinetic chain movement because at least one end (the foot) is free to move. Sequential joint extensions (the thigh rotating forward whilst the shank rotates backwards) during kicking allow fast movement speeds.

to each other. In turn, the use of closed-chain exercises to enhance force production can be coupled with open-chain exercises to enhance the ability to develop high forces initially and then transfer this force through the kinetic chain with increasing velocity as it passes through the body for maximal end point velocity at the end of the movement (such as release of the ball).

Both open and closed kinetic chain movements can be accomplished using one of two movement patterns: push-like or throw-like. Push-like movement patterns are characterized by simultaneous (or synchronous) rotation of the joints, as would occur in the arm when throwing a dart or in the legs when squatting to pick up something from the ground. Because of the simplicity of such movements, push-like movement patterns are typically adopted when high movement accuracy is required. Also, having several joints contribute simultaneously to a movement allows the torque at each joint to sum, which results in a large overall force being applied by the kinetic chain. Therefore, push-like movement patterns are generally adopted when high movement accuracy or large force production is necessary.

Throw-like patterns are characterized by joints changing their angles sequentially, as would occur during a fast overhand throw in baseball, cricket and other sports. The complex, sequential timing benefits high movement speeds but reduces accuracy and maximum force production.

The benefit for movement speed comes from two mechanisms. First, a movement can be initiated using the large musculature around the proximal segments (torso, shoulder, hip); for example, the legs and torso initiate total body momentum, and then the shoulder and pectoral muscles initiate the forward motion of the arm in an overhand throw. The arm therefore has momentum (in fact, it has angular momentum: $H = mk^2\omega$) with the mass distributed about the shoulder joint, which acts as the pivot point, or centre of rotation. Muscle forces then stop the upper arm from rotating, and, because the total momentum of the system must remain constant, the angular momentum is relocated down the kinetic chain. Because the mass of that part of the arm is less than that of the whole arm and the distance from the mass to the pivot point (now at the elbow) is reduced, the angular velocity must increase (i.e., if m and k decrease yet H remains constant, ω must increase). Subsequently, the muscles in the upper arm can be used to stop the forearm from rotating, in which case the angular momentum is relocated to the hand. Both m and k are further reduced and ω has to increase further. As the momentum is transferred down the chain, the angular velocity of the remaining segments must increase. Ultimately, the momentum is transferred to the ball, which is projected at very high velocity. This explanation nicely describes how a throw-like pattern can allow very high speeds in the distal segments (e.g. hands and feet) during throwing- and kicking-type movements.

Nonetheless, if the muscles at the hip are used to stop the upper leg (thigh) from moving during a soccer kick, the final velocity of the foot, and therefore the ball, is reduced. For that reason, among others, a follow-through

Practical Applications

Video analysis of a kick or throw-in allows coaches to slow down the video and watch the order of limb segment movement to determine whether the athlete is using an appropriate movement pattern for the skill being analysed. Push-like patterns should be used when high accuracy is required (e.g., a short pass to a teammate), but a throw-like pattern should be used when high movement speeds are important (e.g., a goal kick or long-distance throw-in).

is important during kicking; it ensures that the thigh segment of the chain is not braked prematurely, which would compromise kicking velocity. So there must be another explanation as to how high speeds are attained using throw-like movement patterns.

This second explanation is that the throw-like pattern allows greater energy storage in the tendons and their recoil contributes to the high movement speeds. During a soccer instep kick, for example, the leg is retracted backwards behind the body in preparation for the kick. Because a kick is a high-speed movement, the player adopts a throw-like pattern in which the thigh is the first lower limb segment to begin the forward (protraction) phase of the kick. At this point the lower leg continues in retraction and the significant knee flexion allows elastic energy storage in the quadriceps tendon (which attaches the thigh muscles to the front of the shin). Later in the movement the lower leg also protracts and the energy stored in the tendon can be released to aid knee extension; this mechanism is similar to that seen in jumping in figure 6.3. The continued hip flexion simultaneous with the rapid knee extension results in very high velocity of the distal segment, the foot. A similar mechanism allows elastic energy to contribute to hand (and therefore ball) speed during a throw-in and to the rapid extension of the ankle in the upward phase of a vertical jump. The combination of a transfer of momentum along the kinetic change and an optimum storage and release of elastic energy provides a dual benefit to the throw-like pattern as far as movement velocity is concerned. So ensuring that joint angle changes occur at the proper time during kicking and throw-in movements is vital for optimum performance.

Projectile Motion

Objects travelling through the air tend to move in a curvilinear (in fact, parabolic) path unless they have flight capability. Of course, a soccer player is a projectile when he or she jumps to head a ball or dives to stop a shot on goal, but the principles of projectile motion are probably most relevant when discussing the flight path of the ball. Several factors influence the flight path of a ball if there is no spin on the ball and we assume that the effects of air resistance are small (the effect of aerodynamic forces, i.e., spin and air resistance, will be discussed later): projection velocity, projection height and projection angle.

Projection velocity depends on the velocity of the foot, which results from the production of internal torques and the transfer of momentum to the foot before striking the ball. The projection velocity is often separated into two components: horizontal velocity and vertical velocity. The horizontal component determines the rate at which the ball travels parallel to the ground, and the distance travelled (i.e., the range) depends directly on the time the ball is in the air. The vertical component determines the height that the ball attains and thus the time that the ball remains in the air (flight time) and is the component that gravity influences to slow the rise or accelerate the fall of the ball. By changing the projection angle, the distribution of vertical and horizontal projection velocity is varied and the range of the flight of the ball is affected.

Typically, the projection height of a soccer kick is zero because the ball is often kicked from the ground (projection height is positive when the ball is kicked from above the ground by a goalkeeper, for example). The angle of projection that elicits the greatest range of a ball projected from the ground is 45 degrees. This angle allows an equal proportion of the projection velocity to be directed in horizontal and vertical directions, optimizing the range travelled. If the projection height is positive, as when the ball is kicked from the hands during a goalkeeper's kick or is thrown from the hands in a throw-in, the optimum angle will be less than 45 degrees because some height was given before the kick and more horizontal projection is required.

Of course, humans can often more easily project objects with horizontal velocity (e.g., we can kick and throw balls horizontally with high velocity), which allows faster projection velocities. Therefore, the optimum angle of projection in kicks and throws is often marginally less than the angle predicted theoretically. Spin that can be placed on the ball also influences the way a projectile travels, which will be discussed in the next section.

Aerodynamics

Fluid dynamics is the area of science that describes how objects move through all fluids, from semisolid materials (e.g., gels) to liquids (e.g., water) and gases (e.g., air). In soccer, the relevant topic is how objects move through air, which is a branch of fluid dynamics referred to as aerodynamics. We can hear air rushing over a ball when it travels at high speed and see that the ball slows down during its trajectory. Both of these phenomena result from drag forces acting on the ball. Two types of drag are important in this context.

Form Drag

Form drag (or profile drag) is the drag associated with the shape of an object. Typically, objects that have a greater frontal surface area (A), are moving at a faster velocity (v) or have a poorer aerodynamic shape (k) experience greater form drag force (F_d). This can be observed in the equation $F_d = kAv^2$, where changes in the velocity of the object (or an increase in the oncoming speed of the air) clearly has the greatest effect on F_d because it increases to the square of velocity.

The drag force is caused by the development of turbulence, which takes energy away from the ball. Consider a ball moving through a mass of air that is moving with constant motion (or is not moving at all), as in figure 6.9. This mass is considered to move as a single entity in nonmixing layers of air, and this air flow is therefore referred to as laminar. The laminar flow is disturbed, however, when the ball passes through this air; the air in front of the ball is pushed out of its path, and some of the air rushes into the

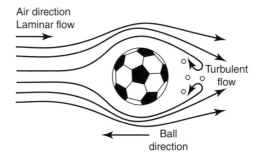

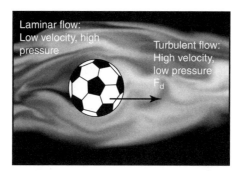

▶ **Figure 6.9** Form drag results from the formation of turbulent flow (top) despite oncoming flow being laminar. Turbulence takes energy away from the ball, slowing it down. During flight (bottom), slower moving, higher-pressure air impacts at the front of the ball, whereas faster, lower-pressure, turbulent air forms behind the ball. The pressure differential results in the formation of form drag (F_d) that slows the ball.

low-pressure zone created at the back of the moving ball. Therefore, the air is accelerated as the ball moves through it, which increases its energy (the kinetic energy of the air is proportional to the square of its velocity: kinetic energy = $\frac{1}{2}mv^2$, where m is the mass of moving air and v is its velocity). The nonlaminar, higher-velocity air is turbulent, and the type of flow is called turbulent flow. But energy cannot be created or destroyed, so this energy must be taken from somewhere. Logically, the energy comes from the moving ball, which now loses energy and thus slows down. The movement of the ball through the air increases turbulence, and thus the kinetic energy of the air reduces the kinetic energy of the ball. The ball must lose velocity because the mass of the ball remains constant.

This occurrence can be conceptualized in another way. The ball collides with the oncoming air as the ball moves; that is, the air exerts a force on the ball. But this air is moving slowly relative to the ball. Behind the ball, air rushes in to fill the low-pressure region that is left behind as the ball moves, and this air travels at high velocity as it is accelerated. According to Bernoulli's theorem (Daniel Bernoulli was a Swiss mathematician and physicist who realized that regions of high-velocity flow were associated with relatively low pressure, whereas regions of low-velocity flow were associated with high pressure; this is referred to as Bernoulli's theorem) a region of high pressure is created in front of the ball and a region of low pressure is created behind the ball. Thus, there is a pressure differential across the ball, and the ball is forced from the high pressure in front to the low pressure behind. This creates a force vector directed from the front to the back of the ball, and this impeding force is the drag force.

In fact, the two explanations are similar in that they require air to move at different velocities and for a pressure differential to exist. The drag force acts on any ball that is moving in air, and it will have a greater effect when the ball is moving rapidly because drag increases to the square of velocity. Of course, the surface area (A) of the ball is also important, but the laws of the game determine the size of the ball so that parameter cannot be changed.

Surface Drag

The second type of drag that acts on a ball is surface (or friction) drag. This retarding force is applied by the air molecules as they contact the ball, causing a friction-like force. This force is relatively small on a smooth soccer ball, but it can vary slightly across the ball because of variations in stitching and panelling. In general, rougher surfaces promote greater surface drag, but it is possible for significant turbulence to be created when the surface is very rough. Because turbulence is characterized by a high velocity of air flow and higher-velocity flows are associated with lower pressure (Bernoulli's theorem), it is possible for balls with a very rough surface to have slightly lower surface drag.

Effects of Velocity on Drag: A Special Case

Form drag increases dramatically as the speed of an object increases (F_d increases to the square of velocity). The drag force is caused by the area of turbulence being created behind the object. In fact, air moving over an object becomes turbulent, which causes surface drag. As the speed of an object increases, the turbulence on its surface increases. The air therefore moves towards the surface of the object because of the lower pressure created, and the total surface area in which there is significant contact between the oncoming air and the object increases; the region of turbulence behind the object therefore decreases. At a critical speed, however, the turbulent region behind the object becomes so small that air moves over it whilst maintaining near-laminar flow. Effectively, the turbulent region is shed from the object. If a ball is kicked at a sufficient speed, drag would be markedly reduced and thus there would be little slowing of the ball in flight. This phenomena can be seen when the ball is struck at very high speeds (the speed at which this occurs depends on the surface characteristics of the ball, the density of the air around the ball and other factors, so this speed varies substantially) and is useful in free-kick situations to minimize the time an opponent has to deflect or stop the ball.

Magnus Effect: Putting Swerve on a Soccer Ball

Because of surface drag, all moving objects (or objects that are stationary in a moving fluid environment) will retain some fluid around them. In the context of a ball moving through the air, some air will move with the ball, much as you can feel the air that moves with a passing train or bus as it goes past you. This moving layer of air is called the boundary layer.

In some cases, a player may apply an external torque to the ball when kicking it to put spin on it. The boundary layer that forms around the ball will therefore also start to spin with the ball. In this case, air on one side of the ball will be moving forward towards the oncoming air and thus be colliding with it. The oncoming air is thus slowed by the collision and deflected away from the ball. Simultaneously, air approaching the other side of the ball will make contact with air moving in the same direction, so its movement is less impaired and it will move past the ball at a relatively higher speed. According to Bernoulli's theorem, the slow-moving air on one side of the ball will be associated with higher pressure and the faster moving (i.e., less impeded) air on the other side of the ball will be associated with lower pressure. A pressure differential results, and the ball is forced towards the side with lower pressure (see figure 6.10). In this case, the spinning of the moving ball has created a condition in which the ball will swerve towards the direction of spin where there is faster moving, lower-pressure air. This effect, and the understanding that it increases as the ball spin rate increases,

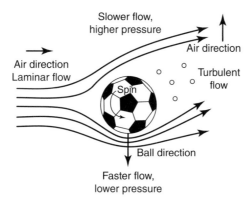

▶ **Figure 6.10** The spinning of the ball during flight causes the boundary layer to spin with it. Thus, oncoming air on one side (top, in this illustration) is slowed significantly, whilst air on the other side is slowed only marginally. The variations in air speed result in a pressure differential across the ball, according to Bernoulli's theorem. A lift force (Magnus force) is created, which is directed from high to low pressure, and the ball will swerve in flight. An alternative explanation is that the deflection of the air around the ball (upward, in this illustration) must be opposed by an equal downward movement, according to Newton's second law. This is the Magnus force.

was first properly described by H.G. Magnus in 1852. It is therefore referred to as the Magnus effect (the force created by the effect, which causes the ball to swerve, is called the Magnus force). This effect is created when any object spins in a fluid environment, but it is particularly noticeable when soccer balls are kicked with sufficient spin.

The effect can be explained in a second way. The collision of air on one side of the ball deflects the air away from the ball. On the other side, air is not deflected and thus has a tendency to be drawn into the low-pressure zone that is left behind the moving ball. Therefore, the spinning of the ball causes a change of direction of the air; that is, the mass of air is accelerated to one side. According to Newton's second law, this acceleration required a force, so an equal and opposite force must be created. This opposing force, the Magnus force, causes the ball to swerve in the direction opposite the moving air. Although Sir Isaac Newton did not use his theories to describe the effect (he did make a note about the curvature on spinning tennis balls before Magnus proposed his theory), we can use his concepts to explain ball swerve. Regardless of the choice of explanation, the idea that a ball will swerve towards the direction of spin is important because it allows a player to determine how much side-, under- or overspin to put on a ball to swerve the ball around or over a wall, or to create an upward lift force on the ball.

Unequal pressures can also be created across a moving soccer ball without spin being placed on it simply because the surface is irregular and the amount of surface drag created by the panels of a soccer ball versus the stitching is

Practical Applications

Placing spin on a ball to produce difficult or unique trajectories can be advantageous, but spin can also be applied unintentionally, resulting in inaccurate kicking. If players use this method to change ball trajectory, repeated practice is needed to ensure reliability, just as players would practice various types of kicks without spin. Practice will ensure that the athlete can reliably perform both types of kicks and minimize the unintentional application of spin.

different. When a ball is kicked without spin, these variations cause the ball to swerve away from higher-pressure regions on the ball. The variations in surface drag will also cause the ball to rotate slightly as it flies, which will expose different regions of the ball to the oncoming air, and the pressure distributions will change. These effects can cause the swerve direction to vary when the ball is in flight. Because these effects are larger when ball velocity is increased, unpredictable swerve can become substantial when a ball is kicked at high speeds. This unpredictability of trajectory can be useful for beating a goalkeeper, although the swerve can also be problematic for accurate kicking.

Friction

The friction force opposes the motion of two objects when their surfaces are in contact. Friction results from bonds being formed between either molecules on the surfaces of the objects (i.e., microscopic level) or small but visible imperfections in a surface (i.e., macroscopic level). The friction force (F_f) depends on two parameters: the friction coefficient (μ), which describes the likelihood of strong bond formation between the surfaces and is unique to each pair of surfaces, and the force pushing the surfaces together, that is, the normal reaction force (R), which acts perpendicular to the surfaces. Thus, $F_f = \mu R$. To increase friction magnitude, the normal force applied to the surface can be increased; in the case of soccer, in which movements are performed on a flat pitch, this force would be the vertical component of ground reaction force.

In some instances, such as when the studs on the boots penetrate the ground and two surfaces interlock, the term *traction* is used. Increasing traction requires the use of longer studs (or optimizing their shape) or the use of a dry, well-grassed soccer pitch to allow the studs to hold without slippage. Thus, the coefficient of traction is affected by the properties of the two surfaces. Although maximizing traction at all times may seem beneficial, it may be problematic when rapid and aggressive changes of direction are required. The lack of movement between the boot and ground ensures that the foot, and therefore the body, is decelerated rapidly and the ankle,

Practical Applications

To improve performance using the concepts of friction and traction, coaches and players can consider both training-based and decision-based opportunities to enhance friction and traction. Training-based changes involve improving the amount of force that a player (through enhancements in strength) can push into the ground that inherently improves the friction that he or she has to push against (or change momentum before slipping). Decision-based changes (that occur on the day of performance) involve making informed decisions with respect to weather and pitch conditions to select the boot that will provide the greatest amount of traction without limiting performance or increasing risk of injury.

knee and hip are placed at increased risk of injury. Therefore, friction and traction should be understood with reference to the correct choice of boot both for boot-to-ball and stud-to-ground interactions.

Conclusion

The laws of physics govern all aspects of soccer performance, from running and changing direction on the pitch to high-speed and high-accuracy kicks and throw-ins. Therefore, playing and coaching performances are substantially influenced by the level of biomechanics knowledge of the player or coach. The ability to improve performance in players who have different body shapes and physical qualities, and who have different skill set requirements, can be dramatically improved by the implementation of biomechanical strategies. When reading the remaining chapters of this book, reflect on the basic knowledge you gained from this chapter.

CHAPTER 7

Refining Techniques and Skills Through Scientific Analysis

—Neal Smith

Soccer play involves a variety of human movement patterns either with or without a ball. These actions can vary from the relatively simple skills of walking and jogging to the hugely complex motor skills of soccer kicking, changing of direction and heading of a soccer ball. This chapter provides some understanding of how to break down these complex skills into phases or subdivisions that coaches and players can understand. Most of these more complex motor patterns occur at high speed, so the human eye and brain cannot take more than a snapshot of the action. In the modern day, however, we are armed with high-quality and sometimes low-cost technology that we can use to help us understand these soccer skills.

The branch of sport science that is concerned with the analysis of sporting technique is called biomechanics. This discipline applies mechanical principles of motion to the biological structures of the body, and its main objective is to improve sporting technique or reduce the potential for injury.

Therefore, in this chapter we will investigate what biomechanical analysis techniques can do for the modern player and coach, provide a summary of the scientific-based knowledge we currently have available this area and attempt to apply it to some of the most common skills required for successful, safe soccer performance.

Sports Analysis

Scientific investigations that have looked into the analysis of soccer skills have often involved highly technological and highly expensive analysis techniques. This chapter is concerned with the interpretation of these complex findings to help us understand the key underlying principles of techniques. Some basic mechanical principles can help us understand the reasons why the body moves and behaves the way it does. The body will not move at all if force is not applied to it, so when we try to unpack the reasons why the body moves in the ways it does, we need to be able to think about which forces are making the various body parts move. Usually we can identify most forces that act on the body to be either muscular (forces applied by the muscles to the skeleton) or gravitational. We can typically try to work this out more simply in picture form (figure 7.1); most people's minds work better this way, in what we call a free body diagram.

If we try to relate this idea to soccer-specific movements, we can start with straight-line running and see that the main way in which the body is propelled forward is through contraction of the lower-limb muscles, which exerts a force on the ground. We can then use Newton's third law of motion, which states that for every action there is an equal and opposite reaction, to see that the ground then exerts an equal and opposite force back on the athlete. The free body diagram shows us that this equal and opposite force comes in two parts: One pushes up vertically (counteracts gravity and propels

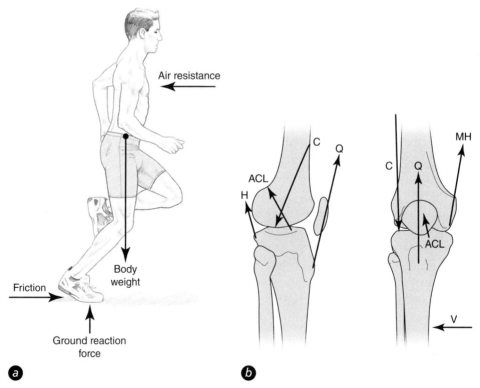

▶ **Figure 7.1** (*a*) Simple free body diagram of an athlete running and (*b*) a complex free body diagram of the knee during a change in direction manoeuvre.

the body into the air), and the other is friction, which serves to propel the body forwards. A player who wishes to accelerate away from an opponent or be first to a loose ball must try to maximize this horizontal (friction) component. Of course, this ability is related to the strength of leg musculature, individual running technique and the optimization of the interaction of the soccer shoe with the turf. Although we can acknowledge these factors here, the individual aspects of strength training, running technique and soccer shoe stud pattern (layout, length, shape, orientation) are beyond the scope of this chapter. These topics are covered in other chapters in the book.

Although the simple free body diagram of running gives us an understanding of the forces acting on a player, this action is performed mainly in two dimensions: vertical and horizontal. Anyone who watches a soccer game knows that motion rarely occurs in a straight line. Take, for example, the idea of a striker making a curved run along the defensive line to maintain forward speed yet also remain onside (figure 7.2).

Research from our own labs has shown that running in a nonlinear path (as seen in figure 7.2) necessitates technical alterations from those of straight-line running. The technical changes also form the basis of cutting-type manoeuvres and turns for change of direction. The key technical changes involve the different roles of the inside and outside limbs during the curved running pattern. Essentially, the body's centre of gravity is lowered by first dropping the hip of the inside leg. This action enables a greater amount of hip motion at the inside leg yet a reduced amount of motion at the knees compared with running in a straight path (Brice, Smith and Dyson 2008). All of this serves to tilt the upper body and hence place the body's centre of gravity closer towards the inside of the curve. This all may help us understand what technically changes with these types of movement patterns, but what implications would that have for coaches or conditioning specialists? These implications are again mainly to do with the generation of forces. In addition to a slightly different movement (kinematic) pattern, the forces generated that push against the ground are also different. Smith, Dyson, Hale and Janaway (2006) showed that a greater force was generated in the outside leg

▶ **Figure 7.2** Highlighting the inside and outside legs of the curved running pattern.

of the curve in terms of the ability to change direction. In other words, this outside leg contributed more force directed inwards, towards the centre of the curve. This would indicate that conditioning of the quadriceps and gluteal muscle groups would be key to changing direction in conjunction with the muscles of the torso. The inside leg of the curve worked in a different way to maintain forward velocity as it provided more force in this direction. The inside leg of the curve would require conditioning of the gluteal, hamstring, and gastrocnemius and soleus muscle groups. In addition, placing the foot in different orientations regarding the direction of travel transmits these different force generation patterns.

Therefore, for successful turning the outside foot of the curve would usually be in total contact with the turf, whilst the inside foot would usually have only a forefoot contact and the foot would be orientated more towards the direction of the next stride.

What became clear from these studies was the need to move the body's centre of gravity into the correct position to initiate the change of direction. Once in the correct position, the correct forces must be applied to maintain the acceleration of the centre of gravity in the desired direction. Body lean in this context serves a double purpose: first, to ease the transition into the next step of the running pattern and second, to oppose the toppling effect of the sideways forces imparted by the foot of the outside leg.

When we understand the role of the inside and outside leg in this type of continuous movement pattern, we can start to examine more abrupt changes in direction such as cutting and turning. Cutting is the rapid change of direction from a single foot plant, which can be performed off either leg. If performed off the inside leg, the movement is called a crossover cut, whereas if it is performed off the outside leg, it is called a sidestep cut. As our curved running studies have taught us, more turning force is generated from the outside leg, so a sidestep cut is likely to be most effective in generating forces by which to change direction rapidly.

Cutting Action

Unfortunately for soccer players, even though cutting (figure 7.3) may be the best way to deceive and evade an opponent, it is also the mechanism by which the knee joint is placed in a position of high loading. One of the most debilitating and potentially career-threatening injuries in soccer is the anterior cruciate ligament (ACL) rupture. Somewhere between 50 and 80 per cent of these injuries result from noncontact situations.

A huge amount of deceleration occurs in the step preceding the cut and the cutting step itself; a large force is generated at the knee from front to back as it flexes on impact. Besier, Lloyd and Ackland (2003) showed that this force is not the dangerous one with regard to injury potential.

▶ **Figure 7.3** Anticipated cutting action.

© *Human Kinetics*

The injury mechanism is more of a three-dimensional issue; the more dangerous loadings appear in the side-to-side (valgus–varus) and inwards–outwards (internal–external) rotational planes.

To make the injury potential even worse for soccer players, the knee joint loading patterns increase almost twofold when the cutting action has to be performed when it is unanticipated (Besier, Lloyd and Ackland 2003). Other research groups have echoed these findings by stating that the loading at the knee is significantly increased when a defensive player is present in the testing environment (McLean, Lipfert and Van den Bogert 2004). Again, the biomechanics research has been able to measure these forces in game-like situations, yet this information is of little use unless we can devise prevention strategies to reduce injury rates.

Studies in this area have informed us that if balance training is incorporated into an injury prevention regime (prehabilitation), then coactivation from hamstring and quadriceps muscle groups improves; they contract more simultaneously on impact with the ground, which has an effect of reducing the valgus (sideways) load on the knee during cutting tasks.

In addition, specific technique aspects of cutting have been found to reduce the loading at the knee (Dempsey et al. 2007). Therefore, coaches and conditioning experts can help in this aspect by training the technique of movement when changing direction. We now know that this knee loading can be reduced by maintaining a more upright posture of the trunk and by placing the cutting foot closer to the midline of the body (not as far to the side). Practically, these technical modifications are difficult to control in a game situation, yet if the technical components are built into training sessions, the incidence of these serious ACL injuries could be reduced.

Heading

We can also apply our knowledge of biomechanics to skills that are more soccer specific than running, accelerating and changing direction. If we take a closer look at specific skills such as heading, we can understand the skill better and make some recommendations from the scientific studies in the area. Heading is an important skill; more than 20 per cent of the goals scored at the 2002 World Cup in Japan and South Korea were scored with the head (FIFA 2004). Our biomechanics objectives of maximizing performance and minimizing injury are prevalent here with the header. Initial worries over the safety of heading a soccer ball were recently refuted by Zetterberg et al. (2007), who showed that there was no neurochemical evidence of brain injury relating to soccer heading with short heading bouts in amateur players. Opposing this, Bamac et al. (2011) showed increases in neurotrophic factors after short bouts of heading in professional players, although the researchers did state that the increase in these levels would not necessarily mean that they came just from the brain; they may also derive from an increased amount of exercise. In general, however, heading a soccer ball (figure 7.4) is not commonly classified as a dangerous activity.

Looking at heading more mechanically, the impact force that a ball has on the head and ultimately the brain is related to the speed of the incoming ball; faster ball speeds generate greater forces at the head. But the force per se on the head does not necessarily lead to injury; it is more the acceleration of the head segment on impact with the ball that would in turn accelerate the brain within the skull. If we then consider the technical aspects from a coaching perspective, players who are instructed to tense the muscles of the neck before impact with the ball will increase the effective mass of the head and neck.

▶ **Figure 7.4**   Typical jumping header sequence from a skilled player.

In other words, the stiff neck then connects the head more rigidly with the whole of the upper body, which has a much greater mass than the head alone, thus minimizing the acceleratory effects of the impact forces on the head during heading (Bauer et al. 2001).

But the stiffness we see at impact around the neck during controlled drills or under experimental conditions does not always hold true in the arena of professional soccer (Kristensen et al. 2004).

Much coaching literature appears to focus on the use of the arms, which many state must be moved backwards at the time the head and torso move forwards to create the optimal heading technique. We can see by the sequence in figure 7.4, however, that the head and neck, whilst flexing, clearly move independently to the torso as it flexes forwards towards ball contact. Kristensen, Andersen and Sørensen (2004) attempted to break down the action by measuring a concept of energy transfer during the header by calculating angular momentum. This concept essentially takes a body part and sees how large it is (its resistance to turning) and then how fast it rotates during the action itself. The product of these values provides a measure of angular momentum for that body part.

If the body parts from the upper body and the lower body are then summed together, a graph is produced (figure 7.5) in which the event D represents ball contact. After the player is airborne, he or she cannot make or lose angular momentum; it can be changed only between one body part and another.

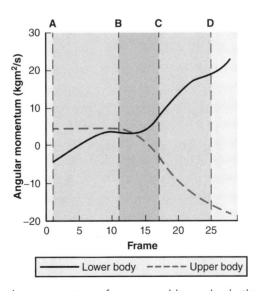

▶ **Figure 7.5** Angular momentum of upper and lower body throughout the jumping header.

From L.B. Kristensen, T.B. Andersen, and H. Sørensen, 2004, "Optimising segmental movement in the jumping header in soccer," Sports Biomechanics 3(2): 195-208. Reprinted by permission of the publisher (Taylor & Francis Ltd.).

This is a good way to highlight the way in which Newton's third law can be applied to angular motion as an action–reaction movement. In other words, we can see the body almost jackknife around the pelvis as the legs move backwards in early flight with the arms and torso. Then the legs begin to come forwards, as the upper body then does up until just after impact with the ball.

Kristensen, Andersen and Sørensen (2004) observed no technical advantage for transfer of momentum by pulling the arms back towards impact, which has been a regular coaching point. If anything, the arms should be pulled downwards and back if the optimum angular momentum transfer is to happen. What ought to be remembered here, however, is that as viewed in figure 7.4 the header is an isolated skill, whereas in practice the arms may have a more tactical role, such as keeping opponents away. From a coaching perspective, optimizing the angular momentum of the torso and legs will have the most benefit to performance. Therefore, the key muscle groups should be trained for this aspect.

Specifically, strength and coordination in the abdominal and hip flexor muscles should be promoted within a conditioning programme to maximize ball speed during the skill of heading.

Throw-In

The skills in soccer that have received the most biomechanical attention have been those that have a definite beginning and end point and are least affected by environmental factors. Typically, that observation directs us to the movements that occur just following a break in play. One of those movements is the throw-in, which not only is required to restart play after the ball has left the pitch but also can frequently have an offensive tactical use if aspects of ball speed and ball trajectory can be optimized.

Two delivery techniques are commonly used; the feet are either placed together (figure 7.6) or staggered (figure 7.7).

▶ **Figure 7.6** Feet-together throw-in.

▶ **Figure 7.7** Staggered-feet throw-in.

We can break down the action of the throw-in into phases

1. Foot contact
2. Maximum ball retraction
3. Trunk and shoulder forward flexion to release
4. Follow-through

In both styles of throw-in, similar sequences of events take place. To begin, the knee joints are extended and a marked pushing of the hips occurs, both forward and upward. This action forms part of an energy storage technique during which the body performs the stretch-shortening cycle; put simply, a group of muscles are stretched to store energy before being strongly contracted and releasing this stored energy. This technique allows the player to increase the power that a muscle group can generate.

For the throw-in, the muscle groups under stretch are primarily the abdominals, the muscles of the shoulder and chest, and the triceps brachii. As the body starts to move forwards, a sequential uncoiling of the joints occurs, which follows a pattern of moving from the larger muscle groups to the smaller ones. The uncoiling moves from the hips, to the shoulders, to the elbows and finally to the wrists and fingers. During this uncoiling motion, each subsequent joint increases in speed from the heavier segments towards the lighter, faster segments that are attached to the ball. This general summation of speed mechanism is something we shall return to later, and it will be noted in the skilled kicking action.

The choice of feet together or feet apart for the throw-in generally comes down to personal preference and comfort, but the choice may depend on the tactical requirement of the throw. A player proficient in both techniques should know that a flatter trajectory is obtained from the staggered feet throw-in and a higher trajectory tends to result from a feet-together delivery style.

Several scientists have investigated the throw-in, and most agree that for maximal speed during the throw-in, the release angle of the throw is approximately 30 degrees to horizontal and the ball reaches speed in excess of 15 metres per second (Kollath and Schwirtz 1988; Levendusky et al. 1985; Messier and Brody 1986). This low release angle may seem incorrect if maximum distance is to be achieved, because projectile theory suggests an optimum angle of closer to 45 degrees. The lower launch angle for a throw-in is recommended because a correctly performed throw will have a controlled amount of backspin imparted to the ball, causing an aerodynamic lift force to be produced on the ball that will increase its flight distance, just as backspin on a golf ball produces a longer flight distance.

Scientists also agree that to attain greatest distance on the throw, players should use a run-up to the throw-in as opposed to a stationary delivery. A study by Lees, Kemp and Moura (2005) attempted to identify just why this phenomenon occurred, because counterintuitively it was discovered that it is not the speed of the ball during the approach that enhances the performance.

The biomechanical mechanism that operates during the throw-in is that in the standing throw-in, the arm must be retracted at the shoulder using just the muscles of the shoulder, whereas in the running approach, the torso moves away from the arm and creates a better stretch around this joint (figure 7.8; Lees, Kemp and Moura, 2005). The greater stretch allows the shoulder to store more energy in its muscles and tendons and subsequently flex forwards with greater rotational force.

Therefore, if players are attempting a long throw-in, they should incorporate a run-up to aid performance. In addition, although strong abdominal and shoulder muscles are needed to perform this skill well, the coordination of these body parts is key. Therefore, regular practice is needed to develop an effective long throw-in.

▶ **Figure 7.8** Forward motion of the torso creates greater stretch at the shoulder joint.

Goalkeeping

Soccer comprises 10 outfield players and only 1 goalkeeper. Consequently, the goalkeeper is most specialized player on the soccer field. Recent advances in player training and equipment have led to new breed of athletic goalkeepers, who use techniques unlike those seen previously. Such techniques enable goalkeepers to deal with the modern game and ball, thus leaving current coaching manuals out of date. Referring to the manuals supplied by the English FA (Wade 1981), the most significant omission from the goalkeeping literature is the coaching of diving saves. Diving saves can occur in open play or from set pieces such as a free kick or a penalty.

Saving the penalty kick was among the first goalkeeper techniques that was analysed by Suzuki et al. (1988). The goalkeeper's centre of mass (COM) was calculated whilst diving to save balls suspended in a laboratory. Data showed that higher-level keepers dived more directly and with greater velocity (4 metres per second) than novice keepers (3 metres per second). As a result, the expert's COM vertical displacements were lower than those of the novice counterparts. In addition, novice keepers failed to use the full stretch-shortening cycle in their preparation in the shape of a countermovement jump (a move downwards before jumping upwards). Naturally, this failure restricted the take-off velocity and reduced the ability to dive directly at the ball against gravitational forces. From a coaching perspective, goalkeepers should be advised to perform a prejump before their final movement to increase the speed of their dive.

During penalty kicks, the keeper often dives too early and fails to make the save. Khun (1988) observed that an early strategy and a late strategy are evident when the goalkeeper dives either before the ball is hit or directly on or just after ball contact.

In European club matches Khun (1988) suggested that the late strategy was more successful, with a 60 per cent chance of success, compared with only an 8 per cent success rate with the early strategy. This finding clearly identifies the most successful strategy for goalkeepers for penalty saves.

A lot of scope remains for scientific investigation regarding the most important cues for a goalkeeper to base his or her decision on to dive left or right, low or high, or simply to stand still. The side to which a keeper dives may also depend on individual preference of handedness or footedness. Spratford, Mellifont and Burkett (2009) demonstrated the difference between goalkeepers diving to their preferred or nonpreferred sides. A difference was evident in a less effective motion to the nonpreferred side. This discrepancy manifested itself through greater rotation to the side of the thorax and pelvis to the nonpreferred side, meaning that the COM travelled more slowly and less directly to the ball. Therefore, knowledge of a goalkeeper's preferred side could be valuable information for a penalty taker. Of course, the nonpreferred side is an area in which extra work and coaching ought to be done for goalkeepers' diving technique.

Goalkeeping manuals suggest that diving should focus on facilitating the learner's ability to attack the ball with both hands (Coles 2003). To do this, goalkeepers are told to dive with the intention of getting their heads behind the ball to act as a second barrier.

Yet when diving at full stretch, the goalkeeper cannot attack the ball with both hands because this would shorten the distance that she or he can reach (Welsh 1999) by using a combination of spinal lateral (side) flexion and shoulder elevation.

Observation of elite goalkeepers shows a variation in the performance of aerial saves. The bottom hand technique (BHT) is the more traditional technique in which the goalkeeper leads with the hand in the direction in which he or she is diving (figure 7.9a). The top hand technique (THT; figure 7.9b) entails the use of the hand initially on the side opposite where the ball is travelling. The arm abducts, often in combination with greater rotation of the hips and trunk, to reach above and around the head to make the save. The absence of these techniques from coaching literature creates difficulties for coaches who attempt to instruct performers in the principles behind each technique and in when they should be used.

Work from our own laboratories by Smith and Shay (2013) concluded that the use of BHT provides a more direct line to the ball in line with traditional coaching technique (Suzuki et al. 1988; Coles 2003). In addition to a trend of increased COM velocity using bottom hand technique, greater horizontal reach was also possible. The authors recommended the coaching and use of the bottom hand technique where possible. Although top hand technique

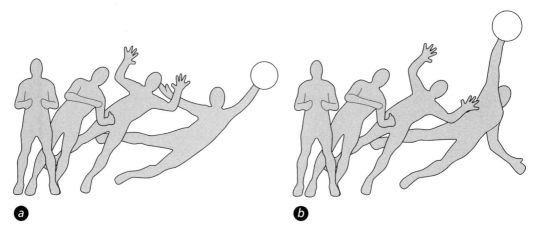

▶ **Figure 7.9** Schema of two saving techniques: (*a*) bottom hand technique; (*b*) top hand technique.

showed that greater vertical height of the hand was possible, it would be recommended only for the top middle goal areas, for situations in which the initial dive parameters determined that the dive occurred either too low or too early to intercept the ball or when late adjustments are required because of altered ball trajectory. Because of the increasing frequency of these saves in the modern game, both bottom hand technique and top hand technique saves should be included within the coaching literature.

Kicking

Although even the most common international name of the sport—football— would provide us with a clue of the main technique required to manoeuvre the ball around the field of play, the actual distance covered during a game with the ball at a player's feet amounts only to 2 per cent of playing time (Reilly and Thomas 1976). Yet the interaction between foot and ball that we know as kicking is still without doubt the most regularly used skill in soccer and, as a result, the most widely studied.

In open play many factors affect the technique required to kick the ball— whether the ball is stationary or moving, the type and construction of the ball, the use of either the preferred on nonpreferred foot and the desired outcome of the kick.

These changing conditions undoubtedly require the introduction of a certain amount of variation into technical practice drills on the training ground from a coaching perspective, yet often they mean that there are too many uncontrollable variables for the study of open play kicking in scientific research. Therefore, the majority of biomechanical research in soccer kicking has focussed on the technique of maximal instep kicking (figure 7.10).

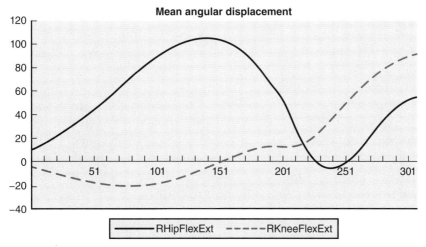

▶ **Figure 7.10**   Maximal instep kick showing changing angles at the hip and knee.

In the scientific literature, the instep refers to the dorsal part of the foot where the laces of the soccer boot are located. This kick is in contrast to a shorter-range push pass that would impact the inside of the foot. Either of these techniques can be seen in a penalty kick. A player who adopts a strategy to kick for power uses the instep kick, whereas the player who wants to place the ball typically uses the inside of the foot. If we look at the fast and complex kicking action, we realize that it involves not only the lower extremities (legs) but also the pelvis, torso and arms. Typically, the maximal instep can be split into three distinct phases, which can be described by looking at the key events that make up the kick.

The four key events seen here entrap the three phases of the kick. The events are toe-off of the kicking leg, landing of the support leg, ball contact and thigh horizontal during follow-through. The kick is made up of three main phases:

1. Leg cocking
2. Leg acceleration
3. Follow-through

These three phases show the main technique for the maximal instep kick, but an approach to the kick takes place before this set of final complex segment interactions. The approach to the kick generally consists of two to four strides (Kellis, Katis and Gissis 2004). If players are allowed to select their own approach, they use a curved approach at an angle of approximately 43 degrees (Egan, Verheul and Savelsbergh 2007). The approach allows players to retract both the kicking leg and the pelvis to a position from which they can optimize the range of motion during leg cocking. Players approach with enough speed to allow this retraction, yet not so much that the strength of the supporting leg cannot cope with the impact.

The angled approach also allows the whole body to be inclined sideways slightly during the kicking action in a manner similar to the technique noted in a curved run (figure 7.2). This sideways lean is required so that the hip joint of the kicking leg is higher than that of the support leg, which enables the foot to swing through and contact under the ball without impacting the ground (Plagenhoef 1971). In other words, the lean allows foot clearance.

When we consider the swing of the kicking leg, we look from a perspective of generating foot speed, because it has been well documented that fast foot speed has the strongest relationship to eventual ball speed (Shinkai et al. 2006). Foot speed is generated from the acceleration of the thigh and shank segments of the kicking leg. As the thigh starts to flex (move forward) from its farthest back position, the knee begins to flex. As the thigh continues its forward motion, the knee is pulled into an even further flexed position. This action reduces its resistance to being swung forward and allows the strong hip flexor muscles to accelerate the hip forwards to its fastest speed, which occurs midway through the acceleration phase.

At this point, the muscles of the quadriceps start to fire and initiate the extension of the knee. From this point during the leg acceleration phase, an interaction appears to occur between the thigh and the shank segments. We can plot the speeds at which both thigh and shank segments move in figure 7.11 and see that after the knee has started to extend, both of the segments continue to rotate forwards until the point where the thigh attains its maximum forward rotation speed.

At this point, the thigh begins to slow down, and the rotation of the shank becomes even quicker. The mechanisms here are complex, but we do know that active muscle contractions do not cause this very fast final rotation of the shank. One mechanism is that of a whiplash effect, similar to the action in which a cowboy brings his arm forwards very quickly and then suddenly stops the movement of the arm. The angular momentum of the arm is passed on to the whip, which is already lagging behind.

A similar effect is noted with the kick, because the thigh is rotating quickly and then begins to slow down towards contact, which has the same whiplash effect of accelerating the shank down towards the ball. This mechanism is combined with a transmission of force from the standing leg passed through the pelvis, which causes an upwards pull on the thigh and, in turn, causes the shank to give extra rotatory force to the segment during its last 90 degrees of movement. This type of force has been identified as a motion-dependent moment (Putnam 1991). The upwards pull from the pelvis to the thigh was also alluded to more recently by other authors (Nunome and Ikegami 2006). Both of these mechanisms serve to apply extra rotatory forces through the connective tissues around the knee to the shank segment. Scientific data have

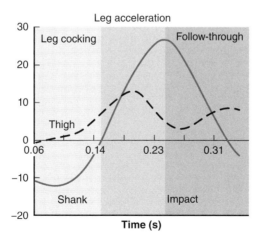

▶ **Figure 7.11**   Angular velocity of the thigh and shank during a maximal instep kick.

shown that during a soccer kick, shank rotation exceeds the force-velocity limitations of the muscles immediately before impact (Shinkai et al. 2006), so the muscular system becomes unable to generate any accelerating force.

Therefore, evidence suggests that the traditional coaching advice of kicking through the ball should be focussed on muscle groups other than the knee, with contributions most likely from hip and trunk muscles (Lees et al. 2010).

Because this very fast action is occurring up to the point of ball impact, the knee needs to be protected from hyperextending after impact to prevent injury. The way that this very fast knee rotation (approximately 2,000 degrees per second) is slowed is by contraction of the hamstring muscle group. By calculating values of joint power during a soccer kick, we are able to identify where certain muscle groups are either generating or absorbing force. This information tells us which muscle actions are dominant during certain phases of the kick (figure 7.12).

To enhance the belief that the hip generates most of the power during a soccer kick, we can see that a large burst of power (positive dotted line A) occurs until a point just before impact, when the hamstring and gluteal muscles slow the movement of the hip (B). Again, power calculations show us an activity of knee extensor muscles in the leg acceleration phase. Then, just before ball impact, we see large energy absorption occurring at the knee joint. This action of the hamstrings serves to prevent the knee joint from hyperextending.

This hamstring action serves not only to prevent injury but also to transmit momentum to the soccer ball. Typical foot speeds in maximal instep kicking are approximately 16 to 22 metres per second and ball speeds are in the

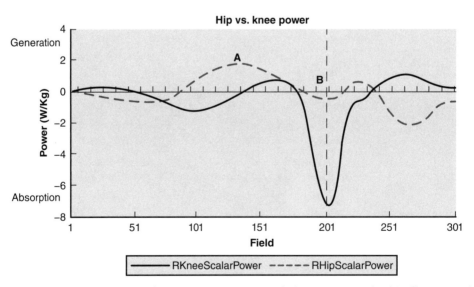

▶ **Figure 7.12** Amount of power generation and absorption at the hip flexors and knee extensor muscles.

range of 24 to 30 metres per second (Lees and Nolan 1998), so clearly the ball travels faster than the foot. The ball-to-foot velocity ratio is greater than one because of a phenomenon known as transfer of momentum.

Momentum is measured by the mass of an object multiplied by the velocity at which it travels, and this momentum present in the player and the ball must be the same both before and after impact. The only difference after impact is that some of the momentum is transferred to the ball. The soccer ball has a fixed mass, so we can multiply this value by its final velocity (about 30 metres per second) to get its momentum. We can also measure the foot velocity before impact (about 22 metres per second), but the mass of the lower limb at impact is based not just on the mass of the foot; it also includes the mass of the shank and thigh.

Obviously, the greater the effective mass of the leg is at impact, the greater is the amount of momentum that can be transferred to the soccer ball. Therefore, the stiffer the leg is at impact, the greater is the amount of leg mass that will be used in the transfer of momentum to the ball. This stiffness is achieved by a strong cocontraction of hamstrings and quadriceps at impact with the ball. The hamstrings dominate at impact, and the large absorption peak occurs near impact, which serves both to increase leg stiffness and to protect the knee joint from hyperextension following impact. Therefore, the training of hamstring musculature can be seen as key to successful performance in maximal instep kicking.

The vast majority of the biomechanical research into maximal instep kicking has focussed on the flexion–extension motion of the hip, knee and ankle, whereas the motion itself is a three-dimensional movement. The curved approach to the ball, whilst enabling retraction of the kicking leg and pelvis, also enables rotation around a vertical axis that passes through the supporting foot. If we pay careful attention to the upper body during the kicking action, we can see that the action of the nonkicking arm provides important information about how the upper body contributes to kicking mechanics. The kicker brings it both forwards and away from the body (Shan and Westerhoff 2005) during the approach to the ball. This action leads the motion of the torso so that the shoulders are rotated in an opposite direction to the pelvis, leading to a trunk twist (Lees et al. 2010) during the preparation phase and an untwisting in the execution phase.

This action is another example of the body using the stretch-shortening cycle to store and release energy during explosive actions. If the kicking action is viewed from above, this stretch-shortening tension arc could be measured by the difference in alignment between the hips and the shoulders; a greater hip–shoulder separation angle gives rise to more energy storage during the stretch phase. Some data presented by Lees and Nolan (2002) showed that the range of hip–shoulder separation greatly increased with increasing ball speed in professional subjects, suggesting that this hip–shoulder separation is an important performance variable. Of course, without sophisticated video analysis equipment, this angle can be difficult to measure, but as noted, the motion of the nonkicking arm can indicate the path that the shoulders are following and could be used as a coaching point.

Despite the large volume of biomechanical research into the maximal instep kick, this type of kick is rarely used in open play. Ball velocity is the main performance outcome for this type of kick, but accuracy and ball flight are also key outcomes during open play. When shooting on goal, players wish to maximize both ball velocity, to reduce the amount of time a goalkeeper has to save the ball, and accuracy, to increase the distance that the goalkeeper has to travel to make a save.

The relationship between these variables has been called the speed–accuracy trade-off. In general, players kick slower when they try to maximize accuracy for their kicks (Sterzing and Hennig 2008), whether they use an instep or a side-foot technique. Conversely, when players try to kick for maximal ball speed, accuracy declines. Therefore, from a coaching perspective, initial ball velocity should be reduced when trying to shoot for goal.

Whilst shooting for goal, imparting some form of spin on the ball is often necessary to evade either the goalkeeper or a defensive wall. Biomechanical studies have shown that ball speed decreases when the amount of spin imparted to the ball increases (Asai et al. 2002) because the player must contact the ball off centre to create spin. In addition to the off-centre impact, an increase in the angle of the foot at impact can generate more ball spin. Therefore, to generate ball spin, players need to strike the ball away from the centre and need to have the foot angled (to the direction of ball travel) to the ball on impact. Note, however, that although a greater foot angle generated more spin, this reached a maximum at approximately 55 degrees.

Because the impact phase of the soccer kick occurs quickly, gaining instantaneous biomechanical measures from such a small duration (about 10 milliseconds) is difficult. Observations during technical practice, however, can be useful to gain objective measures of how an alteration in technique can affect performance outcome. A kick for goal will have three interrelated performance outcomes: ball speed, accuracy and spin. Some modern technologies allow instantaneous calculation of these variables from a single video camera linked with the appropriate software, so that players and coaches can measure the effects of altering each of these variables. All that remains for the coach is to identify some of the technical features discussed in this chapter that will affect technique. The coach will be able to optimize these aspects whilst noting the effect on performance. An example of the outputs of such a system can be seen in figure 7.13, detailing the ball speed, trajectory angle and amount of topspin or backspin, sidespin, and rifle spin, in addition to a calculation of total ball spin.

Recent developments in free-kick taking have seen the rise of kicking techniques that produce highly erratic patterns of ball flight. Top professional

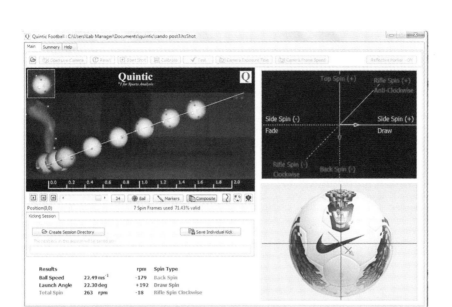

▶ **Figure 7.13** Example of instantaneous output from Ball Flight software.
Neal Smith

players (e.g., Christiano Ronaldo, Didier Drogba and David Luiz) who use either the instep or the side-foot technique are able to apply extreme power to the ball with little or no spin. Because of the effects of extreme turbulence, these deliveries exhibit an unpredictable wobble in flight to create what is termed a knuckleball shot.

Because of a combination of high velocity and little or no spin, the shape and arrangement of the soccer ball panels and the creation of a large turbulent rail of air behind the ball, these shots can be difficult for a goalkeeper to save. Little coaching information is available to date about this technique, yet armed with its key requirements and the ability we now have to track shots instantaneously for speed and spin, the coaching challenge is to develop this technique in our more gifted players.

Conclusion

This chapter has identified some of the key techniques that are essential for soccer performance, and it explained how biomechanical theory can be applied to understand their causation. After we have this understanding, we are able to develop key performance outcomes that can be measured and then implemented within the technical coaching process. Many new skills and techniques will be developed in soccer as players continually push the boundaries and improve their games. With the application of biomechanics, coaches can help players optimize their performance and minimize injury potential during both training and game play.

CHAPTER 8

Biomechanics for Optimal Performance and Injury Prevention

—Martin Haines and Daniel Cohen

In a quest for better performances and results, players must contend with physical demands greater than ever as they compete at local, regional, national and international levels. These demands can take their toll. Increasingly, however, people are recognizing that along with implementing strategies to improve recovery, conditioning programmes must be designed not only to develop and support performance but also to reduce the risk of musculoskeletal injury (Dallinga, Benjaminse and Lemmink 2012). An optimal training programme is personalized, taking into account relevant intrinsic (player-related) factors as well as sport and position-specific demands. Integrating warm-up programmes such as the FIFA 11+, which includes conditioning activities aimed at injury-risk reduction, can lead to significant reductions in injury incidence and improve neuromuscular performance in amateur soccer players (Barengo et al. 2014).

Yet by definition generic programmes are not tailored to the specific biomechanical and neuromuscular profile of the athlete. Pappas et al. (2015) argue that this lack of precision contributes to the inconsistent efficacy of these programmes in the literature and that personalized programmes that address this profile and are guided by individual screening will be both more efficient and more effective.

Within the team sport setting, however, implementing an individualized warm-up and conditioning programme in which each exercise is based on the individual's biomechanical and neuromuscular profile is extremely difficult. An individualized programme needs to be addressed in a conditioning regimen outside team training sessions. In practice, it is often addressed only during rehabilitation from a potentially preventable soft-tissue injury requiring treatment, resulting in a significant loss of playing and training time.

Injuries with recognized modifiable risk factors are estimated to account for approximately 60 per cent of the total time lost to injury in soccer (Hägglund, Waldén and Ekstrand 2009). As McHugh (2009) highlighted, although injuries are often seen as random events and an inevitable part of the game, substantial evidence shows that the risk of some of the most common (hamstring strains) and most severe (anterior cruciate ligament) injuries in soccer can be significantly reduced with prevention programmes (Croisier et al. 2008; Myer, Ford and Hewett 2004; Barengo et al. 2014). Although the importance of risk reduction or corrective programmes is increasingly recognized in both the amateur and professional game, the work of Croisier (2008) demonstrated the important concept of risk screening and rescreening in the process of injury risk. In this study, the researchers found that 16.5 per cent of professional players identified as having bilateral and agonist–antagonist strength imbalances in preseason isokinetic screening but given no corrective training suffered a hamstring injury during the season, compared with only 4.1 per cent in those without these imbalances. A subset of players identified with these imbalances who undertook corrective training aimed at addressing these imbalances had a substantially lower proportion (11 per cent) of hamstring injuries over the season. An even lower injury rate (5.7 per cent) was seen in a group of players who not only initiated the corrective programme but also were rescreened after a period of training to evaluate whether they had reached predetermined criteria.

Those still considered high risk were then given further corrective training and rescreened; the corrective exercises continued until the criteria were achieved.

These findings illustrate that although implementing a cycle of corrective training can reduce injury risk, the normalization of a neuromuscular risk factor is not a guaranteed consequence of a single period of intervention and risk may be reduced further in some people identified by additional screening. The potential value of regular neuromuscular screening is also demonstrated by Schache et al. (2011) in a case study in which a significant change in hamstring muscle strength symmetry observed in a weekly in-season assessment preceded injury to that muscle group. Therefore, it is important to consider such monitoring to quantify the neuromuscular and biomechanical effects consequent to the acute and accumulated fatigue associated with regular training and competition. Nonetheless, the demands of isokinetic screening mean that it is rarely implemented in season in pro soccer. Instead, quick, low-cost and practical means to evaluate the effect of corrective programmes or to identify the development of neuromuscular and biomechanical issues are needed.

Therefore, this chapter provides both a simple means to screen players for biomechanical issues and a corrective prescription route based on its results using activities that can be incorporated into warm-up or cool-down sessions as well as be undertaken between training sessions.

This information is not intended to turn coaches into pseudo-therapists; rather, it is for coaches for whom both the theoretical basis and the exercises and screens themselves are relevant for use in warm-ups and cool-downs as well for players to use in their own time for personal physical development.

What Is Biomechanics?

Many view biomechanics as a complicated science that requires expensive equipment to take detailed measurements and substantial knowledge of maths and physics, so it is one of the least popular of the disciplines within sport and exercise science. Yet a working knowledge of relevant biomechanics provides the coach with practical knowledge of the player and offers an important framework for understanding player weaknesses and areas to work on.

To enable the coach to understand the importance of biomechanics, we should first define it. Mechanics is concerned with the analysis of the action of forces on matter or material systems. Biomechanics is how this is applied to the body. It is often divided into two sections:

- Static refers to the body without movement, such as when a player stands before taking a free kick or a goalkeeper sets him- or herself before a penalty.
- Dynamic refers to the body in motion, which occurs most of the time during soccer training and match play.

The human body and the way in which it moves in mechanical terms can be divided into two areas of study: extrinsic and intrinsic biomechanics. Although the study of the two may overlap, extrinsic biomechanics describes the application of engineering mechanics to biological and medical systems (Hall 1999). This performance aspect is often measured during a kinematic analysis using video in which, for example, movement generated at specific segments and joints is differentiated. This analysis might be used to improve a player's ability to turn quicker in a game or kick a ball farther or in a particular way and is therefore highly relevant to soccer in terms of performance and physical conditioning.

Intrinsic biomechanics, on the other hand, is the study of how the body is able to perform tasks or movements according to the individual's mechanical make-up. Dysfunctional intrinsic biomechanics can have a profound effect on the performance of extrinsic tasks such as kicking a ball and running and the efficiency with which they are executed. Specifically, poor intrinsic biomechanical efficiency can create compensatory movements in gross motor patterns; these intrinsic factors can cause inefficient movements and inappropriate compensations. These compensations may then be repeatedly performed in training and game situations, which can not only manifest as faulty movement patterns and poor execution of skills but also produce inappropriate loading and demands on tissues and muscles, which has implications for injury risk. Therefore, intrinsic factors can have a significant effect on the performance and risk of injury for players at all levels of competition. Cormack et al. (2013) demonstrated the connection between altered neuromuscular and biomechanical (NM-B) function and match performance in professional Australian Football League players. They found that changes in the execution of a countermovement jump 96 hours following a match predicted decreased high-intensity performance in subsequent match play, as indicated by less time spent in higher-speed running and less acceleration as well as a lower subjective assessment of performance by the coach (Cormack et al. 2013).

Players' reflexes and how they adapt to various stimuli appear to have an effect on neuromuscular-biomechanical function, athletic performance and injury risk. According to Lewit (2009) each player has unique, unconditioned (genetic) and conditioned (acquired) reflex codes that determine movement patterns over the course of her or his lifetime. Each player starts with unconditioned codes and during her or his life, for a variety of reasons, begins to acquire conditioned movement codes. These conditioned codes can be acquired from practicing a movement or technique repeatedly, and the good coach ensures that these patterns meet accepted criteria. In addition, each player also picks up her or his own conditioned movement codes from how she or he moves during daily life, which can be influenced by several factors, including how the neuromuscular-biomechanical function compensates for previous injury or posture or from techniques learned in the past.

So the coach needs to consider why each player moves and performs techniques that are not extrinsically biomechanically correct. Does the problem result from innate inability, from conditioned coding from poor coaching (or no coaching) in the past or from neuromuscular-biomechanical compensation for intrinsic biomechanical dysfunction? The coach must be careful when correcting any movements or poor techniques, especially with children through to younger professionals who need technical work, because any changes could work against the way that player has learned to compensate over a lifetime and cause injury because of lack of adaption. For this reason, the coach should first identify and manage any intrinsic biomechanical causes of the conditioned movement codes before teaching any new movement patterns or techniques or new way of executing skills.

In a soccer context, consider the problem of noncontact anterior cruciate ligament (ACL) injuries. One of the extrinsic biomechanical risk factors for ACL injuries is high knee valgus (knee buckling inwards) on landing or when cutting and changing direction, which puts high loads on the ligament and increases risk of rupture (Hewett 2000). Therefore, as part of injury risk screening and risk reduction, assessing jump-landing mechanics and correcting poor foot, knee or hip loading patterns is important to reduce ACL loading. In addition, addressing deficits in hamstring strength may assist in the stabilization of the knee (Alentorn-Geli et al. 2009). But neither technique coaching nor strengthening of the hamstrings would assist in the stabilization of the knee to counter excessive anterior knee translation, which also loads the ACL, if inefficient biomechanics of the hip, spine and foot are not also addressed.

Likewise, coaching techniques would be unable to engage hip lateral rotators if they were inhibited and not able to provide hip stability to minimize hip internal rotation and knee valgus. Establishing the cause of the faulty movement patterns is difficult without first understanding the player's intrinsic biomechanics. This chapter explores this intrinsic biomechanical insight. We look at the possible causes of poor engagement of the hip lateral rotators and hamstrings and their effect on fatigue. We then describe simple techniques that players can be shown to improve their performance of these movements, which could in turn reduce the risk of ACL injury.

Intrinsic Biomechanical System

To prescribe conditioning programmes for people who play soccer (or any sport), the coach must develop the strength, power and muscular endurance of the player's specific muscles and understand that the various soft tissues of the pelvis and spine, including muscles, ligaments and fascia, all interrelate in a highly complex biomechanical kinetic chain. A kinetic chain is a sequence of physiological muscle activations in the upper and lower extremities that enable the execution of an integrated movement. Impairment of one or more kinetic chain links can create dysfunctional biomechanics during movement, leading to pain or injury (Sciascia and Cromwell 2012). In the engineering sense, kinetic chains are composed of a series of rigid links that are interconnected by a series of pin-centred joints. In engineering, the system of joints and links is constructed so that motion of one link at one joint will produce motion at all the other joints in the system in a predicable manner. In the human system of joints and muscles, the same principles apply. In this context, kinetic chain refers to the way in which joints are linked together so that motion at one point in the series is accompanied by motion at an adjacent joint. Understanding the way in which muscles work together in kinetic chains to create movement rather than as individual muscles performing isolated actions (Sciascia and Cromwell 2012; Bryant, Peterson and Franklin 1999) is the basis of understanding functional movement. This complex interaction also means that muscle can respond to traumas, overloads or pathologies, but it can sometimes lead to compromised performance and ultimately pain in a variety of ways. Muscles can become facilitated, overactive and shortened, or conversely they can become inhibited or weakened. The classic example of this is the effect of delayed onset muscle soreness (DOMS), soreness that may follow unaccustomed muscle overload (particularly with exposure to lengthening or eccentric contractions). DOMS, which may last several days, is associated with increase in muscle tone and faulty excitation of muscle (Szymanski 2001; Newham 1988) thought to be related to local inflammation putting strain on microelements of the muscle structure compromising its mechanical integrity and ability to contract and relax normally.

A nonathletic person may more easily avoid a chronic state because he or she does not have frequent and repeated demands for high-intensity work and provides his or her body with adequate recovery. Recovery provides the muscle a normal sensory input and allows it to relax, reducing the risk of aggravating the condition. Because this state is not an injury, players (and coaches) may ignore the continual irritation of the now-shortened muscle, which may then lead to physical changes within the muscle that alter mechanics that are not reversed simply by rest but require biomechanical or even medical intervention (Page, Frank and Lardne 2010).

A shortened muscle will restrict both joint movement and nerve excursion, leading to potential complications within both musculoskeletal and neuro-muscular systems. Typically, the antagonist muscle will become reciprocally inhibited, which may present as a muscle imbalance or muscle weakness and in turn produce abnormal mechanical loads on the joint it crosses, altering biomechanics and generating stress on other joints or body segments.

After muscular dysfunction of this nature has been identified, some evidence shows that submaximal endurance contractions, or antispasm or muscle release exercises, are effective in reducing tension (or spasm) within a muscle and restoring muscle function. Ribot-Ciscar and colleagues (1991) examined the effect of isometric contractions on muscle spindles at rest and in response to a slow stretch. These contractions led to changes in the sensitivity of the muscle spindle to stretch, reducing the stretch threshold and subsequently improving its ability to stretch. They found that a muscle relaxes maximally following submaximal contraction for a prolonged period and referred to this phenomenon as postcontraction sensory discharge.

The way the musculoskeletal system reacts to these changes in neuromuscular-biomechanical function influences the intrinsic biomechanical presentation of the pelvis and spine. Their reaction can result in compromised muscle performance manifesting as muscle weakness or muscle imbalance (Bryant, Peterson and Franklin 1999) somewhere along the kinetic chain.

Current thinking suggests that faulty biomechanics are important risk factors for some of the most common injuries, such as hamstring strains, and some of the most severe, such as ACL ruptures. Therefore, biomechanical evaluation should be part of both primary prevention in those with no history of these injuries and secondary prevention to prevent the recurrence of the pain or injury (Mendiguchia, Alentorn-Geli and Brughelli 2012).

Besides evaluating the directly controlled elements of the muscular system, indirect mechanisms need to be part of the assessment. For example, the shoulder girdle and thoracic spine are physically linked to the pelvis and hamstrings by a connective tissue sheet known as the thoraco-lumbar fascia. This sheet provides the spine the means by which load can be transferred from the thoracic spine to the pelvis, thereby supporting the lumbar extensor muscles in their primary role of spinal stabilisation (Gracovetsky 1985).

The importance of spinal function is well recognized as important to the whole biomechanical system. Therefore, approaches to achieving and maintaining normal spinal function must include exercises that both encourage efficient use of the kinetic chain and promote correct regional movements of the spine that occur simultaneously, known as spinal coupling patterns. The interrelationship between function across the three main elements of the motor system—joint, muscle and nerve—also means that dysfunction in one may promote and manifest as dysfunction in the others, even if the root cause is in another system. Equally, the correction of a dysfunctional pelvis (misaligned sacroiliac joints) could be achieved by reducing a local muscle spasm, and mobilizing the sacroiliac joint could relieve the muscle spasm. Similarly, the function of both the sacroiliac joints and local muscles could be improved by mobilizing the sciatic nerve. The body is an integrated system, and although dysfunction manifests in one screen, it may not be the cause. Therefore, when we implement and interpret the screens that follow at different joints and locations, we need to remember that they are part of the kinetic chain and are interrelated. But isolating and evaluating the capacity of components of the kinetic chain to provide normal function is also important. Therefore, functional screening and training and intrinsic biomechanical screening complement each other and provide a more complete analysis of the player. After the player's capacity to perform biomechanically efficient movements has been evaluated by intrinsic screening and, if necessary, improved with corrective exercise, functional exercises can be introduced safely and more effectively on this biomechanically sound platform, which encourages the systems to work together without dysfunctional compensatory or inhibitory responses. This combination provides the player a powerful performance-enhancing and injury prevention tool with emphasis on evaluating and training movement patterns. Neglecting potential faulty intrinsic biomechanics underlying these functional movements masked by compensatory mechanisms may ultimately lead to injury.

A player could pass a functional movement screen yet still have fundamental intrinsic biomechanical problems. For this reason, a combination of both intrinsic and extrinsic approaches should be adopted. After the intrinsic biomechanical profile has been established and enhanced at specific joints or segments, the evaluation of integrated movement patterns is less likely to be compromised by intrinsic issues.

Application to Sport Performance and Injury Prevention

Many factors affect performance in sport. Neuromuscular-biomechanical function has a profound effect on how movement patterns are performed and compensated for. A player may be excellent technically and athletically but have a poor biomechanical profile that will ultimately either limit development and performance or increase the risk of pain and injury.

For example, an overactive pectoralis minor muscle in the shoulder has been shown to affect thoracic spine function (Bullock, Foster and Wright 2005), which in turn has been shown to affect pelvic function (Gracovetsky 1985) and performance of muscles such as the hamstrings and hip flexors, which are important in high-speed running. Although identifying an overactive pectoralis minor muscle using musculo-skeletal screening or indeed medical screening can be extremely difficult, an intrinsic biomechanical screen can determine it rapidly (Bullock, Foster and Wright 2005).

Many risk factors are associated with injury, including age, sex, body composition, previous injury, joint stability, muscle strength, power, joint mobility, anatomy, alignment, skill level, postural stability and psychological factors (Bahr and Krosshaug 2005). The role of a player's biomechanical function is also thought to be a critical factor, although generally less understood, because the assessment of extrinsic factors often requires expensive technology. Nonetheless, an intrinsic biomechanical screen may highlight deficits in a player's pelvic, shoulder and knee function and identify low-grade muscle spasm in key muscles, which may be restricting both movement and correct joint functioning. In addition, an intrinsic biomechanical screen evaluates aspects of nerve function (in particular the sciatic nerve in the leg and median nerve in the arm), which may promote compensation and breakdown. For example, a tethered sciatic nerve may increase the risk of hamstring injuries in players because it decreases the flexibility of the hamstrings (McHugh, Johnson and Morrison 2010; Méndez-Sánchez et al. 2010).

You will see in this chapter that injury prevention and performance are inextricably linked. You improve one, and you improve the other, partly because not all injuries are traumatic but are chronic, developing over time.

For example, many players are unaware of a rotated pelvis, but it is common and may manifest as a functional leg-length discrepancy (DonTigny 1999), termed as such because a forwards rotation of the pelvis may cause the level of the ilium (pelvic bone) on that side to drop lower compared with the opposite side, which makes that leg appear longer. This alteration in biomechanics can promote a variety of injuries depending on how the player compensates; it can cause lower-back pain, knee pain, shin pain, hamstring injuries, even foot pain (Neely 1998). Upper-back and shoulder problems are also reported to result from this intrinsic biomechanical dysfunction. The effect of a rotated pelvis and resultant leg-length discrepancy on performance should not be underestimated, so evaluation of the biomechanical efficiency of the pelvis is a fundamental screen. If dysfunction is identified, a variety of simple quick-to-perform corrective exercises can improve function.

Intrinsic Biomechanical Screens

The intrinsic biomechanical screens are a joint-by-joint and system-by-system approach that is the focus of the remainder of the chapter.

The intrinsic biomechanical programme provides the building blocks to restore normal function and efficient, biomechanically sound movement in a player by reducing muscle spasm, nerve tethering and joint dysfunction. The intrinsic biomechanics model is derived from data collection spanning 20 years and extensive review of biomechanics literature from authors such as Twomey, Taylor, McGill, Gracovetsky, Vleeming, Nachenson, Hewitt and Janda. To understand the association between intrinsic biomechanics, extrinsic biomechanics and injury, data were analysed from more than 4,000 people with injury records and isokinetic, lumbar motion monitor and video analysis of performance. This analysis and further work identified the manual screens that correlated the highest with the lab tests and the exercises that managed them most effectively. The intrinsic biomechanical screening and corrective exercise process is provides the body with the capacity to perform movements in a way that doesn't require compensations that may ultimately promote pain, injury and reduced performance.

Before the screens and corrective exercises are outlined, the system behind the exercise prescription should be described. A systematic approach is proposed to take a muscle through a series of progressions so that it can become fully functional.

Muscle release (M): First, reduce muscle spasm that may be present so that muscles can engage without compromise.

Stretch (S): If range is still restricted following the muscle release exercises, then stretch the relevant muscle to enable adequate range considering the joint, soft tissues and the activities to be performed.

Antagonist (A): After the muscle can relax and lengthen, the antagonists to that muscle, which have typically been reciprocally inhibited while the muscle has been in spasm (Sherrington 1906), should be reengaged.

Conditioning (C): The muscle that was previously in spasm should be conditioned in line with accepted training principles and optimal muscle ratios around a joint.

This process is followed by each of the screens in this section. After this series of progressions has been completed, the player is better prepared for more functional multijoint movements involving the muscle that was previously in spasm. The MSAC principles apply to those structures that are commonly affected locally by muscle spasm, in particular the pelvis and shoulder. The trunk (core) and the knee, although affected by the pelvis and shoulder, are not commonly locally affected in biomechanical terms by muscle spasm. For this reason, we follow a linear exercise progression using the isolation to integration concept by isolating the relevant muscle groups to ensure they have the capacity to engage and following with more functional movements to promote correct muscle firing patterns, coordination and synchronization.

Various field tests are explored in this chapter. The pelvis, shoulder, knee and spine are the pillars of intrinsic biomechanics. The knee has been included because of the incidence and severity of knee injuries in soccer. A screen and associated exercise prescription for each area is described.

Pelvis

The first screen, called the 4-sign screen, is for the pelvis. Originally a clinical test (Cibulka, Delitto and Koldehoff 1988), it identifies whether the sacroiliac joints were responsible for back or pelvic pain. The 4-sign screen has been largely disproved as a valid clinical test, but it can be valuable in establishing the function of the pelvis. Pelvic dysfunction has been attributed to hamstring injuries, ACL injuries, shin and ankle pain as well as low-back pain, so this test is useful in assessing function of this body part in a simple and timely manner.

4-Sign Screen

Procedure

The player lies on the floor or a therapy table. The player crosses one leg over the other so that the outside of the ankle lies across the opposite thigh, just above the patella (figure 8.1). Ensure that the lateral malleolus (outside ankle bone) is just lateral (to the side) of the lower thigh. Fix the opposite side of the pelvis so that it does not tilt and cause inaccurate readings. Measure the height from the lateral joint line of the knee (just above the head of the fibula) to the floor or table. Switch legs and measure the other side.

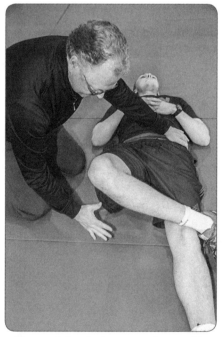

▶ **Figure 8.1** 4-sign screening position.

Martin Haines and Daniel Cohen

Results

Symmetry should be present; the right knee should be the same height as the left. As a guide, the distance from the player's knee to the floor or table should be no greater than the span of the player's outstretched hand. Simply measure the player's hand before the test and use that measurement for a pass or fail.

- A failed test occurs when one knee is higher than the other (asymmetry). The higher side fails the test.
- A failed test occurs when one knee is higher than the distance of the player's hand span from the table or floor to the outside of the knee.
- A pass occurs when symmetry is present and the distance from bench to knee is smaller than the span of the player's hand.

Piriformis Muscle Anatomy and Function

If the player fails the test, the pelvis is likely to be dysfunctional. The player is therefore at higher risk of injury as well as compromised performance. In these circumstances muscles in the pelvic region go into protective spasm, which tends to reduce the function of the pelvis further. These muscles include the piriformis muscle (figure 8.2) in the hip as well as other hip rotators and stabilizers (DonTigny 2005).

The piriformis comes from the anterior aspect of the sacrum. As the muscle leaves the pelvis, some slips arise from the margin of the greater sciatic notch as well as from the pelvic surface of sacrotuberous ligament. The muscle passes out of the pelvis through the greater sciatic foramen. It then attaches to the upper border and medial aspect of the greater trochanter. At this point it may also merge with other tendons including the gluteus

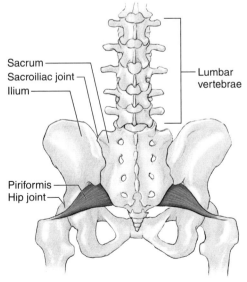

▶ **Figure 8.2** Anatomy of the piriformis.

medius. The piriformis laterally (externally) rotates the hip joint if it is in an extended position and abducts the hip if it in a flexed position. It is an important muscle to control the alignment of the hip and knee.

Exercises for the Pelvis

The work of Ribot-Ciscar and colleagues (1991) shows that low-grade isometric contractions can provide an effective way to achieve muscle relaxation. If the muscle is in a hypertonic state (overactive or in spasm), function can be restored.

Muscle Release (M): 4-Sign Exercise   This exercise can provide an effective means of muscle relaxation for the piriformis. It can be performed first thing in the morning and last thing at night. It also can be used as part of a personalized warm-up and cool-down.

Technique

Sit on a chair with one leg crossed over the other. Place both hands on the inside of the knee. Press the ankle down into the knee of the opposite leg by rotating it inwards at the hip joint (figure 8.3). Notice that the knee lifts if the technique is correct; the hands should be in place to prevent this from happening. This contraction is static, so the leg should not move. Hold for 20 seconds using approximately 20 per cent of maximum effort, just enough to engage the muscles in the hip. Perform four sets on each leg.

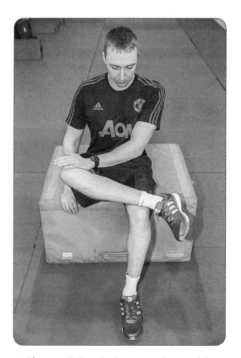

▶ **Figure 8.3**   4-sign exercise position.
Martin Haines and Daniel Cohen

The player should perform this exercise for up to two weeks and then be rescreened using the 4-sign screen. If results have improved (the higher knee has lowered and the knees are becoming more symmetrical), the player should continue using the 4-sign exercise until he or she passes the screen. After the player passes the screen, he or she progresses to the antagonist exercise. If the player does not progress using the 4-sign exercise, a stretching programme can be helpful until the screen is passed. The player then progresses to the antagonist exercise.

Stretch (S): Piriformis Stretch   This stretch is an effective way to increase the range of the piriformis muscle. It can be performed first thing in the morning and last thing at night, and the player can use it as part of a personalized warm-up and cool-down.

Technique

Lie on your back. Lift the right knee up to the chest. Hold that knee with the right hand in the centre of the chest or abdomen. Gently take hold of the right ankle with the left hand and slowly rotate the right hip so that the right ankle moves towards the left elbow (figure 8.4). Maintain the central position of the knee; do not let it move out. Hold for 30 seconds. Do four sets on each leg.

Progression to the next phase of antagonist work is achieved when either of the following criteria is met:

- The player passes the 4-sign screen after using either the 4-sign muscle release exercise or the piriformis stretch.
- Despite working on the 4-sign exercise or piriformis stretch, the player has not passed the 4-sign screen.

▶ **Figure 8.4**   Piriformis stretch.

Martin Haines and Daniel Cohen

Antagonist (A): Hip Adduction Because the piriformis performs horizontal abduction (retraction) of the hip joint, an exercise to work its antagonist involves adduction of the hip joint.

Technique

Lie on your back. Tie a resistance tube around the right knee and bend the knee to 45 degrees. Pivoting on the heel, roll the knee in and out (figure 8.5). Start with 8 repetitions and build up to 20. Perform the exercises on both sides but concentrate on the affected side. Start with two sets and build up to five. Perform once a day.

▶ **Figure 8.5** Hip adduction.
Martin Haines and Daniel Cohen

Conditioning (C): Clam The last progression in the MSAC series is to condition the muscle that was previously in spasm. After one or two weeks of antagonist work, the player is usually ready. The clam is an effective method of working the piriformis directly.

Technique

Lie on the side opposite the dysfunctional pelvis. Tie a rubber band around the knees. Keeping the hips still, lift and lower the top knee by pivoting at the ankles (figure 8.6). Start with 8 repetitions and build up to 20. Start with two sets and build up to five. Perform once a day. Perform the exercise on both sides but concentrate on the affected side.

▶ **Figure 8.6** Clam.
Martin Haines and Daniel Cohen

Many other exercises may be helpful for conditioning. Therapists with an interest in rehabilitation will know other exercises that could help.

Shoulder

Although shoulder injuries in soccer are less common than lower-limb and pelvic injuries, in biomechanical terms dysfunction in the shoulder can affect the function of other body parts, whether from radicular (referred) pain, myofascial pain (muscle and fascia) or merely increased loading through a segment of the body because of overcompensation (Lewit 2009).

Pectoralis Minor Screen

Procedure

The player lies on a table or the floor with the arms by the sides, elbows resting on the table or floor and bent and hands on the lower abdomen (figure 8.7). With the player in this position, measure the distance from the table or floor to the posterior aspect of the acromion process.

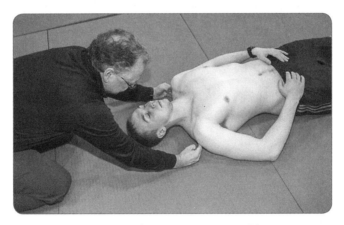

▶ **Figure 8.7** Pectoralis minor screen position.
Martin Haines and Daniel Cohen

Results

Lewis and Valentine (2007) found that when the pectoralis minor muscle is normal length, the distance between a table that the player is lying on and the posterior aspect of the acromion should not exceed 2.5 centimetres (1 inch), or approximately the width of two fingers. A distance greater than this suggests some form of muscle imbalance and a shortened muscle. Symmetry should be present; the right shoulder should be the same height as the left.

- A failed test occurs when asymmetry is noted in which one shoulder is higher than the other. The higher side fails the test.
- A failed test occurs when the posterior aspect of the acromion process is more than 2.5 centimetres (1 inch) from the table or floor.
- A pass occurs when the shoulders are symmetrical and both are within 2.5 centimetres (1 inch) from the table or floor.

Pectoralis Minor Anatomy and Function

A player who has good postural alignment can usually move the arm for 160 to 180 degrees of movement without impingement of soft tissues in the subacromial space. If the player has the classic forward head, rounded shoulders and increased thoracic kyphosis, the scapula rotates forwards and downwards, depressing the acromial process and changing the orientation of the glenoid fossa. In these circumstances as the player attempts to elevate the arm, the supraspinatus tendon or the subacromial bursa may become impinged against the anterior portion of the acromion process. Repeated movements with this dysfunction may accelerate overuse injuries or cumulative trauma disorders and lead to early changes consistent with tendinitis or bursitis (Bullock, Foster and Wright 2005).

This observation is often accompanied by inhibition of the thoracic spinal extensors, which is why the thoracic cage is often rounded. This circumstance also needs to be considered in the player's conditioning; the player should perform exercises to mobilize the thoracic spine and gradually encourage extension.

If the pectoralis minor (figure 8.8) is shortened, anterior tilting of the scapula can result. Ludewig and Reynolds (2009) described shoulder injuries associated with a shortening of the pectoralis minor.

The pectoralis minor lies under the pectoralis major on the front of the chest. This flat triangular muscle comes from the upper ribs to a small bone on the front of the scapula called the coracoid process. The pectoralis minor pulls the shoulder girdle forwards (protraction) and downwards (depression). This action promotes a kyphotic (round-shouldered) posture, which reduces the mobility of the spine and shoulders.

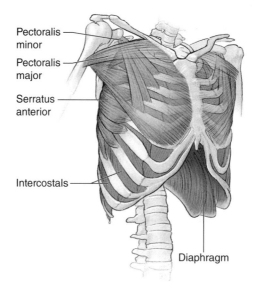

Pectoralis minor
Pectoralis major
Serratus anterior
Intercostals
Diaphragm

▶ **Figure 8.8** Anatomy of the pectoralis minor.

Exercises for the Shoulder

Because the pectoralis minor does not attach to the humerus (arm), the shoulder girdle should be the focus when considering muscle releases and the way to perform them.

Muscle Release (M): Pec Minor   This exercise can be performed first thing in the morning and last thing at night. It can be incorporated as part of a personalized warm-up and cool-down.

Technique

Stand or sit with the shoulders back in a good posture. Place the opposite hand on the front of the shoulder that failed the screen. Press the front of the shoulder into the hand (figure 8.9). Hold for 20 seconds using 20 per cent of maximum effort. Do four sets.

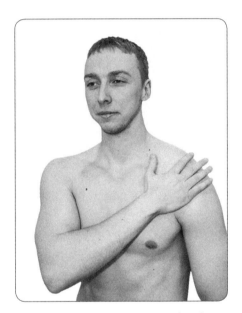

▶ **Figure 8.9**   Pec minor muscle release.
Martin Haines and Daniel Cohen

The players should perform this exercise regularly for up to two weeks and then be rescreened using the pectoralis minor screen. If the player improves (the shoulders are lower and more symmetrical), the player should continue to use the muscle release exercise until he or she passes the test. If the player does not progress, a stretching programme can be helpful.

Stretch (S): Pec Minor This exercise can be performed first thing in the morning and last thing at night. It can be incorporated as part of a personalized warm-up and cool-down.

Technique

Stand and place both hands in the small of the back. Slowly take the elbows back using the hands as a pivot point (figure 8.10). Hold for 30 seconds. Do four sets.

▶ **Figure 8.10**   Pec minor stretch.

Martin Haines and Daniel Cohen

Progression to the next phase of antagonist work can occur when either of the following criteria is met:

- The player passes the pectoralis minor screen from either the pec minor muscle release exercise or the pec minor stretch.
- Despite working on the muscle release or stretch, the player doesn't pass the pectoralis minor screen after three weeks.

Antagonist (A): Backward Shrug The movements that work the antagonists are retraction and elevation. The player performs these movements to help reciprocally inhibit the pectoralis minor muscle.

Technique

Tie a resistance tube around an immovable object close to the floor so that the tube runs at a 45-degree angle from the floor to the shoulders. Adopt a walking stance with one foot in front of the other for balance. Hold the tubing with sufficient tension. Keeping the arms straight, shrug the shoulders back and elevate them slightly (figure 8.11). Start with 8 repetitions and build up to 20. Start with two sets and build up to five. Perform the exercises on both shoulders but concentrate on the affected side.

▶ **Figure 8.11** Backward shrug.

Martin Haines and Daniel Cohen

Conditioning (C): Straight Arm Press-Up Shrug The last progression in the MSAC series is to condition the muscle that was previously in spasm. After one or two weeks of antagonist work, the player is usually ready. The straight-arm press-up shrug is an effective method of working the pectoralis minor directly.

Technique

Get into the upper press-up position. Keeping the arms straight, shrug the shoulders so that the shoulder blades move towards each other and the chest moves away from the floor (figure 8.12). Then press down on the hands and move the chest away from the floor and the scapulae away from each other. Start with 8 repetitions and build up to 20. Start with two sets and build up to five. Perform once a day.

▶ **Figure 8.12**   Straight arm press-up shrug.
Martin Haines and Daniel Cohen

Thoracic Mobility: Shoulder Roll Thoracic immobility tends to be present at the same time as pectoralis minor spasm. Mobility exercises for the thoracic spine are helpful. The shoulder roll is an effective method to increase thoracic rotation. This exercise can be performed first thing in the morning and last thing at night. It can be incorporated as part of a personalized warm-up and cool-down.

Technique

Lie supine with hips and knees bent and feet on the floor. With knees bent and apart, clasp the hands and hold them out in front of the chest. Keeping the hips and knees still, slowly rotate the upper body from side to side (figure 8.13). Make sure that the arms stay straight and the head stays in line with the arms as they turn. Start with 8 repetitions to each side and build up to 12. Start with two sets and build up to three.

▶ **Figure 8.13**   Shoulder roll.
Martin Haines and Daniel Cohen

Knee

Knee injuries are responsible for a large proportion of time loss in soccer. One key test to help mitigate the risk of knee injuries is the drop test or ligament dominance test. Ligament dominance is common among soccer players, especially in adolescent female players and those going through growth spurts. This occurs when a player executes movements such as landing or changes of direction with excessive knee valgus (inward collapse of the knee), hip adduction and hip internal rotation, which puts increased load on the anterior cruciate ligament (Pappas et al. 2015; Hewett, Paterno, and Myer 2002).

Although ACL injury is not one of the most common soccer injuries, its severity and associated time loss, and the substantially higher incidence in female players (Hewett 2000; Waldén et al. 2011) has led to considerable attention in ACL prevention programmes. Common ACL injury mechanisms include single-leg landings, pivots and deceleration (Bahr and Krosshaug 2005), circumstances in which the ground reaction force may control the knee's direction of motion (Winter 1990; Hewett et al. 2005; Myer, Ford, and Hewett 2004; Ford, Myer, and Hewett 2003).

Knee Ligament Dominance Screen

Procedure

Evaluation of a player's ligament dominance can be done using a 31-centimetre box drop jump test as described by Ford, Myer and Hewett (2003). The player stands on the box and jumps from the box. Immediately after landing on the floor, the player bends the knees no more than 30 degrees and goes straight into a maximum vertical jump (figure 8.14).

▶ **Figure 8.14** Knee ligament dominance screen.

Martin Haines and Daniel Cohen

Results

A player who is ligament dominant will display substantial medial knee rotation in the transverse plane on landing. This can be accompanied by loss of balance and a hip drop, in which the level of the pelvis lowers significantly on the contralateral side and awkward arm movements attempt to provide 'artificial' stability to compensate for the lack of control at the knee.

Knee Anatomy and Function

Medial knee rotation may also be related to an overall dynamic knee valgus (femoral adduction, femoral internal rotation in relation to the hip, tibial external rotation in relation to the femur with or without foot pronation). Movement patterns that place a player in positions of high ACL load (excessive external knee abduction moments) combined with a low knee flexion angle may well increase the risk for ligament injury or failure (Lloyd 2001).

The key to minimizing this load is first to understand whether intrinsic biomechanical issues are causing the medial rotation, which may be coming from almost anywhere in the kinetic chain. The 4-sign test will provide an indication of pelvic involvement; if pelvic involvement is indicated, the pelvis needs to be addressed before embarking on the following exercise programme for the knee. Besides the pelvis, the piriformis muscle in the hip is instrumental in maintaining the correct alignment of the knee (figure 8.15) and helping prevent the valgus loads that are known to cause knee injuries. So the function of this muscle must be restored by providing it with the capacity to engage efficiently before strengthening it in a programme for enhancing knee stability.

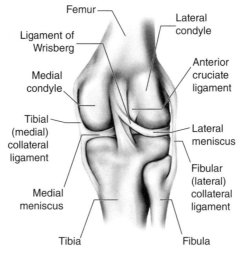

▶ **Figure 8.15** Anterior cruciate ligament (ACL) and surrounding structures.

Exercises for the Knee

The following exercises help control the valgus movement of the knee. In some cases, when the exercises are coupled with player education, they can prevent it altogether.

Start the programme by isolating the relevant muscle groups to ensure that they have the capacity to engage; then follow with more functional movements to ensure correct muscle firing patterns and synchronization.

Besides these exercises, the clam exercise described in the piriformis section can be used. The clam exercise isolates the hip abductors and external rotators, which are another muscle group responsible for helping to prevent hip internal rotation.

Standing Leg Extension   The standing leg extension teaches the player the correct tracking and patterning of the knee movement.

Technique

Attach a band to an immoveable object in front of you and loop the band around the knee as shown in figure 8.16. Allow the knee to bend as shown in figure 8.16 and then straighten it against the resistance of the band. Let the heel come off the floor when the knee is bent and return it to the floor as the knee straightens. Be sure to maintain correct (midline) alignment. Start with 8 repetitions and build up to 20. Perform the exercise on both sides but focus on the affected side. Start with two sets and build up to five. Perform once a day.

▶ **Figure 8.16**   Standing leg extension.

Martin Haines and Daniel Cohen

Hip Hitch   A hip drop occurs when the pelvis drops below horizontal on or shortly after heel strike. The hip drop is part of the process by which ground reaction forces are absorbed, and it should work synchronously with subtalar joint pronation and knee flexion to dampen ground reaction forces on heel strike. The leg transfers the heel strike energy to the spine. It is a mechanical filter (Gracovetsky 1985). Dysfunction in one of these systems can compromise the whole kinetic chain and be one of the causes of what Lewit (2009) describes as conditioned reflexes. The result is often excessive loads around the pelvis, spine, groin and knees. Working the abductor and lateral rotator group in an isolated fashion initially (but still functionally) can help the player control those forces.

Technique

Stand sideways on a step with one foot over the edge of the step and hanging free. The step should be at least 10 centimetres high. Keeping both legs straight, slowly lower the foot of the free leg to a point below the level of the step (figure 8.17) and then lift it above the level of the step. Ensure that the shoulders, spine and pelvis remain in alignment. Hold on to a stable object if necessary until balance improves. Start with 8 repetitions and build up to 20. Perform the exercise on both sides but focus on the affected side. Start with two sets and build up to five. Perform once a day.

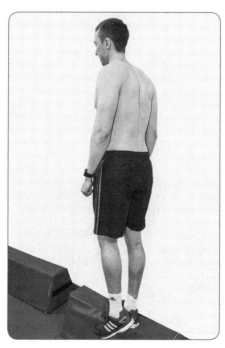

▶ **Figure 8.17**   Hip hitch.
Martin Haines and Daniel Cohen

Single-Leg Squat With Resistance Tubing   After each relevant muscle group has the capacity to engage efficiently, the next progression is to integrate those movements into one functional pattern. The single-leg squat pattern is an effective movement for those who fail the ligament dominance screen. Placing resistance tubing around the lateral side of the knee exaggerates engagement of the lateral hip rotators, thereby encouraging a counterforce to the internal rotation moment at the hip joint. This exercise helps the locomotor system learn to engage the relevant muscles in a synchronous way to mitigate some of the risk factors for knee injuries.

Technique

Stand with resistance tubing tied around the outside of the leg as in figure 8.18. Make sure that the tubing is at 90 degrees to the way you are facing. Lift the nonworking foot. Slowly squat down to 45 degrees at the knee and return to standing. Ensure that the knee stays in line with the foot. Start with 8 repetitions and build up to 20. Perform the exercise on both sides but focus on the affected side. Start with two sets and build up to five. Perform once a day.

▶ **Figure 8.18**   Single-leg squat with resistance tubing.

Martin Haines and Daniel Cohen

Spine

A key biomechanical pillar that links the pelvis and shoulders is the spine (Gracovetsky 1985). If the spine is not functional in terms of mobility, movement and control, associated structures may compensate. A key movement in the spine is rotation. If spinal rotation is restricted, it invariably has an impact on the function of other aspects of the kinetic chain and can compromise performance and increase the risk of injury.

Spinal Rotation Screen

Procedure

The player sits on a chair, places the hands on the shoulders, squeezes the scapulae together and then slowly rotates from one side to the other (figure 8.19). Make sure that the hips stay still on the chair. Make sure that the knees remain still to ensure that the movement comes from the spine and not the pelvis. Expect the player to get to at least 45 degrees of rotation in each direction. The scapulae must stay retracted. As soon as the scapulae start to move and come away from the spine, stop the movement and measure the amount of rotation at that point.

Note

If the scapulae are not retracted during the screen, the rotation movement being measured is not purely from the spine but is a combination of spinal and costo-scapulae movement (the movement of the scapulae around the rib cage). This movement will compromise the results because the spine is the target in this screen.

▶ **Figure 8.19** Spinal rotation screen position.
Martin Haines and Daniel Cohen

Results

A player who can achieve 45 degrees to each side without pain has passed the test. If pain, stiffness or limited movement occurs during the movement or return movement, the player fails the test. The player may experience stiffness or pain at any point in the movement and anywhere in the spine. Note a description of the player's comments and feedback for comparison.

Spinal Anatomy and Function

Spinal rotation is part of many gross movement patterns in soccer, and restrictions have been described as key factors in pain syndromes as well as precursors to injury and compromised performance. Figure 8.20 shows the dominant muscles of the back.

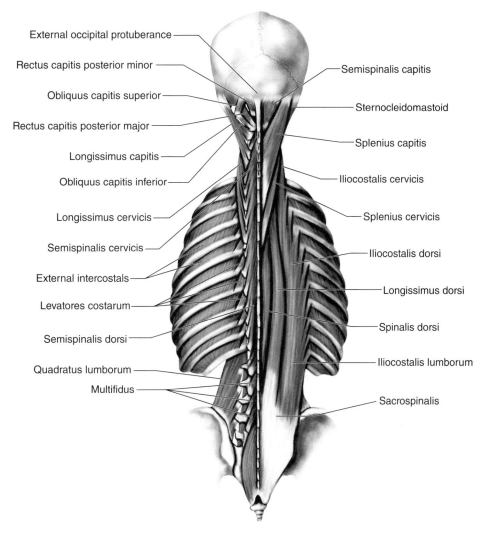

External occipital protuberance

Rectus capitis posterior minor

Obliquus capitis superior

Rectus capitis posterior major

Longissimus capitis

Obliquus capitis inferior

Longissimus cervicis

Semispinalis cervicis

External intercostals

Levatores costarum

Semispinalis dorsi

Quadratus lumborum

Multifidus

Semispinalis capitis

Sternocleidomastoid

Splenius capitis

Iliocostalis cervicis

Splenius cervicis

Iliocostalis dorsi

Longissimus dorsi

Spinalis dorsi

Iliocostalis lumborum

Sacrospinalis

▶ **Figure 8.20** Muscles of the back.

Exercises for Spinal Mobility

Several exercises are used to improve the mobility of the spine in rotation.

The shoulder roll described in the section 'Exercises for the Shoulder' can also be used to improve spinal mobility. Perform shoulder rolls at least once per day and two or three times per day if possible. Start with 8 repetitions and build up to 12. Start with two sets and build up to four.

Trunk Rotation

Technique

Sit on a chair with the feet planted firmly on the floor. Place the hands on the shoulders and hold a broom or stick across the shoulders to help maintain shoulder positioning. Keeping the hips still on the chair, turn the shoulders from side to side (figure 8.21). Do not let the knees glide past each other; keep them fixed. Keep the head in line with the shoulders; do not keep looking forwards. Start with 8 repetitions and build up to 12. Start with two sets and build up to four. Perform trunk rotations at least once per day and two or three times per day if possible.

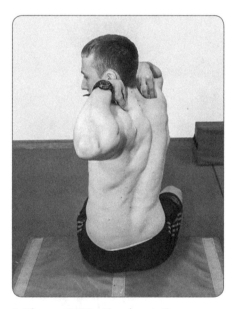

▶ **Figure 8.21** Trunk rotation.

Martin Haines and Daniel Cohen

Leg Roll

Technique

Lie on the back with the knees bent and together. Hold the arms out to the sides at 90 degrees. Keeping the shoulders and arms still, rotate the lower body from side to side (figure 8.22). Do not lift the feet off the floor; simply roll on to the outside border of each foot. Make sure that the knees stay locked together. The hips must come off the floor as the body rotates. Start with 8 repetitions and build up to 12. Start with two sets and build up to four. Perform at least once per day.

▶ **Figure 8.22**   Leg roll.
Martin Haines and Daniel Cohen

Conclusion

Many other screens can be used to assess a player's intrinsic biomechanical profile. Likewise, other exercises can be used to correct flaws. This chapter contains some key screens and interventions that will help the practitioner understand players better by building up a picture of each player's intrinsic biomechanical profile. Although this profile will change over time, the player's current profile can be used in a variety of ways. First, it can be used as a benchmark when a player is returning to play postinjury, providing a clear understanding of preinjury levels. Second, the practitioner can measure the player's key NM-B performance and injury risk factors and compare them with physiological and strength measures to identify red flags. For example, a player who is progressing well in cardiovascular fitness and strength training and is scoring well in movement tests typically would not be at high risk of injury. But if the biomechanical profile shows flaws, which is possible despite a seemingly low-risk status, all the other factors could merely be showing the player's ability to compensate for intrinsic biomechanical flaws, which actually highlights a high risk. Some players can compensate for one or two intrinsic biomechanical flaws, but the more they have, the higher their risk is.

Building any personalized system into a team training session can be challenging, but giving players the responsibility to perform the programme on their own can empower them to look after themselves rather than rely on often overburdened backroom staff. Players who do not have access to the medical and fitness teams of large professional clubs can learn to manage themselves and gain valuable insight into their own health, enabling them to maintain a higher level of performance with less injury over a longer playing career.

The human body is an integrated system, and each of its parts contributes to the performance of the whole. Although an increasing amount of work is being conducted in this field, more is needed. We hope that this chapter contributes to the coach's body of knowledge and provides some insight into how more skills can be added to help players' and ultimately the team's performance and results.

CHAPTER 9

Soccer Boots and Playing Surfaces

—Thorsten Sterzing

Throughout history soccer shoes and surfaces have been discussed for their contribution to victories and defeats, to performance and injuries, and for their general influence on the nature of the game. Thereby, the mutual interaction of shoes and surfaces receives much attention, especially when considering changing surface characteristics because of weather or the development of artificial surfaces, two aspects that soccer shoe design must account for.

Research on soccer shoes is constantly ongoing, covering not only aspects of shoe–surface interaction but also aspects of players' shoe–foot and shoe– soccer ball interaction.

The FIFA laws of the game officially document soccer shoe and surface requirements. The 2011–2012 edition *Law 1—the Field of Play* states that matches may be played on natural or artificial surfaces. Artificial surfaces must meet the requirements of the *FIFA Quality Concept for Football Turf* or the *International Artificial Turf Standard* to be used in official games. *Law 4— the Players' Equipment* states that footwear resembles compulsory pieces of equipment to players, next to jerseys, shorts, stockings and shin guards. It further states that all equipment worn by players must not be dangerous to themselves or to other players. But these two laws provide only a rough framework for the demands on soccer shoes and soccer surfaces. Because the laws leave plenty of room for multiple construction features, this chapter provides insight into the functional criteria when playing soccer. Respective performance benefits and potential injury risks because of player–surface interaction are illustrated, indicating that the right combination of shoes and surfaces provides the best playing characteristics.

The soccer shoe is the most important piece of equipment for the players. Because of its dual function, it likely exceeds the importance of shoes used in other sports. On the one hand, the soccer shoe acts as interface between the player's foot and the surface; on the other hand, it marks the interface between the player's foot and the ball. Athletic footwear companies need to account for the complexity of soccer shoe construction during their marketing, design, development, research and manufacturing processes. Therefore, a remarkable amount of practical considerations, testing efforts and scientific research has been applied to tame the complexity of soccer shoes over the past, efforts that surely will go on in the future.

Such approaches predominantly aim to improve the soccer shoe's two major functions, performance enhancement and injury prevention, which form the main objectives of athletic footwear in general. Thereby, performance enhancement focuses on all areas supporting players in conducting the game. These areas may refer to objective aspects such as acceleration, running and sprinting speed as well as ball-kicking and ball-handling parameters, subjective aspects such as comfort during match and practice sessions, and even psychological factors related to footwear that may affect players' mental condition during games and practice.

Injury prevention aspects aim to keep players injury free throughout match and practice sessions by reducing the physical loads during soccer exposure, such as by providing adequate traction and stability. But for certain aspects, performance enhancement and injury prevention are contradictive requirements of soccer shoes, so compromises need to be reached.

Evaluation of Soccer Shoes

Testing procedures commonly used during the evaluation of general athletic footwear and during the specific evaluation of soccer shoes are based on various areas: computer simulation, mechanics, biomechanics, athletic performance and subjective perception (figure 9.1). Research and testing results provide thorough insight into the complex mechanisms occurring during player–surface and player–ball interaction.

Testing Procedures

Soccer shoes are evaluated for basic properties such as comfort, fit, stability and traction, as well as for more specific characteristics such as lower-extremity loading, agility running, ball kicking and ball handling. Comprehensive analyses combining the various testing procedures describe the overall quality of a soccer shoe. Note that findings based on different testing procedures may complement or contradict each other. For instance, players' subjective perception of soccer shoe features does not necessarily match objective testing observations in all cases. Whereas objective running performance generally reflects subjective perception of players, ball speed during kicking or general ball-handling performance does not always coincide with players' subjective perception. Psychological aspects, such as play-

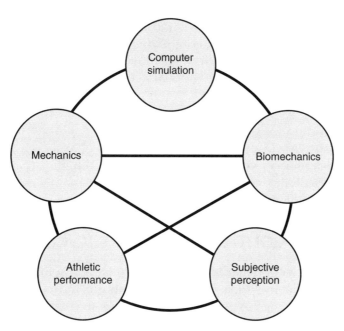

▶ **Figure 9.1** Comprehensive evaluation of footwear.

ers' simply liking a soccer shoe or its outer appearance, should be considered during the evaluation of soccer shoes. Additionally, observations based only on mechanical, machine-driven testing do not necessarily reflect findings from biomechanical testing, which uses human players for measurements. For instance, high mechanical traction values above certain thresholds may indicate unsuitable biomechanical traction characteristics because players' individual biological constitutions may not allow them to use excessively high mechanical traction. Diverse strategies of athletes to adapt to different environmental circumstances are revealed in this context.

Soccer Shoe Properties

Essential information for soccer shoe construction can be derived directly from two main sources: game analyses and player questionnaires. Game analyses deliver walking, running, acceleration and sprinting distances covered by players at different speeds as well as frequency and type of player–ball interaction. Such analyses allow the comparison of general playing styles of teams and individual players, as well as specific subgroups referring to sex, age and skill level, which inspires soccer shoe creation that reflects authentic needs.

Questionnaires provide hands-on information about players' soccer shoe requirements. Applied questionnaire research identified the following shoe properties as most important: comfort, fit, stability, traction and ball sensing.

Thorough understanding of the game characteristics and player requirements is linked to design and development processes applied to soccer shoe manufacturing. Questionnaire findings indicate that the general importance of required shoe properties does not vary considerably in players of different skill levels and only mildly between sexes. But the required degree of certain shoe properties may differ for subgroups and regarding players' general motivation for playing soccer, and this variable should be focused on more extensively in the future. For instance in elite soccer, performance requirements of soccer shoes are naturally ranked higher than in subelite soccer. The following section discusses the main requirements of soccer shoes such as comfort, traction and player–ball interaction.

Functional Comfort of Athletic Footwear

Comfort of athletic footwear is difficult to define in absolute terms because it is a highly subjective measure that accounts for individual preferences and refers to individual experiences that players have with their footwear. Because athletic footwear must fulfil various requirements besides being comfortable, shoe comfort is assessed from a relative, here soccer-specific, perspective rather than from an absolute one. Given the wide range of sports that need specific portfolios of functional properties, measuring comfort in absolute terms is unreasonable. Thus, the recommended approach is to measure comfort of athletic footwear under consideration of its functional usage, referred to as functional comfort. This term indicates that comfort should not compromise other functional requirements of footwear. It should refer to the highest amount of comfort possible after further functional criteria have been sufficiently accommodated.

Soccer Shoe Comfort

Because soccer shoes are typically worn for 90 minutes during games and even longer when considering warm-up or practice sessions, comfort aspects are important. It is reasonable to distinguish between plantar foot comfort, referring to the area underneath the foot, and comfort of the dorsal, medial and lateral foot, referring to the areas above and to both sides of the foot. Whereas the outsole configuration, the shoe plate, midsole and insole affect plantar foot comfort, the shoe upper construction affects comfort aspects linked to the fit of the shoe. Thereby, especially the outsole configuration of a soccer shoe with its characteristic cleat construction calls for adequate cushioning. Nowadays, specific moulding techniques and additional improvements regarding manufacturing processes respond to these needs and are able to reduce plantar pressures. Such techniques have allowed separating considerations of traction and plantar foot comfort to a certain extent. They allow the implementation of a variety of outsole configurations without bringing up concerns regarding excessively high plantar pressures that can potentially lead to discomfort.

Soccer Shoe Fit

The shoe upper in its function to create a good foot–shoe interface aims to provide good fit and stability. Both shoe features have direct influence on comfort perception because poor fit and poor stability would be compromising aspects. Generally, soccer shoes have a rather narrow, tight fit at rearfoot and forefoot, which should not allow relative movement between the foot and the shoe. Partly, these necessities are taken care of by the shaft geometry, referring to shoe upper shape, which depends on the shoe last dimensions, manufacturing procedures and the material used. Final fit adjustments are made by the players themselves using their preferred lacing strategy to accommodate their individual foot morphology. Thereby, some soccer shoes feature regular straight lacing, whereas some feature an oblique lacing shifted to the lateral aspect of the shoe. For the latter the shaft geometry should fit the player's foot morphology well because this type of lacing offers less individual fit adjustment compared with footwear having straight lacings. Straight-lacing arrangements were shown to allow reasonably good individual fit adjustments even when shoe shaft geometry does not entirely match foot morphology.

Traction

Footwear traction refers to the forces counteracting the relative movements of shoe and surface. Traction is based on the material and the geometrical characteristics of the two counterparts. Thereby, the studs of soccer shoes are a paradigm using different geometrical characteristics to configure shoe outsoles for providing suitable traction for players while not putting them at higher risk for injuries. In contrast to court shoes, soccer shoes feature prominent stud configurations. Over the years, stud position as well as geometrical size and shape have been evaluated and discussed intensively.

   Early on, in the first half of the 20th century, plain working shoes, modified street boots, or rather rudimentarily manufactured soccer-like footwear were used for playing soccer because they naturally featured profiled outsole construction (figure 9.2). At that time, soccer shoe cleat positioning was arbitrary and unsystematic. Later on, soccer shoe manufacturers started to implement specifically designed soccer shoe outsole configurations to provide optimal traction to players. Generally, soccer shoe traction is determined by the shoe outsole configuration, the surface conditions and respective loading characteristics. The latter are determined by player anthropometrics such as body dimensions and body weight, the angle of attack of ground contact locomotion patterns and the muscular effort used. Therefore, the amount

▶ **Figure 9.2** (a) Working shoes, (b) modified street boots and (c) soccer-like footwear used for playing soccer in the past.

Franz-Josef Brüggemeier, Ulrich Borsdorf, Jörg Steiner (Hrsg.): Der Ball ist rund. Katalog zur Fußallausstellung im Gasometer Oberhausen. Klartext Verlag, Essen, 2000.

of loading that soccer players experience may differ considerably between players and between movements in various game situations.

Furthermore, surface conditions in soccer are not consistent. Weather has a considerable temporary effect on surface characteristics and may tremendously alter interaction with a given soccer shoe. These observations led to the implementation of different stud types for usage on hard ground, firm ground and soft ground surfaces (figure 9.3).

Some soft ground outsole configurations enable players to change the length of the studs manually by using replaceable screw-in studs. Longer studs are used on wet and muddy surfaces because they penetrate deeper into the ground and thus can reach the firmer, lower surface layers of natural grass pitches. Anecdotally, this mechanism was first meaningfully observed during the final game of the soccer World Cup 1954 in Switzerland, which was played on a wet and muddy pitch. Innovative, longer screw-in studs replaced the studs of regular length and provided the West German players with an edge of advanced performance over the team from Hungary, reportedly contributing to West Germany's eventual victory. After that demonstration, efforts to improve the functional properties of soccer shoe stud configurations received increasing attention.

Good soccer shoe traction is meant to help players avoid uncontrolled slippage, which can reduce performance and lead to injuries, and contribute to a strong push-off in all desired movement directions. Functional traction should balance the relationship of foot translation—the amount of relative movement between shoe and ground during contact—and lower-extremity

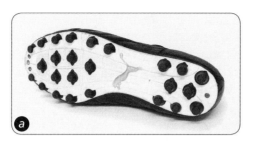

▶ **Figure 9.3**   Soccer shoes for (*a*) hard, (*b*) firm and (c) soft ground natural turf pitches.

Thorsten Sterzing

loading during ground contact of soccer-specific locomotion. The following section illustrates the specific influence of traction characteristics on running performance and on lower-extremity loading. The meaning of different stud configurations for agility running performance and player loading is explained, providing guidance for choosing the right outsole configuration for given environmental circumstances and individual player requirements.

Studs and Running Performance

An important requirement in soccer is fast running performance, incorporating straight acceleration and sprinting, as well as agility running scenarios including multiple changes of direction. Thereby, traction is essential for the propulsive component of locomotion. It is also important for the breaking component during movements that incorporate slight changes of direction, such as cutting, or severe changes of direction, such as turning. A simple method to assess functional traction is the measurement of acceleration, sprinting and agility running times; better traction is identified by shorter times. Running courses that include multiple propulsive and breaking tasks are well suited to distinguish between performances of different soccer shoe outsole configurations. The baseline idea of this testing method is that insufficient low traction would cause slippage, leading to slower running times. In contrast, excessively high traction would cause the foot to lock with the ground, counteracting rotational movements and subsequently reducing agility running performance.

Comprehensive functional traction measurements have been carried out as explained. They examine different outsole configurations and reveal the suitability of various shoe–surface combinations. The most general observation is that stud length influences running performance. The shortening of studs, while maintaining the overall number and arrangement, has led to weaker running performance as indicated by slower speed, especially when changing running direction. Having studs removed completely certainly demonstrates a severe decline in running performance, but cutting the stud length down to half has also been shown to reduce performance considerably. Furthermore, the general stud geometry influences running performance. Bladed stud designs have been found to exhibit better running performance compared with elliptic stud designs, but the benefit was present only in traction courses featuring multiple changes of directions and could not be observed during plain straight acceleration tasks.

Players also subjectively perceived the bladed stud designs to provide better shoe–surface interaction during soccer-specific cutting movements. This result is attributed to the fact that bladed studs, when positioned at the edge of a shoe, provide a greater contact area to the ground in medio-lateral orientation compared with an elliptic stud design (figure 9.4). Subjective perception of running performance in soccer shoes with different traction characteristics in general reflects objective measurements. Therefore, providing optimal traction to players offers benefit for actual athletic performance as well as from a psychological perspective, allowing the strengthening of players' performance confidence.

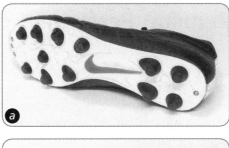

▶ **Figure 9.4** (a) Elliptic and (b) bladed stud designs.

Thorsten Sterzing

Surfaces and Running Performance

Surface characteristics have also been shown to have significant influence for running performance. Surface characteristics may change temporarily because of weather or more fundamentally when different natural or artificial surface types are used. On snow- and ice-layered surfaces, running performance is considerably reduced, which explains the highly different nature of soccer games played on such grounds. When playing on such surfaces, bladed stud configurations are better suited, because they carve into the surface more easily compared with elliptic stud configurations. In contemporary elite sport, most high-level soccer clubs have installed heating systems to prevent such surface conditions from developing.

For artificial surfaces, shoes specifically designed for playing on artificial turf allow better agility running than shoes that were originally designed for natural surfaces. Matching the shoe with the surface is important.

More exposed and prominent stud configurations offered by soft or firm ground stud designs were shown to provoke more cautious cutting and turning movement patterns of players on artificial turf, subsequently reducing agility running performance.

An optimal stud configuration should provide players with a performance edge over opponents in acceleration, sprinting and agility running. Systematic research has shown that agility running performance highly depends on the outsole configuration used for a given surface. Furthermore, in most cases objectively measured shoe performance was matched by players' perceptions. This finding indicates that for outsole configuration and agility running performance, a sound interaction between the cognitive mechanisms and locomotion is present. Moreover, if players do not have the right amount of traction in a certain shoe, their performance decreases, probably because locomotion is executed more cautiously and thus less explosively. Because the relationship between objective measurements and subjective perception of running performance is solid and remarkable, players can make straightforward decisions about which shoes to pick when running performance is considered the most important criterion. Players should simply choose the shoe they feel fastest in, reasonable advice that now has been verified by scientific findings.

Relationship of Mechanical and Biomechanical Traction Characteristics

Whereas it is relatively easy to measure athletic running performance of soccer shoe traction by simple use of timing gates, quantifying respective biomechanical loading effects on the lower extremities of the human body is more complex. Although relationships between soccer shoes and injuries are occasionally referred to in the public discussion, it should be acknowledged that linking specific injury types to soccer shoe traction is difficult from a scientific perspective.

To date, injury surveys do not provide substantial evidence for a clear linkage of sustained injuries to a specific type of soccer shoe. The lack of sufficient quantitative data unfortunately limits respective discussions to anecdotal evidence.

Biomechanical lower-extremity loading can be quantified for various traction configurations with respect to shoe–ground translation (slippage) and loading. Ideally, shoe–ground translation should be minimized because it puts the player in a short passive phase during ground contact. The typical relationship between shoe–ground translation and lower-extremity loading is illustrated for the ankle joint by referring to a turning movement (figure 9.5). Higher amounts of shoe–ground translation coincide with lesser loading of the ankle joint, such as reduced ankle eversion moments. Thereby, higher amounts of shoe–ground translation indicate performance reduction because longer phases of shoe–ground translation force players to remain longer in a state in which they are prevented from propelling their bodies actively in the desired movement direction.

The most pronounced biomechanical movement alterations in response to different footwear take place at the more distal parts of the leg. When players want to reduce or avoid slippage of the shoe relative to the ground, higher traction is required, which in turn increases loading on the lower extremity. As long as players can sustain these loads acutely, avoiding traumatic injuries, and as long as they can sustain these loads repetitively, avoiding overuse injuries, high traction is beneficial.

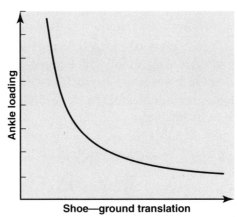

▶ **Figure 9.5** Shoe–ground translation and ankle loading during a turning movement.

Clearly, anthropometric characteristics and the training status of players come into play, because physical status is an important factor to estimate whether a player's loading is not harmful from a physiological perspective. Better training status, indicated, for example, by higher muscular strength of the lower extremities, may prevent injuries that occur because loading characteristics have been only slightly above the person's physiological threshold. Optimal traction has been observed not to be a function of complete minimization of foot translation. This finding indicates that minimization of foot translation below a certain threshold does not lead to increased performance. An excessive increase of lower-extremity loading would counteract players' performance efforts. To avoid injuries, players would use more cautious movement execution patterns if they subjectively perceive that mechanical traction properties of a given shoe–surface combination are too high. In this sense, the resulting traction is based on the player's performance efforts, which in turn depend on his or her ability to cope with the given shoe–surface characteristics.

In situations in which traction properties are reduced (e.g., wet surface conditions), players may compensate for the slippery conditions by altering their movement patterns. Research demonstrates that players aim to increase their initial shoe–surface contact area at foot strike by adjusting the angle of attack, creating a more vertical alignment of the shank and probably the whole body. A larger shoe–ground contact area is produced, which secures more traction. These findings were observed during academic research studies in which studs of soccer shoes were cut off to eliminate the effect of geometrical traction, but similar results were found in more realistic research situations in which wet surfaces decreased traction properties.

In light of these considerations, a functional traction concept was suggested that addresses the relationship between mechanical availability of traction and biomechanical utilization (table 9.1). Whereas the mechanical characteristics of traction are well defined by surface and footwear characteristics, the biomechanical characteristics depend on specific circumstances that may vary substantially between players. In conclusion, traction needs to be optimized, as opposed to maximized, to achieve the best athletic performance.

Table 9.1 Factors Influencing Traction

Mechanical availability	Biomechanical utilization
Material	Anthropometrics
Geometry	Body composition
Interface angle	Motor performance skills
Loading	Training status

Player–Ball Interaction

The interaction of the player's foot with the ball is the defining action in soccer. This interaction includes the standard passing and kicking of stationary and moving balls, using instep, inner instep, outer instep or side foot techniques. It also refers to dribbling, receiving and juggling the ball in various game situations. Therefore, the soccer shoe plays an important role for objectively measurable and subjectively perceivable performance. Performance of ball interaction can be measured by objective parameters such as ball velocity, ball accuracy and ball flight characteristics. Ball velocity and accuracy are aspects that should be maximized by trying to kick as hard or as accurately as possible. Ball flight characteristics are more complex, referring to the amount of spin imparted to the ball or the aim to achieve severely curved or unpredictable flight paths.

The capability of soccer shoes to improve foot–ball interaction has received wider attention over the past two decades. Until then, kicking velocity and kicking accuracy were not regarded to be heavily influenced by soccer shoes but were attributed solely to the players' individual skills. The common belief was that the players' technical skills and anthropometric characteristics were solely responsible for passing, kicking and general ball-handling performance. Confirming this notion, early literature has listed only broad aspects that influence kicking velocity, among them sex, maturation, skill, leg dominance and fatigue. But recent research has shown that soccer shoes can add to the given skills of players in foot–ball interaction. Therefore, two substantially different mechanisms need to be considered: the influence of soccer shoes on the stance foot and their influence on the kicking foot.

During passing or kicking, the player aims to be in a stable and controlled position, which is influenced by stance foot characteristics. Uncontrolled slipping or falling most likely deteriorates the quality of passes and kicks. The influence of the shoe on the kicking foot is even more complex, because it may alter foot velocity, shoe–ball contact location or contact duration, thereby influencing the resultant impact quality. For both the stance foot and the kicking foot, the shoe serves as an artificial interface between the player's foot and the ball.

Fast Kicking

Ball velocity is influenced by kicking technique, including its approach phase characteristics. Regarding the support leg, the outsole configuration of the shoe affects the run-up and the critical foot plant before kicking. Suitable traction characteristics would increase the breaking impulse of the horizontal ground reaction forces generated by the support leg, providing an explosive initiation of the kinetic chain towards the kicking leg as the kicking action unfolds. This would produce a faster swing phase of the kicking leg and contribute to higher ball speed.

Regarding the ball contact phase, high foot velocity, high effective mass of the foot, as the result of the foot coupled to the shank, and short foot–ball contact duration have been shown to be beneficial for fast kicking. Surprisingly, soccer footwear slightly reduces ball velocity compared with barefoot kicking if players can ignore the high pain present during barefoot kicking. The mechanism explaining this phenomenon is referred to as passive forced plantar flexion of the foot, which occurs during the impact phase in shoe kicks. For those kicks, the shoe does not allow players to plantar flex the ankle joint fully and voluntarily just before impact, leading to further, forced plantar flexion during impact.

The absence of this mechanism during barefoot kicking is shown by a high-speed video picture sequence (figure 9.6). When kicking barefoot, players have their foot already fully plantar flexed at the beginning of ball impact, providing a more rigid foot-shank segment and therefore superior collision mechanics through an increase of the effective mass.

Specific features of soccer shoes have been examined for their influence on ball velocity. An increase of the toe pitch, the characteristic upward bended tip of the shoe, has been found to reduce ball velocity. As the foot and shoe at the toe region deform during contact, the initial stiffness of the shoe is reduced, thereby increasing the range for forced plantar flexion (as described earlier) even further. In addition, upper-shoe material friction can affect ball velocity. Moderate friction between shoe and ball material appears to be superior to lower or higher friction when high ball speed is required, possibly because of the amount of spin imparted to the ball during contact. Further characteristics of soccer shoes have not been shown to affect ball velocity.

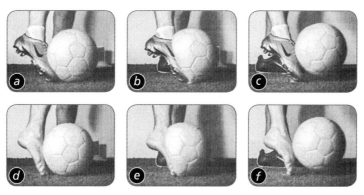

▶ **Figure 9.6** Impact phase of shod and barefoot full instep kicks: (*a* and *d*) initial contact; (*b* and *e*) full contact; (*c* and *f*) final contact.

Thorsten Sterzing

Shoe weight has not been shown to alter ball velocity. Although an increase in weight reduces foot velocity, it does not influence ball velocity. Although the heavier shoe increases the impact mass, this is only a compensatory mechanism for the lower foot velocity present because of increased shoe weight, eventually leaving resultant ball velocity unchanged. Additionally, different outsole stiffness of soccer shoes does not affect ball velocity. Small degrees of outsole stiffness, characterizing a rather flexible outsole, appear to be sufficient to limit the full voluntary plantar flexion of the ankle joint referred to earlier.

Higher outsole stiffness, characterized by a stiff outsole, does not increase ball velocity either, contradicting the idea that a stiff outsole would support the foot during kicking by enhancing transfer of energy.

Research examining the shoe influence on kicking velocity has mainly focused on full instep kicks thus far. It is not known whether shoe features influence kicking velocity during side foot, inner instep and outer instep kicks. Certainly, the latter types of kicking techniques are not meant to exhibit the absolute maximum kicking velocity in soccer. But small performance margins because of certain features of the soccer shoe may also be present and would surely be desirable for players.

Accurate Kicking

Although ball speed, as the more spectacular component of kicking, receives more attention, passing, kicking and ball-handling precision are more important because accuracy affects almost all ball-related actions in the game. In this regard the soccer shoe has been shown to influence ball accuracy. In contrast to its effect on kicking velocity, barefoot kicking has been found to decrease kicking precision. Various soccer shoes evoke different ball accuracy during instep kicking. One proposed mechanism for the improvement of kicking accuracy is to provide players with an almost even shoe–ball contact area, thereby reducing the influence of the anatomical bony prominences of the foot.

The proposed mechanism is in contrast to soccer shoe types on the market, which might sacrifice small accuracy performance margins. Some brands of shoes feature geometrically profiled shoe uppers to affect factors such as ball spin and thus ball control during its flight phases. Because the business demands of manufacturers are driven not only by functional aspects but also by marketing criteria, performance of soccer shoes may be compromised in certain instances.

Specific examination of soccer shoe kicking performance has been taken off the field and into a laboratory environment for better standardization during research studies. Thus, results are well suited to derive general concepts of how soccer shoes should be designed to improve kicking performance. Obviously, these results cannot predict single shots of individual players in a specific game situation. In this sense research on other soccer shoe properties needs to be referred to as well. A huge benefit results from gaining a general understanding of the interactions of the foot, the shoe, the surface and the ball, eventually leading to solid, evidence-based soccer shoe concepts and better soccer performance. But because each player's individual characteristics differ, the optimal personal soccer shoe can be reflected only in a broader sense by such concepts.

Women's Soccer Shoes

Most soccer shoe research and testing efforts have so far been directed to men's soccer shoes. Women's soccer shoes often still resemble scaled-down male versions to some extent instead of being considered authentic sex-specific footwear responding to women's functional needs. In recent years, general soccer research has started to explore sex-specific game characteristics, body characteristics, injury patterns, biomechanical and neuromuscular locomotion patterns, as well as foot morphology. Such research now offers reasonable anchors to transfer female-specific needs into the functional design of soccer shoes.

Although such baseline research indicates functional opportunities to improve soccer shoes for females, general operational implementation is slow. But a steadily increasing number of females around the world engaging in soccer strongly points towards a growing market. Demand is increasing, and manufacturers are seeking to be socially responsible.

This section aims to provide a baseline for the creation of functional women's soccer shoes. Broad areas where innovative functional thinking will improve the quality of women's soccer shoes, and subsequently female soccer players, are summarized graphically (figure 9.7). Based on this, specific necessities of women's soccer shoes are introduced in more detail.

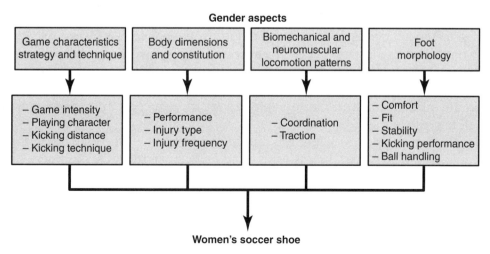

▶ **Figure 9.7** Relevant aspects of women's soccer shoes.

Soccer Game Characteristics Between Sexes

Analysis of general locomotion patterns shows that female soccer teams cover distances similar to those of their male counterparts during a soccer match. Additionally, the overall number of activity-changing movements and game relevant actions per minute are only slightly lower in female soccer. But game intensity in the women's game is remarkably lower than it is in the men's game; women cover only half of the locomotion distance in the high-intensity mode, deemed game decisive, compared with men.

In a comparative analysis of World Cup 2002 (in Japan and South Korea for men) and World Cup 2003 (in the United States for women), it was observed that player–ball interaction differed considerably between the sexes. Women's soccer featured fewer actions characterized as dribbling, ball control, and short passes, and more long passes were observed. In addition, kicking techniques differed between the sexes. Whereas women used inner instep and outer instep kicks more frequently, they less frequently used side foot and outer instep kicks. This difference may be explained by the comparatively lesser muscular strength of female players, although ball size and mass, as well as pitch dimensions, do not differ.

A general recommendation to amend to the observed difference in game characteristics is to reduce the weight of women's soccer shoes in an effort to reduce onset of fatigue during games, which may help lift game intensity of women's soccer closer to the men's level. Of course, reduction of weight must not sacrifice injury prevention properties of the boot.

Female Body Constitution, Injury Occurrence and Locomotion Patterns

Body dimensions and specific body composition form the basis for human locomotion. Besides the notion that on average women are smaller and lighter than men, some less obvious aspects need to be considered. The female-specific muscle-to-fat proportion appears to be less favourable for women in regards to sport performance, indicating a weaker predisposition for women to stabilize and protect lower-extremity joints during explosive locomotion. Moreover, females' generally lower muscle tone and higher ligament laxity contribute to explanations of reduced performance and higher injury risk.

The female-specific wider hip and bigger Q-angle of the lower extremity form the anatomical basis for a more pronounced valgus alignment of the leg, reportedly a risk factor for knee injuries. In addition, knee injury frequency is considerably higher in females than in males, especially regarding anterior-cruciate ligament injuries. Because most of these injuries occur during situations without opponent influence, body predisposition, training status and female-specific locomotion patterns are assumed to be predominantly responsible. Biomechanical and neuromuscular coordination patterns of the lower extremity were shown to differ between sexes for soccer-specific straight running and movements with changes of direction. Differences become more pronounced in movements that are not anticipated well in advance but are reactive in nature, such as when an opponent must be followed after a surprising move or a deflected ball must be followed. Such movements are important and frequently occurring characteristics in soccer and other court sports.

Soccer shoe constructions for women should take into account female-specific body constitution, injury patterns and locomotion patterns. Derived from these findings, investigating the performance and loading characteristics of less pronounced stud configurations for females is clearly worthwhile. Soccer shoe outsole configurations should limit excessive locking characteristics of the shoe during ground contact to reduce the comparatively high risk of knee injury in females.

Female Foot Morphology

Foot morphology is a crucial aspect in soccer shoe construction because it directly affects fit and comfort properties and may affect other performance features as well. For both sexes small feet have been shown to be rather wide and voluminous, whereas long feet are rather narrow and slender. This observation indicates that shoe fit in general is not a linear function for all its measures. Women's soccer shoes often currently resemble scaled-down versions of men's soccer shoes because they use shoe lasts based on male foot dimensions, so female-specific fit properties are not often obtained. When assessed for the same absolute foot length, women have comparatively narrower feet. A less voluminous foot is especially common in the forefoot region. Soccer shoes are often assessed as being too wide in the forefoot, causing slipping of the foot inside the shoe. A narrow and tight anatomical forefoot fit is an important requirement for improving the stability performance of soccer shoes and contributing to higher kicking velocity. Therefore, adequate lasting procedures and fit manufacturing processes based on sex-specific foot morphology need to be established as the norm, not as the exception, in design and development of women's soccer shoes.

Soccer Surfaces

FIFA laws of the game *Law 1—The Field of Play* states that matches may be played on natural or artificial surfaces. This section refers to specific aspects of natural and artificial surfaces and the historical development of artificial surface implementation.

Natural Surfaces

Traditionally, soccer has been played outdoors, predominantly on natural grass surfaces. According to FIFA standards, the main functional criterion that natural grass surfaces must fulfil is to ensure proper interaction with the players and the ball. These standards address biomechanical aspects regarding player–surface interaction as well as ball bounce and roll. The development of these standards took place by observation rather than by prescription. They were derived from measurements taken on pitches regarded by the soccer governing bodies to be of high quality.

Weather can change natural surface characteristics considerably and thereby alter the style of the game. Soccer games on wet and muddy surfaces or on hard and frozen surfaces often develop a different character compared with games played on regular firm grass surfaces. Varying surface conditions influence ball bounce and roll and may weaken the player–surface interaction during locomotion, resulting in decreased performance.

Consequently, tactical considerations regarding game strategy vary too. For example, on hard or frozen surfaces, ball roll is less predictable, so passing the ball to teammates often occurs in a lofted manner. Wet surfaces may encourage players to kick on goal more frequently and try to create ball bounce a short distance from the goal line. Player–surface interaction is also considerably influenced by weather, especially regarding traction characteristics. In response, outsole configurations for playing on natural grass vary considerably. When playing on soft, wet pitches, suitable stud configurations feature fewer but longer studs. Such studs can penetrate deeper into the ground to provide desired traction and avoid slipping, as referred to earlier.

At the same time, usage of fewer studs prevents loose pieces of muddy soil from sticking to the shoe outsole. In contrast, outsole configurations that feature numerous studs provide larger adhesive contact surface for the muddy soil to stick to.

For firm ground pitches, soccer shoes should feature more but shorter stud elements because these pitch characteristics block studs from penetrating fully into the ground. For that reason, players are exposed to unstable stance conditions when studs are too long. A higher number of studs can also distribute body mass more evenly across the plantar foot surface, thus preventing excessively high pressure points under the foot. For hard or frozen surfaces, stud configurations should get even shorter and the number of stud elements should increase further to account even more for the aforementioned aspects describing firm ground pitches. Shorter studs provide improved whole-body balance and stance foot stability to players on hard surfaces, providing important functional support.

Varying surface characteristics require more than the selection of optimal outsole configurations. They also affect the nature of the game by challenging players in other areas. For instance, wet and muddy surfaces increase the general metabolic energy expenditure of players by increasing muscular strength requirements during ground contact, subsequently causing earlier onset of fatigue. Hard, frozen surfaces increase balance and stability demands, which often give the advantage to smaller, lighter and more agile players. But as long as pitch variation remains reasonable and safe, changing surface characteristics should not cause the match to be considered a charade. In fact, some matches in the past have been remarkable because of specific surface conditions.

Artificial Surfaces

FIFA has included suitable artificial soccer turf pitches in the rules of the game since 2004. One of the first artificial turf pitches was installed at the Astrodome in Houston, Texas, United States, in the 1960s. Initially, artificial turf pitches were installed only for American football and baseball. A few years later artificial turf was also used to host soccer games. Since then, the functional characteristics of artificial turf compared with natural turf pitches have been discussed and debated.

Until today, three substantially different generations of artificial turf have been developed with distinctly altered structural characteristics (figure 9.8). The first (1960) generation consisted of a concrete bottom layer covered with a relatively short but densely distributed artificial fibre carpet, featuring no infill. The second (1980) generation featured an elastic bottom layer and longer grass fibres with sand infill. Both of these artificial turf surfaces

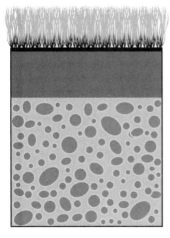
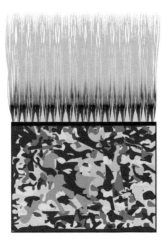
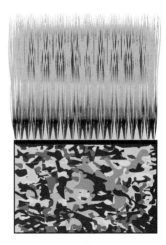

First generation	Second generation	Third generation
1960	1980	1990
Concrete layer	Elastic layer	Elastic layer
No infill	Sand infill	Sand/rubber infill

▶ **Figure 9.8** Structures of artificial turf pitches.

were disparaged for severely changing the nature of the game because they altered ball bounce and roll. Moreover, players commonly experienced skin burns after falls and sliding tackles. Those observations prevented the first two generations of artificial turf from being used regularly as match-play surfaces. Responding to these flaws, the third (1990) generation of artificial turf was developed. It features a two-component sand and rubber infill and improved artificial fibre characteristics that reduce skin friction. The additional rubber infill covering the sand layer provides functional traction to players, creates smoother ball bounce and ball roll, and helps to prevent skin burns. This latest artificial turf structure has been the gold standard of artificial soccer turfs, although manufacturers are developing a fourth generation of artificial soccer turf. Improvement targets include a better, softer and stronger fibre quality, as well as improved infill structures and material developments.

Manufacturers use numerous construction methods and final composing prescriptions to meet the requested quality level of the surface. FIFA certifies only readily installed artificial turf pitches because the subgrade and subbases of pitches are considered as important as the soccer turf itself in ensuring the quality and playability of a pitch. Therefore, the FIFA quality mark is assigned for the installation as a whole, not for the isolated surface as produced in the factory. When meeting respective standards, pitches are assigned either the FIFA 1 star level or the FIFA 2 star level, the latter indicating the highest quality level. Whereas FIFA 1 star refers to the standard for amateur and grassroots soccer pitches able to withstand heavy daily use, FIFA 2 star refers to superior characteristics that guarantee the best quality surfaces at a lower usage frequency. Official top league games are allowed to be played only on FIFA 2 star artificial turf pitches.

Since 2004 some global clubs have installed artificial turf pitches as their home ground. Champions League games and World Championships qualifiers have now been played on artificial turf pitches. The steadily increasing number of FIFA-certified artificial soccer turf pitches around the globe emphasizes the rapid growth and the significant role that artificial turf pitches have today (table 9.2). But this infrastructure development is accompanied by the ongoing controversy about the general quality of artificial turf, including game characteristics and injury occurrence when compared with natural grass surfaces.

Artificial soccer turf pitches are most frequently found in Europe. The reasons for implementation vary, ranging from harsh and long winter weather in the northern countries and some of the eastern countries to the frequent usage demands of soccer pitches in densely populated areas that cannot be sustained by natural grass surfaces. The development of artificial turf installations points towards a general change from natural grass to artificial grass, probably not in the short term but likely in the mid and long term.

Table 9.2 FIFA 1 Star and 2 Star Artificial Soccer Turf Installations

	2010		2011		2012		2013		2014		2015	
	1 star	2 star	1 star	2 star	1 star	2 star	1 star	2 star	1 star	2 star	1 star	2 star
UEFA	109	121	269	245	481	280	686	322	1,049	358	1,194	401
AFC	35	12	48	25	75	17	93	22	129	27	135	38
CONCACAF	29	6	34	35	58	32	76	15	103	18	88	45
CAF	29	4	41	7	58	24	65	9	88	2	90	32
CONME-BOL	10	1	5	5	7	7	15	8	26	8	28	14
OFC	1	0	5	0	7	3	11	2	16	5	22	4
All	213	144	402	317	686	363	946	378	1,411	418	1,557	534

Data from www.fifa.com (accessed between 2010 and 2015).

This change will provide similar and more comparable pitch conditions for soccer games around the globe, which is desirable from a technical point of view. But variable surface conditions add certain challenges and thus an additional degree of excitement to the game.

Referring to the general nature of soccer, game characteristics on the elite level do not show substantial differences between natural and artificial turf pitches, as observed during the U20 Youth World Cup in Canada that was held on both surface types simultaneously. Noteworthy exceptions are sliding tackles, which occur less frequently on artificial surfaces. But subjective assessments of players regarding game characteristics and injury occurrence still differ from objective measurements. Subjective perception remains biased, possibly based on word of mouth or negative experiences with older types of artificial surfaces.

Surfaces and Injuries

Injury surveys comparing first- and second-generation artificial turf surfaces to natural grass surfaces revealed a considerably higher frequency of injuries sustained by players when playing on artificial surfaces. Such injuries on former generations of artificial turf included not only injuries occurring because of inadequate shoe–surface interaction but also general muscular injuries caused by weak shock attenuation properties or skin burns caused by high friction present during sliding tackles or falls. Naturally, this was a major argument to refrain from using artificial surfaces for official games and practice.

In contrast, injury occurrence on the third generation of artificial turf for both sexes no longer differs from injury occurrence on natural grass surfaces in frequency, nature, severity or cause.

Prospective research was carried out during training as well as match play of elite European soccer clubs as well as American college and university teams. Apart from the general neutral findings, only a slight trend showing that injury types may shift towards a higher match incidence of lateral ankle sprains on artificial turfs was reported for elite European players and for young female soccer players. This finding is noteworthy because research showed increased ankle loading when wearing soccer shoes featuring a firm ground stud design instead of a specific artificial turf outsole configuration. Because most players wore outsole configurations designed for firm ground rather than outsole configurations recommended for artificial surfaces, the injury discrepancy observed may reflect inadequate shoe selection rather than genuine difficulties with the surface.

Injury incidence on artificial surfaces was found to be higher for away teams, indicating that familiarization to artificial turf is an issue that needs to be considered. Potentially, teams that are less familiar with playing on artificial turf are more prone to sustain injuries. Therefore, particularly in leagues where both surface types are used, coaches and officials should handle the issue of specific game preparation carefully.

Familiarization should be included in the weekly training and preparation process before upcoming games. The current and short-term future of global soccer is marked by usage of both surface types, so drawing specific attention to familiarization of players when switching between surface types is mandatory.

With artificial turf now more commonly in use, additional scientific research will be carried out to generate better comparisons of game and injury characteristics. Currently, knowledge is lacking about the effect that climate or weather may have on game and injury characteristics on artificial surfaces. Unfortunately, available game and injury research does not report on the footwear used by players who are acutely injured or the type of footwear predominantly worn by players who sustain overuse injuries. The inclusion of footwear characteristics in game and injury surveys would certainly provide important detailed insight into the still unknown relationship of footwear and game characteristics, as well as injury mechanisms.

Footwear for Artificial Surfaces

With the official sanctioning of artificial turf in 2004, the need for adequate footwear became apparent. At that time footwear designed specifically for artificial turf scarcely existed. Soccer shoe manufacturers were not immediately prepared to meet new soccer shoe requirements that responded to artificial surface characteristics. Therefore, players simply used the soccer shoe types they deemed best suited for playing on artificial turf. Players had to compete and train on new surfaces using footwear originally designed and developed to meet natural grass requirements. Players chose from the existing footwear models without the benefit of having recommendations based on scientific research.

Because of individual preference, players have been wearing hard ground or firm ground soccer shoes, and they have widely avoided wearing soft ground soccer shoes. Soccer shoe manufacturers have now directed more attention to specific artificial turf soccer shoes. Systematic research has been done to provide general manufacturing guidelines for artificial turf soccer shoes. Naturally, such research is focused mainly on traction characteristics. Outsole configurations for artificial turf footwear should feature a rather large number of relatively short stud elements. Such stud types are shown to reduce lower-extremity loading while maintaining or even slightly increasing agility running performance. Generally, the characteristics of artificial surfaces are less likely to change because of weather compared with natural grass pitches. Thus, wide variations in outsole configuration to respond to different weather are not necessarily needed on artificial turf pitches, but research is underway.

Conclusion

This chapter has discussed essential aspects regarding the influence of soccer shoes and surfaces on performance and injury prevention when playing soccer. General principles of soccer shoe and soccer surface behaviour have been explained, and these should offer initial guidelines for selecting shoes. The interaction of shoe and surface probably marks the predominant aspect because it determines the traction properties available to the player. General and seasonally changing pitch conditions should govern the selection of the soccer shoe outsole construction.

Only the right combination of shoe and pitch characteristics provides high-level traction to the player and thus high-level movement quality. Moreover, benefits of an ideal match of the soccer shoe upper shape with the individual player's foot morphology have been illustrated. Achieving an optimal fit is a prerequisite for both comfort and stability. Foot morphology is different for each player, and the right combination of shoe and foot helps players attain their best performance.

Academic research has shown to be well suited for deriving conceptual guidelines for soccer shoe manufacturing because findings offer direct opportunities to improve soccer shoe properties. Knowledge about the influence of soccer shoe and surface characteristics on the game will surely be further enhanced through future daily experiences of players and coaches during practice and matches. Academic researchers will contribute to this knowledge base by conducting field and laboratory experiments, and verifying or challenging the assumptions made. Thus, we can expect the quality of soccer shoes and surfaces to increase further, offering the player even better equipment for playing the game in the future.

Acknowledgement

The content of this chapter was retrieved from scientific literature and personal soccer shoe research carried out at the following academic institutions and athletic footwear companies: University of Duisburg-Essen, Germany, and Nike Inc. (United States); Chemnitz University of Technology, Germany, and Puma Inc. (Germany); Li Ning Co. Ltd. (China).

CHAPTER 10

Soccer Ball Dynamics

—Andy Harland and Henry Hanson

Such is the global reach of the game that a soccer ball is one of the most instantly recognizable objects of the modern world. Over 85 million balls are produced each year globally (Waraich 2014). The simplicity of the ball's shape and purpose belies a history of innovation that ensure today's players can enjoy high-quality, consistent products with which to hone and display their skills.

History of Soccer Ball Development

Whilst humankind's instinct to kick objects in games of skill or competition is reported around the world throughout history, it is generally accepted that the origins of modern soccer lie in the games that developed in the United Kingdom during the Middle Ages.

The oldest object bearing resemblance to the balls of today was found above the rafters of Stirling Castle in Scotland in the 1970s. Modern techniques used to date artefacts place it at around 450 years old, likely to have been used during the during the reign of Mary Queen of Scots in the early 16th century.

Popular understanding of 16th-century soccer suggests that rival villages would have used the ball, competing in contests of such savagery and brutality that the game was banned by King Henry VIII because of the casualties it was causing among his military archers. But close inspection of the size, shape and construction of the tanned leather panel and pig bladder assembly suggest that it is more likely to have been used in a delicate, skill-based indoor game also known to have been common during the period.

In 2011 a partnership between the Mary Rose Trust and Loughborough University led to a reproduced replica of the discovered ball being created and assessed, using a range of modern testing methods. Unsurprisingly, the ball failed all but one of the current FIFA standards, and the ball was punctured when kicked by a robotic foot (Hanson and Harland 2012; figure 10.2). Only the air pressure retention of the fresh pig bladder was within acceptable modern tolerances.

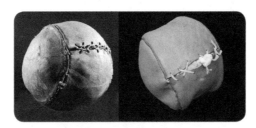

▶ **Figure 10.1**   16th-century ball: original and reproduction.

Andy Harland and Henry Hanson

▶ **Figure 10.2**   Reproduced 16th-century ball punctured during robotic kicking.

Andy Harland and Henry Hanson

Analysis of the recreated ball when filled with a natural pig bladder revealed an obvious lack of sphericity, which suggests that the decision of the Rugby Football Union to preserve the ovoid shape of the ball, eventually specified in the laws of rugby in 1892, was less of a departure from convention than was the decision of the Football Association to specify a spherical ball in 1883.

The ability to specify the shape and dimensions of the ball relied on the materials and manufacturing methods by which they could be realized. Before 1844, when Charles Goodyear (1844) demonstrated the second part of his process by which rubber could be vulcanized to provide a stable, elastic and workable material, the size, shape and properties of the ball were largely determined by the properties of the natural materials and objects from which the balls were formed. With the availability of a material that could be manufactured reliably and repeatedly, the properties of the ball became more uniform. The consistency between balls meant that for the first time, games taking place across the country could be unified with a consistent set of rules.

The effect on the game was marked. Players were now able to control the direction and speed of their passes and be in control of the ball whilst dribbling. Teams now had the opportunity to develop strategy and tactics in their play.

Although the first laws of soccer were written in 1863 (Football Association n.d.), the ball itself was not specified until 1883. In the interim period, balls used in competition were required to be Lillywhites size 5, based on a

Despite countless notable events and decisions in the development of the game of soccer, Goodyear's discovery is arguably the most significant development along the pathway towards the game we know today.

numerical sizing scale of 1 to 5 used by the sports retailer to organize their balls for sale. Although the mass of 12 to 15 ounces (340 to 425 g) specified in 1889 was increased to 14 to 16 ounces (410 to 450 g) in 1937, the specification of the ball, covered by law 2, has remained largely unchanged until today, requiring that the ball be spherical, made of leather or other suitable material, of a circumference of not more than 70 centimetres (28 in.) and not less than 68 centimetres (27 in.), not more than 450 grams (16 oz.) and not less than 410 grams (14 oz.) in weight at the start of the match and of a pressure equal to 0.6 to 1.1 atmosphere (600 to 1,100 g/cm^2) at sea level (8.5 lb./sq. in. to 15.6 lb./sq. in.) (FIFA 2015). Note that none of the static imperial limits is directly equivalent to its metric value; differences vary from 0.8 to 3.6 per cent.

By the end of the 19th century, a standard manufacturing process had been accepted whereby a vulcanized rubber bladder was encased within an arrangement of stitched leather panels. Manufacturers used various arrangements of panels, which were stitched inside out and inverted before the bladder was included and the final join, a heavy leather lace, secured.

The vast majority of arrangements were based on octahedral or cubic configurations, in which six sets of two or three panels were assembled to form the faces of a cube before being stretched during inflation to form a sphere.

The mathematics of spherical polyhedra, whereby certain regular two-dimensional shapes can be tiled to cover the surface of a sphere, have been well known throughout history and are found in naturally occurring structures such as the carbon 60 atom. But not until Richard Buckminster Fuller popularized the geodesic dome within architectural structures in the 1940s and 1950s did soccer ball designers adopt new approaches. Fuller's structure, based on a truncated icosahedron consisting of 12 pentagons and 20 hexagons, offered an elegant method of creating a ball with good natural sphericity, regular distribution of seams and no external lacing.

Around this time, soccer began to be played under floodlights. Experiments that began with balls being painted white led to coloured leathers being used to improve visibility. In 1970 Adidas combined the 32-panel design with white and black panels to produce arguably the first iconic ball design of the modern era, the Telstar (figure 10.3), for the FIFA World Cup in Mexico. Replacing the traditional Slazenger ball that had been used in the 1966 tournament final, the Telstar ball was designed to offer high visibility on black and white television screens.

This ball was also notable because it marked the beginning of a long-standing partnership between FIFA and Adidas to supply the official match ball for the FIFA World Cup. When the current contract expires, the partnership will have lasted 60 years and 16 tournaments, between 1970 and 2030.

Ball sizing based on a five-point numerical scale is still familiar today; certain categories of age-group and sex-specific matches require balls of a certain size. In 2012 the Football Association ratified the recommendations of the youth development review to ensure that game formats, pitch and goal dimensions, and ball sizes were appropriate for respective age groups of players (table 10.1). Variations of association soccer, such as futsal, beach soccer and even blind soccer have developed their own specifications, in which diameter and mass are varied independently.

Because of more detailed specification, ball manufacturers have clear markets for their products. One of the leading ball manufacturers, Forward

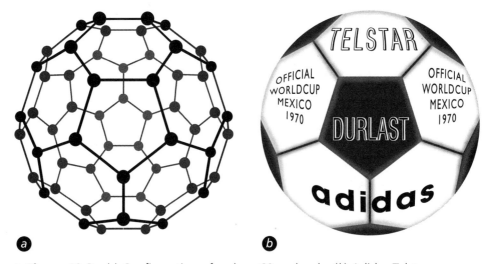

▶ **Figure 10.3** (a) Configuration of carbon 60 molecule; (b) Adidas Telstar.

Table 10.1 Football Association Specifications for Age-Group Soccer

Age group	Format	Pitch dimensions, yards (metres)	Max goal dimensions, feet (metres)	Ball size
U7 to U8	5v5	30 × 20 to 40 × 30 (27.4 × 18.3 to 36.6 × 27.4)	12 × 6 (3.7 × 1.8)	3
U9	7v7	50 × 30 to 60 × 40 (45.7 × 27.4 to 54.9 × 36.6)	12 × 6 (3.7 × 1.8)	3
U10	7v7	50 × 30 to 60 × 40 (45.7 × 27.4 to 54.9 × 36.6)	12 × 6 (3.7 × 1.8)	4
U11 to U12	9v9	70 × 40 to 80 × 50 (64.0 × 36.6 to 73.2 × 45.7)	16 × 7 to 21 × 7 (4.9 × 2.1 to 6.4 × 2.1)	4
U13 to U14	11v11	90 × 50 to 100 × 60 (82.3 × 45.7 to 91.4 × 73.2)	21 × 7 to 24 × 8 (6.4 × 2.1 to 7.3 × 2.4)	4
U15+	11v11	90 × 50 to 100 × 70 (82.3 × 45.7 to 91.4 × 73.2)	24 × 8 (7.3 × 2.4)	5

Sports based in Sialkhot, Pakistan, has a product range of seven ball sizes and a production capacity of 30,000 balls per day. Other markets have also evolved. The One World Futbol project and Soccket have developed original specifications of balls aimed at offering an indestructible and electricity-generating product to third-world countries, respectively.

Materials, Design and Construction

Many constructions are used within the production of modern soccer balls, but each component can generally be categorized within one of four main groups, listed from the inside out: bladder, carcass, foam or outer skin. The bladder is responsible for holding the air, the carcass provides structural rigidity, the foam gives a compliant, tactile feel, and the skin offers durability and waterproofing. Together they combine to allow the ball to hold its sphericity and store and return energy during collisions to ensure appropriate rebound characteristics.

Over the last 50 years, natural materials used in soccer ball manufacture have been gradually replaced with synthetic alternatives. Natural and synthetic latex or butyl rubber bladders are now widely used for their low cost, longevity, ease of manufacture and energy return (bounce) properties. These bladders are typically dip moulded, in a similar manner to rubber gloves. Some are encased in a filament winding to provide structure and are secured with an inflation valve to form an airtight case.

Before the advent of synthetic materials in the 1960s, leather panels were responsible for fulfilling the function of the carcass, foam and outer skin. The Azteca, used in the 1986 Mexico tournament, was the first nonleather ball used in a World Cup. Since that time, development of outer panel materials has continued. Ball panels are now typically constructed from composite layers, which may include polymer films, foams or fabrics.

Through the first decade of the 21st century, the advent of thermal bonding has allowed panels to be premoulded with a spherical curvature before being adhered to a carcass consisting of a bladder encased in a fabric layer that provides the structure of the ball. This method allows the outer panels to offer a softer and more tactile feel because they are not required to be sufficiently stiff to provide structure or accommodate the stitching needed to join adjacent panels. Assembled balls undergo a final forming stage under heat and pressure within a spherical mould where curing is completed.

The low-cost convenience of using woven fabric layers in the construction of either the carcass or outer layer brings potential performance disadvantages. The carcass fabric can be around 100 times stiffer than the bladder and consequently dominates the large-scale deformation of the soccer ball during kicks and collisions. Unlike the bladder material, woven fabrics are typically anisotropic, meaning that their stiffness varies depending on the direction in which they are stretched.

Without careful alignment, the ball might exhibit regions of different stiffness and therefore produce asymmetric deformations depending on which orientation it was kicked in (Price, Jones and Harland 2006).

The most prevalent material used to form the outer skin is thermoplastic polyurethane (TPU), chosen for its durability, water impermeability and ability to hold graphics. Underneath this layer lie the foam panels, often made from polyurethane (PU) or ethylene-vinyl acetate (EVA) foam similar to running shoe midsoles. These foam panels are important in determining the tactile feel of the ball but have a negligible influence on the response of the ball when kicked or during high-speed collisions.

These advances in production methods combined with the desire to create new ball aesthetics have led to unprecedented innovation in the panel shapes used. By curving the edges of standard spherical polyhedral panels, Adidas successfully created the Teamgeist (2006) and Brazuca (2014) based on an octahedral arrangement and Jabulani (2010) based on a tetrahedral pattern.

For many years the grain of natural leather, the stitched seams between panels and necessity of exterior lacing dictated the surface features of a ball. Synthetic materials offered the opportunity to specify and implement more refined and consistent surface features that many brands have taken advantage of. These features have ranged in size and scale from micro-combed textures of a few microns in depth employed by Nike across various balls to larger recessed dimples in the case of the Puma Shudoh. Other brands have chosen protruding pimples or ridges, and Adidas has patented 'aerogrooves'. Rationale for such features has largely been based on their influence on surface-to-surface contacts or flight through the air.

As the soccer community's appetite for technology has grown, the ball has been the subject of inventive modification. Bladders and carcasses have been developed to house electronic components either to allow identification of the ball's position by two of the four FIFA licensed goal-line technology providers or to record and report impact and launch data in systems such as the Adidas miCoach smartball, released in 2014.

The price of soccer balls varies considerably from low-grade recreational balls that retail for a few dollars (U.S.) and highly specified products used in international competition that cost in excess of $150. Price points between these extremes are likely to be dictated by the market rather than the cost of manufacture alone as retailers seek to ensure that product is available to all sections of society.

Manufacturing Processes

In spite of the advanced materials and manufacturing processes, human labour remains an integral part of the assembly process. Carcass panels are stitched by manually controlled sewing machines, and stitched outer panels are sewn entirely by hand. Human intervention allows combinations of bladders and panels to be selectively paired to satisfy the total mass constraints placed on the assembled ball.

Social Responsibility

Because a traditional hand-stitched ball takes as long as four hours to assemble, production facilities have been located predominantly in developing countries because of their low labour costs. In particular, the Pakistani city of Sialkot has long been associated with ball manufacture; facilities there reportedly manufactured over 75 per cent of the world's soccer balls before 2000. Despite overseas competition, Sialkhot remains a significant producer of balls, although estimates of its proportion of production vary wildly from 13 per cent (Nadvi et al. 2011) to 70 per cent (Waraich 2014). Sporting goods revenues from the city in total are valued at more than $1 billion (Mangi 2014). Although some examples of working conditions considered below acceptable standards have been reported, each of the FIFA-licensed manufacturers are now required to comply with the code of conduct specified by the World Federation of the Sporting Goods Industry (WFSGI). This code covers internationally recognized labour and environmental standards, and each manufacturer is required to return a social audit annually. In addition, revenue generated from the FIFA licensing programme is donated to social projects as part of the Football for Hope movement.

Soccer Ball Performance

During play a ball can be subjected to a range of loading conditions, and its response to each will determine its perceived performance. From the earliest origins of association soccer, it has been recognized that consistency in ball specification is crucial to the quality and development of the game. Building on the laws of the game, FIFA introduced the Quality Concept, now the Quality Programme, in January 1996 to specify the quality criteria required for balls to bear the official FIFA markings required for use in FIFA competition matches and competition matches under the auspices of the six continental confederations. This programme was extended to include futsal balls in 2000 and beach soccer balls in 2006.

Tests are carried out by EMPA (the Swiss Federal Laboratories for Materials Science and Technology) at their facility in St Gallen. Manufacturers are required to provide a sample of six balls to certify a particular ball construction through its lifetime of production. Balls accredited with the FIFA-quality mark, which can be applied to size 4 and size 5 balls, are required to pass tests in six categories to certify the weight, circumference, sphericity, bounce, water absorption and loss of pressure of the ball, specified in table 10.2. The more prestigious FIFA-quality pro mark includes an additional

Table 10.2 FIFA Quality Programme Test Criteria

Property	Ball size 5	Ball size 4	
	Quality pro	Quality	Quality
Weight	420 to 445 g	410 to 450 g	350 to 390 g
Circumference	68.5 to 69.5 cm	68.0 to 70.0 cm	63.5 to 66.0 cm
Sphericity	Maximum 1.5%	Maximum 2%	Maximum 2%
Loss of pressure	Maximum 20%	Maximum 25%	Maximum 25%
Water absorption	Maximum 10% (average across sample) Maximum 15% for any single ball	Maximum 15% (average across sample) Maximum 20% for any single ball	Maximum 15% (average across sample) Maximum 20% for any single ball
Rebound at 20 °C **Rebound at 5 °C**	120 to 165 cm Minimum 120 cm Maximum difference between lowest and highest rebound per ball tested: 10 cm	115 to 165 cm Minimum 110 cm Maximum difference between lowest and highest rebound per ball tested: 10 cm	110 to 160 cm Minimum 110 cm Maximum difference between lowest and highest rebound per ball tested: 10 cm
Shape and size retention	Measured after 2,000 kicks, seams and air valve undamaged Maximum 1.5 cm Maximum 1.5% Maximum 0.1 bar		

shape retention test and tighter tolerances on all measured characteristics. Testing is carried out at 20 degrees Celsius and 65 per cent humidity unless otherwise stated.

The weight, or more correctly the mass, is measured using calibrated apparatus on a ball pressurised to 0.8 bar.

The circumference and sphericity are measured using a bespoke machine that rotates a ball along several axes, measuring the radius at 44,000 points. From these data points, an average circumference is determined and the sphericity is calculated as the maximum deviation from the mean as a percentage of the mean.

The pressure loss is determined by the measured reduction in pressure of a ball initially inflated to 1 bar and left in atmospheric pressure for three days.

The water absorption is measured as the percentage gain in mass of a ball compressed and released 250 times at random orientations in a tray with 2 centimetres of standing water. Each ball is required to satisfy the standard as well as an average of the balls sampled.

The rebound is defined as the maximum height of the first bounce of a ball after a drop from 2 metres. Ten drops are completed per ball, and each rebound is required to be within the limits. In addition, a maximum variation of 10 centimetres is permitted across all drops.

The shape and size retention are inspected on balls that carry the FIFA-approved mark only. In the test, a ball is required to pass the pass the pressure loss, sphericity and circumference tests and a visual inspection of damage to the seams and air valves after 2,000 consecutive impacts against a rigid surface at 50 kilometres per hour.

Ball Characteristics Relevant to Play

In addition to the FIFA requirements, a range of additional evaluation methods that better represent the rigours of a game have been investigated by researchers and manufacturers. The game of soccer is dominated by a series of contacts between the ball and other surfaces. Whether with the foot, head, goalkeeper's gloves, goal frame or the surface of the pitch, the manner in which the ball responds to each contact plays an important part in the outcome of the game and the acceptability of the ball in the eyes of the players.

Kicks

The time that the ball is in contact with the foot during kicking typically varies from 8 to 20 milliseconds. Only during this contact can a player exert any influence on the direction, speed, spin rate or spin axis of the resultant kick.

The manner in which a player's kick deforms the outer shell and ball volume and the subsequent response of the ball to this loading determines all the launch characteristics of the kick. The duration of contact is considerably less than the time it would take for the human neural system to sense, feedback, process and adjust, meaning that throughout a kick, a player is unable to modify his or her motion from a predetermined path.

During a kick, the energy of the moving foot is transferred into strain energy within the ball through compression of both the outer layers and the internal air and tension of the outer layers in great circles, or 'hoops', passing around its perimeter (Abeyaratne and Horgan 1984). As the ball recovers its original shape, the strain energy is converted to kinetic energy that propels the ball away from the foot. Not all energy is converted in this way; some is absorbed depending on the elastic characteristics of the materials involved.

In practice, the compression of the internal air and hoop strain dominates the energy storage and return of the ball. The efficiency with which energy can be stored and returned through compressing air is greater than that which is possible by compressing the outer materials, meaning that for a given energy of impact, the maximum outbound ball velocity would be achieved by maximally compressing the air whilst minimally straining the outer material. A sharp toe punt would be a practical example of such a kick, although this theory does not account for the control required of the kick or the discomfort of the player!

The relatively large forces that act at the contact interface between the foot and the ball serve to ensure that little motion occurs between the two surfaces. Little energy is stored and returned through the compression of the materials at the point of impact, meaning that, contrary to popular belief, the portion of the ball that has the least influence in any kick is that in direct contact with the foot.

Bounce

When a ball comes into contact with a surface, the collision can be considered in two phases: the deformation and the restitution.

During deformation, the inbound energy of the moving ball is converted into the same strain energy form as would be the case during a kick. A simple method of analysis is used to characterize the bounce of a ball, a characteristic known as the coefficient of restitution (ε), which is defined as the ratio of inbound energy to outbound energy (Daish 1972). Typically, this characteristic is determined by propelling a ball against a stiff and heavy target that is assumed not to deflect during impact at 90 degrees to the direction of travel, as is the case in the FIFA rebound test. In practice, the efficiency of a collision is known to vary based on factors such as the inbound velocity, angle and spin rate and axis of the ball.

Commonly, even on artificial pitches, variation in bounce is greatly affected by the type and condition of the playing surface. Changes in surface flatness, stiffness of soils or substructures, and frictional characteristics of the turf can all be affected by maintenance, pitch preparation, repeated use or damage, temperature, humidity and rainfall. These variables will affect the bounce of a ball. Many of these characteristics can vary across a pitch, especially where structures such as stadia or buildings cast shadows or where subterranean drainage or heating channels run.

Slip and Roll

In practice, a ball can arrive at a contact surface at any angle, at any speed and with any spin. These, together with the properties and condition of the two interacting surfaces, determine the response of the ball, typically to rebound, slip or roll.

As the force acting in the direction normal to both surfaces is increased, the amount of force required for the surfaces to slip against each other increases. This increase is compounded by the ability of the surface of the ball to deform to accommodate undulations in the mating surface, such as features or seams on the surface of a piece of soccer footwear. This means that the angle of collision at which the surfaces grip or slip is determined by the inbound speed of the ball as well as the material properties of the surface, together with the presence of any lubricant, such as water.

The conditions under which a ball surface slips or grips against the surface it is in contact with generally determines the spin that is applied during the collision. The player cannot do much on the pitch to increase the friction with the ball, other than remove as much possible lubricant as possible from either surface. Some manufacturers include features on the boot or ball designed to improve surface-to-surface interactions, but efficacy studies have not been made public.

Clearly, however, a modern soccer boot upper and a modern ball provide a player with a significantly enhanced ability to grip the ball through increased friction compared with the case 20 years ago.

Evidence suggests that very high and very low amounts of friction can dramatically affect ball velocity. With little friction, the boot and ball can slip, putting the centre of mass and centre of force out of alignment. At the other end of the scale, a high-friction interaction may translate too much of the energy into spin, decreasing the forward velocity.

In practice, elite players will quickly recognize the effect of the complex interaction in various ball–boot combinations and adjust their kicking to achieve a desired outcome, based on observation of ball flight and swerve.

In some cases the surfaces of modern soccer balls have been designed to maintain a certain consistency in wet and dry conditions (Cotton 2007). The inclusion of bumps and ridges, designed to act similarly to the tread on a road tire, aim to direct the water into channels, allowing the raised material to achieve improved connection with the contacting surface. Although these features have been demonstrated to improve consistency, they do not completely solve the problem of water interference.

Slip and roll are known to be sensitive to a range of parameters. For example, an aerial pass hit with backspin may be expected to 'skid' off wet turf, losing little forward velocity, or 'check' on dry turf, bouncing higher and losing forward velocity. Variations in turf length or softness of the ground may cause bounce, slip and roll characteristics to change, and some observed effects are opposite to what may have been anticipated. Skilled teams or players should adjust their tactics or kicking technique based on the local properties of the surface throughout a season or based on the weather.

Heading

Interactions between the ball and other body parts, such as the head, are also important although few studies have been reported. Jeff Astle, an England international who played professionally during the 1960s and 1970s, was known for his powerful headers. Following his death in 2002, the coroner ruled that he had suffered brain damage because of repeated heading (Britten 2002). The balls used during Astle's playing career were known to increase their mass significantly over the course of a match in wet conditions, something that has been addressed by the inclusion of the water absorption limit within the FIFA standards since 1996.

Flight

The manner in which a ball travels through the air has a significant influence on the game. Although the specification of ball dimensions and mass are likely to have been based on examples of balls that travelled with acceptable flight, no further specification is made of any features that are likely to affect trajectory.

The flight of a ball is inherently complex and chaotic; the shape cannot be adjusted to fly with aerodynamic stability the way that an aerofoil or a Frisbee can. Instead, the passage of air over the surface of the ball depends on many variables, which in turn affects the forces that act on the ball and alter its path.

The surface of a ball has been known to affect its flight since the first half of the 19th century, when golfers noticed that used balls with damaged surfaces travelled farther than smooth ones. In 1877 Lord Rayleigh observed the manner by which a spinning tennis ball would deviate from a conventional path, recognizing the effect to be the same as that first reported by Gustav Magnus in 1852. These observations, based on recognition of the interaction between the surface of the ball and its flight, form the basis from which much of today's knowledge of aerodynamics has been developed.

When an object flies through the air, two types of drag slow it down: pressure drag and parasitic drag. The parasitic drag force is caused by the interaction between the air and the surface of the object, similar to friction. Surface roughness determines the parasitic drag. Pressure drag is caused by the need for the ball to displace the air in its path. An object with large cross-sectional area in relation to its direction of travel will have large pressure drag. The shape and dimensions of a soccer ball and its surface features mean that both pressure and parasitic drag are significant and mutually influential phenomena.

The interaction between the air and ball at different speeds produces specific boundary layer conditions, which in turn are responsible for the magnitude of aerodynamic drag. This complicated interplay between interdependent variables and phenomena has been the subject of much scientific study. The general principle can be summarized by stating that as a ball decelerates though the air from high velocity, shown at the far right of figure 10.4, the drag gradually decreases until a critical region is reached, where the drag increases sharply (Passmore et al. 2011).

In many kicks, the action of the ball against the impacting surface induces a spin, which continues, albeit with a gradual reduction in its rate, throughout flight. This spin affects the airflow around the ball and consequently intro-

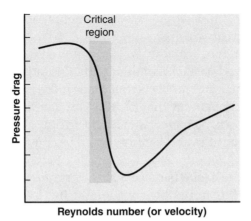

▶ **Figure 10.4** Typical drag of a soccer ball.

duces lateral forces such as topspin, backspin, sidespin or any combination of these that cause the deviation, or swerve, evident to observers since Lord Rayleigh.

Players and spectators have grown accustomed to the manner in which a soccer ball flies through the air. Maintaining certain characteristics of flight is considered necessary to preserve the integrity of the game. Seams are no longer necessary artefacts of manufacture; they are an important aspect of ball design needed to maintain airflow and, consequently, recognizable flight trajectories. Many ball characteristics and features that are known to influence flight are not currently considered within the FIFA Quality Programme, although a recent survey of professional players' attitudes towards balls suggests that many would appreciate more tightly regulated performance in this area.

Match Performance of Soccer Balls

In the early days of the professional game, especially in northern Europe where soccer was played on soft and muddy ground, players had to wear sturdy footwear, coined 'boots', a term still in widespread use today. Early soccer boots offered little opportunity for the player to manipulate the foot with any subtlety during kicking; the action was based solely on the need to give the ball sufficient velocity and loft for it to reach its intended target. Any spin imparted on the ball was modest and unintended. As soccer grew in popularity around the world, players in different climates began to dispense with sturdy ankle boots and use lighter, more flexible shoes. These shoes allowed players more control over the ball contact. They began to notice the effects of imparting spin, especially about a vertical (or near vertical) axis during flight, causing lateral swerve. European players as recently as the 1950s recall being amazed by this movement when first encountering it during South American tours.

Players and spectators are now well accustomed to passes and free kicks being swerved around obstacles in their path. Recently, a generation of players has developed kicking methods that cause more random ball movement during flight. The movement that players are able to achieve from a ball during flight appears to be increasing. Many attribute this ability to changes in ball design, although several factors should be considered before drawing that conclusion.

The omnipresence of television coverage of professional soccer, recorded in high definition, has undoubtedly brought the issue to the attention of the public, and indeed the players, in an unprecedented way. Although TV footage is capable of providing a clear visual account of any ball flight, it is rarely used in scientific analysis because of the sensitivity of any derived path to small deflections in camera orientation. Unless the camera remains in a fixed orientation, small deviations are difficult to observe, appearing to be either exaggerated or minimized by similar deviations in camera alignment.

Imparting and controlling the spin on a kicked ball rely on the interactive properties of the boot and the ball. Because the surfaces of both the ball and the footwear have been developed, the players have more opportunity to affect the spin rate and its axis. Although no evidence shows that players have become more or less inventive over time, the opportunity for players to conceive new kick types has risen sharply as footwear and balls have developed. Indeed, as playing surfaces have improved, allowing ball and footwear surfaces to remain clean throughout a game, the effects of any innovative kick types will likely be more noticeable than they were in previous generations.

From a player's perspective, no longer are large deviations necessary to gain a competitive advantage. For a player approaching a free kick to impart side spin (about a vertical axis), the expectation will be for the ball to swerve accordingly, exemplified by David Beckham in numerous free kicks.

The amount of spin generated is related to the amount of deviation observed, but even with high spin and high swerve, the path of the ball remains within player expectations. More recently, the ability to control spin rate has seen players develop kicking techniques in which spin rates are minimized, sometimes to zero. Cristiano Ronaldo was among the first to deceive goalkeepers with seemingly straight shots that suddenly deviated during flight. This movement is caused by subtle changes in the airflow around the ball. Although the airflow is chaotic and difficult to predict, for most spinning kicks the imbalances are small and change quickly. Therefore, any lateral (side-to-side or up-and-down) forces are small, short in duration and change randomly in direction. So although the ball is subject to continuously changing forces, its path is not noticeably affected. When the ball is travelling without spin, or more likely with a very small spin rate, causing the orientation of the ball to change by a small amount during flight, different airflow can be established on opposing sides of the ball. These differences might be relatively fleeting, but they can cause sufficient force to induce lateral movement of the ball. This movement may happen once during flight, or occasionally more than once, as a ball rotates from a position of left-right imbalance to right-left imbalance.

Many have attributed this movement to modern balls, but when hand-stitched 1960-style leather balls are kicked using a robotic simulator capable of kicking with zero spin, the unstable flight can be more exaggerated than that of modern balls. The fact that this unpredictable flight was not reported when those balls were commonly used is likely because the footwear of the day did not allow players sufficient control. Additionally, such balls regularly increased in mass as they absorbed water during play, so for a given lateral aerodynamic force, the resultant movement of the ball would be lower than that of an equivalent modern ball.

Conclusion

Modern players have substantially more opportunity to control or influence the flight of the ball to their advantage than their predecessors did. More correctly, modern players use equipment that allows them to exploit natural aerodynamic phenomena that have always existed. Nothing should be taken away from the skill level of the modern player, however, because exploiting these effects for competitive advantage is by no means straightforward. Each of the aerodynamic phenomena is highly sensitive to the launch parameters imparted during a kick. The relationship of spin, orientation of the spin axis, speed of the ball and direction of its flight are all crucial in achieving a desired outcome. To unskilled players, many of these effects remain elusive, but to those capable of executing their skills in a highly refined and repeatable manner, the effects can be devastating to opponents.

To some, the ball itself is of little consequence. It is the same for both teams and therefore has no bearing on the outcome of the game. To others, it is the most essential component of any match played at any level and it should be studied and understood. To some, the game has changed because the ball has changed. To others, the ball has changed to keep pace with a rapidly changing game. Whatever your perspective, the lessons of the past and the innovations of the present suggest that the ball will continue to evolve in the future.

PART
IV

Physiological Demands
in Training
and Competition

CHAPTER 11

Targeted Systems of the Body for Training

—Greg Dupont and Alan McCall

The ability to accelerate, decelerate and change direction, as well as to jump high, be strong in contact with opposition players and strike the ball, all require the soccer player to possess high levels of strength, speed, power and technique.

In addition, the recovery periods between high-intensity actions can be brief, which could represent a key performance factor. Players should therefore also possess adequate physical ability to recover quickly between actions so that they can maintain optimal intensity until the end of the match. Thus, physical training for a soccer player is a complex, multifactorial process. Understanding the physiological load imposed on top-level soccer players according to their positional role during competitive matches is necessary to develop a sport-specific training plan that mimics the physiological conditions imposed by matches (Di Salvo et al. 2007).

This chapter outlines the activity profile and physiological demands of high-level soccer players and proposes various conditioning methods to improve the physical qualities required by soccer.

Modern Game Demands

During a soccer match, players cover distances at various speeds and engage in a variety of activities. Most activities performed during the match are at low intensity (e.g., walking, jogging, standing), whereas the high-intensity actions (e.g., high-speed running and sprinting) are less frequent, accounting for around 8 to 10 per cent of the total distance covered (Carling et al. 2008; Rampinini et al. 2007a).

Although high-intensity actions make up a relatively low percentage of the match, these actions cannot be underestimated because they can change the outcome of the match. Therefore, practitioners have to train for these game-breaking moments, such as accelerating to win the ball before an opponent can, outjumping an opponent to score a goal or clear the ball and engaging in brief highly physical challenges with opposing players to retain or regain possession.

In the English Premier League, players covered on average 10.8 plus or minus 1.0 kilometres with a range of 9.9 to 11.8 kilometres (Di Salvo et al. 2013), and a peak recorded at 13.7 to 13.8 kilometres in elite soccer matches (Di Salvo et al. 2007; Dupont, Nedelect et al. 2010a). High-speed running (19.8 to 25.2 kmh) during a match corresponded to 681 to 693 metres and sprinting (greater than 25.2 kmh) corresponded to 248 to 258 metres (Di Salvo et al. 2013; Bradley et al. 2013a). A mean of 11 plus or minus 6 sprints (range 1 to 29 metres) are performed per match (Dupont, Nedelect et al. 2010a). More sprints are performed over a short distance (shorter than 10 metres) than over a longer distance (longer than 10 metres; Di Salvo et al. 2010). Approximately 23 to 30 per cent of sprints are explosive in nature (i.e., rapid acceleration reaching sprint speed greater than 25.2 kmh from standing, walking, jogging or running with time in high speed greater than 0.5 seconds), and 69.5 to 77 per cent can be classified as leading sprints (i.e., gradual acceleration whilst entering high-speed running for a minimum of 0.5 seconds; Di Salvo et al. 2010, 2009). Maximum speeds of about 32.5 kilometres per hour have been recorded during elite match play (Bradley et al. 2013b).

The recovery duration afforded between high-intensity actions during a match varies considerably according to the constantly changing match situation. The recovery time between high-intensity actions (greater than 19.8 kmh) has been shown to be on average 51 to greater than 61 seconds (Bradley et al. 2013a; Carling, Le Gall and Dupont 2012). The majority of the time (98 per cent) is made up of active recovery (e.g., walking, jogging, running; Carling, Le Gall and Dupont 2012). Although the majority of high-intensity actions are interspersed by 51 to 61 seconds or more of active recovery, some are performed with as little as 20 seconds of recovery (Carling, Le Gall and Dupont 2012).

The most extreme play during a match can see players perform up to five high-intensity actions within a 1-minute period (one high-intensity action every 12 seconds) and seven within 111 seconds (one every 15 seconds) (Carling, Le Gall and Dupont 2012).

The frequency of repeated high-intensity bouts (i.e., a minimum of three consecutive high-speed runs at greater than 19.8 kmh and mean recovery time of 20 seconds) is only 1.1 plus or minus 1.1 per match, although these could be match-defining moments.

Positional Activity Profile

Although match analyses reveal an important insight into the global demands of elite soccer match play and yield implications for training, in elite athletes the most important form of training coordinates energy use and biomechanics of an intended competitive performance (Di Salvo et al. 2007). Concerning elite-level soccer, extensive research has shown that differences among playing positions are significant. Understanding these differences is necessary to develop and optimize physical preparation regimes to respond to the specific demands of elite match play (Carling 2013). This section outlines the differences in activity profiles and physiological demands according to playing position, the reasons why these may exist and implications for developing specific training programmes for individual players.

Total Distance Covered

A significantly greater total distance covered (in all speed categories) during elite soccer match play has been shown in central midfielders and wide midfielders (both about 12 to 13 km), whereas central defenders have been consistently shown to complete the least total distance (about 10 km or less) (Di Salvo et al. 2013, 2007). Wide defenders, fullbacks and attackers typically cover 10.5 to 11.5 kilometres (Di Salvo et al. 2013, 2007).

Distance Covered at High Intensity

Differences in high-intensity running distance and combined high-intensity and sprinting distance between positions also exist; the greatest distances are typically performed by wide midfielders (about 900 m and 1,050 m respectively) (Di Salvo et al. 2013, 2009). High-intensity distance and combined high-intensity and sprinting distance run by central midfielders, wide defenders and attackers are 700 to 765 metres and 900 to 970 metres. Central defenders cover the shortest distance at high intensity (mean less than 500 metres) and combined high-intensity running and sprinting (mean less than 700 metres).

Distance Covered in Sprinting

As with high-intensity and combined high-intensity plus sprinting distance, wide midfielders along with attackers cover the greatest distance in sprinting (about 260 to 350 metres) (Andrzejewski et al. 2013; Di Salvo et al. 2010, 2009). Di Salvo et al. (2013) and Andrzejewski et al. (2013) found that central midfielders sprinted the shortest distance (about 140 to 170 metres). Sprinting distance reflects the accumulation of individual sprint distances performed as opposed to the length of the sprint (Di Salvo et al. 2009).

Recovery Between Activities

A study by Carling, Le Gall and Dupont (2012) found that the mean recovery time between high-intensity actions varied among all positions. The longest recovery was seen in central defenders (mean 195 seconds) and the shortest in wide defenders (116 seconds). The most common recovery of greater than or equal to 61 seconds was seen most frequently in central defenders (76.5 per cent). The lowest frequency of consecutive high-intensity actions of less than or equal to 30 seconds and 31 to 61 seconds was observed in central defenders and wide defenders, respectively.

The major challenge is to use these data to help coaches and players make the best choices. So how can these data be useful for coaches and players? Most of the time, these data are sent to the coaches and displayed for the players, but how do they use it? Because the purpose in soccer is not to run the longest distance but to win the matches, is there a link between these two variables?

In other words, do the teams who win the matches run more than the opponents do? Dupont, Nedelec et al. (2010a) reported that high-intensity distance covered in the second half was significantly shorter for the winning team than the losing team, whereas no significant difference was found for the first half. The explanation could be that when a team takes the lead in a game, the target is to maintain that advantage to win the match. To reach that target, the winning team has to try to keep the ball and the losing team has to press the opponent and therefore must perform more high-intensity runs. High-intensity distance would therefore depend not only on the fitness level but also on the match situations and the tactical and technical level. Teams with better technically and tactically skilled players probably cover less distance at high-intensity than the others. Di Salvo et al. (2009) found that high-intensity activity was affected by league position; less successful English Premier League teams covered significantly longer high-intensity distance and sprint distance than their more successful counterparts. In addition, some players have the potential to run longer high-intensity distance during a match, but do not do so if it is not required according to the match situation.

In addition, using the amount of high-intensity distance appears questionable because match-to-match variations are high for all players whatever their position (interindividual coefficient of variation (CV): 42.7 per cent; Dupont, Nedelect et al. 2010a), according to the position (interindividual CV from 24.9 to 40.0 per cent; Dupont, Nedelec et al. 2010a) and for the player who played most of the games at each of the five positions (intraindividual CV from 36.0 to 52.1 per cent).

So this high variability could be linked to a combination of factors including team tactics (Bradley et al. 2011), possession of the ball (Bradley et al. 2013b; Gregson et al. 2010), match status (i.e., match importance, winning or losing) and between leagues (i.e., higher versus lower leagues, premier league of one country versus the premier league of another country; Di Salvo et al. 2013; Bradley et al. 2013a; Delall et al. 2011). Because of the high variability and the poor reliability of the amount of high-intensity running speed, the practical applications of these results need to be interpreted with this in mind.

Nevertheless, these quantitative data can be useful for several purposes:

- To check the effects of a playing system on the distance covered by the team and the player
- To study the evolution of a player throughout a period
- To analyse the fatigue effects at the end of a match
- To analyse the influence of the substitutes, because their objective can be to run a longer relative distance than the starters do

Besides using the quantitative data, practitioners should not underestimate the qualitative data that can come from video analyses. One of the most important qualities for a soccer player is to be at the right place at the right moment. The runs performed are only a consequence to achieve this objective, so training should focus on the optimization of activities to save energy and use it at the right time. Feedback from video analyses and daily correction on the pitch should be encouraged.

Factors Influencing the Differences Between Playing Positions

Several studies have attempted to investigate which factors can influence the physical activity profile of different playing positions. This section discusses some influencing factors that have been identified in the research literature.

One study (Bradley and Noakes 2013) on match analysis investigated the match status (i.e., importance, score line and the introduction of substitutes) on the physical performance. They found that central defenders covered 10 to 17 per cent less running at high intensity when playing in matches that their team won compared with matches that their team lost. Additionally, attackers covered 15 and 54 per cent more high-intensity running and sprinting respectively in matches won compared to matches in which they were defeated. Central defenders and wide defenders were shown to reduce their high-intensity running during the second half of critically important matches. Finally, when a substitute entered the pitch he covered more distance (total and at high intensity) compared with the equivalent period when he completed a full 90-minute match (sprinting activity did not change).

Team possession (i.e., in possession of the ball and without possession of the ball) can influence the high-intensity activity profile of elite players. Di Salvo et al. (2009) found that when a team was in possession of the ball, the high-intensity running distance was greatest in wide defenders (498 metres) and similar to central midfielders and wide midfielders but higher than central defenders (mean 489 metres) and the least in attackers (331 metres). When a team was not in possession of the ball, differences also existed. Attackers covered the greatest high-intensity distance (566 metres), and wide midfielders followed (505 metres). Central defenders covered the least high-intensity distance (179 metres) when out of possession.

Team tactics (formation) can also affect the positional requirements of players. A study (Bradley et al. 2011) comparing the effects of three playing formations (4-4-2, 4-3-3 and 4-5-1) found that although the general team formation does not affect overall physical demands of players, it does have an effect on high-intensity running performance, but only according to whether the team was in possession. In possession, attackers, defenders and midfielders in 4-4-2 playing formation perform significantly more distance in very high-intensity running (more than 19.8 kmh). Out-of-possession attackers playing in a 4-5-1 and 4-3-3 formation ran 37 to 68 per cent more distance at very high intensity than attackers playing in a 4-4-2. A further finding was that out-of-possession defenders and midfielders covered a greater distance at very high intensity compared with when their team was in possession of the ball. In the 4-4-2 formation, the number of high-intensity runs was higher in attackers. Also in a 4-4-2 formation, a decline in peak high-intensity running immediately following the most intense five-minute period during a match was most pronounced in midfielders (58 per cent decline). This decline was 43 per cent when playing in a 4-3-3.

Differences in playing positions can also be influenced by the league the player plays in. A comparison of the English Premier League and the Spanish La Liga (Dellal et al. 2011) highlighted differences for the same playing position in the two leagues. In the English Premier League, central defenders covered significantly more high-intensity running distance than their Spanish La Liga counterparts. Attacking central midfielders and defensive central midfielders of Spanish La Liga covered less high-intensity running distance than players in the equivalent positions in the English Premier League. English Premier League wide midfielders and wide defenders ran a greater percentage of their total distance at high-intensity running speeds compared with players in Spanish La Liga, whereas attacking central midfielders and defensive central midfielders recorded a lower percentage of high-intensity distance than those in Spanish La Liga (2.5 versus 3.1 per cent for attacking central midfielders, 2.5 versus 2.9 per cent for defensive central midfielders). Attacking midfielders in the English Premier League ran similar distance at high intensity in attack and defence, whereas Spanish La Liga attacking central midfielders covered greater high-intensity distance in attacking play compared with defensive play.

Evidently, many factors can influence the global and positional activity demands placed on players. During a competitive match, however, the objective is not to cover a greater total distance or to do more high-intensity running and sprinting or perform more actions than the opposing team or opposing players do. The objective is to win the match. In fact, research and observations into elite soccer suggest that factors other than physical performance, such as technical and tactical effectiveness (Carling 2013), are more important to achieving success. But saying that does not mean that players should not be developed to their optimal physical level. Although players may not always need to perform to the maximum of their physical capacities, the ability to do so is obviously an advantage if they are called upon.

Therefore, the physical training programme of soccer players should prepare them for a worst-case scenario during a match based on position. Some players may also be required to switch position and therefore may need to be able to perform optimally in a physically more challenging or less challenging role, such as wide defender and central defender. A final consideration should be given to substitutes. The training programme of players who do not play regularly needs to be adjusted to make sure that players maintain a match-ready physical condition for when they are called upon.

Physical and Physiological Requirements

During a soccer match, fatigue occurs temporarily after short, intense periods during both halves and progressively towards the end of each half. At these times a fitter team may be able to fatigue the opponent and capitalize by scoring a goal. The total distance and high-intensity activities have been found to decrease following the most demanding 5-minute periods during a match and at the end of the second half compared with the first half (Mohr, Krustrup and Bangsbo 2003). High-intensity running distance has also been shown to decrease at the end of matches (Krustrup et al. 2006). As seen previously, the recovery duration between high-intensity actions during a match varies considerably. In the worst case the most extreme play shows players performing up to five high-intensity actions within 1 minute (one high-intensity action every 12 seconds). Fatigue can be caused by both neural or central factors (e.g., reduced central nervous system drive) and muscular or peripheral factors (e.g., the accumulation of metabolites within the muscle fibres); no one global mechanism is responsible for all manifestations of fatigue (Girard, Mendez-Villanueva and Bishop 2011).

As we can gather from the previous section, a soccer match is characterized by the performance of many actions of varying intensity at unknown time points throughout a 90-minute (and in some cases 120-minute) period according to the match situation. This activity places considerable demand on the players' physiological systems. Accordingly, both anaerobic and aerobic qualities are important for the professional soccer player. This section discusses the requirements and importance of these qualities.

Anaerobic Qualities

In soccer the anaerobic qualities are important physiological requirements for sprinting, jumping, tackling, kicking and holding off opposing players. Although the aerobic system is the predominant energy system used throughout the match, these short, explosive and decisive actions involving a variety of forceful and explosive concentric, eccentric and isometric muscle contractions can ultimately decide the outcome of a match. Players need to accelerate and win the ball before an opponent does, strike the ball and score a goal, outjump the opposing player to head the ball, hold off the opponent in a challenge, tackle and win the ball or keep possession of the ball.

An example of these anaerobic parameters being interrelated is the strong correlation that has been shown for maximal strength and sprint performance and vertical jumping ability in elite international-level soccer players (Wisloff et al. 2004). As outlined in the section on modern game demands, the type and nature of the sprint varies. The majority of sprints in soccer are performed over a short distance (0 to 10 metres and less than five seconds in duration) rather than over longer distances. Therefore, the acceleration capability of professional soccer players should be considered more important than sprint performance over longer distances. But although longer accelerations and sprints are not performed frequently, players do reach maximal or near-maximal speeds during a match and these long sprints warrant consideration for training. Additionally, most sprints are leading in nature (i.e., a gradual acceleration), but explosive sprints (rapid accelerations) are also performed during the match.

Aerobic Qualities

During a 90-minute match, players attain 80 to 90 per cent of their maximal heart rate, which corresponds to 70 to 80 per cent of their maximal oxygen uptake ($\dot{V}O_2$max; Stolen et al. 2005). The soccer player's heart rate during a game is rarely below 65 per cent of maximum (Bangsbo, Mohr and Krustrup 2006), suggesting that blood flow to the exercising leg muscle is continuously higher than it is at rest. All this implies that the aerobic energy system is highly taxed during a soccer match. The ability to recover between repetitions of activities and maintain high intensity during the match is crucial for a soccer player.

High aerobic fitness is therefore important for a soccer player because the player can then sustain intense exercise for longer durations and recover more rapidly between high-intensity phases of the game (Iaia, Rampinini and Bangsbo 2009).

Several authors found significant relationships between $\dot{V}O_2$max and ability to repeat sprints (Aziz, Chia and Teh 2000; Bishop and Spencer 2004; Dupont et al. 2005; McMahon and Wenger 1998). Some authors, however, failed to find significant relationships between $\dot{V}O_2$max and repeated sprint ability (Aziz et al. 2007; Castagna et al. 2007; Bishop, Lawrence and Spencer 2003). The difference in results could derive from the protocol chosen and, more specifically, the number of sprints, the sprint duration, the recovery duration or the intensity of recovery. The aerobic energetic contribution would become higher when the sprints are numerous, long and alternated with brief active recovery periods.

Besides $\dot{V}O_2$max, another important aerobic quality linked to the ability to maintain performance during repeated activities, such as those seen during soccer match play, is $\dot{V}O_2$ kinetics. As suggested by Tomlin and Wenger (2001), a higher $\dot{V}O_2$ during sprinting results in less reliance on anaerobic glycolysis and thus superior power maintenance. A faster $\dot{V}O_2$ adjustment at the onset of exercise could lead to a greater contribution of oxidative phosphorylation and a smaller O_2 deficit. Faster $\dot{V}O_2$ kinetics can allow better adjustment of oxidative processes required when transitioning from rest to work, such as that commonly seen in the intermittent nature of a soccer match (Rampinini et al. 2009). Faster $\dot{V}O_2$ kinetics enables a player to adjust to the energy requirement of exercise more rapidly, resulting in a smaller O_2 deficit (Phillips et al. 1995; Demarle et al. 2001), and it has been shown to be linked to repeated sprint ability in professional soccer players (Dupont, McCall et al. 2010b). In fact, $\dot{V}O_2$ kinetics may be a more important contributor than $\dot{V}O_2$max to a soccer player's ability to perform activities repeatedly during a soccer match. Superior repeated sprint ability has been shown in professional soccer players compared with amateur players (Rampinini et al. 2009); although $\dot{V}O_2$max was similar between professional and amateur players, $\dot{V}O_2$ kinetics was enhanced in the professional group. Therefore, $\dot{V}O_2$ kinetics should be considered an important aerobic-related quality (perhaps more important than $\dot{V}O_2$max) for enhanced ability to repeat activities during a soccer match.

Further support for the importance of aerobic fitness in professional soccer comes from studies demonstrating a significant relationship between aerobic power and competitive ranking, team level and total distance covered during a match (Krustrup et al. 2005, 2003; Wisloff, Helgerud and Hoff 1998; Bangsbo and Lindquist 1992). Additionally, the decline in technical performance is reduced after aerobic training (Impellizzeri et al. 2008; Rampinini et al. 2008).

Training Practices

Professional soccer teams use various methods of training to improve the physical conditioning of their players, including both generic (e.g., continuous, intermittent and repeated sprint running) and specific (e.g., small-sided games, soccer-specific and position-specific drills with the ball) exercises.

Gym-based and field-based exercises are also performed to improve the strength and power capabilities of players. These exercises are not performed in isolation, so practitioners must be able to integrate all these training practices effectively into the overall training programme while considering several important factors:

- Period of the season (preseason, in-season, break, transfer windows, holidays)
- Number of matches per week
- Age of the players
- Status of the players
- Regular starter versus regular substitute
- Injury status

This section discusses the various training practices available to the fitness coach of professional soccer players and ways that these can be successfully integrated into the overall training programme. Conditioning programmes for soccer players will be further addressed in the next chapter.

Generic Training for Soccer

One of the most important training principles is to identify the qualities required to improve and optimize soccer performance in the match. The next step is to propose some exercises that stimulate those qualities.

In this context, some qualities can be improved with generic training, without a ball. For example, improving $\dot{V}O_2$max requires performing exercises that allow the person to attain and maintain a high percentage of $\dot{V}O_2$max (higher than 90 per cent of $\dot{V}O_2$max) for the longest time possible. High-intensity training, characterized by intensities close to or above $\dot{V}O_2$max, performed intermittently, induces peripheral adaptations. Intermittent exercises consist of alternating periods of high-intensity exercise with periods of active or passive recovery. The introduction of recovery periods between periods of intense exercise allows participants to maintain the exercise intensity longer than when the exercise is performed continuously until exhaustion (McDougall and Sale 1981). Intermittent exercises are characterized by the combination of many variables: the period of exercise and its intensity, and the type and duration of recovery. Consequently, one of the difficulties for the practitioner in the design of intermittent exercises is determining the combination of intensity, exercise periods, recovery periods and type of recovery that allow the achievement of the desired objective.

Well-designed intermittent exercise is more effective than continuous exercise in optimizing the time spent at a high percentage of $\dot{V}O_2$max (Dupont et al. 2002). Table 11.1 presents the objectives of the various types of intermittent training sessions.

When the intensity of short-short intermittent exercises is higher than the maximal aerobic speed (MAS), both $\dot{V}O_2$max and anaerobic capacity can be improved. Maximal aerobic speed (MAS) is defined as the critical moving speed corresponding to $\dot{V}O_2$max. In a study involving high-level soccer players performing two sessions per week during 10 weeks (the first session consisted of 12 to 15 40-metre sprints alternated with 30 seconds of

Table 11.1 Classification and Objectives for Intermittent Sessions

Type of session	Exercise phase intensity	Recovery phase	Repetitions	Sets	Effects
Long-long	3 to 10 min. 90 to 100% MAS	2 to 3 min. AR	3 to 5	1	↑ Endurance ↑ $\dot{V}O_2$max
Moderate-moderate	30 sec. to 2 min. 100 to 110% MAS	30 sec. to 3 min. AR	5 to 12	1 to 3	↑ $\dot{V}O_2$max
Short-short	10 sec. to 20 sec. 110% MAS to sprint	10 to 20 sec. AR or PR	10 to 16	3 to 5	↑ $\dot{V}O_2$max ↑ Anaerobic capacity

MAS: maximal aerobic speed; AR: active recovery; PR: passive recovery.

passive recovery, and the second session comprised two sets of 12 to 15 runs at 120 per cent of maximal aerobic speed, about 85 to 90 metres in 15 seconds, alternated with 15 seconds of passive recovery), maximal aerobic speed and sprint speed significantly improved after a 10-week training period using intermittent exercises (an increase of 1.2 kmh for maximal aerobic speed and an increase of 1 kmh for sprint speed over 40 metres; Dupont, Akakpo and Berthoin 2004). A practical example of an intermittent exercise is shown in figure 11.1.

Training based on repeated sprints is also effective in improving aerobic performance, $\dot{V}O_2$max and anaerobic performance (Gaiga and Docherty 1995; McDougall et al. 1998; Rodas et al. 2000). These results can be interesting for practitioners who aim to improve both anaerobic and aerobic performance.

High-intensity training of short duration should be favoured when the time available is limited, because it leads to performance improvements but also reduces the training volume and consequently the risk of overtraining (Bangsbo et al. 2009).

Advantages of generic training include that it is easy to implement, is structured and allows intensity to be well controlled. In addition, this type of training is effective in enhancing aerobic fitness and the ability to increase activities during a match (Helgerud et al. 2001). The disadvantage is that this type of training is not pleasant for most of the players. Generic training comes from the hypothesis that fatigue comes only from running activities. Running performance, however, is probably not the sole cause for post soccer match–induced fatigue (Rampinini et al. 2011; Nedelec et al. 2012, 2013). Other variables such as decelerations, changes of direction, backwards running, jumping, kicking, tackling, contacts and mental fatigue are probably more important in the postmatch fatigue mechanisms than the running activity profile.

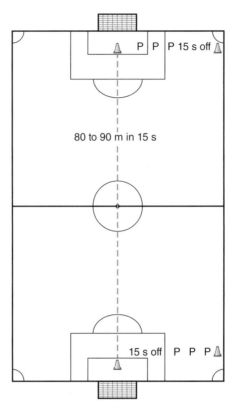

▶ **Figure 11.1** An example of 15 seconds on and 15 seconds off.

Specific Training for Soccer

Exercises specific to soccer have been recommended, and many practitioners use them. This method is advocated because the exercises replicate the specific movement patterns and actions performed by soccer players during match play. They can also be considered time efficient because they train physical, technical and tactical qualities simultaneously. The most popular and most widely researched form of specific training is small-sided games. Specific training can also be made up of soccer-specific and position-specific drills.

A major advantage of incorporating small-sided games is that players need to perform many actions similar to those they perform during a competitive match, such as changes of direction, accelerations, jumps, shots and passes, and have to execute those actions effectively under fatigued conditions. The motivation of players to perform well in small-sided games is also high. Soccer coaches have traditionally employed small-sided games to train technical qualities, but these are now widely accepted and used to train technical and physical capacities simultaneously.

As the name suggests, small-sided games are modified games played on reduced pitch areas, often using adapted rules and involving fewer players than used in traditional soccer matches (Hill-Haas et al. 2011). A variety of small-sided games can be proposed for use in elite soccer players. An example is presented in figure 11.2.

The setup shown in figure 11.2 provides for two situations:

- **First situation:** 1v1, 30 seconds on and 1 minute off, four to six times for one set. To score the goal, individual players have to go between one of the two gates.
- **Second situation:** 2v2, 30 seconds on and 30 seconds off, four to six times for one set. To score the goal, individual players have to go between one of the two gates.

The decision about which type of small-sided games to use depends on factors such as the aim of the training session, the timing during the season (e.g., preseason or in-season) and the timing within the training week in relation to the match (e.g., the number of days separating the match and the training session, in which case a low, moderate, high or very high-exercise intensity may be the target).

The exercise intensity of small-sided games can be manipulated in various ways:

- **Pitch dimension:** The pitch dimensions can be modified so that games are played on a small pitch, medium pitch or large pitch. The larger the pitch dimensions are, the higher the exercise intensity is. One study (Rampinini et al. 2007b) showed that a large pitch for 3v3 and 6v6 resulted in higher heart rate and blood lactate concentrations compared with small and medium pitches.

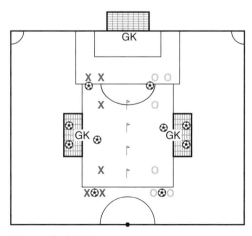

▶ **Figure 11.2** Sample small-sided game.

- **Number of players:** Changing the number of players can affect the exercise intensity. Using a smaller number of players while maintaining the same relative pitch area per player results in a higher training load (Hill-Haas et al. 2009).

- **Addition of a floater:** Adding a floater creates an uneven number (e.g., 3v3 with one additional player, or 7 total). The floater is a neutral player who plays with whatever team is in possession of the ball to create temporary overload or underload situations, typically to focus on attacking and defensive proficiency or to increase the load on the floater (Hill-Haas et al. 2011).

- **Pitch dimension and player number:** A simultaneous manipulation of pitch dimensions and player numbers will further modify the effects on exercise intensity. For example, a simultaneous increase in pitch area and decrease in number of players will increase the exercise intensity of small-sided games (Rampinini et al. 2007b).

- **Rules of play:** Modifying the rules of play during small-sided games also affects the exercise intensity. Imposing rules such as player-to-player marking (Aroso, Rebelo and Gomes-Pereira 2004) can increase the intensity of small-sided games.

- **Goalkeepers:** The inclusion of goalkeepers may have an effect on the resultant exercise intensity, although information on this manipulation is lacking. One study found that inclusion of goalkeepers in 3v3 small-sided games reduced the exercise intensity (Mallo and Navarro 2008), whereas in 8v8 small-sided games the addition of goalkeepers has been shown to increase the exercise intensity (Dellal et al. 2008).

- **Encouragement:** Providing encouragement to players can increase the exercise intensity. Rampinini et al. (2007b) found that coach encouragement resulted in higher heart rate, blood lactate concentration and perceptual responses of players.

- **Duration:** The duration of small-sided games as well as the recovery period can influence the intensity achieved during games. A duration of four minutes per small-sided game has been proposed as optimal (Fanchini et al. 2011). In this study the authors compared 3v3 bouts of two, four and six minutes. A decrease in intensity occurred between four-minute and six-minute bouts. The authors found an increase (although insignificant) in heart rate between two- and four-minute bouts.

Table 11.2 provides some examples of small-sided games strategies and their corresponding exercise intensity that can be used in elite soccer.

Although small-sided games are an effective method for the physical training of soccer players and hold several advantages, this type of training

Table 11.2 Examples of Small-Sided Games Strategies and Their Corresponding Intensity

Number of players	Number of bouts × duration	Pitch dimension (length × width in metres)	Intensity
1v1	1 × 3 min.	10 × 5	Hard
1v1	1 × 3 min.	15 × 10	Hard
1v1	1 × 3 min.	20 × 15	Very hard
2v2	3 × 1, 5 min. (90 sec. recovery)	30 × 20	Moderate
2v2	1 × 3 min.	15 × 10	Moderate
2v2	1 × 3 min.	20 × 15	Moderate
2v2	1 × 3 min.	25 × 20	Moderate
2v2	4 × 2 min. (2 min. recovery)	27 × 18	Hard
3v3	3 × 4 min. (90 sec. recovery)	30 × 20	Moderate
3v3	1 × 3 min.	20 × 15	Moderate
3v3	1 × 3 min.	25 × 20	Moderate
3v3	1 × 3 min.	30 × 25	Moderate
3v3	3 × 4 min. (3 min. recovery)	20 × 12	Hard
3v3	3 × 4 min. (3 min. recovery)	25 × 15	Hard
3v3	3 × 4 min. (3 min. recovery)	30 × 18	Hard
3v3	4 × 3, 5 min. (90 sec. recovery)	32 × 23	Hard
4v4	3 × 6 min. (90 sec. recovery)	30 × 20	Easy
4v4	1 × 3 min.	25 × 20	Easy
4v4	1 × 3 min.	30 × 25	Easy
4v4	3 × 4 min. (3 min. recovery)	24 × 16	Moderate
4v4	3 × 4 min. (3 min. recovery)	30 × 20	Moderate
4v4	3 × 4 min. (3 min. recovery)	36 × 24	Moderate
4v4	4 × 4 min. (2 min. recovery)	37 × 27	Hard
5v5	1 × 3 min.	30 × 25	Easy
5v5	1 × 3 min.	35 × 30	Easy
5v5	1 × 3 min.	40 × 35	Moderate
5v5	3 × 4 min. (3 min. recovery)	28 × 20	Moderate
5v5	3 × 4 min. (3 min. recovery)	35 × 25	Moderate
5v5	3 × 4 min. (3 min. recovery)	42 × 30	Moderate
5v5	4 × 6 min. (90 sec. recovery)	41 × 27	Hard
6v6	3 × 4 min. (3 min. recovery)	32 × 24	Moderate
6v6	3 × 4 min. (3 min. recovery)	40 × 30	Moderate
6v6	3 × 4 min. (3 min. recovery)	48 × 36	Moderate
6v6	3 × 8 min. (90 sec. recovery)	46 × 27	Moderate
8v8	4 × 8 min. (90 sec. recovery)	73 × 41	Moderate

has some limitations that should be taken into account when planning the overall training programme.

First, not all activities performed during a soccer match are replicated during small-sided games (e.g., longer accelerations and sprints). Although shorter sprints are more common than longer sprints during a soccer match, long sprints are nevertheless present. Not performing such activities could have implications for performance or injury and may not prepare the player fully for the worst-case scenario during matches.

Second, the risk of contact injury is increased compared with generic training.

Third, small-sided games can induce different cardiorespiratory adaptations according to the level, engagement and position of the player. Some players may be able to hide during small-sided games and therefore not reach the required intensity to induce physiological and physical improvements. In this instance the objective of the small-sided games should be explained to the players, because typically their objective is not to run more but rather to run at the right times to influence the game. Therefore, if the priority of the small-sided games is to induce physiological adaptations, this goal should be made clear to the players and the strategies mentioned earlier should be incorporated (e.g., coach encouragement and rule changes).

Finally, controlling all the variables to adjust the intensity can be difficult.

Overall, in spite of the advantages presented, small-sided games also present some limits that should be considered when planning the physical conditioning programme for the elite soccer player.

Strength, Speed and Power Training for Soccer

Speed and strength are important qualities in soccer. The product of these two factors corresponds to power, which is probably the most important physical quality for elite soccer players in terms of maximizing performance of explosive actions such as sprinting, changing direction, kicking and striking.

This section provides some examples of how to improve the qualities of strength, speed and power in elite soccer players. Finally, we will show how these activities can be incorporated into the overall training programme.

Strength Training

According to the specific needs of the player, the objective of strength training can be to increase muscle mass (hypertrophy), maximal strength or power. Traditional resistance-training exercises can be implemented to target an increase in muscle mass or maximal strength and power.

Hypertrophy

Hypertrophy training (i.e., increasing muscle mass) in the elite soccer player can be beneficial as a mechanism to increase maximal strength and enhance physical presence in contact situations with opposing players. But the magnitude of muscle mass added by a player must not adversely affect his or her ability to move or change direction.

There are no specific guidelines as to what a sufficient level of muscle mass is for elite soccer players or for different positions. Each player is unique, and all players should be consistently monitored during training. Feedback should be sought from the player and coaching staff to be sure that programmes aimed at increasing muscle mass do not affect mobility on the pitch. Programmes to increase muscle mass typically need four to six weeks before effects become visible. These programmes involve short rest intervals (less than one minute to about two minutes) and may be beneficial in increasing the muscle's ability to resist fatigue.

Additionally, the eccentric contraction mode appears to be particularly potent in terms of increasing muscle mass. These adaptations could be particularly important in the lower-limb muscles where muscle injuries are common in elite soccer players. Resistance to fatigue and greater eccentric muscle strength may reduce injury risk. Specific recommendations for prescribing a hypertrophy programme using traditional resistance-training exercises can be found in table 11.3.

Table 11.3 Hypertrophy Training for an Elite Soccer Player

Sets	3 to 6
Repetitions	6 to 12
Load	70 to 85% 1RM (6RM to 12RM)
Rest	Less than or equal to 1 to 2 min. (2 min. maximum)
Velocity	Eccentric: slow (3 sec.) Concentric: moderate to fast (1 to 2 sec.)
Number of exercises	6 to 8
Frequency	Preseason: 1 to 5 times a week In season: 1 to 3 times a week Rehabilitation: 2 to 5 times a week Nonplaying: 3 to 5 times a week
Programme duration	4 to 8 weeks
Recovery between sessions	Daily if changing muscle groups and exercises
Type of exercises	Traditional resistance exercises
When to perform	After training in the afternoon
Main effects	Increase muscle mass Increase maximum strength Increase resistance to fatigue
Special considerations	Do not perform lower-body exercises in the two days before a match.

Maximal Strength

The most effective method for increasing maximal strength is the use of exercises with heavy loads, typically greater than 85 per cent of one-repetition maximum (one- to six-repetition maximum). Maximal strength gains will be greater in players with less weight-training experience and lower levels of maximal strength at the outset of a programme. As players' strength levels increase, the rate at which they can increase this quality is diminished. Other exercise modalities such as ballistic exercises, plyometrics and Olympic weightlifting (these will be further discussed later) will need to be incorporated. To sustain the intensity required to lift the heavy loads involved for this training modality, longer rest intervals are required to ensure adequate recovery between sets (typically two to five minutes of passive recovery). Additionally, according to the force-velocity curve, force and velocity have an inverse relationship, whereby the greater the force is, the lower the speed is and vice versa. This topic is addressed further in the next chapter.

Lifting heavy loads as performed during maximal strength training means that the velocity of the movement decreases. Players should perform velocities specific to the sport in question, and in elite soccer the velocity of explosive actions can be considered high. Therefore, the intention to move quickly should be encouraged, even if the actual speed is not. Player technique should be sufficient to avoid injury. Lifting heavy weights with poor technique will likely result in injury. Lifts for larger muscle groups (e.g., legs, back, chest) should be performed first in the training programme, and lifts for smaller muscle groups (e.g., arms, shoulders) should be done towards the end. Specific programming recommendations for incorporating maximal strength programmes in elite players can be found in table 11.4.

Power Training

Power training typically involves using lighter loads (0 to 80 per cent of 1RM) lifted at high velocities compared with hypertrophy and maximal strength training. The specific adaptations to expect from this type of training are an increase in muscular power, improved sprinting speed and acceleration, greater jump height and improved ability to change direction. Ballistic exercises, plyometrics and Olympic style weightlifting can also be used to avoid the deceleration phase seen in traditional resistance exercises. Ballistic exercises for the lower body include exercises such as the jump squat, split jump squat (with load or body weight only, single or double leg) and sled tow running.

Plyometric training involves exercises in which the active muscles are stretched eccentrically before shortening concentrically (Ronnestaad et al.

Table 11.4 Maximal Strength Training for an Elite Soccer Player

Sets	2 to 6
Repetitions	1 to 6
Load	Greater than or equal to 85% 1RM (1RM to 6RM)
Rest	2 to 5 min. (3 min. preferred)
Velocity	Eccentric: moderate to slow (2 to 3 sec.) Concentric: fast intention (1 to 2 sec.)
Number of exercises	4 to 6
Frequency	Preseason: 2 to 5 times a week In season: 1 to 2 times a week Rehabilitation: up to 3 times a week Nonplaying: up to 3 times a week
Programme duration	4 to 8 weeks
Recovery between sessions	48 to 72 hours
Type of exercises	Traditional resistance exercises
When to perform	After training in the afternoon
Main effects	Increase maximum strength Increase muscle mass (though to a less extent than hypertrophy training)
Special considerations	Do not perform lower-body training in the two days before a match or in the two days following a match.

2008). Plyometric exercises include repeated jumps and drop jumps from varying heights. These exercises vary from ballistic exercises in that no or little load is used, and they can be highly specific to the demands of the sport (Cormie, McGuigan and Newton 2011).

Olympic weightlifting exercises (e.g., clean and jerk, snatch) and their derivatives (e.g., power clean, hang clean, midthigh pull, high pull and so on) can be particularly specific to elite soccer because their execution requires triple extension at the ankle, knee and hip, as seen in sprinting and jumping. The recruitment of muscle mass required is synchronized in a similar manner to that required for many athletic movements (Hedrick 2004). The full weightlifting exercises (clean and jerk, snatch) should be taught to players because they result in high power output. Specific programming variables for power training can be found in table 11.5.

Speed Training

Here we provide some examples of incorporating speed exercises into the training programme of elite soccer players. As stated previously, most sprints during a soccer match are shorter than 10 metres and come from a combination of explosive (rapid acceleration) and leading (gradual acceleration)

Table 11.5 Power Training Programme for an Elite Soccer Player

Sets	2 to 6
Repetitions	1 to 6
Load	0 to 80% 1RM
Rest	2 to 5 min.
Velocity	Eccentric: fast to moderate (less than 1 to 2 sec.) Concentric: as fast as possible
Number of exercises	4 to 6
Frequency	Preseason: 2 or 3 times a week In season: 1 or 2 times a week Rehabilitation: 2 or 3 times a week Nonplaying: up to 3 times a week
Programme duration	4 to 8 weeks
Recovery between sessions	48 to 72 hours, especially if performing plyometrics
Type of exercises	Ballistic exercises Plyometrics Olympic-style lifts
When to perform	Before training
Main effects	Increase power Increase sprinting and acceleration Increase jumping ability Increase rate of force development Improve ability to change direction
Special considerations	Perform during hardest session of the week, generally three or four days following a match and two or three days before the next match. Can be performed during the day before a game if fewer sets, fewer repetitions and lower loads are used to create activation.

situations. Consequently, improving the acceleration phase seems reasonable. Additionally, many sprints by soccer players can involve a change of direction or nonlinear trajectory. Therefore, the specific speed training of an elite soccer player should target mainly acceleration capabilities from a variety of starting activities with linear and nonlinear trajectories.

Occasionally, elite soccer players sprint up to 40 metres and reach maximum or near-maximum sprint speeds during matches. Therefore, from an injury prevention standpoint they should be conditioned for this activity as well.

Various speed-training exercises can be used in the overall training programme of the elite soccer player. The traditional method is straight-line acceleration and sprint running without a ball. Soccer-specific acceleration and sprint running use explosive and leading starts and nonlinear trajectories (e.g., slaloms, changes of direction) with the inclusion of the ball (running with or without the ball, pass and sprint) as shown in figure 11.3.

Cone Game (figure 11.3)

Two players stand within a small box.

When the coach shows a cone, the players in the small box have to touch the appropriate cone and return to the small box.

Count the points.

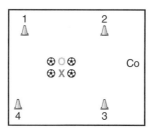

▶ **Figure 11.3**   Cone game: an example of speed training.

Specific resisted-sprint exercises such as sled towing can be used as an additional training modality to introduce variety to the overall programme. Sled towing involves the player running with additional load attached by a harness and sled behind him or her. The mechanism behind sled towing is hypothesized to increase the demand for horizontal force and impulse production of the lower-body musculature during each ground contact. When used over time, the cumulative effect transfers to improved ability to produce horizontal force and impulse during ground contacts, which increases step length during unresisted sprinting (Cronin and Hansen 2005). There is no consensus on the load to be towed during weighted sled running. A load of 30 per cent of body mass has been shown to result in greater values for horizontal and propulsive impulses and therefore requires more horizontal force application and greater demand for horizontal impulse production compared with a lighter load of 10 per cent, which has little effect on ground reaction force (Kawamori, Newton and Nosaka 2014). But in another study (Zafeiridis et al. 2005) a load of about 7 per cent of body mass was shown to improve acceleration over 20 metres. Lighter loads are commonly recommended because heavier loads may alter sprinting kinematics. Therefore, the recommendation is that a range of loads can be used for the elite soccer player from as little as 7 per cent up to about 30 per cent of body mass.

Optimal transfer of strength and power training to sport performance requires the conversion of powerful muscles to a coordinated sport skill (Young 2006). Therefore, speed exercises should be combined in sessions with maximal strength or power training to maximize the training transfer into soccer-specific movements. For example, during a gym-based session for power, a set of 5- to 10-metre accelerations should follow each set of strength or power exercises. Additionally, these training modalities can be combined on the pitch. For example, an on-field session can be performed using a combination of Olympic-style lifts and plyometric exercises, soccer-specific sprints and ball shots and headers. These sessions increase not only the specificity to soccer but also the motivation of the players to perform at optimum intensity. Examples of on-field speed and power sessions are shown in figures 11.4 and 11.5. The specifics regarding sets and repetitions are detailed in table 11.6.

On-Field Speed and Power Session 1 (figure 11.4)

Six hoops and four small hurdles (30 cm): jump side steps with acceleration and cross; 4 to 6 minutes with 25 seconds of recovery between sets.

Bar of 20 kilograms and three hurdles: three to six jumps with the bar, jump with both feet through the hurdles with and without pause, accelerate and shoot; 4 to 6 minutes with 25 seconds of recovery between sets.

Three hurdles and two cones: jump with both feet forward, side, forward, accelerate until the second cone, shift direction to the first cone, shift direction to the goal, shoot; 4 to 6 minutes with 25 seconds of recovery between sets.

Five cones in a slalom: jump side steps, accelerate, cross; 4 to 6 minutes with 25 seconds of recovery between sets.

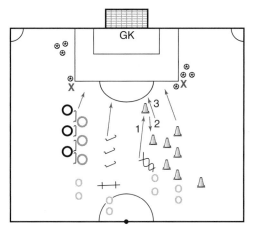

▶ **Figure 11.4** An example of an on-field session combining speed and power with soccer-specific exercise.

On-Field Speed and Power Session 2 (figure 11.5)

Six sets of three reps for squat with 30 per cent of 1RM

Sprint 10 metres

Shoot

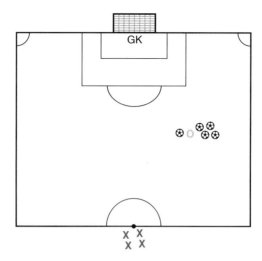

▶ **Figure 11.5** An example of an on-field session combining speed and power training using weight-training exercise and soccer-specific drills.

Table 11.6 Speed Training Programme for an Elite Soccer Player

Sets	2 to 6
Repetitions	1 to 6
Load	0 to 30% body mass
Rest	2 to 5 min.
Velocity	As fast as possible
Number of exercises	4 to 6
Frequency	Preseason: 2 or 3 times a week In season: 1 or 2 times a week Rehabilitation: 2 or 3 times a week Nonplaying: up to 3 times a week
Programme duration	4 to 8 weeks
Recovery between sessions	48 to 72 hours especially if performing plyometrics
Type of exercises	Straight line acceleration (0 to 10 m) Soccer-specific acceleration Explosive and leading starts Sled towing Longer sprint running (20 to 40 m)
When to perform	Before training in conjunction with power training
Main effects	Improve acceleration Increase rate of force development Improve ability to change direction
Special considerations	Perform during hardest session of the week, generally three or four days following a match and two or three days before the next match. Possible to perform the day before a game if using fewer sets, fewer repetitions and less load for activation.

Consider the following recommendations for improving the anaerobic qualities of strength, speed and power in elite soccer players:

- The player has to be strong (i.e., have a high level of initial strength to maximize the effects of speed and power training).

- Exercises for power and speed training should closely mimic the movement patterns specific to soccer. The velocity of execution should be fast during the concentric phase and controlled in the eccentric portion to maximize the training transfer to soccer performance.

- The exercises and programmes prescribed will be determined by the specific needs analysis of each player and should be considered in the overall planning.

Concurrent Training

Soccer requires the development of several qualities such as strength and aerobic performance, but the simultaneous training of these qualities may be incompatible in some conditions. The results obtained in the literature are often conflicting. Although the development of aerobic performance does not appear to be affected by concurrent training, some studies report that strength improvement can be reduced by concurrent training, but not systematically. One of the possible causes of the discrepancies in studies could come from the intensity used in aerobic exercises. Some authors observed that this interference occurred only at intensities close to $\dot{V}O_2$max.

Docherty and Sporer (2000) proposed a model in which some combinations of exercises could increase the probability to generate interference, whereas others could reduce them.

According to the model, when high-intensity interval training is combined with high-load resistance training (lower than 5RM), less interference occurs because the training stimulus in strength focuses on the neural system, not on the metabolic demands on the muscle. Continuous aerobic training at low intensity (lower than 80 per cent of $\dot{V}O_2$max) should also not interfere with strength improvement, whatever the load. Continuous aerobic training at low intensity involves central adaptations mediated by cardiac output and should not impair neural adaptation or muscle hypertrophy.

Interference would be maximized, however, when athletes use high-intensity interval training and an 8- to 12-repetition maximum (RM) multiple-set resistance-training programme. These two modalities of training lead to peripheral adaptations and could be incompatible. Under these conditions, limited change would occur in skeletal muscle cross-sectional area and reduced hypertrophy would occur in individual muscle fibres (Bell et al. 2000). Such interference may be caused by antagonistic intracellular signalling mechanisms, which would inhibit signalling to the protein synthesis (Nader 2006). Alterations in the adaptive protein synthesis changes would be induced by high-intensity endurance exercise or by too-frequent training sessions. Nevertheless, when two sessions per week combining strength and high-intensity endurance exercise were performed, separated by 72 hours, the volume and the time window between training sessions were appropriate for avoiding the interference effect (Silva et al. 2012).

Conclusion

This chapter has outlined the specific demands that can be placed on the elite soccer player during competitive match play from a global perspective and according to the playing position. Many factors can influence the global and positional activity demands placed on players, but the point remains that during a competitive match the objective is not to cover a greater total distance, run more high-intensity sprints or perform more actions than the opposing team or opposing players. The objective is to win the match, and accomplishing this goal requires combining various factors including technical and tactical effectiveness as well as physical performance.

One of the most important qualities for a soccer player is to be at the right place at the right moment. The runs performed are a way to achieve this objective. Training should focus on optimizing activities to save energy and use it at the right time. Nevertheless, developing players to be at their optimal physical level is important. Although players may not always need to perform to the maximum of their physical capacities, the ability to do so is obviously an advantage. Therefore, the physical training programme of soccer players should prepare them for a worst-case scenario during a match based on their positions. Professional soccer teams use various training methods to improve the physical conditioning of players, including both generic (e.g., continuous, intermittent and repeated sprint running) and specific (e.g., small-sided games, soccer-specific and position-specific drills with the ball) exercises. The information presented in this chapter provides the reader and practitioner with the knowledge and tools to design and integrate a physical conditioning programme that complements an overall team training plan aimed at improving all qualities related to performance (e.g., technical and tactical).

The next chapter integrates the science discussed in this chapter and gives practical examples of how physiological principles can be applied to the conditioning of soccer players.

CHAPTER 12

Conditioning Programmes for Competitive Levels

—Tony Strudwick and Gary Walker

This chapter will help coaches and practitioners use the current scientific information in designing conditioning programmes for soccer players. The previous chapter offered an overview of the demands of the game and examined the various components of physical training. This chapter focuses on translating into practice the requirements of soccer, with special insight into planning, training methods and sessions relevant to real working practices in soccer. The role of strength and conditioning is covered to assist in the athletic development of soccer players. In addition, the long-term development of soccer players is addressed with special reference to designing programmes for various age groups.

Here are the four major aims of conditioning programmes in soccer:

- Improve all the relevant capacities of physical performance.
- Enable technical skills to be used throughout a match.
- Allow the players to cope with the game demands.
- Reduce the likelihood of injury.

A comprehensive quantification of the workload that a player experiences during the most intense phases of the game is crucial for understanding the mechanisms taxed and the physiological demands imposed, which have practical implications for the subsequent creation of personalized training programmes. Such an approach, besides being an efficient strategy for maximizing performance, has direct implication on injury prevention because it replicates the high-intensity periods and therefore exposes the players to the fatiguing actions that occur in the game. Thus, before planning fitness training, the individual game requirements need to be clearly understood. Data from match analysis supports this purpose.

Guidelines for Practitioners

Intense exercise is a critical component of soccer performance. The optimization of player ability to perform this type of effort should be a priority in conditioning.

Players should perform high-intensity bouts at maximal intensity (greater than 30 kilometres per hour) during field-based conditioning.

During maximal intensity blocks, players should perform distances of approximately 650 metres in five-minute blocks to prepare them for the most intense phases of match play.

Although conditioning for soccer players should be carried out with the ball, conditioning drills that emphasize small-sided games may not provide appropriate distances or speeds to prepare them optimally for the most intense phases of match play.

High-intensity training is highly demanding and must be followed by extended periods of rest and recovery in a well-planned programme.

Components of Field-Based Conditioning

Many factors need to be considered when designing a programme. Such evaluations should encompass relevant experiences accumulated over the years together with applied research findings.

A programme should not simply be imported, although the development of an appropriate training programme may stem from the results of others. Such a programme needs to be flexible, enabling it to be used as a model of training and easily applied to players with specific characteristics and goals.

Based on the demands of modern games (as discussed in chapter 11), players need to condition themselves and appropriately prepare the necessary energy systems to enable optimal performance. Practically speaking, fitness training is multifactorial and can be divided into components that reflect the physical demands of the game.

For clarification, a common language should be used, and the physiological systems targeted by the various training categories need to be fully understood. Some terminology has been used extensively and is well known, but various other training philosophy descriptors have been introduced over recent years to help translate physiological terminology into a language that coaches can use to put theory into practice. Considerable overlap is seen between training methods that elicit beneficial adaptations in multiple energy systems and methods that contribute to the development of various performance-limiting factors. Having an outline of the physiological pathways reduces the possibility of ambiguity in discussions between support staff and coaches. A clear picture of the training aims can then be adequately presented. Table 12.1 identifies and summarizes the key training categories of field-based conditioning methods that can be used with elite players.

Table 12.1 Methodology for the Main Training Categories of Field-Based Conditioning

| Training category | Aim | Main physiological stimulus or mechanism | TRAINING PROTOCOL | | | | TRAINING MODE | |
			Exercise intensity	Repetition duration	Number of reps	Work: rest	General	Soccer specific
Aerobic low	Recover from intense sessions or matches	Aerobic peripheral	Light: 7 to 11 kmh, <75% HRmax	10 to 30 min.	2 or 3	1:0.1	Bike Jog	Shape Passing routine
Aerobic moderate	Exercise for prolonged periods	Aerobic peripheral	Moderate: 11 to 14 kmh, 75 to 85% HRmax	5 to 30 min.	2 to 8	1:0.2	Straight, shuttle and multi-directional runs	7v7 to 10v10
Aerobic high	Perform repeated high-intensity work	Aerobic central and peripheral Anaerobic	High: 15 to 20 kmh, 85 to 90% HRmax	1 to 4 min.	4 to 10	1:1 1:0.5	Straight, shuttle and multi-directional runs	3v3 to 6v6 7v7 to 10v10 Specific rules, big pitch area
Speed endurance maintenance	Sustain, tolerate and recover from very high-intensity work	Anaerobic lactic capacity Aerobic central and peripheral	Very high or near maximal (>$\dot{V}O_2$max speed)	15 to 90 sec.	3 to 12	1:1 1:3	Straight, shuttle and multi-directional runs	1v1 to 2v2 Individual soccer-specific drills
Speed endurance production	Produce power rapidly and continuously, perform maximal runs more frequently	Anaerobic lactic power	Maximal or near maximal	10 to 40 sec.	4 to 12	>1:5	Straight, shuttle and multi-directional runs	Individual soccer-specific drills
Repeated sprint	Recover and perform repeated sprints	Anaerobic Aerobic	Maximal or near maximal	<10 sec.	4 to 25	1:3 1:5	Straight, shuttle and multi-directional runs	Finishing and skill drills
Speed	React and produce powerful actions and maximum sprinting speed	Anaerobic alactic Neural	Maximal	<10 sec.	4 to 20	1:10	Straight, shuttle and multi-directional runs	Position-specific drills

Aerobic Low-Recovery Training

Aerobic low-recovery training involves low intensities (less than 75% HRmax) and relatively long durations (longer than 10 minutes). This type of training is considered optimal for facilitating the recovery process following high-intensity exercise. The principle of recovery relates to the encouragement of adaptive processes following presentation of the stimulus. An appropriate recovery results in the restoration of physiological and psychological processes so that the player can compete or train again at a suitable level. Active recovery strategies include jogging, walking, swimming and cycling. Because of the mechanical loads associated with intense exercise, these exercises may be performed unloaded.

Aerobic Moderate-Intensity Training

Aerobic moderate-intensity training involves relatively low intensities (less than 85% HRmax) and long durations (longer than 5 minutes). This type of training is considered optimal for producing skeletal muscle adaptations, such as aerobic enzymes, buffering capacity and fuel stores, enabling the muscles to exercise for prolonged periods. These adaptations are critical to minimizing fatigue as a match progresses. They are developed over long periods, but they detrain quickly. Various small-sided games of 7v7 up to 10v10 are ideal for this form of training because they facilitate simultaneous physiological and technical development. These games should be an integral component of early preseason conditioning. They should be delivered in a planned progressive manner to larger-sided games with increased duration to prepare players for 90 minutes of match play. Emphasis on this type of training should decrease during the competition period because adequate adaptations will be attained by high-intensity sessions and match play.

Aerobic High-Intensity Training

This type of work is achieved through both long and short interval work and small-sided games (three to six per side). The aim is to achieve heart rates greater than 90 per cent of maximum. These intensities tax the cardiovascular system maximally and therefore have a considerable effect on specific endurance performance. Adaptations from this training allow players to work at high intensities more frequently and recover quickly from intense periods of play.

Speed Endurance Training

This work involves repeated bouts at maximum or near-maximum pace, ranging from 10 to 90 seconds in duration. These drills are highly exhaustive and psychologically demanding, but the adaptations are critical for elite soccer performance. Speed endurance training significantly improves anaerobic capacities and the systems involved in pH regulation, preserves muscle excitability and develops muscular enzymes involved in aerobic metabolism. The resulting performance adaptation is an increased number of all-out working bouts, reduced short-term fatigue during competition and greater sustainability of very high-intensity exercise. Training typically performed to achieve these adaptations includes various running-based drills and 1v1 to 2v2 games.

Repeated Sprint Training

Soccer involves many repeated high-intensity efforts. Therefore, players must be fast and able to recover quickly so that they can sprint longer and more frequently. One method to train this ability is to perform repeated sprint training (RST), in which short sprints are conducted with a defined rest period. Many soccer-related activities and training exercises (shooting, passing) involve short, fast efforts. If the work time and rest periods are appropriate, soccer-related drills can serve as sprint repetition training. To be effective, these should involve bouts of less than 10 seconds and have a work-to-rest ratio of 1:2 to 1:5. Alternatively, many forms of running training can be used. Training of this type has been shown to improve speed and minimize fatigue between repeated rapid bouts, providing a crossover to some of the aerobic adaptations.

Speed Training

Speed is a key component in the modern game. Components of speed can be broken down into acceleration, maximum speed and agility (decelerating and turning). Small-sided games stress agility; therefore, sprint training will concentrate on developing basic linear speed, using maximum sprints and overload, or overspeed, training.

Several methods of speed training can be used:

- Acceleration runs of less than 30 metres, shooting drills, reaction drills
- Maximum speed runs of 40 to 70 metres
- Agility drills including partner reaction drills and agility courses
- Running mechanics conducted as part of preparation to exercise
- Overspeed training such as downhill running
- Resisted speed and acceleration training with sleds, weighted vests and bungees

In summary, the focus of field-based conditioning from a physiological perspective is to produce stressors that cause the energy systems of players to adapt and become equipped to withstand the competitive demands of the game. The approach is to overload specific areas of physiology in isolation rather than stimulate every component within the same drill.

Translating Theory to Practice

Many components need to be incorporated into field-based conditioning programmes for soccer players. These include a full range of activities, such as activation modalities, injury prevention strategies, individual and team preparation (physiological, technical and tactical), match rehearsal and recovery strategies, in addition to the more obvious training sessions.

In organizing, designing and prescribing the training session, consideration must be given to major conditioning principles, particularly those associated with intensity, duration and specificity. The application of these principles in a planned progressive manner is key to ensuring that the appropriate energy systems are stimulated during physiological preparation. The design of the training session should be based on individual training philosophy and specificity to match performance. Not all training sessions result in the appropriate physiological and performance adaptations. Thus, where possible, specific physiological systems identified as limiting factors to performance should be stimulated, rather than performing holistic training whereby many mechanisms are taxed to lesser degrees.

The consistency and knowledge of workloads during each of the main training categories (see table 12.1) means that three of the most important training principles can be applied during field-based conditioning, namely, specificity, progression and periodization. Specificity refers to ensuring that the appropriate energy systems are stimulated for performance adaptations. Progression refers to increasing the training load gradually over time as fitness gains occur. Periodization can be defined as a logical, phasic method of manipulating training variables to increase the potential for achieving specific performance goals.

Speed Endurance Training

Recently, numerous authors have examined the effects of speed endurance and repeated sprint training in soccer players (Dupont, Akakpo and Berthoin 2004; Ferrari et al. 2008; Hill-Haas et al. 2009). The benefits of conducting frequent sessions of speed endurance training have been well documented (Iaia and Bangsbo 2010; Mujika 2010), but systematic planning of those sessions must follow appropriate guidelines. Failure to follow those guidelines may result in a state of general exhaustion, leading to a decrease in performance and increased risk of injury.

The following outline suggests the number of repetitions that should be performed in relation to when the game is. Adjustment should be made daily depending on the status and individual needs of the players. Special care should be taken with players who do not play much.

- Day before the game: no speed endurance
- Two days before the game: 4 × 15 to 20 seconds
- Three days before the game: 5 or 6 × 15 to 20 seconds
- Four or more days before the game: 7 or 8 × 15 to 20 seconds

Speed endurance training can be incorporated into soccer conditioning programmes using these guidelines:

- The intensity or speed should be nearly all out (about 95% of 1RM over that distance).
- The work-to-rest ratio should be greater than or equal to 1:3 (e.g., 80 seconds of rest after a 20-second bout).
- The speed endurance sessions per week could be either one or two.

As soon as athletes gain experience and get used to training, both the number and the duration of repetitions can be increased (e.g., from 4 × 15 seconds to 6 to 8 × 20 seconds). To minimize the risk of injury and maximize the training-induced adaptation, lower-limb strength training should not be performed in the hours immediately after a speed endurance session.

Small Sided-Games

In recent years a shift has occurred towards using soccer-specific activities (small-sided games and drills) in the preparation of elite players (Little and Williams 2006; Hill-Haas, Dawson and Coutts 2011). The rationale behind using this training mode for conditioning is to facilitate simultaneous physical and technical development with the twinned advantage of enhanced player motivation and greater transfer to match-specific fitness.

With generic-based conditioning, the primary concern is to produce the appropriate intensity for training adaptations, which is usually achieved by specifying distance and duration parameters of the exercise. During soccer-based drills, the voluntary nature of movement in soccer means that the control over intensity is less precise. Nonetheless, with detailed planning and knowledge, practitioners can use small-sided games and position-specific drills containing tactical and technical components associated with the demands of match play.

Methods to control the intensity during small-sided games were presented in chapter 11. Although coaches use small-sided games with the specific intention of fitness training, few monitor the physical components taxed within each drill. A continual system of monitoring is essential to ensure that the correct decisions are made about individual and team requirements. Methods frequently used to monitor soccer players include GPS monitoring, heart rate monitoring, retrospective questionnaires and training diaries.

Figure 12.1 shows an example of a small-sided game, and table 12.2 provides an overview of the key physical match demands that can be used as a guide to evaluate how well conditioning drills overload specific physical aspects of playing soccer.

In summary, small-sided games and position-specific drills containing technical and tactical elements associated with match play have the potential

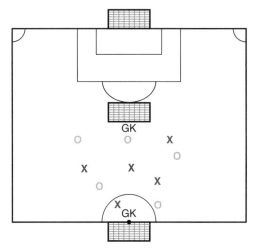

▶ **Figure 12.1** 5v5 small-sided game with two goalkeepers and regular goals. Pitch dimension is 30 by 30 metres, pitch area is 900 square metres, area per player is 75 square metres, and duration of bouts is 5 minutes.

Table 12.2 Physical Match Demands of the Small-Sided Game Shown in Figure 12.1

PHYSICAL PARAMETERS	
Metabolic load	
Total energy expenditure (kJ/kg)	3.4 ± 0.6
Average metabolic power (W/kg)	12.0 ± 1.9
Distance covered from 20 to 35 W/kg (m)	59 ± 18
Distance covered from 35 to 55 W/kg (m)	21 ± 7
Distance covered above 55 W/kg (m)	23 ± 9
Kinematics	
Total distance covered (m)	495 ± 66
Distance covered from 14.4 to 19.8 kmh (m)	43 ± 24
Distance covered from 19.8 to 25.2 kmh (m)	4 ± 6
Distance covered above 25.2 kmh (m)	0 ± 0
Musculoskeletal load	
Number of accelerations of 2–3 m/s²	10 ± 4
Number of accelerations >3 m/s²	2 ± 2
Maximum acceleration m/s²	3.4 ± 0.4
Number of decelerations of 2–3 m/s²	10 ± 4
Number of decelerations >3 m/s²	3 ± 2
Maximum deceleration m/s²	3.8 ± 0.6
Maximum speed kmh	20 ± 2

to produce greater benefits because they allow simultaneous physical and technical development.

Insights Into Planning: Weekly, Monthly, Annual Structures

When planning field-based conditioning for soccer players, the annual cycle should be divided into three stages: transition, preparation and in season. The latter may be further divided into competition and peaking or maintenance. Each of these phases has specific goals and requires different levels of training variation. The use of a planned training programme can allow tighter control of training variables and superior performance enhancements.

Preparation Phase

Starting with a moderate to high volume of low-intensity training, this phase is used to build a foundation for future training. As the phase progresses, training designed to elicit maximal responses are introduced. The preparation phase is designed to increase exercise endurance, positively alter body composition and increase tissue size and tensile strength, resulting in lower injury potential. The preparation phase should be used to enhance soccer-specific fitness. The phase is typically divided into general and specific components. As a guiding principle, players use this period to prepare themselves for the high-intensity demands associated with match play. The workloads during the preparation phase should be closely monitored so that the principle of progression is adhered to.

Moreover, practitioners should allow adequate rest and regeneration, as well as avoid placing unnecessary loads on players by repeatedly performing double field sessions that can increase the risk of overtraining and injury susceptibility.

The length of time spent in the preparation phase depends on the training status and level of the player. The following guidelines are an outline of field-based conditioning over a six-week period:

- Weeks 1 and 2 should encompass soccer activities. Moderate- and high-intensity aerobic drills should be the dominant training category. Speed activities should also be included here in preparation for the work to be conducted in the next period.
- Weeks 3 and 4 should include high-intensity aerobic and anaerobic interval sessions with some quality sprint training as the overall volume decreases.
- Weeks 5 and 6 should include a lower volume of training and an emphasis on high-intensity exercise. The combination of all the training formats discussed and a steady progression in match play exposure is critical in developing soccer-specific fitness.

The preseason schematic presented in table 12.3 shows the relationships among the various types of training used throughout this period. This linear model provides a structured approach to soccer conditioning.

Fundamentally, the challenge for the practitioner is to ensure the following:

- All components of field-based conditioning are incorporated into the training plan.
- Systematic progression occurs from general and soccer-specific endurance to maximal activities.
- All components of the training plan are monitored and evaluated with up-to-date technology.
- Individual thresholds are identified, and the training plan does not use a one-size-fits-all approach.
- Individual players are not overloaded with multiple sessions on any given day.

Table 12.3 Outline of Field-Based Conditioning Priorities Over a Six-Week Preparation Period

Week 1 and 2	Week 3 and 4	Week 5 and 6
General endurance 7v7 to 10v10	Specific endurance 3v3 to 6v6	Specific endurance 1v1 to 2v2
Moderate- and high-intensity aerobic runs	High-intensity aerobic and speed endurance runs	Repeated sprints and speed endurance runs
Quantity		Quality

In-Season Phase

This phase is used to maintain optimal performance throughout the competitive season. The training load should not be dramatically reduced at the expense of training intensity during this phase. Indeed, the management of training intensity is the key, because high-intensity exercise remains a critical component for maintenance or further enhancement of training-induced adaptations. Soccer players need to continue to develop the ability to perform high-intensity exercise repeatedly during the season. They can achieve this by preforming frequent sessions of high-intensity aerobic and speed endurance training specific to the physical, movement, technical and tactical demands of the game (Iaia, Rampinini and Bangsbo 2009).

The key principle during the in-season phase is to ensure that players reach a balance between training and match load and adequate rest and recovery. Continued high-intensity and high-volume training over extended periods may contribute to potentially long-term debilitating effects associated with overtraining and increased occurrence of injury events (Nimmo and Ekblom

2007). Therefore, player performance parameters and actual physiological stress imposed on the athletes need to be carefully monitored. Supplementary recovery sessions as well as reduction in the amount of training should be considered during heavy fixture periods. This concept of undulating periodization, in which changes occur in the volume, intensity and frequency of training, also assists in maximizing physiological adaptations and performance maintenance throughout the playing season.

For squad players who do not play regularly, training load must be sufficient to allow them to cope with the physical requirements of match play. Pronounced mismatches between the demands of match play and training, together with abrupt and severe increases in workload (by switching from nonplay to regular play) may enhance the risk of injury occurrence. Nonregular players, therefore, need to perform additional field-based high-intensity training or engage in practice matches during such periods.

Weekly Planning

The summation of training stimuli plays a key role in the adaptation of each player. To optimize training adaptation and reduce injury risk, players should be exposed to different stimuli daily, thus avoiding monotony or staleness. The inclusion of low-intensity and recovery training together with high-intensity and speed endurance training will help achieve this aim.

In practice, weekly planning is dictated by the number of games as well as the current fitness status of the players, which is often different for each individual. Therefore, a logical approach is to include flexibility in the conditioning programme and tailor weekly templates to the specific requirements of the team and the individual instead of creating a single standard weekly programme. But following some generic guidelines is beneficial in directing the training process. Generally, we face two scenarios: one game per week or two games per week.

One Game Per Week

In this situation a decision needs to be made whether to bring players into training to perform a recovery session the day after a game. A balancing act is required to keep mental freshness amongst the squad whilst also allowing them some quality time with their families and ensuring that they maintain competitive focus during difficult phases of the season. Experience and knowledge of the wellness status of the squad is key in making these types of decisions.

Forty-eight hours after the game is probably the most critical day because muscle soreness tends to be at its highest level and recovery status varies from player to player. Thus, some players can perform moderate aerobic exercise, others may be ready for high-intensity aerobic sessions, and some

Table 12.4 Planning: One Game Per Week

	Playing squad	Nonplaying squad
Sunday	Rest or recovery	High-intensity aerobic, speed endurance
Monday	Moderate- to high-intensity aerobic	Moderate- to high-intensity aerobic
Tuesday	High-intensity aerobic	High-intensity aerobic
Wednesday	Speed endurance	Speed endurance
Thursday	Technical, tactical, individual	Technical, tactical
Friday	Reactive speed, tactical	Reactive speed, tactical
Saturday	Game	Rest

may require a second day of recovery. Coaches may need to monitor and manage all players at the individual level.

The third and fourth days after a game are usually the most demanding ones. Players perform sessions of high-intensity aerobic, strength and anaerobic training. (The inclusion of speed endurance or repeated sprints as part of conditioning work depends on the specific position and individual needs of the player.)

On the two days before the next game, a taper down in volume occurs (sometimes also of intensity with a low-level session implemented), but players frequently carry out either individual conditioning or high-quality, field-based fitness work. For the nonplaying squad, the programme is the same except that during the first two days they may perform additional high-intensity work or specific individual work. Table 12.4 shows an example of a weekly template for both the playing and nonplaying squads.

Two Games Per Week

When two games are played per week, performing physical training in addition to the games becomes more difficult because the majority of time is dedicated to ensuring game readiness and freshness. The day after a game, the playing squad may conduct a recovery session that consists mainly of bike exercise, foam rolling, stretching, upper-body strength training, deep-pool water immersion, ice bath or contrast bathing and massage. When games are three or more days apart, some conditioning work can be conducted, usually consisting of high-intensity aerobic training, but individualized anaerobic specific sessions may also be undertaken.

For the nonplaying squad the day after a game is a crucial conditioning day to ensure that players are well conditioned and physiologically prepared for games. In this situation, training usually consists of additional high-intensity conditioning work through small-sided games or individualized drills. An example of a typical week with two games is presented in table 12.5.

Table 12.5 Planning: Two Games Per Week

	Playing squad	Nonplaying squad
Sunday	Recovery	High-intensity aerobic, speed endurance
Monday	Moderate-intensity aerobic, tactical	Moderate-intensity aerobic, tactical
Tuesday	Game	Rest
Wednesday	Recovery	High-intensity aerobic, repeated sprint
Thursday	Moderate-intensity aerobic, individual	Moderate-intensity aerobic
Friday	Reactive speed, tactical	Reactive speed, tactical
Saturday	Game	Rest

Transition Phase

Following the competitive in-season phase, both physiological and psychological recovery are necessary. Thus, recovery from the in-season should take the form of active rest (AR) in which the volume is kept low and the intensity of training is low to moderate. Some players may benefit from participating in another sport, but at a recreational level. The exact length of time for the AR phase depends on many factors, including training status, injury history and age. The positive effects can include diminished fatigue, injury rehabilitation and psychological recovery. From a negative standpoint, the lower volumes and intensities during this transition can result in loss of sport-specific fitness.

Thus, during the off-season the players should be encouraged to perform regular sessions of moderate-intensity aerobic training to minimize the decrement of fitness that always occurs on cessation of normal training and competition. This regimen will also form a base from which to progress safely to higher work intensities during the preseason. Subjecting players to sudden large increases in intensity can cause stiffness, soreness and demotivation, whilst at the same time running the risk of injury or overtraining.

Strength and Conditioning

The role of strength and conditioning in the athletic development of soccer players is twofold:

- Reduce the likelihood of injury occurrence
- Improve physical performance

The extensive nature of the soccer annual calendar presents challenges to practitioners in terms of planning and periodization of fitness parameters throughout a competitive season. Conditioning programmes therefore must be carefully planned, based on a thorough needs analysis of the sport and athlete and delivered in accordance with the athlete's and coach's goals, together with the fixture schedule.

Needs Analysis

The needs analysis provides the strength and conditioning practitioner with a clear understanding of the demands of the game and the areas most affected by injury. Players require high levels of strength, power, speed and agility to perform explosive movements such as kicking, maximal sprinting, turning, tackling, dribbling and jumping. These decisive actions undoubtedly influence the one-on-one on-field playing duels and ultimately are the actions that decide the important passages of match play. Considerable injury epidemiological evidence has been reported in elite men's soccer, but fewer studies have been conducted in elite women players. In men, injury data from Europe's elite teams show that muscle injuries constituted 31 per cent of all injuries; 92 per cent of injuries affected the four major muscle groups of the lower limb: hamstrings (37 per cent), adductors (23 per cent), quadriceps (19 per cent) and calf muscles (13 per cent) (Ekstrand, Hagglund and Fuller 2011). In women, most injuries occur to the ankle, knee and thigh; women had higher rates of ankle sprains and more serious injuries to the anterior cruciate ligament than men did (Junge and Dvorak 2007). For a more detailed examination of injury frequency in soccer, refer to chapter 15.

The goal of a conditioning programme for soccer players is to improve and maintain an appropriate level of aerobic endurance yet improve the capability of the player to produce explosive actions repeatedly. The ability to remain injury free will allow the player to develop these physical attributes more effectively.

Injury Reduction

The role of injury reduction is the responsibility of all players and support staff within a developmental programme. On- and off-field factors can be monitored and manipulated to reduce the risk of injury to elite senior players. The remainder of this section focuses on the off-field methods that practitioners can use to improve player robustness.

Functional Movement Assessment and Musculoskeletal Screening

The medical department should evaluate all players for musculoskeletal deficiencies during a preseason assessment to guide the fitness and conditioning department in subsequent programme design. This assessment and functional movement screening tools are available for identifying areas of uncontrolled movement, highlight bilateral asymmetry in mobility or stability and detect movement dysfunction. Functional movement assessment is important to assign the correct exercises to each player and to ensure that dysfunctional movement patterns are not inappropriately loaded. For more detail, refer to chapter 8.

Players can be identified as requiring supplementary myofascial release strategies, flexibility programmes, proprioceptive neuromuscular training, movement repatterning or strengthening of specific areas. Programmes should be provided for each player as prehabilitation strategies. Specific programme examples for players identified as having issues with core, hip and shoulder stability are outlined in tables 12.6, 12.7 and 12.8. As technical proficiency and strength increase, programme intensity is increased by adding load or increasing the difficulty of exercise performed. Similarly, exercises are regressed if a player does not have the strength or technical proficiency to perform the exercise correctly.

Table 12.6   Core Programme for Player With Identified Core Weakness (Core Extension Emphasis) Performed Twice Per Week Before Training

Exercise	Sets	Reps
Swiss ball press-up	3	8 to 10
Swiss ball walk (straight)	3	5 to 8 each leg
Plank with alternate arm movements	3	5 to 8 each arm
Plank circuit (front, side, side)	3	Begin with 30 sec. in each position
Tall kneeling rope hold	3	2 × 20 sec.

Table 12.7   Glute Programme for Player With Identified Hip Stability Issue (Glute Med Emphasis) Performed Twice Per Week Before Training

Exercise	Sets	Reps
Miniband walking circuit	3	8 each exercise
Weighted lying abduction	3	8 each leg
Glute bridge (single-leg lift)	3	8 each leg
Lateral single-leg squat	3	6 each leg
Suspension rope single-leg squat	3	6 each leg

Table 12.8   Shoulder Programme for Player With Identified Shoulder Stability Weakness Performed Twice Per Week Before Training

Exercise	Sets	Reps
Swiss ball TYW	3	6 each position
Dumbbell lunge with shoulder flexion	3	6 each leg
Dumbbell circle (thumbs up)	3	10
Slide board flexion and extension	3	8 on specific shoulder
Suspended flexion with fast contraction	3	5 to 8 on specific shoulder

Changing Standard Warm-Ups

Historically, the soccer warm-up has consisted of a jog around the pitch, static and dynamic flexibility exercises, and speed, agility, quickness activity. Expanding on the FIFA F-MARC 11+ warm-up, fitness and conditioning staff may incorporate the 11+ exercises into a standardized warm-up strategy by prescribing an indoor 20-minute squad session before training two or three times per week. (See chapter 15.) A recent study of more than 1,500 youth female players showed that performing the 11+ regularly reduced injuries by 35 per cent compared with performing a standard soccer warm-up (Soligard et al. 2010).

Strengthening Following Injury

Reinjuries constitute 12 per cent of all soccer injuries and cause longer absences than injuries do (Ekstrand, Hagglund and Fuller 2011). Although no definitive evidence suggests that strengthening previously injured areas alone prevents reinjury, it has recently been demonstrated that increasing eccentric hamstring strength was associated with reduced risk of future hamstring injury in a cohort of previously injured Australian soccer players (Opar et al. 2015). Therefore, a prudent approach for the strength and conditioning practitioner is to develop a sustainability programme for soccer players to follow for a period when they return to training and match play following injury. This period depends on each player's injury history and nature. For some serious injuries, the player may continue the programme indefinitely. All programmes should consist of concentric, eccentric and isometric contractions working across the force-velocity continuum. Examples of sustainability protocols for a player who is fully rehabilitated from hamstring, adductor, quadriceps and calf muscle group strains are presented in tables 12.9 to 12.12.

Expanding on this process, more recent evidence measuring electromyographic activity of the hamstring muscles has shown that different exercises activate different components of the hamstring muscle group. For example, kettlebell swings and Romanian deadlifts specifically target semitendinosus, whereas leg curls and Nordic hamstring exercises have higher biceps femoris activity (Zebis et al. 2013). Furthermore, exercises that activate proximal and

Table 12.9 Hamstring Strengthening Programme Following Hamstring Injury Performed Twice Per Week

Exercise	Sets	Reps
Nordic hamstring lowers	2 or 3	4 to 6
Single-leg RDL (resisted)	2 or 3	6 on injured leg
Slide board hamstring curl	2 or 3	8 to 10
Single-leg hamstring bridge	2 or 3	8 on injured leg
Single-leg speed hop	2 or 3	5 × 2 each leg

Table 12.10   Adductor Strengthening Programme Following Groin Injury Performed Twice Per Week

Exercise	Sets	Reps
Single-leg squat	2 or 3	5 each leg
Hip adduction	2 or 3	8 each leg
Eccentric slide board adduction	2 or 3	6 each leg
Kossacks	2 or 3	10 to 12
Side plank with leg movements (top leg support)	2 or 3	8 to 10 with injured leg

Table 12.11   Quadriceps Muscle Group Strengthening Programme Following Quadriceps Injury Performed Twice Per Week

Exercise	Sets	Reps
Single-leg squat	2 or 3	5 each leg
Rear raised lunge	2 or 3	6 each leg
Lateral speed skater hop 'n' hold	2 or 3	10 each leg
Single-leg speed hop	2 or 3	5 × 2 on injured leg
Single-leg 90-degree iso hold	2 or 3	30 sec on injured leg

Table 12.12   Calf Strengthening Programme Following Calf Injury Performed Twice Per Week

Exercise	Sets	Reps
Eccentric calf lower	2 or 3	6 to 8 on injured leg
Calf raise	2 or 3	8 to 10
Low box hold and freeze	2 or 3	8 to 10
Bouncing calf raise	2 or 3	6 to 8 each leg
Single-leg speed hop	2 or 3	5 × 2 on injured leg

distal portions of the hamstring muscles have also been identified, which could have important implications for developing a return-to-training strengthening protocol.

Correcting Bilateral Asymmetry in Force, Velocity and Power

Playing soccer without following an adequate strength and conditioning strategy can lead to a bilateral imbalance in leg strength, speed and power. This issue generally manifests with the nondominant kicking leg being stronger and more stable but slower than the dominant kicking leg. The ingrained movement patterns of training and match play also show players to be more competent when jumping and landing off a favoured leg. Identifying and implementing assessment protocols that highlight players with bilateral asymmetries is important because players with strength imbalance between limbs are at increased risk of injury, which is reduced as a normal strength profile is restored (Croisier et al. 2008).

Improving Physical Performance

In recent years, match analysis data of elite soccer players has clearly demonstrated that the game includes more explosive events than ever before. These increased athletic demands mean that players require the strength, power and speed to perform actions repeatedly, such as kicking, accelerating, maximal velocity sprinting, decelerating, changing direction, dribbling, tackling, jumping and diving. At all competitive levels, these high-powered actions can prove to be the difference between winning and losing. Therefore, practitioners need to prescribe appropriate conditioning programmes that can improve these components.

Players should undergo valid and reliable assessment or testing protocols to ascertain their movement competency, strength and power performance status. Following this, player-specific programmes are prescribed to improve any aspects of movement competency or athleticism, strength and power that a player has a particular weakness or deficit in. Increasing a player's movement competency in key movements such as squatting, lunging (in multiple planes), hip hinging, bracing and rotating is a component of all strength and conditioning programmes and can assist in the important goals of reducing injury incurrence and increasing physical performance. Players who are sufficiently competent in specific movement patterns can then be trained to express force maximally or explosively to improve strength or power as appropriate. Routine monitoring of off-field training using methodologies allows the strength and conditioning professional to determine progress in specific exercises. In addition, regular feedback may improve player buy-in to a particular programme.

Player Assessment

The individual programme prescribed to a player depends on several factors, such as the player's resistance-training age, training status, playing position, injury history, functional screening and physical performance in valid and reliable assessment protocols. As illustrated in the strength and conditioning impact model (figure 12.2), regular assessment every 8 to 12 weeks is used to identify individual strengths and weaknesses and can be used to evaluate the effectiveness of conditioning programmes throughout the season. Assessment generally occurs at the start of preseason, early in the season and at regular intervals thereafter according to the player's playing and travel schedule. Assessment of a player can also be used to indicate readiness to return to training or match play following a period of injury. In addition, in special cases such as a young developmental player leaving the parent club to join another club on loan, the player should be assessed before leaving the club and again on his or her return to evaluate the effectiveness of the prescribed programmes while the parent club's staffs have not been able to deliver the programme.

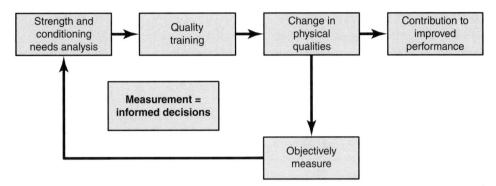

▶ **Figure 12.2** Strength and conditioning impact model.

Off-Field Conditioning

To improve the performance of explosive actions on the pitch, the off-field conditioning aim is to develop the strength and power of a player. To achieve this aim, a sound programme rationale will select appropriate exercises according to an individual's needs analysis and resistance-training history and deliver the programme in accordance with any medical restrictions placed on the player by the medical department. Common components will be prevalent throughout each prescription, but a one-size-fits-all programme should not be used, even when players perform resistance-training sessions as groups or squads. For example, a 28-year-old elite adult player with a low resistance-training age who has never performed Olympic weightlifting exercises may use a different strategy to increase power in the short term than a 16-year-old scholar who uses resistance training as part of a long-term strategy to increase strength and power.

A well-planned resistance-training programme should incorporate exercises that span the force-velocity continuum (figure 12.3), are biomechanically specific to the movements performed in soccer training and match play

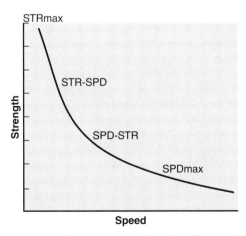

▶ **Figure 12.3** Training strategies encompassing the force-velocity curve.

and incorporate both slow and fast stretch-shortening cycle episodes. Thus, exercise selection should be predominantly based on whole-body, closed kinetic chain exercises performed with one or both legs. Bilateral exercises are generally selected when the goal is to improve strength. Unilateral exercises, although they also develop strength, provide a much greater stability challenge.

Strength Development

Strength development is based on the principle of progressive overload, which is principally achieved by increasing resistance or changing exercise tempo. In general, the goal for each player during a strength development session (lower or upper body) is to perform each exercise with as much weight as possible using correct technical form for the desired number of repetitions. Repetition maximum (RM) testing or estimation is used to prescribe resistance-training loadings with many athletes, but much debate has occurred regarding its suitability for use with soccer players because most have a low resistance-training age. If RM assessment is not performed, close monitoring and recording of each session will allow the strength and conditioning coach to prescribe appropriate loading in subsequent sessions. The length of each strength phase will be player specific, but exercise selection or prescription in terms of repetitions, sets and tempo should be changed at least every six to eight weeks to avoid stagnation. An example of a leg strength session for an elite professional player is provided in table 12.13.

Power Development

A player's capability to generate power is a key goal of many training programmes to improve the performance of explosive movements on the pitch. Training strategies encompassing the force-velocity continuum (figure 12.3) can be used to improve lower-body power in the soccer environment.

Table 12.13 Sample Leg Strength Programme for Senior Player

Complete exercise A before performing B and C as a pair. Rest periods can be used to perform any ancillary or noncompeting individual corrective exercises.

Exercise	Sets	Reps	Rest
A. Trap bar deadlift	3 or 4	4 to 6	3 min.
B. Rear foot elevated split squat B. Single-leg RDL	3 or 4 3 or 4	4 to 6 each leg 4 to 6 each leg	2 min. between pairs
C. Dumbbell lateral lunge C. Nordic hamstring curl	3 or 4 3 or 4	4 to 6 each leg 3 to 6	2 min. between pairs

Developing Power Through Strength

Numerous studies have reported relationships between relative strength, vertical jump power, speed and ability to change direction. In athletes who have done relatively little resistance training, increasing strength through a strength programme may provide both strength and power benefits. This type of approach would be beneficial to a younger player embarking on a long-term periodized strength and power programme or a player playing a highly regimented playing schedule with fixtures known well in advance.

Developing Power Through Strength Speed

Strength speed is defined as the ability to execute a movement quickly against a relatively large external resistance (typically greater than 30 per cent of 1RM). Exercises commonly performed in this category are Olympic lifts and their derivatives. Several factors go into the decision to use Olympic lifts or their derivatives with soccer players, including the player's age, resistance-training background, training priorities and time that can be devoted to learning technique. When Olympic lifts are used, they should be performed from the hang position because this skill is technically easier to master, yet the second pull phase produces the greatest amount of power during the lift, so the player receives a large benefit for effort. The value of Olympic lifting derivatives in athletic performance gives further credence to the support for technique development work during a soccer player's formative years.

Developing Power Through Speed Strength

Speed strength is defined as the ability to execute a movement quickly against a relatively small external resistance (typically less than 30 per cent of 1RM). Exercises commonly performed in resistance programmes in this category are squat jumps, loaded bilateral and unilateral countermovement jumps, resisted sprints and medicine ball power exercises. Both strength speed and speed strength exercises are known to increase the ability of an athlete to develop force quickly (rate of force development), an important characteristic to develop for soccer actions such as sprinting, jumping and changing direction, in which ground contact times are short.

Developing Power Through Speed

Plyometric exercises such as repetitive jumping, hopping, bounding and depth jumps have repeatedly been shown to increase power performance in athletes, in which the emphasis is on attempting to jump or move as high or far as possible with minimal ground contact time. Care must be taken to start plyometric exercise safely and progress volume and intensity sensibly, beginning with having the athlete demonstrate the ability to land and develop eccentric contraction.

This phase is particularly important for female soccer players because they suffer more ACL injuries than male players do when cutting and landing from jumps in noncontact situations. Furthermore, neuromuscular jump-landing training with correct coaching has been shown to cause a dramatic reduction in the risk of injury occurrence in this population.

A classification of plyometric exercise intensity is shown in figure 12.4. Players who are joint compromised should not use high-intensity plyometric exercises, but plyometric activity for those players can be performed in the swimming pool environment to reduce body load while still emphasizing minimal ground contact metrics.

Combination Power Programmes

The type of power programme that a player is prescribed depends on many factors together with his or her performance assessment profile. For example, an adult player identified as having a large window of adaptation for a certain component (e.g., unloaded power) will be provided with exercises that encompass the velocity end (speed strength and speed) of the force-velocity continuum, whereas a player identified as having a loaded power weakness will be prescribed both strength speed and speed strength exercises as appropriate. Players who need to improve all aspects of power may be prescribed three-way combination power programmes, in which a strength speed exercise is followed by a speed strength exercise and then a plyometric exercise, performed as a cluster set. Table 12.14 provides an

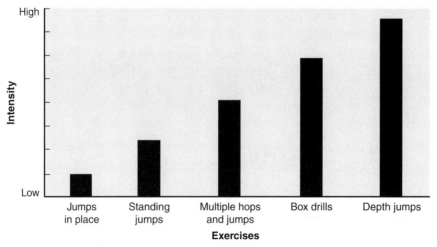

▶ **Figure 12.4** A classification of the intensity of plyometric exercises.

Table 12.14 Sample Leg Power Programme for a Senior Player

Circuit A is conducted as a cluster set with short rests after each component to develop bilateral power. Circuit B develops unilateral power. Circuits can be used independently or combined depending on training goal.

Exercise	Sets	Reps	Rest
A. Barbell squat jump	2 to 4	3 to 5	30 to 60 sec.
A. Box jump	2 to 4	3 to 5	30 to 60 sec.
A. Two-foot microhurdle jump	2 to 4	6 to 8 × 2 (short rest after 6, repeat)	3 min. rest after each circuit
B. Loaded single-leg box jump	2 to 4	3 to 5 each leg	30 to 60 sec.
B. Single-leg bench drive	2 to 4	3 to 5 each leg	30 to 60 sec.
B. Single-leg speed hop	2 to 4	5 × 2 each leg (short rest after 5, repeat)	3 min. rest after each circuit

example of leg power programmes to develop both bilateral and unilateral leg power in adult players.

Planning

The extensive nature of the soccer annual calendar presents challenges to the strength and conditioning practitioner at the macro-, meso- and microcycle levels. Professional male players of Europe's elite teams participate in more than 200 training sessions and up to 60 competitive matches per season and have extensive national and international travel commitments. Seasonal variations in fixture scheduling expose the players to periods of matches every 3.3 days over a five-match period. Therefore, the off-field training load is clearly dictated by the fixture schedule, which is divided into preseason and competition phases.

Historically, the preseason period was regarded as the only time for soccer players to perform off-field strength and conditioning to improve strength. The hope was that this conditioning would provide a protective benefit lasting into the season. Players now commonly perform structured strength and conditioning programmes throughout the competitive phase of the season. The challenge in season is to maintain or improve strength and power qualities when having limited time to perform strength and conditioning and with accumulating levels of fatigue (Yule 2014). Residual fatigue can develop throughout the training and playing week and accumulate in players over prolonged periods of training and playing. During these periods, the strength and conditioning practitioner needs to 'plan but write in pencil,' because things change constantly and appropriate adaptation is required. Throughout all, the strength and conditioning practitioner must have good liaison with the technical coaching staffs to combine off-field strength and conditioning work with on-field physical, technical and tactical training.

Preseason

The two general aims for player preparation in preseason are to increase soccer-specific endurance and to improve whole-body strength. Because of the time constraints in preseason, concurrent training of these fitness components is unavoidable. Therefore, the strength and conditioning practitioner must adopt specific practices to reduce interference between the competing components and maximize training adaptation:

- Strength sessions should be scheduled on days when lighter on-field sessions are planned. Good communication and planning among coaches will help to achieve this goal.
- If strength sessions and vigorous on-field sessions must occur on the same day, schedule as long a gap as possible between sessions; challenge the traditional soccer culture and extend the training day. Attempt to set up areas where players can rest, relax or sleep between sessions to optimize quality training in each session.
- Ensure that players follow appropriate nutritional and recovery strategies to maximize adaptation.

An example of a six-week preseason plan and an individual off-field conditioning session are outlined in tables 12.15 and 12.16.

Competition

The major goal of this period is to maintain optimal on-field performance. A player's ability to remain injury free throughout the competitive season will increase his or her opportunity to perform at a high level.

On- and off-field training load is largely dictated by the fixture schedule. Therefore, precise monitoring and careful manipulation of training, playing load and recovery is required for each player. A one-size-fits-all approach will not work. The weekly microcycles of playing and nonplaying squad members will differ, but during this phase players must continue to develop the ability to perform high-intensity exercise repeatedly. This aim can be achieved by manipulating frequency, intensity, duration and volume of sessions.

Off-field conditioning goals will vary depending on individual player needs, but players should at least maintain strength and power throughout a competitive season. With the congested fixture schedule, a nonlinear, undulating periodized programme design may be more suitable for these players, and the strength and conditioning practitioner may occasionally have to be creative with the loading approach. But a younger developing player who is

Table 12.15 Sample Off-Field Conditioning Plan for Preseason Phase

This plan is flexible and is subject to change, depending on on-field training and playing schedules.

	Mon	Tues	Wed	Thurs	Fri	Sat	Sun
Week 1	Whole-body strength (2 sets)	Injury prevention circuit (3 sets)		Injury prevention circuit (3 sets)	Whole-body strength (2 sets)		
Week 2	Whole-body strength (3 sets)	Injury prevention circuit (3 sets)		Injury prevention circuit (3 sets)	Whole-body strength (3 sets)		
Week 3	Whole-body strength (3 sets)	Injury prevention circuit (3 sets)		Injury prevention circuit (3 sets)	Whole-body strength (3 sets)		
Week 4	Whole-body strength (3 sets)	Injury prevention circuit (3 sets)		Injury prevention circuit (3 sets)	Whole-body strength (3 sets)		
Week 5	Power transition (2 sets)	Injury prevention circuit (3 sets)		Power transition (3 sets)			
Week 6	Power transition (3 sets)	Injury prevention circuit (3 sets)		Power transition (2 sets)		First match of season	

Table 12.16 Sample Preseason Session Aimed at Developing Whole-Body Strength

The player works fully through a circuit, indicated by same letter, and then rotates to the next one. Completion of two or three sets of all four circuits is a total-body strength workout. The players should perform the session twice a week during preseason. This organization would allow a squad of players to train simultaneously.

Exercise	Sets	Reps	Rest
A. Trap bar deadlift	3	6	
A. Single-arm shoulder press	3	5 each arm	
A. Band rotation	3	8 each direction	2 min. and then move to B
B. Dumbbell high box step-up	3	5 each leg	
B. Wide grip pull-up	3	6	
B. Front plank	3	Begin with 45 sec	2 min. and then move to C
C. Dumbbell lateral lunge	3	5 each leg	
C. Bench press	3	6	
C. Single-leg glute-ham bridge	3	5 each leg	2 min. and then move to D
D. Supine pull	3	6	
D. Romanian deadlift	3	6	
D. Side plank	3	Begin with 30 sec. each side	

participating in one match or fewer per week may follow a linear periodized model to increase strength and transfer to power production over a greater period. To increase player buy-in to any particular programme, the strength and conditioning practitioner needs to develop good relationships with the player and coaching staff, conversing with them about the physical areas they believe need improvement to aid on-field performance. Providing the player specific assessment feedback can help in identifying areas of weakness and developing programmes to improve the highlighted deficiencies. If the player agrees with this direction and the way that it relates to on-field performance, then programme adherence will improve significantly. A specific player assessment feedback report is illustrated in figure 12.5. When it is not possible to conduct regular player assessments, routine monitoring of the player during off-field conditioning exercises is used to determine how the player is responding to the training programme. Monitoring tools are available, such as contact mats to determine jump height or reactivity, linear encoders to measure power output through bar velocity and timing gates to measure speed, but the details of their usage is beyond the scope of this

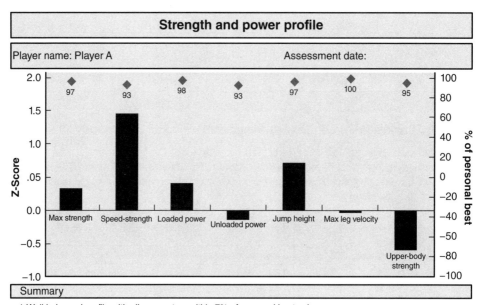

▶ **Figure 12.5** Specific player assessment feedback report. This sample report provides details relating the score to previous assessments and performance in relation to a particular squad.

Based on an unpublished figure created by R. Hawkins. Used with permission.

chapter. Routine monitoring and feedback enhance player motivation and effort during training sessions.

Lower-body strength or power programmes should be performed during the lightest on-field training days, and upper-body strengthening should be performed on postmatch recovery days to aid recovery.

Torso strengthening is scheduled on days according to the player's preference and is designed to improve the player's ability to transfer force from the ground to the extremities, whilst preventing uncontrolled movements of the spine and pelvis. The exercises stabilize and strengthen the torso, hips, shoulders and upper back to help protect against injury and increase movement efficiency. Programming includes antiextension exercises (movements of the arm and leg with limited movement of the torso), antirotation and antilateral flexion exercises (resisting against a rotational or lateral force) and rotational exercises (producing and controlling a rotary force). These exercises use a variety of postures such as planks and stances that are progressed from half kneeling to tall kneeling, squat, split and single-leg stances that challenge the player to control movement within three planes of motion as strength and technical proficiency increases. Torso strengthening should also be incorporated into the group injury prevention warm-up circuits performed before training.

Sample scenarios for players participating in one and two matches per week are presented in tables 12.17 and 12.18. Note that these examples do not represent all players; some players will conduct more or less work depending on their ongoing subjective and objective assessments. During a heavy fixture schedule that allows limited time for off-field conditioning, players need to perform low-level injury prevention strategies or corrective exercise programmes as appropriate. Furthermore, the strength and conditioning practitioner should look for windows within the season such as injury, suspension or free weeks to maximize off-field conditioning opportunities.

Table 12.17 Sample Off-Field Training Scenario for Player With One Match Per Week: Focus to Improve Strength and Power

Session	Mon.	Tues.	Wed.	Thurs.	Fri.	Sat.	Sun.
Leg strength		X				Match	
Leg power				X			
Upper-body and torso strength			X				X
Group injury prevention warm-up	X			X			
Individual prehabilitation	X		X				

Table 12.18 Sample Training Scenario for Player With Two Matches Per Week: Focus to Improve Leg Power

X indicates potential session depending on subjective and objective monitoring of player. In this scenario, no work is performed on the day before the match, but if the player is comfortable, then upper-body strength, lower-body explosive work or individual prehabilitation is possible.

Session	Mon.	Tues.	Wed.	Thurs.	Fri.	Sat.	Sun.
Leg strength							
Leg power	X				X		
Upper-body and torso strength			Match	X			Match
Injury prevention warm-up	X				X		
Individual prehabilitation				X			

Development of Young and Youth Soccer Players

It has been suggested that to achieve excellence, more than three hours of deliberate practice daily for 10 years is required (Ericsson, Krampe and Tesch-Römer 1993). Although hours of practice and performance are highly correlated, the current fascination with 10,000 hours is misplaced. Practice at that volume does not guarantee world-class performance. Nonetheless, the research by Ericsson, Krampe and Tesch-Römer (1993) has brought attention to the importance of experience and structure in the development of expertise as opposed to some innate talent that is often assumed to be beyond training.

More important, to implement the concept of deliberate experience appropriately in the development of soccer players, a long-term plan is necessary. From a physiological perspective, the general goal in the development of an elite soccer player should be split into improving the mechanisms for producing and reducing force and improving motor control. All aspects of soccer conditioning should contribute to the enhancement of one or both of those areas.

The appropriate implementation of training programmes is essential in the optimal development of soccer players. Without the necessary planning from an early age, the full potential of any player may never be realized.

Coaches and practitioners need to adopt a long-term approach in the development of soccer players. The training principle of progression (referred to earlier in the chapter) is often neglected in the training programmes of young players; instead, adult training regimens are often applied to children. Such practices must be avoided. Moreover, if young athletes are exposed to highly intensive training before they build a solid base, then issues will ultimately arise with short-term burnout and increased injury risk. Soccer may be considered a late specialization sport that requires an athletic foundation for successful performance.

Critically, multilateral development is required from an early age to develop a variety of fundamental skills. The focus should be on the development of general athletic abilities such as running, tumbling, balancing and coordination. This process of development improves overall training adaptability and facilitates the progression towards the demanding training that will be introduced in later years.

The development of a soccer player can be divided into four phases:

- Fundamental phase
- Training to train
- Training to compete
- Training to win

These phases provide only a guideline about the types of training that should be undertaken and where the bias should lie. Consideration must always be given to individual differences and the chronological, biological and training age of the players. Invest in the long-term planning of soccer players. Elite players do not develop by chance.

Fundamental Phase (5 to 11 Years)

The fundamental phase of development is a multilateral phase that builds the foundation on which complex motor skills can be developed. Agility, balance, coordination and speed are the key areas, together with fundamental aspects of running, throwing and jumping. As many sports and skills as possible should be introduced to this age group. The focus should be on maximum participation and fun in all activities.

Practitioners working with this age group should focus on these aspects:

- Developing basic skills
- Developing speed, power and endurance using fun games
- Slowly progressing in hopping and jumping activities
- Introducing strength training through exercises that use the child's own body weight and medicine balls with a focus on technique development
- Emphasizing coordination and body awareness through activities and games, integrating gymnastic and athletic movements
- Emphasising training and playing together

Training to Train Phase (11 to 14 Years)

During this phase of development, athletic formations begins to take place in the body and its capacities develop rapidly. Sport-specific skills are emphasized together with fun games. Instead of competition, the perfection of technical skills is the key during this phase. Children are encouraged to play soccer in all positions, although position specificity is introduced towards the end of the stage. In addition, the ability to concentrate on specific tasks should be improved as more complex skills are introduced to offer progressive challenge to the athlete.

Practitioners working with this age group should focus on these aspects:

- Developing sport-specific skills
- Developing knowledge of warm-up, cool-down, stretching, hydration, nutrition, recovery and concentration
- Continuing to develop speed with specific activities during the warm-up, such as agility, quickness and change of direction
- Refining some previously learned skills because limb growth will affect technique
- Emphasizing flexibility training because of the sudden growth of bones, tendons, ligaments and muscles
- Learning correct lifting techniques

During this phase, only short-duration anaerobic activities are recommended. Competition is structured, and a 70:30 practice-to-competition ratio is recommended.

Training to Compete Phase (14 to 20 Years)

The greatest changes in training occur during this phase of training. The exercises undertaken are aimed at high-performance development, and the intensity and volume of work gradually increase. Sport- and position-specific skills are emphasized, and player programmes become individualized. Developing the aerobic system is a high priority because players pass through their period of peak growth. Strength development increases as levels of testosterone rise in the body. The volume and intensity of anaerobic activities progressively increase throughout this phase. Therefore, careful monitoring of the adaptations and workloads is necessary to ensure optimal programme implementation and to reduce risk of injury. Indeed, the incidence of injury because of load mismanagement here can have negative consequences for performance potential.

Practitioners working with this age group should focus on these aspects:

- Developing the aerobic and anaerobic systems and training them for maximum output
- Implementing soccer-specific energy system training
- Maximizing strength and power routines to improve overall strength development and optimize neuromuscular training

- Devoting 50 per cent of the available time to the continued development of technical and tactical skills
- Devoting 50 per cent of the available time to competition
- Continuing a gradual progression in training overload throughout this phase
- Tailoring conditioning programmes to the player's needs

Training to Win Phase (20 Years and Older)

The focus in this phase is exclusively on elite performance. The emphasis moves to high-intensity training and position-specific training. During the competition period, maintenance of the established physical and physiological capacities is critical, requiring constant changes to the training programme in terms of volume, intensity and frequency. Prophylactic breaks will also ensure optimum regeneration. Efficient programming is required throughout the various stages of the season depending on the playing programme. For recommendations on effective planning, see the aforementioned section on programming.

Practitioners working with this age group should focus on these aspects:

- Maximizing performance because the player's physical, technical, tactical, mental, personal and lifestyle capacities should now be fully established
- Incorporating the most advanced physical training techniques and programmes to ensure maximum adaptation and minimal risk of injury
- Using state-of-the-art scientific knowledge and sports medicine information to formulate training programmes
- Conducting appropriate medical and sport science monitoring
- Using a training-to-competition ratio of 25:75, with the competition percentage including competition-specific training activities

Conclusion

Practitioners can employ methods to reduce injury risk and improve the physical performance of soccer players of all ages and both sexes. Both on-field and off-field conditioning strategies should be individualized, based on a needs analysis and planned in accordance with the playing calendar and match demands. Regular assessment is used to educate and motivate players to modify conditioning programmes appropriately throughout a season. This, together with strategic objective and subjective monitoring of player workload will maximize the training adaptations of players.

Throughout the past decade, a shift has occurred towards systematic methods of preparing soccer players for matches. Contemporary practitioners have been exposed to scientific approaches of preparing teams for competition. In general, the coaches who have adopted a strategic approach have been rewarded with success by gaining an advantage over competitors.

It has taken some time for the accumulation of scientific knowledge to be translated into a form usable by coaches. Efforts are now being made to compile scientific information and make it accessible to the soccer world. This chapter contains special insight into translating into practice the physiological requirements of soccer. Reference was made to planning, training methods and conditioning guidelines for all ages, including practices relevant to elite soccer.

CHAPTER 13

Environmental Stressors

—Donald T. Kirkendall

Athletes can play soccer in nearly every conceivable environment, from above the Arctic Circle to the Namibian deserts. FIFA World Cups in the United States (the 1994 men's and 1999 women's tournaments) and Spain (1982) were contested in oppressive heat (greater than 38 degrees Celsius, or 100 degrees Fahrenheit). In Mexico (1986) some games were played at altitude (at nearly 9,000 feet, or 2,700 metres) in heat, polluted air or both. In Korea (2002) the excessive humidity (in excess of 85 per cent at times) was extremely challenging. At the 2008 men's Olympic final in Beijing, the temperature at kick-off was so high that FIFA's medical committee took the unprecedented action of instituting a water break midway in each half. Qualifying matches and professional league games in northern Europe can be played in cold weather. Tromsø, a city 350 kilometres north of the Arctic Circle, is in the top Norwegian division and has an average February temperature of −4 degrees Celsius.

The size of the United States and its range of environments mean that many conditions are possible, especially for the travelling team that participates around the country. A team from a northern state such as Vermont (average April temperature of 6 degrees Celsius) that travels to a spring tournament in Houston, Texas (average April temperature of 27 degrees Celsius), will encounter far hotter conditions than they are prepared for. The prestigious USA Cup in Blaine, Minnesota, has been played in oppressive heat and humidity (heat index over 37 degrees Celsius). The average high temperature in July for Doha, Qatar, site of the 2022 FIFA World Cup, is 41 degrees Celsius. Delhi averages 38 to 40 degrees Celsius in the summer. Daily February temperatures in Moscow range from −3 to −9 degrees Celsius. The time of year and the location of the match mean that a player may have to perform in any of these conditions.

This chapter summarizes the influence of the environment on exercise, specifically soccer.

Training and Competing in Heat and Humidity

Heat and humidity are the environmental conditions that most soccer players will experience and are of greatest concern to coaches, players, parents and medical personnel.

Body temperature is a closely regulated balance of heat production and heat loss. Normal body temperature is around 37 degrees Celsius (98 degrees Fahrenheit). Humans live close to their thermal boiling point; daily body temperature is close to the temperature that can lead to problems. A far greater difference in temperature exists between basal temperature and the temperature that is dangerously cold.

Living close to boiling point presents a problem during exercise. Body temperature rises during exercise. Without some mechanisms to lose heat, people would quickly boil over. Thankfully, the human system is adept at keeping temperature below the dangerous boiling point.

Normal temperature largely comes from the breakdown of ATP to maintain basal metabolic function. During exercise, working muscles break down ATP at an incredibly fast rate, meaning that a great deal of heat is being built up. The amount and intermittent nature of running inherent in soccer (intermittent running creates a more challenging thermal load than does continuous running; Kraning and Gonzalez 1991) elevate the core body temperature. Adding this to the basal temperature means that the body's temperature rises above resting temperature.

Luckily, the body has ways to rid itself of excess heat to avoid overheating:

• **Radiation**: Radiant energy waves move from the higher heat source to the lower source. Consider a simple example—snow melting on a sunny though sufficiently cold day. The snow melts as the radiant heat from the sun moves to the colder surface of the snow.

• **Conduction**: Place your hand on a cool surface and note that the cool surface gradually warms. Heat moves downhill from the direct contact of the warm surface of the hand to the cooler surface. Think of being sprayed with water, jumping into a pool or draping a cold towel over the head. Clearly, swimmers benefit from conductive heat transfer.

• **Convection**: Heat is lost to the cooler air molecules as they pass over the skin. This process is similar to the notion of standing in front of a fan or air conditioner. Likewise, cyclists do not appear to be sweating a great deal because convective heat loss is occurring as they speed through the cooler air. But when they stop and no longer have the benefit of convective heat loss, they begin to sweat profusely.

• **Evaporation**: This mechanism is the primary way that we lose heat during exercise. Muscle contraction requires energy, and core body temperature rises from all the heat produced by the muscles. This heat is transferred from cell to cell and then to the blood. This warm blood is transported back to the heart and then out, and some of it passes over the thermostat of the brain (the hypothalamus). The hypothalamus senses a rise in temperature and signals the blood vessels of the skin to dilate. Blood is diverted away from the warm core to the cooler skin, where sweat is produced. The actual loss of temperature is evaporation of the sweat to the environment, not from dripping sweat. Anything that hampers evaporation reduces the ability of the body to lose heat.

Each millilitre of water evaporated results in a loss of 0.6 kilocalories of heat energy. A recreational athlete might lose up to 1 litre of sweat in an hour, but the highly competitive athlete might lose up to 2 litres of sweat or more in that hour. Therefore, minimizing any barriers to evaporation (e.g., clothing, humidity) is critical.

The American College of Sports Medicine (ACSM) has proposed limits on exercise and competition based on the radiant heat, humidity and ambient temperature measured as the wet bulb globe temperature (WBGT; American College of Sports Medicine 2007). The formula is as follows:

$$\text{WBGT} = (0.1 \times \text{ambient temp}) + (0.2 \times \text{black globe temp}) + (0.7 \times \text{wet bulb temp})$$

Where

- ambient temp is the environmental temperature measured with a standard exterior thermometer,
- black globe temp is the temperature measured by a standard exterior thermometer inside a black, metal globe (for radiant temperature), and
- wet bulb temp is the temperature measured by a standard exterior thermometer with one end of a cotton wick over the mercury reservoir (the measuring tip) and the other end in water (for humidity).

The WBGT is heavily influenced by humidity (the 0.7), so the higher the humidity, the more challenging the conditions. Any medical personnel attending (not just covering) a match should know the temperature and humidity. Most modern smartphones have a weather application, so coaches and practitioners should ensure that it is activated and displaying the current conditions.

The ACSM has recommended that sport participation be suspended if the WBGT exceeds 32 degrees Celsius. Unfortunately, suspending an event may not be possible when mass-participation events (e.g., marathons or other fun runs) or spectator events (league matches, tournaments and so on) are scheduled in advance because of time, economic or media constraints. For example, during group play at the 1994 FIFA World Cup in the United States, the Norway versus Republic of Ireland match in Orlando, Florida (28 June

1994), was scheduled for 4:00 p.m. local time (the hottest time of the day) for an evening television broadcast in Europe. Therefore, the attending medical staff must be prepared to treat heat illnesses, to players and spectators alike.

Heat Injury

Medical issues that arise from excess heat and humidity can range from mild to fatal. Everyone who cares for athletes, including physicians, coaches, trainers, parents and the players themselves must be aware of the signs, symptoms and initial treatment.

Heat Cramps

Heat injury is probably the main concern of trainers and medical staff during summer preseason training. Some consider the term *heat cramps* to be a misnomer. The thought was that imbalances of water and electrolytes (mostly sodium) caused heat cramps, but this relationship has not been proven. Muscle cramps can occur at rest or during exercise. Successful use of fluid and electrolyte therapy for exertional cramps may just be coincident with rest.

Regardless of the cause, cramping requires some treatment: passive stretching, massage or both by a trainer or physical therapist and ingestion of a sport beverage that has some electrolytes. Ice has been used successfully by some athletes as well. Occasionally, intravenous fluids (normal saline or Lactated Ringer's solution) are used.

Heat Exhaustion

A more serious condition is heat exhaustion, which, if left untreated, may progress to heatstroke. The player suffering from heat exhaustion may be irritable, light-headed, nauseated (with or without vomiting) and weak. The player likely will have a rapid heart rate, low blood pressure, goose bumps and reduced urine output and will be sweating profusely. Core temperature will be high but less than 40.6 degrees Celsius (105 degrees Fahrenheit). Dehydration and the loss of blood volume are major factors in heat exhaustion. Thankfully, heat exhaustion does not seem to be a big problem in soccer (see the sidebar 'Catastrophic Injuries in Soccer').

Electrolyte loss, particularly sodium, is a contributing factor. Treatment for heat exhaustion requires swift cooling to get the core temperature to 38.9 degrees Celsius (102 degrees Fahrenheit) or less. The recommendation is to escort the player to a cool location and spray him or her with cool or lukewarm water to speed evaporative and conductive heat loss. In addition, a fan can increase convective heat loss.

Oral rehydration is the preferred method of fluid replacement, but severe nausea or vomiting may require the medical staff to consider intravenous fluids. Again, normal saline or Lactated Ringers solutions are the physician's choice.

Catastrophic Injuries in Soccer

The public may not be aware of a decades-long project on catastrophic injury in sport at the University of North Carolina. The research team scours newspapers, press releases and the Internet in the United States for word of the most serious injuries in sport: paraplegia, quadriplegia and death. During the summer of 2001 several heat-related deaths occurred in American football, so I asked a member of the research team whether any heat-related deaths have occurred in soccer. I was told that no heat-related deaths have occurred in soccer to date in the United States. But the environment has been a factor in death on the soccer field; lightning has killed many players. An open field is no place to be during an electrical storm.

Heatstroke

Heatstroke, a complete collapse of the body's ability to dissipate heat, is a medical emergency and requires immediate care. Rectal temperature is very high, 40.6 degrees Celsius (105 degrees Fahrenheit) or greater. The reduced blood volume and constriction of blood vessels at and near the skin hamper the body's ability to transfer heat to the environment.

Signs and symptoms of exertional heatstroke include hypotension, fast heart rate, reduced urine output, vomiting and diarrhoea. In extreme cases, the player may go into shock, which can lead to kidney failure. Disorientation and delirium happen frequently, and bleeding into the brain may even occur. Seizures and coma have been reported. Other organ systems can fail including the hematologic system, liver, muscles, and lungs, and myocardial infarction may occur. Treatment is designed to get body temperature below 38.9 degrees Celsius (102 degrees Fahrenheit) as rapidly as possible by ice water immersion to take advantage of conductive heat loss. People with exertional heatstroke are extremely sick, so ice water immersion should be done only in the presence of emergency medical personnel who can monitor the player. Most medical areas at local soccer competitions or tournaments are not equipped to treat heatstroke, so athletes with heatstroke usually need to be quickly transported to an emergency facility.

Cooling should begin before transport. An effective first treatment is to pack the body in towels that have been soaked in ice water; the more skin that is in contact with cold water, the more effective the heat loss. An older remedy was to place ice packs over the large vessels in the groin and armpits, but that method may result in a reflex vasoconstriction, so it should be avoided. Spraying cool water on the skin and fanning the air may also be beneficial. Competitive venues must not forget that they may have to treat spectators as well because spectators aren't likely to be as acclimatized as the players are.

Preventing Heat Illnesses

The risk of heat illness can be minimized through acclimatization to the heat and by the ingestion of fluids. And the rules of a tournament have occasionally been modified to address heat illnesses (see Beijing Olympics, discussed earlier).

Acclimatization is the gradual process of adapting to the local conditions. The process, while rapid, can still take upwards of 14 days of repeated exposure to the new, hotter conditions. With adaptation, sweating begins earlier, the sweat is more dilute (allowing the body to conserve sodium), and the sweat rate is higher. All these changes increase the efficiency of heat loss while conserving sodium (see table 13.1).

For decades, fluid ingestion recommendations have been available for coaches and practitioners. Any team management personnel (coaches, managers, trainers, doctors, parents) who restrict fluid intake during training may be courting a charge of negligence.

Thinking that fluid ingestion during a soccer match is not possible because of the running clock is inaccurate. Remember that the ball is in play for only 60 to 70 minutes of a 90-minute match, and less in severe environmental conditions. The wise placement of fluids around the pitch and use of injury stoppages and other times when the ball is out of play allow plenty of time for fluid intake. As mentioned earlier, a fluid break in each half was instituted for the men's Olympic final in Beijing. At the 2012 women's U20 championships, the same policy was in place when conditions were extreme. Many youth leagues have modified their rules to include a fluid break. Coaches and practitioners should not use the rules as a reason to withhold fluids in extreme heat.

Plastic bottles can be placed in the goals, along the touchlines and at the corners or be carried out to the players during injury stoppages. During

Table 13.1 Adaptations to Training in the Heat

Adaptation	Exercise in the heat
Earlier onset of sweating	Major
More heat loss through radiation and convection	Major
Increased plasma volume	Major
Lower heart rate	Major
Lower core body temperature	Major
Lower skin temperature	Moderate
Altered metabolic fuel utilization	Major
Decreased oxygen consumption	Major
Improved running economy	Moderate

Adapted, by permission, from L.E. Armstrong, 1998, Heat acclimatization. In *Encyclopedia of sports medicine and science*, edited by T.D. Fahey for the Internet Society for Sport Science. [Online]. Available: www.sportsci.org/encyc/heataccl/heataccl.html.

Accommodating Sudden Heat and Humidity: The USA Cup of 1995

In July 1995, 500 youth teams from around the world participated in the USA Cup tournament in Blaine, Minnesota. Unfortunately, the heat and humidity were unusually oppressive, far above normal morning temperature and humidity. In the first two days of competition, 15 players were treated for heat illnesses. After two days of competition and many treatments for heat, Dr Bill Roberts, the head of the medical team, met with his group to discuss the heat problem. They recommended that the tournament organizers shorten each half by 5 minutes and add those 10 minutes to halftime. Playing time would be a little shorter, and the time between halves would be longer, allowing time to rehydrate with no change to the overall match schedule. At first the organizers decided not to make any changes. Dr Roberts and his staff said they would walk out of the tournament if the recommendations were not adopted. Faced with no medical coverage in dangerous weather, the organizers relented and put the modifications in effect. The number of heat problems dropped dramatically over the rest of the weeklong tournament.

tournaments in which postmatch drug screening is to be performed, each team should lay out water bottles in their team colours to avoid a declaration of a contaminant.

Other strategies to help keep players cool in the heat include the use of ice towels. This practice is often employed in American football; teams keep a big water jug filled with ice water to soak towels that are draped over the head. Substantial heat loss occurs through the scalp, making cold towels on the head an effective means of conductive heat loss.

Note here the distinction between cooling for comfort versus cooling to lower elevated body temperature. Cooling the face and neck with cold towels, face fanning and so on will achieve the former rather than the latter. Whole-body cooling is best achieved by enhancing evaporative cooling using, where applicable, artificial sweating and whole-body fanning. Hand immersion also works and can be combined with the ingestion and holding of cold slush fluids in suitable containers (the bigger the volume, the better, within reason).

In general, the maintenance of normothermia (normal body temperature) before participation is recommended. Predampening clothing (artificial sweat) with misted water using a simple liquid spray dispenser before games and training means that evaporative cooling will begin immediately without waiting for sweat to saturate the clothing. When possible, players should remove shirts because evaporative cooling is most effective when it occurs next to the skin. Modern technical soccer shirts are constructed from suitable material to facilitate sweat wicking and evaporation. Those at rest (substitutes) should need cooling only for comfort, because the major cause of heat strain even in warm environments is the metabolic heat production associated with exercise. Shade is important for those waiting on the touchline to play. In addition, a reduction in the normal warm-up routine is also recommended.

At the elite level of play, a cooling station can be set up in the changing room or on the touchline, if rules permit. This station can include shade, whole-body fanning, hand cooling and ice slush drinks. If conditions are particularly humid, dehumidification will enhance evaporative cooling. Some consideration should be given to identifying players who are susceptible to the heat and therefore at greater risk of heat exhaustion. Finally, acclimatization to conditions as close as possible to those to be experienced is important. Players can be monitored for their achievement of acclimatization.

Some leagues have free substitution, so opportunities to keep players cool are adequate. And some teams make their own mist tents or purchase liquid spray dispensers. Tournament organizers have been known to set up mist tents like those seen at outdoor concerts to duplicate the misting fans seen on the sidelines of NFL and college American football games. These tents are most effective when the fans are blowing hard; the home-grown methods may achieve cooling for comfort but do not have the same effect as the commercial products.

Here are specific cooling recommendations for game management:

- **Pregame:** Changing rooms should not be especially cool; keep them at about 19 to 21 degrees Celsius to avoid vasoconstriction (narrowing of the blood vessels) and cold-induced diuresis (increased or excessive urine output). Do not precool by immersion or by any other means for the same reason. Have cool drinks to ensure euhydration (normal state of body water content).

- **Warm-up:** Reduce intensity. Aim to return body temperature to normal (not precool) on early return to the changing room. Set up a cooling station in the changing room.

- **During game:** Have cool drinks available pitch side. Do not use ice vests with substitutes; instead, keep substitutes shaded, at rest and hydrated. Try to get some air movement (fanning) over the substitutes' bench if possible. Hand-held fans and misting (clothes dampening) will help maintain comfort.

- **Halftime:** Use cooling strategies in the changing room as in pregame.

- **Postgame:** Avoid cold-water immersion; tepid water (30 to 33 degrees Celsius) immersion or showering is much less stressful. Maintain peripheral blood flow to deliver heat to skin rather than clamp it beneath a vasoconstricted shell. The goal here is to return body temperature to normal. Ensure fluid replenishment; see the sidebar 'ACSM Recipe for Fluid Replenishment'.

ACSM Recipe for Fluid Replenishment

Position statements from the American College of Sports Medicine include a recipe for fluid replenishment before, during and after exercise. The most recent statement (2007) suggests the following:

Preexercise

Any preexercise hydration should begin several hours early to allow fluid absorption and stabilization of urine output. Salted snacks or small meals can both stimulate thirst and help retain fluids.

During Exercise

Athletes need to develop a customized replenishment pattern to keep fluid losses to less than 2 per cent of preexercise body weight. Fluids with electrolytes can help sustain fluid and electrolyte balance and aid performance.

After Exercise

If time is sufficient, normal food and fluid intake will replenish body fluids. For more rapid replenishment (no time factor was presented), drink 1.5 litres per kilogram of weight lost (1.5 pints per pound). Doing this takes some time, so don't try to replenish all fluids lost in an hour. Consuming salty fluids, snacks or both can help by stimulating thirst and encouraging the body to retain ingested fluids. Intravenous fluids should be limited to conditions of extreme dehydration when medically necessary and supervised by a physician.

The available evidence provides abundant practical advice for the coach to minimize the potential issues of exercising in the heat. All coaches, athletes and parents need to be educated about heat illness.

Thirst is a poor indicator of dehydration, so fluid intake must be encouraged even when the player does not feel thirsty. Drinking to satisfy thirst may hold off dehydration, but it will not be enough to replace what has been lost.

Dehydration limits performance. Players lose strength and endurance with as little as 2 per cent weight loss because of dehydration, which can occur even before the player feels thirsty. Weigh before and after exercise to determine just how much fluid needs to be ingested.

Remember that humidity decreases the ability to lose heat. Sweat evaporates down a gradient. The greater the gradient is from the wet skin to the dry air (as in the desert), the faster the evaporation is. The smaller the gradient is (as experienced in humid areas such as the south-eastern United States, Southeast Asia, the Indian subcontinent and many others), the slower the heat loss is and the greater the rise in body temperature is, causing more oppressive playing conditions.

Fluid replacement takes time, sometimes 24 hours or more. Athletes who don't make the effort to rehydrate are at risk of being marginally dehydrated before they step on the field the next day. Research has shown as many as 40 per cent of players are dehydrated before training begins. Overloading the player with water, however, can dilute body sodium, which can be a real problem. Thinking that a player can prepare for the heat by drinking a lot of water before playing is a mistake.

Consuming extra salt is not necessary. Most athletes naturally salt food according to taste. Offering salt tablets or encouraging their consumption is unnecessary.

Choice of drink matters. Drinks with carbonation, such as commercial sodas, should be avoided. The carbonation makes people feel fuller sooner, so they consume less fluid. Choose water or a commercial fluid replenishment drink. Carbohydrate replenishment drinks are to be ingested following training. Discourage the use of so-called energy drinks that contain a lot of caffeine. High caffeine intake stimulates urination. Make water freely available during training and schedule fluid breaks every 15 to 20 minutes. Let the players drink until they quench their thirst. Don't force more volume. Instruct players to watch their urine colour. Closer to the colour of lemonade is good. Closer to the colour of apple juice means that more fluids are needed.

Wearing light clothing (in colour and weight) is recommended. Athletic clothing made of moisture management materials is common and is effective at helping the body evaporate sweat and speed heat loss. Old-style 100 per cent cotton clothing is a relic of sporting history. See 'High Tech Sports Clothing'.

High Tech Sports Clothing

For the January 1, 1969, Rose Bowl American football game, the Ohio State University team showed up wearing mesh jerseys. The university had done some research that showed how much their standard uniforms inhibited evaporative heat loss. Playing the end of their season in the cool Midwest meant that the players had lost much of the heat tolerance they gained in the hotter weather early in the season. The temperature in Southern California was hot that year, so Ohio State came prepared with jerseys that would help the players deal with the brief exposure to the California heat.

Since then, clothing has been modified to aid evaporation. The newest generation of clothing is made from moisture management fabric because the fluid evaporates from the new fibre faster than it does from cotton. The fibre has channels along its length (cotton is a round fibre) that expose far more (as much as 40 per cent more) surface area to the air, allowing faster evaporation of sweat. Coolmax and Dri-Fit are two of the most familiar of these new materials, but there are others. Although a little expensive, kits made from these materials are worth the cost. Today, athletic clothing made with 100 per cent cotton is rare because most major suppliers have shifted to one of the more modern materials.

Monitoring Training Intensity

Measuring the intensity of soccer is difficult; some work is extremely hard, and at other times the player is stationary. Running while dribbling is more intense than running the same speed without the ball. Heart rate or perceived exertion (Foster et al. 1996) can be used to monitor intensity. Both can be affected by external temperature. These methods are most accurate when training at temperatures of 15 to 25 degrees Celsius (about 60 to 75 degrees Fahrenheit). At higher temperatures, physiological and perceptual intensity tend to be higher; the same work feels harder when the heat leads to fluid lost in sweat. This upward drift varies significantly among people. When training at higher temperatures, expect heart rate and perception of effort to any exercise level to be higher. Adequate fluid replenishment during training is essential to avoid any impairment of training quality.

If possible, during spells of high heat or humidity vary the practice time to avoid the hottest and most humid times of the day, typically late afternoon. When temperatures are greater than 27 to 29 degrees Celsius (81 to 84 degrees Fahrenheit), reduce the volume and intensity of training. When temperatures are greater than 32 degrees Celsius (90 degrees Fahrenheit), consider cancelling training.

Acclimation to the heat can take up to 14 days. During this time, gradually increase training duration and intensity. About 75 per cent of the adaptation to heat occurs in the first 5 days. Encourage players to be active outdoors in the weeks preceding arrival to training camp. Ideally, they should be well adapted on arrival to the start of training, but make no assumptions. Begin slow and easy.

All these problems are magnified in children and the elderly. The symptoms of heat illness occur earlier in children and the elderly than in adults.

Training and Competing in the Cold

Normal body temperature is much closer to the body's thermal boiling point than it is to its thermal freezing point. Therefore, more emphasis is rightly placed on heat problems. In colder situations, behavioural choices (e.g., clothing choices and shelter) are effective at preserving heat. Most heat loss in the cold is conductive and convective, but other environmental factors, such as wind speed, solar radiation, and humidity, can influence heat loss. No single index indicates cold exposure like the WBGT does for heat exposure, but the wind chill index (WCI) is a familiar measure of cold stress. The WCI estimates the rate of cooling of a surface from the combined effects of temperature and wind. The 2014 chart from the National Oceanic and Atmospheric Administration (NOAA) in the United States displays two zones that show the ambient temperature and wind velocity that could cause exposed tissue to develop frostbite within 5 to 30 minutes (http://www.srh.noaa.gov/ssd/html/windchil.htm). By this chart, the danger of frostbite is small when the wind chill index is –22 degrees Celsius (–8 Fahrenheit) or higher.

The concept of wind chill might be sound, but the formulas are constantly debated and revised. Despite this, the WCI helps when making clothing decisions. The body responds to cold with overall peripheral vasoconstriction to shunt blood to the warmer core, and it increases the production of metabolic heat by shivering. But exercise increases metabolic heat production far more than shivering does. An odd dilation of the blood vessels of the extremities because of oscillating skin temperature makes the fingers and toes susceptible to cold injury, so gloves are common accessories for players. In addition, cold contributes to a decline in manual dexterity. Cold weather can also stimulate urine production (cold-induced diuresis) in part because of the redistribution of blood to the core. With the increased urine production, players need to be encouraged to drink fluids in the cold months, too. During exercise, blood is diverted away from the kidneys, helping to minimize this diuresis, but that mechanism doesn't negate cold-induced diuresis.

Another factor to consider is body fat, which acts as an insulator and limits heat loss. Those with more body fat tolerate cold better than their leaner counterparts do. In spite of the higher relative fat mass in women, they seem to have limited capacity to tolerate cold. As with heat, the elderly and the very young have a lower tolerance for the cold. See table 13.2.

From a practical viewpoint, matches played in the cold require players to make some decisions. Although Law 4 does not mention anything about clothing to accommodate play in cold weather, most referees make allowances for match conditions. For example, many players may choose to wear a ski band to protect the ears and gloves to protect the hands and fingers. Players usually reject a stretchable cap because it can be a nuisance during

Table 13.2 Adaptations to Training in the Cold

Adaptation	Exercise in the cold
Lower core temperature at the onset of sweating	Moderate
Increased heat loss through radiation and convection (skin blood flow)	Major
Increased plasma volume	Moderate
Decreased heart rate	Major
Decreased core body temperature	Moderate
Decreased skin temperature	Moderate
Increased sympathetic nervous system outflow (efferent)	Major
Increased oxygen consumption	Major
Improved exercise economy	Minimal

Adapted, by permission, from L.E. Armstrong, 1998, Heat acclimatization. In *Encyclopedia of sports medicine and science*. Edited by T.D. Fahey for the Internet Society for Sport Science. [Online]. Available: www.sportsci.org/encyc/heataccl/heataccl.html.

heading. Players may also want to wear a layer or two of clothing underneath their club jerseys; some modern high-tech athletic clothing has such a layer as part of the jersey. The layer closest to the skin should be made of a material that wicks sweat away from the skin to avoid excess skin cooling. Long training pants or running tights are not normally worn, but they do show up on some goalkeepers and referees.

Those most at risk for problems with the cold are the spectators who may dress improperly (insufficient clothing or not dressing in bulk), fail to drink or drink the wrong beverages (e.g., alcohol, which will accelerate the diuresis), are not exercising and may be relatively stationary for long periods in the cold.

Cold air affects heart rate response. When training at temperatures below 15 degrees Celsius (about 60 degrees Fahrenheit), the heart rate limits are reduced by about 1 beat per minute for each degree. An activity that leads to a heart rate of 170 becomes 160 when training at 5 degrees Celsius.

This reduction needs to be considered by teams that train using heart rate monitors. The poorly informed practitioner may see the lower heart rates as reduced effort by the players and try to raise the training stimulus. Knowing how the players view the training impulse (e.g., by perceived exertion) would support effort of training in spite of the lower heart rate.

Training and Competing at Altitude

Any increase in altitude leads to a reduced partial pressure of oxygen. The percentage of air that is oxygen remains the same, but the molecules are farther apart. Soccer can be contested at high altitudes such as Mexico City (approximately 2,500 metres above sea level) and La Paz (approximately 3,800 metres above sea level). During one group match in Toluca during the 1986 FIFA World Cup, the ball was in play for just over 45 minutes because of the combination of altitude and unusually high temperature. See table 13.3.

If the time in play is reduced, then the distance covered by players and teams is probably also reduced. At FIFA World Cup matches played at or above 1,200 metres, the distance covered both with and without the ball

Table 13.3 Defining Altitude

Altitude (metres above sea level)	Description	Impact
0 to 500	Near sea level	None
500 to 2,000	Low altitude	Minor impact on aerobic performance
2,000 to 3,000	Moderate altitude	Acclimatization necessary, acute mountain sickness possible
3,000 to 5,000	High altitude	Acclimatization required, acute mountain sickness likely for some, considerable reduction in aerobic performance
>5,000	Extreme altitude	Progressive deterioration with long exposure

declined by about 6 per cent, but top running speed was unaffected; when players want or need to sprint, they do. But they will need more time to recover between those high-speed runs because of the reduced oxygen consumption at altitude (Nassis 2013).

Altitude affects more than just the time in play and running performance; it can also affect the outcome of the match. McSharry (2007) compared 100 years of national team matches within South America to see just how much altitude affected soccer results. For example, when two South American national teams compete, the odds of the home team winning are 0.54, slightly better than 50–50. When the difference in altitude between home team stadiums is around 3,500 metres—for example, when Brazil (the altitude at Rio de Janeiro is 5 metres) travels to Bolivia (the altitude at La Paz is 3,760 metres)—the odds of a win by Bolivia increase to 0.825. But when Bolivia travels to Brazil, the odds of a win by Bolivia fall to 0.21. The goal difference in a match played by two teams from the same altitude (e.g., Brazil versus Argentina) is around 0.7. When Brazil travels to Bolivia, the goal difference favours Bolivia by about 2.2. In general, if the altitude difference is greater than 2,000 metres, the home side has a distinct advantage (Gore et al. 2008).

Altitude leads to a reduction in air resistance (or drag) and a reduction in oxygen transport by the blood, and it requires an acclimatization process. Endurance capacity begins to be affected at about 1,200 metres. With increasing altitude, the driving pressure of oxygen into the blood drops, reducing the amount of oxygen carried by the blood, the subsequent unloading of oxygen (because of a left shift of the oxyhaemoglobin curve) and the eventual delivery of oxygen to the working muscles. In a game like soccer, which has a large endurance component, the overall work output and intensity are affected.

10 Highest Altitude Capitals

La Paz, Bolivia: 3,760 metres (12,335 feet)

Quito, Ecuador: 2,850 metres (9,372 feet)

Bogota, Columbia: 2,580 metres (9,372 feet)

Addis Ababa, Ethiopia: 2,390 metres (7,841 feet)

Asmara, Eritrea: 2,340 metres (7,677 feet)

Thimphu, Bhutan: 2,300 metres (7,546 feet)

Sana'a, Yemen: 2,260 metres (7,415 feet)

Mexico City, Mexico: 2,230 metres (7,316 feet)

Kabul, Afghanistan: 1,800 metres (5,906 feet)

Johannesburg, South Africa: 1,770 metres (5,807 feet)

Highest Professional Soccer Stadium in the World

The highest stadium in the world is the Estadio Daniel A. Carrion in Cerro de Pasco, Peru. This stadium is located at an incredible 4,380 metres (14,370 feet) above sea level, and the temperature is rarely above 0 degrees Celsius (32 degrees Fahrenheit). Despite the altitude, the site is in a vibrant area of 70,000 people that supports a professional soccer team.

People can acclimate to altitude, but some planning is required. Realize first that exercise responses and time to acclimate vary significantly among people. One player might have some difficulty with moderate altitude (around 1,500 metres), whereas another might have little problem. One player might quickly adapt to altitude, but another might take twice as long. Fitness is no guarantee of protection against altitude sickness.

People can acclimate to altitude in a several ways. One is to arrive well in advance of competition to allow the body time to adjust to the lower partial pressure of oxygen. FIFA suggests that a team arrive one to two weeks in advance of competition (Bartsch, Dvorak and Saltin 2008). Living and training 24/7 at altitude will provide the most comprehensive stimulus for the body to adapt and minimize the potential effect of altitude.

But given club and country obligations, this travel schedule is impractical for all but long tournaments such as the FIFA World Cup. Some observers have advocated the separation of living and training altitudes. 'Live high, train low' suggests that athletes spend their resting hours at altitude and travel down to a more accommodating altitude for training. This way, training intensity can be maintained. Others have suggested the opposite so that the athlete's sleep and recovery periods are not limited. Currently, the best research evidence supports the 'live high, train low' programme (Levine and Stray-Gundersen 1997; Levine 2002).

A practical problem with such approaches is transit to and from training because the distances can be extreme, so attempts have been made to reproduce full or partial exposure to living at altitude with the use of so-called hypoxic tents or even hypobaric living conditions in specially constructed and pressurized structures that simulate altitude. Although these methods have shown promise, availability and expense tend to make such options impractical for all but the wealthiest clubs.

Chronic exposure to altitude stimulates the body to produce more erythropoietin to increase red blood cell production and improve oxygen carriage, delivery and use that ultimately improve exercise performance. Ventilation, haemoglobin concentration, capillary density, mitochondrial number and myoglobin (muscle's version of haemoglobin) all adapt to improve oxygen use. See table 13.4.

Table 13.4 Adaptations to Training at Moderate Altitude

Adaptation	Exercise at moderate altitude
Increased submaximal heart rate	Moderate
Increased submaximal ventilation	Moderate
Increased lactic acid production	Moderate
Increased red blood cell mass	Moderate to major
Reduced aerobic capacity	Major
Earlier onset of fatigue	Moderate
Poor sleep quality	Minimal to moderate
Increased thirst	Moderate

Adapted from L.F. Hallagan and E.C. Pigman, 1998, Acclimatization to intermediate altitudes. In *Encyclopedia of sports medicine and science*, edited by T.D. Fahey for the Internet Society for Sport Science. [Online]. Available: www.sportsci.org/encyc/heataccl/heataccl.html.

In general, on arrival at altitude, training volume and intensity should be reduced initially but be gradually increased over the following days and weeks. Players should be advised to get plenty of rest, drink plenty of fluids (the excess ventilation even at rest blows off extra water, and the humidity is usually low so sweat evaporates quickly) and eat (some will experience a transient reduction in appetite on arrival to altitude).

Collectively, the adaptations improve submaximal performance. As previously mentioned, the time to adaptation varies greatly among players. Most adaptations occur within one to two weeks, but some players may take much longer, and adaptations take longer at higher elevations.

Because acclimatization improves performance at moderate altitude, the team should arrive at the site of competition one to two or more weeks early. This practice will maximize adaptation while minimizing the potential detraining that can occur with reduced training intensity. But if time for acclimatization is not available, some players find that arriving close to the start of competition and then leaving right afterward seems to minimize the potential acute effects of altitude. This procedure has not been scientifically tested.

Other environmental factors (heat, humidity and so on) and changes in ballhandling and ball flight because of differences in aerodynamics may also play a role in reduced performance of players who live at sea level or low altitude and play at moderate to high altitude. The reverse is true for players who live at moderate or high altitude and play at lower elevations.

F-MARC recommended that teams arrive one week before matches to be played at moderate altitude (2,500 metres, or 8,200 feet) and two weeks before matches to be played at altitudes higher than 3,000 metres (9,800 feet) to adjust to the thin air. The *Scandinavian Journal of Medicine and Science in Sports* published the presentations in August 2008 (volume 18, supplement 1).

International Soccer at High Altitude

High altitude has been a thorn in the side of teams from Brazil for years. The Brazilian Football Confederation complained that national team matches in La Paz, Bolivia, left their players gasping for breath while the Bolivians seemed largely unaffected. CR Flamengo (Rio de Janeiro) said they would boycott matches at altitude after supplemental oxygen was required for players in a Copa Libertadores match at 4,000 metres (13,100 feet) in Bolivia. Other Brazilian clubs said they would follow Flamengo's lead.

In May 2007 FIFA issued a statement that effectively banned international matches at elevations above 2,500 metres (8,200 feet) because of concerns about player health and the unfair advantage benefitting the team acclimated to the higher elevation. As a result, countries like Bolivia, Ecuador and Columbia, among others, would no longer be able to host FIFA World Cup qualifying matches in their capitals. The ban was not well received. All CONMEBOL member nations except Brazil said they would ignore the ban and continue to schedule matches in locations at their own discretion. FIFA then raised the limit to 3,000 metres; La Paz was now the only capital above this revised limit.

In response to these complaints and association reactions, F-MARC (the FIFA Medical Assessment and Research Centre) convened the F-MARC Consensus Meeting on Football and Altitude in Zurich on 25 to 27 October 2007 and brought together international authorities on altitude and physical performance. This group concluded that players living at sea level or low altitude and competing at moderate to high altitude

- will have to cope with reduced aerobic performance,
- will find that their performance is affected beginning at 500 metres and that substantial impairment occurs at 3,000 metres and above and
- should not experience much effect on a single sprint but will require longer recovery periods between repeated sprints.

In addition, players living at moderate to high altitude who travel to compete at sea level or low altitude might experience some improvement in aerobic performance but disadvantages in the first days at sea level or low altitude.

CONMEBOL nations continued to protest, and FIFA suspended the ban in May 2008 to gain the opportunity to examine the effect of environmental extremes (e.g., altitude, heat, humidity, cold, air pollution).

A further consideration is training at altitude to enhance performance at sea level. Athletes have been known to train for a time at altitude and then go directly to sea level for competition. The thought is that the altitude training would enhance endurance performance at sea level. Researchers in studies have tried to determine the best mix of training and altitude on subsequent sea-level performance. Currently, the best model appears to be what is referred to as the 'live high, train low theory'. This concept combines the best of the adaptations from living at altitude (approximately 2,500 metres) with the ability to continue to train without reducing intensity at lower altitudes (at 1,250 metres or lower).

The logistics of daily travel make implementing the model challenging. In addition, some athletes may have sleep difficulties at moderate altitude. An alternative is the so-called hypobaric house, an airtight house at sea level in which the inside environment is controlled to simulate altitude. Training is then performed outside at sea level. Some people have tried a hypobaric tent that simulates moderate altitude for sleep. Research is continuing on this concept to determine the optimal time exposure to altitude. FIFA published the results of their consensus conference on altitude and soccer in the 2008 supplement to the *Scandinavian Journal of Medicine and Science in Sports* (volume 18, supplement 1).

Training and Competing in Air Pollution

Matches frequently occur in major cities, so another factor for the medical staff to consider is air pollution (table 13.5). Pollutants have both acute and chronic effects from mobile (e.g., vehicles) and stationary (e.g., industry) sources. Ozone, sulphur dioxide, carbon monoxide, lead and fine particulate matter all can affect normal respiration and exercise performance.

Although sensitivity to these various pollutants varies with the individual, players with a history of asthma or exercise-induced bronchospasm will likely be most susceptible to some respiratory reaction. And given the current estimates on the prevalence of asthma (about 8 per cent of the U.S. population; the figure varies by country) and exercise-induced bronchospasm (as high as 40 per cent of athletes in some studies), coaches are very likely to have players with one or the other at some point during their coaching careers. Therefore, an understanding of the effect of airborne pollutants is warranted (Rundell 2012). As surprising at it may sound, no research appears to have been published on the effects of air pollution on the performance of intermittent exercise, much less soccer specifically.

Table 13.5 Major Cities and Their Pollutants

City	Pollutants
Los Angeles, Sao Paulo, Mexico City, Houston	Ozone
Pittsburgh, Seoul, Prague, Beijing, Mexico City	Sulphur dioxide
Beijing, Shanghai, Bangkok, Mumbai	Particulate matter
Los Angeles, Athens, Mexico City, Moscow	Nitrogen dioxide
Mexico City	Carbon monoxide

Ozone

Ozone is the result of a photochemical reaction of the products of internal combustion engines. Ozone exposure can lead to coughing, sore throat, substernal pain with a deep breath and a tight feeling in the chest. Static lung function tests and exercise performance tests show decreased results at values well below the daily ozone values seen in cities such as Mexico City, Los Angeles and other locations that have a high density of automobile traffic. An inverse, curvilinear relationship is present between ozone concentration and the fraction of a maximal exhalation performed in one second (FEV1). Exposure to ozone does not appear to aggravate athletes with exercise-induced asthma, so the player with exercise-induced asthma should not expect to be affected by ozone any worse than other players are.

Carbon Monoxide

Carbon monoxide is also a product of internal combustion engines, as well as fires. Carbon monoxide combines with haemoglobin about 250 times faster than oxygen does, so loading oxygen onto haemoglobin is more difficult. The amount of oxygen carried, transported, and unloaded decreases, reducing endurance performance.

Sulphur Dioxide

Sulphur dioxide is the result of the combustion of fossil fuels (e.g., at coal- and oil-fired power plants) by refineries and by pulp and paper mills. Sulphur dioxide also forms acid aerosols and acid rain, but exposure to typical levels has little effect on respiration even in athletes working at very high intensities. Those with asthma, on the other hand, will likely experience bronchoconstriction and wheezing even with just a few minutes of exposure. Coaches and medical staff need to know which athletes have been diagnosed with asthma and be prepared for possible problems when they are exposed to sulphur dioxide.

Nitrogen Oxide

Nitrogen oxide is an exhaust emission that participates in the formation of ozone. On any given day, the levels have little, if any, effect on respiration or exercise performance. But exposure to nitrogen dioxide does increase respiratory illnesses in children.

Ozone and carbon monoxide can impair normal lung function and exercise performance. For those with asthma, other pollutants can trigger wheezing and reduce exercise performance, require frequent substitution (if allowed) or force cessation of exercise. The exposure to air pollutants that are a result of vehicular traffic is the highest near highways and dissipates with distance from traffic. When planning training (or competition, if possible), find a site distant from major highways and factories and train at periods of the day away from local rush hours. The body does not adapt to air pollution as it adapts to heat or altitude.

Travel Fatigue and Jet Lag

The human body operates on a 24-hour internal clock, or circadian rhythm, that is driven by external environmental cues such as sunlight and darkness. The clock guides feelings of alertness in the mornings and sleepiness at night, and it regulates bodily functions such as hunger and temperature. Travelling disrupts that rhythm because the environment and our internal schedule are not synchronized, leading to jet lag.

Soccer players are regularly called on to travel large distances to participate in competitive games. Teams may also participate in closed-season tournaments or friendly games overseas as part of preseason training. Such engagements are made possible by the speed of contemporary air flight. Although international travel is routine for many elite performers, it is not without issues for the travelling player, a circumstance that should be recognized in advance.

Circadian Rhythms and Sleep

In human beings a variety of physiological functions such as body temperature and heart rate undergo distinct rhythmic changes in the 24-hour period. Generally, the values are at their lowest during the night and reach their peak in the afternoon. This phenomenon is known as the circadian rhythm.

Humans often experience travel fatigue during long journeys. Even without crossing time zones, which brings about jet lag, fatigue can occur because of boredom or stiffness from unfamiliar seating and poor posture. Teams may want to travel several nights before competition to avoid fatigue and the detrimental effects of jet lag.

Because of the disruption of biological rhythms, jet lag arises mainly from crossing time zones. The body's rhythms on arrival try to retain the characteristics of their point of departure, but the new environment forces new influences on these cycles, the main factors being the time of sunrise and the onset of darkness.

Players may experience several jet lag symptoms:

- Fatigue during the new daytime yet inability to sleep at night
- Decreased mental performance
- Decreased physical performance
- Loss of appetite, as well as possible indigestion, nausea and bowel disturbances
- Increased irritability, headaches, mental confusion and disorientation

Generally, circadian rhythms affect performance, and the coach or practitioner must consider this when planning training and competition. Physical conditioning work should take place in the afternoon, leaving the morning session for skill work, especially because arousal levels and activities that depend on the central nervous system tend to peak around midday. A graded warm-up is useful in the morning to prevent injury to stiff joints and muscles (which are not yet at their optimum temperature).

Although people differ in the severity of symptoms they experience, many people simply fail to recognize how they are affected, especially in tasks requiring concentration, situation awareness and complex coordination. Therefore, wellness and performance monitoring should be built into the training schedule.

Internal (endogenous) circadian rhythms such as core temperature and other measures are relatively slow to adjust to new time zones. Complete adaptation of core temperature requires about one day for each time zone crossed. Sleep is likely to be difficult for a few days, but external (exogenous) rhythms such as activity, eating and social contact during the day help to adjust the sleep-wake rhythm. Arousal state adapts more quickly than does body temperature to the new time zone. Until the whole range of biological rhythms adjusts to the new local time and resynchronizes, players' performance may be below par.

The severity of jet lag is affected by factors besides individual differences. As the number of time zones travelled increases, the difficulty of coping with changes increases. A two-hour phase shift may have marginal significance, but a three-hour shift (e.g., British teams travelling to play opponents in Russia or American players travelling coast to coast within the United States) will cause desynchronization to a substantial degree.

In such cases the flight times—time of departure and time of arrival—may determine the severity of the symptoms of jet lag. Training times might be altered to take the direction of travel into account. Such an approach was shown to be successful in American football teams travelling across time zones within the United States and scheduled to play at different times of day (Jehue, Street and Huizenga 1993).

When journeys entail a two- to three-hour time-zone transition and a short stay (two days), staying on home time may be feasible. Such an approach is useful if the stay in the new time zone is three days or less and adjustment of circadian rhythms is not essential. This approach requires that the time of competition coincide with daytime on home time. If this is not the case, then adjustment of the body clock is required. A European team that is to compete in the morning in Japan or in the evening in the United States will require an adjustment of the body clock because these timings would otherwise be too difficult to cope with.

The administration of sleeping tablets or drugs (melatonin) does not provide an easy solution to preventing jet lag, and a behavioural approach can be more effective in alleviating symptoms and hastening adjustment (Reilly, Waterhouse and Edwards 2005).

The timing of exposure to bright light is key in implementing a behavioural approach. Light demonstrates a phase-response curve, opposing the effects of melatonin (Waterhouse, Reilly and Atkinson 1998). Exposure to natural or artificial light before the trough in core temperature promotes a phase delay, whereas a phase advance is encouraged by light administered after this time, meaning 'body clock time'.

Exposure to light at 10 p.m. in Los Angeles following a flight from London would promote a phase advance on the first night rather than the required phase delay, administration occurring after the trough in core temperature (Waterhouse et al. 2007). Where natural daylight cannot be exploited, artificial light from visors or light boxes can be effective for phase-shifting purposes. These commercially available devices have been used in treating seasonal affective disorder found among natives of northern latitudes during the winter seasons when the hours of daylight are limited.

Focusing on the local time for disembarkation can help in planning the rest of the daily activity. Natural daylight inhibits melatonin and is the key signal that helps to readjust the body clock to the new environment. Other environmental factors may need to be considered, such as heat, humidity and even altitude.

The direction of travel influences the severity of jet lag. Flying westward is easier to tolerate than flying eastward. On flying westward, the first day is lengthened and the body's rhythms can extend in line with their natural environment. A phase delay of the circadian rhythm is required after travelling westward, and visitors may be allowed to retire to bed early in the evening. Early onset of sleep will be less likely after an eastward flight. In this case, a light training session on that evening will add local clues into the rhythms.

Training in the morning is not recommended after a long haul, eastward flight because it exposes the person to natural daylight and could delay the body clock rather than promote the phase adjustment required in this circumstance.

Here are specific training and coaching recommendations for travel and jet lag:

- Exercise should be light or moderate in intensity for the first few days in the new time zone because training hard while muscle strength and other measures are impaired will not be effective.

- Skills training requiring fine coordination is also likely to be impaired during the first few days. Strenuous technical training sessions might lead to accidents or injuries.

- When a series of tournament engagements is scheduled, having at least one friendly competition before the end of the first week in the overseas country is useful.

- Naps should be avoided for the first few days because a long nap when the person feels drowsy anchors the rhythms at their former phases and therefore delays adaptation to the new time zone.
- Some precautions are necessary during adjustment to the new time zone. Alcohol taken late in the evening is likely to disrupt sleep and is not advised.
- Normal hydration levels may decline following the flight because of respiratory water loss in the dry cabin air, so fluid intake should be increased.
- A diet recommended for commercial travellers in the United States entails the use of protein early in the day to promote alertness and carbohydrate in the evening to induce drowsiness. This practice is unlikely to gain acceptance among soccer players, although they could benefit from avoiding large evening meals.

By preparing for time zone transitions and the disturbances they impose on the body's rhythms, the player can reduce the severity of jet lag symptoms. The disturbances in mental performance and cognitive functions have consequences not only for players but also for training and medical staff travelling with them, who are also likely to suffer from jet lag symptoms.

Air Travel and Fatigue

The long periods of inactivity during a plane journey may lead to the pooling of blood in the legs and cause deep-vein thrombosis in susceptible people. Moving around the plane periodically during the journey, perhaps every two hours, and doing light stretching exercises are recommended. Travellers should also drink about 15 to 20 millilitres of extra fluid per hour, preferably fruit juice or water, to compensate for the loss of water from the upper respiratory tract attributable to inhaling dry cabin air (Reilly et al. 2007). Without this extra fluid intake, the residual dehydration could persist into the early days in the new time zone.

Finally, flight strategies before departure, during the flight and on arrival should be implemented to ensure peak performance for the travelling soccer player. The following guidelines offer the player a suitable strategy:

Strategies before departure

- Practice drinking extra water during the week before departure. This regimen will form good habits as well as ensure that you are optimally hydrated before departure, which is crucial because you will experience some dehydration during the flight.
- Be sure to consume a high-carbohydrate diet during the week before departure. Doing so will help you optimize your body's carbohydrate

stores, which will be essential to enable you to complete the training and match schedule. Failure to do this may lead to mental and physical fatigue, as well as related symptoms such as muscle and stomach cramps, nausea and lack of concentration.

- Because the meals offered on the aeroplane may be limited, some snacks should be provided for you throughout the journey. You may wish to carry some snacks in your hand luggage.
- Bring plenty of things to occupy you on the trip to prevent boredom and boredom eating. Occupy yourself with books, games, magazines, music and films.
- Make sure that you pack any supplements or medication in your hand luggage so that you have enough for the entire journey.

Strategies during the flight

- Set your watch to local destination time as soon as you board the plane. This practice will enable you to tune in mentally to the new local time and adjust accordingly.
- Try to do activities that are appropriate for the destination time; you will need to wake up before landing. Mentally prepare yourself to do this, because your desire will be to sleep rather than wake up.
- Dehydration is a real problem during air travel, so you need to increase fluid intake throughout the flight. Avoid drinks containing caffeine, such as coffee, tea and colas during the first phase of the flight.
- You may feel stiff or cramped during the flight. You can perform some exercises whilst in your seat, but you should also walk down the aisle of the plane and do some flexibility and stretching exercises. You should do these sensibly for safety purposes and out of respect for the other passengers on the plane.
- Try to consume a high-carbohydrate meal as soon as possible on the flight. This meal will help to maintain your body's store of carbohydrate and increase sleepiness.
- If you are hungry or thirsty during the flight, ask one of the flight attendants or a member of the staff.

Strategies on arrival

- On arrival at the destination, mentally tune in to the new local time and adjust accordingly.
- If you arrive at the destination early in the evening, you should try to remain awake; otherwise, you will not be able to sleep during the night.
- When travelling eastward, avoid early morning light (6:30 to 10:30 a.m.). You should be exposed to light during the middle part of the day.

- Continue to keep hydrated by drinking plenty of fluid. Avoid caffeine during the evenings.
- Consume a high-protein meal and a cup of tea or coffee at breakfast on the first couple of days to promote alertness. Foods such as scrambled, boiled or poached eggs, yoghurt, milk, peanut butter, baked beans and porridge are all high in protein.
- During the first two or three days try to avoid prolonged (45- to 60-minute) naps in the afternoon because taking a nap may affect your ability to sleep at night.

Conclusion

Overall, no one can do much about the environment on any given training or match day. But several strategies, some behavioural, some physiological, can prepare players for training or competition in extreme environment conditions. The key is planning and advance preparation. By doing so, player health can be maintained and negative influences on physical performance can be minimized. Players and teams that do not plan will be approaching upcoming competitions with inadequate preparation and will be less likely to achieve a successful outcome. Plan and be rewarded.

CHAPTER 14

Nutritional Needs

—Mayur Ranchordas

The unique demands placed on players during soccer performance necessitate an adequate supply of energy for fuelling muscular activity as well as restoring metabolism during periods of formal and informal rest. The patterns of activity in soccer are characterized not only by an intermittent high-intensity workload but also by the contribution of motor skill performance and cognitive functioning. These psychomotor tasks are vital components of match play, and their successful execution often determines the result of the game. In addition, prolonged soccer exercise can cause pronounced thermoregulatory strain and induce considerable sweat losses that can lead to dehydration. Such an occurrence of dehydration may also result in deterioration in the performance of cognitive, attentional and psychomotor tasks. At the behavioural level, as mental and physical fatigue accumulates, the consequences of mistakes may also lead to increased risk of injury.

Following evidence-based nutritional practices can enhance athletic performance and recovery in soccer players. Because the physiological demands of soccer are challenging and vary greatly depending on the nature of training, environmental conditions, travel and playing schedules and intensity of play, sound evidence-based dietary practices should not be overlooked. Otherwise, performance and recovery may be compromised.

Coaches and soccer players are often assumed to have sufficient knowledge of nutrition to support training load, growth and development. The nutritional practices of a sampled group of young soccer players, however, demonstrated inadequate ability to fuel performance throughout training and match play (Russell and Pennock 2011). The authors recommended that youth soccer players ensure that their diets contain adequate energy through increased total caloric intake and derive the optimal proportion of energy from carbohydrate.

Note that this chapter is by no means exhaustive. Various performance nutrition areas can be expanded on in more detail. Nevertheless, this chapter covers the following:

- An overview of the energy requirements for training and match play
- Macronutrient and micronutrient requirements
- Fluid and electrolyte recommendations
- Special requirements for youth players
- The importance of nutrition for illness and injury
- Special circumstances such as nutrition for travel
- Special requirements for weight management
- Special requirements for youth players
- An overview on periodized nutrition
- The use of supplements and sport foods for soccer players

Practical recommendations on implementing some of the evidence in a professional setting will be provided along with some recommended menu plans.

Energy Expenditures

Energy expenditure in soccer varies greatly depending on the type of training being carried out, player position, environmental conditions, tactics and the nature of the match. Although the measurement of energy expenditure is complex and values vary depending on the methods used, several studies have estimated and measured total energy expenditure in soccer players using doubly labelled water, heart rate and activity record monitoring (Reilly and Thomas 1979; Rico-Sanz et al. 1998; Ebine et al. 2002; Ogsnach et al. 2010).

Mean energy expenditure for a match has been estimated to be approximately 4.63 megajoules (MJ) (Ogsnach et al. 2010), and 14.4 to 16 megajoules per day for daily training (Rico-Sanz et al. 1998; Ebine et al. 2002). See table 14.1. Note that energy expenditure varies greatly depending on factors such as size, body weight, type of training, environmental conditions and time of season. The use of heart rate monitors and, more recently, GPS systems

Table 14.1 Energy Expenditures in Professional Soccer

Study	Level	Participants	Conditions	Method	MJ	kcal
Rico-Sanz et al. 1998	Puerto Rican Olympic team members	n = 8 17 ± 2 years 63.4 ± 3.1 kg	Intense training	Activity record	16.0 per day	3,821 per day
Ebine et al. 2002	Japanese League professional players	n = 7 22.1 ± 1.9 years 69.8 ± 4.7 kg	Competitive season	Doubly labelled water	14.8 per day	3,535 per day
Ogsnach et al. 2010	Italian Seria A professional players	n = 399 27 ± 4 years 75.8 ± 5.0 kg	Competitive season	Theoretical model	4.63 per match	1,106 per match

can provide some estimation of energy expenditures (based on algorithms) for players during training. But accuracy can vary greatly among systems, and values should be interpreted with caution.

Full-time youth academy players (16 to 21 years) in many professional soccer clubs may have slightly higher energy expenditures than those reported in table 14.1 because they tend to train twice daily. The energy demands of training are augmented by the energy demands needed for growth and maturation. More recently, Russell and Pennock (2011) investigated the nutritional and activity habits of professional male soccer players who played for the youth team of a UK-based Championship club. All players recorded their seven-day dietary intake and activity habits during a competitive week that included a match, four training days and two rest days. In addition, players wore accelerometers 24 hours a day to estimate energy expenditure. Results from the study revealed that during heavy training (two sessions per day), a mean energy deficit of approximately 650 kilocalories per day was apparent. Therefore, the nutritional practices of these players were inadequate to support performance.

Coaches and practitioners must understand the amounts of work that players are undertaking. Underperformance may be caused by energy deficit and fatigue. A more appropriate understanding of energy demands of training, match play and general growth and development are required. Youth soccer players must have education support to sustain performance.

Here is a summary of some practical guidance to ensure that players are meeting energy needs.

Catering

Most professional soccer clubs provide breakfast and lunch to players, but little guidance is usually given on portion sizes and the amount of food to be eaten at meal times. A practical way to help players consume the correct number of calories daily is to present examples of correct portion sizes for breakfast and lunch. In addition, the chef could be instructed to provide meals and snacks that contain more carbohydrate 24 hours before a match. For recovery days after matches, the meals would contain more protein and carbohydrate.

User-friendly food labels or cards could be provided at the buffet to help educate players on which foods they should be eating. This approach is especially helpful at the academy level to educate and nurture younger players and encourage them to become more autonomous as they become older professional players.

A picture of what a typical plate should look like and information in the canteen can be varied depending on the type of training done that particular day. Special pictorial guidance can also be provided in the canteen for players who want to gain muscle mass or lose fat mass. Similarly, special guidance can be provided to injured players.

With the technological advances today, a high-definition TV in the dining hall can be used to educate players with specific nutrition messages tailored to the time of the week, such as to increase carbohydrate intake on match day.

Recovery Drinks and Snacks

For days when higher energy expenditures are present (i.e., two training sessions per day), players should be provided with additional snacks and recovery drinks to meet energy needs. These can be placed in the locker room or changing room.

Some players are poorly educated and prone to gaining fat mass. Appropriate education should be provided to these players.

Chef

Communication with the team chef is of paramount importance. Often the chef is not a sport nutrition expert. The sport nutritionist should establish a good working relationship with the chef. The support staff must coordinate with the chef to prepare the food provided based on the training done.

A close working relationship between the team chef and sport nutritionist can ensure that the catering meets the needs of the players. Players eat with the eyes, so the presentation of the food can be important in relation to what foods they chose to eat. This point is especially important for buffet-style catering.

Macronutrient Requirements

Macronutrient requirements for soccer players vary depending on the situation. A periodized approach to macronutrient intake is discussed in this section. For example, carbohydrate intake may be higher during preseason when players engage in two training sessions per day. Similarly, carbohydrate intake may be higher one day before a match. When training volume or intensity drops, however, carbohydrate intake should be lower. Similarly, protein requirements may be higher during periods of intense training, after a match, or when looking to increase muscle mass. Dietary fat typically remains unchanged, although it could be manipulated to alter energy balance when required.

Carbohydrate

Carbohydrate has four main roles in the body. The first is to act as a main energy source during high-intensity running in which glycogen is broken down into glucose (a process called glycogenolysis). Glucose is then used to create ATP through the process of glycolysis (oxidized to form water and carbon dioxide), which provides energy to the working muscle (Jeukendrup

2004). Second, carbohydrate helps to preserve important tissue proteins that are essential for muscular maintenance, repair and growth. Third, it provides an uninterrupted supply of fuel to the central nervous system as the brain metabolizes blood glucose. Finally, carbohydrate acts as a metabolic primer for fat oxidation (Burke, Kiens and Ivy 2004). The readily available carbohydrate sources are fairly limited (1,500 to 2,000 kilocalories), so this becomes a restrictive factor in the performance of prolonged training sessions (greater than 90 minutes) of submaximal or intermittent high-intensity exercise (Burke, Kiens and Ivy 2004).

The diet of elite soccer players must include strategies to fuel and refuel between matches and training sessions. The greater the intensity of the training session is, the more carbohydrate is required (see the section 'Periodized Nutrition' later in this chapter). The following recommendations have been adapted from Burke, Loucks and Broad (2006):

- Daily intake for recovery from training of low-intensity and moderate duration is 5 to 7 grams per kilogram per day.
- Daily intake for recovery from endurance training of moderate to heavy duration is 7 to 10 grams per kilogram per day.
- Intake one day before a match to increase muscle glycogen stores in preparation for the game is 8 to 10 grams per kilogram per day.

The total amount of carbohydrate that the athlete consumes per day is the most important dietary factor for replenishing glycogen stores. The following strategies are recommended to optimize carbohydrate intake and glycogen repletion:

- Before a training session or match, players should consume a high-carbohydrate meal (two to four hours beforehand) or a carbohydrate snack if this is not possible (30 to 60 minutes beforehand).
- During exercise lasting longer than one hour, players should consume 30 to 60 grams of carbohydrate per hour, which can be met by consuming a commercially available sports drink (discussed in the section 'Fluid and Electrolytes' later in the chapter).
- The highest rates of muscle glycogen storage occur in the first few hours (zero to four hours) following exercise. Therefore, 1 to 1.2 grams of carbohydrate per kilogram of body mass should be consumed each hour immediately after exercise.
- Foods with a high glycaemic index (GI) replenish glycogen stores more rapidly than low GI foods do, but the form of carbohydrate (solids or liquids) does not affect glycogen resynthesis.
- Under these recommendations, a 60-kilogram player would require 60 to 72 grams of carbohydrate per hour, which could be met by consuming

one litre of sports drink, four slices of white bread with jam, a bagel and a banana or two large bowls of cereal.

- If recovery time between sessions is limited, the coingestion of carbohydrate and protein (e.g. flavoured milk, beans on toast or tuna sandwich) may enhance glycogen storage, particularly during the first hour of recovery.

- Glycogen in fast-twitch Type IIa and Type IIb muscle fibres takes longer to replenish in comparison with glycogen in slow-twitch muscle fibres. Therefore, players should increase carbohydrate intake to 8 to 10 grams per kilogram of body mass per day on days when heavy training sessions are undertaken and after matches.

Fat

Although carbohydrate is the predominant source of fuel that is used during soccer, fat oxidation will also contribute to energy provision, particularly at the lower intensities. Although no studies have investigated the effects of high-fat diets on soccer-specific performance, other well-controlled studies do not support the use of high-fat diets (i.e., about 70 per cent of total energy intake) on performance (Muoio et al. 1994; Lambert et al. 1994; Burke and Kiens, 2006).

Conversely, no evidence supports the use of very low-fat diets (i.e., lower than 20 per cent of energy intake from fat). Moreover, avoiding or drastically reducing dietary fat consumption over the long term may compromise an athlete's health. Furthermore, low-fat diets can compromise the absorption of fat-soluble vitamins and reduce glycogen storage in the muscle.

The recommended amount of daily fat intake to ensure adequate intramuscular triglyceride stores for an athlete is 20 to 35 per cent of total energy intake. Approximately 10 per cent should come from saturated fat, 10 per cent from monosaturated fat and 10 per cent from polyunsaturated fat (Holway and Spriet 2011; Rodriguez et al. 2009). Dietary survey studies from soccer players on the proportion of energy from fatty acids have been reported to be 26 to 42 per cent (Holway and Spriet 2011).

The type of dietary fat intake should also be given some consideration. Athletes often neglect polyunsaturated fat, and some evidence suggests that in today's Western diet, the ratio of omega-6 to omega-3 fatty acids ranges from 10:1 to 20:1, which can be prothrombotic and proaggregatory, resulting in excess inflammation and impairment of postexercise recovery (Simopoulos 2007). Thus, players should aim for a diet that provides a ratio of omega-6 to omega-3 fatty acids of 1:1 to 2:1. This ratio can be achieved by minimizing foods high in omega-6 and increasing the consumption of foods high in omega-3, such as oily fish and nuts. A regular supply of foods high in omega-3 should be part of the daily menu plan.

Protein

Protein is made up of a combination of amino acids. Some protein, such as alanine, serine and glutamic acid, can be synthesized within the body. But we are unable to synthesize many essential amino acids, such as leucine, lysine and tryptophan. Therefore, adequate protein must be ingested in the daily diet to maintain protein synthesis and adequate recovery. Protein is used primarily to promote muscle fibre repair, regeneration and growth (Tipton and Wolfe 2004), but it can also be used as an energy source if carbohydrate and fat sources have been reduced significantly.

Protein is essential for muscle growth and repair, a functional immune system (Nieman and Bishop 2006; Tarnopolsky 2004) and a host of other physiological functions. The vast majority of athletes, both male and female, consume protein in excess of their biological requirements (Rosenbloom, Loucks and Ekblom 2006). The recommended dietary protein intake for endurance athletes is 1.2 to 1.4 grams per kilogram per day and is 1.2 to 1.7 grams per kilogram per day for strength and speed athletes (Stear 2006). Soccer players routinely undertake all these training practices, and dietary intake studies have reported that female soccer players consume protein in adequate amounts (1.3 to 1.4 grams per kilogram per day) throughout the preseason and competitive season (Clark et al. 2003; Mullinix, Jonnalagadda and Rosenbloom 2003). Providing that energy needs are met, reaching the recommended protein requirements is not difficult, and they can be met through food alone in most cases. Nonetheless, if the diet is severely restricted, either in energy intake or dietary variety, then there is a risk that protein needs may not be met (Stear 2006).

The timing of the consumption of protein can affect the ability of an athlete to adapt to a training stimulus. Resistance-training adaptations may be more effective if a small amount of protein (approximately 6 to 10 grams) is ingested immediately (within 15 minutes) before the session (Stear 2006). Thirty grams of lean meat or poultry, 200 grams of yogurt, 300 millilitres of milk or three slices of bread can provide 10 grams of protein.

Protein is also required following training and match play. Research has reported that the window of opportunity is wider for protein recovery than it is for glycogen repletion to promote a positive nitrogen balance across the active muscles and to stimulate protein synthesis (Tipton and Wolfe 2004).

Menu Plans

The following menu plans have been created to provide practitioners practical examples on how to achieve appropriate macronutrient requirements for training and match play. The menu plans provide a wide selection of the foods required to fuel performance. These recommendations are relevant in a team setting and may be used as templates that can be delivered on the road and in a hotel environment. Educational materials such as posters, banners and even printed plates that outline portion sizes can help educate players on what portions of macronutrients to choose. These materials can be tailored to the nature of the training session carried out.

Menu 1: Standard daily breakfast

Selection of fresh juices

Selection of bran-based, no-sugar cereals (Special K, Weetabix, Bran Flakes or Oaty Bix; no chocolate coated or puffed cereals)

Wholemeal bread, toast, grilled mushrooms, low-sugar baked beans, Bircher-style ready-mixed muesli (with milk already added), hot porridge

Cooked smoked ham or parma ham, marinated chicken pieces, smoked salmon slices

Fresh green salad

Fresh sliced or whole fruit or fruit salad in natural juice, natural yogurt, honey, low-fat yogurts (0 per cent fat Greek style)

Low-sugar jams, marmalade, selection of nut butters, organic butter

Drinks station: green tea, peppermint tea, coffee, tea (breakfast), jugs of cold low-fat milk

To be alternated daily: omelettes, scrambled eggs with spring onions and spinach, poached eggs

Equipment: blender

Menu 2: Evening meal the night before a game

Minestrone soup with smoked bacon

Salmon and cauliflower bake

Thai green chicken curry

Honey roasted vegetables with pesto and pine nuts

Sweet potato mash

Asparagus, green peas and carrots

Mixed leaf salad with chopped salad items

Thai prawn salad with Asian vegetable and sweet chili sauce

Cold meat platter to include ham, turkey, pastrami and pickles

Fresh fruit salad

Baked bananas with pistachios, sultanas, and low-calorie custard

Basket of wholemeal and granary bread

Extras: olive oil, parmesan cheese, light salad dressings, classic vinaigrette, tabasco sauce, tomato ketchup

Menu 3: Pregame meal

Roasted carrot soup

Mixed prefilled (choice of two wet fillings) wholemeal tortilla wraps

Fresh ham and sliced light cheese (edam, gorgonzola) platter with green salad and salad items with homemade light dressings and vinaigrettes

Foil-cooked parcels of chicken breasts with bok choy or other Asian vegetables

Wholemeal pasta and two sauce choices (one tomato and one meat, such as chunks of chicken as a meat base); sauces served in separate dishes to the pasta

Wholemeal pancakes with syrup, natural yogurt and dried fruits

Whole fruit (apples, bananas)

To be available: wholemeal toast and butter, mixed spreads including peanut butter

Drinks station: herbal tea, coffee, breakfast tea, jugs of cold water with slices of lime on tables

Menu 4: Early kick-off game-day menu

Cereal station: selection of bran-based, no-sugar cereals (Special K, Weetabix, Bran flakes or Oaty Bix; no chocolate coated or puffed cereals)

Wholemeal bread, toast, wholemeal pita breads or seeded bagels

Bircher-style ready-mixed muesli (with milk already added) and hot porridge with honey and dried fruits

Accompaniments: high-quality jams, Manuka or organic honey, marmalade, cottage cheese with walnut halves added and organic butter

Cold meat and self-serve area: cooked smoked ham or parma ham, Thai or coconut marinated chicken pieces and smoked salmon slices; all cold meat served on a bed of fresh salad with homemade salsa in the middle in a manikin bowl

To be available: extra virgin olive oil and aged balsamic vinegar, fresh fruit salad (limit citrus fruits), Greek yogurt, selection of Trek Bars and Muller Rice

Hot service area: omelettes or scrambled eggs with light crème fraiche and chives (cooked on demand in the eating area on a mobile unit), grilled mushrooms and grilled tomatoes

Drinks station: organic flavoured milkshakes or For Goodness Shakes, green tea, peppermint tea, coffee, tea (breakfast), jugs of cold low-fat milk, pots of espresso or one-touch easy-to-operate espresso machine; no fruit juices

Micronutrient Requirements

Vitamins and minerals play an important role in the body because many are precursors for various processes. Potential deficiencies can compromise performance. There is no evidence to suggest that soccer players have an increased requirement for micronutrients; therefore, if players are following an adequate and balanced diet, additional vitamins and minerals are not required. In special circumstances, such as for players who are following a negative energy balance for weight management purposes or for players who avoid or eliminate large food groups, use of a standard multivitamin supplement that is batch tested under the guidance of a qualified sport nutritionist or dietitian may be appropriate over a short period to ensure that 100 per cent of the recommended dietary allowance (RDA) for all micronutrients is met.

In a study of youth soccer players, Russell and Pennock (2011) reported that the intake of fibre was significantly lower than the recommended nutrient intake (RNI) values, whereas all other analysed micronutrients met or exceeded recommended values. This finding supports the concept of providing more structure to these players using education about types of foods consumed in snacks, pre-event fuelling and postrecovery meals. The provision of nutrient-rich foods as well as adequate carbohydrate and protein is therefore essential in facilitating optimal performance in young athletes.

Soccer players commonly eat breakfast and lunch at their training grounds. Therefore, certain food provision strategies such as making fresh fruit and vegetable juices available for breakfast and providing an adequate supply of a variety of vegetables and salads at lunch can encourage players to increase the micronutrient content of their diets. Note that most breakfast cereals are fortified; a medium bowl of breakfast cereal would typically provide approximately 40 per cent of the recommended daily micronutrients.

Soccer players also normally have blood tests during preseason. Certain important micronutrients should be measured, such as iron stores and vitamin D. Indeed, micronutrient deficiency, particularly vitamin D, has attracted growing interest in recent years (Owens, Fraser and Close 2015; Moran et al. 2013). Vitamin D is primarily synthesized endogenously following exposure to ultraviolet radiation. Apart from its effect on calcium homeostasis and bone metabolism, vitamin D has been found to influence physical performance and muscle strength (Owens, Fraser and Close 2015; Moran et al. 2013). It follows that vitamin D would have an effect on soccer performance such as repeated sprints, jumps, turns and explosive changes of direction. Paradoxically, a growing number of studies report a high prevalence of vitamin D deficiencies even in regions with extensive sunlight (Hamilton 2010; Maïmoun et al. 2006). Given that soccer is played over a long season that includes large fluctuations in sunlight, players should be screened regularly. When necessary, diets should be supplemented with appropriate doses of vitamin D (see also the section 'Vitamin D').

Fluid and Electrolytes

Fluid balance and electrolyte balance are crucial factors for optimal exercise performance, including soccer performance. Because soccer is played in a variety of climates and environmental conditions, sweat rates and electrolyte losses vary greatly (see also chapter 13).

Providing specific fluid and electrolyte recommendations is challenging. Furthermore, interindividual variability is large. A one-size-fits-all approach is not recommended. Nonetheless, this section will provide an overview of the fluid and electrolyte recommendations for soccer players.

Maughan and colleagues (2004) recorded sweat losses of 2,033 plus or minus 413 millilitres in 24 professional Premier League players from England over a 90-minute preseason training session during which the temperature was 24 to 29 degrees Celsius and the relative humidity was 46 to 64 per cent. Electrolyte losses were measured using sweat patches across four sites; mean sodium losses were 49 plus or minus 12 millimoles per litre, potassium losses were 6.0 plus or minus 1.3 millimoles per litre, and chloride losses were 43 plus or minus 10 millimoles per litre. This equates to a salt loss of 5.8 plus or minus 1.4 grams. In a similar study, Maughan and colleagues (2005) reported mean sweat loss of 1,690 plus or minus 450 millilitres during a 90-minute training session in cool conditions (5 degrees Celsius, 81 per cent relative humidity) in 17 elite soccer players from the Dutch Premier Division. Mean sodium and potassium losses in sweat measured by sweat patches was 42.5 plus or minus 13 millimoles per litre and 4.2 plus or minus 1.0 millimoles per litre, respectively, and mean total salt lost was 4.3 plus or minus 1.8 grams. When 31 players from the English Premier League were measured in a similar cool environment of 6 to 8 degrees Celsius and relative humidity of 50 to 60 per cent, mean sweat losses of 1,680 plus or minus 400 millilitres were recorded (Maughan et al. 2007). Sweat sodium concentration was 62 plus or minus 13 millimoles per litre, and total sweat sodium loss was 2.4 plus or minus 0.8 grams.

In warmer conditions when temperatures of 32 plus or minus 3 degrees Celsius and relative humidity of 20 plus or minus 5 percent were recorded, sweat rates of 2,193 plus or minus 365 millilitres have been reported in 26 male professional soccer players during a 90-minute preseason training session (Shirreffs et al. 2005). Mean electrolyte losses collected by patches for sodium, potassium and chloride were 67 plus or minus 37 millimoles per litre, 3.58 plus or minus 0.56 millimoles per litre and 8 plus or minus 2 millimoles per litre, respectively.

In the studies in which fluid balance has been measured, consistent findings suggest that players do not ingest fluid to match sweat rates, indicating that from a practical perspective, players should try to rehydrate after training but also start training hydrated. Because sweat rates and electrolyte losses vary among players, a practical strategy would be to weigh players appropriately (in underwear to account for sweat absorbed on clothing) before and after training, taking into consideration fluid intake. Ideally, electrolyte losses would be measured by suitably qualified sport science personnel. But if the team budget does not permit use of this procedure, "salty" sweaters can typically identify salt residue visible on the training kit.

Hydration status can be measured in various ways, including hematocrit, plasma osmolality and urine osmolality. Some of these tools, however, are not practical in the real world. Although plasma osmolality remains the most accurate physiological biomarker to measure hydration status, it is not practical in the field. Other noninvasive methods such as urine osmolality can be useful tools if the data are interpreted appropriately by suitably qualified sport science personnel.

From a practical perspective, the sport science support team needs to create an environment that offers players the opportunity to ingest fluid, such as by placing water bottles around the training ground.

Table 14.2 summarizes some practical guidance to ensure adequate hydration levels are maintained on a daily basis.

Table 14.2   Practical Recommendations for Fluid and Electrolyte Intake

Scenario	Practical recommendations
Opportunities to rehydrate	Place individual water bottles in player lockers so that players have an opportunity to ingest fluids while dressing. During hotter temperatures, such as preseason training (typically in July), this drink may contain additional electrolytes. Provide access to drink bottles in various rooms around the training ground such as the gym, treatment rooms, canteen and changing rooms. During training, individually labelled drink bottles allow support staff to gauge the amount of fluids ingested by a player and minimize the occurrence of sharing bottles, which can spread the risk of infection. This procedure can also allow a bespoke rehydration strategy whereby players with greater sweat or electrolyte losses could have an individualized drink.
Measuring hydration status	Players could be randomly spot checked before training by providing a urine sample measured by a portable osmometer. Support staff could check hydration status 24 hours before a game and advise players on their fluid intake.
Sweat testing	Various field methods are available such as sweat patch testing and portable devices. Although various issues arise with validity and reliability, guidance from a suitably qualified sport nutritionist and physiologist can help ensure that data are collected accurately. This testing can be scheduled during the preseason, and data on sodium, potassium and magnesium can be used to provide bespoke drinking guidelines.
Types of drinks	Add effervescent electrolyte tablets to water bottles. Use flavoured water. Coconut water contains high levels of electrolytes and can be used before and after training. Coconut water may also be used during travelling. Isotonic drinks (6 to 7 per cent carbohydrate) can be used during training sessions that last 90 minutes or longer. Hypotonic drinks (2 to 4 per cent carbohydrate) can be used before, during and after training sessions because these drinks typically contain electrolytes but lower amounts of carbohydrate.

Young Soccer Players

Most professional teams run soccer academies at which young adolescent players ages 6 to 18 years are coached and nurtured through the age groups. Although providing specific nutritional guidance for the various age groups is complex and limited research has examined the recommendations for academy players, this section discusses certain specific requirements that should be considered.

Nutrition requirements for young adolescents should not be overlooked because meeting appropriate dietary needs is central to growth, maturation, recovery from training and, ultimately, optimal performance. A poor diet in conjunction with increased energy expenditure and an arduous training schedule can significantly increase the risk of injury, impair adaptation to training, increase fatigue and negatively affect growth and maturation.

The following recommendations provide practical guidance to ensure appropriate nutrition for young soccer players.

Educating Players, Parents and House Parents

Young soccer players should receive education through engaging interactive workshops delivered throughout the season. An educational curriculum should run throughout various age groups during the season and cover various aspects of sport nutrition including hydration, recovery nutrition, fuelling for training and matches and eating like a professional athlete. These topics are central to creating an autonomous and educated young player.

Parents and house parents (if players are away from home) commonly provide snacks, pack school lunches and produce evening meals. Therefore, they need to understand the dietary needs of the young soccer player. Educational workshops, booklets and newsletters that explain important points can be used to educate parents and house parents.

Feeding and Hydrating Academy Players

Full-time academy players (16 to 21 years old) are usually provided with breakfast and lunch at the training complex. Sport science support staff should ensure that a selection of breakfast cereals, porridge, milk, yogurts, eggs, bread, fruit and nuts is available for breakfast. Similarly, adequate good-quality portions of protein, carbohydrate and fruits and vegetables should be available for lunch. The macronutrient composition of the menu can be changed depending on the training or match schedule.

Promoting the Use of Milk

Educating young soccer players on the importance of milk for growth, recovery and hydration can help their development through the academy. Often young players train twice daily, and lunch is typically provided, but provision of food after the second training session may be limited. In these cases, strategic use of milk and milkshakes can be an effective strategy to promote recovery (James 2012; Cockburn, Bell and Stevenson 2013; Volterman et al. 2014), muscle growth (Phillips, Tang and Moore 2009) and rehydration (James 2012) because milk is high in protein, carbohydrate and electrolytes.

Nutrition for Illness and Injury Prevention

Players can lose several weeks of the year through illness and injury. Sport science staff should provide the necessary education and support to players to reduce the incidence of illness and injury and help support players in recovering from injuries with evidence-based nutritional interventions.

Upper respiratory tract infections (URTIs) can be detrimental to soccer players because they impair training time, volume and intensity and could cause players to miss important matches. Although preventing players from

Other Interventions

Use of Antibacterial Hand Gel

Infectious bacteria can remain on door handles and surfaces for extended periods. Using antibacterial hand gel before and after contact with public places can help kill some of the bacteria.

Provide antibacterial hand gels around the training ground to ensure adequate hand hygiene. Use antibacterial hand gels when travelling. Educate players and staff regarding the importance of washing hands regularly and the link between hand hygiene and spreading of infections. Players and staff should not share drinks bottles or any other items such as toiletries that can spread the risk of an infection.

Sleep

Evidence is conflicting regarding sleep and immunity in athletes, but there does seem to be some agreement that sleep deprivation over prolonged periods will suppress the immune system (Irwin et al. 1994). The evidence indicates that acute bouts of sleep deprivation (i.e., three consecutive days) will not increase the incidence of getting an infection, but little is known about longer-term sleep deprivation.

Some evidence indicates that sleep deprivation suppresses the immune function. Typically, players suffer from poor sleep patterns on match days, particularly for games that have an evening kick-off time. Similarly, soccer players travel frequently, and the hectic nature of travel can disrupt sleep. The day after an evening match, players could report for a recovery session later in the day to promote more hours of sleep. Montmorency cherry juice consumption may increase melatonin levels, thus promoting sleep (Howatson et al. 2012).

getting ill is impossible, many interventions can reduce the risk of getting infections and enhance health.

Probiotics

Emerging evidence suggests that probiotics may help protect immunity in athletes (West et al. 2009). Some research conducted in athletes has demonstrated promising results, but more data are needed. An important feature of probiotics is that the effect is strain specific. In other words, not all probiotics have the same effect. West et al. (2009) reported that 11 weeks of probiotic supplementation reduced the number of episodes, the duration and the severity of infection in males but not in females. These authors found that taking a probiotic drink containing the L-Casei Shirota strain (one in the morning and one in the evening) over a 4-month period in the winter helped protect the immune system in athletes. Note that this study was well controlled because 84 well-trained endurance athletes took part and the group receiving the probiotic drink had 50 per cent fewer episodes of infection (probiotic 1.2 plus or minus 1.0, placebo 2.1 plus or minus 1.2). This result suggests that taking two servings of a probiotic drink containing the L-Casei Shirota strain over the winter months may be beneficial in promoting immune function.

Certain probiotics can be made available for players during intense periods of training such as preseason or during weeks when back-to-back matches are played. These probiotics can be made available in the canteen area.

Carbohydrate

The evidence supporting the use of carbohydrate is convincing (Walsh et al. 2011). When blood glucose levels fall during exercise, stress hormones rise, which can impair immune function. Maintaining blood glucose levels during exercise can lower stress hormones and thus immune dysfunction. When exercising for longer than 45 to 60 minutes, 60 grams of carbohydrate should be consumed for every hour of exercise. This intake of carbohydrate can dampen the immune inflammatory response. Carbohydrate consumed through either a sports drink or solid foods such as cereal bars should be sufficient. Similarly, a recovery drink should be consumed immediately after training. For most activities lasting 60 minutes or longer, a 250-millilitre serving of low-fat milk or a low-fat milkshake is appropriate.

Players should ingest 30 to 60 grams of carbohydrate during intense training sessions to reduce the incidence of infections during heavy periods of training and matches.

Vitamin D

Some evidence suggests that athletes have insufficient levels of vitamin D (Hamilton 2010; Maïmoun et al. 2006). Moreover, clinical studies have provided evidence on the association of vitamin D insufficiency and respiratory tract infections (Ginde, Mansbach and Camargo 2009). Athletes should have their vitamin D levels tested and take an appropriate supplement dose to correct any insufficiencies. Practical advice regarding vitamin D is complex, so coaches and practitioners alike should seek professional advice regarding vitamin D.

Zinc

A recent systematic review by Singh and Das (2011) found that taking zinc syrup, tablets or lozenges might lessen the severity and duration of the common cold. These authors conducted a systematic review of the available scientific evidence and reported that taking zinc within a day of the onset of cold symptoms facilitates recovery. They also found that zinc could help ward off colds. A note of caution here is that long-term zinc use can become toxic and excessive amounts of zinc can cause nausea, vomiting, abdominal pain and diarrhoea. Therefore, sensible advice is to take zinc lozenges at the onset of cold symptoms. The amount of zinc added to lozenges is unlikely to be excessive. Note that the recommended upper limit of zinc is 11 milligrams per day. Also note that taking zinc in amounts higher than the RDA is not recommended. In other words, taking more zinc through supplements may not necessarily prevent an infection, but it could be toxic.

The following supplements have been shown to have no effect on immune function and are therefore not supported by sound clinical evidence in preventing illness:

- Vitamin C: no better than a placebo
- Vitamin E unless there is a deficiency
- Multivitamin: not supported in the literature
- Glutamine: conflicting evidence
- Branch chain amino acids (BCAA)
- Herbal supplements (e.g., ginseng, echinacea).
- Fish oils and omega-3

Large increases in training volume and intensity are also linked to immune dysfunction. Therefore, coaching and sport science support staff should consider this point when devising training schedules.

Some foods and other factors may compromise immune function:

- Constant temperature changes
- Poor basic hygiene
- Poor sleep
- Being around ill people
- Dehydration

- Sharing drinking glasses or bottles
- Cakes, biscuits, pastries, fast food (especially during recovery periods)

Nutrition and Travel

Soccer players are frequent travellers because of the nature of the fixture list, and professional soccer players who play in major international competitions will face weekly trips that may involve long travel times that can cause fatigue. Having access to nutritious balanced meals and adequate fluid can be challenging, but ample planning of meals, snacks and fluids can enhance a soccer player's diet when travelling.

The pressurized cabins on an aeroplane can cause more fluid than normal to be lost from the lungs and skin, which increases the risk of dehydration. Water or no-added-sugar squashes are generally the best choices for most athletes. Moreover, athletes should always take their own supply of fluids on board rather than rely on cabin service.

A change in climatic conditions can also upset normal eating and drinking patterns. Therefore, athletes should be encouraged to keep to their usual routine as much as possible.

Finally, long hours of travelling can upset the digestive system. Low-fibre meals combined with humid conditions and being seated for long periods can cause the gut to become sluggish. To minimize constipation, athletes should be encouraged to drink lots of fluid and eat fibre-rich foods such as fresh fruit, breakfast cereals and vegetables.

Infection and Illness

Travelling increases the risk of infection and gastrointestinal disturbance, more so if traveling abroad. Using antibacterial hand gels and washing hands often can minimize some risk. In addition, the use of probiotics can also be useful in some instances.

Catering

Each hotel and kitchen has its own way of preparing meals, and the result may not match expectations. Communication about menu plans, possible recipes and specific snack items may be useful. Team chefs should travel with teams to look after the food provision and to liaise with the chefs at the team hotel.

Food and Water Hygiene

In some countries, drinking tap water is ill advised, and foods such as fruit, vegetables, salads and ice cubes could pose a risk. Players should stick to drinking sealed bottled water and avoid swallowing water when brushing teeth or showering. Food should be washed with clean water that is not contaminated.

Eating on the Move

Travel poses uncertain issues such as delay and availability of food. Therefore, the team should ensure that snacks and meals are preplanned. Communicating with travel companies and hotels and prepacking food items are important.

Weight Management

The principles of weight management remain the same regardless of the sport. This section focuses on general methods for weight gain or weight loss, but they will be put into the context of soccer and the best way to achieve weight management in the soccer environment.

Note that weight change is best accomplished during the off-season or a period outside competition to prevent any potential adverse effects on performance. Manipulating body composition takes time, so the practitioner needs to devise appropriate weight management goals with athletes.

During periods of heavy training, players must consume adequate energy to replenish muscle glycogen stores. Some players lose weight if they consume inadequate energy during periods of intensive training. The following sample menu plan illustrates the type of meals needed for times of hard training.

Menu for Hard Training

Breakfast

Day 1: super berry porridge and protein shake

Day 2: scrambled egg on toast

Morning Snack

Day 1: smoked salmon and cream cheese bagel

Day 2: recovery shake

Lunch

Normal balanced meal, such as chicken breast with new potatoes and steamed vegetables

Afternoon Snack

Day 1: recovery shake

Day 2: fruit smoothie with 20 grams of whey protein

Dinner

Day 1: beef and super vegetable stir-fry

Day 2: Mediterranean fish stew

Supper

Day 1: casein shake

Day 2: low-fat yogurt

Weight Gain

Weight gain through increasing skeletal muscle mass (hypertrophy) is often advantageous in soccer for certain players. To increase weight, an athlete must achieve a positive energy balance; muscle hypertrophy occurs only when muscle protein synthesis exceeds the rate of protein breakdown for a prolonged period (Koopman et al. 2007). Off-season or periods of less endurance training might be the best time to increase muscle mass.

The two principle determinants of skeletal muscle protein synthesis in adults are physical activity and nutrient availability (Atherton and Smith 2012).

Increasing protein ingestion to approximately 2 grams per kilogram per day and performing the appropriate training, particularly resistance exercise, promotes an optimal anabolic environment in skeletal muscle compared with either stimulus alone (Breen and Phillips 2012). The addition of protein ingestion following a bout of resistance exercise has repeatedly been shown to augment the stimulation of muscle protein synthesis, which, over a period of resistance training with increased protein consumption, can lead to muscular hypertrophy. The anabolic effects of nutrition are driven by the transfer and incorporation of amino acids captured from dietary protein sources into skeletal muscle proteins. The amino acid leucine has been highlighted to be particularly important in stimulating protein synthesis and appears to have a controlling influence over the activation of protein synthesis (Volpi et al. 2003). As such, rapidly digested leucine-rich proteins such as whey, in conjunction with resistance exercise, is advised for those wishing to increase muscle mass. In terms of protein quantity, 20 to 25 grams of high-quality protein with at least 8 to 10 grams of essential amino acids (Phillips 2011) has been shown to maximize exercise-induced rates of muscle protein synthesis in healthy young adults (Moore et al. 2009). In total, athletes are advised to consume about 1.6 to 2 grams per kilogram per day consumed as four meals while attempting to gain weight by increasing muscle mass (Phillips and van Loon, 2011).

To increase muscle mass, athletes should perform two or three resistance sessions in the afternoon to stimulate protein synthesis. Immediately after resistance training, 25 grams of whey protein with 3 to 4 grams of leucine should be consumed. Athletes should take 25 grams of casein protein before bedtime to stimulate protein synthesis. Each main meal (i.e., breakfast, lunch, dinner) should contain 25 grams of protein. Taking 5 grams of creatine supplementation can enhance muscle hypertrophy. A positive energy balance of 500 kilocalories per day is required, and protein intake should be about 2 grams per kilogram per day.

Menu for Hypertrophy

Breakfast

Day 1: super berry porridge, two pieces of toast with honey, protein shake

Day 2: scrambled eggs on toast, glass of milk, two pieces of fruit

Training Morning and Afternoon

Gatorade during sessions

Morning Snack

Day 1: salmon and cream cheese bagels

Day 2: recovery shake

Lunch

Normal meal such as chicken breast with new potatoes and steamed vegetables, fruit juice or milk to drink, fresh fruit and yogurt for dessert

Afternoon Snack

Day 1: recovery shake

Day 2: fruit smoothie with 20 grams of whey protein

Dinner

Day 1: lentil soup, beef and super vegetable stir-fry, brown rice protein pancakes

Day 2: chicken salad, Mediterranean fish stew, potatoes, fruit and low-fat custard

Supper

Day 1: casein shake

Day 2: low-fat yogurt

Weight Loss

Weight loss is not an uncommon goal for soccer players, and performance issues are often the motivation. Excess fat is usually detrimental to performance in soccer because players are engaged in activities requiring the transfer of body mass either vertically (such as in jumping) or horizontally (such as in running). Excess fat adds mass to the body without providing any additional capacity to produce force. Excess fat can also be detrimental to performance through increasing the metabolic cost of running, which requires movement of the total body mass. Moreover, excess body fat places an increased load on the joints, particularly during activities that involve a sudden change of direction. Therefore, players should not carry unnecessary body fat.

Weight loss occurs when a negative energy balance is created. Thus, weight loss can be achieved by restricting energy intake, increasing the volume and intensity of training or, most often, a combination of these strategies.

Athletes and coaches need to recognize that with extreme energy restrictions (i.e., less than 1,500 kilocalories per day), losses of both muscle and fat mass may adversely influence an athlete's performance (Murphy, Hector and Phillips 2015).

Therefore, in most cases, the player wants to preserve fat-free mass during periods of weight loss. A growing body of evidence suggests that a protein intake greater than the 1.7 grams per kilogram of body weight recommended by the ACSM during energy restriction can enhance the retention of fat-free mass (Helms et al. 2014; Josse et al. 2011). A reduction in dietary fat and carbohydrate may allow athletes to achieve higher protein intake without excessive restriction of a particular macronutrient. Current recommendations advise athletes who are aiming to achieve weight loss without losing fat-free mass to combine a moderate energy deficit (about 500 kilocalories per day) with the consumption of 1.8 to 2.0 grams of protein per kilogram of body weight per day in conjunction with performing resistance exercise (Phillips 2011).

To lose body fat, a negative energy balance of 500 to 700 kilocalories per day is required. Additional high-intensity workouts may be required to increase energy expenditure. Increasing protein intake to 2 grams per kilogram per day will preserve muscle mass. Periodizing carbohydrate intake throughout the day so that carbohydrate is consumed after training will promote glycogen resynthesis, but carbohydrate intake should be reduced at other times.

Menu for Fat Burning

Breakfast

Day 1: smoked salmon and omelette

Day 2: ham and cheese frittata

Morning Snack

Day 1: protein shake

Day 2: grilled chicken salad

Lunch

Normal balanced meal such as chicken breast with new potatoes and steamed vegetables

Afternoon Snack

Day 1: grilled prawns and yogurt dip

Day 2: protein shake

Dinner

Day 1: beef and super vegetable stir-fry

Day 2: Mediterranean meaty fish stew

Supper

Day 1: casein shake

Day 2: low-fat yogurt

Special Considerations for Female Players

Two micronutrients of concern in exercising females are iron and calcium. An adequate intake of calcium and vitamin D is essential for bone health (Maughan and Shirreffs 2007). Because soccer training and match play impart stress in the form of weight-bearing exercise, female soccer players have higher bone mineral density than sedentary women do (Sundgot-Borgen and Tortsveit 2007).

Although most female soccer players are healthy, a recent study on Norwegian elite female soccer players showed that soccer players are dieting and experiencing eating disorders, menstrual dysfunction and stress fractures (Sundgot-Borgen and Tortsveit 2007). Dieting behaviour and lack of knowledge of the energy needs of the athlete often lead to energy deficit, menstrual dysfunction and increased risk of bone mass loss.

Although dieting, eating disorders and menstrual dysfunction are less common in soccer than in many other sports, being aware of the problem is important because eating disorders in female athletes can easily be missed. Therefore, players, coaches, administrators and family members should be educated about the three interrelated components of the female athlete triad—disordered eating, menstrual dysfunction and low bone mass—and strategies should be developed to prevent, recognize and treat the triad components (Sundgot-Borgen and Tortsveit 2007).

Dairy products are the best source of calcium, but many female athletes with body image issues may avoid them because of their fat content. Female soccer players should be encouraged to consume dairy products that are low in fat, such as milk, cheese and yogurt.

The effects of iron deficiency anaemia on performance are well documented, because low levels of haemoglobin are associated with reduced exercise performance and capacity (Landahl et al. 2005). Fallon (2004) monitored the haematological parameters of 174 elite female athletes, of whom 33 were soccer players. The study reported that 58 per cent of the soccer players had an abnormal haematological profile. Further alarming evidence is provided by Landahl et al. (2005), who determined the prevalence of iron deficiency and iron deficiency anaemia among Swedish elite female soccer players selected as part of the national squad for the 2003 Women's World Cup. Fifty-seven per cent of the selected female soccer players had iron deficiency and 29 per cent had iron deficiency anaemia in the six months before the World Cup. This finding suggests that all elite female players should be routinely screened for iron deficiency. Any athlete diagnosed by a doctor as having iron deficiency anaemia should take iron supplements. But iron supplementation should not be initiated on a just-in-case basis because excess iron may be harmful to the athlete (Maughan and Shireffs 2007).

Practical nutritional strategies to increase iron intake are recommended, such as ensuring that the diet contains sufficient red meat, fortified foods such as breakfast cereals, as well as eggs, wholegrain bread and green leafy vegetables.

Periodized Nutrition

The concept of periodized nutrition is simple, but athletes, particularly soccer players, usually execute it poorly. Periodized nutrition refers to altering the macronutrient content of the diet in relation to the training and competition schedule. More specifically, by periodizing nutrition programmes, the progressive cycling of training stressors is reflected. Because training goals differ between phases, nutrition should be tailored to meet those requirements. During preseason training, for example, the timing and amount of carbohydrate and protein consumption are important. Because of the increased volume and intensity during this training phase, players should increase their carbohydrate and protein intake to match the requirements. Similarly, on rest days, players should decrease carbohydrate intake accordingly by 25 to 30 per cent because energy expenditures and muscle glycogen utilization will drop. The oscillation of training volume and intensity will affect both energy requirements and metabolism. Table 14.3 provides a summary on how to alter macronutrient intake based on training phase.

Dietary Supplements and Sport Foods

The use of sport foods and dietary supplements in soccer is widespread. Many products, however, are not effective and lack evidence for improving soccer performance. Moreover, many supplements have been found to be contaminated and could increase the risk of a positive doping test (Maughan 2005). Therefore, players, coaching staff and sport science and medical staff should ensure that dietary supplements are batch tested for contamination before use. This section, as well as table 14.4, provides an overview of certain supplements that may be beneficial for soccer players.

Table 14.3 Macronutrient Guidelines for Soccer Players Based on Training Phase and Day

	Dietary goals	CHO g/kg	Protein g/kg	Fat g/kg
Rest day and off-season	Reduce energy and carbohydrate intake to its lowest level, approaching that of sedentary people. Protein consumption should be reduced unless the rest day follows a match. Dietary fat consumption should be at the lower end during periods of inactivity to reduce total energy consumption.	3 or 4	1.2	1 to 1.5
Day before match and match day	Provide sufficient carbohydrate to increase muscle glycogen prematch. Protein intake should be moderate with a high protein feeding (i.e., 30 g) after the match. Dietary fat should be at the lower end of the guidelines because carbohydrate intake is the main goal before a match.	7 or 8	1.4 to 1.6	1 to 1.5
Day after match	Provide sufficient carbohydrate to replenish muscle glycogen and increase protein to enhance recovery. Increase protein intake by 25 per cent to promote recovery. Increase fat to the upper end of the guidelines to ensure adequate consumption of energy.	6 or 7	1.7 to 2	1 to 1.5
Preseason or heavy training	Provide sufficient energy and macronutrients to support high-volume training and adaptation. Increase protein up to two grams per kilogram to ensure adequate recovery during intensive training periods. Increase fat to the upper end of the guidelines to ensure adequate consumption of energy.	8 to 10	1.8 to 2	1 to 1.5
Tournament	Provide sufficient energy and macronutrients to support training and recovery and prepare for several matches and adaptation. Protein intake should remain high throughout this period, because muscle damage will increase during competition. Increase fat to the upper end of the guidelines to ensure adequate consumption of energy.	6 to 10	1.6 to 2	1 to 1.5

Creatine

Creatine supplementation increases intramuscular phosphocreatine stores and appears to enhance performance in activities that primarily involve repeated short bouts of high-intensity exercise that require energy from the ATP–PC energy system. Although the use of creatine supplementation in soccer is widespread, few studies have been conducted and findings to support its use are mixed.

Table 14.4   Dietary Supplements That May Enhance Performance

Supplement	Ergogenic benefits	Practical implications	Considerations
Beta-alanine	Increases carnosine muscle content. Because beta-alanine is an essential rate-limiting precursor of carnosine (β-alanyl-L-histadine), when ingested as a supplement, it can act as an intracellular acidosis buffer and enhance high-intensity exercise.	Six grams per day in three two-gram doses consumed with meals or in recovery drinks. Consuming beta-alanine with a meal will enhance uptake. Making it available at breakfast and lunch is an effective strategy.	Can cause paraesthesia. Therefore, ingest with meals or use slow-release products at lower doses. Up to nine weeks are required to maximize carnosine stores, so players need to learn that this is a long-term strategy. After carnosine stores are maximized, however, eight or nine weeks will pass before carnosine stores return to baseline. Therefore, missing a dose is not a problem.
Creatine	Increases intramuscular phosphocreatine stores and appears to enhance performance in activities that primarily involve repeated short bouts of high-intensity exercise that require energy from the ATP–PC energy system.	A traditional loading phase is not required. Consuming five grams daily with recovery drinks or carbohydrate-containing meals can be a useful strategy throughout the season. This supplement can be added to the recovery drinks.	Can increase body mass by one to two kilograms within a few weeks. A creatine loading phase may not be needed. A five-gram dose daily can be taken throughout the season.
Nitrates	Dietary nitrate supplementation can reduce the oxygen cost of submaximal exercise and can improve exercise tolerance and performance.	Eight millimoles per day for two to three days before kick-off and 90 minutes before kick-off.	Acute loading over two to three days may be more beneficial.
Polyphenol antioxidants	Can reduce delayed onset muscle soreness, reduce inflammation and preserve muscle function.	Tart cherry or pomegranate juice and NAC supplementation could be used acutely for tournament situations or back-to-back matches.	Chronic use can impair training adaptations.
Vitamin D	An inadequate amount of vitamin D can lead to bone loss and injury because it has a crucial function in bone growth, density and remodelling.	Vitamin D_3 supplementation taken daily or weekly depending on vitamin D status.	Vitamin D should be monitored every three months throughout the season. Very dark and very pale-skinned players may be at increased risk of deficiency.
Caffeine	Can reduce perception of fatigue, improves reaction time and can enhance exercise capacity.	Three milligrams per kilogram taken 45 minutes before kick-off (depending on the form of caffeine). Lower doses of one to two milligrams per kilogram may be taken at halftime.	Certain players may be more sensitive to caffeine, so an individualized approach should be taken. Any form of caffeine can be beneficial, including drinks, gels, powders and gum.
Carbohydrate	Provides exogenous fuel to the working muscle and central nervous system.	Thirty to 40 grams after the warm-up and again at halftime.	Can be taken in various forms from gels, bars and drinks. Carbohydrate mouth rinsing may also be beneficial.

Redondo and colleagues (1996) found that creatine supplementation with glucose had no benefits on three repeated 60-metre sprints separated by two minutes of recovery in 18 university-standard men and women. More recently, Williams, Abt and Kilding (2014) examined the effects of 20 grams per day of creatine supplementation for seven days on performance on a 90-minute soccer-specific test (BEAST test) in 16 amateur male players. Performance levels decreased by 1.2 to 2.3 per cent and by 1.0 to 2.2 per cent in the creatine and placebo groups, respectively. These studies suggest that acute creatine supplementation had no positive effect on soccer-specific performance.

In contrast, Mujika and coworkers (2000) found that 20 grams per day of creatine (5 grams four times per day) and maltodextrin supplementation for six days enhanced the time to complete six repeated 15-metre sprints separated by 30-second recovery in 17 well-trained male soccer players by 2.9 per cent. No benefit was observed for repeated countermovement jumping or on intermittent endurance tests. In another study, Cox and coworkers (2002) investigated the effects of 20 grams (5 grams four times per day) of creatine supplementation over six days on an exercise protocol simulating soccer match play that consisted of multiple blocks of sprints interspersed by agility runs and shooting in elite female players. Body mass significantly increased by an average of 0.7 kg in the creatine group, and no change occurred in the placebo group. Performance was enhanced in 9 of the 55 sprint runs, but no improvements were observed in kicking accuracy. Ostojic (2004) examined the effects of creatine monohydrate supplementation (three 10-gram doses) for seven days on a series of soccer-specific tests in younger male soccer players aged 14 to 19 years. Although no improvements were observed in an endurance shuttle run test, creatine supplementation did enhance vertical jump performance, dribbling and sprint times.

Creatine supplementation appears to be safe in people without pre-existing health complications. But some side effects have been reported, such as acute increases in body mass of one to two kilograms in the initial two weeks (Bishop 2010). An issue appears to remain about creatine, dehydration and muscle cramps, but data are sufficient to suggest that creatine supplementation enhances performance in hot or humid conditions and, if used correctly, does not cause muscle cramps (Dalbo et al. 2008).

From a practical perspective, creatine loading (i.e., five grams taken four times per day) is not required because the competitive season takes place over several months. Therefore, five grams taken daily with high glycaemic index carbohydrate at the start of preseason is sufficient to increase phosphocreatine stores over the course of several weeks.

Antioxidants

The use of antioxidant supplements is controversial because the evidence supporting its use is mixed (Gross, Baum and Hoppeler 2011; Peternelj and

Coombes 2011) and emerging data suggest that antioxidant supplement may be counterproductive (Paulsen et al. 2014; Gomez-Caberera et al. 2008). Single vitamin supplements such as vitamin C and vitamin E or even an antioxidant cocktail of supplements such as vitamin C, E, beta-carotene and selenium combined in one way or another is not recommended because little evidence supports its use. Moreover, vitamin C and vitamin E have been found to impair endurance training adaptations, increase oxidative stress and in some cases increase mortality (Gross, Baum and Hoppeler 2011; Peternelj and Coombes 2011; Draeger et al. 2014). Therefore, the use of these supplements is not warranted. N-acetyl cysteine (NAC) supplementation has also been found to preserve performance on the Yo-Yo Intermittent Recovery Test Level 1 after damaging exercise in comparison with a placebo (Cobley et al. 2011), although it does cause mild gastrointestinal discomfort in some athletes. When players play back-to-back matches with little time for recovery or participate in tournament situations in which adaptation to training is inconsequential, certain antioxidant supplements derived from food concentrates or NAC supplementation may be beneficial for recovery. Note that antioxidant supplements should not be used over the long term because of their detrimental effects on endurance-training adaptations.

Beta-Alanine

Beta-alanine is a nonessential amino acid found in small quantities in meat. Beta-alanine supplementation has received a great deal of attention because numerous studies have now shown its effectiveness at enhancing high-intensity intermittent sprint-based activities. Beta-alanine supplementation increases carnosine muscle content, and because beta-alanine is an essential rate-limiting precursor of carnosine (β-alanyl-L-histidine), when ingested as a supplement it can act as an intracellular acidosis buffer and enhance high-intensity exercise performance (Harris et al. 2006).

Although several studies have investigated the effects of beta-alanine on exercise performance, few have done so in relation to soccer-specific performance. Saunders and colleagues (2012) investigated the effects of 3.2 grams of beta-alanine supplementation over a 12-week period using a parallel design in 17 amateur male soccer players. The players performed the Yo-Yo Intermittent Recovery Test Level 2 at the start and end of the supplementation period. No significant improvements were observed in the placebo group, but players in the beta-alanine group significantly improved by 34.3 plus or minus 22.5 per cent.

In contrast, Sweeney and colleagues (2010) found no ergogenic effects of beta-alanine supplementation over a five-week period on two sets of 5-second sprints with 45-second recovery separated by 2 minutes of active recovery. No change in blood lactate was reported in 19 physically active university-standard men. One of the limitations of this study was that the sprints were carried out on a motorized treadmill, thus reducing the validity of the test.

Saunders and colleagues (2012) examined the effects of 6.4 grams per day of beta-alanine supplementation over four weeks on the Loughborough Intermittent Shuttle Test in 16 elite and 20 nonelite team sport players. Although blood lactate was elevated during the test in both groups, no differences were found in sprint times between groups, suggesting that beta-alanine supplementation produced no performance gains. Note that the elite participants in this study were hockey players and the nonelite participants were a mixture of hockey and soccer players, so the findings of this study are not directly applicable to soccer players.

Although few studies have examined the effectiveness of beta-alanine on soccer performance, it does seem to have some beneficial effects on high-intensity repeated sprint performance. Thus, its performance-enhancing effects could certainly benefit soccer players (Harris and Sale 2012). With the exception of paraesthesia (tingling sensation), no other deleterious side effects of beta-alanine supplementation have been reported (Sale et al. 2013). Note that paraesthesia is exacerbated when beta-alanine powder is consumed in doses higher than one or two grams or ingested on an empty stomach. Consuming beta-alanine capsules or using a slow-release beta-alanine supplement can minimize paraesthesia. Some evidence suggests that consuming beta-alanine with a meal that contains some carbohydrate can both enhance the absorption of beta-alanine and reduce the effects of paraesthesia (Stegen et al. 2013). Insulin may play a role in stimulating muscle carnosine loading, so a sensible strategy might be to use low doses of beta-alanine supplementation of around two grams in recovery drinks after training or in conjunction with meals up to three times daily. To maximize muscle carnosine levels, beta-alanine supplementation of around six grams per day (in three two-gram doses) over 12 weeks is required, and this level can be achieved gradually over the course of the season. To maintain muscle carnosine levels, a lower dose of two to three grams per day should be sufficient. Evidence suggests that muscle carnosine levels drop gradually over 12 weeks (Stellingwerff et al. 2012).

Therefore, if players missed a dose on rest days or match days—not an ideal situation but common amongst soccer players—muscle carnosine levels would not decline acutely. More studies on beta-alanine supplementation on soccer-specific performance are needed in well-trained players, and no studies have investigated the effects of beta-alanine on female players. Nevertheless, some promising evidence suggests that beta-alanine supplementation can enhance high-intensity intermittent exercise despite causing mild side effects such as paraesthesia.

Vitamin D

Awareness about the role of vitamin D in athletic performance is rising. Vitamin D is an essential nutrient that contributes to bone health, muscle functionality and calcium regulation in the blood. Recent studies have shown that soccer players have inadequate levels of vitamin D (Galan et al. 2012; Morton et al. 2012; Kopeć et al. 2013) because it is difficult to source and acquire the recommended daily amount. The principal source of vitamin D is ultraviolet B radiation in sunlight.

Vitamin D has been found to play an active role in many physiological processes in the body (Ogan and Pritchett 2013). First, vitamin D is well known for its active role in osteoclast activity and absorption of calcium in the intestine (Larson-Meyer and Willis, 2010). An inadequate amount of vitamin D can lead to bone loss and injury because it has a crucial function in bone growth, density and remodelling (DeLuca 2004). Low status of this vitamin can also impair calcium and phosphorus homeostasis, resulting in a restricted calcium absorption rate in the small intestine (Heaney 2003). Metabolic processes, neuromuscular activity and bone health are compromised when calcium absorption is insufficient, further stressing the importance of maintaining adequate vitamin D status. Optimal levels of serum 25-hydroxyvitamin D for athletes may be 100 to 175 nanomoles per litre, and lower levels may impair performance (Larson-Meyer et al. 2013).

Galan and colleagues (2012) measured serum 25-hydroxyvitamin D in 28 professional soccer players in Spain and found that only 14.3 per cent had levels above 100 nanomoles per litre. In October 93 per cent of players has levels greater than or equal to 75 nanomoles per litre, and in February 64 per cent of the players' levels had dropped below 75 nanomoles per litre. These findings suggest that in two-thirds of the players measured, vitamin D levels had dropped to insufficient levels in the winter months. Similarly, Morton and colleagues (2012) reported that mean serum 25-hydroxyvitamin D levels in 20 FA Premier League players had dropped from 104.4 plus or minus 21.1 nanomoles per litre in August to 51.0 plus or minus 19.0 nanomoles per litre in December, indicating that 65 per cent of the players were classed as insufficient in the winter months. These findings are also consistent with Kopeć and colleagues (2013), who investigated seasonal changes in serum 25-hydroxyvitamin D, calcium and bone turnover markers in 24 Polish professional soccer players. Measurements were taken in two training phases, after the summer period and after the winter period. Only 50 per cent of the players measured after the summer period had normal levels of serum 25-hydroxyvitamin D. After the winter period the proportion of players who had normal levels dropped to 16.7 percent, suggesting that vitamin D levels fall during the winter season when exposure to sunlight is inadequate.

These data suggest that first, serum 25-hydroxyvitamin D levels should be routinely measured in soccer players at various time points throughout the year, and second, if vitamin D levels are insufficient or deficient, then vitamin D_3 supplementation should be used to correct shortfalls. Vitamin D_3 is more commonly used than vitamin D_2, and absorption is significantly enhanced when taken with lipids because vitamin D is a fat-soluble vitamin. Thus, depending on serum 25-hydroxyvitamin D levels in players, the sport science and medical team should consider vitamin D_3 supplementation ingested during the largest meal of the day.

Caffeine

Caffeine has well-documented ergogenic effects on performance in sport (Burke, Desbow and Spriet 2013). Caffeine is one of the most commonly used supplements. Its main mode of action is to block the adenosine receptors found in tissues throughout the body, such as those in the brain, heart and skeletal muscle. Moreover, caffeine has also been shown to enhance fat oxidation, improve energy status and increase secretion of catecholamines (Graham 2001).

Caffeine supplementation in doses of six milligrams per kilogram of body weight has been shown to improve passing accuracy and jump performance without any negative side effects during a simulated soccer protocol (Foskett, Ali and Gant 2009). In another study by Gant, Ali and Foskett (2010), a caffeine (3.7 milligrams per kilogram) and carbohydrate beverage improved sprinting ability, countermovement jumping performance and the subjective experiences of soccer players. These findings have been replicated in other studies in which an energy drink containing caffeine in a dosage of three milligrams per kilogram of body weight enhanced repeated sprinting ability, high-intensity running distance covered during a simulated soccer game and jump height in semiprofessional players (Del Coso et al. 2012). The ergogenic effect of caffeine on running performance appears to be similar in female players; Lara and colleagues (2014) found that caffeine supplementation in doses of three milligrams per kilogram increased total running distance, number of sprint bouts and high-intensity running distance covered during a simulated soccer match. Caffeine supplementation also appears to enhance cognitive performance and perceptual responses in female players (Ali et al. 2015). These findings suggest that caffeine supplementation in doses of around three milligrams per kilogram may provide meaningful improvements in soccer performance during match play. But be aware that not all studies investigating the ergogenic effects of caffeine on soccer have found positive effects on performance variables (Andrade-Souza et al. 2015; Pettersen et al. 2014; Astorino et al. 2012).

Studies have shown that caffeine taken in doses of three milligrams per kilogram may be just as effective as six to nine milligrams per kilogram (Cox et al., 2002; Kovacs, Stegen and Brouns 1998). Thus, practitioners working with soccer players should avoid doses higher than three milligrams per kilogram because caffeine may negatively affect sleep postmatch, particularly for evening kick-off. Regarding when to take caffeine, most studies have examined the effects of caffeine ingested 30 to 45 minutes before exercise; therefore, caffeine ingested either before or after the warm-up may be an effective strategy. As with any supplement, players should practice the intended supplementation strategy in training to ensure that they tolerate it before taking it on match day.

Nitrates

Over recent years, the use of dietary nitrates has become popular in soccer. Supplements such as concentrated beetroot shots, nitrate-containing gels and bars now available are purported to enhance performance. Despite the rise in the use of nitrate supplements, few studies thus far have investigated the effectiveness of nitrates on soccer performance.

Wylie and colleagues (2013) found that dietary nitrate supplementation in the form of concentrated beetroot juice in doses of about 8.2 millimoles of nitrate ingested several days before completing the Yo-Yo Intermittent Recovery Level 1 Test elevated plasma nitrite levels by about 400 per cent and improved performance by 4.2 per cent in comparison with the placebo. No differences were observed for blood lactate, but blood glucose was lower in the supplementation group at the end of the test, suggesting that nitrate could have facilitated greater muscle glucose uptake. Note that although performance in the Yo-Yo Test improved, the participants were recreational rather than elite athletes. In contrast, however, Martin and colleagues (2014) found that acute supplementation of dietary nitrate in the form of concentrated beetroot juice in doses of 0.3 grams of nitrate ingested two hours beforehand had no effect on repeated sprints lasting 8 seconds separated by 30-second recovery periods in team-sport athletes. Possible reasons for finding no ergogenic benefit in the study conducted by Martin and coworkers (2014) could be that an acute dose of nitrate was taken just two hours before testing whereas in the study conducted by Wylie and colleagues (2013) nitrate was taken several days before testing, which may have allowed the plasma nitrite level to become greater. Moreover, Martin and colleagues (2014) did not measure plasma nitrite levels, so it is uncertain whether the 0.3-gram acute dose was sufficient. In addition, sprinting was carried out on a cycle ergometer rather than performed as a running-based exercise.

The research on dietary nitrate is in its infancy, and although further research on high-intensity intermittent team sports such as soccer is necessary, it appears to be a promising dietary supplement.

Contamination of Supplements

Many sport foods and dietary supplements are in the sport nutrition market, and various products purport to enhance performance and promote recovery. Unfortunately, many do not work as suggested, and evidence to support their effectiveness is poor. Players and support staff should acknowledge that many supplements have been found to be contaminated with substances on the WADA list of prohibited substances. If ingested, these supplements could result in a positive doping test (Maughan 2005; de Hon and Coumans 2007). Several professional soccer players have inadvertently tested positive and been subsequently banned from competition. Therefore, players should seek advice from appropriately qualified sport nutrition professionals before ingesting supplements. Further, laboratories commonly test supplements for contaminants, and many brands offer certificates to demonstrate that supplements have been tested and are safe. Nevertheless, there is always a danger that a dietary supplement can cause a positive doping test. The key message to soccer players and support staff working with athletes is that food always comes first and that safe batch-tested supplements can offer some benefit when used appropriately.

Conclusion

Sound performance nutrition is important for soccer players from youth all the way up to the professional level. A periodized nutrition approach whereby diet is tailored to the type, duration and intensity of players' training can enhance performance and accelerate recovery. Carbohydrate requirements are increased for the preseason period, days on which two training sessions are performed and the day before a match (greater than 7 grams per kilogram of body weight). Similarly, protein requirements are increased after strenuous training sessions and up to two days after a match (greater than 1.7 grams per kilogram of body weight). During these periods an aggressive and targeted recovery nutrition approach is needed. Sweat rates and electrolyte losses vary greatly among players and change depending on environmental conditions, but sport science personnel can measure these parameters and give bespoke advice to players. Creating an environment around the training ground that offers players the opportunity to take appropriate fluids can enhance fluid uptake.

Youth players have increased energy expenditures. During certain periods of high-intensity training, players may need greater levels of carbohydrate (more than 8 grams per kilogram of body weight) and protein (1.7 grams per kilogram of body weight). Educating youth players by offering a curriculum on the various aspects of performance nutrition is extremely important in developing knowledgeable and autonomous athletes. Soccer players are frequent travellers because of the nature of the competition schedule, but appropriate planning and communication with catering staff at hotels can ensure that sound, nutritious food is available.

Certain dietary supplements and sports foods such as carbohydrate drinks, gels and bars; vitamin D; dietary nitrates; caffeine; beta-alanine; creatine and polyphenol antioxidants used strategically at the right times and at the correct dosages can enhance performance and recovery.

CHAPTER 15

Injury Frequency and Prevention

—Mario Bizzini and Astrid Junge

Playing soccer requires various skills and abilities, including endurance, agility, speed and a technical and tactical understanding of the game. All these aspects will be instructed and improved during training sessions, but playing soccer includes a certain risk of injury. Injury prevention is an important task of the Medical Committee of the Fédération Internationale de Football Association (FIFA). The development and implementation of measures for injury prevention should follow the four-step sequence proposed by van Mechelen, Hlobil and Kemper (1992). After having established the extent of the injury problem (step 1) and analysed the aetiology and mechanisms of injuries (step 2), possible preventive measures should be introduced (step 3). Finally, the effectiveness of the preventive interventions is assessed (step 4) by repeating step 1.

At best, randomized controlled trials (RCTs) should be performed to investigate the preventive interventions (Sackett, Strauss and Richardson 2000; Scherrington 2012). The following review presents a brief summary on the most relevant literature on injuries, an update on preventive interventions and a special focus on the FIFA 11+ injury prevention programme for amateur soccer players.

Incidence of Injuries

Most studies in the literature have been conducted in male players; research in female and youth players is still deficient (Junge, Chomiak and Dvorak 2000; Peterson et al. 2000; Junge and Dvorak 2004, 2007). Match and training injury data are available for tournaments such as World Cups, national elite (or professional) leagues, and lower and junior leagues (Nielsen and Yde 1989; Inklaar 1994; Hawkins and Fuller 1998, 1999; Hawkins et al. 2001; Junge and Dvorak 2004, 2007; Dvorak et al. 2007; 2011). Recently, the influence of the playing surface (natural versus artificial turf) has also been investigated (Fuller et al. 2007a, 2007b; Ekstrand, Hagglund and Fuller 2011; Williams, Hume and Kara 2011). In 2006 a consensus paper on the injury definition and methods of data collection procedures in studies of soccer injuries was published simultaneously in three major sports medicine journals (Fuller et al. 2006a, 2006b, 2006c).

The injury incidence of male elite players ranges from 16 to 42 match injuries and 1 to 6 training injuries per 1,000 exposure hours. For elite female players the injury incidence is 14 to 24 match injuries and 1 to 8 training injuries per 1,000 hours. At the World Cup tournaments since the mid-2000s, we have observed an increase in injuries of female players and a decrease in male players (Junge and Dvorak 2007; Dvorak et al. 2011). This may be explained on one side by stricter refereeing in the men's matches, and on the other side by the fast-growing intensity and competitiveness in high-level female soccer (Junge and Dvorak 2007; Dvorak et al. 2011).

In low-level players, lower incidences of injury have been reported. For youth players, the injury rate appears to increase with age. The 17- to 18-year-old age group has a similar or even higher injury incidence than their adult counterparts (Junge and Dvorak 2004). Froholdt, Olsen and Bahr (2009) reported that organized soccer (small-sided games, 5v5 or 7v7 games) for children 12 years or younger is associated with a low risk of injury (1.4 to 2.3 injuries per 1,000 playing hours).

Recent studies of soccer injuries on artificial turf (third generation) and natural grass showed no significant differences in the injury incidence for both male and female elite players (Fuller et al. 2007a, 2007b; Ekstrand, Hagglund and Fuller 2011; Williams, Hume and Kara 2011).

Characteristics of Injuries

Most soccer injuries affect the lower extremities. The most frequent locations are the ankle, knee and thigh. Sprains, strains and contusions are the most common types of injury.

Specifically, ankle and knee ligament injuries and hamstring muscle lesions are the most often documented injuries in soccer players. Hamstring strain is the most common muscle injury in male players (Arnason, Sigurdsson et al. 2004; Arnason et al. 2008), whereas noncontact anterior cruciate ligament (ACL) tears have been found to be more prevalent in female players (Renstrom et al. 2008; Alentorn-Geli et al. 2009a; Brophy, Silvers and Mandelbaum 2010).

Epidemiological data on ACL injury rates show that female athletes have a 2- to 10-fold higher incidence of ACL injuries than their male counterparts (Brophy, Silvers and Mandelbaum 2010).

Junge and Dvorak (2007) reported that head injuries (especially concussions) were more common in women's tournaments than in men's top-level tournaments. Although the distribution of injuries per body location appears not to be age related, younger players sustain more contusions than adult players do whereas adults suffer more strains and sprains (Junge and Dvorak 2004).

About two-thirds of traumatic injuries are caused by the action of another player, and 12 to 28 per cent of all injuries are caused by foul play (Junge and Dvorak 2004). The percentage of noncontact injuries (e.g., during running, twisting, cutting, landing from a jump) varies from 26 to 59 per cent (Junge and Dvorak 2004). Overuse injuries (e.g., tendinopathies, low back pain) account for 9 to 34 per cent of all injuries. This figure could be higher, considering methodological problems with the injury definitions used in many studies (Bahr 2009).

About a quarter of injuries are reinjuries of the same type and location.

Risk Factors and Injury Mechanism

Risks factors can be classified as intrinsic (e.g., age, gender, level of play) or extrinsic (e.g., surface, weather, equipment) or as modifiable (e.g., strength) or nonmodifiable (e.g., age) (Meeuwisse 1994; Bahr and Holme 2003). Because many factors may interact simultaneously in the cause of injury, research in this field is challenging (Drawer and Fuller 2002; Bahr and Holme 2003).

Previous injury, possibly combined with an inadequate rehabilitation, is the most important risk factor for soccer injury (Arnason, Sigurdsson et al. 2004; Hagglund, Walden and Ekstrand 2006; Meeuwisse et al. 2007; Alentorn-Geli et al. 2009a). Specific knowledge on the studied risk factors for injury is warranted to develop targeted preventive interventions for soccer players (Dvorak et al. 2000). Detailed information on the injury mechanism (e.g., ACL tear after landing in a knee valgus position; figure 15.1) can additionally help in designing prevention exercises or programmes, focusing on neuromuscular control (e.g., landing with neutral knee alignment) (Bahr and Krosshaug 2005; Alentorn-Geli et al. 2009b).

Consequences of Injuries

Most injuries are not severe, and the player can return to play on average one to two weeks after injury (Nielsen and Yde 1989; Inklaar 1994). But sometimes players have a longer absence from the pitch, such as after an ACL tear and subsequent surgery and rehabilitation (Brophy, Silvers and Mandelbaum 2010). Acute injuries or chronic problems also cause retirement from professional soccer (Drawer and Fuller 2001); osteoarthritis (OA) is one of the major causes (Lohmander et al. 2004; Kuijt et al. 2012). Soccer injuries

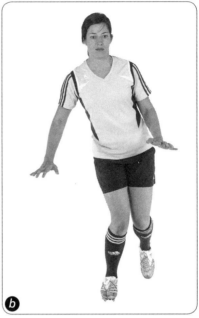

▶ **Figure 15.1**   Body positions: (*a*) optimal; (*b*) destabilized.

Courtesy of FIFA.

also have a socioeconomic effect in terms of health care costs (Dvorak 2009; Junge et al. 2011).

Injury Prevention

To date, approximately 30 publications on the effectiveness of injury prevention measures in soccer players can be found in the literature. Most studies were conducted in youth and nonprofessional male and female players.

Following the first RCT study by Ekstrand, Gillquist and Liljedahl (1983), almost 20 years elapsed before Junge et al. (2002) published a controlled trial on injury prevention in soccer. Both studies showed that a multimodal intervention programme (comprising adapted equipment, warm-up routine, prophylactic ankle taping, controlled rehabilitation, specific stabilization and coordination exercises for the trunk, ankle and knee joints) was effective in reducing overall incidence of injuries by 75 per cent in male senior teams (Ekstrand et al. 1983) and by 21 per cent in male youth teams (Junge et al. 2002). A preseason neuromuscular training programme (cardiovascular conditioning, plyometrics, strength, flexibility) was found to reduce the number of overall injuries in female youth players (Heidt et al. 2000). Lehnhard et al.

(1996) reported a reduction of overall injuries (47 per cent) when a one-year progressive strength-training programme was performed in a male college soccer team. Similarly, Emery and Meeuwisse (2010) reported the positive preventive effects of a neuromuscular programme for injuries in general and the acute onset injury in youth male and female players.

A simple injury prevention programme (FIFA's the 11) implemented in a four-year countrywide campaign in Switzerland showed a 12 to 25 per cent reduction in injuries in male and female amateur players of different ages and levels of play (Junge et al. 2011). With its consequent effect on the health care costs, this study demonstrated how injury prevention in soccer may have significant socioeconomic impact. Soligard et al. (2008) in a cluster RCT study showed how an injury prevention programme (FIFA 11+) reduced the incidence of injuries by 30 to 50 per cent in youth female soccer players performing this so-called complete warm-up at least twice a week. Additionally, the importance of compliance, a crucial aspect for the effectiveness of the prevention programme, was evaluated in the aforementioned study (Soligard et al. 2010).

The results showed that players with high compliance had a significant lower risk of injury and that positive coach attitudes towards prevention were correlated with high compliance and lower injury risk (Soligard et al. 2010).

Although the aforementioned research has been aimed at reducing the incidence of soccer injury in general, other research has focused on specific types of injuries. A large percentage of the research dealing with preventive strategies and specific types of injury studies has addressed ankle sprains (Handoll et al. 2001). Balance training (on unstable surfaces) and the use of semirigid ankle orthoses were effective in reducing (by about 80 per cent) the recurrence of ankle sprains in previously injured male and female players, but not in healthy players (Tropp, Askling and Gillquist 1985; Surve et al. 1994; Sharpe, Knapik and Jones 1997; Mohammadi 2007).

Specific hamstring eccentric strengthening exercises were found effective in reducing hamstring strains (by about 30 per cent) in male elite and amateur soccer players (Askling, Karlsson and Thorstensson 2003; Arnason et al. 2008; Petersen et al. 2011), whereas Croisier et al. (2008) described how the restoration of normal strength decreased the incidence of hamstring injuries in professional male players. Hölmich et al. (2010), however, did not find significantly fewer groin injuries in amateur players performing a specific strengthening and core stability programme.

Several studies have addressed prevention measures for ACL and severe knee injuries. Caraffa et al. (1996) reported a significant reduction in ACL injuries in male professional and amateur players with balance board proprioceptive training, but Sodermann et al. (2000) found no preventive effects with the same intervention on the incidence of acute knee injuries in female adult players. Neuromuscular programmes, including plyometrics, strength and stabilization training, were specially developed to target the high incidence of noncontact ACL injuries in female soccer players (Hewett et al. 1996). Hewett et al. (1999) published the first paper in this field and reported a trend towards reduction in knee injuries in young female players performing such programmes. Two studies (Mandelbaum et al. 2005; Gilchrist et al. 2008) evaluated the PEP (prevent and enhance performance) programme and found that it was effective in reducing noncontact ACL tears in female college players. Walden et al. (2012) reported similar findings in a large RCT in adolescent female players with a 15-minute neuromuscular warm-up programme. By implementing an adapted programme (warm-up, balance, strength, and core stability), Kiani et al. (2010) documented an impressive reduction of acute knee injuries and noncontact knee injuries in youth female players. Hägglund, Walden and Ekstrand (2007) showed how a 10-step progressive rehabilitation programme for injured players was able to reduce (by 66 to 75 per cent) recurrent injuries in those same players following this programme.

Fredberg, Bolvig and Andersen (2008) found no preventive effect with specific eccentric exercises in the prevalence of Achilles and patellar tendinopathy in male professional players.

A study by Johnson, Ekengren and Andersen (2005) reported a lower injury frequency with training in mental skills (cognitive-behavioural training) among high-risk elite male and female players, whereas no effects on acute injuries were found with an educational video-based injury awareness programme.

Back in 2006, and after F-MARC research (Andersen et al. 2004; Arnason, Tenga et al. 2004; Fuller et al. 2004; Fuller, Junge and Dvorak 2005), the International Football Association Board (IFAB) decided that any incident of elbow to the head should be sanctioned with a red card (as IFAB did for tackles from behind and two-footed tackles from the side). The consequent application of these decisions helped in reducing the number of head injuries (including concussions) and ankle injuries caused by elbowing and dangerous tackles.

Data from previous FIFA World Cups (2006, 2010) proved that the reinforcement of the Laws of the Game and the subsequent stricter refereeing during competitions were crucial in protecting the health of the players (Dvorak et al. 2007; Dvorak 2009; Dvorak et al. 2011).

Exercise-Based Injury Prevention Programmes

Between 20 and 50 per cent of all noncontact soccer injuries can be prevented with exercise-based prevention programmes (Junge et al. 2002; Mandelbaum et al. 2005; Gilchrist et al. 2008; Soligard et al. 2008; Emery and Meeuwisse 2010; Walden et al. 2012).

Based on the current evidence, the key elements of effective injury prevention programmes are core stability and strength, neuromuscular control and balance, eccentric training of the hamstrings, plyometrics and agility.

Core Training

The core is a functional unit that includes the muscles of not only the trunk (abdominals, back extensors) but also the pelvic and hip region. The preservation of core stability is one of the keys for optimal functioning of the lower extremities (especially the knee joints). Soccer players must have sufficient strength and neuromuscular control in their hip and trunk muscles to provide core stability. Growing scientific evidence suggests that core stability has an important role in injury prevention (Borghuis, Hof and Lemmink 2008; Hewett et al. 2010).

Neuromuscular Control and Balance

Neuromuscular control does not represent a single entity, but complex interacting systems integrating different aspects of muscle actions (static, dynamic, reactive), muscle activations (eccentric more than concentric), coordination (multijoint muscles), stabilization, body posture, and balance and anticipation ability. Strong empirical and growing scientific evidence indicates that sport-specific neuromuscular training programmes can effectively prevent knee and ankle injuries (Hupperets, Verhagen and van Mechelen 2009; Verhagen and Bay 2010).

Plyometrics and Agility

Plyometrics are exercises that enable a muscle to reach maximum strength in as short a time as possible. Eccentric muscle contractions are rapidly followed by concentric contractions in many sport skills. Consequently, specific functional exercises that emphasize this rapid change in muscle action must be used to prepare athletes for their sport-specific activities. The aim of plyometric training is to decrease the amount of time required between the yielding eccentric muscle contraction and the initiation of the overcoming concentric contraction. Plyometrics can train specific movement patterns in a biomechanically correct manner, thereby strengthening the muscle, tendon and ligament more functionally.

Plyometrics and agility drills were the important components of the programmes, which were shown to be effective in the prevention of ACL injuries as well as other knee and ankle injuries (Hewett et al. 1996; Hewett et al. 2010).

FIFA 11+ Complete Warm-Up Programme for Amateur Players to Prevent Injuries

The FIFA 11+ injury prevention programme was developed by an international group of experts based on their practical experience with various injury prevention programmes for amateur players aged 14 or older. The FIFA 11+, the advanced version of the 11, integrates the basic characteristics of the PEP programme. It is a complete warm-up package that should replace the usual warm-up before training for amateur teams (Bizzini, Junge and Dvorak 2011).

In a scientific study (RCT), youth female soccer teams using the FIFA 11+ as a standard warm-up had significantly lower risk for injuries than teams that warmed up as usual. Teams that performed the FIFA 11+ regularly at least twice a week had 37 per cent fewer training injuries and 29 per cent fewer match injuries (Soligard et al. 2008). Recently, a large RCT in male soccer players (NCAA Divisions I and II) found significantly fewer training and match injuries in teams practicing the FIFA 11+ as a warm-up routine (Silvers, Mandelbaum et al. 2015).

Two studies in Italian male amateur soccer players showed that the physiological warm-up effects of the FIFA 11+ are similar to or even better than a standard warm-up routine and that it enhances neuromuscular control (core, lower extremity) and knee flexor strength (Bizzini et al. 2013; Impellizzeri et al. 2013). Other authors have found improvements in static and dynamic balance and thigh muscle strength in male soccer and futsal players after they performed the FIFA 11+ programme (Brito, Figueiredo and Fernandes 2010; Daneshjoo et al. 2012a, 2012b; Reis et al. 2013). In a RCT study on Canadian youth female soccer, Steffen and colleagues (2013) found that players with higher adherence to FIFA 11+ showed significant improvements in functional balance and reduced injury risk.

The FIFA 11+ has three parts:

- Part 1: Running exercises at a slow speed combined with active stretching and controlled partner contacts
- Part 2: Six sets of exercises focusing on core and leg strength, balance, and plyometrics and agility, each with three levels of increasing difficulty
- Part 3: Running exercises at moderate to high speed combined with planting and cutting movements

The FIFA 11+ should be completed as a standard warm-up at least two to three times a week and takes approximately 20 minutes to complete.

The key point of the programme is to use the proper technique during all the exercises. Players must pay full attention to correct posture and good body control, including straight leg alignment, knee-over-toe position and soft landings.

For further information on FIFA 11+ see the review papers by Bizzini, Junge and Dvorak (2013) and Bizzini and Dvorak (2015) and visit www.f-marc.com/11plus.

Motivation and Compliance

The coach should be aware of the importance and efficiency of injury prevention programmes. Not all soccer injuries can be prevented, but knee injuries, ankle sprains and overuse problems can be significantly reduced by the regular performance of preventive exercises (Soligard et al. 2008). See table 15.1.

The players are the essential assets of the club and the coach. If key players are injured, coaches have fewer possibilities to select the squad and the team usually gains fewer points. Therefore, injury prevention strategies should be part of every training session.

The coach should motivate the players to learn the FIFA 11+ and perform the exercises regularly and correctly. Research has shown that compliance is the key factor for efficiency. Teams that performed the FIFA 11+ more often had fewer injured players than other teams. The easiest approach is to perform the FIFA 11+ as a standard warm-up at the beginning of every training session and to perform parts I and III as a warm-up before matches (Soligard et al. 2010).

How to Teach the FIFA 11+

The coach should start by highlighting the importance of injury prevention: All players should clearly understand this message. Only then should the coach begin the explanation and instruction of the exercises.

The key for efficient teaching is to start at level 1 and focus on the correct performance of the exercises. The coach should carefully correct all mistakes. Good body positioning is crucial to promote better neuromuscular work and

Table 15.1   Injury Incidence Following Implementation of FIFA 11+

Percentage of injured players	Performed FIFA 11+	Warmed up as usual	Reduction
All injuries	13.0%	19.8%	34.3%
Acute injuries	10.6%	15.5%	31.6%
Overuse injuries	2.6%	5.7%	54.4%
Knee injuries	3.1%	5.6%	44.6%
Ankle injuries	4.3%	5.9%	27.1%
Severe injuries	4.3%	8.6%	47.7%

Data from T. Soligard, G. Myklebust, K. Steffen, I. Holme, H. Silvers, M. Bizzini, et al., 2008, "Comprehensive warm-up program to prevent injuries in young female footballers: Cluster randomized controlled trial," *BMJ* 337:a2469.

more efficient training. When the players are able to perform the exercises correctly, the duration and the number of repetitions can be raised to the proposed intensity.

The following steps are helpful in teaching the exercises:

- Explain briefly and demonstrate one or more (usually no more than three at a time) exercises.
- Instruct the players to practice the exercise and provide general feedback or corrections.
- Discuss with all players some of the problems and demonstrate the exercises again (perhaps with one player who performs it well).
- Instruct the players to perform the exercise again and provide individual feedback and corrections.

This method is particularly recommended for the six exercises of part 2. The running exercises of parts 1 and 3 may need shorter explanations and consequently less learning time. Usually, at least two training sessions will be needed until the players are able to perform all exercises of the FIFA 11+ (level 1) correctly.

Progression to the Next Level

Players should begin with level 1. Only when the player can perform an exercise without difficulty for the specified duration and number of repetitions should he or she progress to the next level of the exercise.

Three options are viable:

- Ideally, progression to the next level is determined individually for each player.
- Alternatively, all players can progress to the next level for some exercises but continue with the current level for other exercises.
- For simplicity, all players can progress to the next level of all exercises after three or four weeks.

Note: For all exercises, correct performance is of great importance. Therefore, the coach should supervise the programme and correct the players if necessary.

Field Set-Up

A simple set of cones (six pairs of cones placed in parallel lines about five to six metres apart) is necessary to prepare the course (figure 15.2). Two players start at the same time from the first pair of cones. They jog and perform the exercises along the inside line of cones and then run back along the outside after reaching the last cones (speed may be increased as players warm up).

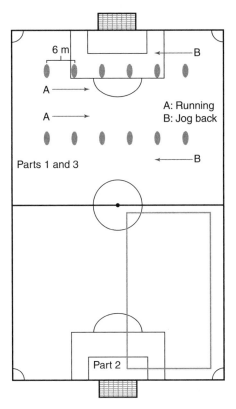

▶ **Figure 15.2** Field set-up.

FIFA 11+ Programme

Instructional video of all exercises can be viewed on www.f-marc.com/11plus. The poster, a detailed manual and other educational material can be downloaded from that website. The material is available in seven languages.

PART 1: RUNNING EXERCISES

1. Straight Ahead   Jog straight to the last cone. Make sure you keep your upper body straight. Your hip, knee and foot are aligned. Do not let your knee buckle inwards. Run slightly more quickly on the way back. Perform two sets.

2. Hip Out   Jog to the first cone. Stop and lift your knee forwards (figure 15.3). Rotate your knee to the side and put your foot down. Repeat the exercise on the other leg at the next cone. Repeat until you reach the other side of the pitch. Perform two sets.

▶ **Figure 15.3**   Running: hip out.

Courtesy of FIFA.

3. Hip In Jog to the first cone. Stop and lift your knee to the side (figure 15.4). Rotate your knee forwards and put your foot down. Repeat the exercise on the other leg at the next cone. Repeat until you reach the other side of the pitch. Perform two sets.

▶ **Figure 15.4** Running: hip in.

Courtesy of FIFA.

4. Circling Partner   Jog to the first cone. Shuffle sideways towards your partner (figure 15.5). Shuffle an entire circle around one other (without changing the direction you are looking) and then shuffle back to the first cone. Repeat until you reach the other side of the pitch. Perform two sets.

▶ **Figure 15.5**   Running: circling partner.

Courtesy of FIFA.

5. Jumping With Shoulder Contact   Jog to the first cone. Shuffle sideways towards your partner. In the middle, jump sideways towards each other to make shoulder-to-shoulder contact (figure 15.6). Land on both feet with your hips and knees bent. Shuffle back to the first cone. Repeat until you reach the other side of the pitch. Perform two sets.

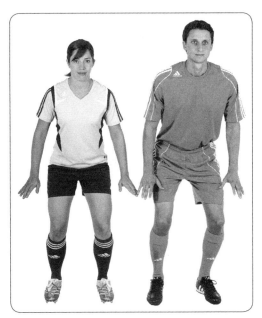

▶ **Figure 15.6**   Running: jumping with shoulder contact.

Courtesy of FIFA.

6. Quick Forwards and Backwards Sprints   Run quickly to the second cone and then run backwards quickly to the first cone, keeping your hips and knees slightly bent. Repeat, running two cones forwards and one cone backwards until you reach the other side of the pitch. Perform two sets.

PART 2 STRENGTH, PLYOMETRICS AND BALANCE

7. Bench

Level 1: Static Bench

Lie on your front and support your upper body with your forearms. Your elbows should be directly under your shoulders. Lift your upper body, pelvis and legs until your body is in a straight line from head to feet (figure 15.7). Pull in the abdominal and gluteal muscles and hold the position for 20 to 30 seconds. Perform three sets.

   Note: Do not sway or arch your back. Do not move your buttocks upwards.

▶ **Figure 15.7**   Static bench.

Courtesy of FIFA.

Level 2: Bench With Alternating Legs

Lie on your front and support your upper body with your forearms. Your elbows should be directly under your shoulders. Lift your upper body, pelvis and legs until your body is in a straight line from head to feet. Pull in the abdominal and gluteal muscles. Lift each leg in turn, holding for a count of 2 seconds (figure 15.8). Continue for 40 to 60 seconds. Perform three sets.

   Note: Do not sway or arch your back. Do not move your buttocks upwards. Keep your pelvis stable and do not let it tilt to the side.

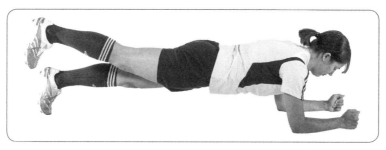

▶ **Figure 15.8**   Bench with alternating legs.

Courtesy of FIFA.

Level 3: Bench With Single-Leg Lift and Hold

Lie on your front and support your upper body with your forearms. Your elbows should be directly under your shoulders. Lift your upper body, pelvis and legs until your body is in a straight line. Pull in the abdominal and gluteal muscles. Lift one leg about 10 to 15 centimetres off the ground and hold the position for 20 to 30 seconds. Repeat with the other leg. Perform three sets.

Note: Do not sway or arch your back. Do not move your buttocks upwards. Keep your pelvis stable and do not let it tilt to the side.

8. Sideways Bench

Level 1: Static Sideways Bench

Lie on your side with the knee of the lowermost leg bent to 90 degrees. Support yourself on your forearm and lowermost leg. The elbow of the supporting arm should be directly under the shoulder. Lift the pelvis and uppermost leg until they form a straight line with your shoulder (figure 15.9). Hold the position for 20 to 30 seconds. Repeat on the other side. Perform three sets.

Note: Keep your pelvis stable and do not let it tilt downwards. Do not tilt shoulders, pelvis or leg forwards or backwards.

▶ **Figure 15.9**   Static sideways bench.

Courtesy of FIFA.

Level 2: Sideways Bench With Hip Lift

Lie on your side with both legs straight. Support yourself on your forearm. The elbow of the supporting arm should be directly under the shoulder. Raise your pelvis and legs until your body forms a straight line from the uppermost shoulder to the uppermost foot (figure 15.10). Lower your hips to the ground and lift them again. Continue for 20 to 30 seconds. Repeat on the other side. Perform three sets

 Note: Do not tilt your shoulders or pelvis forwards or backwards. Do not rest your head on your shoulder.

▶ **Figure 15.10**   Sideways bench with hip lift.

Courtesy of FIFA.

Level 3: Sideways Bench With Leg Lift

Lie on your side with both legs straight. Support yourself on your forearm and lower leg. The elbow of the supporting arm should be directly under the shoulder. Raise your pelvis and legs until your body forms a straight line from the uppermost shoulder to the uppermost foot. Lift the uppermost leg (figure 15.11) and slowly lower it again. Continue for 20 to 30 seconds. Repeat on the other side. Perform three sets.

 Note: Keep the pelvis stable and do not let it tilt downwards. Do not tilt the shoulders or pelvis forwards or backwards.

▶ **Figure 15.11**   Sideways bench with leg lift.

Courtesy of FIFA.

9. Hamstrings

Level 1: Beginner

Kneel with your knees hip-width apart. A partner pins your ankles firmly to the ground with both hands. Slowly lean forwards while keeping your body straight from the head to the knees (figure 15.12). When you can no longer hold the position, gently take your weight on your hands and fall into a press-up position. Perform three to five repetitions.

Note: Do the exercise slowly at first. After you feel more comfortable, speed it up.

▶ **Figure 15.12** Beginner hamstrings.

Courtesy of FIFA.

Level 2: Intermediate

Perform the exercise as described for the beginner level but increase the number of repetitions to 7 to 10.

Level 3: Advanced

Perform the exercise as described for the beginner level but increase the number of repetitions to 12 to 15.

10. Single-Leg Stance

Level 1: Hold the Ball

Stand on one leg with the knee and hip slightly bent. Hold a ball in both hands (figure 15.13). Hold your balance and keep your body weight on the ball of your foot. Hold for 30 seconds and repeat on the other leg. Make the exercise more difficult by lifting the heel from the ground slightly or by passing the ball around your waist or under the knee of the lifted leg, Perform two sets on each leg.

Note: Do not let your knee buckle inwards. Keep your pelvis horizontal and do not let it tilt to the side.

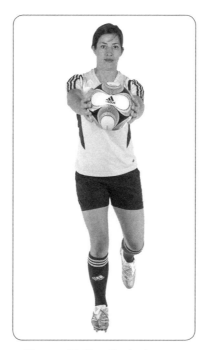

▶ **Figure 15.13**　Single-leg stance with ball hold.

Courtesy of FIFA.

Level 2: Ball Throw With Partner

Stand on one leg. Face a partner who is two to three metres away. Keep your balance while you throw the ball to each another. Hold in your abdomen and keep the weight on the ball of your foot. Continue for 30 seconds and repeat on the other leg. Make the exercise more difficult by lifting the heel from the ground slightly. Perform two sets on each leg.

  Note: Do not let your knee buckle inwards. Keep your pelvis horizontal and do not let it tilt to the side.

Level 3: Test Your Partner

Stand on one leg at arm's length from your partner. Keep your balance while you and your partner in turn try to push each other off balance in different directions (figure 15.14). Continue for 30 seconds and repeat on the other leg. Perform two sets on each leg.

  Note: Do not let your knee buckle inwards. Keep your pelvis horizontal and do not let it tilt to the side.

▶ **Figure 15.14** Single-leg stance with partner test.

Courtesy of FIFA.

11. Squat

Level 1: Squat With Toe Raise

Stand with your feet hip-width apart and your hands on your hips. Slowly bend your hips, knees and ankles until your knees are flexed to 90 degrees (figure 15.15). Lean the upper body forwards. Then straighten the upper body, hips and knees and stand up on your toes. Then slowly lower again and straighten up slightly more quickly. Repeat for 30 seconds. Perform two sets.

Note: Do not let your knee buckle inwards. Lean the upper body forwards with a straight back.

▶**Figure 15.15** Squat with toe raise.

Courtesy of FIFA.

Level 2: Walking Lunge

Stand with your feet hip-width apart and your hands on your hips. Lunge forwards slowly at an even pace. Bend your hips and knees slowly until your leading knee is flexed to 90 degrees (figure 15.16). The bent knee should not extend beyond the toes. Perform 10 lunges on each leg and complete two sets.

Note: Do not let your knee buckle inwards. Keep your upper body straight and pelvis horizontal.

▶ **Figure 15.16** Walking lunge.

Courtesy of FIFA.

Level 3: Single-Leg Squat

Stand on one leg and loosely hold on to a partner. Slowly bend your knee until it is flexed to 90 degrees, if possible (figure 15.17), and straighten up again. Bend slowly and then straighten slightly more quickly. Repeat on the other leg. Perform 10 squats on each leg and complete two sets.

Note: Do not let your knee buckle inwards. Keep the upper body facing forwards and pelvis horizontal.

▶ **Figure 15.17** Single-leg squat.

Courtesy of FIFA.

12. Jumping

Level 1: Vertical Jump

Stand with your feet hip-width apart and your hands on your hips. Slowly bend your hips, knees and ankles until your knees are flexed to 90 degrees. Lean the upper body forwards (figure 15.18). Hold this position for 1 second and then jump as high as you can and straighten your whole body. Land softly on the balls of your feet. Repeat for 30 seconds. Perform two sets.

   Note: Jump off both feet. Land gently on the balls of both feet with your knees bent.

▶ **Figure 15.18**   Vertical jump.

Courtesy of FIFA.

Level 2: Lateral Jump

Stand on one leg. Bend your hips, knee and ankle slightly and lean your upper body forwards (figure 15.19). Jump from your supporting leg approximately one metre to the side on to the other leg. Land gently on the ball of your foot and bend your hips, knee and ankle. Hold this position for about 1 second and then jump to the other leg. Repeat for 30 seconds. Perform two sets.

Note: Do not let your knee buckle inwards. Keep your upper body stable and facing forwards and pelvis horizontal.

▶ **Figure 15.19** Lateral jump.

Courtesy of FIFA.

Level 3: Box Jump

Stand with your feet hip-width apart. Imagine you are standing in the middle of a cross. Jump with both legs forwards and backwards, from side to side, and diagonally across the cross. Keep the upper body leaning slightly forwards. Jump as quickly and explosively as possible. Repeat for 30 seconds. Perform two sets.

Note: Land softly on the balls of both feet. Bend your hips, knees and ankles on landing. Do not let your knee buckle inwards.

PART 3 RUNNING EXERCISES

13. Running Across the Pitch   Run approximately 40 metres across the pitch at 75 to 80 per cent of maximum pace and then jog the rest of the way. Keep your upper body straight. Your hip, knee and foot should be aligned. Do not let your knees buckle inwards. Jog easily back. Perform two sets.

14. Bounding   Take a few warm-up steps and then take six to eight high bounding steps with a high knee lift. Then jog the rest of the way. Lift the knee of the leading leg as high as possible and swing the opposite arm across the body (figure 15.20). Keep your upper body straight. Land on the ball of the foot with the knee bent and spring. Do not let your knee buckle inwards. Jog back to recover. Perform two sets.

▶ **Figure 15.20**   Bounding.

Courtesy of FIFA.

15. Plant and Cut   Jog four or five steps straight ahead. Then plant on the right leg, cut to change direction to the left (figure 15.21) and accelerate again. Sprint five to seven steps at 80 to 90 per cent of maximum pace before you decelerate and plant on the left foot and cut to change direction to the right. Do not let your knee buckle inwards. Repeat the exercise until you reach the other side of the pitch and then jog back. Perform two sets.

▶ **Figure 15.21**   Plant and cut.

Courtesy of FIFA.

Conclusion

Scientific evidence shows that injury prevention programmes such as FIFA 11+ can reduce the incidence of noncontact injuries 30 to 50 per cent in amateur male and female soccer players. Coach and player compliance and adherence are key factors in ensuring the preventive effects of such exercises.

As studied, a (neuromuscular) warm-up format of the programme can enhance adherence and facilitate its integration into the overall training plan. Note that research has not been done with some age groups (i.e., children) and at the professional level.

Despite the available evidence, the implementation of injury prevention in real practice still represents a major challenge. The willingness of clubs and teams (and national soccer associations) is crucial in prioritizing the commitment towards the health of the soccer players.

PART

V

Psychological and Mental Demands

CHAPTER 16

Psychology and Elite Soccer Performance

—Geir Jordet

What do we know about the psychology of elite soccer players? This chapter presents the status quo from research on psychology and elite soccer performance.

Psychology is often defined as the science of behaviour, referring to observable actions, and the mind, referring to processes such as perceptions, memories, thoughts, motives and emotions (Gray 2007). Psychology is based on systematic analysis of objectively observable data and not on folk knowledge or laymen's claims about the workings of the mind. The core of this chapter is soccer-specific psychology, that is, the scientific knowledge we have about soccer players' behaviours and minds. This foundation will be supplemented by anecdotes, both from well-known players and coaches and from the author's 15 years of experience as a sport psychology consultant in professional soccer in Europe.

> *The last 10 years, we have been in the physical and in the technical area. The next 10 to15 years we will move forward in the mental area. Not only related to the desire to win, but to perception and quick understanding. This is certainly the new area of development for our sport.*
>
> *Arsene Wenger (2010)*

Elite soccer performance is ultimately related to reaching and performing at the professional level. In 2007 the total number of soccer players registered with a club or team in the world was reported to be 38 million, of which 34 million were male (FIFA 2007). This number is increasing, but the number of male professional players in the world remains fairly stable, at around 110,000. Therefore, only 0.3 per cent of all registered male players are professional (FIFA 2001, 2007), showing clearly how difficult and challenging it is to make it to that level (Haugaasen and Jordet 2012).

This chapter is about the specific psychological requirements of making it into the top professional level. Most of the available research has focused on male soccer players, and this body of knowledge is the foundation of this chapter, but the principles are likely to be similar for men and women.

A search for peer-review research articles with the keywords 'soccer' and 'psychology' in the leading sport science database Sport Discus produced 1,167 article hits (May 2014). Although closer inspection reveals that not all of these articles are directly relevant to psychology and elite soccer performance, the number of articles suggests that the scientific basis for psychology in soccer is considerable. This chapter reviews a selection of those studies.

The 11-Model

The chapter is structured into 11 key types of behaviours that are hypothesized to develop, facilitate or support elite soccer performance. Philosophically, this structure rests on ecological (e.g., Gibson 1979; Bronfenbrenner 1979) and phenomenological (Merleau-Ponty 1962) foundations. Actual experiences and behaviours, and the context within which these take place, serve as the starting point. With that said, each of these behaviours is driven or facilitated by a series of psychological (i.e., cognitive, motivational or emotional) processes, and this chapter reviews the most prominent of these processes as they relate to each behaviour. Each type of behaviour is displayed as a player in a soccer team starting line-up (see figure 16.1).

The following sections briefly describe each of these characteristics, starting with the back four, proceeding up the field and finishing with the goalkeeper.

Passionately Play the Game

Players who freely play and enjoy soccer are autonomously and passionately involved in the game. Many of the world's best soccer players anecdotally refer to the joy and pleasures they derive from the game. For example, the Argentinian legend Diego Maradona stated in his autobiography, 'To play soccer gave me a unique calm. And this feeling—just the same feeling that I've always had and still have: Give me a ball and I am enjoying myself' (Maradona 2005, 11). Similarly, Cristiano Ronaldo said, 'I feel so lucky, doing what I like the most' (Ronaldo 2007, 11).

> *He used to skip school and play football at the waste disposal area and come back dirty and full of scratches. We tried everything, but then there was a time when he had broken his hand but didn't care and wanted to go back to the pitch to play again—that is when my husband and I realized that we would never be able to kill the footballer in our son.*
>
> *Lyubov Shevchenko, mother of former AC Milan and Chelsea FC player Andriy Shevchenko (Christensen 2005, 51)*

▶ **Figure 16.1** The 11-model of performance psychology in soccer.

The hypothesis of this section is that intrinsic motivation is the foundation for elite players' participation in the game. This idea has lately been linked to self-determination theory, whereby high levels of self-determination refers to intrinsic or autonomous motivation and low levels of self-determination refers to external or controlled regulation of motivation (Deci and Ryan 2000). Further, the theory puts forward that people have certain basic needs, among them the need for autonomy (i.e., need to have control over one's actions), need for relatedness (i.e., need to feel connected with other people) and need for competence (i.e., need to have a positive effect on outcomes and surroundings). Fulfilment of these needs is associated with a series of positive outcomes in sport, among them positive well-being, good health and increased performance (Ntoumanis 2012).

What do we know about these processes in soccer players? In a study of U15, U17, U19 and senior professional soccer players in English soccer clubs, the authors found that the players' self-determined motivation remained high even for the more elite groups (i.e., the U19 and first-team players) (Forzoni and Karageorghis 2001). This finding suggests that intrinsic, self-determined motivation can be sustained when elite athletes progress through age and performance levels, even as their involvement in soccer becomes more serious. But this is not always the case. In a more recent study, it was found that the more time U17 players had spent in Scottish top clubs' academies, the lower their self-determined motivation was and the higher their levels of extrinsically controlled motivation were (Hendry, Crocker and Hodges 2014). The researchers discuss whether the highly competitive academy system, with its elaborate day-to-day involvement and potential focus on external rewards, may have had detrimental effects on the players' levels of self-determination over time.

Other studies have shown that young elite soccer players with high self-determined involvement in the game indeed enjoy a series of psychological benefits. For example, a study of UK elite academy players showed that the players high on self-determination (i.e., their needs of autonomy, relatedness and competence are satisfied) have more positive energy, vitality and ultimately well-being than players who are lower on self-determination (Adie, Duda and Ntoumanis 2012). A similar study, with another group of UK academy players, found that self-determined involvement is positively linked to processes such as goal setting, leadership, responsibility and emotional regulation (Taylor and Bruner 2012), all processes associated with optimal development of performance. Thus, we can conclude that there is indirect evidence for self-determined involvement in the game to be a foundation for players who make it into the professional ranks in soccer.

Players who feel actively in control over their own actions, feel connected to others and feel that they have a positive effect on their surroundings are more likely to develop high performances than those whose involvement is less self-determined.

Passion refers to a strong inclination towards an activity that a person likes or loves and finds important, in which significant time and energy is invested (Vallerand 2012). Although some studies in nonsoccer samples link higher levels of passion to deliberate practice and to better performance (Vallerand et al. 2008), different types of passion seem to affect people in different ways.

Typically, harmonious passion can be found in players who freely choose to participate in soccer, with no sense of obligation. Obsessive passion can be found in those whose intense feelings about soccer are equally strong but whose drive comes from internal pressure, a feeling that the person 'has to' train, play and so forth. Both types of passion can lead to high performance. Although some evidence from ice hockey suggests that obsessive passion can be more adaptive than harmonious passion in elite sport contexts (Amiot, Vallerand and Blanchard 2006), athletes with obsessive passion run a higher risk of maladaptive consequences such as exhaustion, overtraining and burnout (Vallerand 2012).

Coaches can stimulate intrinsic, self-determined motivation and harmonious passion in their players by providing an autonomy-supportive environment (Adie, Duda and Ntoumanis 2012; Felton and Jowett 2013; Taylor and

Bruner 2012). Coaches can create an autonomy climate by allowing players' motivational needs (for autonomy, relatedness and competence) to be met; by taking players' perspectives, desires, feelings and choices seriously; and by establishing safe and genuinely good relationships with players by demonstrating concern for them and by being approachable and trustworthy.

Relentlessly Pursue Performance

Passionate play is not enough. In a study of successful youth elite players (academy level or playing for their country's youth national team), all players referred to the love of the game as their primary motivation (Holt and Dunn 2004). But in a study by the same research team, this time with players at about the same age who were about to be cut from their club (hence, likely not reaching a professional career and here labelled 'unsuccessful'), the players also all referred to the love of the game as their core motive (Holt and Mitchell 2006). Both the successful and the unsuccessful players refer to the same motive. Clearly, something else differentiates those who reach the professional level from those who do not.

The successful players (Holt and Dunn 2004) pointed to one element that the unsuccessful players (Holt and Mitchell 2006) did not—the determination to succeed.

> *From the moment I first remember seeing a picture of him holding the European cup, I wanted to copy his success.*
>> *Paolo Maldini, former AC Milan and Italy player, referring to his father Cesare Maldini's European cup victory (Kuper 2011, 93)*

> *He still surprises me every day with his quest to always improve and to look inside as well.*
>> *Cesare Maldini, about his son, Paolo Maldini (Kuper 2011, 93)*

In interviews, 10 expert development coaches working at academies for English Premier League or Championship clubs identified several factors as necessary to reach the top professional level in soccer (Mills et al. 2012). Among these were goal-directed attributes such as desire and passion, determination, work ethic, professional attitudes and focus. Further, a central part of a professional attitude was to be self-disciplined and ready to make sacrifices for a career. What more do we know about these processes specifically in soccer?

Researcher Nico Van Yperen gathered data in the beginning of the 1990s on 65 young elite players from the Ajax Amsterdam academy. When this sample was revisited 15 years later, 18 players had played at least 10 years for a professional premier league soccer club. These highly successful players could be distinguished from the relatively unsuccessful players on several factors (Van Yperen 2009). One such factor was their level of goal commitment. The players who ultimately became successful were more invested in their goals of becoming professional players. This characteristic may have caused them to put more effort into reaching the goals, to pursue them more persistently and to be more reluctant to lower or abandon them when faced with adversity.

Thus, although many players are likely to seek success, they may differ in the extent to which they want success, think about success, are driven by the prospect of success and ultimately follow up with day-to-day actions.

Players who intensely strive for success are not only highly committed to reaching their goals but also exert high levels of effort, invest much energy and mobilize all their resources to get where they want to go.

This behaviour corresponds with approach motivation (wanting to achieve success), which is hypothesized to be more adaptive than avoidance motivation (wanting to avoid failure) (Elliot 1999; Roberts, Treasure and Conroy 2007). Striving for success is also consistent with hope theory, in which both wanting to achieve something and identifying the pathways to success are important (Snyder et al. 2002). The unsuccessful players in the Holt and Mitchell (2006) study reported having high career aspirations but little or no strategic planning of the pathways to excellence. Another relevant concept is grit, a trait-based perseverance and passion for long-term goals, which entails working strenuously towards challenges and maintaining effort and interest over a long period despite failure, adversity and plateaux in progress (Duckworth et al. 2007).

Although no research has documented the effect of grit in sport, it has been linked to high performance in several nonsport samples (Duckworth et al. 2007) and is likely to distinguish successful soccer players.

Finally, in the study by Holt and Dunn (2004), the authors found that successful elite youth players referred to the concept of delayed gratification (i.e., sacrifice now, achieve rewards later). None of the unsuccessful players referred to this concept (Holt and Mitchell 2006). This ability can be labelled self-control (or self-discipline or willpower). In one of our studies, we found that dispositional self-control was significantly higher in our 644 Norwegian professional players than in the general population, and the players at the highest professional league level or with senior national team experience had higher scores than the others did (Toering and Jordet 2015). Further, higher self-control was negatively associated with sleep but positively associated with time playing video games or surfing the Internet. Thus, players with high self-control may be able to resist the desire to engage in activities that they know may not be good for their overall performance (such as staying up late at night, excessively surfing the net or playing video games). Consequently, they end up recovering and resting with higher quality than other players do.

In conclusion, the extent to which players are relentlessly pursing their long-term goals may be where other players fall short. Coaches need not only to encourage players to set high goals but also to help them identify the exact paths through which they can achieve their goals and to support them in making daily sacrifices to reach their long-term career goals.

Regulate Total Load

To become an elite soccer player, a young player needs to engage in large amounts of quality, deliberate soccer practice (see Ford and Williams 2012; Haugaasen and Jordet 2012; Haugaasen, Toering and Jordet 2014).

> *I spent at least an hour and a half warming up, strengthening muscles: I still keep it up almost every day—never quit, never think you've got it made. This requires a serious personal investment.*
>
> Didier Drogba (2009, 245)

This commitment requires considerable mental and physical effort. Hence, athletes need to balance the work they put down with sufficient recovery to avoid burnout or overtraining (Ericsson, Krampe and Tesch-Romer 1993). World-class athletes, across multiple studies, refer to the importance of long- and short-term recovery for the development of their performance (MacNamara, Button and Collins 2010a; Orlick and Partington 1988), combined with a sense of life balance (Durand-Bush and Salmela 2002).

What do we know about the psychological correlates of such processes in soccer?

If too little or the wrong recovery accompanies too much load, soccer players risk injuries, illness, overtraining, overreaching, sleep disturbance, emotional disruption, loss of motivation and ultimately stagnation or decrease in performance (Brink et al. 2014, 2010, 2012). For example, one study identified symptoms of overreaching in 30 to 50 per cent of high-level Belgian soccer players during a competitive season (Naessens et al. 2000). These symptoms can have psychological underpinnings. In a study of professional adult German players, Faude and colleagues (2011) showed that stress and lack of recovery accumulated across a season, causing players to score significantly higher on various indices of stress at the end of the season compared with before the season started. Those particular stress elevations, however, were not associated with physiological changes. Other studies show that signs of stress are potential early markers for overreaching (a stage that precedes overtraining and burnout) or overtraining. For example, a study of 94 young Dutch elite academy players showed that players with high levels of emotional stress, lower general well-being and less sleep were vulnerable to symptoms of overreaching over a period of two seasons (Brink et al. 2012). Measures of emotional stress, physical recovery, general well-being and sleep quality seemed most predictive.

In a recent study, we found a considerable difference in coaches' planned training intensity and young elite soccer players' perception of training intensity (Brink et al. 2014).Players tended to perceive training as harder than what was intended by the coach (when the coach planned for low or intermediate intensity), which suggests the importance of carefully planning and monitoring training intensity levels to prevent the accumulation of exhaustion and fatigue that can lead to overreaching, overtraining and burnout. Furthermore, some players are more at risk for these syndromes than others. In one study, young elite players who conditioned their self-worth on issues such as achievement experienced more perfectionism and were more vulnerable to burnout than players whose self-worth was more stable and less conditioned on such factors (Hill et al. 2008). Although obsessive passion and burnout do not seem to be directly related, researchers still suspect that obsessive passion can indirectly predispose young soccer players to exhaustion and burnout (Curran et al. 2011, 2013). On the other hand, high levels of harmonious passion are associated with higher levels of self-determination and seem to protect young soccer players against burnout (Curran et al. 2011, 2013).

Other studies demonstrate that soccer players are more prone to injury when they experience different types of stress in their lives. For example, in a study of 53 Dutch elite academy players, Brink and co-workers (2010) found that physical stress and psychosocial stress led to more incidents of illness and injury. Moreover, in a study of 56 Swedish professional soccer players, trait anxiety, stress from negative life events and daily hassle were associated with significantly higher injury rates (Ivarsson, Johnson and Podlog 2013). Other, more personality-based psychological variables, such as trait anxiety, stress susceptibility and trait irritability, have also been shown to predict injury occurrence in soccer players (Ivarsson and Johnsson 2010). Overall, researchers in this area agree that the reduction of stressors and daily hassles combined with more effective coping with stress can considerably reduce injury risk.

Together, all these research findings suggest that coaches and fitness staff should incorporate psychosocial factors such as social activities, well-being and sleep when working to prevent overreaching, overtraining and injuries and to facilitate optimal performance. Coaches should also monitor psychological factors and their role as early markers of overreaching or overtraining and as risk factors for injuries. Careful monitoring of training load, equipping players with various ways to cope with stress and creating an autonomy-supportive climate are all measures that are helpful in this regard. In addition, creating specific targeted psychological interventions can help players prevent maladaptive responses to total load. In an intervention study with young soccer players, a brief psychological skills-training programme significantly lowered the number of injuries (Johnson, Ekengren and Andersen 2005). The intervention consisted of somatic and cognitive relaxation, stress management, goal setting, attribution and self-confidence training, and identification and discussion of critical incidents related to soccer participation and situations in everyday life.

Self-Regulate Learning

We have some knowledge about how much and in what way elite and professional soccer players practiced in their youth years (for a review, see Haugaasen and Jordet 2012). For example, most players start engaging in soccer before the age of 10, and some evidence suggests that elites start earlier than nonelites do (e.g., Ward et al. 2007), although there are also reports that players at the Portuguese national team started playing as late as age 14 (Leite, Baker and Sampaio 2009). Furthermore, the total number of accumulated practice hours seems to differentiate both elite youth (Ford et al. 2009; Ford and Williams 2012; Ward et al. 2007) and senior (Helsen, Starkes and Hodges 1998) players. On the other hand, a recent study with a large sample (745 players) using a new and possibly better statistical procedure, did not find such a difference between professional and nonprofessional players (Haugaasen, Toering and Jordet 2014).

Thus, a large quantity of soccer-specific practice seems to be necessary to reach high levels of performance, but it may not be sufficient. In this section, the focus is on the quality of learning that players can extract from practice.

> Almost always, I think about the mistakes that I have done. What can I improve? Always, always, I bring something that I can use from practice or games, and this is tiring. I never become fully pleased, not even when I should, but this helps me to be in development.
>
> Zlatan Ibrahimovic (Ibrahimovic, Lagercrantz and Urbom 2013, 45)

From achievement goal theory and research, we know that athletes whose goals are based predominantly on task mastery, learning, improvement and effort (task orientation) enjoy a long series of positive benefits compared with athletes whose goals are based on winning, beating others and looking good in front of others (ego orientation) (Roberts 2012). In a study of Ajax academy players, data were gathered to examine the characteristics of the players who most improved their performances across a single season (Van Yperen and Duda 1999). The results showed that the players who were most task oriented had the largest progress in the season that the study lasted.

Self-regulation of learning has been defined as the extent to which people are meta-cognitively, motivationally and behaviourally proactive participants in their own learning process (Zimmerman 2006).

Self-regulation of learning can be linked to processes such as planning, reflection, evaluation and self-monitoring (Toering et al. 2009). In interviews with elite youth soccer coaches about the characteristics of the players who make it into the professional level, the coaches referred to the capacity to reflect, assimilate and adapt (Mills et al. 2012). The researchers concluded that self-regulation of learning seems to be a critical factor for successful players. In a series of studies, we find that young Dutch elite players, the top 1 per cent of players in their age group in the Netherlands, consistently score higher on these qualities compared with both lesser-skilled players (Toering et al. 2009) and other boys in the same age who do not play soccer (Jonker et al. 2010). In addition, players who score high on self-regulation of learning also engage more in learning-productive activities in practice, such as focusing, communicating and coming early to practice (Toering et al. 2011). Researchers have also found that world-class professional soccer players from Manchester United are students of 'their game' and engage in active self-regulation of their learning (Horrocks 2012), and that self-regulation seems to distinguish elite from less-elite female youth soccer players (Gledhill and Harwood 2014).

In conclusion, evidence suggests that the better players engage more in self-regulation of learning than others do, which indicates that players may benefit from doing this. Coaches are advised to encourage their players to plan their practice; set individual learning goals for each practice; self-monitor their focus and performances during practice; evaluate their practice; and reflect on their development, what they need to work on and what they need to do to progress in their careers.

Manage Relationships

An emerging top player has to manage and capitalize on a series of relationships with other people, on and off the field.

> *When I look back at my soccer career, I can conclude that my learning orientation and coachability made the difference.*
>
> Wim Jonk, former Ajax, Inter Milan and
> Netherlands player (Van Breukelen 2011, 184)

Expert development coaches claim that social competence and interpersonal skills are critical for players' ability to navigate the various relationships and groups of a soccer club environment (Mills et al. 2012). One of the coaches in the study expressed it like this: 'The type of player that I find is successful in the modern game is the person who is socially switched on, the one that is able to interact really effectively with everybody' (Mills et al. 2012, 1599).

In the study of young Ajax players, seeking out social support was one of the major factors predicting success (Van Yperen 2009). The players who became top professional players as adults reported that they sought support from their parents when they were in the academy significantly more than did the players without such careers. Similarly, in the study series by Holt and colleagues (Holt and Dunn 2004; Holt and Mitchell 2006), both the successful and unsuccessful players sought out social support, but only the successful players received tangible support (e.g., help to drive to and from practice) from their parents.

Teams in which players often communicate positive and supportive messages to each other are likely to be more successful than teams in which players communicate less in this way. In one of our studies on major tournament penalty shootouts, we found that even when we controlled for the relative standing in the shootout (which team was up or down), players who visibly celebrate their individual goals with various physical actions are more likely to end up on the winning team than players who celebrate their goals less visibly (Moll, Jordet and Pepping 2010).

We believe this happens because emotions are contagious. When a player on your team exhibits strong, positive emotions after his or her performance, you are more likely to experience similar (performance-enhancing) emotions, and ultimately your performance may improve.

Similar effects have been found across an entire season in the Israeli professional league, where teams whose players celebrated their goals together with their teammates (i.e., ran towards their teammates instead of their fans following a goal) ended up higher on the table at the end of the season (Bornstein and Goldschmidt 2008). Likewise, a study from NBA basketball showed that teams whose players engaged more in early-season touch behaviour (e.g., hugs, head grabs and high fives) had higher performance both as individuals and teams later in the season (Kraus, Huang and Keltner 2010).

These studies taken together suggest that players can positively affect their team's performance with the intensity of their communication (Moll, Jordet and Pepping 2010), the direction of their communication (Bornstein and Goldschmidt 2008) and the type of their communication (Kraus, Huang and Keltner 2010).

Players, however, do not always engage in such communication naturally or spontaneously, and they may need help. Several intervention studies have shown that various aspects of communication indeed can be altered and improved, and the consequence is increased soccer performance. For example, discussion of team functioning and mutual sharing in a soccer team gave a positive effect on team communication, cohesion and performance (Pain and Harwood 2009). This study is a part of a series of studies that first showed how team cohesion was an important success factor for youth England national teams (Pain and Harwood 2008), then that cohesion can be influenced positively (Pain and Harwood 2009) and finally that these processes can be monitored and affected over time (Pain, Harwood and Mullen 2012).

My experience is that much can be achieved by explicitly addressing the manner by which soccer players communicate, cooperate and help each other to perform better. This purpose can be achieved by asking each player to reflect on the following:

- With whom do you communicate (entire team, a specific group of players, only the players in close proximity on the field)?
- When do you communicate (first five minutes of each half, first five minutes after a goal, when someone does something well, when someone makes a mistake, during natural breaks)?
- How do you communicate (actions, physical touch, eye contact, body language, words)?

In this way, even players who are not natural communicators may get the competence and confidence to take more part in such communication. A statement from goalkeeper Edwin van der Sar illustrates how communication can be a learned skill, as much as an inherent personality characteristic: 'On the pitch, I am always talking and telling people where to go. But off the pitch I am a very quiet and shy lad' (Henderson 2011).

Adapt to New Contexts

Recent research on talent development shows that athlete development follows complex and nonlinear pathways and that many transitions occur between phases (Gulbin et al. 2013; MacNamara, Button and Collins 2010b).

Thus, an emerging elite soccer player will experience a series of transitions to new contexts—new teams, new relationships, new venues, new levels of performance, new countries, new cultures and new languages. The ability to cope with and adapt to new contexts seems crucial.

Although making it through these types of transitions appears crucial for the outcome of a career in professional soccer, little research specifically addresses it. But one area that has received some interest is the migration of players between clubs and countries. From 2004 to 2005 and 2008 to 2009, foreign players made up 40 per cent (n = 3,551) of the total player population (n = 8,785) in the big five European soccer leagues (i.e., Premier League, Ligue 1, Bundesliga, Serie A and La Liga) (Littlewood, Mullen and Richardson 2011). In addition, clubs in Europe are now looking to recruit young players earlier to ensure that they will get status as home-grown players (Littlewood, Mullen and Richardson 2011). When such young players are relocating, they are extremely vulnerable to experiencing culture shock, which may include isolation, self-doubt, homesickness, fear, helplessness, irritability and disorientation (Littlewood and Nesti 2011).

To study players who have relocated from another country to play soccer in England, semistructured interviews were conducted with 14 foreign professional players at different clubs from the four English Football League divisions (Donaldson 2006). Among the findings were that most of the players struggled in the first few months at the new club and country. Difficulties could be found at a surface level (food and weather) and at a deeper level (basic values and assumptions of British society). The latter proved most difficult to cope with. Having external support networks outside soccer made a positive difference, and coming from a culture with high perceived cultural closeness to Britain also helped.

In a similar recent study, researchers examined the experiences of five young players of different nationalities related to their entry into an English Premier League club (Richardson et al. 2012). All these players experienced a series of challenges on cultural, social, personal and game-related levels, such as the new playing style, game demands, coaching style, language and general homesickness. Some of the players indeed experienced culture shock and felt fear, loneliness and helplessness, and they had nobody on the inside of the club to confide in. The researchers concluded that much proactive work needs to be done with players in these situations to help them deal with all these new challenges.

Coaches are advised to be particularly sensitive to the psychological challenges that arise when players transition through different contexts. Players will probably need extra help and support to cope and adapt effectively.

Following the work of Nesti (2010), helping players adapt to new contexts should follow a holistic approach that focuses on the identity of the player with respect to every aspect of his or her life (i.e., family, relationships, education, culture and lifestyle). Simply teaching coping techniques or psychological skills is insufficient.

Cope With Adversity

The question is not whether an elite soccer player will experience adversity. Even the best players will undoubtedly experience setbacks, mistakes and failure at multiple points in their careers. The question is, How do they cope with this adversity? What are elite soccer players doing when they experience failure? Are they 'winners' when they 'lose'? This section touches on these questions.

> *What makes you grow is defeat, making mistakes. It is what keeps you alert. When you win, you think: 'Great, we won!' And even if we certainly did some things wrong, you relax. The only thing that winning is useful for is a good night's sleep.*
>
> *Pep Guardiola (Balague 2012, 128)*

English academy coaches refer to resilience as one of the critical factors for making the step to the professional level. Their answers can further be grouped into confidence, optimistic attitude, coping with setbacks and coping with pressure (Mills et al. 2012). Further, elite soccer players sometimes struggle with the prospect of experiencing adversity and failure. In a study of English academy players (Sagar, Busch and Jowett 2010), 81 players were first surveyed about their fear of failure. The entire sample experienced low to moderate levels of fear of failure, and fear of experiencing shame and embarrassment following failure was the highest rated type of fear. Four of the players who reported high levels of fear of failure were then interviewed about their experiences. Their perception of failure typically included not performing well, obtaining an undesirable game outcome and not receiving recognition or acknowledgement. They also experienced several aversive consequences of failure, such as emotional cost, reduced self-image, uncertain future, reduced social status, punishment from others and letting down important others.

In the study of young elite Ajax academy players (Van Yperen 2009), no difference was found between successful and unsuccessful players on the extent to which they experienced stress as young players. But these two groups of players coped with stress in different ways. The players who became successful employed more problem-oriented coping strategies than the others did. Problem-oriented coping strategies are strategies that attempt to alter or manage the situation that causes the stress (Lazarus and Folkman 1984). These results indicate that the successful players took more control over the stressful situation instead of just trying to deal with the emotions that came from the stress (which would be labelled emotion-oriented strategies) or attempting to disengage emotionally or behaviourally from the stress (avoidance-based strategies).

A problem-oriented coping approach is in line with several anecdotal reports about highly elite players not shying away from addressing and processing their failures. Goalkeeper Edwin van der Sar said in an interview,

> Making a mistake upsets me more now than it did in my youth. It doesn't bother me during a game, but afterwards I run a mistake over in my head. It is terrible. I replay mistakes more than victories and the good saves.
>
> (Henderson 2011)

Running through these situations and experiencing the emotions may be unpleasant and difficult, but doing so may be necessary to continue to develop and get better. In contrast, the non-elite players interviewed about their fears of failure (Sagar, Busch and Jowett 2010) reported responding to their fear of failure with mostly avoidance-based coping strategies; few reported using problem-focused coping strategies.

With that said, the coping process is complex, and one specific type of strategy may not fit all players. In the studies of English and Canadian youth players, the successful ones reported having a series of coping strategies to deal with obstacles and stress (Holt and Dunn 2004), whereas unsuccessful players seemed to lack such strategies (Holt and Mitchell 2006). Thus, elite players may simply have a wider repertoire of coping strategies to choose from. In other studies, elite players report using different strategies. In a qualitative study of female players' experiences with stress and coping at the World Cup, the players used reappraising, social resources, performance behaviours and blocking (Holt and Hogg 2002). In interviews with professional goalkeepers about coping with media stress, the most popular strategies were problem-focused strategies, social support and avoidance (Kristiansen, Roberts and Sisjord 2011). Thus, players can use many different strategies, and certain strategies are not necessarily always better than others.

The best bet for coaches and practitioners working with individual players is to educate them about different strategies and experiment with them to find what works for them in specific situations. Ultimately, the goal for players is to work through adversity, setbacks and failure so that they can have the same or more focus and energy in practice and games as they would have had without encountering the adversity.

Cope With Success

A 16-year-old player who performs at a high level on the soccer field will quickly receive attention and recognition from peers, media, agents, scouts and bigger clubs. The decisive question is whether this young player can continue to work hard and focus on the right things. The interviews with English expert development coaches gave some statements related to these processes (Mills et al. 2012). The coaches reported meeting players whose lack of emotional maturity led them to display a 'made it already attitude', which would not help them develop as effectively as they might.

> We had 22 players in the squad and at least 10 of them overestimated themselves in China. You crash into a brick wall when that happens.
>
> Foppe de Haan, Dutch U21 national team coach,
> about his team's unsuccessful 2008 Olympics (de Haan 2008)

Several potentially destructive or debilitative psychological processes may be involved here, such as arrogance, narcissism and hubris. For example, psychology researchers have recently started distinguishing between authentic pride and hubristic pride (Tracy and Robins 2007a).

Authentic pride derives from specific accomplishments and is often focused on the efforts made towards that goal, whereas hubristic pride refers to global beliefs about skills, abilities and strengths, which can be reflected in statements about oneself such as, 'I do everything well' or 'I am naturally gifted' (Tracy and Robins 2007b). In general, authentic pride seems to be an adaptive emotion that is correlated with higher self-control, whereas hubristic pride is less adaptive and related to measures of impulsivity and aggression (Carver and Johnson 2011). Experiencing authentic pride after successful sport performances is surely not wrong. The problems may start when a player's self-image grows out of proportion and he or she starts to feel entitled to a series of other benefits because of his or her accomplishments. This latter tendency may be a sign of hubristic pride. Certain young soccer players, when they experience early success and recognition, may adopt hubristic types of pride that have potentially negative consequences for their continued achievement behaviours.

Unfortunately, little research has been done on these processes in soccer or in other sports, but interviews with successful athletes from various sports have highlighted the ability of world-class athletes to respond to success with an increased drive for more success, realistic expectations and a willingness to move out of their comfort zone and seek fresh ideas from coaches and teachers (MacNamara, Button and Collins 2010a, 2010b).

In practice, coaches may want to address this area with their players and sensitize them to the potential challenge of becoming arrogant and developing hubristic tendencies. Coaches can share stories about successful players and the way they dealt with their success. Players should learn how to cope with their status in adaptive ways.

Cope With Pressure

Coping with pressure is about performing your best in situations that are important. In this section, I will use the case of the penalty shootout to illustrate a series of psychological mechanisms that are involved when elite soccer players perform under pressure. First, from our research, we see that many players underperform when pressure peaks. For example, on high-pressure penalties when a miss will instantly produce a loss, players score on only about 62 per cent of their attempts. In contrast, on penalties when a goal will secure a win, players convert 92 per cent of their attempts into goals (based on every shot in shootouts in the World Cup, European Championships, and the Champions League between 1976 and 2006; Jordet and Hartman 2008).

> *When we were in the midcircle I became incredibly nervous. I thought it showed on television that my legs were shaking, that is how nervous I was.*
>
> *Professional player participating in a penalty shootout in the 2004 European Championships (Jordet and Elferink-Gemser 2012, 81)*

This difference clearly illustrates the effect that thinking about positive or negative consequences has on performance for international-level soccer players. In all types of pressure situations, the smart approach for the player is to fill her or his head with either task-involved thoughts or positive thoughts.

Coping with pressure is in essence coping with high expectations. When John Terry stepped up to take Chelsea's fifth shot in the 2008 Champions

League final penalty shootout, one specific piece of statistic told us that he had a 25 per cent chance of scoring. In penalty shootouts, the most internationally recognized players (i.e., players who have won a prestigious individual award) tend to score considerably fewer goals (65 per cent) than players with equal levels of skill but with lower status (89 per cent) (Jordet 2009a). High-status defenders, such as John Terry, flop even more in these situations and score on only 25 per cent of their attempts. The explanation may be that many high-status defenders have obtained their high status because of excellent duelling, tackling and leadership, qualities far different from those required in a one-on-one with the goalkeeper from 12 yards away. Thus, when people expect players to deliver in situations where they may not have the corresponding skills, the pressure becomes incredibly high, and many of them fail.

To prepare players for pressure moments, a coach needs to reduce the expectations that players feel by, for example, publicly taking responsibility for the outcome.

Pressure is by nature uncomfortable. When exposed to it, humans typically look for a way out, for a way to escape. In his autobiography, Gareth Southgate said about his missed penalty in the 1996 European Championships game against Germany, 'All I wanted was the ball: Put it on the spot, get it over and done with' (Southgate, Woodman and Walsh 2004, 191). He is not alone in thinking like this. Our video analyses show that players prepare their shots twice as fast as normal when they take extreme-pressure, if-I-miss-we-lose kicks (Jordet and Hartman 2008).

Interestingly, England has the fastest penalty takers in the world: English players take, on average, 0.28 seconds to react to the referee's whistle and run towards the ball (Jordet 2009b). Although research has shown that players with quick preparation times miss more shots than those who take a second or two extra (Jordet, Hartman and Sigmundstad 2009), players in penalty shootouts are not necessarily advised to stretch the time they use to prepare their shots because this can potentially lead them to choke in various ways (Masters 1992). Rather, each player needs to find the most comfortable and natural preparation time for him- or herself, where he or she feels the most in control over him- or herself and the situation.

In general, however, players should be made aware of the tendency of soccer players to rush decisions and actions under pressure. This circumstance can happen when a team is in a counterattack, with lots of space to play in. The player with the ball can be affected by the pressure and make the wrong decision too quickly, when just holding the ball for one more second would have helped the player see the right decision. Or a goalkeeper sees the corner kick come in, feels the pressure to act quickly and wrongly leaves the goal line with no real chance to get to the ball. After players become aware of the manner in which they act on these tendencies, they can engage in deliberate work to regain control.

Several years ago, Michael Jordan nailed an adaptive philosophy related to coping with pressure in a Nike commercial:

I've missed more than 9,000 shots in my career. I've lost almost 300 games. Twenty-six times I've been trusted to take the game-winning shot, and missed. I've failed over and over and over again in my life—and that is why I've succeeded.

Being comfortable about making mistakes can bring athletes far in dealing with the fear of making mistakes. Perhaps we should learn from industries in which making a mistake costs not merely a lost game or a lost championship but human lives.

Examples of such organizations are airlines, hospitals, nuclear power plants and aircraft carriers. The best of these organizations focus on quickly reacting and coping with mistakes instead of avoiding them completely, and then learning from the mistakes (Weick and Sutcliffe 2007). Furthermore, they acknowledge that mistakes will indeed occur under pressure. Rather than attempt to prevent individual mistakes altogether, they put the focus on collectively coping with the consequences of these mistakes. I used this approach with a national team going into a penalty shootout in a U21 European Championships. In a team meeting before the tournament, we addressed potential failure and, more important, discussed strategies for dealing with it if it happened. We had plans for each player to deal with his missed kick and for the group to support the unlucky players who had missed. The team then did take part in a penalty shootout. The preparation seemed to have taken some of the edge off the high-pressure situation, and the shootout ended with a victory, despite several missed shots.

In general, for (nonpenalty) high-pressure games, coaches and players should work to do the following:

- Reduce the pressure of the high-stakes situations (e.g., accept that errors sometimes occur and have a plan for dealing with failure)
- Normalize emotional distress (e.g., accept that tension and uncertainty are natural parts of performing at a high level)
- Optimize self-regulation (identify strategies that give each player a sense of control over him- or herself and the situation and practice these strategies so that they become automatic)

Prospectively Control Game Dynamics

In the interviews with 10 expert academy coaches, another factor emerging as important for players making the transition to the professional level of play was sport intelligence (Mills et al. 2012). Four of the coaches discussed sport intelligence as having 'heightened game awareness', which one identified as having to do with seeing or perceiving a situation differently from others, a quality that would separate the elite from the subelite.

Prospective control refers to successful anticipatory regulation of future actions (Adolph et al. 2000; Jordet 2005a), anticipating what will happen two to five seconds into the future and acting accordingly.

In a functional magnetic resonance imaging (fMRI) study comparing elite (semiprofessional) soccer players with nonelite players and novices on anticipation of an opposing player's action (Bishop et al. 2013), it was found that elites were not only superior in anticipation but also used different brain processes than the nonelite players and novices did. This finding suggests that elite soccer players' anticipation skills (which would be an underlying cognitive process of effective prospective control of actions) are associated with superior brain function in these situations.

A central component of prospective control is visual perception. Some studies find that skilled players fixate their gaze less frequently but with longer durations, which may imply that they are able to extract more information from each individual visual fixation (e.g., Canal-Bruland et al. 2011). Other studies find that skilled players fixate their gaze more frequently but with shorter duration (Roca et al. 2011). A reason for this disagreement may be that these studies employed different types of laboratory designs in which players are asked to respond to either static photos (e.g., Canal-Bruland et al. 2011) or filmed game sequences (e.g., Roca et al. 2011).

In a more ecologically valid research protocol of visual perception, we have obtained close-up video images of players in actual games, which are then edited together with a smaller overview image of the general game events and the ball.

Such footage makes it possible to examine what we call visual exploratory behaviour (VEB), which refers to the manner in which players physically move their bodies and heads to perceive their surroundings more efficiently before receiving the ball, so that they can start preparing their actions with the ball (prospective control). We have conducted a series of studies with this methodology (Jordet 2005a, 2005b; Jordet, Bloomfield and Heijmerikx 2013). The results suggest that VEBs and performance are positively related; the more skilled players explore more frequently than the less skilled players do, and players who explore more frequently are able to reach their teammates with a greater number of successful passes (Jordet 2005a; Jordet, Bloomfield and Heijmerikx 2013).

The findings have major implications for both what scouts look for in players and how coaches work to improve players' soccer skills. Scouts can look at the quality of players' VEB to learn about how they take in information and how well they prospectively control the game dynamics. And coaches can encourage their players, particularly in the period before receiving the ball, to engage in more frequent VEB and to optimize it to each specific role and situation.

These behaviours are relatively easy to work with in practice. In an intervention study, two of three professional players quickly (after one to two weeks) increased their VEB frequency through deliberate visual imagery training (Jordet 2005b). Full integration in everyday exercises is probably more effective and functional. In general, players have to learn to adapt their VEB to each situation, learn the ideal points in time for implementing it and, most important, learn to extract information out of VEB and use it to control their actions prospectively.

Innovatively Advance the Game

One of the most influential accounts of expert performance is the theory of deliberate practice introduced by psychologist Anders Ericsson (Ericsson et al. 1993). What has received less attention from Ericsson's original work is his description of the most eminent level of expert performance, in which people go beyond the level of their teachers to 'make a unique innovative contribution to their domain' (Ericsson et al. 1993, 369).

> I am a fanatic about the game and I am constantly looking for explanations, just as a professor who is always looking to expand his knowledge. For me, football is first of all a science. Just like a physicist that throughout his career is trying to break the scientific codes, I try to solve all the mysteries in football.
>
> Yaya Toure (SkySport 2013)

When experts attain this level, they not only reproduce available knowledge and technical skill but also contribute something important and new to their field that ultimately advances the field.

Ericsson refers to eminent chess players who discover new versions of chess openings and advance the knowledge of chess and to eminent musicians who contribute new techniques and distinct interpretations of existing music.

In soccer, at the highest level, eminent players are those who have left a legacy to the game itself by defining a new skill, role or playing style. Some notable examples (obtained from Jonathan Wilson's *History of Football Tactics*, 2008) are Franz Beckenbauer's attacking libero–sweeper role (p. 272), Rinus Michel's and Johan Cruyff's total football (pp. 218–234) and, perhaps a more contentious pick, Luca Modric's new style of playmaking—*fantasistas*—with robustness and tactical discipline (p. 334). Clearly, innovation comes in many forms, some on the global stage and some on a more local scene. The point is that some players are able to strike out on a new path, which involves a certain level of innovation and transformation that advances not only the player's performances and career but the game itself.

Not much research has been done on the psychology behind these types of accomplishments in soccer. The players at this stage are different, they stand out, and as the expert English academy coaches might express it, they have something that makes them able to outshine their rivals (Mills et al. 2012). But this level of accomplishment is about much more. It requires a deep respect for the game, an interest to study it and the will to contribute to it and advance it. In an existential, phenomenological study of the soccer feint, it has been shown that creative players transcend the established views of performance and that this necessarily needs to be analysed on the basis of the expectations that already exist in the game (Aggerholm, Jespersen and Ronglan 2011). Players need to know the game first before they can innovatively contribute to it. An interesting case in that respect is the former Dutch player Dennis Bergkamp, who in his biography goes into his deep admiration, love and respect for the game. His manager at Arsenal describes Bergkamp like this:

> *I believe that Dennis was one of those who had such a high idea of the game and such a respect for the game that he wanted that to be above everything. I believe that the real great players are guided by how football should be played, and not by how football should serve them.*
>
> *(Bergkamp and Winner 2013, 168)*

Bergkamp expresses some of his ambition in this way: 'To do something that others don't do or don't understand or are not capable of doing. That's my interest; not following, but creating your own thing' (Bergkamp and Winner 2013, 16).

This type of expertise requires creativity, or divergent thinking. Creativity can be defined as 'the ability to produce work that is both novel (i.e., original, unexpected) and appropriate (i.e., useful)' (Sternberg and Lubart 1999, 3).

In sport, creativity often refers to originality and flexibility in game situations (Memmert and Roth 2007). In a longitudinal study of the development of convergent and divergent thinking in soccer game situations, large individual differences seem to occur in the extent to which divergent tactical thinking (creativity) is developed in young soccer players (Memmert 2010).

With respect to how these processes can be developed, coaches should help their players widen their attention. This purpose can be accomplished by not offering too much specific advice on what concrete decisions are the right ones to make so that players do not lock on what others say or do (Memmert 2011).

This recommendation is consistent with Dennis Bergkamp's thinking about how to educate young players in his role as coach at the youth academy of Ajax Amsterdam: 'Be special. Be unique. That's what we want. You can't be unique if you do the same thing as the 10 other players. You have to find that uniqueness in yourself' (Bergkamp and Winner 2013, 20). On a personal note, in a training session that I recently witnessed, Everton FC manager Roberto Martinez encouraged the young players he was coaching not just to react instinctively but to think and find solutions for themselves. Thus, during a 30-minute session, at least 20 times, he told individual players, just as they were about to receive the ball, to think. Not just do, but think. 'Think! Think! Think!'

Conclusion

In this chapter I have attempted to describe some of the empirical knowledge we have on the psychology of elite soccer performance. The 11-model of performance psychology in soccer outlines a series of performance development behaviours; each is driven, facilitated or supported by different psychological mechanisms. Although many of these factors are logically derived from research and practice with elite soccer players and most of the psychological mechanisms underlying them are documented with empirical research, the model is still in an early stage of development.

Nevertheless, the model may already be used as a practical tool in several ways. First, the 11 behaviours point to important areas of soccer performance that psychology will influence. Thus, the model constitutes a functional checklist of important behaviours that can help both players and coaches become more aware of the directions that their daily work on psychological dimensions can take. Second, with each of the 11 behaviours as goals for psychological work, both coaches and players should be mindful that the path to that goal might take different directions and complex trajectories, depending on the specific idiosyncrasies of both player and situation. Thus, knowledge about the psychological mechanisms that potentially can be involved in each of the 11 behaviours is critical. This chapter has attempted to provide some rudimentary insights into those mechanisms. Third, the 11-model can be used to profile or screen and monitor players to make the day-to-day work on psychological factors more systematic.

We have developed self-report and coach observation–based profile (Profile of Performance Psychology in Football, PPPF) and monitoring tools (Monitoring of Performance Psychology in Football, MPPF) (Jordet and Toering 2014) that we are currently piloting with elite players at both the professional first-team level and elite youth level in different European countries. With the research base that now exists on the psychology of elite soccer performance, the model presented in this chapter and the practical implications that arise from it, soccer players and coaches can take more competent and active responsibility for effectively developing the psychology of elite performance.

CHAPTER 17

Mental Interventions

—Matt Pain

In the fast-paced, high-stakes modern game, mental skills are critical to making good decisions under pressure and coping with increasing demands on and off the pitch. How well players step up in managing these demands can define how far they go and how much they achieve in the game. The ability to cope effectively reflects the person's level of mental toughness and the psychological climate around her or him, which includes coaches, teammates, parents and fans.

When you see resilient, composed and mature responses, both on and off the pitch, you know that the player is benefitting from mentally sound intervention and advice. Equally, if a player freezes under pressure, switches off at a crucial moment or punches an opponent, a part of you asks why and searches for reasonable and proactive answers.

> *A poor player isn't poor because he tends to kick the ball in his own goal. It's because when you put intense pressure on him, he loses control. So you have to increase the tempo of the game and he'll automatically give the ball away.*
>
> *Johan Cruyff*

This chapter helps coaches, psychologists and others gain an increasing sense of responsibility for the psychological development of their players. It focuses on the five Cs of mental toughness, which is the framework adopted by the Football Association (FA) in England when working with teams and, increasingly, by professional academies and grassroots clubs. See figure 17.1 and table 17.1.

Mental interventions can take many forms. This chapter provides case study examples of one-to-one work with players, coaching interventions and team practices designed to develop mental returns.

Commitment

Commitment is the central characteristic of the five-C framework. It underpins the development and performance of the other Cs and drives the

▶ **Figure 17.1** Successful, confident players have developed all five Cs of mental toughness.

© Human Kinetics

Table 17.1 Defining the Five Cs of Mental Toughness

Commitment	Quantity and quality of motivation; desire to achieve goals
Confidence	Belief and trust in abilities and a feeling of self-assurance
Concentration	Ability to focus on the right thing at the right time by switching attention effectively
Control (emotional)	Regulation of thoughts and emotions to manage the quality of performance
Communication	Ability to send and receive useful visual and verbal information

technical and physical corners of player development. In a recent interview, Dave Brailsford (2013), head of Team Sky and, at the time, GB Cycling, talked about two prerequisites for world-class performance: 'You need two things to succeed, one is talent, the other is commitment. If you've got commitment but not talent you can still go a long way, but if you've got talent and no commitment, not for me'.

You are just switching on, you're thinking, who am I playing against, right, what does he do, what do I need to do? Do I need to watch a video of him, what do I need to practise in training tomorrow? Is he quick and jinky? Do I need someone to run at me? Is he physical? So I practise my heading. That's the sort of preparation I do which is what I call more specific.

Gary Neville, Horrocks et al. forthcoming

Commitment concerns energy, direction and persistence. It is valued because of its consequences and the motivation it produces. Commitment is a key concern to managers, teachers, coaches and parents, all those involved in mobilizing others to act. But people are motivated to act by various factors, which can produce highly varied experiences and consequences.

Players may value an activity or participate only because of strong external coercion. They can be urged into action by curiosity and interest or by a bribe. They can behave from a sense of personal commitment to excel or from a fear of being criticized.

Core Behaviours of Commitment

Broadly speaking, players should show four core behaviours:

1. Mental and physical effort will not only be high in sessions and matches but also be consistent in intensity of effort across time.
2. Player engagement in tasks, drills, games and challenges will be high. These players are in the game for intrinsic reasons and love being part of the action. This enthusiasm for involvement is tangible on the pitch.
3. Players will approach rather than avoid new challenges and difficult tasks that stretch their current skill levels. They will actively look to improve themselves and won't shy away from embracing the development of a new skill.
4. When learning a new skill, these players will demonstrate persistence in the face of mistakes and errors. They will see mistakes as offering necessary information about how to refine the skill further.

Understanding the Motivations of Players

The key to developing committed players is to understand their motivations for playing the game—the why. With young players the relationship between effort and ability is not always clear. Feelings of competence and self-worth stem mainly from trying hard and enjoying a growing sense of self-mastery and skill. Young players are not yet in the trap of comparing themselves with others at everything they do. At this age, players get on with it and tend not to react in an overemotional manner to mistakes and setbacks.

For adolescents (which in modern Western society now extends well into the 20s) peer pressure and comparison can exert a strong positive or negative effect depending on the culture and commitment of the group. At its best, a committed group of peers can drive each other to new heights in training and matches (witness the class of '92 at Manchester United); on the other hand, a fear of failure and hiding behaviours can emerge if the banter is too sharp and the group is more interested in other distractions. The coach has the job of shaping the overall motivational climate so that peer influence is a positive force, not a negative one.

All players need to remain grounded and develop a growth mind-set, doing all they can to be the best they can be technically, mentally and physically, and not being too concerned with others despite the competition for starting places and, later, contracts. Maintaining this approach can be hard because results alone often become the benchmark of success. Current ability should still be seen as something that is improvable, and a sense of satisfaction and achievement stems from the players' efforts to stretch their pool of skills further. These improvements are also the most stable source of confidence. This point is explored later in the chapter.

Developing Committed Players

In soccer, which has a strong emphasis on proving superior ability, coaches need to continue nourishing and feeding a development perspective in their players. The coach's role is to promote the four core commitment behaviours (see table 17.2) and openly value effort, skill learning and personal improvement, as well as develop feelings of ownership and social support. In doing so, the coach will be producing players who are more committed as part of the team.

Self-determination theory (Deci and Ryan 1985) is the most influential theory of human motivation. The theory suggests that people are funda-

Table 17.2 Observable Commitment Behaviours in Soccer

Player with excellent commitment	Player with poor commitment
Shows him- or herself for teammates, especially when they find themselves under pressure from an opponent	Tracks back poorly throughout the game
Is eager to engage in the match with a first touch as early as possible, whether home or away	Gives up intensity of runs, tackles or winning of second balls when things go wrong
Renews effort and intensity after a goal has been scored for or against	Fails to renew efforts when needed
Does all that the coach asks in training and matches, approaching 100 per cent compliant	Is distracted by things outside the game

mentally driven to function effectively, to feel a sense of personal initiative in doing so and to feel connected to others. Deci and Ryan (1985) describe these three basic needs as competence, autonomy and relatedness. Literally thousands of studies have shown them to be essential for personal well-being, optimal functioning and constructive social development. Evidence suggests that the following strategies are the most effective in fostering intrinsic motivation and commitment:

- Reward effort, attitude and intention over outcome. The coach encourages persistence after mistakes and cultivates a positive peer climate.
- Provide skill-specific feedback and personalized recognition when earned. Use individually chosen goals and targets.
- Use competitive games in practice with targets, individual and team bests and clear fact-based evidence of improvements (link with performance analysis).
- Give players ownership within practices and a voice in team functioning—voice and choice.

How the coach brings these strategies to life in the team is a personal decision, but in general the more the coach can involve the players in the process and develop two-way communication channels, the more they will develop strong intrinsic motivation and the commitment required to reach the highest levels of the game. Preseason training camp can be a good time to start this process by working on team and individual goals, defined primarily by the players and then aligned skilfully by the coach and any specialist support staff.

Reigniting Commitment: A Case of Goal Setting

John came to me as a second-year academy scholar who'd just been offered a pro contract. His progress had recently stalled a little, and the coach had observed that he wasn't putting in the extra effort required to really kick-on as a pro. A chat with John revealed that he had lost focus on his own development and intrinsic motives because of the growing importance placed on the team outcomes and concerns. He had been involved in a successful youth cup run, was on the fringes of the first team but was yet to start a game. This circumstance is common as academy players rise through the system. Personal development objectives can be lost in messages about winning and team success.

So the core of our work involved redefining his personal targets and objectives using a detailed goal-setting process (see figure 17.2), which, crucially, still aligned with the team directives.

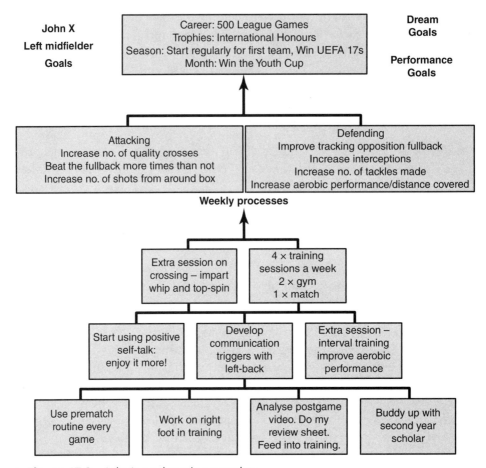

▶ **Figure 17.2** John's goal-setting template.

As a result of the goal setting, in particular defining for the first time his long-term career ambitions (dreams), John started to focus more on what he wanted to achieve in games and in training. He became committed to working on all aspects of his development, becoming fitter, more technically rounded and more integrated with the first-team squad, all vital steps to reaching his long-term targets.

Concentration

Concentration plays a key role in regulating the quality of a player's performance. It reflects a player's ability to sustain and switch attention effectively during play (table 17.3). Two factors determine the quality of concentration:

Table 17.3 Observable Concentration Behaviours in Soccer

Player with excellent concentration	Player with poor concentration
Is aware of the movements of teammates, movements of opponents and use of space	Is easily distracted by external or internal factors
Adopts the right positions in open play and refocuses quickly after a break in play	Drifts out of position
Helps others to stay focused and organizes tasks	Fails to refocus quickly after a mistake or break in play
Is able to vary the intensity of concentration in response to transitions on the pitch	

1. Attentional focus—where the focus of attention is placed. Is where the player looks and what he or she thinks or says to him- or herself relevant to the task?
2. Attention span—the ability to remain focused or hold attention on certain objects, people, thoughts or feelings for a required period without being distracted.

What people don't realize is that it's obviously a physical game, but after the game, mentally, you're tired as well. Your mind has been through so much. There are so many decisions you have to make through your head. And then you're trying to calculate other people's decisions as well. It's probably more mentally tiring than physically, to be honest.

Wayne Rooney

Developing the Focused Player

Figure 17.3 (Nideffer 1989) is a simple way to explain where a player's attention could be placed at any given time, and the description could be useful in helping to target concentration in training. As players mature, they should be comfortable working in each of the four channels and be able to switch quickly from one channel to another, even when under severe pressure (e.g., from ball to teammates).

Focusing on the Right Thing at the Right Time

Players with superior attentional skills develop a clear understanding of what is happening in the game around them (pictures), as well as how they can make a difference. This game intelligence is a hallmark of the elite modern professional, as shown by the Germany World Cup 2014 team, who rarely played a blind pass and had a record completion rate approaching 90 per cent. Jordet, Bloomfield and Heijmerikx (2013) have shown that frequency of

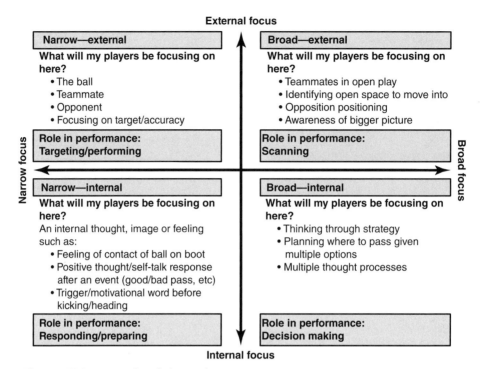

▶ **Figure 17.3** Attentional channels.

Adapted from R.M. Nideffer, 1989, Attention control training for athletes (New Berlin, WI: Assessment Systems International).

visual exploratory behaviours (VEBs) is closely correlated with pass completion and, even more important, with *forward* pass completion. Teams need the ability to break lines because they frequently face a mid or deep block. The ability to complete forward passes is the hallmark of creative midfielders like David Silva and Xavi Alonso.

Nevertheless, players can suffer from poor attentional focus. They focus on things that are essentially irrelevant to their immediate performance, such as ball watching, arguing with the referee or simply lacking vision for what is around them. Concentration coaching trains the players' focus of attention so that they can consistently optimize performance and not be disrupted by negative distractions.

Coaching Focus

Commitment to train attentional focus systematically and to sustain focus on the right things in training will help a player to maximize the robustness of his or her concentration in a match. Concentration is most tested under pressure, so it needs to be conditioned to hold up against pressure in training and matches.

The following strategies have been shown to be effective for developing concentration in players:

- Use game-realistic, opposed practices that challenge players to scan and switch focus effectively between ball, space and key players (i.e., tight areas).
- Highlight the cues and triggers that a player should be focusing on when on and off the ball.
- Use practices that challenge players to play head up—for example, to control the ball with peripheral vision only and to play a pass while keeping eye contact with the receiver.
- Randomly select players to close their eyes then ask them, 'Where are your nearest teammates or opponents?'
- Overload and stretch player concentration through distraction training by extending practice when players are fatigued or bored.
- Use consistent individual, unit and team trigger words to reinforce concentration cues, such as press, squeeze, drop.

Drill 1: Trigger Word Small-Sided Game With a Concentration Theme

Setup

Set up a playing area of 40 by 25 yards with a goal at each end and a halfway line marked (figure 17.4). Amend the size of the area as necessary according to the age and ability of the players in the group. Create two teams of four players, each with a goalkeeper.

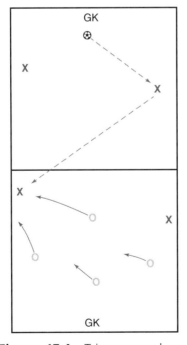

▶ **Figure 17.4** Trigger word small-sided game with a concentration theme.

Procedure

Designate one player per team as the team captain. Play a normal match. When a team loses possession of the ball, the team captain must decide whether the team is to defend in the attacking half or drop and defend in the defending half:

- If the team captain decides to defend in the attacking half, he or she shouts, 'Press!' The whole team then must defend in the attacking half.
- If the team captain decides to defend in the defensive half, he or she shouts, 'Drop!' The whole team then must defend in the defending half.

Goals count double if the defending team occupies both halves of the pitch.

To Add Concentration

- Develop the use of the trigger words 'press' and 'drop', making sure that the players use them at the appropriate moments.
- Practise without oral communication. The players have to react to the actions of the first defender and read the cues as to whether they can pressure the ball or not.

Communication

Communication involves the sending and receiving of information between two or more people. The quality of this process has psychological effects because it can directly influence the thoughts, feelings, actions or performance of one, both or all people involved. As the opening quotation illustrates, communication links closely to concentration, and it can either improve or interfere with performance depending on the efficiency of the process.

> *There should be no unnecessary yelling of instructions. The coaching of a teammate is only then necessary when he is not able to observe something, for example when he is being attacked by an opponent from behind. Especially when observing British teams, you can experience an unbelievable chattering. This only leads to a rushed and too hurried execution, increasing the chances for mistakes.*
>
> *Rinus Michels (2001)*

Types of Communication

In coaching and training sessions, communication by the coach and between players can be of several types:

- Verbal in the form of specific feedback, praise, encouragement or instructions
- Nonverbal in the form of physical responses, such as a reaction of dismay to a player's mistake or a positive or negative gesture, or a positive run in behind that acts a visual trigger to the player in possession
- An action, decision or behaviour that represents what one person thinks or feels about another, such as not passing the ball to a teammate who is the best option or turning around and walking off when being talked to

Communication can often be inefficient between players because only some players send information or because players have no agreed understanding of the information provided. Alternatively, they might send information in an overaggressive, overemotional and unhelpful manner. Most players are not very aware of their communication. Some players are not good receivers of information, typically those who think that others are criticizing them, those who can't take commands or constructive criticism, those who will not accept any information sent from a player they don't respect and those who simply need information to be explained more clearly. The key communication behaviours are summarized in table 17.4.

Developing Communication Skills

Communication needs to be practised both on and off the pitch and at all times. Opportunities for practicing positive communication and effective interactions with teammates are everywhere. If these opportunities are consistently taken, the team begins to form a cohesive group who begin to understand the strengths and limitations of others and work with them effectively.

The first step is to heighten player awareness of communication patterns. Several strategies can help in practice:

Table 17.4 Observable Communication Behaviours in Soccer

Player with excellent communication	Player with poor communication
Gives positive, constructive information and feedback to teammates	Stays quiet and gives no visual or verbal information to teammates
Listens to instructions from teammates and coaches	Fails to give praise and reinforcement to a teammate who has done something well
Shows positive body language	Blames or criticizes teammates in front of others
Provides clear visual triggers on the pitch (e.g., run behind, first man to press, and so on)	

- Develop a specific practice that assesses communication (e.g., only two players can talk, swap every minute, silent soccer) to highlight its importance.
- Include conditions that develop communication (e.g., putting a name on a pass, use of trigger words 'press' and 'drop', silent soccer to emphasize nonverbal communication).
- Recognize and reinforce when a player gives good praise, body language, feedback, information or instruction to a teammate.
- Recognize and praise when a player acknowledges or listens to a teammate.

On top of these, you can do specific work to develop the common triggers between units of players. Good instruction or information always relates to the team tactics or game plan, and the players clearly understand it. For example, if the plan is the play out from the back, screaming, 'Get rid!' as soon as you regain possession is not helpful. But if you're the central midfield player and your team plays a pressing game, yelling, 'Press!' would be appropriate when you're looking to regain possession.

These instructional team triggers must be coordinated with the playing philosophy and game plan; otherwise, everyone will be shouting different and possibly conflicting instructions. This problem is common in teams when players don't know the game plan well enough or their role in the team.

Table 17.5 has been helpful in my work with teams to agree to a common language within and between units.

Repetition is key to embedding the triggers within training sessions and reinforcing them in match reviews when things often get lost in translation under intense pressure.

Table 17.5 Common Language Between Units

Situation	Instruction
Midfield press hard to win ball back	'Press!'
Defensive line push up	'Squeeze!'

Drill 2: Support Play Possession Practice With a Communication Theme

Setup

Establish an area of 35 by 35 yards with four scoring squares, one in each corner (figure 17.5). Amend the size of the area as necessary according to the age and ability of the players in the group. Set up two teams, one team of six players (Xs) and one team of four players (Os). Two target players (Ts) operate between two scoring squares each. Rotate roles every few minutes.

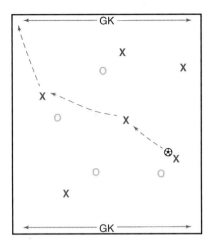

▶ **Figure 17.5** Support play possession practice with a communication theme.

Procedure

The teams compete for possession. To score, one of the target players must receive a pass in a scoring square. If a goal is scored, the ball returns to the attacking team, and they look to score in a different square. After a designated period, replace the target players with two Xs. The two target players join the Os, so now the Os play 6v4 against the Xs.

To Add Communication

- Run the practice without verbal communication to force the players to communicate nonverbally.
- Introduce combination play triggers, such as '2s' to indicate that the player wishes to perform a 1–2, or 'Sid's' and 'Fred's' to indicate that the receiving player is letting the ball through his or her legs for another player or performing a takeover.
- Develop communication triggers between defending players (e.g., 'Press', 'Show inside', 'Drop').
- Allow the target player to dictate which scoring square to attack by pointing to the desired square.
- Allow the target player to dictate which scoring square to attack by calling the square to attack.
- When the players are allowed to communicate verbally, draw their attention to what they are saying. How useful is their communication? Are they praising teammates? Are they offering useful information and instruction? Are they providing important feedback to help future performance? Are they encouraging and motivating teammates?

Confidence

The most noticeable characteristic of confidence is that it is a positive, forward-moving energy. As a force within the player, it never ever goes backwards. It allows the player to approach the challenges of the situation as opposed to avoiding them, and it gives the player the power to take opportunities and make decisions that less confident players might view as risks or threats to themselves and the team. These confidence behaviours, both positive and negative, are referenced in table 17.6.

> *Before the game I sat by myself listening to my own music. I didn't really talk to the lads and just tried to think to myself that I'm going to be the best on the pitch. I focused on how I was going to play; I kept going over the basics of how they wanted me to play. I pictured my positive moments from previous games and saw it all coming together and tried not to think negatively.*
>
> *Academy player before his first-team debut*
> *(Reeves, Nicholls and McKenna 2009)*

The fundamental challenge with confidence is that it can fluctuate between and within matches and sessions if it is not built on a sound foundation of three key positives, based on the seminal work of Bandura (1977) on self-efficacy: positive accomplishments, positive support and positive attitude.

Positive Accomplishments

Regardless of any coach intervention, if players get plenty of time on (and off) the ball to try new things, to experiment freely and to reach new targets and goals, they will achieve the small successes that add up to becoming confident players.

Coaches need to design sessions that offer consistent and frequent opportunities to develop new skills and reinforce old ones. Pitching the level of the challenge should be done at an individual level when possible (differ-

Table 17.6   Observable Confidence Behaviours in Soccer

Player with excellent confidence	Player with poor confidence
Involves him- or herself in receiving the ball under pressure	Allows his or her head to drop
Maintains positive body language at all times, even after mistakes	Shows poor body language
Demonstrates inventive or creative play as opposed to making cautious decisions	Hides from the game
Pushes him- or herself out of the comfort zone in training and games	Wants to offload the ball as quickly as possible

entiation) because success that is earned does far more for confidence than success that comes easily. The coach can develop a sense of accomplishment within the players by setting appropriate and progressive challenges and goals at an individual level. He or she should allow plenty of experience of success and time for higher perceived competence to develop by moving from simple to harder and more complex challenges. The coach literally builds the player's confidence through progressive task achievements, because every success matters and should be built upon. By setting individual achievable and realistic goals that are written down and ticked off when completed, the player gets to see real progress, which helps to reinforce each success and build further confidence. Dave Alred, who worked with Johnny Wilkinson, calls it 'fact-based practice'.

The same is true for games. Meeting individual challenges and objectives can mean that confidence grows (or is at least protected) even if the team doesn't win. Far too often, individual, self-referenced achievement is lost in group- or team-level judgements.

Performance analysis is an excellent tool for this purpose. Players I've worked with have built confidence from seeing things they're working on in training reflected in improvement in their stats over time (number of passes, completion percentage, shots on target and so on).

Positive Support

Positive support refers to social persuasion, in other words, positive and negative feedback. In my experience, this plays a major role in maintaining the confidence of a soccer player in what is an insecure industry. The coach can play a significant role (for better or worse) in this area. Most people can remember times where something said to them significantly altered their confidence, particularly when it came from a highly respected source.

Whereas positive feedback increases self-efficacy, personal criticism (which is different from constructive feedback) decreases it. Decreasing someone's confidence is much easier than increasing it. If a player is often told, however innocently, that she or he is 'not so good on the left foot', the player will come to believe it, putting an artificial limit on confidence and development.

Generally, delivering specific feedback ('great body shape when holding off the defender') is much more effective than offering general comments such as 'well done' or 'good effort'. This environment of positive support helps players want the ball more even after a poor execution. In a nonsupportive climate that creates a fear of mistakes, some players may hide because their low confidence causes them not to risk showing incompetence.

In my experience I've found that players are often starved of positive feedback. So I aim to remind them consistently of past successes, especially if confidence dips. Coaches can do this when reviewing a session by highlighting examples of skill in the video and asking the player to recall the things he or she did well. By logging these in a training diary, the player has a constant source of confidence information to refer to. If a player is struggling for form, remind him or her of good performances and recall specific successes. If video is available, show the best moments. I've had great success with preperformance montages set to the player's favourite music (see Pain, Harwood and Anderson 2011).

Positive Attitude

'If she can do it, I can do it as well'. When players see someone else succeeding at a skill, their confidence will increase. This process is more effective when the player is of similar ability. Therefore, using video footage is more effective for building confidence if the players performing are within similar ability range. Although not as strong as personal experience of success, modelling is particularly helpful when a player is unsure of her- or himself.

Picking out good examples of skill during practice and alerting the group to watch is an effective way to model behaviour and build confidence through use of capable peers. The same process can be used postmatch, individually and as a group. This method is especially powerful if video is available.

A positive effect can also result from acting as if you are a confident player, so role-modelling for younger players and taking a positive posture despite how you may feel can help shape a positive attitude.

When players can draw on these three qualities—positive accomplishments, positive support and positive attitude—they are more likely to develop a shield that protects them from experiencing any more than simple minor fluctuations in the power of their belief. This self-belief is vital in the professional game, where many factors can potentially affect confidence (e.g., being loaned, first-team debut, injuries, unrealistic expectations of self from others, including fans and media). Coaching sessions, therefore, need to tune in to developing an environment in which players regularly experience these three positives. Several confidence strategies can be used in practice:

- Use the player's first name when giving praise and specific feedback on individual accomplishments.
- Scaffold the coaching session so that players gain success at a challenging level. Use personal bests, targets and competition to embed success. Remember that little improvements lead to big steps.
- Copy confidence. Set up players to train like the confident player, copying her or his qualities, responses and body language. Reinforce whenever a player behaves like the confident role model.
- Use imagery so that players can mentally rehearse success, good execution and positive responses.

- Create a no-failure climate. Encourage players to express themselves, to be creative and to keep trying new things even after making mistakes.
- Offer players the chance to do their feel-good drills and practices to hone their strengths.

Confidence Intervention Case Study

In my experience, building confidence in the short term is not as easy as improving the other Cs. Confidence takes time to grow, and a robust confidence must be based on real achievements, as noted previously, and cannot be magically put into players. Often it is more a case of removing the barriers to confidence, such as negative self-image and negative self-talk, that are blocking a player's natural confidence and positivity. Unhealthy perfectionism and unrealistic expectations are often underlying factors here, and they help explain why some of the technically best players can still struggle with fragile self-confidence. The perfect game never happens, so such players often find it hard to bank for themselves any positive accomplishments even when from the outside it looks as if they've done well.

Aidan was a technically gifted midfielder at a Championship club but was extremely hard on himself when things did not go exactly as he wanted in training and games. Although his perfectionism was certainly driving high levels of commitment, the frequent negative self-talk ('You stupid idiot, you should do better there!', 'I always mess up!') was slowly draining his confidence, and the poor emotional control was also draining the energy of his teammates, who also felt the force of his frustration.

My intervention had three main components. First, I asked Aidan to become more aware of his self-talk in training and games. This step involved his keeping a simple diary in which he wrote down the things he had said to himself and his thoughts straight after sessions. We used this record as the basis for discussions. I challenged some of the unrealistic and damning messages and had him shift over time to more rational responses using a rational emotive behaviour therapy (REBT) framework to challenge his basic musts. For example, 'I must win' became 'I really want to win'; 'I must win the approval of others' became 'It's nice but not essential to gain their approval'; 'It's terrible to fail' became 'Failure won't kill me'; 'I should've scored there' became 'I could've score there'.

The second step was to make Aidan pick at least three positives from every game, even when he felt there had been none. He wrote these down in his diary as part of a postmatch review. This exercise helped take him away from dwelling on the negatives and mistakes and gave some closure to each game to prevent negative rumination, which often interfered with his sleep after games.

The third step built on the positives by developing a prematch ideal performance DVD. Done in collaboration with the club's performance analyst, this project involved finding clips of Aidan's performance of key skills in games (passes, tackles, interceptions, scoring goals) and cutting them to music that he associated with an ideal performance state and that he was connected to emotionally.

It took six weeks to put these steps into action and a further three months with weekly reinforcement before Aidan's game-day psychology and outlook began to change significantly. But over time he became less self-critical and was able to find more positives in his performances, which kick-started the process of building a more stable self-confidence. His response to disappointment became more rational and balanced. This change helped take the edge off his perfectionism, which then drove him in a more positive way towards his goals.

Control

Soccer can be a physical, volatile and unpredictable sport characterized by gamesmanship, hostility and inconsistent officiating. When a match is meaningful to players and the consequence of the result is important to the team, prematch anxieties and highly emotional responses to game events that go for or against the team are common.

> *I learned that if you don't control yourself psychologically, there comes a time when words like 'love', 'determination' and 'emotion' are not enough. You need to have that ability to stop and think.*
>
> *Dante (2014), Brazil and Bayern Munich central defender reflecting on Brazil 1, Germany 7 at the FIFA World Cup 2014*

These responses can include positively oriented emotions such as joy, happiness, elation, excitement and often relief when individual and team goals are met (e.g., scoring a goal, making a string of successful contributions, winning the game or saving a penalty). Players can also experience negative emotions such as excessive anxiety or fear, anger, frustration, shame, embarrassment and dejection when they fail to reach their own expectations or those that others have of them, or when key decisions go against the team.

Developing the Controlled Player

For every player, being able to control and manage emotions is a fundamental psychological skill. This skill is highly visible on a soccer pitch. Repeated examples of costly responses and poor coping at the highest levels reinforce to all coaches and players that being able to control emotions is important. On the pitch, teaching and coaching self-control demands attention to the physical and mental components that will influence composure, levels of

Table 17.7 Observable Control Behaviours in Soccer

Player with excellent control	Player with poor control
Responds swiftly and positively after an error or setback	Shows excessive aggression to an opponent, referee or teammate
Controls arousal levels so that she or he can perform optimally	Freezes under pressure
Minimizes blaming and arguing and maximizes positives	Blames other players for mistakes for which she or he was partly responsible
Remains composed during key periods and phases of the match (game management)	

arousal and a state of readiness. Table 17.7 illustrates the key positive and negative behaviours associated with emotional control.

Introducing players to breathing strategies and using command words, phrases or images when adversity challenges them will help them keep their nerves or anger in check and commit to the next opportunity. In addition, working on their physical image and body language can be productive in helping players command a consistent physical presence, particularly after mistakes, and seamlessly detach them from the past event. Here are strategies that can be used in practice:

- Highlight to players a negative emotional reaction—anger, self-criticism, bad body language, slow recovery, worry or negative thoughts—and its effect on performance.
- Allow players to practise switching from a negative reaction to a positive response (quick, involved, alert and so on).
- Use bad calls, consequences for losing control and pressure simulation ('ugly zone') in games.
- Encourage players to detach themselves from mistakes quickly by using a simple refocusing routine such as breathing, saying 'I'm back' or 'Next chance' or giving a thumbs-up. Note who recovers quickest.
- Reinforce the use of a mental preparation routine for pregame, breaks in play and at set pieces—breathe, visualize or use a trigger word (for both taker and receiver).

Given that soccer can incite emotions, coaches need to help players master their emotions so that they conserve and manage their energy. Often coaches and players leave self-control and stress management skills to chance. Players then suddenly reach a level at which they lack the coping skills to manage their own mental state and arousal levels. The journey ahead then becomes frustrating when all they had to do was spend time understanding their feelings and practicing the optimal ways to behave as players as they master new challenges. The following case study provides examples of how coaches can help players stay calm under pressure and in control of their emotions when they make mistakes and things don't go to plan.

Case Notes for Andy Field (U14 Player in Northern Academy)

03/08: Andy seems to sulk when things aren't going his way, often then lashing out at teammates (e.g., late and dangerous tackles, intentional fouls).

05/09: Andy played very well today, performing as a true leader out on the pitch, setting a fantastic example for all the others to follow in terms of his attitude to never be beaten, be strong in the tackle and generally be a disruptive influence on their attacking play. He showed great bravery in putting his foot in time after time (often against bigger, stronger boys) and maintained his discipline when it might have been expected for him to react to potentially bad-tempered incidents. In terms of improvements, I'd like to see Andy work on his speed of movement to receive the ball from his backline and his general passing (long and short, on floor and through the air).

12/09: Andy stepped in to play as a central defender today (in George's initial absence), doing an accomplished job for the half of the game he played in this position. His reading of the game and corresponding positional play is naturally good, enabling him to get into positions to make tackles and interceptions. His fantastic attitude towards fully committing himself to tackles then allows him to regain possession for his team in most of the situations in which he gets involved. I think, as was more apparent when Andy moved into midfield during the second 25-minute period, he will greatly improve as a player if he can develop his speed over short distances and increase the accuracy of his short passing in particular (although his longer-range passing, in the air and along the floor, also requires further work). He's done very well so far this season (showing excellent leadership skills, as well as attentiveness and deliberate effort to learn) and will continue to accelerate if we can provide him with specific practices to develop him.

19/09: Because Sam arrived late, I decided to start Andy as our central striker, thinking that his physical presence and direct play could help us to cause them problems. Unfortunately, Andy turned his nose up at this a little; when I was telling him that this was where he was going to start, he turned his head from me, and when I did get eye contact with him again, he seemed as if he could be close to tears. I wasn't expecting this reaction, thinking that he'd probably enjoy this role. But he did play there for the first 25 minutes before moving into midfield for the remainder of his time on the pitch. His performance on the pitch was generally very good, especially when he moved into midfield. In addition to the three goals that he scored—a nicely taken header, a nice strike from outside the box and a free kick into the top corner—he got highly involved in our build-up and possession play, linking well with teammates. Again, though, he could be heard criticizing teammates after they made mistakes or didn't do what he wanted them to.

26/09: Having started Jamie on the bench last week, he needed to start this week. In wanting to create a balance within our midfield (in terms of physical presence and attacking and defensive qualities), I therefore decided that I wanted Andy to sit out for the first period so that he could come on and be our primary source of attacking threat for the second period. As with last week, though (and following up on a similar incident during a practice session this week), Andy didn't respond in the understanding manner that I would have hoped. As I try to do with players on the sideline anyway, I spoke with Andy about the events that were occurring within the first period that were of relevance to him and his second-period performance, but I didn't feel as though Andy was listening. Perhaps because of his frustration, Andy didn't get as involved in the game as I would have liked. His movement as part of the midfield unit was limited (i.e., few, if any, rotations to create space for himself or others). Instead, he played as more of an individual, staying high up the pitch and too often overdribbling when he did get on the ball. That said, he did carry a threat.

03/10: Injured (sore hamstring); did not play.

10/10: Because Andy was injured last week and only just returned to training yesterday, we decided to rest him for the first third of the game and then play him for two consecutive periods before resting him again for the final period. His introduction to the game provided the team with some obviously lacking energy and bite; we started the second period in a much more positive and assertive manner. A lot of this was down to Andy's aggression in making tackles and generally playing on the front foot to pressurize opponents. I've previously commented on how his distribution was an area of concern, but this was an area of strength today, because he played some very accurate and well-weighted passes (that were more often forward than usual). But the feedback on this could have been even more positive had his decision making in the final third on two particular occasions not let him down. Twice in the second period he attempted to shoot (first time it was from 30 yards with no pace already on the ball, second time was from 20 or 25 yards on his left foot) when he would have been much better off passing because he had teammates in better positions. One final comment to make on Andy's performance today relates to his self-discipline and ability to control his emotions. He got very obviously frustrated at one particular moment (not sure what the source of this was, but it seemed to relate to the pressure we were under at the time and some ongoing personal battles he was involved in—I need to ask him about this further), leading him to swear at the top of his voice, make a quite cynical foul on the edge of our area and cry when he was no longer able to suppress his anger and frustration. His current inability to control his emotions in these situations needs to be worked on, because it will continue to cause both him and his team problems until he is able to channel this appropriately.

17/10: After starting the game in a 4-4-2 formation, with Andy playing as one of the central two midfielders, we reverted to 4-3-3 for the second period after a period during which Andy, like the rest of our midfield and defence, struggled to cope with the movement and passing game of our opponents. Although Andy was not the only player failing to cope, the speed of movement from some of their players exposed Andy's lack of pace over short distances. He was able to control this much better in the second period, finding it easier to drop a little bit deeper and anticipate forward passes (enabling him to intercept or challenge for those), and the extra body in midfield also made it more difficult for them to pass through us. He played the final 12 1/2 minutes as a central defender and did a good job of providing cover for his partner, sweeping up any balls in behind that needed covering.

31/10: Andy seemed to be pumped up for today's game with a desire to do well against Leeds, meaning that he was particularly driven. Although in many ways this can be a good thing, it seemed to have a bit of an unsettling effect on Andy (particularly in the early stages of the game), meaning that some of his play lacked a composure that would have helped him make better decisions. As the game progressed, though, he returned to be much more his normal self, winning tackles and setting up attacks for us. Overall, though, while he had some good moments in the game, the game passed him by for long periods (in terms of the contributions he was able to make to our possession). For his long-term development, he really needs to get on the ball much more than he did today.

What would you do? Given what you now know about mental game interventions, how would you help Andy?

Mental Intervention

The initial approach with Andy was to educate him on how his lack of control over his emotions was leading to the negative outcomes he was experiencing (and had been experiencing for several years). The next step was to teach him that he could control his emotions and therefore stop this from happening in the future.

We did this by speaking to him about how he felt and what sort of thoughts were going through his head during these moments when he first started to feel angry, frustrated or annoyed. Helping him understand those feelings was a starting point for him to begin recognizing them when they happened in the future, which would act as a trigger for him to do something to interrupt them.

We spoke about how, when he recognized those thoughts or feelings, taking slow, deep breaths would enable him to slow down his heart rate and regain control of the frantic, overwhelming feelings that were leading him to explode (red mist) and, more often than not, lash out and cry.

We spoke again (to remind him why it was important) about these same strategies on a few occasions, sometimes when he was in the middle of a meltdown and at other times when he was much more relaxed and open to receiving the information.

Over time he could be seen to be starting to use the breathing technique during stressful moments in practice sessions and games. I could see that he was doing this because he would walk off on his own and have his head down (and his long hair would be covering his face), but you could see his shoulders rise and fall with each breath in and out.

During opportune moments, I would speak quietly with Andy to let him know that I could see that he was having a go at doing the stuff we had spoken about and that I was proud of his willingness to give these techniques a go. Also, I would remark on the positive effect it was having on his ability to control his emotions, making sure to refer to specific moments within recent games and sessions when it might have been easy for him to lose his cool.

One of the other kid's parents spoke to me about how Andy's dad was a key source of those issues. I had heard him on the far touchline cheering when Andy made crunching tackles. He seemed to be encouraging Andy to throw his weight around and demonstrate the physical side of his game. Being 12 or 13 and not too good at controlling his temper, Andy sometimes mistimed his tackles, but the positive reinforcement he was getting from his dad in those moments seemed to be conflicting with how he was giving away free kicks and getting told off by referees. But when it came to parent evenings, his dad would say that he didn't understand where Andy's meltdowns came from. He also spoke about not understanding why Andy kept looking over at him after making a mistake (saying, 'It's as if he thinks I'd be annoyed with him', which he said he made sure not to give any indications of).

So I spoke with Andy's dad about how, in my view (and he knew that I had a background in psychology), Andy seemed to be putting himself under pressure that was unhelpful to his game. I spoke about how this pressure was holding back his development. His fear of failure, evidenced through his recurring glances towards his dad every time he made a mistake, put him off taking risks. I spoke about how, as a midfield player, Andy needed to receive the ball from his goalkeeper or back four in quite risky areas of the pitch. A fear of failure about giving the ball away in those areas would limit his progress as a player. So I said that it was important for Andy to overcome this pressure and to play with more freedom (in a more relaxed state). I spoke with his dad about these issues to educate him on the things that I thought were holding Andy back, without challenging him about the role that he might have been playing in it (because I'm pretty certain that he wouldn't have received this too well).

Andy continued to improve his emotional control over the course of the season and only occasionally lost control in the final two to three months of the season. And when he did, he tended to regain control quickly. Earlier, those same incidents would lead to him needing 10 to 15 minutes out from the game or session to calm down, stop crying and get himself together again. One of the parents of another kid in the group told me at the end of the season that he regarded the work I had done with Andy to be my biggest success story from the season. He explained that he had seen Andy 'lose his rag' on a consistent basis over the previous few seasons, which had often had a negative effect on the other boys. So he was pleased for both Andy and the other kids that this was becoming less of an issue.

Conclusion

In this chapter I described the five Cs framework of mental toughness in soccer. I have also tried to give a flavour of various types of intervention that can help players develop the five Cs. These included one-on-one work with the player off the pitch (e.g., goal setting, REBT), integration of mental skills on the pitch (e.g., use of process goals, relaxation, self-talk), coaching sessions specifically designed for mental returns (e.g., concentration sessions with triggers) and interventions linked to parental involvement.

As mentioned in the introduction, the England youth teams and many professional academies in England have adopted this framework and now have programmes to develop the five Cs in their players. Experience suggests that linking different support structures can be difficult, especially making the connections between off-pitch work with the psychologist and on-pitch practices of the coach. Doing this on a systematic rather than ad hoc basis requires clear planning and coordination of action (see figure 17.6).

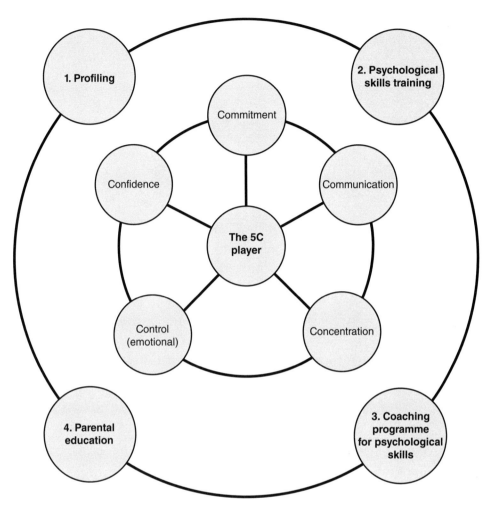

▶ **Figure 17.6** Systematic support for the five Cs.

In addition, the technical syllabus must be linked with the development of the five Cs (see Harwood and Anderson 2015). When you add parents into the mix at the youth levels, you can begin to see the work involved in providing joined-up support to target the needs of individual players. Nevertheless, the five Cs provide a common language and a set of clear behavioural outcomes to work towards. These elements lay a strong foundation to making a positive and tangible impact with mental game interventions.

Acknowledgement

Many thanks to Dr. Gareth Morgan for his support with this chapter.

CHAPTER 18

Performance Mind-Set

—Mark Nesti

This chapter identifies the type of psychological issues that sport psychologists and coaches have to deal with when providing sport psychology support at first-team levels in elite-level and professional soccer. Some of these issues relate to narrow and specific concerns that the player or member of the staff must address on match days or on the training pitch. Others are more about the kind of factors that emerge from the range of issues commonly found in soccer at these levels, such as coach–athlete relationships, transition and retirement, deselection and broader life concerns that can indirectly affect performance.

The concepts and theory referred to in this chapter are not meant to represent a comprehensive account of all that may be encountered from a psychological perspective in professional soccer. Instead, the aim is to highlight the most important issues that players face and suggest how these can be understood in relation to research and theory in psychology and sport psychology.

Four key topics have been identified as important for sport psychologists and coaches working in professional soccer:

- Anxiety
- Identity
- Critical moments
- Life beyond the training ground

Anxiety and identity have been extensively studied in sport psychology, although rarely in relation to professional sport and soccer. The effect on motivation and confidence of being dropped from the team or starting line-up and the effect of broader life concerns on performance have not been adequately covered in the literature despite their importance in the lives of professional players, especially in team sports.

One of the major challenges in addressing this topic is the limited amount of research done on the psychological factors associated with elite-level and professional soccer. A few studies have been done on psychology and coaching practices (Potrac, Jones and Cushion 2007), perceptions about sport psychology and sport psychologists in soccer (Pain and Harwood 2004) and organizational practices (Relvas et al. 2010), but this work has been concerned with youth rather than first-team levels. One of the problems with this focus is that the culture and psychological demands on players and the importance of developmental issues are very different between senior first-team soccer and soccer at academy or youth stages. Therefore, sport psychologists or coaches who have carried out applied work in senior professional soccer have often had to borrow ideas and concepts from other professional sports or from nonprofessional elite amateur sport environments.

To approach the topic from a different direction, this chapter is mostly informed by my applied experience rather than by research studies. I worked for nine seasons delivering sport psychology support four days a week on average at first-team levels at several English Premier League (EPL) clubs. During almost two decades of work with staff or players at high-level and professional soccer at clubs like Newcastle United, Bolton Wanderers, Hull City, Everton, Leeds United and Chelsea, I have been able to reflect on my approach to applied practice in sport psychology. This process, alongside feedback from coaches and managers, has helped shape my views about which psychological factors are most important at this level of soccer and what the coach or sport psychologist can do to begin to address these issues. In addition, much that is discussed in this chapter is derived from supervising or collaborating closely with sport psychologists, performance coaches and directors of performance who have worked for many years inside some of the most successful clubs in English professional soccer. In summary, the material written about here owes much more to practice than research, and it is arguably more relevant to higher levels than to lower levels of the sport.

Given the roles that some of these highly successful practitioners have adopted and my own experiences inside two of the EPL clubs I have been involved with, some of what is included in terms of theory could better be described as organizational psychology. This branch of psychology is established in the business world but has been slower to emerge in sport psychology despite being of central importance to the work of many sport psychologists operating in elite and professional sport (Fletcher and Wagstaff 2009; Nesti 2010). This topic is briefly examined in this chapter and guidance for further reading is provided to help stimulate new research and prepare applied practitioners to meet the reality of working in a demanding environment.

The focus of this chapter is on working one-on-one with players and coaching staff. Group-based activities can be a valuable and highly effective method of delivering sport psychology support, especially if the aim is general education and team-building exercises. But at higher levels and within the culture of professional soccer, especially in the UK (Roderick 2006), there are very real limitations to engaging in this form of work. Some of these are discussed. A more complete account of where it is useful and appropriate to carry out these types of activities can be seen in the work of Nesti (2010).

Although mental skills training is mentioned throughout the chapter, the main approaches to practice discussed here are those of existential phenomenological psychology and person-centred perspectives. These are used to inform and guide an applied approach that may best be described as personalist sport psychology counselling (Nesti and Littlewood 2011). This approach is based on closely related philosophically informed perspectives grounded in various strands of humanistic, existential and transpersonal psychology. Practice that is derived from this type of psychological theory is less effective in environments where strict confidentiality cannot be assured or where trust is difficult to develop. The reasons behind this limitation are examined in this chapter, and suggestions are offered about how to achieve this within elite-level and professional soccer club environments.

Finally, the mode of delivery used must be appropriate to the needs of the athletes and the type of challenge they face (figure 18.1). As the task becomes less about mental skills training, interaction should move from a more teaching-focused approach to a broader educational and more athlete-led scenario. I have referred to this approach as mentoring, which conveys that the relationship is on an equal footing. Any solutions should emerge more from the player than from the coach or sport psychologist.

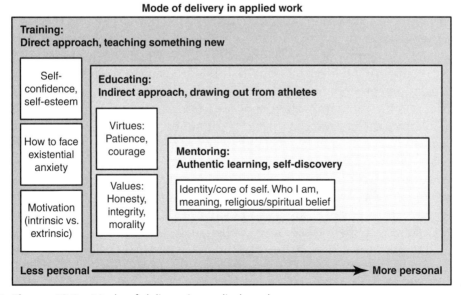

▶ **Figure 18.1**   Mode of delivery in applied work.

Anxiety

Anxiety in sport is one of the most studied areas in the academic discipline of sport psychology. Almost every book on sport psychology contains a chapter on anxiety and stress. But a closer inspection of what is usually meant by anxiety in sport reveals a rarely noted fact. Sport psychologists have not really been interested in theorizing and researching anxiety per se. Rather, their focus has been on the more specific and narrow concern of competitive anxiety, defined by Martens, Vealey and Burton (1990) as the feeling of nervousness before a competitive event or situation. This type of anxiety is related to fear of failure in competitive situations like those found in sport.

Competitive anxiety in sport has been described in terms of its symptoms. The cognitive psychology approach describes this in terms of cognitive anxiety and somatic anxiety. From the perspective of somatic anxiety, interest has been directed at how the physical manifestations of competitive anxiety such as tension, shaking or butterflies interfere with performance. The same concern has guided research into the effects of cognitive symptoms, where attention has been on how worry, lack of focus and fear of failure can undermine sport performance. These symptoms have usually been measured using the competitive state anxiety inventory (Martens, Vealey and Burton 1990). Recently, research has moved away from identifying intensity of the emotion to concern with its meaning. Researchers have begun to acknowledge that competitive anxiety can facilitate good performance for some athletes and that not everyone views anxiety symptoms negatively (Jones 1995)

But few researchers in sport psychology appear aware that there is more than one way to conceptualize anxiety and that competitive anxiety is not the only type of anxiety experienced in sport. The reasons behind this failing are many. For example, researchers have considered anxiety only in terms of what the cognitive approach offers despite the extensive discussion of the topic of anxiety in older and equally influential approaches to psychology. For example, psychoanalytical and existential approaches have identified anxiety as the most important concept in psychology (Nesti 2004). These perspectives differ from cognitive accounts by considering the meaning of anxiety rather than focusing on its symptoms and do not conceptualize anxiety as always being negative.

Returning to competitive anxiety, the experiences of many sport psychologists and coaches who have worked in professional soccer are that players often view this type of anxiety as a positive, especially where they feel fully prepared to face the forthcoming challenge. In some ways we could argue that the theoretical literature in traditional sport psychology has finally caught up with practice, because we now have a directional scale added to the Competitive State Anxiety Scale-2 (CSAI-2) (Jones 1995). This scale allows researchers to identify whether athletes view their somatic or cognitive symptoms as a hindrance or a benefit to performance. This development suggests that some sport psychologists are finally beginning to recognize that the cognitive account, which explains anxiety as always a negative emotion, is incorrect.

In my experience carrying out applied sport psychology with high-level professional players, I would often hear them inform me that they liked to feel anxious because it was a sign that they cared about the outcome and that they were ready to perform well. They explained that they had performed poorly in the past when they had no or little pre-event anxiety or when they had too much. Of course, the particular anxiety levels were related to their own preferred states rather than scores and norms derived from psychological inventories. For that reason, players must be dealt with as individuals. Some I have worked with feel positive about experiencing intense levels of anxiety before they compete, and they resist any attempt to alleviate their anxiety. Often these players would describe that they feel anxiety and excitement simultaneously. Some researchers (e.g., Hanton, Neil and Mellalieu 2008) have questioned whether this is possible and have suggested that these players are confused. They claim that positive anxiety is really another name for excitement. This position appears to be at odds with the empirical data that have emerged from applied practice with professional soccer players; it goes against the idea that the athlete knows him- or herself and is usually able to identify the different feelings associated with anxiety and excitement.

From a more theoretical perspective, Nesti (2004) has proposed that this restricted view of anxiety and excitement results from limitations of the cognitive approach, which assumes that a person can process only one emotion or cognition at a time. In contrast, a phenomenological psychology approach rejects this because no method can identify whether a person can feel two or more emotions or thoughts at the same time. The phenomenological view is that because it is impossible to examine inside someone's brain to discover precisely what he or she is thinking or feeling, the best solution is to ask the person to describe what is taking place. For psychologists who hope that neurophysiology may offer an answer here, it is worth repeating what May (1977) pointed out many years ago. He stated that a precise recording of activation in the brain is in itself unable to inform us that a particular cognition is taking place or that a specific emotion is being felt. To achieve this, we must ask the person what he or she is thinking or experiencing at a given moment. After all, the neurological and biochemical activity that occurs in the brain for the different emotions of anxiety and excitement are impossible to differentiate.

Competitive anxiety can be a problem when a player is facing a difficult experience, like coming back from injury, returning from deselection or facing heightened expectations. Sometimes the anxiety felt may be more closely associated with physical symptoms. On other occasions the symptoms could be more mental than physical. But this does not mean that anxiety can be either a physical or a mental phenomenon, because it clearly always originates in the mind.

Professional soccer players adhere to various physical relaxation strategies or other forms of mental skills because they quite sensibly believe that these methods may help calm their minds, which could have the added benefit of relaxing their bodies at the same time. This practice has been demonstrated in research studies, such as the work of Maynard and Cotton (1993). They tested the matching hypothesis, which proposes that interventions should be tailored to deal with the specific emotion that is causing the problem. They found that tennis players benefitted from either physical or mental interventions to control their cognitive and somatic anxiety symptoms. They interpreted these results to mean that matching the intervention to the specific symptom was not necessary to achieve a positive effect. Their finding strongly suggests that anxiety is always about mental worry first and that various types of symptoms follow from this.

So, can we say that measures like the CSAI-2 should not be employed in applied work with professional soccer players? I would argue that as long as it is not used in isolation and that it is mainly used to help the player reflect on how he or she deals with the symptoms of competitive anxiety, this psychometric test can be useful for sport psychologists and coaches. The CSAI-2 could also assist with the design of mental skills training for anxiety control when this is warranted and needed. But in relation to this, an important though rarely cited paper by Corlett (1996) warned that sport psychologists may be acting inappropriately by teaching mental skills to 'manage anxiety symptoms away, because the problem may not be with the anxiety but with the sport' (p. 87). He argued that the sport psychologist or coach might sometimes need to support the athlete to deal with anxiety associated with issues like being dropped from the starting 11, receiving negative feedback from key staff, heightened expectations and many other experiences unrelated to competitive anxiety per se. He also points out that attempting to remove the anxiety is often unnecessary because it is a frequently experienced and inevitable part of participation in sport. The challenge is to face up to this reality and perform despite the uncomfortable feeling of anxiety.

In developing the idea of Corlett (1996) but from an existential psychology framework, Nesti (2004) has argued that beyond competitive anxiety a serious problem may result from attempting to teach skills to remove or reduce anxiety. The existential view is that anxiety often accompanies a challenge; it proposes that the athlete will benefit psychologically by accepting or even embracing feelings of anxiety. According to the existential psychology perspective, anxiety can be understood as being an emotion that we experience when facing choices. Anxiousness arises because we are unable to know in advance what the outcome of our choices will be. The task facing the player is to persist in the face of this anxiety. In this way the player becomes ever more ready to consider her or his choices when next confronting difficult moments and challenges. The player is prepared to choose and act despite feeling anxious.

Professional soccer players can experience this kind of anxiety daily and weekly over the season and across their careers in the game, especially when they still care about what they are doing and remain concerned about their future achievements in soccer. For example, when a player joins a new club or plays under a new manager and coaching team, he or she may feel the need to prove him- or herself. This situation is common in a sport where at the top level, squads comprise up to 30 players, several of whom are competing for the same position on the team. Players who decide to move to a new club may also experience existential anxiety. This transition can be even more challenging if the team is at a higher level or is in another country and has a high profile. Anxiety here may relate not only to concern about being a success on the pitch but also to apprehension about being immersed in a new culture, learning a new language, playing a different type of soccer or wondering whether their families will settle.

A sport psychologist or coach working with a player facing these challenges should help the player confront the anxiety that is inevitably associated with being in a challenging situation in which the outcome cannot be known in advance. High-level sport and professional soccer is replete with these experiences. Fortunately for sport psychologists and coaches, high-level and professional players are usually well aware that making choices, and that trying to learn, develop and improve in anything, will often be accompanied by anxiety.

The role of the sport psychologist or coach is to help the soccer player clarify and understand the choices being considered. The focus should be on thinking through what each choice could mean for the player and identifying which choice seems to be the best for personal growth, fulfilment and achievement. The player may need to revisit long-term plans and examine what is important to her or him as a professional athlete and person.

Identity

The topic of identity has been studied in sport psychology from theoretical approaches (Balague 1999). But as in the study of anxiety in sport, the majority of research studies in sport psychology have adopted a cognitive psychology perspective. This work has led to some interesting and useful findings, especially in relation to understanding transitions like retirement from sport.

Most of the research has attempted to measure athletes in relation to athletic identity. This construct identifies how strongly someone views him- or herself as an athlete. Research in professional soccer (Brown and Potrac 2009) has revealed that most youth players tend to have a strong athletic identity. They see themselves as being youth professional soccer players rather than as young people with a broad self-identity that includes that of elite soccer player.

Undoubtedly, as Brown and Potrac have argued, this type of restricted identity can contribute to serious problems for the players given that so few eventually make it to the professional ranks. In addition, when young players view themselves exclusively in terms of their soccer role, their motivation to acquire further education and qualifications is undermined, which is obviously a serious issue if they do not make the grade.

According to Parker (1995), many coaches in professional soccer are likely to encourage young players to devote themselves fully to the task of becoming a professional soccer player. Although not from a soccer context, research suggests that many high-level youth athletes possess an exclusive athletic identity (Brewer, Van Raalte and Linder 1993). This work also describes the process that many young athletes experience as they become more committed to their sport. Rather than continuing to explore other roles and identities for themselves, these athletes begin to construct a narrow and exclusively sport-based self-identity. This process, referred to as foreclosure, is viewed as a potentially negative phenomenon for two reasons. First, foreclosure is a risky strategy to adopt for young athletes like youth soccer players. Few of them will progress to full professional levels, and they may experience this failure and rejection more forcefully given their view of themselves as professional soccer players in the making. Second, a foreclosed identity could also significantly reduce young players' motivation to develop other skills and acquire experiences beyond their soccer lives. Encouraging foreclosure is ethically problematic because it could hinder the overall development of the player. For example, foreclosure could reduce the player's desire to broaden his or her knowledge about sport science support and how to manage broader life issues.

Identity is also an important term in other approaches in psychology. Indeed, one of the most famous psychologists ever, Abraham Maslow, claimed that the concept of identity was the most important topic in psychology. As the founder of humanistic psychology, Maslow (1968) followed the earlier work of European existential and phenomenological psychologists in emphasising that meaning, and discovering personal meaning, was ultimately the most important foundation for mental health and human flourishing. Although the literature (for example, May 1977) dealing with these topics can appear complex and obscure at times, it provides a very different perspective to the more traditional cognitive or behavioural perspectives around the topic of identity.

These theoretically rich and in-depth accounts of meaning and identity provided by humanistic and existential perspectives have been more useful in guiding the practice of some highly experienced sport psychologists and coaches operating in elite professional soccer (Nesti 2010). The weakness of the traditional sport psychology conceptualization of athletic identity is that few elite professional soccer players define themselves solely in terms of their identity as professional soccer players. Players often describe themselves as being equally committed to their professional role and to other important roles, such as that of spouse, father, mother, brother or sister. During my applied experience I have frequently come across successful and high-achieving professional soccer players who are equally proud of their identity as role models for young people or as advocates and high-profile supporters of important charitable, philanthropic and humanitarian projects.

These people often discuss the importance of being more than a soccer player. They have explained that having a broader and more complex personal identity has helped them become more successful and better professional soccer players. They have benefitted from being able to deal more constructively with setbacks and disappointments in their professional lives; they understand that who they are is based on much more than one particular and current role. This broad self-identity allows them to engage fully in the demands of professional soccer and to maintain greater levels of emotional equilibrium and consistency of behaviour during the good times and the bad. They are able to maintain a performance focus, one in which they are able to lose themselves in the task and perform at their best. Research based on the extensive studies on optimal performance and sport by Jackson and Csikszentmihalyi (1999) suggests that this ability is commonplace with high-level sport performers. From an applied perspective, this was memorably described to me by one former African player of the year based at one of the clubs at which I worked, as being, 'able to give your all to your football, by knowing that football is not your all!'

The semifictional vignette that follows is based on applied work with a young high-level professional soccer player who was facing a challenge associated with existential anxiety and identity. Despite performing well during training and reserve matches alongside established first-team professionals, many of whom were international players, he was no longer progressing into the team. An opportunity to go on loan emerged. This move was to a lower-level professional club that was currently facing relegation from the division. The manager had conveyed to the young player that although he believed the loan experience would be good for the player, the final decision rested with the player himself. The sport psychologist had been working closely with this player during the previous 18 months and had developed a trusting relationship. All sessions were fully confidential. The manager and coaching staff were informed that meetings were scheduled, but no detail was provided about the issues discussed. The extract provided here represents an important example of this type of dialogue between the player and the coach or sport psychologist.

Sport psychologist (SP): I know that you are feeling very confident about the successes you have had so far this season in being able to match the standards of the first-team guys when you have trained with them and played in the reserves. The hard data on your fitness statistics, pass completion rates and all the other performance-related information that the sport science team gives you let you have some robust evidence to back up your own feelings around confidence.

Young professional player (P): I feel great about how I am performing at the moment. I feel as though I could easily break in to the first-team squad at any moment. The only worry I have is whether I have left it a little too late. We are getting to the business end of the season, and although I feel that Coach X would give me a shot on the bench against Sunderland or home to City, I'm not sure that the Boss feels the same way. And now they've asked me about this loan deal. It's to a huge club, but they are in a really horrible situation right now. I'd love to play in front of 25,000 to 30,000 people each week, but I'm not sure it's the best choice for me right now.

SP: What are the choices you have, and how do you feel when you think about them?

P: Well, I can stay here, keep working hard and wait for my chance. It's been a long, brutal campaign, and maybe there will be a need for some fresh legs and extra energy in the team before the end. I have seen players go out on loan before, and it sometimes seems as if they can get forgotten about. Especially at important stages of the season like this, you can be kind of 'out of sight and out of mind'. After all I've achieved since coming to this country as a 17-year-old nearly 3 years ago, I don't want to miss out because I'm not in the building! I'm also edgy when I think about how garbage the facilities are at the other club. I know they have a great stadium and brilliant fans, but from what I hear they don't have a sport science programme and all the fantastic support that we have here. I don't want to lose my sharpness, my focus or drop my standards just so I can have the experience of three or four first-team games.

Clearly, the young player in this example dialogue is dealing with anxiety associated with important choices he must face. In addition, this excerpt clearly shows that he is discussing his identity in terms of how he currently sees himself, how others may view him and what and who he hopes to be in the future.

These types of experience typically occur repeatedly in the dynamic and ever-changing environment of high-level and professional soccer. We now look more closely at how these experiences occur in the lives of players and the challenge they present.

Critical Moments

Nesti and Littlewood (2011), currently the most experienced university academics and qualified sport psychologists to have worked one-on-one with players inside the English Premier League, have criticized the concept of transitions in sport. They argue that the reality in EPL professional and youth team levels is that players constantly face difficult moments rather than transitions. They suggest that the term *transition* conveys the idea of smooth, carefully managed and relatively easy change.

Their applied experiences inside EPL clubs challenge this view. According to Nesti and Littlewood, players must be prepared to deal with the anxiety associated with critical moments. They continually face such moments during a professional soccer career. These events relate to dealing with deselection, being sent on loan, being sold to other clubs, dealing with increased expectations, moving to a new club, being ignored by senior coaching staff, handling media interest and other similar challenges. In terms of the psychology associated with these critical moments, considerable effect on a player's identity is likely to occur.

At a deeper level, the case can be made that these issues are really about isolation, choice, responsibility and courage. For example, players may find themselves out of the team after a period of prolonged involvement. This can occur for many reasons. The player may be losing form, other more talented and experienced players may have returned from injury and be available for selection, other players who play in their position may have joined the club, or the coaching staff may be dissatisfied with some aspect of the player's performance. The player may have failed to meet the required standards in terms of physical output, tactical requirements or technical skills. The precise reasons for being dropped are often not explained to the player. This failure may be the result of the traditional communication practices in professional soccer (Nesti 2010), the belief that the player should already know the reasons for deselection and will work to overcome these on his or her own and a tendency to use this mechanism as a way to coerce individual players to improve performance.

When a player has been dropped from the starting 11, especially if this extends for a considerable time, the sport psychologist or coach will have an opportunity to assist the player in his or her effort to return to a place in the team. A range of reasons, from the easy to identify to the more complex, can be behind the failure to be in the starting team.

The sport psychologist or coach must initially spend time with the player identifying the range of possible reasons and describing each in as much detail as is possible. This task can be very difficult to pursue given that the player will usually feel frustrated and even angry about the situation. When someone is prevented from carrying out his or her work by the decision of someone else, the normal psychological reaction is to place the blame completely on someone else. Therefore, the first and most important stage in this work, guided as it is by the existential phenomenological psychology ideas around freedom, choice and responsibility, is for the individual players to be able to accept that they have in some, perhaps only small, way contributed to the situation they are now in. This process is not infrequently surrounded by anxiety. This anxiety is connected to the difficulty we face as human beings in having to acknowledge that we are rarely without some measure of responsibility for our failures and missed opportunities.

The sport psychologist or coach needs to stay with the player in a particular way at this critical stage. The psychologist or coach must support the player as the player begins to separate the things she or he is responsible for from those that she or he has not contributed to.

Someone encountering this level of existential anxiety can easily fall into one of two false and unhelpful positions—either denying all responsibility and blaming everything on circumstances completely out of one's control or descending into self-pity and accepting total responsibility for all that has happened!

After this process has been completed, the sport psychologist or coach must work with the player to identify ways to begin addressing the issues that the player has some control over. Frequently, the player in this situation will talk about lack of motivation. This deficiency could be affecting performance in training and competitive play, and may extend to behaviours in the rest of his or her professional and personal lives. Enquiry may reveal that the player has become immersed in extrinsic rewards and is able to see achievement only in those terms (Deci and Ryan 1985). This change can take place after a period of success when the player has featured in the starting 11 for many games and has begun to measure success and achievement exclusively in terms of extrinsic motivation. This attitude can easily develop when the positive and negative comments in the media begin to play a major role in how the player perceives success or when the player begins to place unrealistically high expectations on him- or herself. The sport psychologist or coach will frequently hear the player describe in his or her own words feeling guilty about losing focus on the basics, not doing the job and being distracted by opinions and pressure from others. The player will also usually complain about not enjoying this final phase of matches and being torn between trying to do ever more to satisfy the demands of others whilst knowing deep inside that those demands are unrealistic and unhelpful.

When the player has begun to suggest actions that she or he can take to reignite intrinsic motivation, a deeper level of anxiety sometimes emerges. This experience may be quite different from the positive anxiety associated with feelings of excitement that the player had previously felt during the prolonged run in the team. A closer examination of this uncomfortable anxiety that can emerge during the dialogue between the sport psychologist or coach and the player may reveal that being deselected from the starting 11 is also seen as a threat to the person's identity. In other words, for a professional soccer player a source of crushing anxiety and despair is that she or he is unable to do one of the most important things in her or his life. What the player does is play sport for a living; she or he engages in this activity because invariably it is both a passion and a central and important source of self-identity and personal well-being. For some professional soccer players, their relationship with the sport can no longer be described in those terms; extrinsic motives may have become the complete justification for their involvement, and they no longer feel any love (intrinsic motivation) for their profession. This situation has been precisely described in Deci and Ryan's elegant and scholarly account of self-determination theory. They provide an organismic cognitive psychology explanation of how, and in what ways, extrinsic motives can undermine intrinsic motivation.

Where the sport psychologist or coach is working with a player for whom professional soccer is still an important part of his or her identity, an opportunity to look again at what this means may arise. This exercise can be effective when the player is able to express in his or her own words what he or she loves about being a professional soccer player and how this is a central part of his or her identity. A highly experienced professional player often reflects on personal history in the game and articulates how important being a soccer player has always been. The player might be able to describe this in rich detail as being something that brings great meaning to life and in a deeper way has defined him or her.

Dialogue with a coach or sport psychologist about identity and meaning can be incredibly inspiring for the player, especially when facing difficult and complex situations such as those associated with critical moments. This process may allow some degree of peace and help galvanize the player to begin to bring intrinsic and extrinsic motivation back into a more psychologically healthy balance. From a more narrow perspective, this regeneration of who the player is and what is important to her or him can provide the necessary structure and opportunity for the player to assess the use of mental skills and identify where improvements and practices need to take place.

Life Beyond

Considerable evidence from the applied literature dealing with professional soccer (Nesti 2010) and from research studies (Fletcher and Wagstaff 2009) confirms that especially for serious and higher-level sport performers, the major sources of stress they encounter are not confined to the competitive event, training or matches. This empirical work points to the need to view performance as being something related to the athlete's whole life, which can equally include personal and professional issues.

The recent debate between Andersen (2009) and Brady and Maynard (2010), who argue that sport psychology must be only about athlete care or that performance enhancement is the sole concern, is rejected here on two counts. The approach from mainstream psychology, which guides my work, does not rest on a dualist account of human identity. In other words, when sport psychologists or coaches adopt a holistic perspective (Freisen and Orlick 2010), they view the player as a person, not in narrow terms such as soccer player, athlete or youth professional. It is argued that because what happens in our personal lives affects our professional roles, and vice versa, choosing either a caring or a performance-enhancing agenda is not necessary.

Our role as sport psychologists and coaches who provide psychological support to players is to work with the whole person in front of us and acknowledge that everything we do with that person affects performance, including caring for her or him as a fellow human being.

Consistent with this approach, the sport psychologist or coach should encourage the player to lead the session and direct the content of meetings. As will be seen in the case study vignettes, the issues raised can often be about broader matters that indirectly affect overall performance. The holistic and personalist approach also requires the sport psychologist or coach to demonstrate genuine care for the athlete as a person in all the work done (Gilbourne and Richardson 2006). The psychologist or coach expresses this care through the authenticity and directness of communication and the building up of mutual respect. The key features that must be in place to facilitate effective encounters between players and sport psychologists or coaches have been described in detail by Nesti (2004) in discussing how existential psychology perspectives and counselling can be used in high-level sport environments.

Sometimes the sport psychologist or coach will find that the player may be having difficulties on the field of play that are closely related to challenges she or he is facing outside the competitive sport arena. In the vignette that follows, the player is unable to address the problems through use of mental skills training; rather, the player needs to clarify the broader life issues he is facing and begin to consider choices he can make to move forward.

SP: OK, so we have looked again at how you are dealing with your emotions and reactions to mistakes in the match. Keep working on these and we will follow up next time we meet. But just to change things a bit, Eddie, what are things like away from the training ground in the rest of your life at the moment?

P: Funny that you should ask that because to be honest things are very different to how they usually are. You know me well enough to know that I like things to be mellow and calm at home, so I can rest and take it easy with the family and take my mind off professional soccer and recuperate properly. But this past three months it has not been like that, to be honest with you. I suppose it has crept up on me and my wife. She has had some health issues, and it is making her really homesick. Her parents back in France are trying to help, but they are elderly and not well themselves. We have been really struggling with the huge support that she has to give to her sick elderly parents. Their condition has become much worse recently, and this puts a big strain on us—you know time, energy and from an emotional point of view. It means that I feel emotionally tired at home, which is not good, you know.

SP: How much control do you have over how much is happening to you in this situation, and what have you been feeling during this time?

P: To be honest, I feel a bit guilty and selfish. What I mean is that I am not sharing the load properly and I leave my wife to do most of it, including looking after our two young children. That is not how I like to see myself; it's not what I'm about! My family is my rock; you know it is really them that make everything else make sense. I suppose I have been pretending to myself that I can somehow separate out what goes on in matches from the tough things we are dealing with in our outside lives. I am not sure what to do about it, and to be honest, I think I have put my head in the sand a bit over it all. I know some people seem able to get by like that, but not me. I always like to feel in control.

SP: And how much control do you feel you have at the moment?

P: Hardly any. It has never been like this for me that I can remember. This is new, and I don't like this feeling. I know I can't perform my best like this. Something has to give, and at the moment it's my performance.

SP: What do you feel you could maybe do to help these matters?

P: I could help my wife more with this incredible burden, or try to forget about it more. After all, there are doctors and all sorts of other people able to help them. Maybe what I need to do is become a bit more self-ish in a professional way, you know, and make sure I focus properly on what I need to do. After all, my whole family and our life is based on me continuing to perform and do well as a professional player, so this is maybe where my energies should go.

SP: What do you think about those choices, and how do they make you feel when you imagine yourself carrying them through?

P: It is OK to say these things and important for me to put them on the table. I think I have not been doing this lately, and talking about it now, I realize I should have done this before. There is only one option there that I could imagine doing, one that fits in to what I think is important, and that is to help my wife more fully and find a way to help her to cope.

It's funny really because I waste lots of time sitting and worrying about what I am not doing and thinking about how little I really do to help her, when I really should have been doing more rather than thinking more!

SP: These are difficult things that you are talking about, and you must not be too harsh with yourself. After all, you're right in saying that if you don't perform, it is not only you who will eventually suffer but those closest to you as well. I think you have been really courageous in describing what you really face and trying to come up with something practical that can help. This is not an easy thing to do.

P: Just thinking about what I have been saying has made me feel much better already, even though I know this is going to be tough to carry out. But it feels right to me, and that's very important. Because I can't act things—it's not what I'm like. At least this way I will be more of a help to others, and I think this in turn will help me to feel ready to begin to put my mistakes in some perspective and stop overreacting to things.

In summary, getting to this level of dialogue with a professional or high-level player may be very difficult unless he or she knows that sessions will be fully confidential (Andersen 2005).

Conclusion

The approach discussed in this chapter is based on the belief that a professional soccer player will be less likely to engage in a deep, meaningful and searching dialogue if he or she is unable to perceive that the sport psychologist or coach cares about him or her as a person, not just a high-achieving professional athlete. This point is consistent with what Martens (1979) demanded of sport psychology more than 35 years ago. He suggested that we need to see the person alongside the athlete, and that best practice, from both an ethical and a performance enhancement perspective, should be based on a philosophy of the person first, the athlete second.

PART

VI

Tactics and Strategies

CHAPTER 19

Popular Systems and Styles of Play

—Jens Bangsbo and Birger Peitersen

A top-class team is well organized and has a clear style of play. The coach designates player positions and roles to give the team the best options for striking the balance between defensive solidarity and attacking fluidity. This formation is expressed by a system that denotes how many players are in the defensive zone followed by the number of players in the midfield area and then the number of players in the attacking zone (the goalkeeper is not considered as it is given). An example is 4-4-2. This notation represents the formation on which the play is based. The formation is not fixed, and it may change several times during a game.

Throughout the history of playing systems, the trend has been to withdraw players from the attacking line to strengthen the defence. Going back to the early days, when England played Scotland in 1872, the teams appeared with one goalkeeper, one fullback, two midfielders and seven attackers, that is, a 1-2-7 system in modern context (figure 19.1*a*).

In today's structure, the emphasis is turned upside down. In recent years some clubs, such as FC Barcelona, have even fielded a 4-6-0 formation (figure 19.1*b*). For most people, systems like 4-4-2 and 4-3-3 are familiar, whereas fewer know about 4-2-3-1 or 4-1-4-1, even though most top teams are using those formations.

In this chapter we describe the most popular systems that national and top club teams have used in recent years, focusing on how some well-known managers and their teams have developed successful team tactics using different systems and strategies. Before the most popular systems are described, brief outlines of various attacking and defensive styles are explained. Some of them will also be referred to in the description of well-known teams and their chosen systems.

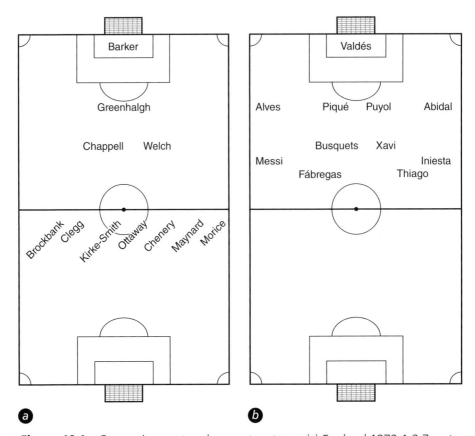

▶ **Figure 19.1** Comparing past and current systems: (a) England 1872 1-2-7 system; (b) FC Barcelona 4-6-0 system.

Style of Play

The way that a coach wants the team to perform tactically in a given system is known as style of play (Bangsbo and Peitersen 2000a). It is the characteristic way that the team and the individual players handle the tactical demands and options in both the offensive and defensive areas.

Attacking Styles

The two distinct types of attacking styles are possession soccer and direct play (Bangsbo and Peitersen 2000b). Possession soccer is based on a systematic and meticulous buildup consisting of many passes and movements between defence and midfield. Through keeping possession of the ball in a kind of weaving process, the team pushes many players forward and establishes the game in the last third of the pitch. The team keeps the ball patiently to wait for the right opening to be created through a sharp or often risky combination. In recent years the soccer world has witnessed two remarkably successful teams that use the possession style: FC Barcelona and the Spanish national side, the latter of which won the 2010 World Cup and the 2008 and 2012 European Championships. In Spain, this is called tiki-taka style. The name seems to refer to the sound of two pieces of wood knocking together, reflecting the rhythm of the rapid continuous passes between players across short distances.

The philosophy of possession soccer can be traced to the 1970s Dutch team, which performed a quasi-rotational passing scheme between midfield and attack called total soccer. The players, spread out widely, switched positions during the buildup and made it difficult for the opposition to mark them. The stress placed on the defence became particularly clear when the opposition was playing with man-to-man marking.

In contrast to the possession strategy, direct play means that a team, when getting the ball, quickly plays the ball forward to the opposition's third and often tries to finish the attack rapidly. Direct play, also called the long-ball approach, aims to get the ball in the box as fast as possible and put the defence under pressure. Thus, the aim is to challenge the defending team in its own penalty area and be searching to get the ball, returning when the defenders clear the ball.

The style is often linked to British soccer; historically, the most notable teams that used this approach were Wimbledon FC and Watford FC in the 1980s and 1990s, when the teams surprisingly won promotions. In today's Premier League few teams use direct play as their only playing style, but on occasion Sunderland, among others, choose this style. On the continent, Athletic Bilbao under Marcelo Bielsa adopted the direct style with high intensity. The team's speed and directness surprised many international opponents.

Defensive Styles

Defensive styles include pressing and defensive safety (Bangsbo and Peitersen 2000c). Pressing is an offensive style of defence in which the team collectively tries to win the ball aggressively. One or two players put pressure on the player with the ball, while the others cover space to prevent the player with the ball from making a proper pass.

When pressing, all players in the team must move as a unit. Pressing is physically demanding and can be performed only during parts of a game. In high pressing, the team tries to win the ball back as quickly and as close to the opposition's goal as possible. The strikers are the first to press, while the defensive line (back four) pushes forward to reduce space in midfield and make the opponent's attackers offside. In low pressing, all players move back to their own half when the team loses the ball. They build a compact block and do not start pressing until the ball has reached the halfway line. They wait for an opportunity to capture the ball and make a counterattack (see figure 19.2). Because the pressing and the counterattack action are demanding, some players appear to become temporarily fatigued, illustrated by the

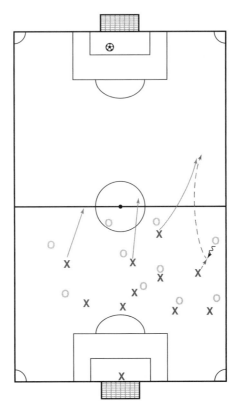

▶ **Figure 19.2** Low pressing with rapid transition from defence to offence.

fact that high-speed running in a period following the most intense exercise period is reduced in comparison with the average of the other periods (Mohr, Krustrup and Bangsbo 2005; Mascio and Bradley 2013).

Defensive safety is used by teams that are satisfied as long as the opposition does not score. Italian top teams from the mid-1960s, such as AC Milan and Inter FC, became known for their defensive safety, named *catenaccio*, meaning 'bolt' or 'lock' in Italian.

When teams adopted this strategy, they positioned a player behind their four-man defence as a guard. The task was to cover whenever an opponent with the ball broke through the defensive row. The back four could then put full pressure on their direct opponent, knowing that they always had backup. The teams made sure that the defensive and the midfield sections formed a compact wall that used every means (fair or foul) to prevent goal-scoring opportunities from arising. Because international tournaments in their final rounds include head-to-head home and away meetings, some teams apply defensive thinking that resembles the *catenaccio* approach when playing away.

Transition

Over the last few years, transition has become a crucial tactical concept in the game plan of many teams. Teams are focusing on taking advantage of situations when they regain the ball, because the opposition's defence often is disorganized at that moment. Gaining possession of the ball calls for immediate forward-seeking actions. Teams such as FC Barcelona and Athletic Bilbao are using this approach; players focus on winning the ball back and moving the ball intelligently and quickly forward. An aspect of transition is included in another offensive tactical concept known as counterattacking. By deliberately keeping the team back and letting opponents come far up the pitch, space is available to overplay several opponents rapidly when the ball is won back. The focus is on the first pass after regaining the ball. It may be a long pass to an attacker in an open space combined with fast forward running by teammates to support the player who receives the ball (see figure 19.2).

Basic Systems

Looking through the FIFA technical reports and statistics for the World Cup tournaments in 2002 (Korea and Japan), 2006 (Germany), 2010 (South Africa), and 2014 (Brazil) offers a full perspective on the dominating playing systems in the world of soccer (www.fifa.com). The most used system is clearly 4-2-3-1, and a few teams use the 3-5-2 and 4-3-3 systems. The same tendency was observed at the European Championship 2012 (Euro 2012), where only two teams used another system, namely Greece and, in some games, Italy, who played 3-5-2. In the World Cup in Brazil in 2014 most teams (12 out of 32) played 4-2-3-1. Four teams played 4-4-2, four teams played 4-3-3, including the world champion Germany, and two teams played 3-5-2 (www.fifa.com).

This section describes the basic 4-4-2 and 4-3-3 systems and the way that some of the top-class coaches have developed these systems into 4-2-3-1 and 4-1-4-1. In addition, other popular systems and the way that top teams use them are described.

4-4-2

The orthodox 4-4-2 line-up was founded around the mid-1960s. Most systems are variations of this system. The distribution of players in this system provides width and depth on the pitch, and the well-defined positions bring balance to the team that allows players to cover essential space and create options for ball distribution within the team.

Normally, the back four are organized in a line across the pitch, that is, the 'flat back' concept with two fullbacks and two central defenders. Their defensive work is organized by zone marking (Bangsbo and Peitersen 2000c; www.zonalmarking.com). The four players move forward and back as a unit and focus on maintaining balance in defensive situations. During buildup the two fullbacks provide width, and one of the fullbacks often moves down the flank.

The midfield can be organized in various ways: diamond structure, line structure, 2-2 positions and 3-1 arrangement (figure 19.3). The choice of mid-

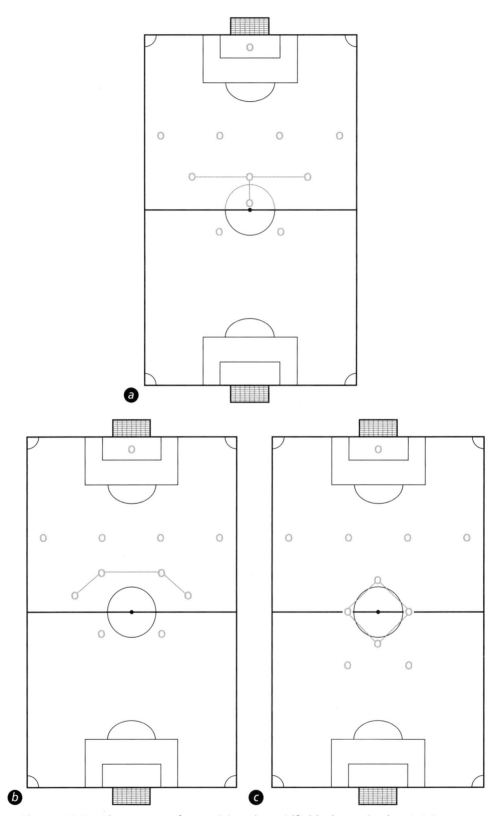

▶ **Figure 19.3** Three ways of organizing the midfield players in the 4-4-2 system: (*a*) 3-1 shape; (*b*) bowl shape; (*c*) diamond shape.

field formation depends on the coach's evaluation of the team's offensive and defensive resources as well as abilities.

Organizing the midfield in a line usually strengthens defensive coherence as long as the space between the back four and the midfielders remains short. A diamond formation, on the other hand, often better dictates the opposition's buildup of play when the offensive midfielder and the two attackers close certain areas. The diamond formation has a player just in front of the back four to shield the defence, known as the holding player. In the transition from defence to attack, a diamond formation is an advantage because it generally is easier to find a quick passing option after winning the ball.

The two attackers work as a pair to close specific areas for the opposition's buildup. In their offensive moves, they have to be fully aware of each other's position to be able to coordinate the runs and cause trouble for the opposition, as well as create space for penetrating midfielders.

4-4-2: Manchester United in the 1990s

As one of the truest and most successful followers of the 4-4-2 systems, Manchester United in the 1990s provides a good illustration of how this system is characteristically played. In 1999 Manchester United achieved the unthinkable. They won the Premier League Championship, the FA Cup and, in a dramatic match, the European Cup against Bayern Munich. In his first years at Manchester United, manager Sir Alex Fergusson, because of his British upbringing, had selected a traditional British style of play that focused on playing the ball forward quickly to the opponent's third and trying to finish rapidly. Manchester United's shape was a traditional 4-4-2, and the style was direct play.

The most frequent team line-up in the 1998–99 season was Peter Schmeichel in goal and a back four of Gary Neville and Denis Irwin as the fullbacks and Ronny Johnsen and Jaap Stam as the central defenders (see figure 19.4). The midfield players were David Beckham on the right side, Roy Keane and Paul Scholes in the centre and Ryan Giggs at the left flank. Up front were Andy Cole and Dwight Yorke.

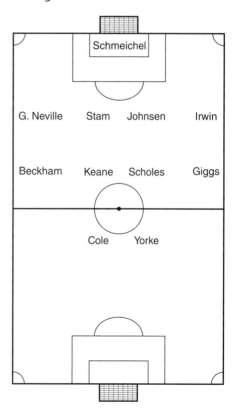

▶ **Figure 19.4** Manchester United 1999 playing 4-4-2.

(continued)

4-4-2: Manchester United in the 1990s, *continued*

The United style focused on quick and precise passing, thereby playing at such a pace that their opponents had difficulties keeping their defence well organized. The key elements in the buildup were to use the wide players and get the ball to the fullbacks, who created width and made contact to the midfield player on the flank. The team focused on penetration from the wings, making room for Neville or Irwin farther up the field. The crosses from David Beckham became a strong attacking strategy. On the left side of the pitch, Ryan Giggs used his speed to challenge and often went from the outside to the inside to connect with the pair up front. The two central midfield players concentrated on supporting the wide players and penetrating through the middle to challenge the penalty area. Keane and Scholes worked simultaneously and took advantage of the freedom to drift around. In York and Cole, United had a successful partnership up front. They worked with each other with an instinctive and unselfish understanding. Often they had a nearly telepathic collaboration when crosses—high or flat—entered the penalty area. With their split runs, they also opened for the midfield players to give them shooting opportunities.

Defensively, Ferguson formed a solid central defence. The bowl formation in midfield with Keane and Scholes just in front of the central defenders invited opponents to play through the middle. United always put hard, aggressive pressure on the opponent with the ball and relied more on individual defensive work than on a sophisticated collective system.

All successful team have synergies among players, a common understanding of each other's strengths and weaknesses as well as willingness to compensate for a teammate's mistakes and lack of ability.

A trademark of United was their determination to attack opponents, both home and away, and enter the risk zone in pursuit of their challenge. A prime example is the extra-time goals against Bayern Munich in the Champions League Final in 1999. After scoring 6 minutes into the game, Bayern Munich took the lead and twice hit the woodwork, but it all turned around within 3 incredible minutes at the end of the game. United substitute Teddy Sheringham scored a late equalizer and as Bayern Munich seemed to wait for extra time, United kept trying to win. In the 91st minute of the game, another substitute, Ole Gunnar Solskjaer, volleyed the ball into the roof of the net and Manchester United completed the unique treble.

As a proof of the determination of the team effort, manager Sir Alex Ferguson recalls the unique situation like this:

> I have since watched the match on video, and although it can be argued we were lucky to score such late goals after the Germans had twice hit the woodwork, I thought we were the better side and deserved to win because we tried to win. Bayern relied on their old belief that what you have got you don't give away. They put their trust in their organization and the machinery of performance, but at the end of the day it was not quite enough. We brought a greater adventure to the final and I think fate rewarded us.
>
> *Ferguson (2000)*

4-3-3

The 4-3-3 formation has four players in defence, three midfielders and three attackers (see figure 19.5). The midfield can be arranged in four variations: a linear or a triangular shape, offensive or defensive in character. The shape of the triangle varies among coaches, but the most common line-up involves a defensive midfielder (a holding player) and two attacking midfielders. The attackers normally position themselves so that the opposition's defence is spread as widely as possible.

This system, with its three attackers, is offensive in character. The ball should ideally be played quickly up to the attackers so that the game is taken into the opposition's defensive zone. Support should come quickly from the midfield players and the fullbacks. When the team conquers the ball, the three attackers should move to get into positions where they can receive the ball, and they may change positions to confuse the opposition's defenders. The wide attackers (wingers) should be speedy, allowing the midfield players to make deep passes to them. Another penetration strategy is overlap created by the fullbacks. The forward should be in constant movement and sometimes move back to receive a pass and create space for a midfield player, who can penetrate and utilize the free space.

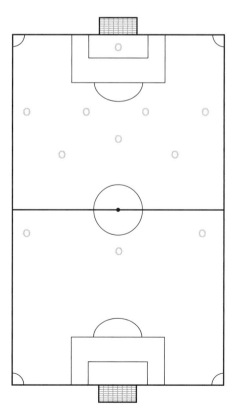

▶ **Figure 19.5** The 4-3-3 system.

The vulnerable part of the system in defence is the midfield. The back four normally use zone marking with close collaboration between the two central defenders. A team may play with a flat four-man defence or with a sweeper or libero, as Ajax player Danny Blind did in the successful years in the mid-1990s, but it is rarely used nowadays. The fullbacks have to attack

4-3-3 the Chelsea Way

Successful manager José Mourinho has been a strong supporter of the 4-3-3 system over the years and used it in the clubs he has coached. To illustrate how he has used the system, the focus will be on Chelsea FC. The most frequently used team line-up in the Chelsea 2005–06 season was Petr Cech in goal and a back four of William Gallas and Del Horno as the fullbacks and John Terry and Ricardo Carvalho as the central defenders (see figure 19.6). The trio in midfield was organized in a 1-2 shape, with Claude Makélélé behind, Michael Essien on the right side and Frank Lampard on the left side. In the attack Arjen Robben was at the right wing position, Damien Duff was at the left, and the centre striker was Didier Drogba.

Chelsea liked to defend deep where they were constantly putting pressure on the opposition. Makélélé as the holding player covered a crucial and disciplined role. Often the two wingers were called back to create a 4-5-1 for-

▶ **Figure 19.6** Chelsea 2005 playing 4-3-3.

mation when defending. Building on a compact defence allowed one of the central defenders to bring the ball forward, where especially Carvalho often created two-against-one situations.

In attack, the wingers created width high up the pitch, and Chelsea focused on getting their fullbacks forward to support the attacking players and grab opportunities to make crosses to Drogba, the physically strong forward. The wingers, particular Robben, created space for the fullbacks by entering the field, thereby moving the opponent's fullback. The wingers often changed sides, and, in combination with players penetrating from the midfield, Frank Lampard in particular made it difficult for the opposition to defend properly.

their opponents aggressively when receiving the ball, even in the opponent's half, to reduce the pressure on the midfield. To protect the back four, most coaches favour a centrally placed (holding) midfielder who is strong in physical contests and stays behind the other two midfield players. The player focuses on picking up the opponent's creative key player. To support the player, one of the central defenders may move forwards to cover the space in the central midfield area. The wingers have important defensive work. They need to follow the opposition's fullbacks and pressure the ball when the opposition controls it in its own defensive zone.

In line with this, studies of the English Premier Leagues have observed that the external midfield player covers the most high-intensity running distance (Carling et al. 2008). These players also often have the best intense intermittent exercise capacity (Ingebrigtsen et al. 2012).

Tactical Evolution: Breaking the Bands With the 4-2-3-1 or 4-1-4-1 Systems

The game has evolved. As an example, Williams, Lee and Reilly (1999) highlighted major changes in English Premier League games since 1992, which was the start of the rule of not allowing the goalkeeper to take a pass from a teammate with his hands. The authors found that contemporary matches include more passes, runs with the ball, dribbles and crosses than before 1992, which suggests a significant increase in the tempo of the game. Generally, the defensive line has moved closer to the midfield line, reducing the available space, which was one of the reasons for leaving the old three-band systems and adjusting to a more flexible and tactically demanding 4-2-3-1 or 4-1-4-1 system (see figure 19.7).

After winning the Champions League in 1999, successful manager Sir Alex Ferguson realized that the increased pace of modern European soccer made it necessary for his team to include more tactical flexibility to master some of the big clubs on the continent. Therefore, he changed to a 4-2-3-1 formation (see figure 19.8) to make room for more possession soccer and allow a more cautious approach when playing away in the Champions League. For Manchester United the tactical change after the 1999 success meant that they played with a lone striker and a three-man line behind him (see figure 19.8). Nowadays, 4-2-3-1 and 4-1-4-1 formations are the most used systems.

The defensive demands on the back four in the 4-2-3-1 system are the same as they were in the older systems. The five-man midfield is made up of two defensive players who screen the back four and support the three advancing midfielders, who line up as two wide players and a central offensive midfielder, who is withdrawn from the striker. The two defensive players pick up the opponent's offensive midfield player or withdrawn attacker to reduce that player's space and prevent passes to the player. The two function

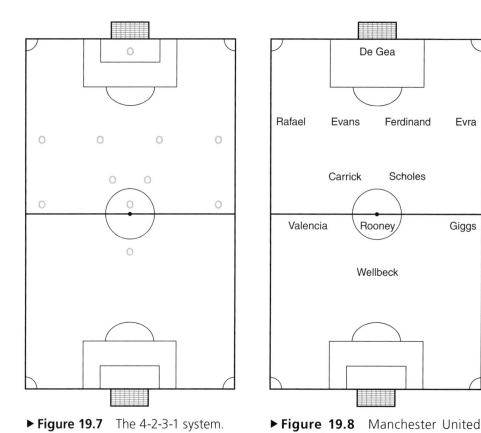

▶ **Figure 19.7**   The 4-2-3-1 system.

▶ **Figure 19.8**   Manchester United 2012 playing 4-2-3-1.

as a unit rather than only one of them having defensive responsibility. Thus, communication and improvisation between the two are vital.

In the defence, the three offensive midfielders have to collaborate to win the ball back high up. The main defensive work of the striker is to put pressure on the opponent's defenders and make the forward work hard in the defence. Actually, in a study of 5,938 Spanish La Liga and English Premier League players, forwards covered the longest high-speed running distances (Dellal et al. 2011).

In the attack, several passing opportunities are offered. The external midfield players push forward to support the striker. Besides running along the sideline and making crosses, they should seek goal-scoring positions by cutting in. Their outside–inside runs leave space for overlap by the full-backs. Often a left-footed player is positioned on the right side (e.g., Dutch player Arjen Robben) and vice versa to get a shot with the strong leg when approaching the penalty area. The central offensive midfield player often has a free role, acts as the nearest support to the striker and combines with the wide players.

To take full advantage of a five-player midfield, the interaction between the players should be natural and effective. Their cooperation should not follow schematic and predictable schemes; defending against a team is difficult when the midfielders make runs into the box.

The lone striker serves as a target player. This player is under constant pressure from the central defenders of the opposing team. When receiving the ball, he or she has to control and distribute it mainly to forward-coming teammates. The target player may also use the free space behind the opponent's fullbacks and receive balls played deep from the midfielders. Some managers use a physically strong target player who can keep the ball, but others prefer a striker with high speed and challenging movements to spin away from defenders and stretch the opponent's defence. Although central defenders are almost always tall, the physical characteristics of forwards vary significantly (Bangsbo 1994).

When a team has a holding central midfield player in their squad, they often play with two box-to-box midfielders ahead of him or her, making it a 4-1-4-1 system. The holding player is usually a physically strong player who makes defensive actions just in front of the defence line. This player is often described as a destroyer. Normally, the holding player makes easy, short passes. For example, the Spanish national side in the Euro 2008 final played with Marcos Senna as the holding player and with Andres Iniesta, Cesc Fabrégas, Xavi Hernández and David Silva behind striker Fernando Torres.

4-2-3-1 the Real Madrid Way

When moving to Real Madrid, José Mourinho changed his 4-3-3 system to a 4-2-3-1 formation. In most Real Madrid matches in La Liga, emphasis was put on the key elements of the system. The fullbacks were extremely offensive, in particular left back Marcello. In midfield the triangle was turned around (4-2-3-1) so that Xavi Alonso and Sami Khedira made up the defensive wall, and from their deep positions they performed diagonal passes to the flanks. Mesut Özil was the playmaker and drifted around searching for opportunities to execute his penetrating passes to the attackers, centre forward Karim Benzema, right winger Di Maria and left winger Cristiano Ronaldo. The two wingers played asymmetrically. On the left the threat from the remarkably fast and skilled Ronaldo often made opponents pull over more players to cover that side. Di Maria was more an outside–inside player who had a special ability to make precise crosses and initiate fast, penetrating combinations.

4-2-3-1: Spain, 2012 European Champions

Spain's record-winning three-title sequence started with Euro 2008 followed by the 2010 World Cup and a title at Euro 2012. As evidence of the development and reassurance of the playing style (tiki-taka) of the team, the average number of passes per match in the three tournaments grew each tournament. The team had 501 passes in 2008, 588 in 2010 and 707 passes in 2012.

Throughout this period the national side had mainly relied on a 4-2-3-1 or 4-2-4-2 system. Their line-up in the 2012 final had Ilker Casillas in goal and a flexible back four of the two offensive fullbacks Álvaro Arbeloa and Jordi Alba in combination with midstoppers Sergio Ramos and Gerard Piqué (see figure 19.9). In front of them were Sergio Busquets and Xavi Alonso to coordinate the necessary defensive tasks and basic ball distribution. The offensive initiatives mainly came from David Silva, Xavi Hernández and Andrés Iniesta, who integrated with Cesc Fábregas as the front player in their attack.

A constant interchange in positions was a key element in their playing style. The team used six midfielders in conjunction with a back four. Most noticeable was that they most often did not have a striker. Thus, in the final against Italy, they played with midfield player Cesc Fabrégas as the front player.

▶ **Figure 19.9** Spain 2012 playing 4-2-3-1 system.

A typical buildup had the central defenders starting with the ball and passing to a central defensive midfielder, who combined with a central offensive player before making a pass to an advancing external midfield player or fullback. Spain's strength was in the midfield and attacking with the fullbacks, especially on the left side with Jordi Alba's aggressive runs. The space was opened as the external midfielders moved inside. The fullback made many long, high-speed runs and was one of the players who covered the most distance at high speed in this playing style (Bradley et al. 2011). The controlling passes in midfield include playing sideways and passing in small triangles, showing patience for the right moment of change of pace and penetration. The change comes with a combination of rapid passing and constant runs in behind the defence. The team's offensive work is part of their defensive work. Their passing patterns bring players in close contact, thereby making it possible to put pressure on the opponent after losing the ball (see figure 19.10). That switch comes with aggression, and high pressure as an important part of the defensive strategy.

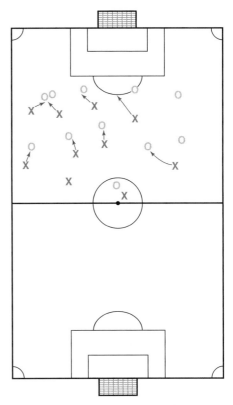

▶ **Figure 19.10** Pressuring the opponent after losing the ball (high pressure).

Other Popular Systems

Other playing systems have been used successfully. Often they have been based on a manager's strong belief in prioritizing either an offensive or a defensive organization within the actual well-known systems. The background for a distinct change of an established system could be the qualities of the squad or the strength of individual players as well as the basic tactical approach to succeeding within a shorter or longer period. This section briefly describes other systems and the teams that used them with good success. To supplement the text and obtain more detail, see Jonathan Wilson's *Inverting the Pyramid* (Wilson 2009).

4-3-2-1: The Christmas Tree

A coach who prefers 4-3-3 but focuses on defence may arrange a formation shaped like a Christmas tree: four players in defence, a midfield divided into bands with a three-player line just in front of the defenders, two offensive central midfield players and a striker (the star in the tree).

The French 1998 World Cup winners used this formation and turned the defensive approach into an offensive version by solving the tactical challenge in accommodating their creative star and elegant playmaker, Zinedine Zidane. He was given free role as one of the two offensive midfielders and was paired with another offensive-minded player. When the French team gained the ball, players ran forward to obtain a penetration pass from Zidane. Another top team, AC Milan, found a different way of integrating a playmaker successfully in this system.

4-3-2-1 the Milan Way

The Champions League winners of 2007, AC Milan, played in a Christmas tree shape (see figure 19.11). In their line-up they had a solid four-man defensive block with two experienced central defenders, Alessandro Nesta and Paolo Maldini, and two attacking fullbacks in Massimo Oddo and Marek Jankulovski.

The three players in the centre of midfield had cooperated effectively with Gennaro Gattuso and Massimo Ambrosini as two hard-working, ball-chasing teammates, leaving creative André Pirlo to do intelligent ball distribution. The two offensive midfielders, Clarence Seedorf and Kaká, drifted in good receiving positions and showed skilful passing to the deep-running striker, Filippo Inzaghi. The Milan five-man midfield had a unique collaboration. The players were capable of roaming and finding the right balance in their positions in relation to defensive demands and offensive opportunities.

▶ **Figure 19.11** AC Milan 2006 playing 4-3-2-1.

The team's defensive approach was different from the high-tempo pressing philosophy of the team's successful years under Arrigo Sacchi in the late 1980s, when they played a 4-4-2 system. Instead, a low-pressure tactic was applied. In the defence the tactic was based on the strength of a player chasing the ball and squeezing space in the midfield.

3-4-3

The Dutch influence on the style of soccer, since the days of total soccer, has especially been spread by Ajax, Amsterdam, with their successful team in the mid-1990s playing 3-4-3. In later years the same offensive attitude was expressed by FC Barcelona, starting when icon and Dutch international Johan Cryuff influenced the playing style, both as a player and later as a coach. In recent years FC Barcelona has developed that playing style and made it more sophisticated. At the World Cup 2014 in Brazil, Costa Rica demonstrated the qualities of 3-4-3 by reaching the quarterfinal.

The basic philosophy of the 3-4-3 formation is to play the game in the opponent's field (see figure 19.12). The team begins its defence in the middle of the opposition's half so that they can get a scoring opportunity within a few passes after capturing the ball. The three defenders play with zonal marking and switch to man-to-man marking when the opposition gets over the halfway line. They do not have fixed roles, so any of the three can act as a supporting player. One of the defenders often takes a position in front of the two other defenders. The organization of the midfield is crucial in supporting the defenders. The four midfielders form a diamond. One of them, a holding player, is close to the defence's line. The holding player operates defensively according to the situation and goes deep in the defence on one

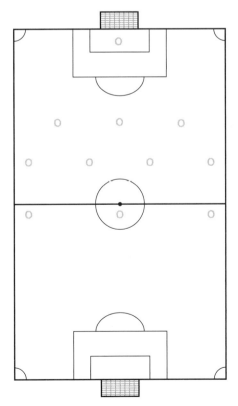

▶ **Figure 19.12**   The 3-4-3 system.

3-4-3 the FC Barcelona Way

The 2009 season was a remarkable year for FC Barcelona. It was the only club in the world to win six major titles: the Spanish Copa del Rey, the Spanish League (La Liga), UEFA Champions League, the Spanish Supercup, the European Supercup and FIFA Club World Cup. From a historical perspective, FC Barcelona is now the team with the most European trophies (15), and the club's playing style has contributed to the development of soccer tactics for decades. The philosophy of the Barcelona team was rooted in the concepts of total soccer. The team formation shifted from the original 4-3-3, which was the structure when Josep (Pep) Guardiola took over as manager in 2007, to a more offensive, flexible 3-4-3 formation, and at times the remarkable 3-7-0 structure.

The team's standard line-up consisted of three players at the back. Two midstoppers, Carles Puyol and Gerard Piqué, were assisted by either one of the wide defenders or by the holding player, Sergio Busquets, who occasionally dropped into the back line (see figure 19.13).

▶ **Figure 19.13** AC Barcelona 2011 playing 3-4-3 system.

The midfield had two offensive wide players, Daniel Alves at the right flank and Eric Abidal at the left flank, and Sergio Busquets playing just in front of the back three. The wingers, like Pedro and Alexis Sanchez, stretched the opposition and kept moving in and out of the spaces created by the two central playmakers, Andres Iniesta and Xavi Hernández. In front, two players alternated as the player closest to the opponent's goal—Lionel Messi and Thiago or Cesc Fabrégas. They were in ever-moving actions in relation to the possibilities of the two playmakers.

The pass was the calling card of the Barcelona team, and their passing quality made them feel comfortable. Through possession they controlled a game. They could speed up the game and slow it down whenever they wanted, and they had the patience to wait for the right penetrating pass. They aggressively attacked the ball after losing it (high pressing) so that they could win it back and promptly play it to a running teammate breaking through.

One of the team's greatest moments was when it won Club World Cup in 2011 by beating Brazilian Santos. Barcelona's second goal, scored by Xavi

Hernández, was assisted by every other outfield Barca player and comprised 32 Barcelona passes.

As one of the consequences of the possession style and the vital runs from midfield, coach Guardiola surprised the soccer world at the start of the 2011 La Liga season by fielding a team without a proper centre forward and winning 5-0. His team was composed almost entirely of midfield players, and their constant interchanging gave the opposition's defence major problems. It created a new tactical term, the false nine, a striker who no longer acts in the normal way but moves around like an offensive midfield player. Because of the lack of a designated striker, the new version of the 3-4-3 was described as a 3-7-0. Other teams have also experimented with not having a normal striker, like AC Roma playing in a 4-6-0 shape with Francesco Totti as the most offensive player.

Barcelona's style has also influenced the successful Spanish national team, which included seven players from Barcelona. The Spanish coach wisely used that style of play and the players' knowledge of each other, which had been established through many years at FC Barcelona.

side if it looks as if the opposition will break through. When the opposition is in control of the ball, the midfielders try to position themselves so that the opposing team can attack on one side.

This system puts heavy physical demands on the two wingers in the defence, because they have to block the advancement of the opposition's fullbacks and, in addition, cover the midfield players on the opposite side. When the opposition starts its buildup, the central attacker falls back to disturb passes from the back line.

The two external attackers are positioned wide in the attacking play. They have to avoid getting too close to the opposition's defenders, and they have to create and find free space to receive passes. They are often fast, and by moving back a bit just before receiving the ball, they can create an opportunity to turn with the ball and gain speed when challenging the defenders. The system is based on well-developed teamwork between the fullbacks, outer midfield players and wingers, and likewise between the central attacker and midfield players. Midfield cooperation and maintaining the winger's width creates shooting opportunities from distance. An essential part of the success of the 3-4-3 system is the high degree of interchangeability. The players have to be able to do the work of each other technically, tactically and physically.

3-5-2

During the late 1970s some coaches started wondering why they were playing with a traditional four-back line when the opponent played with two attackers. In response, they created the 3-5-2 formation (see figure 19.14) in which the defensive line was reorganized by placing the former fullback's position 15 to 20 metres farther up the pitch, joining the three midfield players. In defence the team plays with two man markers and a sweeper. The two attackers are positioned well up the pitch.

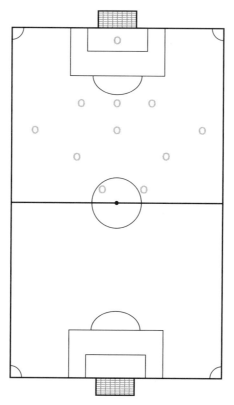

▶ **Figure 19.14** The 3-5-2 system.

3-5-2: A European Champion Winning Formula

The two biggest shocks in European Championship tournament history were the wins of Denmark and Greece in 1992 and 2004, respectively. Both teams used a 3-5-2 system and were well aware that they were not able to dominate the games. Instead, they adopted a strategy based on a strong, hard-working defence with a focus on utilizing counterattacks; for example, Greece played with a striker who was a strong header, placed a creative and offensive midfield player just behind him and relied on breaks from the wide players.

The success of the Danish team in 1992 was created over several years. In the tournament the team had a base of five players playing for the same Danish team, Brøndby, which qualified for the semifinal in the European Cup in 1990. To these were added players from various teams in Europe, but all had been playing together in the national team for many years. The team was selected only 10 days before the tournament because Yugoslavia had been banned for political reasons. Several players had already been on holiday for more than two weeks. These players went through a specific fitness programme, and even though they were not optimally prepared, they were able to contribute to the first game against England, which ended in a draw. As the tournament progressed, their fitness level increased and their contributions became greater. Nevertheless, it was mainly the playing style and team spirit that created the Danish success.

The 3-5-2 system is still a valid option. The Italian national coach at the Euro 2012 finals, Cesare Prandelli, started the first match against Spain in a 3-5-2 shape and changed later in the tournament to his favoured 4-3-1-2 formation (see figure 19.15). One of the reasons for his introductory line-up was an injury to key defender Andrea Barzagli in the last friendly game before the tournament and three successive defeats in the last few friendly games. Over the preparation period Italy had tried two different systems as part of their tactical flexibility, and the coach was confident that his team could adapt depending on which team they played against and which players were available.

FC Barcelona is another example of a team that switches formations for a specific match. In La Liga 2009–10 Barcelona played Real Madrid at Estadio Bernabéu and lined up in an unexpected 3-5-2 formation.

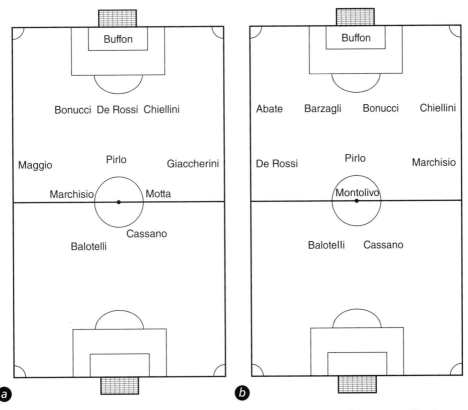

▶ **Figure 19.15** Italy Euro 2012 playing (a) 3-5-2 (first match); (b) 4-3-1-2 (final).

The offensive play of the backs led to the coinage of a new word in the vocabulary of soccer tactics, namely wingbacks. Wingbacks should control the corridor area in both defence and offence. In the buildup, the sweeper should be available for the goalkeeper. The two central defenders should go wide and create space for the sweeper. The two wingbacks should position themselves farther up and create width in the game. The buildup can also be initiated with a wingback going back to receive the ball and then dribble forward to the halfway line. If challenged, the wingback can play the ball back to the sweeper, who makes a diagonal pass to the other side, where free space is often available for the other wingback.

In the offence the wingbacks should constantly try to penetrate the corridor at the side and get to the goal line to make a cross. The strikers should position themselves centrally. Because the wingbacks often make crosses, the two strikers have to look for free space in the box, often finishing with a header. They are also expected to do diagonal runs towards the sideline when the buildup is created.

The defensive organization with a five-player midfield often forces the opposition to play through the centre, where the team normally allocates its strongest players. The three players in the central midfield are positioned either in a line or in a triangle, with one defensive midfield player who is strong in one-on-one situations. The central defenders mark the attackers, whereas the sweeper behind has the role of controlling the defensive organization and closing any gaps. This player is also the initiator of any offside traps.

Developing a System

Game strategy and style of play has changed in the past few years. Having players maintain their positions has been replaced by a more flexible approach in which players can interchange positions at any time. This approach requires a certain game intelligence by players, which has to be developed through training and coaching.

Young players have to be educated on how to be multifunctional. Science also has to contribute to the coaching manual, especially in relation to physical parameters and game observation, leading to new training methods and more sophisticated tactical reflections.

For example, the analysis of the individual demands on a player during a game provides useful information about how to train each player in the team, even in a team session (Bangsbo and Mohr 2014). Assessment of loading, such as by measuring intensity with GPS on players during training and using the information in the planning of training, will be valuable in the future (Cummins et al. 2013).

The style of play and the team system influence the demands on individual players. In a recent study the effect of the playing formation on high-intensity running and technical performance of English FA Premier League teams was analysed (Bradley et al. 2011). No differences were observed in total distance covered or amount of high-intensity running between 4-4-2, 4-3-3 and 4-5-1 formations, but players in a 4-5-1 formation performed less very high-intensity running when their team was in possession and more when their team was not in possession compared with the 4-4-2 and 4-3-3 formations. These differences may be related to the attacking and defensive characteristics inherent to those playing formations. A 4-5-1 is a more defensive system than a 4-4-2 and a 4-3-3 because of the reinforcement of the midfield zones at the expense of a forward player. Not much difference was observed in the individual positions, except that attackers in a 4-3-3 performed about 30 per cent more high-intensity running (greater than18 kilometres per hour) than did attackers in the 4-4-2 and 4-5-1 formations.

The attacker in a 4-5-1 system does significantly less high-intensity running in the second half, which was not observed in the other systems. It may be that the 4-5-1 formation requires marked physical work by the attacker, because the player is often isolated and, in the defence, has to put pressure on the opponent's back line. Overall ball possession did not differ between 4-4-2, 4-3-3 and 4-5-1 formations, but the number of passes and the fraction of successful passes were highest in a 4-4-2 compared with the 4-3-3 and 4-5-1 formations.

Generally, the results suggest that playing formation has only a limited influence on the overall activity profiles of players, except for attackers, but it has an influence on high-speed running with and without ball possession and on some technical elements of performance.

Since the 1950s quantitative analysis of soccer has been constantly growing. Development of new video-recording technology in the last decade has allowed the study of all 22 players for each one-sixth of a second during the entire game. Almost every top team in Europe now uses observational systems. Managers and their assistants analyse the data in various ways to find the key success factors in their game. Scientists also uncover new knowledge about the many aspects of the game, which leads to more grounded discussions about various performance-related soccer issues. But in the tactical area, more complex methodological questions still limit the search for a winning formula. When English FA's former director of coaching and education, Charles Hughes, published the book *The Winning Formula* in 1990, soccer coaches for the first time were able to learn about data-based arguments for a specific style of play. The book highlighted the importance of a direct style of play for successful performance, as opposed to a strategy based on possession soccer (Hughes 1990).

Since then, many scientific observations and studies have focused on central tactical factors for success in soccer (e.g., playing style). Possession play, contrary to Hughes's belief, is now widely considered the most effective way of performing on the field (Lago 2009), although newer studies including assessment of opponent interactions have more varied results depending on the opponent's defending situation (Carling 2011; Bradley et al. 2013).

Results from multiple regression analysis show that counterattacks and offence tactics are more effective than elaborate attacks (possession style) when playing against an imbalanced defence, but not against a balanced defence (Tenga et al. 2010a, 2010b). Hence, assessing the opponent's style of play is crucial when evaluating the probability of producing a scoring opportunity with a particular offensive playing tactic. But none of the studies in this area seems to appreciate the importance of the intricate interrelationships that exist in relevant physical, situational and psychological parameters. A contextual problem is also inherent in most studies, because information has been constrained to a few domestic leagues.

A more complex methodological approach to scrutinizing the game's tactical challenges is needed, which includes a call for broader comparative studies to account for intercultural variations in the style of play (Collet 2013).

In the search for clarification and inspiration, a coach may look to various media. In today's comprehensive TV coverage of top soccer matches, several impulses will hit a coach, which may lead to reflection and inspire the coach to find or to remodel a system and style of play. Traditionally, the system of a team that wins one of the important tournaments serves as a basis for many coaches and federations. The copycat effect is at work here. But this inspiration is often not useful because the success of a system depends on the quality of the players.

A system has to be coherent, practicable and flexible in relation to the goals of the team. Its foundation must be within the capacities of the players in the squad. When choosing a system, the coach has to clarify his or her vision on how the team will play. The philosophy should be present in both the long-term perspective and the desire to win the next match.

In some clubs a certain system is prioritized, and players are thus developed to fulfil the roles in the system or they are selected because they have certain qualities. Ajax and FC Barcelona are examples of clubs that have a clear strategy and well-established academies for youth players. Experienced coach Louis Van Gaal (formerly at Ajax and the Dutch national team, now at Manchester United and with experience at Barcelona and Bayern Munich) said,

> The overall concept must be clear. The concept in Ajax is that we have to sell a product, and that product is attacking and attractive football. The best system for doing this is 3-4-3 because the players and the coaching staff fully support it. We agree on things together and then we implement them together.
>
> (Kormelink and Seeverens 1997)

As a consequence, Ajax puts about €4 million into their academy every year for talent, and they only want players from the outside who can and will adjust to the club's culture. Their belief is that no player is more important than the philosophy.

Top teams need even more tactical work in implementing a broad tactical foundation. Personal experience from Juventus with Carlo Ancelotti and Marcello Lippi tells us the importance of being well prepared in the tactical area. We created a tactical foundation on which different tactical strategies could be explored. In Juventus, we often started one way, changed to another strategy during the game and finished with a third strategy, all prepared in the training before the game.

Conclusion

Most top teams are playing with one striker in a 4-2-3-1 or 4-1-4-1 system with two external midfield players who have good dribbling qualities and high speed, as well as a creative offensive midfield player behind the striker. Other teams play with two attackers in a 4-4-2 or 3-5-2 system, as Italy and Greece did during Euro 2012. Both teams were successful; Italy reached the final and Greece made the quarterfinal. Sometimes teams play without a striker, such as the brilliant FC Barcelona team. Thus, no one system is superior to the others. Both the team system and style of play have to be developed in light of the qualities of the players.

As this chapter has documented, a single winning formula or a right way of playing does not exist. Navigating the selection among various types of systems and playing styles is largely in the hands of the coach or manager. The coach's perception of how a good team should perform and the realistic chances of achievement always create a dilemma. This is the challenge of being a coach.

The head coach and fitness coach have to evaluate what the chosen tactical strategy and style of play require of the technical and physical aspects of each player, as well as whether the players have the necessary qualities (Bangsbo 2007; Bangsbo and Mohr 2014).

Physical and technical testing can provide important information for evaluation. If individual players do not have the needed capacity, team tactics may have to be modified or training programmes that take into account individual needs may have to be implemented (Bangsbo and Mohr 2014). In all cases such a process requires that all coaching staff have sufficient understanding of all important aspects of performance in a game. For example, the head coach needs to know the basic principles and effects of fitness training, and the fitness coach must be aware of the technical and tactical aspects of the game.

Daily training and match analysis can provide useful feedback to the coach and allow tactical adjustments. Systematic, precise interpretation and presentation of the data to the head coach and the players are needed. The magnitude of available game data may overwhelm some people, but for others it is most welcome. In an interview with UEFA, André Villas-Boas made his view clear:

> *Some coaches are obsessed by their computers and the data they receive. I am not that way, because I favour the emotional human aspect of the game and the cultivation of the players' talent. Sometimes players can't express their quality because they are restricted by rigid systems.*
>
> *(Roxburgh 2011)*

Nevertheless, many coaches have had success with a different approach. Sir Alex Ferguson expressed his view in an interview a few years ago: 'Sports science, without question, is the biggest and most important change in my lifetime'.

CHAPTER 20

Optimal Preparation for Defensive Play

—Sam Erith and Gary Curneen

Several references to the match demands of soccer appear in this book. Contributors have stated that the physical demands of the game appear to be on the increase and that tactical trends are constantly evolving. These developments generate new technical challenges for players and coaches alike.

This chapter demonstrates how science contributes to the training and preparation of defensive players. In doing so, it examines the role of the modern fullback and central defender and identifies the specific physical demands for these positions. In addition, the principles of defending are explored so that you can understand the key features of applying defensive pressure. Clearly, these components need careful consideration when planning training, and they should be integrated into the coaching process to optimize the preparation of defensive players.

Motion Analysis

Motion analysis entails determining work-rate profiles of players within a team and classifying activities in terms of intensity, duration and frequency (Reilly 1994). In this way, an overall picture of the physiological demands of soccer can be gathered. The application of motion analysis to soccer has enabled the objective recording and interpretation of match events, thus describing the characteristic patterns of activity in soccer.

The advent of computerized notation systems has facilitated sophisticated analysis of movement and patterns of play leading to key events during match play. Used for real-time or postevent analysis, these systems provide qualitative and quantitative information. Improving performance is the central purpose of the coaching process, and detailed knowledge at the behavioural level of performance is essential for almost all stages of the training programme.

To date, motion analysis has been used to investigate soccer performance of teams and players at various time points across leagues throughout the world (Bangsbo, Norregaard and Thorso 1991; Anderson, Ekblom and Krustrup 2007; Mohr, Krustrup and Bangsbo 2003; Di Salvo et al. 2007). In addition, motion analysis research has yielded some valuable insights into factors that may influence physical outputs during competitive games including training status (Krustrup et al. 2003), fatigue (Mohr, Krustrup and Bangsbo 2003; Krustrup et al. 2006), the effect of playing formation (Bradley et al. 2011) and playing position (Bradley et al. 2009). These results have important implications for the integration of match analysis in evaluating performance and driving action at the behavioural level of the coaching process.

In the literature, characteristic work-rate profiles have emerged in relation to playing position. Midfield players are observed to cover a greater percentage of their total distance jogging; forwards cover a greater percentage of their distance sprinting; and central defenders cover a greater percentage of their distance moving sideways or backwards (Bangsbo, Norregaard and Thorso 1991; Rienzi et al. 2000).

The increased distance covered moving backwards for defensive players is a reflection of the specific positional requirements. Defenders are frequently required to retreat towards their own goal whilst facing the direction of play, either jockeying an individual attacker or adjusting their position in relation to the attacking team's movement. Therefore, practitioners should include such modes of movement in the training drills for defensive players.

Overall, central defenders cover less total distance and perform less high-intensity running than players in other positions do (Mohr, Krustrup and Bangsbo 2003). The reduced distance covered by central defenders may be linked to the aerobic capacity of the players. Thus, the greater distances covered at lower intensities by the central defenders may be connected with their having the lowest $\dot{V}O_2$max values among all outfield players (Strudwick 2006). Additionally, the higher $\dot{V}O_2$max capacities of fullbacks and midfield players could be attributable to their having to perform more high-intensity activities throughout a match. A high $\dot{V}O_2$max is correlated with greater distances covered in a match (Reilly 1993) and has been shown to influence the number of sprints attempted during a game (Smaros 1980). This suggestion is supported by published results from an intermittent endurance test with elite-level male soccer players that demonstrated a correlation between distance covered in this test and the positional role of the players (Bangsbo and Michalisk 2002).

The central defender's work-rate profile is characterized by sudden bursts of high-intensity exercise interspersed with low-intensity recovery periods that seem to indicate a lack of direct involvement in the play. Practitioners need to include high-intensity training to complement matches and tactical work of central defenders to ensure maintenance of fitness throughout regular match play. Moreover, when playing 11v11 games becomes the major stimulus for physiological conditioning, some amount of detraining may occur during the season. Therefore, training loads of players should be monitored to ensure that appropriate loads are achieved.

Bradley et al. (2009) analysed English Premier League games to determine the activity patterns for players in various playing positions. Twenty-eight English Premier League games were analysed during the 2005–2006 competitive season (n = 370). Fullbacks and central defenders covered 2,605 metres and 1,834 metres at high speeds, respectively. This distance was significantly lower than that covered at high speed by wide midfielders (3,138 metres). Central defenders did significantly less high-speed running than players in all other outfield positions did. This study also reported that fullbacks covered a greater distance sprinting than central midfielders, attackers and central defenders did. These data have been further supported in the literature (Di Salvo et al. 2007). Collectively, these findings suggest that the demands placed on modern fullbacks are extremely high. The following qualities may be displayed by contemporary elite fullbacks:

- High aerobic capacity ($\dot{V}O_2$max values around 64 millilitres per kilogram per minute)
- Ability to sustain repeated bouts of long sprints throughout match play
- Ability to accelerate, decelerate and jump
- Quickness over short and long distances
- Ability to work closely to their full performance capacity
- Ability to recover quickly from repeated speed endurance bouts

Many view the attacking fullback as an integral position within the modern game. The attacking fullback is a demanding position because of the high number of sprints associated with the role. These players have to be able to attack and defend throughout the game, which is demanding not only physically but also mentally. In addition, the influx of unorthodox wingers (i.e., a right-footed winger playing on the left side and working inside or vice versa) has added even more need for fullbacks to provide width and penetration when attacking. Practitioners and coaches must therefore ascertain whether certain players can fulfil the physical and tactical requirements of this role.

A further interesting finding from motion analysis research is that central defenders and attackers experience the largest drop-off in high-speed running immediately following the most intense five-minute period of the match (Bradley et al. 2009). It is unclear whether this decline results from a physical limitation of central defenders or simply a reduced tactical need to perform high-speed actions at that time.

Most practitioners use match analysis technology to gather information about the physiological strain imposed on players during match play. Although this approach yields an overview of the physiological strain during competition, much of the qualitative information during the most critical phases of the match may be overlooked. Moreover, although the total distance covered at various exercise intensities offers a global measure of the physiological strain imposed on players, the most intense five-minute blocks of match play offer more detailed information that can be better used in the design of field-based conditioning drills. In addition, recent research has indicated a fairly high variability (20 to 30 per cent) from game to game (Gregson et al. 2010), suggesting the occurrence of large fluctuations in game demands. In this regard, several factors such as the positional role, the level of the opponent, the result of the game and the tactical system played have marked effects on the amount of high-intensity work performed during a match (Bradley et al. 2011). Taken together, these studies provide sufficient evidence to suggest that global measures of match data may not always be optimal key performance indicators when designing conditioning programmes.

A common observation in motion analysis research is that the physiological responses to competitive soccer match play depend on the position in the team. The greatest work rate demanded by the game is imposed on midfield players because of the linking role they play between defence and attack, which requires more sustained running. On the other hand, central defenders have more periods of low-intensity work, which may allow a greater degree of recovery. What is not clear is whether it is the game per se or the physiological characteristics of the individual players that dictate the work-rate profile. Performance in soccer is the result of a variety of independent factors. Players may or may not be taxed to the limit of their physical capacities during a soccer match because of the tactical responsibilities and situational conditions. Nonetheless, given the observed reduced work rate over the duration of competitive match play, all players, regardless of tactical assignments, may experience temporary and cumulative fatigue over the duration of a game. Therefore, to ensure the optimization of player ability to perform intense exercise, this type of effort should be a priority in conditioning programmes.

Work-Rate Profiles of Elite Players

At a behavioural level, the specific demands of soccer determine the relative importance of the various aspects of physical performance required to be successful. Therefore, practitioners should concentrate on the work-rate profiles of elite players and interpret the unique demands of participation through these profiles. The average distances covered by fullbacks and central defenders at various speeds during Premiership games over three competitive seasons are presented in tables 20.1 and 20.2. These profiles can be used to set benchmarks for individuals and groups and develop normative values on which assessments can be made. These profiles also provide

Table 20.1 Average Distances Covered by Fullbacks at Various Speeds During Premiership Matches Over Three Seasons

Season (number of matches analysed)	HI distance (sprint distance plus high-speed distance)	Sprint distance (total distance covered at >25.2 kmh)	High-speed running (total distance covered at 19.8–25.2 kmh)	Average sprint length (>25.2 kmh)
2011–2012 (274 matches)	916 m	268 m	649 m	7.2 m
2012–2013 (366 matches)	1,026 m	307 m	720 m	7 m
2013–2014 (361 matches)	1,032 m	300 m	731 m	7.1 m

Table 20.2 Average Distances Covered by Central Defenders at Various Speeds During Premiership Matches Over Three Seasons

Season (number of matches analysed)	HI distance (sprint distance plus high-speed distance)	Sprint distance (total distance covered at >25.2 kmh)	High-speed running (total distance covered at 19.8–25.2 kmh)	Average sprint length (>25.2 kmh)
2011–2012 (282 matches)	566 m	146 m	420 m	6.7 m
2012–2013 (376 matches)	630 m	163 m	468 m	6.4 m
2013–2014 (369 matches)	630 m	156 m	473 m	6.4 m

valuable information at the behavioural level regarding the physical performance of players and provide assistance in the evaluation, modification and prescription of training programmes.

Combined data from current and historical literature suggest that fullbacks exhibit the greatest variation in overall distance covered (Reilly and Thomas 1976; Mohr, Krustrup and Bangsbo 2003). This variability is believed to be a function of the tactical flexibility applied to fullbacks in each game; lower values are recorded when the players are directly confronted by an attacking opponent, and higher values are seen in players who have been converted from a midfield role (Reilly 1994). This information is critical in determining selection of appropriate players for the particular tactical role in the team and against a variety of opponents. Moreover, the sport science staff and coaches need to communicate and work collectively to organize information and deliver an appropriate game plan. This task is critical when coaches decide to play central defenders out of position, through either necessity or tactical choice. The role of the sport science staff is then to ascertain whether the player can fulfil the physical requirements of the new position.

Integration of Scientific Evidence

Practitioners and coaches need to consider the variety of movement patterns and short high-intensity bursts of activities that defenders must execute during competitive matches. Players execute a high number of short accelerations, decelerations, jumps and tackles (Mohr, Krustrup and Bangsbo 2003). As previously discussed, defenders perform a greater proportion of backwards, lateral and shuffling movements when compared with players at other positions (Bloomfield, Polman and O'Donoghue 2007). Various situational moments in matches can have a significant effect on the work that defenders are required to do. One further consideration is that when the team loses possession of the ball in an unbalanced situation (when the team formation is out of shape) and their opponents launch a direct counterattack, the defenders often need to cover more ground at high speed and make quick, tough decisions about what action to take (for example, attempt to delay the attack, tackle immediately, and so forth).

These critical moments involve many visual, cognitive and decision-making challenges under high pressure. The wrong execution of decisions at these moments can influence the outcome of the match. These demands are hard to replicate in the training environment but need to form part of the overall training programme for defenders whenever possible. Moreover, practitioners and coaches alike must prepare defenders for the most intense phases of the game.

General Training Objectives

Many components need to be incorporated into the training programme of soccer players. These elements include a full range of activities such as recovery strategies, individual and team preparation, match rehearsal, activation modalities and injury prevention strategies, in addition to the more obvious training session. Therefore, detailed and intimate cooperation between the sport scientist and coach is crucial.

For coaches to undertake the increasing sophistication of tasks expected in elite contemporary soccer, they need to have well-developed knowledge and understanding of physiological principles. For sport scientists to have an effect on the coaching process, they need to be able to translate detailed statistics and key messages to coaches. This interpersonal relationship must be established and respected. For example, the sport scientist must decide what information should be delivered to the coach to make it clear that a fullback may be too fatigued to make repeated overlapping runs beyond the wide player as a result of accumulated playing and training exposure within the past seven days. In this context the physical capabilities of the individual athletes must be matched to the demands of the upcoming game.

Clearly, the design of the programme should be based on training philosophy (as established by the coach and sport scientist) and specificity to match performance per se. The need to isolate match performance components and to control workload intensity is achieved by a series of activities conducted within the training session. It is in the context of this systematic planning process that the coach and sport scientist must collaborate and decide

- the duration of training and respective drills,
- the intensity of training and respective drills and
- the frequency of training.

The application of these principles in a planned progressive manner is the key to ensuring that the appropriate energy systems are stimulated during physiological preparation. Moreover, if coaches (through lack of interpersonal communication with the sport scientist) increase duration, intensity and frequency of training without understanding the planning process, they will increase the risk of underperformance or injury to the athletes.

General Aims of Physical Preparation

A physical preparation plan should have several purposes:

- Ensuring that the athlete is physically capable of implementing the tactical blueprint
- Ensuring that the athlete has the necessary physical capacities to execute the technical requirements of his or her role in the team
- Ensuring that the athlete enters matches as injury resistant as possible
- Ensuring that the key physical attributes required for the player's role are developed effectively through a periodized plan

Opinion has always been divided among coaches and fitness staff about whether position-specific training needs to take place as part of or in addition to the generic team training. This debate has prompted practitioners to develop exercise protocols that attempt to match the physiological demands observed during specific moments during games. Such procedures may then facilitate the development of position-specific fitness.

A common practice is to incorporate small-sided games within the conditioning process. This approach has been highlighted throughout the book. The manipulation of pitch size, numbers and work–rest times all affect the training stimuli, and small-sided games have been shown to be an effective method to condition players (Little and Williams 2007). When this work is carefully integrated with more expansive team drills and games, achieving a balanced training programme is possible.

But on some occasions it may not be appropriate to expose players to expansive practices like 9v9 or 11v11 to achieve the appropriate training dose for fullbacks and central defenders. Examples of these occasions include periods of congested fixture schedules when certain personnel in the squad are not getting match exposure or when reconditioning players are returning to training after an absence because of injury. At these moments fullbacks and central defenders need carefully planned training to ensure they are exposed to key physical components of their positional demands, such as longer high-speed running, significant change of direction and sprint distances. Furthermore, position-specific training could prove an effective way to prepare players for the most intense periods of competition.

Therefore, preparing players for these highly taxing periods makes sense to minimize the subsequent effect on team performance. Here are some examples of the types of drills that can be used effectively to supplement team training at the appropriate time. The drills target the aerobic and anaerobic energy systems, and practitioners should decide on the most appropriate timing and planning of these drills.

Position-Specific Repeated Sprint Drill The player starts from the middle of the penalty area (figure 20.1) and performs a maximal acceleration zigzag sprint between the box and the base line. The player performs repetitions on a rolling 20-second clock (approximately 5 seconds of work and 15 seconds of rest), performing a total of five repetitions per set (approximately 90 seconds). When possible the player should perform multiple sets with 90 seconds of rest between sets.

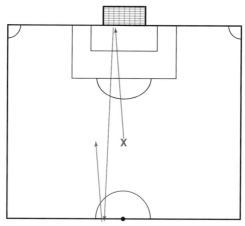

▶ **Figure 20.1** Position-specific repeated sprint drill

Position-Specific Speed Endurance Drill The player performs a shuttle run at full maximal speed from the edge of the box to the halfway line and back to the box (figure 20.2). The player performs repetitions on a rolling 50-second clock (approximately 10 seconds of work and 40 seconds of rest). One set should contain a minimum of three repetitions. When possible the player should perform multiple sets with 3 minutes of rest between sets.

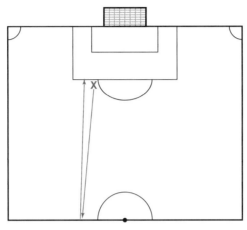

▶ **Figure 20.2** Position-specific speed endurance drill.

Position-Specific Aerobic Endurance Drill The player begins on the touchline and performs a three-quarter paced run to the halfway line (figure 20.3), covering the distance in 9 or 10 seconds. The player immediately turns and jogs back to the touchline in 20 seconds before repeating the process. Each hard run should start on a 30-second rolling clock. The player should complete 10 repetitions.

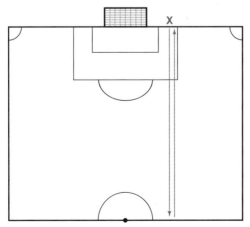

▶ **Figure 20.3** Position-specific aerobic endurance drill

Position-Specific Drill for a Fullback The player shuffles in and out of the poles (figure 20.4). The player volleys the ball from the coach, turns and receives an overhead throw. The player turns and drives with the ball, playing through the cones to the coach. The player drives around the poles, receives the ball and crosses first time into the goal. The player then turns and drives back to the start line. The player should complete the course in 30 seconds maximum and then rest for 1 minute. The player performs three sets of six repetitions with 2 or 3 minutes of rest between sets.

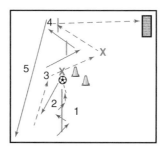

▶ **Figure 20.4** Position-specific drill for a fullback.

Position-Specific Drill for a Central Defender 1 The player runs out from the cone to receive the ball (figure 20.5). The player heads the ball back to the coach over the mannequin and then runs back to the cone. The player runs to the second coach and receives the ball. The player heads the ball back to the coach. The coach passes the ball down the pitch and the player turns to chase the ball. The player passes the ball back to the coach and sprints back to the start cone. The player performs 20 seconds of work and 30 seconds of rest for six repetitions. The player alternates sides.

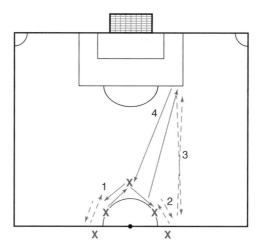

▶ **Figure 20.5** Position-specific drill for a central defender 1.

Position-Specific Drill for a Central Defender 2   The player drives out to the pole and plays a contested 1-2 (figure 20.6). The player backpedals and spins out to receive the ball down the channel from the coach. The player recovers back to the start position. The player repeats to the opposite side. The player performs three runs with a 1:2 work-to-rest ratio.

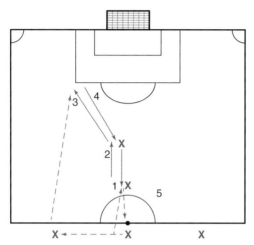

▶ **Figure 20.6**   Position-specific drill for a central defender 2.

Coaching Philosophy and Principles of Defending

Regardless of coaching level, success is not possible without an organized and effective defensive strategy. Although the importance of stopping the opposition may not have changed in the past 50 years, both the demands and ways of coaching it certainly have. As a result, we have seen a transformation in the area of defending over the past decade. We no longer see teams relying on a simple central defender pairing to hold off the opposition. Instead, teams have to work together to earn those priceless shutouts and clean sheets.

The World Cup 2014 in Brazil demonstrated the importance of teams over individuals. Chile, Costa Rica, Colombia and Mexico all overachieved because of systems centred on successful defensive organizations. We have also seen a change in the demands on defenders in the modern game. If you watch any analysis of any game in any league in the world, the chances are you will find criticism of defending. Whether the criticism is directed at individuals, team shape or marking on set pieces, defenders always seem to be under fire. So with increased demands along with heightened criticism, how can we address defending with our teams? First, we must understand that the key for successful teams is not only to be good at defending but to excel at it.

Winning teams understand its importance and are willing to place a premium and focus on it. Only when every player embraces his or her role and the concept of team first defensively can the group become successful.

The principles of defending have evolved in recent years and now incorporate the following:

- Compactness: Space is the most important commodity required for teams to attack effectively. Therefore, from a defensive viewpoint, the primary aim is to reduce space in key areas throughout the game.

- Delay: Remember the days of scathing tackles from players like Gentile, Stiles, Hunter and Goikoetxea? They are long gone! As referees clamp down on tackling, defenders have to delay forwards and wait for support.

- Adaptability: With detailed scouting systems now implemented at almost every level, the defensive unit will likely face a different challenge every week. One team may try to exploit space behind, whereas the next opponent may look at wide areas to attack. Successful defensive systems must be able to cope with different questions every game.

- Balance: Cover and balance are at the foundation of a team's success. When players go to press, players also go to cover. Defending is not simply about chasing the ball as individuals; it is more about providing cover for each other.

- Discipline: The two types of discipline in the game today are mental discipline and physical discipline. Mental discipline is centred on tactics and positioning. Physical discipline is about directing controlled aggression towards winning the ball and competing. At the top level, a foul is considered a mistake, so the best teams have disciplined players who can consistently perform and make good decisions for 90 minutes.

- Communication: With intricate attacking systems centred on movement and rotation, defenders must give information to their teammates at all times. The volume of a defender usually reveals the intensity in which he or she plays. Effective communication can create role awareness, promote refocussing, build trust, solve problems and give teams a winning edge.

- Recovery: The best indicator of a defensively solid team is how quickly they can recover into defensive shape after losing possession. Some of the reasons that teams do not recover defensively include arguing a referee's decision, assuming a teammate will do it or not fearing repercussions from the coach or team captain.

Four Dimensions of Defending

With countless variables at elite levels of play, coaching defence one dimensionally in the modern game is impractical. Before planning defensive exercises, coaches and practitioners must look at how their defenders will be challenged during games, which may change because of playing level, the opponent's playing style or their own team's playing style, but in many ways the fundamental demands will always be similar.

At the youth level, defenders usually excel in the physical side of the game. When players progress to the elite level, however, the best defenders are proficient in technique, possession, decision making and concentration because the modern game demands it. Working solely on one dimension of defending without a link or progression to the big picture will not develop individuals or teams. Clearly, some defenders will need work in certain areas, but keeping the four-dimensional approach present in the majority of coaching sessions will ensure improvement in competitive games.

Technical

The speed of the modern game punishes defensive mistakes quickly and with no mercy at the highest level. In the modern game, defenders require almost faultless technique. Balance is important because defenders have to restrict the space of attacking players, but at the same time they have to be careful not to get too tight because forwards can spin off, turn and be difficult to catch if they get away.

One of the most important technical elements of modern defending is being able to stop opposing players without leaving the feet and committing to the tackle. The defender who goes to the ground with a slide tackle in today's game runs the risk of free kicks, penalties and yellow cards. In possession, the demands on modern defenders are higher than ever.

The increased attacking qualities demanded for an elite defender have also evolved. No longer is it enough for a fullback to be a solid 1v1 defender or for a central defender to be unbeatable in the air. The modern game demands fullbacks to push forwards, combine with wide attackers and deliver in the final third. Likewise, central defenders are asked to bring the ball comfortably out of defence and provide a range of passing similar to that of a central midfield player.

The English Premier League has appointed Opta as their official media data collection and distribution source. Live Opta soccer data include every single on-the-ball action in a match, and more than 1,600 individual pieces of information are recorded from every 90 minutes. Every action incorporates an x, y pitch coordinate and time stamp, detailing when and where it occurred on the pitch. Data from Opta figures demonstrated that defenders averaged 63 ball touches per 90 minutes in the 2010–11 Premier League season, midfielders 73 touches and forwards 51 touches. These figures demonstrate that defenders must be able to perform high-quality distribution. Strength in the air is still an important skill, and the ability to be brave and block shots is an asset that goalkeepers and coaches appreciate from any member of their back four, but the modern defender has to be competent in possession.

Tactical

Systems of play and formations today demand that all players defend together as one unit rather than simply leave it to the back four to do all the dirty work. To win in the modern game, all 11 players must be committed to the defensive side of the game. Moreover, teams can no longer have passengers on their team. Players who are unwilling to work for the cause have found themselves as disposable assets regardless of their attacking qualities. Coaches only have to look at Lionel Messi's work rate to see how attackers have become the first line of defence.

The other tactical advances in the game today are the concepts of pressure and counterattack defending. Defending has become more complex because teams now look to keep the space between their back four and their farthest attacking player as compact as possible. Playing against this type of team is difficult. Defending in the modern game is not simply about what you do without possession. Pep Guardiola supports the philosophy that teams can also defend when they have the ball: 'Sometimes you have loads of possession but do not create chances, just to defend and defend, because when you have possession, you have the ball and it is impossible for the opponent to score a goal' (Defendingwiththeball.com).

Physical

To stop teams from scoring in the modern game, the physical demands on both the team and individual players have increased enormously. Can you imagine the fitness levels needed to pressure teams relentlessly as Barcelona does for 90 minutes? A vast amount of energy, stamina and aerobic capacity is needed to do this effectively. Clearly, the interaction of the coach and sport science staff is important when devising a tactical and training plan for teams. The following elements need careful consideration:

- A defensive strategy needs to facilitate defending from all areas of the field.
- Defending by its very nature presents players with a wide variety of stresses that need to be appreciated, quantified and confronted.
- The capability of the players to meet those demands must be evaluated.
- Teams and individuals need to be prepared for the most intense phases of defensive pressure.

The concept of speed has also changed with regards to defending in the modern game. Coaches used to be concerned with having players who were quick enough to recover and deal with the space behind the back four. Today, however, coaches focus more on the space in front of the back four because time and space have become such important commodities. As the physical demands on players and teams have evolved, so too has the type of physical training required to defend effectively in the modern game. Physical training needs to focus on covering shorter distances and changing direction multiple times at maximum speed with minimal time for recovery.

Mental

The mental and physical components go hand in hand when discussing defending in the modern game. A mental error can be just as costly as a physical one. As fatigue sets in towards the end of the game, mental mistakes are never far away. If one player does not fulfil his or her defensive responsibility, space can open up, and this can prove costly. Defenders are also asked to multitask in today's game, both offensively and defensively. They have to take on more information, use the ball well, constantly be aware of shape in and out of possession and communicate with their defensive partners on who is picking up whom, among a host of other responsibilities. Opportunities for defenders to rest are rare, because as soon as they win a corner or a set piece, they usually have to travel to the opposition penalty area and fulfil an attacking role. Because of the many demands during the game, concentration has become an essential asset for a top-class defender. Although maintaining full concentration for 90 or more minutes is virtually impossible, defenders must be able to focus for short periods, break and refocus again quickly.

Other mental challenges include knowledge of the opponent, anticipation, alertness and judgement. If the training environment can reflect the same challenges that a game will bring, defenders will be conditioned to focus and refocus at the right time, hence reducing the likelihood of focus breaks happening during a game.

Developing a Coaching Philosophy

Like all coaches, I have altered my philosophy as I have gained more experience working with players and as the importance of results has increased. I believe that you must find a coaching style that is consistent with your personality. Reading the work of John Wooden, Pete Carroll, Tony Dungy and Phil Jackson gave me a clear vision of what I wanted to stand for as a coach, person and leader. All these coaches instilled in their players enthusiasm and traditional values such as hard work, respect, and timekeeping, basic principles that are sometimes overlooked in today's world.

I believe that your goals as a coach should be to get the most out of each player and to win. The win-at-all-costs model can be misleading. Winning is not just about getting a result; it is about maximizing your potential regardless of the opponent and looking for that edge to get better. Therefore, developing and winning go hand in hand. The first step in winning is a foundation built on a strong defence and even stronger work ethic. Those two factors have lifted many teams from mediocrity to success. I have realized that for a team to become strong defensively, the base of energy and attitude would have to come from me.

The foundation of my philosophy is the importance of practice. I want my teams to develop a competitive advantage by how they train, and I relentlessly pursue that goal. By placing a premium on training, I believe I make a statement to my team every day. Practice is where habits are developed, and in the pressure of a game, a player will always become those habits. My training principles are tempo, game-realistic exercises, detailed organization and competition. With consistently competitive practices, players ultimately reach a point where they can perform in the absence of fear. Therefore, they will always be accountable for their own performance.

Pressure, Delay, Depth and Balance

High pressing has been one of the main tactical trends over the past five years. Pep Guardiola led this defensive trend with his great Barcelona team. He believes that the rewards of regaining possession higher up the field favour his team's attacking ability: 'Pressuring high limits the amount of running players must do. When you win back the ball, there are 30 metres to goal rather than 80' (theguardian.com, 28 May 2009).

Therefore, pressing is certainly a high-risk, high-reward method of team defending. Before instructing the team to pressure, however, a coach needs to understand the functional components of pressing. Every player should understand pressure, delay, depth, balance and the responsibilities of the defender with proximity to the ball.

Legendary Italian coach Arrigo Sacchi said it best when it came to pressure: 'Pressing is not about running and it's not about working hard. It's about controlling space' (Brian Pink, keepitincoaching.com).

Before deciding to play a system that involves high pressing, a coach must be aware of why he or she is trying to pressure the ball. Effective pressing offers several advantages:

- Controls the tempo of the game
- Breaks attacking patterns of the opposition
- Speeds up the opponent and forces them to play at a tempo that they are not comfortable with
- Can change the focus of the opponent so that they are more concerned about keeping possession than they are about starting an attack

The reward for pressuring effectively is huge! Winning the ball higher up the field allows you to be closer to the opponent's goal with their defensive unit unorganized.

Pressing is not limited simply to the physical work. Without making decisions, a player who presses relies solely on speed and aggression. Before deciding to press, each player must make the following decisions:

- Which player do I leave so that I can go and press?
- What angle do I approach from?
- What is the risk–reward trade-off of going to press?
- Where do I recover to after pressing?

Individual Roles in Pressure, Cover and Balance

In pressure and delay, the first defender slows down the attack and puts the attacker's head down so that he or she cannot see options. The first defender only attempts to win the ball if the attacker makes a mistake. This action makes play predictable and slows them down on one side. The first defender must be patient.

For depth, the second defender supports the first defender by covering the space behind the first defender, judging appropriate distance based on the attacker's speed and skill. The second defender must communicate well with the first defender.

For balance, the rest of the team picks up any other attackers who may get the ball and cuts out passing lanes. They must be aware of attacking players moving into space in forward positions and be ready to assume the roles of first or second defender as the play progresses.

Aggressive pressing and putting numbers around the ball is ineffectual if you fail to achieve balance. Lack of balance will expose your team against good players. Jürgen Klopp developed a hugely effective pressing style with Borussia Dortmund and highlighted transition as key: 'The best moment to win the ball is immediately after your team just lost it. The opponent is still looking for orientation where to pass the ball' (Paul Waring, footballspeak. com, 16 May 2013).

Ways to Train Defensively

Coaches can use three different types of defensive training exercises:

- Functional: individual roles and responsibilities as well as teams within teams
- Transitional: a team's reaction to defending when the ball has just been lost
- Tactical: team shape and the way that each player's role changes in relation to the ball

Functional Exercises

The real teaching part of defending is establishing roles and responsibilities and emphasizing the importance of providing cover and distances. Here is an example of a functional defending exercise.

Functional Defensive Training Exercise 1: Team Defending When Out-numbered   Three defenders play against four attackers in a 20-by-44-yard area (figure 20.7). The defenders start the exercise by passing to the attackers and then sprinting out to cut off the space in front. The objective of the four attackers is to score in any of the four minigoals ahead. If the defenders win the ball, they can transition and score in the four minigoals on the other side.

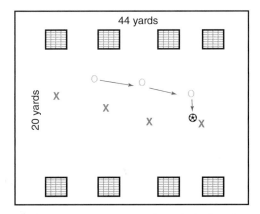

▶ **Figure 20.7**   Functional defensive training exercise 1: team defending when outnumbered.

Coaching points can be addressed in exercises like this. The role of the first defender; the supporting distance of the second and third defenders; and the importance of staying compact, communicating, and dealing with situations in which the attacking team interchanges are all areas that defenders need to apply in a game. The exercise also challenges defenders to deal with overloads, which is a huge part of the modern game.

Functional Defensive Training Exercise 2: Penalty Area Defending Another functional exercise designed by Neil Adair takes place inside the 18-yard box. Four defenders and a goalkeeper stand on the goal line opposite four attackers, each with a ball, who are named A through D (figure 20.8). The exercise begins when the coach calls one attacker, who dribbles and has 5 seconds to create a shot against the opposite defender. After that ball, those two players stay inside the 18-yard box and the coach calls another player who brings the ball in to create a 2v2. The pattern continues as the exercise develops into a 3v3 and finishes with a 4v4.

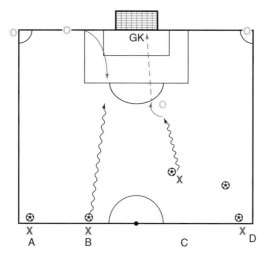

▶ **Figure 20.8**   Functional defensive training exercise 2: penalty area defending.

Because the exercise takes place inside the penalty box and has a time restriction on the attacking team, the defenders need to apply pressure quickly and delay the attackers. The basics of defending and communication are necessary for success because the players who react quickest to the coach's call will most likely be successful. The relationship between goalkeeper and defender is also highlighted. This exercise helps teams establish a winning defensive mentality.

Transitional Exercises

Transition is a popular word in today's game. Coaches emphasize its importance to players, and experts continually attribute it as a reason for goals at the highest level. Successful coaches train their teams to become defensively solid in transition and even use it to their advantage.

Transitional Exercise: Jürgen Klopp Transitional Exercise   This exercise was used by Jürgen Klopp and his Borussia Dortmund team. It takes place 10 yards on either side of the halfway line. The field is split into four areas; each area is occupied by a defender and an attacker directly opposite. As they match up together, two additional attacking players are on the outside sidelines. A goalkeeper is behind the four defenders on one side, and a coach acts as a server behind the attackers on the other (figure 20.9).

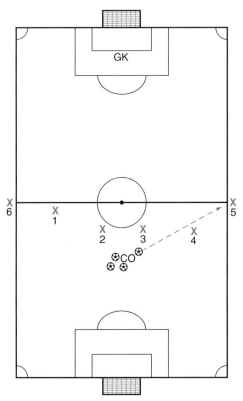

▶ **Figure 20.9**   Transitional exercise: Jürgen Klopp transitional exercise.

The first part of the exercise involves the four defenders and the four adjacent attackers. The two wide attackers are not part of this. All players stay in their own areas. The attacking players pass the ball square. Each time the ball arrives at an attacker's feet, the defender directly opposite steps up to apply pressure. As the attacking player passes the ball square and the ball leaves the area, the same defender retreats to his original line. It is a simple exercise of pressure, shifting and covering, but it allows defenders to pick up cues where they will be able to see the ball arriving by the body shape of the passer. These cues can be hugely important in games because the defender can then apply pressure quicker and reduce the options of the attacker.

On the coach's signal, the exercise transitions into a 6v4 towards goal. The ball used in the first defensive positioning exercise is now out of the exercise. The coach triggers the ball to one of the wide players to start the attack towards goal.

The first role of the defenders is to retreat towards goal but also to stay balanced (figure 20.10). The goal of the Dortmund back four is to defend from the inside out, which means they stay compact and push teams out to wide areas. You can also see that, although retreating is important, they are unwilling to drop into their 18-yard box. This coaching point is critical because after a back four drops into that area, they are unable to apply any pressure on the ball towards attacking players and they are vulnerable to crosses.

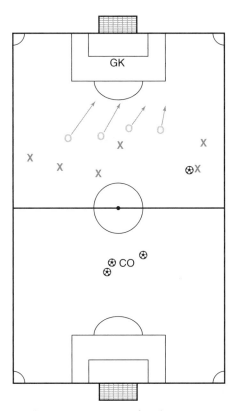

▶ **Figure 20.10** Defenders retreat towards the goal.

Tactical Exercises

Players need to be able to see the relationship between training and the game itself. This section contains a tactical exercise that coaches can adapt based on a team's playing style or even coaching philosophy.

Tactical Exercise: Pep Guardiola Defending Exercise   Pep Guardiola used this exercise with his Bayern Munich squad to work on pressing the ball high up the field. The simple setup features an 8v8 game played from one 18-yard box to the other and two floating players who play with the team in possession. Teams can score in three goals: one team scores in goals 1, 2 and 3 and the other team scores in goals 4, 5 and 6 (figure 20.11). The tactical element of the game is centred on the location of the outside goals. The position of the goals creates an incentive for teams to press high and in wide areas. If the team is organized in a 3-2-3, the outside forwards can press aggressively high up the field.

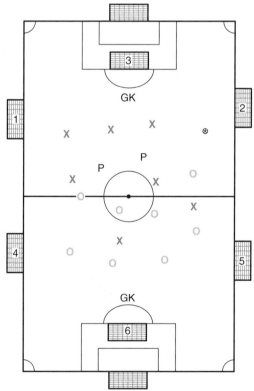

▶ **Figure 20.11**   Tactical exercise: Pep Guardiola defending exercise.

The two floating players create an overload for the attacking team so that the defenders cannot simply play man-to-man and instead have problems to solve. This element, along with the size of the field, means that defenders have to make decisions quickly and effectively. In an exercise like this, ineffective pressure will result in the attacking team using their numerical advantage and exposing another area of the field, just like in a real game.

Conclusion

In the preparation of soccer players, the training programme must be well planned. It needs to be specific and objective, taking into consideration the player's potential and physiological capabilities. Furthermore, the training programme should be simple and flexible, enabling modification at any stage. Many factors need to be accounted for when addressing the requirements of contemporary soccer. Without detailed planning, achieving any of the short- or long-term objectives is unlikely.

To develop a successful training programme, the physical demands of training and competition need to be fully understood. The physiological requirements of match play are highly individual and may vary from match to match, depending on playing position, tactical role and level of competition, among other situational factors. A system of continual monitoring is therefore essential to ensure that all players perform the required volume, intensity and frequency of training. Training load should be prescribed individually based on each player's physical, movement, technical and tactical requirements of match play, but daily adjustments should be made depending on the health, physiological and subjective status of each player. Careful planning between the coach and sport scientist allows the optimization of the training process, maximizing a player's potential and reducing the risk of injury occurrence, detraining or overtraining.

Clearly, individual philosophy (agreed between coach and sport scientist) will ultimately shape the outcome of how a training session, weekly plan or annual plan will look. Regardless of how practitioners decide to plan their training schedules (position-specific elements or generic team drills), the key to success will be ensuring that players are exposed to the right training dose at the right time. The advancements in tracking technology, coach education and employment of specialized staff within soccer clubs have all contributed to make the systematic monitoring of individual sessions commonplace and the information generated appropriately contextualized.

CHAPTER 21

Key Transitions and Midfield Manoeuvres

—Dave Tenney and Sigi Schmid

The preceding chapters of *Soccer Science* show that the modern game of soccer has evolved over the last few decades in the style of play, the methods used for quantifying athlete performance and the manner in which soccer players are trained. At the elite level of soccer, the next decade will see improved coach education, sport science knowledge and player management. In addition, elite soccer teams will move towards high-performance environments where the development of systematic performance models and advanced training regimens are commonplace. Therefore, player preparation has to be sharper and better informed. These factors call for better understanding of the demands of the game and changing athletic qualities of the participants. In the coming years, expanded systemic and tactical variety in the game of soccer may include these developments:

- 11 technical players
- Increased positional interchanges and rotations
- Evolution of the midfield sweeper
- More wrong footers playing in wide positions
- More teams building and attacking centrally
- More teams passing into and inside the penalty area to produce strikes
- More counterattacking teams playing at maximal speed
- Multipurpose wide midfielders
- Faster transitions

To cope with these tactical changes, players must have the physical resources to perform the high work rates and critical actions required during match play. Several shifts in the game may occur:

- All physical attributes will continue to be enhanced.
- Power and speed will be the dominant attributes.
- Training will be administered to reach full genetic potential.
- Individual positions will need unique and specific training programmes.
- Players will sustain higher work capacity and intensity for longer periods.
- Sport science support will be a significant and stellar factor in performance success.

In line with these observations, practitioners need to have knowledge and understanding of the physical and physiological demands of soccer in relation to specific positions and individual players. Moreover, training certain positions and evaluating the performance required for such positions are critical responsibilities for both the head coach or manager and the sport science staff.

Although the game of soccer includes various positions, this chapter focuses on the physiological aspects of midfield players and considers principles of performance planning that should be incorporated into coaching practice. In doing so, the chapter explores several questions related to preparing midfield players:

How do training methods apply specifically to midfield players?

Should a coaching and sport science staff apply a training stimulus that meets or exceeds the physical requirements of specific positions during a particular week?

How should a coaching staff train a group of midfield players over an entire season? What changes does the coaching staff make in the week-to-week, month-to-month or year-to-year perspective?

A high-level sport science support staff can aid a coaching staff in addressing these questions. The aim of this chapter is to inform the reader how a coaching staff and sport science department may interact in the applied setting daily to make real interventions in training methodology, fatigue management and player selection for midfield players.

The modern game seems to be dictated tactically by two distinct approaches: One focuses on possession play over longer durations to pull defenders out of position, and the other focuses on playing quickly in transition by having deeper-lying midfielders play the ball forward early and attack quickly after the opponent has lost possession.

Although both approaches seek to attack the opponents while they are unbalanced defensively, the manner of creating such unbalanced situations tactically is quite different. As a result, the training demands and methodologies may also differ significantly. This chapter explores how the modern coach and sport scientist can collaborate to choose a particular playing style and create long-term and short-term methodologies that promote physical and technical training to optimize that style.

This chapter focuses on the relationship of the sport scientist and manager or coach in determining training content. The aim is to display how evidence-based ideas from scientific research can inform practitioners on how to drive the coaching process at the elite end of soccer. In addition, information presented will facilitate an understanding of the characteristics and attributes of midfield players, systems and organization that will help inform practitioners at all levels of soccer play.

Qualities of Midfield Players

Midfield players possess various qualities that support the requirements of their roles:

- The ability to pass accurately, both long and short
- Excellent vision and awareness
- The physical resources to work hard and press the ball when not in possession
- A good first touch to maintain possession
- The ability to receive the ball and turn under pressure
- An understanding of how to make penetrating runs beyond the attackers
- The capacity to run from box to box for 90 minutes
- The ability to be creative when in possession of the ball

Although this list gives an indication of the generic requirements of midfield players, midfield players must fulfil several important defensive and offensive functions. In addition, the roles and responsibilities of central midfield players differ from those of wide players or wingers. Defensively, central midfield players function as a screen for the central defenders and create a strong defensive block in the middle of the field. Depending on the individual qualities of the players or the preferred midfield organization adopted by the coach, one, two or three players can be used to provide this screen and defensive block. For example, in a diamond midfield shape, one player is assigned to this task. Contemporary models for this role include Gattuso, Busquets, Makélélé, De Jong and Mascherano. The requirement is to patrol the space between the midfield and defensive units and intercept passes into opposition attacking players. Offensively, central midfield players act as a link between defenders and attackers and between the right and left sides of the field. The speed at which these players change and adjust their angles of support is a key determinant in the team's ability to maintain possession in midfield.

Wide midfield players usually fit into one of two mutually exclusive categories. The player is either a traditional winger or he or she is not. Wingers are players who combine exceptional 1v1 abilities and the technical qualities to deliver accurate crosses into the box. As such, they are most comfortable and dangerous playing in very wide and large spaces. Because of the amount of distance they cover and the frequency of 1v1 duels, these players must possess exceptional fitness, creativity and confidence. Arjen Robben and Nani are good examples of natural wingers. Wide midfield players without those characteristics are typically more effective if they play from a more central position where they can combine more with central midfield players and thus not be exposed physically.

Clearly, the physical, technical and mental characteristics of the individual players determine their tactical role and the selection of midfield organization employed by the coach.

Principles in Guiding Functional Organization of the Midfield

In line with these descriptions, coaches must select an appropriate organization to suit the physical, technical, tactical and mental characteristics of the individual players within the system. For example, although many variations of midfield organization are used in a 4-4-2 system, the midfield can generally be arranged in one of two basic ways: in a line of four (figure 21.1) or in a diamond (figure 21.2). The coaching staff needs to understand the characteristics of the players available for selection to resolve the decision of whether to play in a line of four or in a diamond.

Clearly, when the team has two dominant wingers, a line of four will be considered. This shape allows the wingers to play in spaces where they will be able to exploit their athleticism and 1v1 talent. In contrast, when the team has players with average or below-average speed, a diamond shape should be considered. This tighter shape hides the defensive weaknesses of these players because they will be less vulnerable defensively and in transition. In addition, the diamond shape may be used when the team has several technical players with average speed who can use their technical ability to combine with other players in small spaces.

Midfield players have defensive and offensive functions within the team. From a coaching perspective, teams can adopt a particular team formation based on the talents of individual players. Alternatively, teams can select appropriate players with the individual talents to fit into the designated philosophy or team shape. Defensive and offensive functions of midfield players are described in table 21.1.

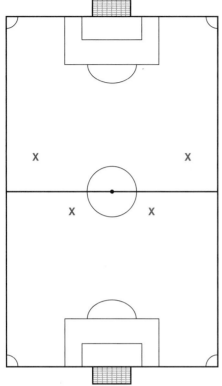

▶ **Figure 21.1** Line of four midfield organization.

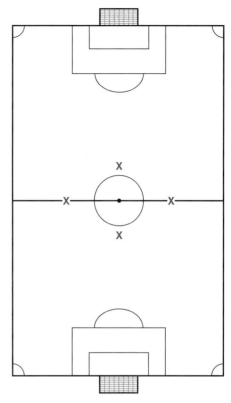

▶ **Figure 21.2** Diamond midfield organization.

Table 21.1 Defensive and Offensive Functions of Midfield Players

Defensive functions	Offensive functions
Transition immediately to defence	Transition immediately to attack
Communicate with fellow midfielders, defenders and forwards	Offer support behind and in advance of the ball
Start in goal-side positions and make recovery runs to get behind the ball	Use total team support to seek penetration
Delay the attack and apply pressure on the ball	Create width and space for self and teammates
Track opposing players	Read the game
Use controlled aggression to recover the ball	Change the point of attack
Use man-to-man or zone marking	Finish from close and long range
	Be successful in 1v1 duels

Differences in Physical and Technical Demands of Midfield Players Based on Tactical Approach

A common assumption is that a team who allows the opponent to have the ball, thus choosing a low-possession style of play, often demands more running of their players than a team that chooses a possession-based style. Bradley et al. (2013) examined closely the difference in technical and physical demands among various positions depending on the playing style (high-percentage possession team versus low-percentage possession team) in the English Premier League.

When looking purely at technical data, players in a high-percentage ball possession team performed 44 per cent more passes than those in a low-percentage ball possession team. This trend was also evident for successful passes, received passes, touches per possession, shots, dribbles, tackled events and final-third entries (Bradley et al. 2013).

Although players in a high-percentage ball possession team had marginally lower demands in variables such as the number of high-intensity actions and running distance, the effect was trivial.

Thus, the percentage of ball possession does not appear to influence the overall activity profile of the team. Nonetheless, although teams playing against possession-based opposition should not expect a more physically demanding match, they should be prepared for all eventualities, particularly plenty of high-intensity running to regain the ball. Given that this chapter deals specifically with midfield play, the coach and sport science staff must assimilate the current scientific evidence available and formulate a strategy to select an appropriate style of play and a training programme to maximize individual fitness characteristics associated with match strategy. Coaching drills for midfield players that integrate high-intensity actions with and without the ball would prepare the players appropriately. See the sidebar 'Coaching Drills'.

Coaching Drills

Possession-based approach: Select drills for midfield players that stimulate high-intensity running with ball possession and passing ability.

Low possession-based approach: Select drills for midfield players that stimulate high-intensity running to regain the ball and quick counterattacking actions.

Work-Rate Profiles of Midfield Players

Midfield players cover greater distances during competitive match play than other players do (Rienzi et al. 2000; Bradley et al. 2009). This greater distance may be attributed to tactical or physiological factors or a combination of both. In theory, the most successful players should have the physiological characteristics best suited to their particular roles, and differences in physiological characteristics should emphasize the important aspects of performance physiology. Given that midfield players are characterized by higher $\dot{V}O_2$max levels than other players, coaches are more likely to select those with higher $\dot{V}O_2$max values than those with lower $\dot{V}O_2$max values (Strudwick 2006). Moreover, such high $\dot{V}O_2$max values would allow those players to sustain higher work rates and make them less susceptible to the reduction in work rate associated with fatigue (Rienzi et al. 2000). Indeed, the extent that fatigue is experienced by players has been shown to be negatively related to $\dot{V}O_2$max (Reilly 1990). Self-selection of players into specific positional roles may be common when they possess the appropriate physiological characteristics. The main physical qualities associated with world-class midfield players are summarized in figure 21.3.

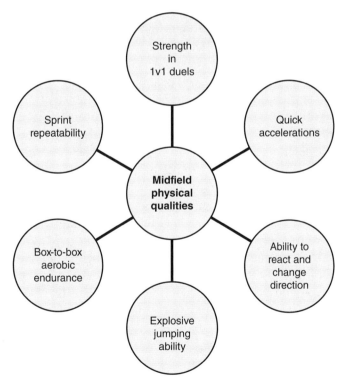

▶ **Figure 21.3** Physical attributes of midfield players.

Elite-level soccer for midfielders appears to be a mix of aerobic qualities (ability to cover greater distance) and the ability to perform repeated bouts of high-speed running. Research indicates that such high-intensity work may be a more valid way to distinguish players at differing levels of play. According to Bradley et al. (2009), wide and central midfield players cover a greater total distance than fullbacks, attackers and central defenders do (11,491 plus or minus 996 and 11,411 plus or minus 486 versus 10,763 plus or minus 627, 10,504 plus or minus 1,090 and 10,057 plus or minus 582 metres, respectively). Wide midfield and centre midfield players also cover significantly more high-intensity distance than players at the other positions do. At very high-intensity velocities, the demand made on the wide midfielders is significantly higher ($p < 0.01$) than it is for any other position.

Interaction Between Soccer Coach and Sport Scientist: A Case Study

As of 2016, Sigi Schmid (head coach) and David Tenney (sport scientist) are in their sixth year of working together at the professional level with Seattle Sounders FC in Major League Soccer (MLS). The two have evolved their collaboration to integrate sport science data and ideas more efficiently into the daily, weekly and monthly management of the athletes and team. Before Schmid joined the Sounders as head coach, he won one MLS Cup with the Columbus Crew (2008) and one with the LA Galaxy (2002). When it comes to using sport science to aid in the development of a playing style, Schmid notes that, contrary to conventional thought, it may be easier to play a possession-based style of play with success in MLS than a counterattack style.

With the athleticism and speed of the younger American players and a lack of squad depth because of the smaller salary cap, it becomes harder to play with the technical precision required of a true counterattacking style with a deeper-sitting midfield, good striker hold-up play and fast wingers capable of performing high-intensity workloads weekly over an entire season.

According to our experiences in this league, a possession team may be more successful in MLS because it is more oriented towards playing in the opponent's half and is geared towards pressing an opponent after possession is lost. Coaches and fans often speak about possession teams or counterattack teams, but we believe that a possession team will focus on possession in the offensive phase of play and opt for a pressing strategy when the opponent is in possession. We do not see the possession style as simply aiming to have possession of the ball for as long as possible, because we know that this task is difficult, particularly with the hectic pace of our league. We see the possession style of play as a tactical goal of focusing on possessing the ball in the opponent's half and then regaining it in the opponent's half rather than allowing the opponent to have it. As a result, our staff believes that the style is a possession-pressing style, rather than the deep-lying counterattack style.

With the interaction of sport science support systems, Seattle Sounders has evolved its style from a counterattacking team in 2009 and 2010 to a possession-pressing team in recent seasons. We also take into account the American player when determining tactical style. The mentality of the American athlete is to try to dominate an opponent and put them under pressure for as long as possible. At the international level, this approach may appear naive, but MLS is a league in which an aggressive possession-pressing mentality has paid dividends. Some argue that Sporting KC won the 2013 MLS Cup with this sort of strategy. To play within this particular strategy, teams in MLS must opt for midfield players who excel in winning balls and regaining possession.

With the Columbus Crew, Schmid effectively applied more of a counterattacking style in a 4-4-1-1 tactical shape with a lone striker (Alejandro Moreno) and underneath striker (Guillermo-Barros Schelotto) in front of three offensive midfield players and one holding midfield player, all of whom were capable of performing high volumes of high-intensity running. The issue with this style is that it requires a central attacker and an underneath, or withdrawn, attacker with high technical qualities. Within the context of MLS, if such a player is injured, replacing him is difficult. All these issues put the onus on the sport science staff to provide the coaches with data, which may help keep such athletes healthy over the course of the season, and aid the head coach in creating position profiles that may be used when recruiting new players to play the coach's chosen tactical system.

Training Methodology

Seattle Sounders have opted to use a training model similar to Impellizzeri's internal load–external load model (Impellizzeri et al. 2004). Currently, many clubs throughout the world use global positioning system (GPS) technology to quantify the external load. While there is often some scepticism about the validity and reliability of such external load data and technology, the latest research (Varley, Fairweather and Aughey 2012) seems to indicate that the most up-to-date GPS hardware (10 Hz) may be as much as six times more accurate in measuring instantaneous velocity than previous 5 Hz units. Currently, Seattle Sounders are using GPS devices, as well as heart rate systems and session RPE, to assess external and internal load markers.

The goal of such a training model is to derive an external physical load imposed on each athlete and then to discern the physiological cost of such a load through the heart rate response. Over time, the sport science staff can provide adequate feedback to the coaches about the cost of various exercises and which players may be experiencing a higher than normal cost because of fatigue.

When it comes time to sit down as a staff and agree on what exercises may be appropriate for training midfield players specifically over the course of the week, the science and technical staff have been able to evolve ideas over the course of the last three years because of some of the recent research by Casamichana, Castellano and Castagna (2012) and Castellano and Casami-chana (2013). The biggest area of evolution in training methodology has been in comparing the movement patterns of various exercises and recognizing which ones may elicit higher velocity demands on athletes and which ones may lead to increased numbers of intense accelerations and decelerations (which we call eccentric loading). Research comparing typical small-sided training games and full-field 11v11 exercises (Casamachina, Castellano and Castagna 2012) indicates that although data taken from semiprofessional athletes playing small-sided games (SSGs) such as 4v4, 5v5 and 7v7 display global indicators of work intensity that are significantly higher ($p < 0.01$) (with the exception of maximum velocity) in comparison with a full-sided training match, the frequency, quantity and duration of higher-velocity work (greater than 21 kilometres per hour) is significantly greater in the 11v11 exercises ($p < 0.01$).

The question comes up among staff about the appropriate volume of small-sided activity over the course of the week. When we consider specifically the demands placed on midfield players and ways to prepare them optimally over the week, the coaching staff must take into account these specific external load demands placed on midfield players. Through experience, we know that we need to look specifically at wide and central midfield play-ers in the postgame period to assess the level of accumulated fatigue when prescribing the weekly exercises. At Seattle Sounders, we have found that the higher levels of accelerations and decelerations found in smaller games such as 5v5 may lead to an overload in some of our fatigued central midfield players. As a result, in the athlete-monitoring system using GPS, we need to quantify acceleration and deceleration, even if it is with the use of triaxial accelerometers, which allow us to assess the instantaneous changes in veloc-ity in such exercises (Varley, Fairweather and Aughey 2012). Sole reliance on velocity in this case seems to underestimate the amount of high-intensity work performed and does not take into account the eccentric loading that may accumulate with the high numbers of decelerations and changes of directions inherent in small-sided games. Therefore, we should adopt an approach similar to that of many teams in Europe by viewing exercises in relation to demands on power, as well as velocity.

Gaudino et al. (2013) reported convincingly that the loads in SSGs are underestimated when looking only at high-intensity speed thresholds and not power thresholds (metabolic power estimated as the combination of run-ning speed and acceleration). This research seems to reinforce what we have found with the Sounders; relying solely on velocity from a loading perspec-tive can lead to underestimation on certain positions. Although midfielders are typically not the underestimated position (central defenders seem to be most underestimated), early on in the process we recognized that we were overloading central midfielders in the attempt to load the other positions appropriately. The continued evolution of an advanced sport science structure at Seattle Sounders has allowed us to optimize the ability to quantify external load better and find the right balance.

Especially when it comes specifically to finding the appropriate type of training stimulus for midfield play, we can use GPS technology to determine whether certain athletes rely more on maintaining high-speed velocities over a game or whether they rely more on shorter, sharper changes of direction (anterior eccentric loading).

So what is the right balance of different-sized SSGs? What is the best approach for training wide midfield players, who we know must be able to sustain longer periods of high-intensity work than other players on the field (Bradley et al. 2009)? Research reveals that peak velocities achieved during small-sided games rarely approach those performed in competitive matches. As a result, athletes are unlikely to be overloaded during the week (if an overload is required) by the use of smaller (4v4 to 6v6) small-sided games. The type of exposure and volume prescribed for this type of high-velocity work during a weekly training rhythm remains a critical job of the sport science support team. If too many exercises are used that do not elicit higher-velocity patterns in wide midfield players, we believe that these players will exhibit an underload effect over time, potentially making them more susceptible to hamstring injuries in games.

Typical Training Exercises for Midfield Players

These examples were designed to prepare midfield players to meet the physical and technical demands of MLS.

Passing Pattern　These passing pattern exercises are aimed at high-intensity running and high-speed dribbling for a longer time. Duration of work per set is 3 minutes. Each player should be able to complete four rounds in 3 minutes. Rest between sets is 90 seconds, and the number of sets is three or four.

Explanation

These passing pattern exercises simulate some of the passing lengths and distances covered by midfielders within match play. The exercise can be done by seven players on either side of the field (see figure 21.4). Each cone is approximately 18 to 20 metres from the adjacent cones. If the goal is to elicit more high-speed running, increase the spacing between the cones. If the aim of the exercise is to elicit more of a cardiovascular training effect, you may have fewer players at a certain pattern or prescribe longer bouts of the activity. Performing this exercise over four stations can provide a training stimulus for up to 28 players.

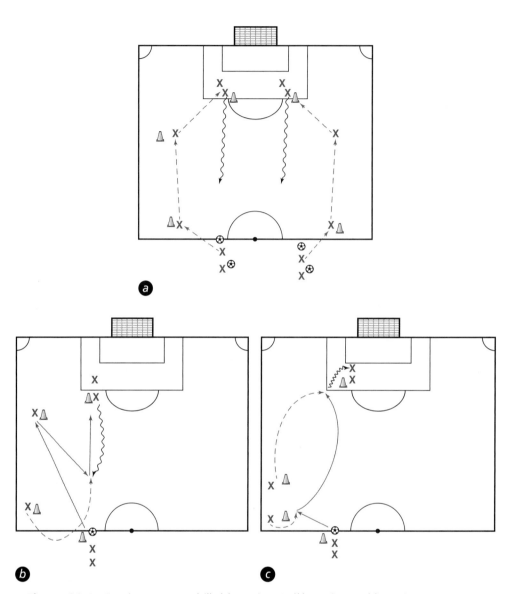

▶ **Figure 21.4** Passing pattern drill: (*a*) version 1; (*b*) version 2; (*c*) version 3.

Version 1

Players perform a simple pattern of three 20-metre passes along the ground, followed by a ball into space for the final player to dribble back to the original starting point as quickly as possible. Two balls should always be in play during this time; the second ball starts when the fourth player (dribbler) is about to receive the ball.

Version 2

This version uses the same form as version 1, except that the second player shows for the ball, does not receive, but spins off to receive a ball laid back from player 3. This short-short-long pattern often occurs in the midfield areas in high-level soccer.

Version 3

This exercise is a short ball to feet (15 metres) followed by a ball into space (the third player makes a 20-metre sprint to get to the ball and dribbles to the end of the line). This exercise can be done with eight players at a time. Players move up to the next cone after playing the ball. The ends (where the balls start) are approximately 40 metres from each other. This exercise elicits a good volume of short accelerations and receiving the ball at speed, actions typically required of high-level midfielders.

7v5 Pressing Game   A group of seven players plays one or two touch (figure 21.5). The team gets a point after completing eight consecutive passes. A group of five players attempts to win possession of ball and can score in any of the four goals for a point. Duration of the game is two to three minutes or first team to 3 points. Rest between sets is one minute. Number of games is two or three sets of games before tactical or larger small-sided games.

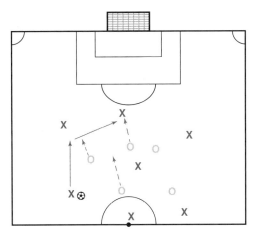

▶ **Figure 21.5**   7v5 pressing game.

6v5 Pressing Game The team of six players may take only one or two touches while the team of five players have unlimited touches (figure 21.6). The five must press the ball and try to score as quickly as possible after winning possession. You can also make the six-player team a goal up—they can't score unless they give up a goal—to train the team of five how to press as a group. Game duration is three minutes. Recovery time is one minute. Number of games is two to four.

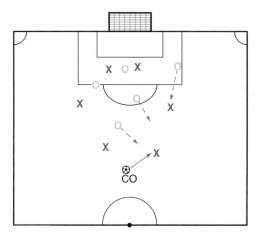

▶ **Figure 21.6** 6v5 pressing game

9v9 Large-Sided Game This exercise is aimed at pressing and regaining possession quickly. Teams may have two touches in their own half but unlimited touches in the attacking half (figure 21.7). Duration of sets is 6 to 10 minutes. Rest is 2 minutes. Number of sets is one to three.

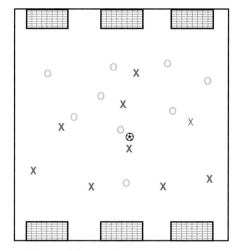

▶ **Figure 21.7** 9v9 game

Fatigue Management and Heart Rate Variability

The support staff at Seattle Sounders uses heart-rate variability (HRV) as a tool to assess the fitness and fatigue equilibrium of the players and then prescribe the appropriate training stimuli over the course of the training week. Research has suggested that HRV and the state of the autonomic system (ANS) is an easy, noninvasive method of athlete fatigue management (Buchheit et al. 2007).

The advantage of using HRV in the fatigue management process is that we can easily assess the effect of all the stressors imposed by the league—extensive travel (including time zone changes), different surfaces and large differences in weather—on athletes on a daily or weekly basis (two or three times per week is advised). Also, because HRV is a noninvasive measure, taking only approximately five minutes per day, physiological markers of fatigue and ability to adapt to training can be assessed and then passed on to the coaching staff by the sport scientist before daily training even begins.

The goal of any athlete-monitoring system should be to provide coaches with data as quickly as possible, giving both staffs the opportunity to collaborate and search for interventions that may avoid injury and promote increased adaptation to training loads.

As supported in the scientific literature, staff at Seattle Sounders have discovered that the application of heavy loads (match periods) may result in increased sympathetic activation of the ANS, leading to a compromised ability to recover (Boullosa at al. 2013). When viewing the response to loading over a longer period (week to week), the ability of athletes to achieve an appropriate parasympathetic reactivation will result in improved recovery ability. Typically, as also seen by Buchheit et al. (2010), athletes who experience increased HRV values with an associated parasympathetic nervous system (PSNS) activation also display a concurrent aerobic adaptation to exercise. Our experiences over six years and collection of injury patterns over this time suggest that central midfield players in particular are loaded from a cardiovascular perspective far more than most other players. As a result, HRV assessments take on even more value for our central midfield players to avoid soft-tissue injury. At Seattle Sounders, the sport science support team works in close cooperation with the medical staff in sharing these HRV data to individualize recovery protocols aimed at improving a PSNS response in the postgame period, because we know that a moderate pressure massage may elicit an increased PSNS response in our athletes, aiding their ability to recover (Diego and Field, 2009).

Beyond soft-tissue therapy, at Seattle Sounders we also look to use cold-water immersion therapy (CWI) to promote improved recovery with our players during specific days or weeks. Cold-water immersion therapy and ice baths have become a controversial topic among professional athletes and coaches in all sports. The data we have from our sport science research are similar to those seen by other sport science professionals (Buchheit et al. 2009), showing the efficacy of CWI in promoting improved PSNS activation. In fact, a protocol consisting of just six to eight minutes of CWI resulted in both increased PSNS activation and increased self-reported sleep and recovery scores in our midfielders during the 2011 season.

Everything described here gives the reader an indication of some of the work conducted behind the scenes not just between the sport science staff and coaching staff in quantifying fatigue in the postgame period but also between the sport science staff and the medical staff during this same period in measuring the recovery ability of midfield players, as well as other players. The technology we have chosen to assess fatigue allows us to obtain real-time feedback about the readiness state of each athlete before training. Such information can be useful before a training session in preventing players from entering a nonfunctional overreaching state. In this area more than any other, the coaching staff and sport science staff need to be on the same page regarding the importance of the data provided. We have been able to build up a large level of trust in this area after several campaigns in the CONCA-CAF Champions League and four deep runs in US Open Cup competition. In instances of fixture congestion, we use our fatigue management model.

A critical determinant in the successful interaction of the sport science support structure is that the coaching staff must trust the validity of the data provided and the sport science staff must trust that the coaching staff will provide the correct intervention in training or squad rotation from the fatigue analysis provided.

Training Periodization

Major League Soccer is similar to many other leagues in the world in season length and number of games. The season runs from March until October, and the playoff extends through the first week of December. As a result, the coaching and sport science staffs must organize the optimal weekly (microcycle), monthly (mesocycle) and season (macrocycle) training plans. At Seattle Sounders, we are currently able to use GPS and heart rate technology to quantify training load daily and apply the appropriate training stimulus daily and weekly.

Microcycles

We could say that over the course of the week we adhere to the model shown in figure 21.8 when planning the training process.

Typically, our starting point is the response to the game demands. Gregson et al. (2010) provided us with some insight that large variability can exist in the match-to-match physical outputs across all positions in elite-level soccer

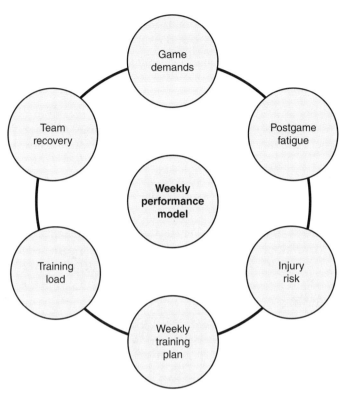

▶ **Figure 21.8** Weekly performance model for planning the training process.

matches. As a result, when planning the weekly training prescription, the sport science staff notifies the coaching staff of the physical demands for a particular match (using MatchAnalysis stadium tracking data). Because MLS also experiences variability in travel demands, surface (in 2014, 4 of the 19 teams had full-time artificial grass pitches), game-time temperatures and time zone changes, the use of athlete management tools such as heart rate variability technology is important in quantifying the levels of fatigue in response to game loads. We believe that the physiological response to the match load (inclusive of travel and extrinsic conditions surrounding the match) may be more important than the actual quantification of the game loading (physical work performed). When assessing this specifically for midfielders, we see that the four midfielders are usually among our at-risk fatigued group. Our data show us that our wide midfielders are among the top of the group on the field in high-speed running (greater than 5.6 metres per second) and that our centre midfielders cover the most total distance.

At Seattle Sounders, we have also recently used injury-prediction algorithms to attempt to predict injury risk based on such postgame response, along with the injury history of each player. In the past, we have attempted to use a three-week loading, one-week unloading scheme to maintain an optimal loading pattern. But because of the highly variable individualized response to game demands and associated fatigue, we have found that weekly microcycles such as the one shown in table 21.2 should be planned according to these weekly data.

This model is relatively simple, but our experience is that it creates a common language and context that our coaching staff and sport science staff can understand. The research of Akenhead et al. (2013) has reinforced for us the need to use smaller SSGs such as 5v5 or 6v6 one day per week, because our data suggest the need to maintain the ability to sustain higher volumes of accelerations and decelerations over the course of a game. The intensity of this work can be so metabolically demanding, however, that an overload of this type may prevent an athlete from fully recovering before the next game. In fact, our injury data over the last two years with centre midfielders suggest that imposing such a stimulus on a fatigued centre midfielder may result in increased injury risk and lowered probability of an optimal performance.

Because of the sport science knowledge at Seattle Sounders, we know that wide midfield players require the ability to sustain longer bouts of high-speed running. Internal data indicate that wide midfield players often surpass 2,000 metres of high-speed running per match (match analysis data, greater than 5.6 metres per second). As a result, we need to create exercises for one day in the week that overload this facet of the game through large-sided training games like 9v9 to 11v11. That being said, if the injury risk metrics indicate that wide midfield players are unusually fatigued from a match, we may choose to alter this plan and not do a normal volume of such work. Beyond this large-sided game volume, such physical work can be supplemented with passing pattern exercises or maximal aerobic speed (MAS) work as discussed within research by Buchheit and Laursen (2013). We frequently programme our wide midfield players (especially those not playing regularly) with bouts of 15 to 30 seconds of work and 15 to 30 seconds of rest, depending on the precise intensity required for that day. Such

Table 21.2 Typical Weekly Plan for Seattle Sounders

0/–7	Saturday	Game day	
+1/–6	Sunday	Travel	
+2/–5	Monday	Regeneration training	Low-intensity activities, biking or swimming, light weights
+3/–4	Tuesday	Heavy training load	Smaller SSGs such as 5v5 or 6v6 (heavier acceleration and deceleration day), afternoon strength-training session
+4/–3	Wednesday	Off	
+5/–2	Thursday	Tactical (moderate load)	11v11 and larger SSGs (7v7 to 9v9), light strength-training session
+6/–1	Friday	Prematch training (low load)	Small-field 9v9 to 11v11, set plays
0/–7	Saturday	Game day	

30-30, 30-15 or 15-15 high-intensity training (HIT) is performed at a velocity that sufficiently taxes the anaerobic system.

At Seattle Sounders, the midfield players must also be able to sustain high volumes of changes of direction (accelerations and decelerations) while also covering longer distance of lower-velocity running. As a result, the smaller SSGs seem to correspond with the match demands of a centre midfield player when it comes to duration and average length of short sprints and work-to-rest ratio. But because of the high anterior eccentric stress of SSGs (adductor complex, hip flexors and quads), the volume of such work should be monitored for a centre midfielder who may be red-flagged through our fatigue management process.

Although the season in MLS is similar in length to seasons in the rest of the world, the big difference is in the length of the off-season period (table 21.3). In most of our past years, our off-season has been about 2 months long (approximately 9 or 10 weeks), during which many athletes leave the Seattle area. Although this period is long enough to allow full recovery from the demands and stresses of the season, it is also long enough for players to become substantially deconditioned if they do not perform strength or aerobic maintenance training.

At Seattle Sounders, we have also used this period to make some changes in specific athletic qualities among our team, especially in maximum strength and power development. Although some of the new players have been hesitant to perform heavy strength training during the off-season, we have found some massive improvements in strength, speed and power with this type of periodization model by those who are fully compliant.

This training can be especially useful for our midfield players who have played many minutes over the course of the season. The high metabolic demand of centre and wide midfielders often result in a degradation of strength and power over a long season. Without the ability to address this loss of power with appropriate loading in the weight room, these midfielders may experience a loss in power over the course of their careers.

Table 21.3 Sounders FC 2013 Year

Week	Date	Note
1	January 25	First day of preseason
7	March 8	First MLS match
40	October 25	Final MLS match
42	November 8	End of first playoff series
42–45	November 9 to 30	Recovery period
46–48	December 1 to 20	Maximum strength block
49–52	December 21 to January 17	Nonspecific metabolic prep

Conclusion

The purpose of this chapter was to give insight into the planning, organization and communication that must take place between a head coach and sport scientist in a league such as MLS. Professional soccer is currently in a dynamic space in regards to the evolution of tactical and physical changes occurring in all leagues around the world. The game continues to make increasing demands on the speed and power capabilities of players in all positions. This chapter looked specifically at those demands on midfielders, including the effects of the various tactical variations (flat four with wingers versus diamond shape) and strategic variations (high pressure versus lower pressure) selected by the coach. The coach and sport scientist must consider all these variations as they decide how their group will train daily, weekly and yearly to optimize performance.

Secondary to the developments on the field come the developments beyond the field. Technology and the ability to measure physical activity performed in training and games will only continue to improve in validity and reliability. We hope that this chapter will serve to reinforce the role of the sport scientist in merging research and science with the tactical ideas of the head coach to create an optimal training model for an elite-level club.

In our specific situation at Seattle Sounders, we have used Impellizerri's training-load model to inform the coaches of the internal and external load demands placed on athletes daily. After six years of collaboration, we have created a daily communication surrounding each of these internal and external metrics of workload that allows us to make informed decisions regarding weekly training rhythms. When it comes to the technology used daily, we have decided as a club to be early adopters in MLS of tools such as GPS and HRV technology to reduce injury risk as much as possible. MLS is a difficult league because of the large variations in field surfaces (turf versus grass), climate and time zones. As a result, our midfielders have historically been the most overloaded athletes over the course of the season. Added to this is the fact that MLS tends to be a league in which coaches opt for the possession or pressing style of play, which leads to a frenetic pace that allows little time for recovery or breaks for our midfielders over a match. Although these factors have made our job difficult and the collaboration among the staff extremely important, they have also led to the template of working that we have presented in this chapter.

CHAPTER 22

Essential Elements of Attacking Soccer

—Richard Hawkins and Darren Robinson

The primary role of the soccer coach is to maximize individual and team performance. This goal is achieved by appropriate training and instruction. In many circumstances, coaches may operate without the benefit of specialist support personnel. Therefore, coaches need to have sufficient knowledge and understanding of the principles of the coaching process. In soccer, the coaching process can be grouped into four categories:

1. Technical
2. Tactical
3. Physical
4. Psychological

These components need careful consideration when planning training and should be integrated into the coaching process to provide the best possible service to the players. Information presented in this book should enable coaches to recognize these independent components. To achieve effective coaching, practitioners should train all these components simultaneously. Moreover, contemporary coaches are now encouraged to adopt this four-dimensional approach, in which effective communication and integration of the technical, tactical, physical and psychological aspects are supported in game-realistic drills and exercises.

This chapter demonstrates how science plays a role in the training and conditioning of attacking players. In doing so, it validates how soccer science is informed by or serves to inform an attacking philosophy from the training process to the competitive match.

The chapter addresses the key physical training components for attacking players, more specifically, centre forwards, attacking central midfield players and wingers. The various options available to practitioners are addressed, including examples of the types of drills to use in training at an elite level, consideration being given to both the physical and tactical requirements of teams and players to enhance attacking play.

Six key areas of consideration are covered:

1. Principles of attack
2. Attacking tactics
3. Physical qualities of attacking players
4. Coaching philosophy and planning considerations
5. Drills for the physical development of attacking players
6. Tactical and physical development of attacking play

Establishing the best ways to train the physical attributes of players is constantly debated among practitioners the world over. Opinions differ depending on foundational philosophies; even the simple question of whether position-specific conditioning is required is a subject of debate. Differences have been identified in the movement activity profiles of various positions (Bloomfield, Polman and O'Donoghue 2007; Di Salvo et al. 2010; Carling, Le Gall and Dupont 2012), suggesting that players would benefit from greater specificity in training. But it has also been reported that physical output varies significantly from game to game (Gregson et al. 2010), implying that several factors are influential in addition to playing position.

Regardless of opinion, few argue that the physical qualities of players are not important because in the pivotal moments of games, physical dominance or inefficiency is often highlighted as being a key determinant in the outcome.

Physical seasonal trend data (Prozone, personal communication) and contemporary physical activity analysis (Reilly 2007; Di Salvo et al. 2007) highlight the change in physical qualities and increased demands imposed on players over the past decade. Therefore, the development of the physical capabilities of players appears to be a necessity in the modern game.

The physical qualities of players are trained either in isolation or in combination with technical and tactical work, depending on individual philosophy. Reliance on skill and tactical training alone, however, has been shown to lead to deterioration in various physical abilities over the course of the season. Therefore, additional drills or sessions that focus on overloading specific physical components are advised (Hervert, Sinclair and Deakin 2013). The best method depends on the priorities of the session and the characteristics of the players being trained, such as age, experience and level. The soccer science practitioner, supported by the use of appropriate technology, has the role of informing coaches of the type of additional drills that can be implemented to support the physical training process.

Principles of Attack

The principles of attack will help a team in possession of the ball react to any situation during soccer. These principles apply regardless of the system of play and formation played by the team, and they will always apply, no matter how the game evolves. The principles of attack apply when a team is looking to keep possession of the ball, move the ball forward into an attacking position and create chances to score a goal. Principles of attack include the following:

- Penetration
- Support
- Width
- Mobility
- Improvisation and creativity

Penetration (figure 22.1) is the ability to play through or behind the opposition. Penetration is achieved by exploiting space with good on- and off-the-

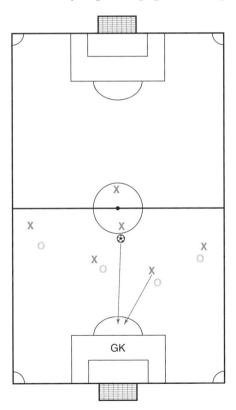

▶ **Figure 22.1** Penetration.

ball movement. A key facet behind the principle of penetration is to encourage players to look forward and exploit the space behind the opponents.

To maintain possession and move the ball down the field, the player on the ball needs support (figure 22.2). Forward, back and side support facilitate attacking options. When in possession, support requires good dispersal to spread the field. Angles, distance and timing of passes also become important.

Stretching the defence to create width (figure 22.3) should always be in the minds of the attacking team. Opponents can be stretched vertically or laterally. The ability to stretch opponents laterally across the field provides the opportunity for penetration through wide areas. Correct positioning also gives opportunities to switch the play to exploit the weak side.

Individual speed and the ability to interchange positions, or mobility (figure 22.4), are important in contemporary soccer. The ability to interchange positions and provide good movement to support the play creates attacking opportunities. Movement on and off the ball can create space for the first attacker or other players.

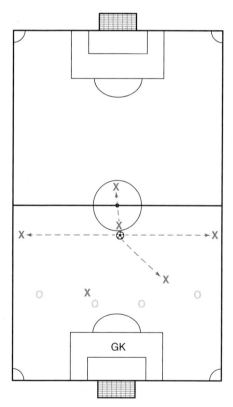

▶ **Figure 22.2** Support.

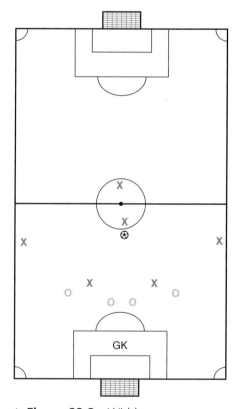

▶ **Figure 22.3** Width.

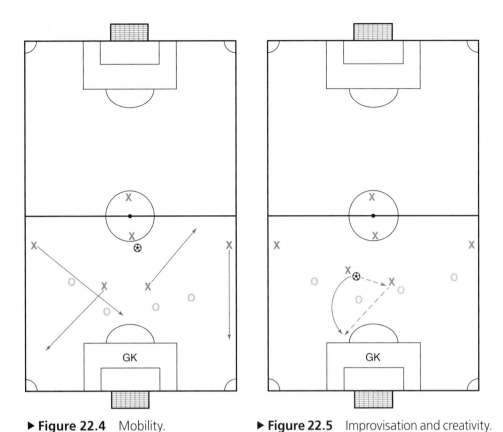

▶ **Figure 22.4** Mobility.

▶ **Figure 22.5** Improvisation and creativity.

Improvisation and creativity (figure 22.5) are the most exciting principles. They represent the ability to provide inventive and unpredictable play achieved through either individual skills or small-group combinations, such as one-on-one plays, one-two passes, overlaps or feint movements, to create attacking opportunities.

The events that occur immediately after regaining possession often determine the outcome of a competitive match. A fast, positive response at this time can catch teams off balance and in poor defensive shape. Transition should be discussed as part of the strategy and tactics of a team, and the principles covered in this section should be used.

Attacking Tactics

To use the attacking principles, players need to understand how to create space, both as individuals for themselves and others and as a team to make the pitch as big as possible. Creating the environment for players to make good decisions should be an integral part of the training sessions. As a first thought, can the players be positive and look to play or advance the ball forward quickly, trying to penetrate the opposition? If this isn't possible, then the players need to keep possession and be patient.

Training sessions should encourage youth soccer players to change play and the point of attack to maximize penetrative play. Selling a team on improving their attacking play can be an easy task, because it is often the more enjoyable aspect of soccer training and match play. Nevertheless, coaches can benefit from understanding statistical analysis of what contributes to winning performances. Statistics are now ubiquitous within soccer. Recent findings show that since 2006–2007 in the UEFA Champions League, the team that creates the most chances is 54 per cent more likely to win, hence promoting the concept of attacking play within your team's playing style.

This section describes 11 key attacking tactics: pass and move, combination passing, attack switch, the through ball, the long through ball, use of the space between the opponent's defensive line and midfield fine, triangular movement, swapping the wide player, strong side overloads, use of a target player and one loose.

Pass and move is the most basic team tactic. As soon as the ball has come into possession of the player, he or she needs to be quick to decide whether to pass it or not. If the player doesn't pass it immediately, he or she needs to move with it; if the player does pass it, he or she needs to create space for teammates, following the general ball movement but often moving in advance of the player receiving the ball. This basic tactic can also be used to denote that after passing the ball, the player does not remain stationary but moves into a position where he or she can receive the ball again and give more options to the player in possession.

Combination passing is essentially the same as pass and move and is an integral part of the target player style of play. The player in possession of the ball plays a pass to a teammate and then immediately seeks to move into space. If the player who passed the ball can lose her or his defensive marker (through either pace, movement, superior fitness or lack of awareness on the part of the defender), she or he can then be free to receive a return pass and advance towards and possibly threaten the goal. A ball played by the receiving player immediately back to the first player is known as a one-two.

Using a square or cross pass across the whole width of the pitch to a player in plenty of space is an effective way of both relieving pressure and building a fresh attack. This tactic is known as switching the attack. The defending team must adjust its positions and in doing so usually creates spaces that can be exploited. Switching play can include setting a pass off a central striker from a wide position and changing the point of attack by passing to the opposite side, often to a winger or an advancing fullback. Alternatively, fullbacks often switch the attack by using support from behind the ball, passing to a central defender, who then changes the play to an opposite winger or fullback. A good example of this is from the 2011 Champions League final when Barcelona played a central midfielder, Javier Mascherano, in the central defensive position. His role as a pivot player helped Barca win the final; changes of play were a key feature of their attacking play. Indeed, Eric Abidal, the left-side defender, had his strongest passing relationship with the right-side defender, Sergio Busquets, making 16 passes across the field. Alternatively, the switching of play from right to left was direct as Mascherano played his part by making 16 passes out to Abidal.

The through ball is a pass between defenders into the open space between the fullbacks and the goalkeeper. The idea is that a forward will beat the defenders to the ball. Passes into this area have many benefits. If an attacking player reaches the pass, taking care to avoid being offside, he or she may get a one-on-one challenge with the goalkeeper or be in an excellent position for a flank attack. Typically, teams that have attackers faster than the opponent's defenders will try to challenge this space. In these cases the defending team will want to keep their defenders low when defending to give away as little space as possible between the defenders and the goalkeeper.

The long through ball is a long and often high pass from a team's own half over the heads of the other team's defence. The attacking players need to chase the ball, but they have to remain in an onside position until the ball is kicked. This tactic works best with strong and fast attackers who have a good chance of winning back the ball, taking control of it and eventually getting a shot on goal. A real-life example occurred in the 2014 World Cup when Robin Van Persie timed his run perfectly to head home first time an aerial long ball from Daley Blind. Similarly, Arjen Robben's late winning goal for Bayern in the Champions League Final resulted from a 40-metre Jerome Boateng pass dropped in behind Dortmund's defensive line. A long through ball can also be played along the ground. Using the principles of attack, the supporting players create space with good movement and open up gaps in the defensive line, allowing an attacking player to run onto the ball from a penetrative through ball.

A common buildup of an attack is to pass the ball into the space between the opponent's defenders and midfielders. This tactic is often referred to as playing between the lines. Normally, an attacker with her or his back to the goal receives the pass. The player seeks to turn with the ball to continue forward momentum or distribute it to a player facing the goal, who optimally also is in front of the opponent's midfielders or even on the move into the space behind the opponent's defenders. The enhancement of tactical formations and systems of play in recent years has now seen a team create more layers of units within the team structure. A 4-2-3-1 formation is a good example of this in comparison to 4-4-2. The role of the number 10 playing ahead of the midfield unit and behind the central striker also promotes the use of space between the opponent's defensive and midfield lines. Indeed, during the 2013–2014 Champions League campaign, 19 out of 32 teams played the 4-2-3-1 formation in the group stages of the competition, demonstrating that clubs are playing with more flexible units and systems of play. Additionally, offside decisions dropped by 21 per cent during the same campaign, suggesting that defences are playing deeper to protect the space behind the defensive line.

Triangular movement is a movement tactic that allows safe and quick shifting of the offensive flanks while maintaining control of the ball. In a triangular play, the ball is passed among three players who form a triangle. The triangle is then shifted to a different position when a new player is added. Many triangles can be created with various combinations of players. The intention is to move the ball slowly forward and never really compromise possession. This tactic works well when trying to gain control in the midfield, but it can also be used for pure attacking purposes. The effectiveness of this tactic lies in the fact that defenders are unable to adapt quickly and recover to the other attacker's style of play.

Sometimes a team with two flexible (position wise) wide players will allow them to interchange as the game progresses. This tactic is known as swapping the wide player. The aim of this tactic is to allow the winger to attack the defenders by cutting inside towards goal rather than attacking space on the outside. By having wide players cut inside, fullbacks can push on and overlap to create space in wide areas. Also, if the wingers are different types of players (for example, one favours crossing from a deep position whereas the other is prone to trying to dribble past his or her marker), then the tactic might be used to exploit a weakness in the opposing defender.

An offensive attack can pressure the defence onto one side of the pitch by running most of its attackers and midfielders to one side, letting a wing player or defender come to the opposite side with little or no coverage. This tactic is called a strong side overload. The ball is then crossed or passed to that unmarked player for a free or near-free shot. This style of play uses the switching of play form as discussed earlier.

Using a target player is useful when the team possesses a quality striker who has the ability to take on the whole defence alone. This player usually occupies two defenders, thus making the defence more vulnerable. When the team has two fast wingers, this tactic may give the flat back four defence problems. The team may also benefit from a target player at set pieces. The target player can also use give-and-go tactics, attempt to knock down high passes to teammates or simply try to overpower and outmuscle opposition defenders to create scoring opportunities for him- or herself.

The one loose tactic is useful when the team possesses a quality winger or attacking fullback. The midfield unit often has three central players with one winger player loose in a much wider position. Consideration needs to be given to the strengths and capabilities of each team member, but this formation allows an offensive winger to attack from an advanced position on one side and a deeper-lying fullback to attack down the flank on the opposite side.

Role of the Coach

For coaches and practitioners to make effective use of the time available, a series of steps must be followed. First, the coach must appreciate the movement patterns and tactical elements of successful performance, including technical considerations and time on task (a critical function of sport science guidance). Second, the coach needs to translate this information into soccer-specific training drills. Third, the organization, design and prescription of relevant training methods must consider the major conditioning principles (namely, specificity and overload). The application of these principles in a planned manner is the key to effective physiological preparation, enhanced motivation and improved execution of technical performance.

At an elite level of participation, the coach builds co-operation between sport scientists and soccer players. Moreover, the coach assimilates information, analyses the effectiveness of the training programme and constructs the training sessions. This approach will maximize the training effect of time spent in specific preparation.

Information is the fuel that drives the coaching process. Planning, decision making, monitoring and performance analysis all depend on the availability of the necessary information. In addition, information on player and team performance provides the platform for interaction among coaching staff personnel, players and sport science practitioners.

For example, the data produced from match analysis may identify a reduced high-intensity output from a striker in the second half compared with the first half. Although situational variables such as quality of opposition, game location and congested fixture periods must be taken into consideration, a trend may be identified. This information will then act as a catalyst for discussion among key stakeholders in the coaching process. Possible causes can then be examined, and physical, technical and tactical recommendations can be executed to reduce such effects, as in these examples:

- Sport science practitioners can focus on increasing the ability of the player to sustain high-intensity bouts through speed endurance training.
- Technical coaches can work on when and where to execute high-intensity runs so that the player will maximize successful events and avoid unnecessary onset of fatigue.

- The match analysis team may identify areas of high-intensity runs to look at performance traces to ensure that match preparation strategies are evident at the behavioural level of performance.

Clearly, the interaction among all personnel is critical in understanding why physical demands may vary throughout games.

The coaching process includes several potential variables for interaction and discussion:

- Quantitative match analysis: distance covered, percentage of high-intensity running, sprint distance, number of accelerations, high-intensity bouts, first half versus second half, five-minute periods, work following the most intense phase
- Qualitative match analysis: number of passes, crosses, shots, tackles, headers, passing accuracy
- Targets for performance: variables that are position specific
- Squad rotation: identifying periods of intense fixture periods and allocating necessary changes to ensure repetition of high-level performance; player appearances and expectations based on previous performance; integration of young players based on readiness to perform at the senior level
- Objective performance scores: physical and technical elements to execute match strategy

Improvement in performance is the central purpose of the coaching process, and a detailed knowledge at the behavioural level of performance is essential for almost all stages of the performance management model, from promotion of recovery after training and competition to preparation and the training programme. These processes have great potential for assisting coaches and practitioners alike in making decisions about future performance. The key here is to move the role of performance analysis from a descriptive to a prescriptive function.

With the advent of GPS technology, practitioners can now plan the physical workloads imposed on the players during the training programme to ensure that the appropriate loads are achieved during the weekly schedule. Although normative values do not always ensure successful performance, they nonetheless act as appropriate markers and can be used in a platform with the coaching and sport science staff.

For example, the information presented in table 22.1 may be used as reference values for weekly training targets. The sport science staff and coaches can then engage in meaningful decision making to ensure that each player is optimally prepared. Moreover, those who play regularly are not overworked, and those who are not playing receive the appropriate loads to maintain fitness. Successful preparation involves a complex interaction of art and science.

Table 22.1 Weekly Reference Values for Physical Parameters

Parameter	Weekly target
Duration	300 to 350 min.
Total distance	20,000 to 28,000 m
High-intensity distance	1,000 to 1,500 m
Sprint distance	150 to 300 m
High accelerations	100 to 150
High decelerations	100 to 150

Coaches should be prepared to understand data and information, and sport science staff should endeavour to provide appropriate feedback in a meaningful way to ensure that coaches buy into the scientific process. Clearly, this process involves understanding the requirements of presenting information in a detailed and informative system.

Sport Science Interaction in the Design of Drills

The cooperative process of the coach and sport science practitioner must also translate into meaningful delivery of individual coaching drills. Coaching drills should have a physical, technical, tactical and psychological purpose. When this process is achieved, the potential for successful coaching is optimized. For example, the session Purposeful Possession and Switching Play can be used to emphasize purposeful possession and positive attacking play and maximize time spent in preparation.

The biggest advantage to effective movement and smart switching of the ball in competitive games is that fullbacks can be exposed in one-on-one situations. This element of attacking play must be practised because coaches can be guilty of putting on possession drills for their own convenience. Expansive passing and attacking moves should be an integral part of a team's play because positive possession leads to the creation of good goal-scoring opportunities.

Physical Qualities of Attacking Players

Attacking players possess various physical qualities that support their technical capabilities. Players do not usually excel in all areas, but they tend to have an outstanding physical attribute that makes them stand out from the rest at the elite level. Over the past decade, with GPS technology now common at the elite level, a more in-depth objective analysis of the physical demands of players and specific positions has been possible (Coutts and Duffield 2010). The main physical qualities associated with world-class attacking players are summarized in figure 22.6.

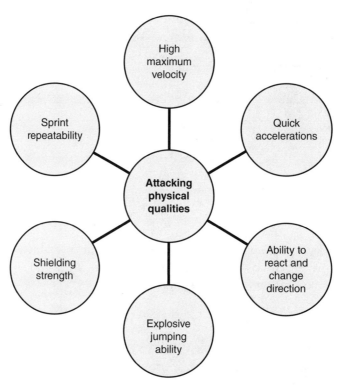

▶ **Figure 22.6** Physical attributes of attacking players.

The physical components highlighted involve a range of physiological systems, predominantly neurological, musculoskeletal and metabolic, all to varying degrees. The qualities do not include all the abilities of attacking players, but they do contain the major components that tend to be targeted at some point during training. Many points need to be considered when designing drills, and concentrating on every quality all the time is not possible. Priorities will change with different players and positions, and team tactical requirements are likely to become a factor.

Coaches need to establish what is required at the competitive level. A recent review by Carling and Court (2013) provides a succinct summary of the physical match demands imposed on players and the influence of factors such as playing position, tactical formation and game duration. Research of this nature provides a platform from which the physical requirements of players can be established. However, this information can provide only a generic framework for developing the physical attributes of players. The individual characteristics of players, their unique playing style and the requirements from a tactical perspective should be influential in guiding effective practice.

Coaching Philosophy and Planning Considerations

An elite soccer player's training should include some essential elements regardless of position. These are combined in various ways to achieve the following:

- Preparation: prepare players for competition
- Prevention: increase resistance to potential injuries
- Progression: develop physical qualities

Methods of devising a weekly template and producing a schedule that achieves these three principles are outlined in chapter 12. Depending on the individual player, the requirements to develop a specific attribute will differ. Longitudinal monitoring of player activity using the various technological systems available informs practitioners of what players have done, thereby

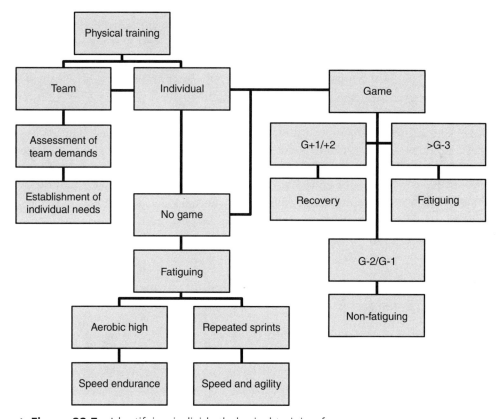

▶ **Figure 22.7** Identifying individual physical training focus.

assisting in the determination of what training is required. Multiple decisions of this nature are constantly undertaken to identify what specific players need in the next session.

The decision tree in figure 22.7 shows the potential thought process that practitioners go through when planning specific drills and sessions. First, the proximity to the previous game and the next game dictates the template for the session. Practitioners need to understand the expected physical demands of the technical and tactical work planned. Following this, they can make decisions for individuals. Players who are not involved in the next game are usually returning from injury and tend to require greater emphasis on developing the various energy systems and explosiveness, whereas those involved in games possibly fit into fewer categories, as shown. Greater load can be exerted on players in the early part of the training week, whereas when the next competitive game is within 48 hours, the emphasis is on quality rather than inducing an overload.

Planning for G-2 and G-1

In season, because of the scheduling and the number of games that players are preparing for, significantly developing all physical attributes is often difficult. Such qualities, however, can be honed with minimal exposure to prepare players for competition. Moreover, players can be stimulated physically without undue stress, ensuring a suitable level of readiness going into competition. A key role of the scientific support models adopted at the elite level is to inform this process, assuming that the knowledge of what players need is in fact correct. On this note, the player's own opinion should not be neglected; players at the elite level often know what they need to prepare themselves for the next game. From a training perspective, any form of overload is difficult, but short, explosive, high-intensity drills with small groups or individuals can provide a suitable stimulus, both mentally and physically.

Planning for G-3 and Greater

When players are more than 72 hours before a game, targeting any physical component is usually possible. Depending on the content of the technical and tactical work undertaken, knowledge of individual player profiles and individual needs analysis will direct the practitioner to the appropriate quality to overload. Explosiveness, which is fundamental at the top level, is associated with many of the attributes represented in figure 22.6. Targeting such qualities with high-speed, explosive-orientated drills is more logical than having players perform traditional steady-state running, even when energy system development is required. Desirable adaptations can be attained by repetition of high-speed runs as described by Iaia and Bangsbo (2010). This type of training ensures that speeds more representative of the high-intensity movement patterns reported at the elite level are replicated. The training also incorporates high accelerations and decelerations, both of which have a role in injury prevention (Carling, Le Gall and Reilly 2010).

Drills for the Physical Development of Attacking Players

The drills presented in this section are explosive, aimed at matching intensities demonstrated by players in competition. Movement patterns can be adjusted to suit specific players and mimic individual game actions. However, the fundamental principles outlined in chapter 12 remain consistent. Drills of an individual nature tend to fall into two categories: pure conditioning, which focuses on overloading a physical component, and functional conditioning, which incorporates technical skills as well as specific physical qualities. The former can support a club's monitoring strategy with the repetition of specific drills being used to assess a player's status by comparison with previous drill outputs. The latter, if implemented effectively, encompass position-specific cognitive components, which can provide added benefit as long as the physical emphasis is not compromised. Each type has its place, but by considering the variables discussed earlier, the most suitable drills can be identified.

Note that many of the individual drills presented are performed at the end of team training sessions, unless individual or unit work is implemented as part of the main session. Therefore, the work completed and the demands of the planned drills need to be considered to ensure that sufficient quality and explosiveness is possible. Sometimes the physical requirements for players may change because of what has been completed in the main session, requiring the practitioner to make adjustments. The examples that follow illustrate the nature of functional drills commonly performed by elite attacking players in season.

The two qualities highlighted in figure 22.6 that are not targeted specifically in these drills are jumping ability and shielding strength. The development of both of these qualities depends on the off-the-field strength and power development sessions (see chapter 12). From a functional perspective, these qualities are generally put under a degree of stress daily by possession practices and games. Additional overload will rarely be used unless a player requires technical assistance.

High-Intensity Aerobic: Attacking Midfield Run   The player begins on the halfway line and drives forward with the ball to the edge of the centre circle. The player plays a short pass into space and moves quickly around the cone, moving onto the ball to dribble past the pole and pass out wide to a coach (figure 22.8). The player continues a run into the box to receive a return pass and shoot. The player immediately turns, strides back to the start and repeats, working to the opposite side. The player continues for two minutes and then rests for one minute. The player completes four to six repetitions.

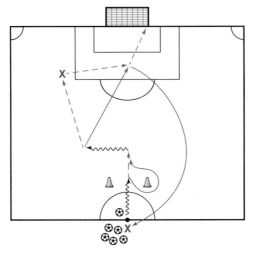

▶ **Figure 22.8**   Attacking midfield run.

High-Intensity Aerobic: Individual Repeated Finishing   The player starts by one goal and strides out towards the opposite goal, moving onto the ball played diagonally across the goal by a server, finishing first time (figure 22.9). The second goal is placed on the halfway line. The pace of the run is slowed slightly around the back of the goal and the sequence is repeated into the other goal. The player continues for 45 seconds and rests for 15 seconds to complete one repetition. The player does four to six repetitions to complete one set. For multiple sets, have a 2-minute break and vary the ball delivery and skill requirement for the player. The player completes up to six sets.

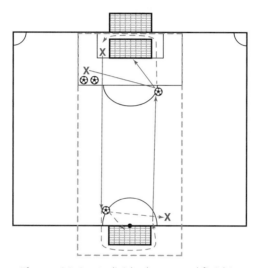

▶ **Figure 22.9**   Individual repeated finishing.

Repeated Sprint Finishing   Player receives the ball in a four-by-four-metre square and reacts by controlling and moving the ball through the gate number called by the coach (figure 22.10). The player accelerates into space, passes the ball into a small goal and immediately sprints back to repeat. The player performs two or three minirepetitions in 5 to 7 seconds, repeating on a 20-second rolling clock. The player performs four to six repetitions to complete one set.

The second set can be varied by having the player sprint around the nearest mannequin following the shot and back into the square (figure 22.11). Only two mini repetitions are possible in the 5- to 7-second period.

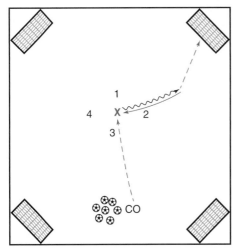

▶ **Figure 22.10**   Repeated sprint finishing.

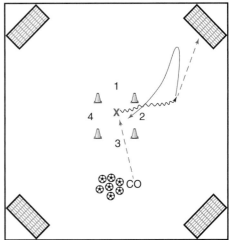

▶ **Figure 22.11**   Screen 2.

Repeated Sprint Shooting   This finishing drill (double shot) with small numbers ensures peripheral overload. The player begins by passing the ball into the server and sprinting onto the return pass to dribble and shoot. The player immediately sprints around the pole on the edge of the box to finish a second shot first time (figure 22.12). Two players can work at the same time, aiming to complete the repetition in five to eight seconds. Up to three pairs can work in rotations, ensuring a work-to-rest ratio of approximately 1:3. Players perform four to six repetitions to complete one set, and they do two to five sets.

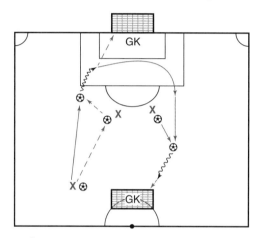

▶ **Figure 22.12**   Repeated sprint shooting.

Speed Endurance   The player begins in his or her own half, tracks back around the pole to the ball and dribbles 5 to 10 metres before passing out wide to the server (figure 22.13). The player continues a maximal run to receive the return pass from the server, shoots first time and immediately turns to sprint back through the gates. Each repetition should be 15 to 20 seconds and repeated on a 90-second rolling clock. The player does four to six repetitions to complete one set.

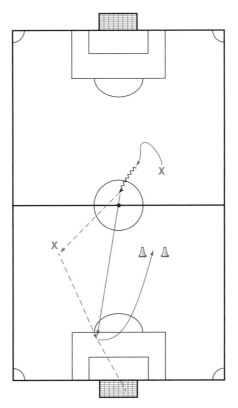

▶ **Figure 22.13**   Speed endurance.

Speed Endurance Full Pitch   In groups of three or four, players sprint the length of the pitch, combine passes with the option of using a coach in the centre circle and aim to score within 10 seconds (figure 22.14). After the first group clears the pitch, the second group works the other way. Players continue for four to six runs to complete one set. The aim is for each group to do approximately 10 seconds of work followed by 30 seconds of recovery.

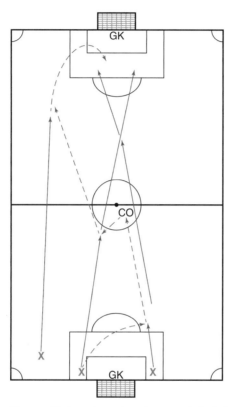

▶ **Figure 22.14**   Speed endurance full pitch.

Maximum Speed Finishing   The first player accelerates with the ball maximally towards the edge of the box, shoots and then makes a recovery run around to the opposite side (figure 22.15). Immediately after the first player shot, the second player begins his or her run. The sequence continues for 6 to 10 shots per player to complete a set. For multiple sets and variations in skill, reduce set repetitions to six. Players aim for full recovery and maximum effort.

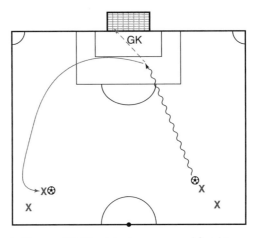

▶ **Figure 22.15**   Maximum speed finishing.

Short Counter Sprints   The drill starts with player 1 passing to player 4. Players 1, 2 and 3 immediately sprint in support to attack the goal and try to score within six seconds (figure 22.16). The defending players start slightly behind the attacking players so that they have slightly greater distance to cover. Emphasis is on shooting as quickly as possible and making accurate passes to maintain high speed. Players walk back and change roles, ensuring full recovery between repetitions. Players perform 6 to 10 repetitions to complete one set.

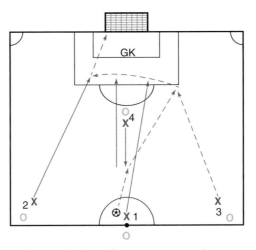

▶ **Figure 22.16**   Short counter sprints.

Acceleration Finishing Players work in a group of three. Player 1 passes the ball to player 2, who comes off the line and plays a one-two with player 3 (figure 22.17). Player 2 sprints to the touchline to cross first time, whilst players 1 and 3 continue their respective runs into the box to finish. Groups of three can work both sides. Players perform 12 to 16 repetitions with full recovery.

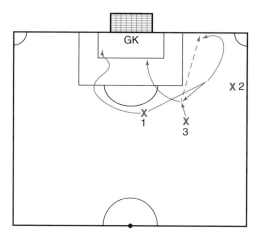

▶ **Figure 22.17** Acceleration finishing.

Shoot and Defend Player 1 dribbles at maximal speed with the ball and shoots once past the pole, 15 metres from the touchline (figure 22.18). After player 1 shoots, player 2 immediately repeats the process, being put under pressure by player 1, who tracks back to try to block the shot. The routine should be continuous; using 10 or more players allows sufficient recovery. Players perform four to six repetitions per set. They repeat from the opposite side for multiple sets.

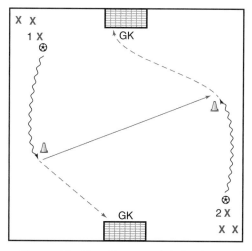

▶ **Figure 22.18** Shoot and defend.

Mannequin Reaction   Set up mannequins randomly inside the penalty area. The player receives a ball from the coach and manipulates it quickly to get a shot on goal (figure 22.19). The player receives a series of three balls and jogs slowly to the edge of the box and back into the mannequins. The player repeats twice more for a total of nine shots to complete one set. Set variations include two-touch finish, one-touch finish and reacting off a mannequin ricochet.

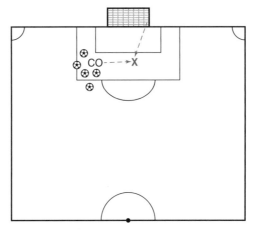

▶ **Figure 22.19**   Mannequin reaction.

Rebound Board Reaction   The player stands with her or his back to the goal facing the rebound boards. The coach drives the ball against one of the boards at random. The player reacts to the ball movement and manipulates the ball to get a shot off quickly, aiming for one of the corners (figure 22.20). The player receives a series of three balls and slowly jogs to the goal line and back into the start position. The player repeats twice more for a total of nine shots to complete one set. Players perform two to four sets with variation in the rebound board position to replicate different attacking scenarios.

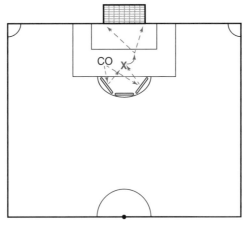

▶ **Figure 22.20**   Rebound board reaction.

React and Pass   The player reacts to the visual stimulus of a pass towards a mannequin, accelerates to the ball, passes back to the server and jockeys back into start position (figure 22.21). The player repeats for three mini repetitions.

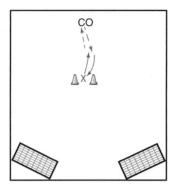

▶ **Figure 22.21**   React and pass.

After the third mini repetition, the player opens up and moves around the outside pole, always facing the ball, and initiates a sprint to the ball after the coach plays the ball into space (figure 22.22). The player accelerates onto the ball and passes first time into one of the small goals. This completes one repetition. The player performs four repetitions to complete one set. Players can perform one to three sets varying their movement.

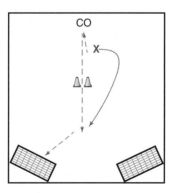

▶ **Figure 22.22**   Peel off, accelerate and finish.

Tactical and Physical Development of Attacking Players

Training generally follows a consistent pattern throughout the season, although the overall volume of work is manipulated at times to vary the overall stimulus. The nature of training sessions tends to follow a pattern dictated by the number of days that have passed since the previous game and the proximity to the next game. Because of scheduling, coaches often have only one or two days to work on the tactical requirements of players for the next match. Coaches may adopt strategies that maximize the qualities their players possess, organize them to target the weaknesses of the opposition or, most likely, incorporate a combination of the two whilst also minimizing the threat from the opposing team's strengths.

Although match strategy is not a key focus of this chapter, it should be considered because many practitioners in the modern game incorporate several aims within the same drill to maximize the value of the limited time available. Coaches want to work on tactical demands whilst also servicing the physical requirements of players. Also, because of typical staff-to-player ratios, providing one-to-one service is not always possible. This type of approach is a useful vehicle for targeting physical qualities with holistic soccer conditioning methods.

Conclusion

Tactical training provides an opportunity for simultaneous physical overload, but the required stimulus for development of physical qualities is not always achieved. By using drills with suitable volume and intensity and manipulating work-to-rest ratios accordingly, both physical and technical player qualities can be developed whilst at the same time increasing the tactical capabilities of a team.

The practitioner must understand the demands of technical and tactical-biased sessions, and incorporate specific physical drills into the daily training plan at the appropriate time when necessary. Although real-time monitoring systems will aid this process in the future as they become more reliable and less intrusive in the field, knowledge of the needs and capabilities of individual players remains important. Advances in soccer science will continue to support these processes, but practitioner experience and at times intuition will continue to play a role in identifying practices that support the physical development of players.

The integration of all required components requires effective communication among support staff. Training implemented in the smartest possible way can help to achieve the desired multiple outcomes from sessions. This approach ensures that the position-specific needs of players are met and that readiness for competition is optimized, thus maximizing the potential for success.

Match Performance and Analysis

CHAPTER 23

Player and Team Assessments

—Rob Mackenzie and Chris Cushion

The use of performance analysis technology alongside video review sessions as part of weekly training programmes has established analysis as a key part of the coaching process within professional soccer.

Professional clubs worldwide employ people to provide analysis support, but insight into the workings of analysis in soccer is limited. This chapter addresses this issue with insights from the inner world of soccer analysis. The chapter considers the role of analysis and the analyst in top-level professional soccer and contrasts this with work at the international level. This subject includes discussion of issues surrounding the delivery of information to coaches and players within review sessions and the role of analysis in scouting. The principles of practice used at an elite performance level are discussed, where possible, in relation to application for coaches working at all levels of the game.

Soccer is a complex game in which multiple factors, including chance, influence performance and contribute to the final outcome. These factors present significant challenges for both players and members of the coaching team. The smaller the difference in performance levels is, the smaller the margin for error. Therefore, teams are constantly looking for areas to develop that can give them the competitive edge. Successful coaches are willing to explore various resources that may assist in this process.

Performance analysis can be an important resource to equip both players and coaches at all levels of the game with the tools and skills to help in navigating these challenges.

Soccer tactics vary markedly. For example, some coaches still use direct play and long-ball tactics. This approach is largely based on research suggesting that goals are commonly scored following fewer than four passes (Reep and Benjamin 1968). More recently, possession-based approaches, such as FC Barcelona's current playing style, have come to the fore. But within these broad playing approaches, teams commonly adopt different tactics from game to game or even within games. The result is that both players and coaches are challenged to adapt to the situation they find themselves in.

Role of a Performance Analyst

To complement the fluctuating needs of players and coaches effectively, it is important to acknowledge the varying functions and purposes of performance analysts within a backroom team environment. Although roles may differ from team to team and situation to situation, performance analysis is predominantly used

- to establish and allow the evaluation of player roles and responsibilities within a team,
- to analyse the execution of match-specific game plans,
- to analyse the effectiveness of training in line with the desired outcomes from that specific session,
- to analyse the strengths and weaknesses of forthcoming opponents and
- to evaluate a series of performance indicators of players from other clubs (prospective signings) over time.

Although applied with significant depth and detail within the professional game, these functions could be adopted within any level of soccer depending on need and resources.

Player Roles and Responsibilities

For any team to be successful, the members of the team need to be made explicitly aware of their roles and responsibilities within the team. Research has found that if role ambiguity is high, that is, if players are uncertain about their roles in the team, their confidence may be lower than if they were aware of what is expected of them (Eys et al. 2003). Such uncertainty may then, in turn, contribute to detrimental performance (Beauchamp et al. 2002). Subsequently, in conjunction with the management team, performance analysis can be used to establish roles and responsibilities within a team at any level of the game with the ultimate aim of improving performance. For example, a manager may have a specific preference for his or her fullbacks to make a high number of crosses per game. With this information, an analyst may compile video evidence of when the players execute this specific event during a game. Additionally, an analyst may be able to record and analyse instances in a game when the fullbacks have an opportunity to execute this type of action but do not.

Giving feedback to a player either statistically or visually enables their contribution to performance to be evaluated. Moreover, position-specific data recorded over a prolonged period alongside information relating to the context of the match (such as match result, opposition, venue, opposition formation and so on) allows emerging trends and patterns to be used and may inform team selection. This approach could be applied at all levels of the game. Basic analysis of player performance can be made, with or without video. In the example here, that measure is the number of crosses made by a fullback. That measure may be linked to player goal setting during training and games. In addition, such a process would allow players to reflect on the information gathered in the context of their games. The coach would have added detail and points of reference to help players understand how they might approach improving their play (see figure 23.1).

Professional soccer academies may seek to compile videos and analyses of their first team squad (if applicable) carrying out position-specific roles and responsibilities. This product may then act as a blueprint for what is expected from their younger players whilst also providing them with some guidance about areas that they may seek to improve.

To develop this notion further, the club could invite young players from their academy to observe live home games and conduct basic notational analysis on position-specific actions carried out by the players playing their

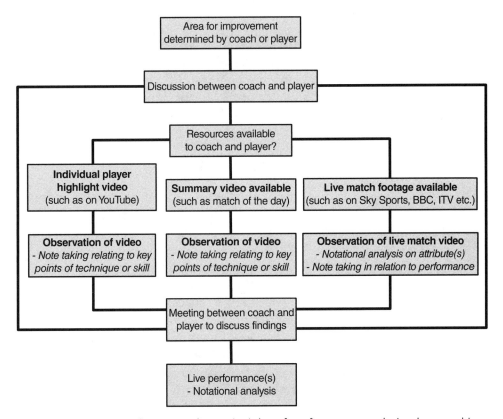

▶ **Figure 23.1** Coaches may adopt principles of performance analysis when working with players at a sub-elite level.

position. Youth players at any level of the game can adopt this methodology. Coaches can offer direction about observing position-specific role models regularly executing the desired skills.

Coach's Approach

For analysis to be used effectively (irrespective of the level of expertise), a significant amount of guidance is required from the manager or coach about his or her approach to the game. This direction enables an analyst to consider the salient aspects of performance to be scrutinized. But this statement from a respected professional soccer manager suggests that the reality can be somewhat different: 'Managers can sometimes go through the motion of letting analysts produce complicated documents or reports which ultimately have little effect on the coaching process' (Mackenzie 2014).

In short, for analysis to complement the coaching process and influence professional practice, a line of communication needs to be an open between the analyst and the coaching team. This interaction ensures that the analysis undertaken is meaningful and accurately represents the coach's approach towards the game.

Time Constraints

Performance analysts are required to provide flexible analysis and insights capable of adapting to changes in tactics and personnel. Analysis is required over a prolonged period, often a series of games, although it could be just for a 90-minute game. A key challenge for the performance analyst is contact time. This time will vary greatly between international and club teams and depends as well on the standard of competition at club level.

Working at the Elite Club Level

At the elite club level, playing three competitive games in a seven-day period is now common. Subsequently, the opportunity for interaction with players and for coaches to conduct tactical training sessions in preparation for each game can be limited.

Elite players who monitor their own performances over time in line with the manager's approach can increase their chances of being successful and selected regularly. Another important key to success is to be able to switch attention and focus to a different opponent every week. Consequently, in alignment with the needs of the players, the analyst at club level must be able to provide relevant postmatch information on the performance of her or his team and analyse the strengths and weaknesses of the forthcoming opposition within a tight time frame.

Working at the International Level

In contrast, at the international level the time between competitive fixtures is often substantial. An analyst usually has far more time to prepare the analysis on the upcoming opposition. The analysis can be more detailed and can include more previous performances than is feasible for club analysts working within strict time constraints. Conversely, analysts at the international level face a different challenge with postmatch information. The majority of players rejoin their club sides immediately after the final game during an international break and become immediately involved in preparing for their club's next fixture.

To use performance analysis effectively at the international level, both analysts and coaches have to find alternative means of providing performance feedback to players other than face-to-face interaction or structured coaching sessions.

In addition, the needs of the players at the international level are arguably different from the demands at club level. Players coming into an international environment are usually required to operate within a different style of play or for a manager who has a different approach. Therefore, as with club players, their chances of individual and collective success are often determined by their ability to execute the manager's strategic plan. Therefore, an important role of the performance analyst working at the international level is to help make this transition as smooth as possible.

Working at Other Levels

Practitioners working at other levels of the game have even less contact time. For example, amateur teams commonly train once or twice a week on an evening and play one competitive game at the weekend. But if principles of performance analysis can be implemented with such groups of players, even if only at a basic level because of time and resource constraints, player development and collective team operation may still be enhanced.

Notational Analysis: Manual Coding Versus Computer Tracking

The analysis of specific individual player or team events can be performed in real time or postgame. In its simplest form, match events can be recorded to produce a frequency count of specific preselected actions, such as team shots, crosses, set pieces and so on. The report could be as advanced as a log of every time each player touches the ball, accompanied by a description of where on the field the action took place, action type, (e.g., long pass, short pass, tackle and so on) and the outcome of the action (e.g., successful or unsuccessful).

Technological advances over the last few years have led to the introduction of low-cost digital video–based analysis solutions with self-designed manual coding templates. These allow multiple on- and off-the-ball events to be indexed and then reviewed. Solutions now entering the market even allow the filming and analysis of a game to be performed with only an iPad or PC tablet (for a more detailed description of match evaluation tools, see chapter 25). The cost of equipment no longer prevents clubs from starting to use basic digital video–based analysis systems. Clearly, this area will develop rapidly in the forthcoming years. Furthermore, clubs may be able to forge links with sport science departments at universities. Students can gain valuable hands-on experience by providing performance analysis support to a club's coaching and playing staff, whilst the coaches and club can gain the potential benefits.

The obvious advantages of digital video–based match analysis systems compared with notational analysis are that they allow a multitude of on- and off-the-ball parameters to be not only statistically recorded and analysed but also visualised. Digital video–based analysis systems are obviously dependent on the availability of match footage. Here the extra resources available in elite soccer allow better video quality (e.g., broadcast quality) and often a better camera angle (or multiple camera angles) compared with other levels. A professional coach today may have access to four or more camera angles when viewing a specific event. Thus, referring back to the original example of analysing the number of crosses that a fullback makes during a match, a single wide-angle view or a multiple- camera feed will allow the position of teammates and opponents to be considered.

In professional soccer, semiautomated computer tracking systems have emerged over the last decade. Current computer tracking systems in soccer offer a range of services. For example, reporting of all technical on-ball game events (more than 2,000 per game) is available within 24 hours postmatch, as is a comprehensive description of each player's movement patterns at a sampling rate of two times per second. Such data offer detailed insights into physical performance that is not otherwise available during competitive games. In theory, all the technical game events generated by computer tracking systems can also be generated by manual coding of the game. But this task is extremely time consuming, possibly requiring eight hours of work!

In reality, only professional teams can implement a computer tracking solution because of the relatively high installation and game-to-game costs. Furthermore, most professional clubs and national teams that employ third-party service providers to analyse their games using the computer tracking methodology still use manual coding systems to complement these data (Mackenzie and Cushion 2013). They do this for several reasons. First, the processing time for semiautomated computer tracking systems is currently

12 to 24 hours (although this may change in the near future because real-time tracking systems are currently being developed). Therefore, a manual coding system is needed for real-time and immediate postgame statistical and visual feedback of key on- and off-the-ball events. Members of the coaching staff positioned in close proximity to the performance analyst during a game can then review events immediately after they have occurred and feed information directly to a coach or manager pitch side or at half time. Either way, such information can be used to aid decision making during the game itself.

A second reason is that manually coded events can be self-defined. The analyst can devise and implement match- or training-specific coding templates that can be quickly adapted. Custom definitions can be refined to include a degree of subjectivity in line with the requirements of the manager or coaching staff. Rigid predefined computer-generated definitions may not always give a true reflection of the performance of an individual player or team. In some cases, certain parameters of a player's performance may be perceived as poor when in reality the player may have executed the coach's game plan to great effect. If such a scenario were to arise, the player's confidence in the work of the performance analyst may be greatly diminished.

A simple example can illustrate this point. Suppose that the primary attacking tactic of a team is long ball, or direct play. They want to play a long ball deep into the opponent's territory and, if possession is lost, win the ball back as quickly as possible. With such tactics, the timing of the long ball and the area to which the ball is played may be of more interest to a manager or coach than whether possession was directly retained, that is, whether the pass was completed or not. In this scenario, a manual coding system could allow for the passer of the long ball to be judged on the choice, timing and quality of the pass as opposed to the more commonly used pass completion statistic. Furthermore, incidents can be indexed when the ball carrier had the option to play a long ball but chose another option or when the ball carrier was looking to play a long ball but did not have the support of appropriate movement by teammates or correct team shape. Subsequently, a manual coding approach can allow the quantification of nonobjective aspects if players know what is expected of them in specific situations.

Manual coding also allows indexing of off-the-ball events, an area where important insights can be gained. For example, a key component of a game plan may be for both strikers to stretch opposing central defenders apart with runs into the channel. If the coding is restricted solely to technical, on-the-ball events, a striker would get credit for making such a run only when he or she received the ball. A performance analyst who is familiar with the game plan would be able to recognize such tactical runs and code them accordingly.

At a professional level, tactical training can also be analysed by manual coding in the same manner and with the same coding template as the match performance itself. By adopting this approach, the effectiveness of training in preparing the players to carry out a specific game plan can be quantified, as can the actual training performance of players in relation to their ability to execute their roles within the game plan. By analysing these scenarios, players who are continually failing to execute their roles within the team's proposed game plan may receive extra training or may be replaced by more effective performers.

Several important issues need to be considered when a manual coding approach is adopted with custom definitions that incorporate a degree of subjectivity. For example, it can be erroneous to make statistical comparisons with data generated outside the club where similar terminology may have very different definitions. The event terminology used throughout the team and preferably the club should be consistent. Clear definition guidelines should be drawn up not only to aid the analyst when coding the game but also to ensure reliability and accurate interpretations of the statistics. The analyst must be proactive and adopt a multidisciplinary approach in which members of the coaching staff and potentially the players themselves are involved to ensure that everybody is aware of event definitions (see figure 23.2).

An obvious question concerns the depth of game knowledge required by an analyst who codes a game. What is the ideal skill set of a performance analyst? In an ideal world, a performance analyst would be a qualified coach and IT specialist with good analytical and communication skills. Although a person who has this combination of skills is rare today, the recent introduction of specialized three-year degree courses in performance analysis may make such people more available in the future. The reality is that some element of all four components is needed, the balance of which will be determined to some extent by the needs and expectations of the manager. Some may consider the preference of the manager quoted here a dream, whereas others may think that it stretches beyond their capabilities:

> I prefer an analyst who is prepared to be proactive in their approach to processing and analysing the information. There is a need for attention to detail, which could encourage debate. Good 'people skills' are imperative to tweak the thought processes of managers or coaches, by challenging any aspect of performance and offering options.
>
> (Mackenzie 2014)

Whatever form of analysis is adopted—manual coding or a computer tracking solution through a third-party service provider—the evaluation of a team's ability to execute a predetermined game plan or patterns of play is a pivotal aspect of an analyst's role.

With so much data available to be collected following each performance, another aspect of the analyst's role is to store the vast volumes of data and engage in longitudinal analysis. Such analysis takes into account contextual

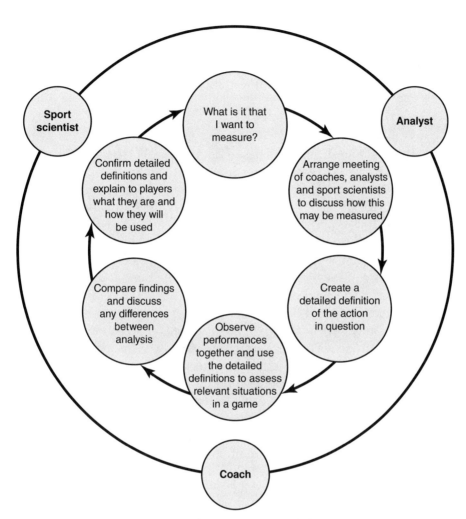

▶ **Figure 23.2** A guide to establishing transparent definitions.

variables surrounding each match in its entirety. Meaningful insights can then be provided to the club's management team that may influence coaching practice or team selection (Groom, Cushion and Nelson 2011).

Clearly, analysis can contribute to accurate and efficient decision making within a professional soccer environment. For example, at the international level where a team's squad is not predetermined and can change between matches, an analyst can provide both statistical and visual insights (in line with the manager's approach) into fringe players who may be considered for a call-up. Similarly, the manager can use the information provided by an analyst to assess how the current players compare with those who have not been selected previously. In this way, analysis may influence future team selection. Moreover, given the lack of contact time that players have with both coaches and the backroom staff at the international level, a performance analyst can provide information and insight into how the manager wants the team to play to both established and recently called-up players to prepare them for their transition. In short, an analyst at the international level may be able to influence changes in player behaviour from how they are required to play at club level to what their international manager will expect of them.

Data Usage

Despite the vast and different types of data now collected regularly during and following a professional soccer match, little is known about how that information is used or fed back to coaches and players by the analyst.

One reason for this lack of knowledge is likely the reluctance of clubs and organizations to reveal their trade secrets, alongside an insular culture that precludes access by other organizations (including educational institutes) to their clubs. The issue here may be a spurious notion of confidentiality about the nature of the work that goes on and the perceived implications if that work was made publicly accessible. But the way in which the analyst transfers information and data collected to players and coaches has significant implications for the strength of its influence on behaviour and practice.

Performance analysis is a tool aimed specifically at improving future performances through the analysis and dissemination of information relating to previous training and match performances to an athlete or player (Hughes, Cooper and Nevill 2002). On this basis, its implementation may seem straightforward. But because of the multifaceted nature of soccer performance, identifying any one aspect of a player's preparation that contributed most to successful performance is difficult. We propose that if a player learned something new or meaningfully analysed a previous performance as part of a novel learning experience, she or he is more likely to perform successfully than if she or he had not learned anything. If this is true, we can identify principles of practice to follow when delivering performance analysis.

The most meaningful learning experiences for people are those in which they have ownership over the process (Moon 2004). Subsequently, one of the roles of the analyst may be to provide a specific selection of clips relating to an aspect of a player's performance that has been identified by the player. The player could then review aspects of his or her performance that are specifically meaningful to him or her. The role of the coach in this situation would be to ask reflective questions of the player relating to the selected aspect of his or her performance. The coach would not offer a response and perspective until the player has given his or hers. Such an approach would ensure that the players have firm ownership of the situation and would improve information retention along with motivation to reflect on and subsequently improve that aspect of their performance (Dewey 1933). If an analyst manually codes meaningful instances within a game in line with the manager's practice and tactical approach, the ability to provide players with this kind of footage and information is enhanced. In contrast, if a club uses a third-party data analysis provider, some of the instances that a player is interested in may not involve direct contact with the ball.

Coaches working at other levels or in youth soccer can adapt this principle of player-led reflection by assigning players a homework task to watch whatever soccer they have access to (live match or a highlight show) and to observe players playing in their positions. The players note what they think their counterpart is doing successfully (or perhaps unsuccessfully) and how this contributed to (or hindered) overall performance. Players may gain another perspective on being effective in their positions, and they would have discussion points to talk about with the coach.

Understandably, given that soccer is a team game, performance analysis is usually conducted with the full team or a select group of players as opposed to one player. Despite the increase in the number of people involved in the session, research suggests that the principle of ownership within the learning process remains the same (Dewey 1933). The use of performance analysis with groups of people who share the same end goal and outcome is likely to strengthen their commitment to the process and enhance their overall experience because they perceive the analysis to be meaningful to them (Lave and Wenger 1998).

With specific reference to people maintaining ownership over the process, an approach in which players actually lead video or analysis sessions and choose the content of the session is suggested to be one positive adaptation of performance analysis. In such an environment, players are able to discuss pertinent issues openly and honestly in a nonthreatening manner that involves all members of the group and subsequently provides the best opportunity to influence their future behaviour.

If analysis is delivered more formally by a manager in a group environment, such as with the full first-team playing squad, the challenge of making the information meaningful is more complicated. Subsequently, the manager and the coaching staff need to create a balance in which the players receive relevant information and have an opportunity to provide their perspective on the analysis but the manager is still able to exert authority and maintain a position of power (Foucault 1972; Potrac, Jones and Cushion 2007). Irrespective of the situation in which performance analysis is used with players, a balance must be achieved that complements the learning requirements of the players at the club.

Scouting Prospective Players and Opponents

One of the more recent adaptations of performance analysis is to the field of scouting, both in analysing forthcoming opposition and in assessing prospective signings.

Because of the heightened availability of match footage of upcoming opposition through both third-party service providers and resourceful analysts exchanging footage with colleagues at clubs who have recently played the opposition, more information can now be accessed than ever before. For example, traditional subjective scouting reports provided by a club's scouts can be supplemented with objective analyses of the same game, done either in house by a club's analyst or by using the information and data provided by a third-party service provider. Similarly, video evidence of opposing teams' common patterns of play, strengths and weaknesses (among other things) can be presented to a team's management staff as well as to the players themselves. With an increase in the number of games being analysed, the consistency of an opposing team's play and patterns of play over a significant number of games can also be assessed. Therefore, how a team approaches a game and the team that is selected for that game can be more informed than ever previously possible.

Similar to scouting upcoming opposition, scouting players who may be considered as a future signing was traditionally a subjective process before the emergence of performance analysis. Now, should a club's resources allow, statistical data are available for individual players across the world, because of the vast number of games that are processed and analysed. Subsequently, position-specific key performance indicators can be assessed and compared with those of similar ability and standing as well as against a club's own players. Therefore, scouting departments are able to gauge whether a prospective signing is currently outperforming other recommended players or players in the current squad. Such a process can minimize risk associated with signing new players because their ability to fit in with a club's playing style can be assessed before signing.

But some issues may arise when using independently produced data about potential signings. For example, if a manager's position-specific demands of a player are not fully analysed, the data may be misleading or misrepresentative of the player's overall contribution. For example, a manager may be looking for a dominant central defender who is strong in the air. Typically, data provided independently consider only successful ball contacts (headers) and do not show the number of aerial duels that a player was involved in and the number of successful or unsuccessful outcomes. With this in mind, a club's technical scout or recruitment analyst may opt to analyse manually with coding software if footage is available. In this way, the analyst can provide a representation of the player that is directly aligned with the needs of the manager and the requirements of that player's position in the team.

An in-house approach to analysing prospective players using computer-coding software or programmes as part of the scouting process is not without its limitations. For example, depending on the complexity of the position-specific coding template used, the time required to code games manually can be extensive, resulting in fewer games being analysed than by other means. Subsequently, the data produced by in-house player analysis may be less reliable and inconsistent because of small sample size. Moreover, if a club or organization chooses to adopt their own definitions and selection of coding events, they would be unable to compare their data to that of other clubs or organizations not using the same criteria. This issue may prove a problem when trying to benchmark both position-specific and generic averages across competitions.

Irrespective of which approach is adopted, a universal, club-wide approach must be adopted towards performance analysis to ensure that the data are comparable across departments. This approach allows members of the current playing squad and prospective signings to be compared with each other in the knowledge that the data have been collected using the same definitions and parameters.

Conclusion

Performance analysis is firmly rooted in the coaching process within professional soccer. This chapter has given an insight into the role of analysis and analysts in the professional game and has provided examples of how principles of good practice can be adapted by those working at other levels. These insights are important because the process of performance analysis should not be treated in a unidimensional way, nor should the analyst be viewed in that way. This chapter has illustrated that analysis used broadly, alongside the role of the analyst, is both multifaceted and multidimensional.

Although the chapter raises issues related to the process of analysis and with the nature of data generated, remember that analysis is embedded in a broader coaching process, itself subject to social and cultural pressures and constraints. So although the possibilities for analysis in soccer are almost limitless, the application in reality will be governed by the prevailing approach and culture in any given context. Perceptions and understanding towards analysis may not be based on evidence but on experience and tradition. Therefore, the application of analysis often mirrors the wider coaching process in soccer and is largely coach led. The players are passive receivers of information. In turn, they are expected to transfer that information seamlessly into improved performance. The stumbling block then becomes not the what and how of analysis itself but the application of the information created. Thus, questions about the delivery process of analysis information, some of which have been raised in this chapter, seem vital to maximizing its use.

CHAPTER 24

Match Evaluation: Systems and Tools

—Chris Carling

Over the last decade or so, professional soccer has been characterized by a more systematic approach towards training and preparation for competition than traditionally employed. Reflecting this evolution, the analysis of match play and subsequent evaluation of player performance has gained widespread acceptance across the professional soccer community.

Most professional clubs now formally employ performance analysts to perform match analysis in one form or other. In addition, extensive statistical analysis during media coverage of elite soccer competition has raised interest in coaching practitioners and players across other standards of play. But at all competitive levels, the dynamic and random nature of soccer play frequently leads to incomplete or inaccurate recollection of various aspects of performance. Therefore, practitioners are often unable to make an objective appraisal of how an individual player or team has performed.

The primary function of match analysis is to provide an objective, factual and permanent record of events regarding physical, technical and tactical performance during competition (James 2006).

Information derived from analyses provides an opportunity to appraise how players are performing and is the foundation for feedback to coaches and players. Areas of match performance deemed successful can be subsequently built on in practice, and identified weaknesses can be remedied. Data can aid team selection and choice of team tactics as well as inform the player recruitment process. Large datasets can be mined to identify key trends in performance across games and seasons. For a review of the major findings derived from match analyses of physical, tactical and technical performance in elite soccer competition, refer to the research of Carling and Court (2013) and Sarmento et al. (2014).

Research to refine and improve techniques and instruments for observing, measuring and evaluating match performance has been ongoing for many years, initially by coaches, later within academic institutions and more recently by commercial organizations. Simple hand notation systems later combined with analogue video recordings of play were initially developed and employed by coaches at all levels as a way to evaluate competitive performance. At elite standards, these methods have been phased out over the last two decades or so, primarily because of the emergence of information technology, digital video and electronic sensor devices.

Advances in technology have provided innovative mediums for analysis that lead to more efficient collection, processing and transmitting of data. Information is now obtained on a massive scale, leading to unprecedented opportunities to profile and benchmark match performance. Unfortunately, problems related to cost, convenience and measurement error are still common. Indeed, both developers and operators of analysis systems face many challenges, including ergonomics, size, battery life and usability (Intille et al. 2012). Similarly, any analytical technique must comply with basic quality control specifications including accuracy, objectivity, reliability and validity to create an objective and error-free account of match performance (Drust, Atkinson and Reilly 2007).

This chapter describes the analysis techniques used to collect and evaluate information on match performance. These methods include simple manual techniques and the latest in state-of-the-art computer and video technologies and portable electronic tracking devices currently employed at elite levels. The workings, strengths and shortcomings of each respective methodology are discussed.

Manual Techniques

Practitioners have employed hand-based or manual techniques since the 1950s to analyse singly or in combination, technical, tactical and physical performance in soccer match play. Before the evolution of digital video technology and computer-aided techniques for analysing performance, the most commonly employed systems were pen and paper based and involved a form of shorthand notation of match actions using tally marks or codes to represent playing actions.

Some form of shorthand was frequently required to record actions because occurrence in competition was too rapid for them to be noted manually with any degree of accuracy. Early systems generally focused on the players engaged in direct activity with the ball and covered technical and tactical aspects of performance. Information was mainly collected on three key factors: the player, the type of action and its outcome (e.g., shot on target, uncompleted pass). Positional data were often recorded on schematic pitch representations broken into numbered zones, and time was noted from a clock or stopwatch. This process generated pertinent datasets on frequencies and success rates in actions such as passing and shooting and information on attacking sequences of play that led to goals. Later on, coaches employed analogue television recordings and films of performance on videotape to review performance postmatch. Similarly, running commentaries of match events were sometimes recorded on analogue audio cassettes and subsequently transcribed for collation and analysis.

Early attempts to record physical performance involved tracing soccer player movements on a scaled plan of the playing surface to estimate distances covered. Later, manual methods included subjective assessments of distances and exercise intensities recorded manually or orally onto an audiotape recorder. A map of pitch markings was used in conjunction with visual cues around the pitch boundaries to aid the observer. Other methods employed match-play video recordings to analyse soccer player movements after individual locomotor characteristics had been preestablished according to runs performed at various exercise intensities. The time for the player to pass markers and known distances was used to quantify the speed for each activity of locomotion.

In general, manual techniques for collection of match data are relatively cheap. If they are correctly designed and observer experience is high, they can provide reliable and pertinent data sets for dissemination (Carling and Williams 2008). The development of digital video has provided small and low-cost cameras, so use of video recordings for hand-based analysis is convenient and affordable for most analysts and coaches. Manual coding methods are generally within reach of standard coaches. They are adaptable and provide information that can answer many of the questions posed about match performance.

Three early but definitive studies using manual data collection techniques greatly increased understanding of the physical (by time motion analyses of physical activity; Bangsbo, Norregaard and Thorsoe 1991; Reilly and Thomas 1976) and tactical (analysis of sequences of play leading to goals scored; Reep and Benjamin, 1968) elements of elite soccer performance. Note that manual time motion analysis techniques are still frequently used to assess running performance in elite soccer competition (Andersson et al. 2010; Mohr, Krustrup and Bangsbo 2003; Mohr et al. 2008).

Recent technological developments on earlier manual time motion analysis techniques include Sportstec's Trakperformance system (www.sportstec.com) and the TimeMotion touchscreen application (http://itunes.apple.com) created for Apple's iPhone device. Despite using contemporary technologies, these devices still require manual input from a trained operator. The former system enables a single player to be followed mechanically throughout training or competition using a computer pen and tablet on a scaled version of the playing field. Ground markings and cues around the pitch are used as reference points for tracking the players. The miniaturized playing field is calibrated so that a given movement of the mouse or mouse-pen corresponds to the linear distance travelled by the player. An early study conducted on elite soccer match play showed this system to be accurate. Real-time analysis is possible, although high levels of operator skill and experience were indispensable (Edgecomb and Norton 2006).

The TimeMotion smartphone application (figure 24.1) allows an observer to analyse physical activity profiles manually in real time. The observer simply records the time spent by players in up to six categories of running speed during a match or training session. The derived data can then be used for example to determine exercise-to-rest ratios for use within player fitness regimens (e.g., high-intensity to low-intensity exercise ratios). The application automatically collates and embeds data in a summary table and subsequently allows the user to share and visualize results, notably through contemporary information mediums such as email, SMS or Twitter.

The capture of match data through manual coding methods has its disadvantages. Coding game events is generally considered by performance analysts to be tedious, labour intensive and therefore time consuming especially if information on many actions is to be collected. Real-time analysis using pen and paper methods can be difficult because of the speed at which data can be recorded. Attention is required to make an entry on the sheet, and time is required to collate results. Early analyses of performance using analogue video footage also required slow manual searching (rewinding and fast forwarding) across recordings to visualize specific game actions. These systems had limited capability to produce edited sequences of attacking and defensive plays.

To a certain extent, manual data collection processes are also subject to inaccuracies, notably when attempting to record positional information. Moreover, manual time motion analysis techniques do not allow accurate quantification of transitional changes in running speeds such as acceleration and deceleration movements, and analysis is limited to coverage of a

▶ **Figure 24.1** The TimeMotion iPhone application interface.

Reproduced with permission from Grant Abt.

single player at a time (Carling et al. 2008). Efficient analysis, collation and archiving of data for future analysis are also difficult, especially because records are often stored on simple sheets of paper. Finally, work is necessary to transform manually collected raw data into simple but attractive and meaningful presentation formats to aid in getting the message across to practitioners. For additional examples of manual coding systems and information on the strengths and shortcomings of these processes and presentation of data, refer to books by Carling, Williams and Reilly (2005) and Hughes and Franks (2004).

Computerized and Digital Video Technologies

The use of digital video and computer technology to analyse performance in match play and more recently in training is now prominent in contemporary elite soccer. Indeed, a plethora of commercial computerized game analysis systems and software exist for soccer. A nonexhaustive list of the different types of technology currently available is presented in table 24.1. Additional information on the workings and applications of these systems can be obtained on the website of each company or in the references provided.

In general, innovations in technology over time have streamlined the entire match analysis process. Although manual logging of the majority

Table 24.1 Contemporary Commercial Soccer Match and Motion Analysis Systems

VIDEO MONTAGE OR STATISTICAL ANALYSIS SOFTWARE				
Company or institution	Country	System	Website	Research publication
Noldus Information Technology	Netherlands	Observer XT	www.noldus.com	Bloomfield, Polman and O'Donoghue 2007
Dartfish	Switzerland	Dartfish	www.dartfish.com	
Elite Sports Analysis	UK	FocusX2	www.elitesportsanalysis.com	
MasterCoach Int	Germany	PosiCap	www.mastercoach.de	
Match Analysis	US	Mambo Studio	matchanalysis.com	
Nacsport	US	Nacsport Pro	www.nacsport.com	
Performa Sports	UK	Performa Sports	www.performasports.com	
Platosport	UK	Platosport	itunes.apple.com	
Scanball	France	Scanfoot	www.scanball.com	
Sportstec	Australia	Sportscode	www.sportstec.com	
Statzpack	UK	Statzpack	www.statzpack.com	

(continued)

Table 24.1, *continued*

Company or institution	Country	System	Website	Research publication
PLAYER TRACKING TECHNOLOGY: DIGITAL VIDEO				
Cairos Technologies AG	Germany	VIS.TRACK	www.cairos.com	
Feedback Sport	New Zealand	Feedback Football	www.feedbacksport.com	
Prozone Ltd*	UK	ProZone 3	www.pzfootball.co.uk	Di Salvo et al. 2009
Spinsight Ltd	UK	Spinsight K3	www.spinsight.com	
Sport-Universal Process SA*	France	AMISCO Pro	www.sport-universal.com	Randers et al. 2010
STATS LLC	US	SportVU	www.stats.com	
Tracab	Sweden	Tracab	www.tracab.com	
University of Campinas	Brazil	Dvideo	www.unicamp.br	Barros et al. 2007
Venatrack	UK	Venatrack	www.venatrack.com	Redwood-Brown, Cranton and Sunderland 2012
PLAYER TRACKING TECHNOLOGY: GLOBAL POSITIONING SYSTEMS				
Catapult Sports#	Australia	Minimax	www.catapultsports.com	Castellano et al. 2011
GPSports#	Australia	SPI Elite	www.gpsports.com	Castagna et al. 2009
K-sport	Italy	K-sport	www.k-sport.org	
Real Track Football	Spain	Real Track Football	www.realtrackfutbol.com	Pino et al. 2007
VX Sport	New Zealand	VX340	www.vxsport.com	Buchheit et al. 2014
Statsports	Ireland	Viper	www.statsports.ie	
PLAYER TRACKING TECHNOLOGY: WIRELESS TRIANGULATION SENSORS				
CSIRO	Australia	WASP	www.csiro.au	
Inmotio Object Tracking BV	Netherlands	LPM Soccer 3D	www.inmotio.nl	Frencken, Lemmink and Delleman 2010
Fraunhofer Institute	Germany	RedFIR	www.iis.fraunhofer.de	
ZXY Sport Tracking AS	Norway	ZXY Sport Tracking	www.zxy.no	Pettersen et al. 2014
PLAYER TRACKING TECHNOLOGY: OTHER WEARABLE DEVICES				
Adidas	Germany	MiCoach Speed_Cell/X_Cell	www.adidas.com/us/micoach	Porta et al. 2012
Orthocare Innovations LLC	US	StepWatch	www.orthocareinnovations.com	Feito, Bassett and Thompson 2012
Polar	Finland	Polar s3+	www.polar.fi	Grigg, Smeathers and Wearing 2011
PLAYER TRACKING TECHNOLOGY: MANUAL SYSTEMS				
Sportstec	Australia	TrakPerformance	www.sportstec.com	Edgecombe and Norton 2006
Grant Abt	UK	TimeMotion	itunes.apple.com	

*Companies have now merged.

#GPSports recently acquired by Catapult Sports.

of technical match actions is still necessary (e.g., shots, passes, tackles), advanced user-friendly software interfaces are now routinely employed to speed up the coding and collection of performance-related data. Touchscreen devices, voice recognition technology and personal tailoring of software interfaces to restrict the quantity of data inputted according to the specific demands of coaches all play a part in reducing the time necessary to code match performance.

Live real-time analysis of match performance (see figure 24.2) on small mobile devices such as tablet computers and smartphones (e.g., see Statz-pack and Platosport on itunes.apple.com) is now a reality, and coaches can benefit from immediate access to statistics at any time during the game. The advantage of real-time analysis is the availability of data on which the coaching staff can confirm their gut feelings and make tactical changes or substitutions over the course of matches using objective evaluations of performance. The portability, ease of use and substantially lower cost of portable smartphone and tablet-based game analysis systems in providing comprehensive game analyses compared with other contemporary systems has led to their widespread adoption at elite levels.

The development of video-based semiautomatic tracking systems such as AMISCO Pro (www.sport-universal.com) and Prozone 3 (www.pzfootball. co.uk) nevertheless revolutionized the analysis of player performance in professional soccer competition in the late 1990s. These pioneer systems (the two companies have now merged) were designed to counter the problems commonly encountered when coding technical or physical performance using footage from a single camera source (e.g., television coverage, camcorder). Indeed, such analyses are generally limited to the player in possession of the ball or at best to those in close proximity to the ball. Their development was aimed at providing a means for monitoring the movement and positions of every player over the entire course of games in an unobtrusive manner. Players are passively tracked on video footage obtained from a fixed set of cameras positioned strategically to cover the entire pitch. Some manual intervention is required by an operator as interruptions in tracking processes occur because of occlusions that come about when multiple players cluster in restricted playing areas, such as in the penalty area during a corner kick. Technical actions performed by each player are concomitantly coded by operators, and results are generally available 12 to 24 hours postcompetition.

Recently, similar passive vision technologies such as Tracab (www.tracab. com) have developed enhanced image recognition algorithms that enable tracking of player activity on video in real time. The Venatrack system reportedly monitors player movements at a frequency of 25 measures per second. Accuracy rates for player identification operate at 98 per cent, and player position tracking is at 98 per cent as well (Redwood-Brown, Cranton and Sunderland 2012).

▶ Figure 24.2   The Sportscode match analysis software interface.
Reproduced with permission from Sportstec, Australia.

Four frequent inconveniences of multiple-camera vision systems are their inability to perform real-time tracking with sufficient levels of accuracy, inability to detect and track players in extreme weather conditions (e.g., during snowfall), lack of portability and relatively high cost.

Regarding the lack of portability, most teams that use these configurations nevertheless sign reciprocal agreements to share match data when playing in each other's stadiums. Unfortunately, data are unavailable when playing matches in stadiums not equipped with the same technology. Therefore, various commercial companies have developed transportable systems that, in theory, enable player performance to be monitored anywhere. The VisTrack (www.cairos.com) and Spinsight K3 (www.spinsight.com) camera systems reportedly provide real-time player tracking using portable camera configurations. The latter, for example, merges three video images into one to provide a panoramic view of the match. These portable configurations also have implications for use in monitoring training contexts. In addition, the use of the same system for training and match play analyses will eliminate discrepancies across datasets derived from different tracking technologies (Harley et al. 2011; Randers et al. 2010). Recent research attempts to provide calibration equations that allow the interchangeability of the various tracking technologies used in soccer (Buchheit et al. 2014). For additional information on workings, strengths and weaknesses and applications of these and other vision tracking systems, see the work by Barris and Button (2008); Carling, Bloomfield, Nelsen and Reilly (2008); and Leser, Baca and Ogris (2011). For a review of published time motion analysis research using computerized tracking systems (Amisco and Prozone) to analyse match running performance, see the review by Castellano, Alvarez-Pastor and Bradley (2014).

Portable Electronic Tracking Devices

Sport scientists and fitness practitioners in elite soccer clubs often quantify player movements using global positioning system (GPS) technology. GPS devices are mainly employed in training environments but are also frequently used by elite-standard clubs in preseason friendly matches and, especially, in youth competitions. These devices provide data on distance run and speed of movement through triangulation of signals emitted from satellites. Concomitantly, the devices record heart rate responses to exercise. The information derived from GPS is particularly useful for monitoring and manipulating the intensity of daily practice. The data can be used to verify whether there are imbalances in the intensity of training sessions versus the physical demands of match play. Recent versions transmit data on an entire squad of players through a wireless connection to a laptop computer or smart phone, enabling second-by-second analysis, evaluation and feedback. In addition, integrated triaxis accelerometers are used to record detailed information (currently at more than 100 measures per second) on the frequency and intensity of accelerations, decelerations and impacts between players, such as tackles and collisions. Collectively, this information enables an objective evaluation of the global physical and physiological stresses that players are subjected to during play.

The data-sampling rates used to measure distance travelled and running speed in the most recent GPS models have greatly increased—15 measures per second at the time of this writing—although some GPS reportedly use algorithmic interpolation of data collected at lower sampling rates. Increasing sampling rate has been shown to improve device validity and reliability for providing accurate assessments of running performance (Castellano et al. 2011), although contrasting evidence exists (Vickery et al. 2014). Indeed, concerns about precision and reliability subsist even in the latest models, notably in recording short bursts of high-intensity running and locomotor actions involving changes in direction (Jennings et al. 2010; Akenhead et al. 2014). Also, interunit reliability concerns, especially with earlier models, have led researchers to recommend that players wear the same device (Duffield et al. 2010). Comparisons of data collected using GPS made by the same company but sampling at different rates should not be performed (Johnston et al. 2014). Nevertheless, the size (length less than 80 millimetres), weight (less than 50 grams), logging capacity (300 hours of data), battery life (6 hours) and robustness of current devices have greatly improved since their introduction into professional soccer at the start of the last decade. For additional information on objectivity, reliability and validity in measurement issues related to time motion analysis, see Drust, Atkinson and Reilly (2007).

Other shortcomings of GPS devices include loss of satellite signals and therefore potentially incomplete datasets. Accuracy also depends on the number of available satellites and their constellation in relation to the GPS receiver. GPS devices typically do not work indoors (sports hall, stadium with closed roof), although real-time wireless transfer of accelerometer and heart rate data is currently being addressed (see statsports.ie/technology). Finally, these systems remain relatively expensive to purchase and are generally inaccessible to practitioners at lower levels of the game, although some companies propose a loan service or sell lower-frequency GPS devices (e.g., one to five measures per second) as a cheaper alternative to the latest models. For additional information, refer to the websites of two major manufacturers (Catapult at www.catapultsports.com and GPSports at www.gpsports.com) and to a paper on limitations and applications of GPS in monitoring performance by Aughey (2011).

An alternative to GPS is a local wireless tracking system that uses signals sent from small lightweight microchip transmitters worn by players. Such a setup enables real-time data acquisition, evaluation and presentation. Configurations such as the RedFIR (www.iis.fraunhofer.de) and Local Positioning Measurement system (LPM, www.inmotio.nl) collect information on the movements and positions of every player and the ball up to several hundred times per second. Signals from the electronic tags are picked up by antennas placed around the playing area under observation. Receiver units process the collected signals and determine their time of arrival. Based on a calculation of the differences in propagation delay, each transmitters position is then continuously determined. Independent testing of the LPM system capacity to measure positional information, distances and changes in running speed has demonstrated high levels of accuracy in static and dynamic movement situations (Frencken, Lemmink and Delleman 2010; Stevens et al. 2014).

Although these systems also enable the collection of data on heart rate responses to exercise, current competition rules restrict their usage to training contexts, friendly matches and youth competitions. In addition, up until recently, the system required a fixed installation of base receiver stations linked by a fibre optic cable network around a single training pitch. When players trained on a different pitch in their training facility, game activity could not always be monitored. Cost is also again a major issue, although research is currently being conducted internationally to develop similar yet lower-priced transportable local wireless systems (see www.csiro.au).

Alternatively, note that time motion information on physical effort can be captured (rules permitting) at a relatively lower cost to GPS or local wireless systems using small accelerometer-based devices strapped unobtrusively to the athlete. For example, physical activity monitors strapped to the ankle have been used to monitor and record the number of steps performed over set time intervals. Subsequently, the duration and intensity of work bouts in amateur soccer match play were determined (Orendurff et al. 2010). Running sensors (for example the Polar s3+, see www.polar.fi) can be attached to or, as in the case of Adidas miCoach (see www.micoach.adidas.com), placed inside a specially designed cavity in adapted footwear. Information on movement speed and distance travelled is transmitted, stored and displayed in real time on compatible wrist-held computers or smart phone devices. The price of these sensors is now within the reach of clubs and players at lower standards, although research is needed to determine their scientific legitimacy for measuring physical performance both accurately and reliably. For additional information on contemporary sensor technologies, see a recent review paper (Intille et al. 2012) and online research performed by the Elite Sport Performance Research in Training group (see www.uksport.gov.uk).

End-User Software

Irrespective of the technology employed to collect information on match performance, most contemporary systems provide end user software that enables seamless integration, collation, analysis and attractive graphical output of results. Numerous presentation possibilities exist including simple table summaries. Graphs and spatial pitch representations such as heat maps are available at the click of a button. Contemporary tracking systems also provide an opportunity to create two-dimensional animations of match play to recreate the game in its entirety combined with simultaneous digital video recordings (figure 24.3). Some also enable novel three-dimensional representations that allow virtual embedding of the user in the game and visualization of play from the player's or coach's viewpoint.

During the coding process, automatic event indexing with the digital time code allows analysts and coaches to access and visualize any action over the course of a game instantaneously. Edited high-quality digital video compilations of defensive and attacking plays can be readily produced. Dedicated digital video training applications such as Dartfish (www.dartfish.com) also provide opportunities for high-quality, slow-motion playback and the creation of special effects such as synchronized split-screen visualisation,

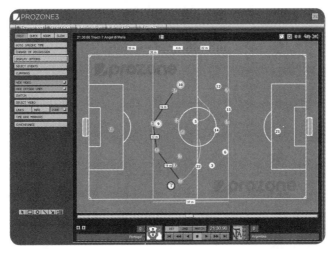

▶ **Figure 24.3**   A two-dimensional recreation of play using the ProZone player tracking system.

Reproduced with permission from Prozone, UK.

image blending and drawing effects to break down and compare actions. Game analysis software such as Sportscode (www.sportstec.com) allows immediate uploading of exported data or video compilations onto the world wide web or for use in commercial multimedia presentation programmes. Raw data outputs can easily be imported into other spreadsheet or statistical analysis software. Similarly, compatibility across end-user platforms allows information on physical performance (e.g., distances covered and heart rate data) derived from portable electronic tracking devices such as GPS or wireless transmitters to be imported, synchronized and visualized simultaneously with technical and tactical data and video compilations of game events.

Database technologies (for example, the Trend online database software on www.prozonesports.com) provide possibilities to create benchmarks and monitor trends in performance using physical, technical and tactical data for teams and individuals. Data can readily be compared, cross-tabulated and visualized in numerous formats such as time (e.g., total time spent in possession in opponent's half), distance (e.g., distance run at high intensities), speed (e.g., mean and peak sprinting speed), counts (e.g., total number of final-third entries), percentages (e.g., proportion of completed passes) and ratios (e.g., number of set plays in relation to goals scored directly from set plays).

Databases enable the user to search, cross-tabulate, compare and display results across a defined number of games, such as over the last five matches or an entire season, or perform a cross-seasonal analysis. Similarly, online databases aid in player recruitment by allowing the mining of technical and tactical data combined with edited digital video compilations of performance (for examples see www.sport-universal.com, info.scout7.com and www.optasports.com). Detailed statistical information on a potential recruit can be compared against benchmark data for a club's own players or against league averages internationally for players in the same playing position. This facility is especially useful if a club is looking for a specific type of player to strengthen its squad and for an objective assessment of how the player might perform and adapt to the demands of a new league.

Conclusion

This chapter covers techniques used in collecting data on match performance, including sensors attached to equipment (e.g., stride sensors) or to the player's body (e.g., GPS receivers), technology embedded in the local environment (e.g., multiple-camera approach) and hand-based game analyses. Current match analysis technologies are constantly being supplanted by new or improved devices, especially in terms of size and convenience and the quantity and variety of data they provide. Smart clothes and footwear in which performance sensors are embedded are a major step in this direction, although their scientific legitimacy has yet to be satisfactorily established. The lower cost of many emerging and existing technologies has also increased their availability to coaches at all standards of the game. Future developments will likely involve real-time simultaneous capture of information from multiple sensors (biochemical information, heart rate and brain wave patterns, muscle activity, joint speed, contact forces and running speed) combined with intelligent systems that analyse and interpret the masses of complex data to aid the feedback and decision-making processes.

CHAPTER 25

Statistical Evaluations in Soccer

—Ron Smith

The analysis of soccer performance can be undertaken in several areas. For example, physiological analysis may focus on the performance of the cardiovascular system or yield information concerning the efficiency of the energy systems during the same performance. A psychological perspective might relate to the mental preparedness of a player or yield information concerning coping strategies during competitive match play. Although each type of analysis differs in the theoretical basis from which enquiries are generated, one critical element remains invariant. They all converge on one behavioural outcome that has meaning within the context of the sport performance under examination (McGarry and Franks 1994). Quantitative analysis describes the performance at this behavioural level of analysis. It involves the objective evaluation of a player's performance during match play.

A considerable amount of research into soccer performance has been devoted to establishing the need for quantitative forms of analysis (Franks and Miller 1986, 1991). As the sophistication of technological notation systems has increased, so has the depth of analysis, to the point that complex playing patterns and tactics can now be traced and analysed.

Analysis of soccer performance usually infers that the competitive situation includes some inherent organization and predictability. An assumption is also made that the events being analysed have a certain amount of structure and follow one another in a sequential manner. If these assumptions are false, then anything is possible. Nonetheless, the game of soccer appears to have a certain amount of organization. Several lines of research into match analysis have provided evidence to suggest that the events of soccer are not completely random (Reep and Benjamin 1968; Bate 1988).

Because the events of soccer have a certain amount of organization, identifying patterns of play that yield favourable profits will provide the coach with valuable information concerning match strategy.

In soccer play, scoring a goal is usually regarded as the most important feature of the game. Therefore, the majority of match analysis and tactics employed in soccer have been related to attacking play. This chapter further develops the area of goal analysis and identifies the critical parameters that precede goals being scored. Analysis is performed from the viewpoint of technique and tactics, and a different strategic element is introduced, which is supported by data from international and English Premier League soccer. The information concerns the key factors responsible for successful performance in soccer. In addition, previous data are critically examined and integrated with current analysis.

The take-home messages provide suggestions to players and coaches on interpreting the available research to improve individual and team performance. The information detailed in this chapter has been drawn from various sources and produced by respected analysts. Tables provide an in-depth analysis of the material. These data will appeal to people involved in analysis support or research. Comparisons are made between past and more recent analysis on events that precede goal scoring because monitoring known variables can confirm consistencies in performance or identify changes that occur over time, however subtle they might be.

Useable Information

At an elite level of play, an enormous amount of data about a team's performance is constantly generated. Some coaches now have first-hand experience using sport analytics to improve player and team performance. Sports analytics are the extensive use of data, statistical and quantitative analysis, explanatory and predictive models and fact-based management to drive actions and decisions (Davenport and Harris 2007).

The methods by which analytics have been collected have varied from a simple tick or cross to a complex notation system that has to be decoded post event. Clearly, a critical feature of the analytics process is the management and use of the data. For data to be useful, the practitioner must be able to understand and make use of the information. Data gathering can be expensive, time consuming and futile unless it is used to drive the coaching process. In the past, match analysis has tended to focus on characteristics of soccer match play that are simple, objective and interesting, but not always the sort that a coach might be able to apply in a practical way. For example, analysis shows that more goals are scored with five or fewer passes, but would that information discourage you from keeping possession for more than six passes? In addition, analysis can inform us when goals are scored during different periods during the game, but would you plan to score just before half-time rather than in the opening 15 minutes?

In this sense analysis provides information that can be categorized as either useful or useable. The information that many goals are scored in the 15 minutes before half-time is useful and might encourage a higher level of concentration during this period in a match, but it's not practical to implement at training. The information that approximately 80 per cent of goals in open play are scored from inside the penalty area and with one or two touches is useable information that can be implemented at training by setting the same conditions in practices.

With the useable concept in mind, new criteria were employed in the formulation of this research to analyse the goals scored in open play in international tournaments and the English Premier League (EPL) for the 2011–2012 season. The criteria distinguished three types of goals:

1. Goals scored from passing the ball behind the opposing defence or to a player level with the last defender
2. Goals scored from in front of defenders or by dribbling past the last line of defence
3. Goals scored from crosses, which were defined as coming from outside the penalty area and within 18 metres of the goal line

A critical element in the research was to determine whether passing the ball behind the defence was the dominant method of scoring goals and, if so, which area of the field provided the most final passes. This strategic information could be implemented at training within any soccer philosophy and system of play, making it highly useable. In short, this information can drive decisions and actions and therefore improve player and team performance.

For the purpose of the research, data were collected from the World Cups from 1998 to 2014, the European Championships from 2004 to 2012, the Asian Cup in 2011 and the EPL in 2011–2012 to make comparisons between the various tournaments and between international and club soccer. The analysis presented is primarily on goals scored in open play, but some information is also provided on goals scored from set plays.

The conclusion provides a summary of the analysis, some comments for coaches to consider when doing match analysis and some specific comments about the application of the research outcomes, which are logical deductions from the evidence provided in the text. In addition, practices are included for coaches and players to implement the useable information at training.

Common Research Topics and Procedures

Match analysis tends to focus on aspects of play that can be counted, measured or timed because the results are based on evidence, not opinion. Historically, goals have been separated into two categories: open play and set play. However, the reporting of information has often included results from goals in open play and set play, which can be slightly misleading, as will be demonstrated later in the chapter.

Analysis has provided detailed information such as the number of passes made before a goal was scored, the time in possession before each goal was scored, the time during the match when each goal was scored, the number of touches taken by the goal scorer and whether the scorer was inside or outside the penalty area.

Other topics have focused on where possession was regained in terms of the thirds of the field, the areas of the field where the final pass was made and how many goals were scored from crosses, a topic that will be referred to in detail later in the chapter. The characteristics of successful and unsuccessful teams have also been given considerable attention.

A common practice is to repeat the analysis of particular topics in World Cup tournaments to see whether the nature of soccer has changed or whether predictions can be made about what is likely to happen in the future.

A Case for Separating Data From Goals in Open Play and From Set Plays

Analysis of events preceding goals scored in open play and from set plays shows a noticeable difference. For example, goals scored with one touch in open play have a wide range, from 44 per cent (World Cup 1998 the lowest) to 82 per cent (Euro 2008 the highest), but a much tighter and higher range from 81 per cent (Euro 2004) to 100 per cent (Euro 2008) from set plays.

Goals scored with headers in open play range from 12 per cent (Euro 2004 and World Cup 2014) to 21 per cent (Euro 2012) but much higher, from 33 per cent (Asia Cup 2011) to 75 per cent, from set plays. The 75 per cent recorded in the Euro 2012 was an exception; the average was 46 per cent for all the other tournaments. If headed goals from open play and set plays are combined, the range is 20 to 30 per cent, which represents a different picture completely.

The number of goals scored in open play from moves of five or fewer passes ranges from 62 per cent (Euro 2012) to 82 per cent (Euro 2004). If set plays are included, the figures rise by 5 to 10 per cent because most goals from set plays are scored with fewer than five passes, such as direct free kicks into the goal and penalties, or from one-pass moves, such as corner kicks and free kicks played into the penalty area. See table 25.1.

Table 25.1 Summary of Match Analysis From International Tournaments

Open play (OP) Set plays (SP)	World Cup 1998	World Cup 2002	World Cup 2006	World Cup 2010	World Cup 2014	Euro 2004	Euro 2008	Euro 2012	Asia Cup 2011
One-touch goals OP	49; 44%	78; 68%	46; 49%	62; 58%	70; 57%	31; 63%	49; 82%	35; 57%	38; 60%
One-touch goals SP	36; 86%	31; 97%	52; 96%	25; 86%	30; 91%	17; 81%	13; 100%	11; 92%	17; 94%
Total without penalties	85; 55%	109; 74%	98; 75%	87; 64%	100; 64%	48; 68%	62; 85%	46; 63%	55; 68%
Total with pens	102; 60%	123; 76%	111; 75%	97; 67%	112; 67%	55; 71%	66; 86%	49; 64%	64; 71%
Inside pen. area	137; 89%	123; 84%	106; 79%	99; 73%	138; 88%	66; 94%	67; 92%	64; 88%	68; 84%
Outside pen. area	17; 11%	24; 16%	28; 21%	36; 27%	18; 12%	4; 6%	6; 8%	9; 12%	13; 16%
Excluding pens and including set plays	154 17; 90%	147 14; 85%	134 13; 81%	135 10; 75%	156 12; 89%	70 7; 95%	73 4; 92%	73 3; 88%	81 9; 86%
Including pens in total	171	161	147	145	168	77	77	76	90
Open play	112; 65%	115; 71%	93; 63%	106; 73%	123; 73%	49; 64%	60; 78%	61; 80%	62; 69%
Set plays	42; 25%	32; 20%	41; 28%	29; 20%	33; 20%	21; 27%	13; 17%	12; 16%	19; 21%
Penalties	17; 10%	14; 9%	13; 9%	10; 7%	12; 7%	7; 9%	4; 5%	3; 4%	9; 10%
Total	171	161	147	145	168	77	77	76	90
5 or fewer passes in OP	88; 79%	61; 73%	72; 77%	78; 77%	87; 71%	40; 82%	46; 77%	38; 62%	46; 73%
4 or fewer passes in OP	80; 71%	55; 66%	62; 67%	70; 66%	83; 67%	37; 75%	44; 73%	34; 56%	41; 65%
Goals from regain possession in OP: Back third	33; 29%	34; 30%	21; 23%	26; 25%	41; 34%	16; 33%	15; 25%	17; 28%	17; 27%
Own half, M 3rd	26; 23%	22; 19%	32; 34%	27; 25%	31; 25%	10; 22%	27; 45%	9; 15%	13; 21%
Their half, M 3rd	30; 27%	23; 20%	15; 16%	33; 31%	25; 20%	15; 29%	8; 13%	18; 29%	16; 26%
Midfield total	56; 50%	45; 39%	47; 50%	60; 56%	56; 45%	25; 51%	35; 58%	27; 44%	29; 47%
Attacking third	23; 21%	36; 31%	25; 27%	20; 19%	26; 21%	8; 16%	10; 17%	17; 28%	16; 26%
Crosses: two areas	18; 16%	32; 39%	12; 13%	14; 13%	21; 17%	7; 14%	17; 28%	12; 20%	10; 16%
Headers in OP	14; 13%	20; 17%	12; 13%	18; 17%	15; 12%	6; 12%	8; 13%	13; 21%	10; 16%
Headers in set plays	18; 43%	15; 47%	18; 44%	10; 34%	19; 58%	11; 52%	7; 54%	9; 75%	6; 33%
No. as % of all goals excluding penalties	32; 20%	35; 24%	30; 22%	28; 21%	34; 22%	17; 24%	15; 20%	22; 30%	16; 20%

If analysis for regained possessions in the final third includes goals scored from set plays, the results are significantly higher than percentages in open play. For example, the figure for regained possessions in Euro 2004 increases from 16 per cent (table 25.1) to 44 per cent, so distinguishing between the figures is important when using them as a point of reference. See table 25.2.

For analysing events that precede goals scored, differentiating between open play and set play is important so that coaches can make appropriate comparisons.

Table 25.2 Percentage of Goals Scored From Regained Possession in Back Third, Middle Third and Final Third of the Field Including Set Plays

	World Cup 1998	World Cup 2002	World Cup 2006	World Cup 2010	World Cup 2014	Euro 2004	Euro 2008	Euro 2012	Asia Cup 2011
Regained in final third	82; 48%	80; 50%	74; 50%	54; 37%	71; 42%	34; 44%	26; 34%	32; 42%	43; 48%
Open play	23	36	25	20	26	8	10	17	16
Set plays	59	44	49	34	45	26	16	15	27
Regained in middle third	56; 33%	47; 29%	52; 36%	65; 45%	56; 33%	27; 35%	36; 46%	27; 36%	30; 33%
Regained in back third	33; 19%	34; 21%	21; 14%	26; 18%	41; 25%	16; 21%	15; 20%	17; 22%	17; 19%
Total goals	171	161	147	145	168	77	77	76	90

NB. Two set plays regained outside final third in World Cup 2002.

Five set plays regained outside final third in World Cup 2006 and 2010.

Two set plays regained outside final third in Euro 2004 and one in 2008.

One set play regained outside final third in Asia Cup 2011.

Number of Passes Preceding Goals

Charles Reep developed the classical methodology for data collection and statistical analysis in soccer in the 1950s. Reep developed a comprehensive shorthand system for recording events and outcomes of match play. The Reep system was primarily developed to break down the continuous movement of a soccer game into a series of discrete on-the-ball events. Data on passing movements for professional soccer teams in England were compiled over a 15-year period. With the accumulation of so much data, Reep and Benjamin (1968) revealed compelling evidence for the probability of certain behaviours, such as number of passes and shots at goal, to adhere to a well-established mathematical function (negative binominal). The general finding from their analysis was that random chance plays a significant role in determining match outcome. This conclusion led Reep and Benjamin to the reasoned assumption that the patterns of play most likely to yield favourable probabilities should be maximized to the exclusion of the less profitable actions. The patterns of play identified by Reep and Benjamin have had profound implications on the development of match strategy in soccer play.

The number of consecutive passes that a team made before scoring was analysed by Reep and Benjamin (1968). They found that 98 per cent of all goals scored in the English Football League from 1953 to 1967 were scored from passing sequences of three or fewer passes. These findings have remained impressively stable over time. Bate (1988), in conjunction with Charles Hughes, collected data on international games in the 1980s. He reported that 94 per cent of goals scored at all levels of international soccer were scored from movements involving four or fewer passes. Bate further recommended,

> *Whilst there may be times in games that a team deliberately attempts to keep possession at all costs, if the aim is to score goals then the ball must be played forward into the attacking third regularly, accurately and as economically as possible with regard to the number of passes made in each passing movement.*
>
> (Bate 1988, 298)

The evidence that most goals are scored with a low number of passes has continued to fuel the debate regarding the merits of direct play and possession-based soccer and has prompted analysts to look at frequencies of events. When the number of attempts at goal from 'moves of five or fewer passes' are compared with the number of attempts at goal from 'moves of six or more passes', the former is higher, as might be expected, because most teams have more possessions of five or fewer passes than possessions of six or more passes. But when the frequency of events is normalized, at per thousand possessions, the results demonstrate that more attempts at goal are produced from longer passing sequences. The fact remains that during a game, more possessions consist of five or fewer passes, so more goals are scored with fewer passing moves.

Goals Scored With Five or Fewer Passes

The general finding from much of the early work on quantitative soccer analysis was that random chance plays a significant role in determining the outcome of a match. Data on goal scoring showed that most goals were a result of three or fewer passes and from regained possessions in the attacking third, partly because defenders had difficulty clearing long forward passes into the goal-scoring area. The adoption of playing the ball quickly into the goal-scoring area from long distance has come to be known in English soccer as direct play.

In 1990 Charles Hughes, the FA director of national coaching, produced a book and series of videotapes in an attempt to identify the common denominators of the best teams. *The Winning Formula* provided evidence to show that a large percentage of the total goals scored at all levels of international competition are scored from passing sequences of five or fewer passes. Hughes reasoned that although soccer is concerned with passing sequences, the achievement of a long sequence of passes is not the most effective strategy in the scoring of goals. For Hughes, the most effective strategy for scoring goals is to play the ball forward as regularly and as soon as possible. Moreover, Hughes maintained that when possession is gained, the ball should be played into the opposition's danger area, because they will be at their most vulnerable when they have just lost the ball.

Direct play often involves long forward passes into spaces behind the opposing defenders. The important factor here is that not only are long passes made behind defenders but also that other team members are in positions to receive the ball or are in positions that will allow them to challenge for the ball. Teams that adopt this direct style of play tend to have a high level of fitness because all members strive to keep play compact. The reason for maintaining compactness is that data have also shown that if teams win possession in their defending third of the field, they have a higher probability of losing that possession in their own half of the field if opposing players can apply pressure. The concept of regaining possession is further examined later in the chapter.

Much of the impetus for direct play has originated from descriptive statements of analysis concerning how goals are scored. But a coach who reads into descriptive statements concerning how goals are scored will not necessarily have the blueprint for successful soccer performance. Before implementing tactics and strategy, the coach must carefully think through all the ramifications of these descriptive statements.

Not surprisingly, direct play recommendations have been met with a great deal of resistance, especially from coaches who advocate a possession-based approach to soccer. The merits of possession-based soccer are supported by the fact that international teams such as Brazil, the most successful team in World Cup history, have adopted a possession-based style of soccer. The fact that Brazil scores more goals from five or fewer passes has done little to diminish support of this style of play.

Could it be that Hughes had discovered something that happened in soccer, that most goals were scored from five or fewer passes, regardless of how it was played? Hughes (1990) reported that 87 per cent of goals scored in open play and from set plays were from passing sequences of five or fewer passes in matches analysed before and during the 1980s. In the five World Cups since 1998 the figures were 85 per cent, 86 per cent, 86 per cent, 81 per cent and 79 per cent. Similar trends can be seen in European Championships. The point is that regardless of playing style 80 per cent or more goals are likely to be scored with five or fewer passes if set plays are included. See table 25.3.

In Hughes' analysis of 84 goals, 42 per cent were scored in open play with five or fewer passes. The figure has increased in most international tournaments since 1998 with a range of 49 per cent (WC 2006) to 60 per cent (Euro 2008) with one exception when the figure was 38 per cent (WC 2002).

Note that the percentage of goals scored in open play from passing sequences of six or more also increased from around 14 per cent in tournaments up to 2006 to an all-time high of 30 per cent in Euro 2012. These figures show a definite upward trend for goals scored from longer passing sequences.

Table 25.3   Goals Scored From Five or Fewer Passes

	Hughes 1990	World Cup 1998	World Cup 2002	World Cup 2006	World Cup 2010	World Cup 2014	Euro 2004	Euro 2008	Euro 2012	Asia Cup 2011
Open play	84; 42%	85; 50%	61; 38%	72; 49%	78; 54%	87; 52%	40; 52%	46; 60%	38; 50%	46; 51%
Set plays	92; 45%	59; 35%	78; 48%	54; 37%	39; 27%	45; 27%	28; 36%	17; 22%	15; 20%	27; 30%
Sub-total	176; 87%	147; 85%	139; 86%	126; 86%	117; 81%	132; 79%	68; 88%	63; 82%	53; 70%	73; 81%
6+ passes	26; 13%	27; 15%	22; 14%	21; 14%	28; 19%	36; 21%	9; 12%	14; 18%	23; 30%	17; 19%
Total	202	171	161	147	145	168	77	77	76	90

Possession and Success Rates

For many coaches and players the risk of playing possession soccer in their own half is too high because losing the ball near your own goal often leads to conceding goals. Therefore, players are encouraged to employ a pragmatic approach and play the ball up field rather than through the midfield.

One of the negatives that arise from analysing isolated events from different matches is that frequencies of events from a whole match are rarely included and for good reason. Assessing frequencies of events like success rates of moving the ball from the back third through midfield to the final third involves considerable time and effort, so the analysis is not often done.

Personal research conducted of Spain and Brazil in the Confederations Cup Final in 2013 to calculate success rates of playing from their back third and own half to the final third of the field revealed close to 30 per cent for both teams. Similar figures came out of the analysis of Bayern Munich versus Borussia Dortmund in the final of the European Championship in 2013.

For two top national teams and two top clubs in Europe, achieving a 30 per cent success rate is surprising, but how many regained possessions in the match occurred in their back third and how often did either team try to play through midfield?

For coaches who want to analyse their team's performance in any aspect of play, success rates and the number of attempts should be included as well as the actual numbers associated with the event. Obviously, doing this is easier and more efficient using computer software, but using a pen and paper can still be effective.

After you start to record where you regained possession of the ball, you will ask yourself, How do I define having possession? Does winning a header from a long ball constitute having possession, or is it more than that?

Having control over the ball might be a better definition, and that could include first-time passing as long as there is intent, which is a judgement call. If you want to record the attempts to play from the back third to reach the final third, the key components that need to be identified are where you play in each third of the field. See table 25.4.

By ticking the boxes or writing a letter (e.g., B to indicate the third of the field where possession was regained and a tick in B3 to indicate play in the back third, followed by play in own half), calculations can be made quite easily to ascertain the number of regained possessions in each third of the

Table 25.4 Sample Record Sheet for Regained Possession and Play in Each Third of the Field

Time	Third of field	Long ball	B3	OH	TH	F3	<5 passes	6+ passes	Notes
1	B	/							Goal kick
3	OH		/	/	/		/		Throw-in
4	B		/	/	/	/		/	Shot saved
5	OH	/	/	/			/		
7	B		/	/	/	/	/		Counter, won corner
8	TH			/	/	/			Goal

B3: back third; OH: own half of midfield; TH: their half of midfield; F3: final third field, the number of attempts to play through midfield and the success rates of reaching the opponent's half of midfield or the attacking third. If you want to record the number of long balls and where they were played or count the number of passes in each possession, just add a column. A note can indicate what happened when the ball goes out of play.

The critical issue with using pen and paper methods to do match analysis is the limited extent to record information, which is why computerized systems are so much more efficient. Computers also allow you to view the selected incidents if you just want chunks of the game to review before getting into the finer detail to see why you lost possession.

Goals Scored From Regained Possessions in the Attacking or Final Third

Imagine a situation in which possession is regained in the final third. Think of one before reading any further.

I have asked hundreds of coaches to do this exercise, and without exception they described a situation in open play. In the aforementioned research by Hughes, it was reported that 52 per cent of goals were scored from regained possessions in the attacking or final third of the field, thus advocating a defensive strategy of pressurizing opponents as quickly as possible to win back possession. The strategy was based on the goal-to-regained-possession ratio in each third of the field, in which the final third had the highest return of 1:34.

Unfortunately, the ratio of goals to regained possessions in the final third makes no distinction between regained possession in open play or from set plays. Penalties and free kicks are a result of fouls by the opposition, not a result of pressuring opponents. Similarly, few corners are conceded when a team has possession of the ball. So facts can easily be misinterpreted because we all make assumptions about what we think has happened. If it makes sense, we don't question our decision; it's a function of the cognitive processes within the brain. See table 25.5.

Table 25.5   Goals and Regained Possessions in Open Play and Set Plays

	Goals scored in 109 matches, including 92 from set plays Total = 202	Goals scored in open play Total = 110
Regained in attacking third	106; 52%	14; 13%
Regained in middle third	60; 30%	60; 54%
Regained in back third	36; 18%	36; 33%

Assuming that all 92 goals scored from set plays restarted in the attacking third, which is most likely, then only 14 goals, 13 per cent, were scored in open play from regained possession in the final third. The difference between 13 and 52 per cent is considerable.

Like the coaches whom I asked to imagine a situation in which possession was regained in the final third, I visualized a situation in open play. I realized I had mistakenly assumed that all the goals had been scored in open play only through doing match analysis of the topic. The difference in results was so great it motivated me to find out why.

Hughes' figure of 13 per cent is slightly less than the proportion of goals scored from regained possessions in the final third in open play in more recent international tournaments, where the range is 16 to 31 per cent. See table 25.1.

Although the trend in this category is upward in international soccer, remember that Hughes' analysis included a mixture of club teams as well as youth and senior international teams.

Calculating Percentages

Note the manner in which percentages are calculated. For example, 36 of 161 equals 22 per cent of the total goals scored, including set plays, but 36 of 83 equals 43 per cent of all goals scored in open play, which is almost double the original figure.

Figures quoted to players to encourage pressuring in the opposition's back third should be realistic and relevant to the competition the team is in; an average of 26 per cent of goals scored in open play have come from regained possession in the final third in World Cups since 1998. See table 25.6.

In the World Cup 2010, Spain scored seven goals in open play but didn't score from a regained possession in the final third. Comparing individual teams with the results of all teams can highlight differences, which drives more analysis.

Goals From Regained Possession in the Back and Middle Thirds

Table 25.1 shows that in international soccer the number of goals scored in open play from regained possessions in the back third ranges from 23 to 34 per cent. A greater variation can be seen in the middle third, where the range is 39 to 58 per cent. In the EPL in 2011–2012 the figures for each third of the field were 25, 41 and 34 per cent, respectively, all within ranges similar to those in international soccer. See table 25.7.

The fact that the majority of goals are still scored with five or fewer passes and that roughly 25 per cent originate in the back third shows that quick forward movement of the ball by passing or running with it is a key indicator of successful play. Therefore, practices that facilitate quick transition from defence to attack, that is, with direction, will be more meaningful

Table 25.6   Goals Scored From Regained Possession in the Final Third (F3)

Competition	Goals regained in F3	Goals regained in F3 as % of total	Goals regained in F3 in open play as % of total goals in OP	Goals regained in F3 in open play as % of total goals
World Cup 1998	42 (SP) + 17 (P) + 23 (OP) = 82	82/171 = 48%	23/112 = 21%	23/171 = 13%
World Cup 2002	30 (SP) + 14 (P) + 36 (OP) = 80	80/161 = 50%	36/83 = 43%	36/161 = 22%
World Cup 2006	36 (SP) + 13 (P) + 25 (OP) = 74	74/147 = 51%	25/93 = 27%	25/147 = 17%
World Cup 2010	24 (SP) + 10 (P) + 20 (OP) = 54	54/145 = 37%	20/106 = 19%	20/145 = 14%
World Cup 2014	33 (SP) + 12 (P) + 26 (OP) = 71	71/168 = 42%	26/123 = 21%	26/168 = 15%
Euro 2004	20 (SP) + 7 (P) + 8 (OP) = 35	35/77 = 45%	8/49 = 16%	8/77 = 10%
Euro 2008	12 (SP) + 4 (P) + 10 (OP) = 26	26/77 = 34%	10/60 = 17%	10/77 = 13%
Euro 2012	12 (SP) + 3 (P) + 17 (OP) = 32	32/76 = 42%	17/61 = 28%	17/76 = 22%
Asia Cup 2011	18 (SP) + 9 (P) + 16 (OP) = 43	43/90 = 48%	16/63 = 25%	16/90 = 18%

SP: set plays; P: penalties; OP: open play.

Table 25.7   Goals Scored in Open Play From Regained Possession in Each Third of the Field for the EPL in 2011–2012

	Regained in back third	Regained in OH of midfield	Regained in TH of midfield	Total regained in midfield	Regained in final third	Total goals in open play
EPL 2011–2012	201; 25%	151; 19%	175; 22%	326; 41%	265; 34%	792
Man Utd	15; 22%	8; 11%	15; 22%	23; 33%	31; 45%	69
Man City	22; 32%	12; 17%	16; 23%	28; 40%	19; 28%	69
Arsenal	16; 24%	14; 22%	13; 20%	27; 42%	22; 34%	65

OH: own half of midfield third; TH: their half of midfield third.

than practices that only emphasize keeping possession. See the possession practice with direction drill.

Possession Practices With Direction

Objectives

- Create a numerical advantage, such as 5v2, and provide direction.
- Encourage forward passing, forward runs and quick transition.
- Encourage supporting positions so that players are level with as well as outside opponents and can see players at the other end of the grid.

Rules

- In a group of nine players, five keep possession against two opponents in one end of the grid while an attacker and a defender stay at the other end (figure 25.1). The size of the grid can be changed to suit player ability.
- After three or four passes, the ball and some of the players (one of the defenders and four of the attackers) move into the other end to make 5v2 again. This activity repeats for 60 to 90 seconds, and then three defenders change with three attackers.
- If the defenders win the ball or kick it out of play, a new ball is given to the attackers and play continues.

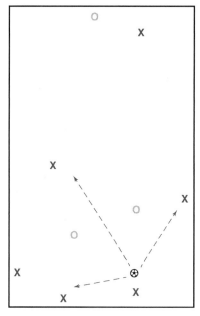

▶ **Figure 25.1** Possession practice with direction.

Variations

- Increase the number of players to 10 with 2v1 at the other end or to 11 players with 2v2 at the other end.
- Make the area bigger or introduce one- or two-touch or other variation.

Progressions

- Start with 4v2 or 5v2 in each end (12 to 14 players). The aim is to take the ball from one end to the opposite end zone to score (figure 25.2).
- Passing or taking the ball over the halfway line allows players to run into the other end to make 5v5 to reach the end zone.
- If defenders win the ball in their own half and pass quickly to the other end when the odds are 2v2, they can attack with a 3v2 advantage; that is, defenders are not allowed back into their own half (quick transition).
- Play 5v3 in each half and use one or two goalkeepers.
- Increase the size of the end zone or use a portable goal at one end or both ends.

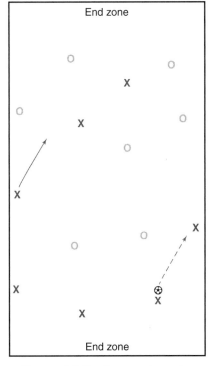

▶ **Figure 25.2** Progression of possession practice with direction: 12 to 14 players (4v2 or 5v2).

- Allow players to drop into the end zone to start the practice without too much pressure to pass forwards or run forwards with the ball.
- Defenders in the opponent's half cannot press in the end zone or drop into the 10-metre zone near the halfway line before a pass is made.
- If a pass goes between the defenders in the opponent's half, the midfield player Y1 can go over the halfway line to challenge R1 (figure 25.3).
- Introduce two midfield players for both teams, with one in each half.
- Allow midfield players to defend in the opponent's half of the field to exert more pressure and increase realism.
- Give the player starting the practice the choice of playing a long pass to a teammate in the opponent's half.
- Encourage players to look for opportunities to pass the ball into the end zone.

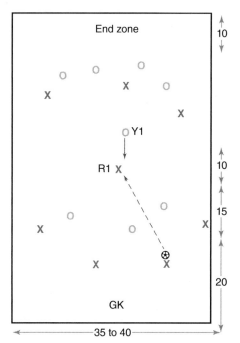

▶ **Figure 25.3** Progression of possession practice with direction: going over the halfway line to challenge.

Analysis shows that successful teams in World Cup finals (top eight teams) are better at maintaining possession, making more consecutive forward movements with the ball, dribbling, scoring goals from regained possession from any area of the field and playing through the central areas of the field. They have a better ratio of goals to strikes at goal, usually less than 1:10.

The ability to play through central areas of the field, particularly in the opponent's half, where space is often limited, may indicate superior passing, dribbling and receiving technique or supporting players moving more quickly into position.

Most goals are scored from inside the penalty area, so attention has focused on the areas of the field where the final pass is made. Dividing the field into 18 equal parts and monitoring where the final passes are made shows that the area just outside the penalty area, referred to as Zone 14, is the most productive.

Scoring From Behind or in Front of Opponents and From Crosses

Research analysed where the final pass was made, although with the number of areas reduced from 18 to 7. See figure 25.4.

The analysis considered the position of the last line of defence because goals are scored from either side of it. The last line of defence can be anywhere between the halfway line and the goal line. To consider this, a new area was created and referred to as zone 14+.

One of the critical objectives was to determine the success of playing the ball behind the opposing back line or to a player level with the last line of defence who could shoot or take the ball forwards. The term *playing the ball behind a defender* has more than one interpretation. As play gets closer to the goal line, there is less space between the last defenders and the goal line, so a pass over a defender's head into the space between defenders is interpreted as going behind the last defender.

To determine where the passes were made from, the seven areas of the field were described as own half (OH), wide right (WR), wide left (WL), left crossing area (LC), right crossing area (RC), zone 14+ (Z14+) and inside the penalty area (IPA).

The crossing areas are from outside the penalty area and up to 18 metres from the goal line on each side of the field. The wide left and right areas are from outside the width of the penalty area and from the end of the crossing area to the halfway line. Zone 14+ includes the area from the halfway line to the edge of the penalty area and within the width of the penalty area. Inside the penalty area (IPA) is the final area.

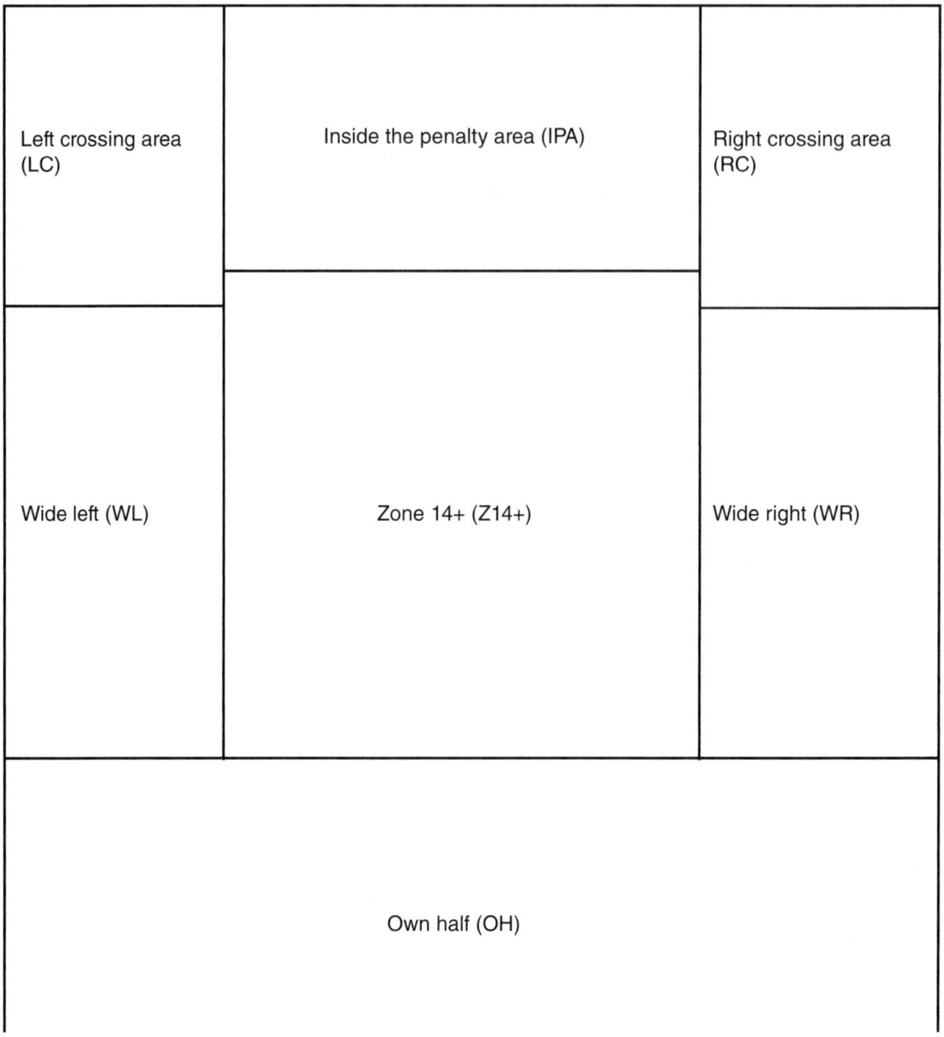

Left crossing area (LC)	Inside the penalty area (IPA)		Right crossing area (RC)
Wide left (WL)	Zone 14+ (Z14+)		Wide right (WR)
	Own half (OH)		

▶ **Figure 25.4** Location of the final pass leading to a goal.

The goals in open play were put into the following categories:

- A pass behind the last line of defence followed by a strike at goal or to a player in line with the last defender, who could shoot or take the ball forwards (ball behind and strike, or BB&S).
- A pass behind the defence or to a player level with the last defender, followed by a pass or header inside the penalty area, followed by a strike at goal (ball behind pass and strike, or BBP&S).

- Any other method of scoring, such as shooting from in front of the defence, dribbling past the last line or intercepting a back pass, categorized as other methods (OM).
- Crosses from the right (RC) or left (LC) and up to 18 metres from the goal line. A ball passed into the penalty area was recorded as passed in from the crossing area (PCA).

Pass Behind the Defence Followed by a Strike at Goal

In the first category, two considerations apply. A goal from passing the ball to a player who is level with the last defender but onside and without a defender to beat is included because a player cannot always continue making a forward run because of the offside rule. Second, when a player receives a pass or takes the ball forwards behind the last line of defence, a covering defender usually tries to block the shooting opportunity. When this happens and the attacker evades the challenge before either scoring or passing to a teammate to score, the goal is included in BB&S or BBP&S rather than being recorded as a dribble past the last line of defence and allocated to other methods.

Goals From Passing the Ball Behind the Defence

Table 25.8 shows the number of goals scored from each category in open play in international tournaments as well as from the matches in the EPL in the 2011–2012 season. As might be expected the total goals scored from tournaments indicates a trend with some exceptions. The range of goals from passing behind the defence in the last three European Championships was 49 to 57 per cent, and the range for World Cups from 1998 and 2014 was 48 to 51 per cent. The Asia Cup in 2011 was slightly lower at 46 per cent, and the lowest overall figure was in the EPL with 39 per cent.

Spain scored an amazing 82 per cent of goals—9 goals out of 11—in Euro 2008 followed by 80 per cent of goals in 2012 from playing the ball behind the opposing defence or to a player level with the last defender. But in the World Cup 2010, which they also won, Spain scored only 2 out of 7 goals, 29 per cent, from that method, a massive drop compared with the European Championships.

Playing the ball behind the defence becomes harder when the opposition defends in numbers around the penalty area, a situation that successful teams face regularly and that Spain did at the World Cup. In the World Cup 2010, Spain's five other goals came from other methods, none from crosses.

Table 25.8 Goals Scored From Playing the Ball Behind the Last Line of Defence: Other Methods and Crosses

	BB&S	BBP&S	Total from ball behind	Other methods	Crosses	Total goals in open play
Euro 2004	17	9	26; 53% (0)	16; 33% (5)	7; 14% (4)	49 (9)
Greece	1	0	1; 33% (0)	2; 67% (1)	0	3 (1)
Portugal	0	1	1; 20% (0)	3; 60% (1)	1; 20% (1)	5 (2)
Euro 2008	23	11	34; 57% (2)	9; 15% (5)	17; 28% (3)	60 (10)
Spain	7	2	9; 82% (0)	0	2; 18% (0)	11 (0)
Germany	2	2	4; 57% (1)	1; 14% (1)	2; 29% (0)	7 (2)
Euro 2012	21	9	30; 49% (3)	19; 31% (11)	12; 20% (3)	61 (17)
Spain	4	4	8; 80% (0)	2; 20% (2)	0	10 (2)
Italy	2	0	2; 67% (0)	0	1; 33% (0)	3 (0)
World Cup 1998	53	9	30; 49% (3)	32; 31% (11)	18; 20% (3)	112 (17)
France	4	2	6; 75% (0)	1; 12.5% (2)	1; 12.5% (0)	8 (2)
Brazil	6	1	7; 70% (1)	2; 20% (1)	1; 10% (0)	10 (2)
World Cup 2002	41	8	49; 48% (8)	34; 39% (20)	32; 13% (8)	115 (36)
Brazil	6	1	7; 54% (1)	4; 31% (1)	2; 15% (0)	13 (2)
Germany	3	1	4; 40% (0)	0	6; 60% (0)	10 (1)
World Cup 2006	36	9	45; 48% (12)	36; 39% (12)	12; 13% (1)	93 (25)
Italy	2	1	3; 60% (1)	2; 40% (1)	0	5 (2)
France	3	0	3; 60% (1)	2; 40% (0)	0	5 (1)
World Cup 2010	39	15	54; 51% (9)	38; 36% (7)	14; 13% (4)	106 (20)
Spain	2	0	2; 29% (0)	5; 71% (0)	0	7 (0)
Holland	3	1	4; 36% (2)	5; 45% (1)	2; 19% (0)	11 (3)
World Cup 2014	47	14	61; 50% (10)	41; 33% (0)	21; 17% (5)	123 (15)
Germany	2	3	5; 42% (1)	3; 25% (0)	4; 33% (0)	12 (1)
Argentina	2	0	2; 40% (0)	3; 60% (0)	0	5 (0)
Asia Cup 2011	19	9	28; 46% (7)	23; 38% (6)	11; 16% (3)	62 (16)
Japan	2	3	5; 45% (2)	3; 27.5% (1)	3; 27.5% (0)	11 (3)
Australia	3	3	6; 60% (1)	3; 30% (1)	1; 10% (0)	10 (2)
EPL 2011–2012	226	81	307; 39% (67)	350; 44% (155)	135; 17% (43)	792 (265)
Man Utd	15	7	22; 32% (8)	34; 49% (16)	13; 19% (6)	69 (30)
Man City	20	14	34; 49% (8)	30; 44% (11)	5; 7% (1)	69 (20)
Arsenal	28	8	36; 55% (10)	20; 31% (11)	9; 14% (2)	65 (23)

Number of goals from regained possession in the final third in brackets ( ).

BB&S: goals from a ball behind the defence or to a player level with the last defender.

BBP&S: goals from a ball behind the defence or to a player level with the last defender followed by a pass inside the penalty area.

In the EPL, Man Utd scored 32 per cent from playing the ball behind the defence, which is lower than the overall figure of 39 per cent. Man City scored 49 per cent, and Arsenal scored the most, 36 out of 65 goals, which is 55 per cent. Each of the three teams scored over 50 goals in open play, so it's not surprising that there were differences in the categories, which reflect the success rate of scoring a particular way or the most consistent method of trying to score.

Success Rate of Passes Behind the Last Line of Defence or to a Player Level With the Last Defender From Different Areas of the Field

The breakdown of where the final passes were made in table 25.9 shows clearly that zone 14+ was the most productive by a huge margin over the other four areas of the field. In every tournament at the international level

Table 25.9   Areas Where Passes Were Made Behind the Defence or to a Player Level With the Last Defender

	BB&S	BBP&S	Total	Own half (OH)	Wide right (WR)	Zone (Z14+)	Wide left (WL)	Inside penalty area (IPA)
Euro 04	17	9	26/49 = 53%	3	2 (0)	15	3 (1)	3
Greece	1	0	1/3 = 33%				1 (0)	1
Portugal	0	1	1/5 = 20%					
Euro 08	23	11	34/60 = 57%	4	3 (0)	18	7 (3)	2
Spain	7	2	9/11 = 82%	2		6	1 (1)	1
Germany	2	2	4/ 7 = 57%			3		
Euro 12	21	9	30/61 = 49%	3	2 (0)	22	3 (1)	
Spain	4	4	8/10 = 80%	2		6	2	
Italy	2	0	2/ 3 = 67%	1		1		
World Cup 1998	53	9	62/112 = 40%	10	5 (1)	36	8 (0)	3
France	4	2	6/8 = 75%	1		3	1 (0)	1
Brazil	6	1	7/10 = 70%			6	1 (0)	
World Cup 2002	41	8	49/115 = 43%	4	6 (1)	30	5 (0)	4
Brazil	6	1	7/13 = 54%		1 (0)	3	2 (0)	1
Germany	3	1	4/10 = 40%		1 (0)	2	1 (1)	
World Cup 2006	36	9	45/93 = 48%	5	3 (1)	31	2 (0)	4
Italy	2	1	3/5 = 60%			2	1 (0)	
France	3	0	3/5 = 60%			3		
World Cup 2010	39	15	54/106 = 51%	5	8 (5)	32	6 (3)	3
Spain	2	0	2/7 = 29%		1	1	1	1
Holland	3	1	4/11 = 36%			2		
World Cup 2014	47	14	61/123 = 50%	7	5 (3)	36	4 (3)	9
Germany	2	3	5/12 = 42%	0	0	4	0	1
Argentina	2	0	2/5 = 40%	0	0	2	0	0
Asia Cup 2011	19	9	28/63 = 44%	5	2 (1)	18	2 (2)	1
Japan	2	3	5/11 = 45%	1	1 (0)	5	1 (1)	
Australia	3	3	6/10 = 60%			3		
EPL 2011–2012	226	81	307/792 = 39%	28	22 (5)	189	24 (4)	44
Man Utd	15	7	22/69 = 32%	1	2 (1)	10	1 (0)	8
Man City	20	14	34/69 = 49%	1	1 (0)	23	4 (1)	4
Arsenal	28	8	36/65 = 55%	1	5 (1)	25	2 (0)	3

Goals scored with headers from wide right and wide left areas in brackets.

and in the EPL 2011–2012 season, the contribution from Z14+ to goals from passes behind the defence was over 50 per cent, with the exception of Man Utd, who had 10 out of 22 goals, or 45 per cent.

Although the figures speak for themselves, note that 6 of the 9 goals that Spain scored in winning Euro 2008 and 6 of the 8 goals they scored in 2012 came from zone 14+, as did 5 of 5 by Japan in winning the Asia Cup in 2011. In the EPL, 23 of the 34 goals scored by Man City, 68 per cent, and 25 of the 36 goals scored by Arsenal, 69 per cent, were from the central area. The results suggest that Arsenal and Man City placed more emphasis on playing the ball behind opponents from Z14+.

The overall figures for international tournaments and for individual teams show that the success rate of scoring goals from playing the ball behind opponents from WR, WL, OH and IPA was quite low out of the total number of goals scored in open play. Table 25.10 shows that the number of goals from passing the ball behind the opposing defence from inside a team's own half (OH) in international tournaments was constant at 5 to 9 per cent. The overall figure in the EPL in 2011–2012 was 4 per cent, and Man Utd, Man City and Arsenal recorded close to 2 per cent. The combination of goals from WL and WR produced a low of 5 per cent in World Cup 2006 and a high of 17 per cent in Euro 2008. In the EPL the overall figure was 6 per cent. Man Utd, Man City and Arsenal recorded 4, 9 and 11 per cent, respectively.

Goals Scored From Other Methods

In the other methods category, the range in international tournaments was quite narrow, from 31 per cent (WC 1998) to 39 per cent (World Cup 2010). The exception was 15 percent in Euro 2008. See table 25.8. The overall figure in the EPL in 2011–2012 was 44 per cent. Man Utd and Man City recorded 49 and 44 per cent, respectively. Arsenal was much lower at 31 per cent.

Table 25.11 includes a breakdown of goals scored with shots from outside the penalty area. The distance was calculated perpendicular to the goal line from the edge of the penalty area up to 21 metres and from 21 metres and beyond. In general, less than 10 per cent of goals are scored from outside 21 metres in open play.

Other methods also includes goals from zero passes. Examples of zero-pass goals include players being caught in possession, back passes being intercepted, passes given straight to opponents and clearances from the penalty area.

Goals scored after saves by the goalkeeper or shots blocked right in the goal by defenders or after rebounds off the posts or cross bar were not included as zero-pass goals in this analysis.

Table 25.10 Contribution of Goals in BB&S and BBP&S From Own Half (OH) and Wide Right (WR) and Wide Left (WL) Combined as Percentage of Goals Scored in Open Play

	Own half	WR and WL total
Euro 2004	3/49 = 6%	5/49 = 10%
Euro 2008	4/60 = 6%	10/60 = 17%
Euro 2012	3/61 = 5%	5/61 = 8%
World Cup 1998	10/112 = 9%	13/112 = 12%
World Cup 2002	4/115 = 3%	11/115 = 10%
World Cup 2006	5/93 = 5%	5/93 = 5%
World Cup 2010	5/106 = 5%	14/106 = 13%
World Cup 2014	7/123 = 6%	9/123 = 7%
Asia Cup 2011	5/62 = 8%	4/62 = 6%
EPL 2011–12	28/792 = 4%	46/792 = 6%
Man Utd	1/69 = <2%	3/69 = 4%
Man City	1/69 = <2%	6/69 = 9%
Arsenal	1/65 = <2%	7/65 = 11%

Table 25.11 Goals From Crosses and Headers, Shots From Outside the Penalty Area, Goals Scored Inside the Penalty Area and Total Goals in Open Play

	Crosses and headers	Headers in OP and SP	Shots 16–21 m	Shots 21m+	Goals inside PA	Total goals OP
Euro 2004	7 (2)	6; 11	6	6 = 12%	41; 84%	49
Euro 2008	17 (4)	8; 7	4	0	56; 93%	60
Euro 2012	12 (6)	13; 9	6	2 = 3%	53; 87%	61
World Cup 1998	18 (9)	14; 19	8	5 = 4%	99; 88%	112
World Cup 2002	32 (12)	20; 15	11	4 = 3%	100; 87%	115
World Cup 2006	12 (5)	12; 18	8	10 = 11%	75; 81%	93
World Cup 2010	14 (5)	18; 10	9	10 = 9%	87; 82%	106
World Cup 2014	21 (5)	15; 19	5	8 = 4%	110; 89%	123
Asia Cup 2011	11 (2)	10; 6	8	6 = 10%	48; 77%	62
EPL 2011–2012	135 (53)	97; 95	92	52 = 7%	648; 82%	792
Man Utd	13 (6)	11; 7	7	6 = 9%	56; 81%	69
Man City	5 (2)	4; 7	9	7 =10%	53; 77%	69
Arsenal	9 (4)	6; 3	5	2 = 3%	58; 89%	65

Goals Scored From Crosses

The range of goals scored from crosses in international tournaments was 13 per cent (WC 2002 and 2006) to 28 per cent (Euro 2008), which was exceptionally high. See table 25.8.

The figures for each category of goals in table 25.8 are expressed as a percentage of total goals scored in open play. In the EPL in 2011–2012, the overall figure for crosses was 17 per cent. The comparison of teams shows that Man Utd scored 19 per cent, Man City scored 7 per cent, and Arsenal scored 14 percent.

In Euro 2008, Spain scored 2 of their 11 goals in open play from crosses, but in 2012 they did not score any. Italy and France, who were finalists at the World Cup 2006, didn't score from a cross, and the finalists in 2010, Spain and Holland, recorded 0 out of 7 and 3 out of 11, respectively. In 2014 Argentina did not score from a cross, but Germany scored 1 out of 12.

The figures may represent the successful outcome of attempts to score goals from crossing the ball or reflect the way in which teams actually try to score in other ways, such as through attacking centrally in preference to attacking from the flanks. A team's style of play may suit the technical and physical attributes of its players. For example, a team with more short players than tall players may attempt to score by passing the ball centrally through the opposing defence rather than trying to score from crosses and headers.

Table 25.11 shows the number of goals from crosses that were scored with headers (in brackets). In every category the figure was 50 per cent or less. This figure suggests that crosses played in low or passed into the penalty area are just as effective as crosses in the air but will include goals scored from a header to set up a shot or after a save was made, possibly from a header at goal.

What about the other wide areas of the field, between the halfway line and up to the crossing area? These areas were defined as wide left (WL) and wide right (WR) to look specifically at the success rate of balls played behind the defence from what might traditionally be called a crossing area.

Table 25.9 shows the number of goals scored from headers from the wide left and wide right areas, which are low in number to start with. The figures are typically 1 out of 5 (Euro 2004 and 2012) when WR and WL scores are combined, which represents 20 per cent. The overall figure for the EPL was 9 out of 46, which is 20 per cent. Man Utd, Man City and Arsenal recorded 1 out of 3, 1 out of 5 and 1 out of 7, respectively. The two exceptions were in the Asia Cup (3 out of 4 goals were scored with headers from WL and WR combined, which represents 75 per cent) and in the WC 2014 (6 out of 9, which is 67 per cent).

Note the low figures recorded in the EPL over a whole season and the low success rate of the top teams. Although the overall figure for the Asia Cup was high (75 per cent), the total was 3 out of 4 goals from the wide areas, from 62 goals scored in open play.

Goals Scored From Set Plays With Headers

Table 25.1 shows the number of goals scored from headers in open play and from set plays in international tournaments. The percentage of goals scored from headers at set plays is more than double the percentage of goals scored from headers in open play, which highlights the importance of heading as the most prolific way of scoring from set plays. The average for headed goals in open play is 15 per cent, whereas the average from set plays is 48 per cent. The average percentage of goals scored from headers from all goals scored, with the exclusion of penalties, is 23 per cent. Table 25.12 shows the goals scored from set plays. The number scored from headers is in brackets.

The greatest difference in headed goals from set plays, if penalties are not included, was between Man Utd, with a figure of 64 per cent (7 out of 11), and Man City and Arsenal, who recorded 44 per cent (7 out of 16) and 43 per cent (3 out of 7) respectively.

The final practice allows all the aspects of the current research to take place, if some variations are made to the basic setup. The box practice is designed

Table 25.12   Goals From Set Plays, Headers in Brackets

	Corners	Free kicks	Throw-in	Penalties	Total goals
Euro 2004	10 (7)	11 (4)	0	7	28
Euro 2008	5 (3)	7 (4)	1 (0)	4	17
Euro 2012	6 (4)	6 (5)	0	3	15
World Cup 1998	20 (11)	20 (7)	1 (0)	17	58
World Cup 2002	17 (12)	15 (3)	0	14	46
World Cup 2006	15 (10)	23 (7)	3 (1)	13	54
World Cup 2010	11 (6)	17 (4)	1 (0)	10	39
World Cup 2014	21 (13)	12 (6)	0	12	45
Asia Cup 2011	7 (4)	11 (2)	1 (0)	9	28
EPL 2011–2012	113 (61)	79 (31)	8 (3)	74	274
Man Utd	8 (6)	3 (1)	0	9	20
Man City	14 (6)	2 (1)	0	7	23
Arsenal	5 (3)	2 (0)	0	2	9

to replicate situations that arise in zone 14+, to keep play compact and to encourage moves that result in passing the ball behind the opposing defence. The opportunity to allow crosses is just an extension of the original practice.

The Box

Rules

- The drill requires 12 to 18 players and 2 goalkeepers.
- Play 6v6 within the central area and either rotate a third group every four minutes or have a recovery period.
- Play starts from a goalkeeper. Attacking players are allowed to drop to receive the ball without pressure so that the practice can start.
- Opponents do not try to win the ball outside the box (figure 25.5) and must retreat to the central area when possession is lost. Otherwise, the game gets stretched over 50 or more metres, a counterattacking mentality takes over, and the whole purpose of the practice can easily be forgotten.

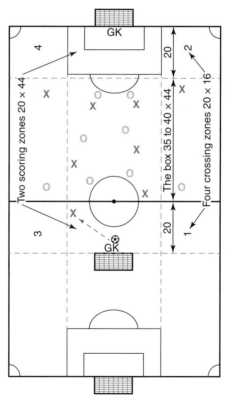

▶ **Figure 25.5** The box: coaching practice to support zone 14+ play.

- Defenders can go anywhere in the box and in front of their own goal, but attackers cannot enter the scoring zone before a pass is made.
- If an attacker passes the ball back into the box, all players in the scoring zone must go back into the box before the ball can be played into the scoring zone again. This rule keeps players moving and coming back level with the ball, desirable behaviour near the goal.
- Attackers can dribble the ball into the scoring zone.
- After the ball is in the scoring zone, any other attacker can enter.
- Extra players for each team can be stationed outside the central area and allowed to run forwards to provide a cross and support the attack.
- Shots can be allowed from just outside the scoring zone.
- The full width of the field can be used to involve 8v8 or 9v9.

Conclusion

The point of allocating goals to different categories was to determine whether one strategy for scoring goals might be more successful than any other. To keep the analysis as simple and useful as possible, the number of categories was kept to a minimum.

The evidence produced in table 25.8 shows that in nine international tournaments since 1998, the most dominant method of scoring goals in open play was from passing the ball behind the last line of defence or to a player level with the last defender (BB&S and BBP&S), with a range of 46 to 57 per cent.

In eight of the nine tournaments, the category for second place was other methods, with a range of 31 to 39 per cent. The exception was Euro 2008, when 28 per cent of goals were scored from crosses compared with 15 per cent from other methods. Goals from crosses ranged from 13 to 20 per cent in the other eight tournaments. These figures show a high degree of consistency in the way goals were scored overall in international tournaments, but the data aren't normalized.

The most dominant method in the EPL in 2011–2012 was from other methods with 44 per cent. Goals from BB&S and BBP&S were at 39 per cent, and crosses were at 17 per cent. Although many teams in both levels of competition follow the overall trend, not all do. In Euro 2008 and 2012 Spain won and scored 82 per cent and 80 per cent in open play from playing the ball behind opponents. In 2010 Spain was the favourite and won the World Cup but scored only two out of seven goals, 29 per cent, with the same strategy. Did Spain change their way of playing in 2010, or did they adapt to solve the problems they faced in another way? Spain may not have changed their strategy at all. The point is that analysis cannot provide answers to such questions unless frequency of actions is recorded, so analysts put forward logical suggestions. For example, Spain probably forced teams to defend in large numbers in the back third, so they found it much harder to play the ball behind the defence. As a result they scored more goals from in front of the defence or by dribbling past the last line of defence. In 2014 Spain scored only three goals and failed to go beyond the group stage, but they scored all three goals from playing the ball behind opponents.

Another benefit of allocating goals to different categories is that over time, analysis of one particular team should indicate a preferred method of scoring goals, such as from playing the ball behind opponents, other methods or crosses.

Man Utd followed the overall trend in the EPL by scoring the most goals with other methods, 48 per cent, followed by 31 per cent from BB&S and BBP&S and 21 per cent from crosses. Arsenal didn't follow the overall trend. They scored 55 per cent from BB&S and BBP&S and 31 per cent from other methods. Arsenal scored only two goals from outside 21 metres, which suggests they might look to play the ball behind the defence as a priority from such distances, rather than shoot at goal.

If, as some believe, the success of a team has more to do with the quality of the players in the squad, more analysis should be done on what successful players actually do in the game. Questions might include the following: Where, when and why do they make forward runs in the game, and how do they do so? Do players have a preferred method to receive the ball? Why? Decision making is fundamental to the game, so what do top players look at or look for? Do they have priorities? If passing the ball forwards and behind the last line of defence is a key to successful attacking play, is there a preferred way of positioning the body on the field to facilitate forward passing?

Here are some general considerations for coaches. Analysis is specific to the standard of soccer being played and the type of competition. For example, the World Cup produces different outcomes compared with the EPL. Percentages are often used to compare results from different tournaments, but the small samples can be misleading. Results show trends over time, which lead to expectations in the future, such as scoring more than 80 per cent of goals in open play inside the penalty area. Interpreting results in the absence of video footage can be misleading. For example, a goal from a cross may have different meanings to different people, so operational definitions are essential. Comparing evidence from the same tournaments over many years can help identify trends or inconsistencies. When reviewing evidence, keep open play and set plays separate to produce more accurate and useful information. When setting tasks for players, make sure they are appropriate and realistic to avoid feelings of failure. For example, pressing opponents in the final third will make it easier for players in midfield or the back line to win the ball, but strikers need to know they might not win the ball in the whole game but can still do a great job for the team.

Based on logical deduction and from figures provided in this chapter, up to 10 per cent of goals in open play are scored outside 21 metres, so the other 90 per cent are scored just outside and inside the penalty area, which makes soccer highly predictable. The majority of goals from a pass behind opponents come from the central area zone 14+, that is, within the width of the penalty area and between the halfway line and the edge of the penalty area. When players are more than 21 metres from goal and have time on the ball, encourage them to look for opportunities to pass to a player closer to goal before shooting unless they have a good record of scoring from distance. Most goals are scored with one or two touches and from inside the penalty area, so practise finishing that way. Most forward passes from central areas are made when players are facing forwards or able to see the goal. Encouraging players to take up supporting positions where they can face the opponent's goal and see the ball will encourage forward passing, forward runs and one-touch finishing. When supporting players can see the goal and the ball, they can usually see their immediate opponent as well. A player in possession cannot pass the ball to the back of the defence unless players off the ball make forward runs, so encourage players to make forward runs when the player on the ball can pass it forwards. Crosses from outside the penalty area and within 18 metres of the goal line provide 10 to 20 per cent of all goals in open play. Generally, 70 to 80 per cent of goals in open play are scored from sequences of five or fewer passes, so when possession is regained encourage players to look, run and pass forwards as a priority. Practise defending and attacking at free kicks and corners because 20 to 30 per cent of goals are scored this way.

This information should encourage coaches to think differently about how their teams score goals and how they can use that information to design appropriate practices at training. Note that throughout the chapter and in all the references to analysis, no mention was made of systems of play.

Epilogue

The Future of Soccer Science

—Tony Strudwick

The features of *Soccer Science* provide an appropriate understanding of the scientific parameters that affect the performance of soccer players. Given the extensive nature of the topic area, the coverage is broad. This final section, therefore, is a postscript that brings some coherence to the themes throughout the book and situates this with a personal interpretation of the issues that will shape soccer science and the future of soccer coaching.

Several critical components that affect player performance management are discussed throughout *Soccer Science*. Although many of the components overlap, future success in soccer will be achieved by providing scientific models appropriate to soccer. The application of these models has a self-evident role in improving elite performance. Features of the model, such as devising training programmes, monitoring performance, establishing preparation for competition and evaluating sport-specific analyses, are informed by such knowledge.

The general message from *Soccer Science* is that high performance is being taken seriously, priorities have been recognized and a coordinated approach is essential for success at the elite end. We can assume that genuine endeavours are now being undertaken to improve coach education, knowledge of soccer science and professionalization. Organizational and cultural factors that have been conspiring against a move towards high-performance environments (i.e., reluctance to embrace change, coach education, professionalization, accountability and the development of scientific framework) are now being overcome.

Ultimately, the roles of the support staff will be examined more closely, to the benefit of the soccer profession. The increase in qualification-led employment will lead to an examination of the traditional role of the head coach. To facilitate these changes, a new era of performance directors and performance managers will arise. These practitioners will have the skills for appreciating the coaching process and its associated elements. This concept is based on the belief that preparation in the modern era is more important, more influential and more intelligent than in previous decades.

Scientific principles are used in maximizing individual performance and player well-being. Contemporary coaches should be trained and educated to think and work in a multidisciplinary environment. Above all, coaching is about problem solving. Therefore, coaches must appreciate the vital role of specialist support personnel.

Successful soccer performance is undoubtedly multidisciplinary in nature. Contemporary coaches need to be aware of the physiological, biomechanical, psychological, nutritional, medical and the other types of issues that can affect competition. When all these factors work as an integrated system, excellence in high-performance soccer is possible. Coaching is all about problem solving. Coaches who are trained to think critically about all aspects of performance will gain an advantage over competitors.

If the role of the coach is to assimilate information and drive the coaching process, then the role of the soccer scientist is to monitor, record and deliver performance insights. Just as modern coaches need to be familiar with the significant contributions that sport science can offer, soccer scientists need to be familiar with the specific demands of soccer and the appropriate methods of communicating with athletes and coaches.

Soccer scientists provide information for the subsequent action by both coach and athlete. To achieve this, the athlete, coach and soccer scientist should be well versed in the procedures involved. Engagement of all parties is critical to improving performance. In the coming years, soccer scientists will link specific testing and monitoring procedures to the coaching process. The coach is then responsible for making appropriate interventions and modifications to the overall training plan.

The spiralling costs of purchasing players on the transfer market will reinforce the need for professional soccer clubs to put appropriate talent identification and development structures into place. Identifying soccer potential at an early age will ensure that players receive specialist coaching to accelerate their talent development. With the need to develop young, talented players, soccer scientists need to identify the key parameters and talent pathways that are required for elite performance participation.

Talent may be characterized by properties that are genetic and partly innate. Although talent may not be evident at an early age, trained practitioners can identify some early indicators, which may provide a basis for predicting those players who are more or less likely to succeed at some later stage. Soccer scientists will therefore need to understand genetic profiling as well as performance testing in the quest for more informed decision making. As a result, the future of talent identification will use genetic information alongside an adequate environment to maximize the pursuit of excellence.

The traditional bases of soccer competition are eroding fast. Innovation in products and services is more challenging by the day. Expectations continue to rise. Organizations have more data on hand but far less room for errors in execution, so their decision making has to be sharper and better informed. Overall, these factors call for superior analytics and deeper insights into what makes an organization work. Analytics will involve the extensive use of data, statistical and quantitative analysis, explanatory and predictive models and fact-based management to drive decisions and actions (Davenport and Harris 2007).

The analytics may be input for human decisions or may drive fully automated decisions. Analytics and intuitive decision making need not represent two diametrically opposed paradigms. Nonetheless, contemporary coaches and practitioners will have first-hand experience of how the intelligent use of analytics can improve asset acquisition and management, talent management, operational performance and even injury prediction.

Finally, all those involved in athlete preparation need to consider how much is too much. Even though we will have sophisticated protocols, technology and analytics, we need to remember that professional sport participation is a human pursuit. At what point do all these advanced methods become overwhelming and transform athletes into machines who become too mechanical and lose their enthusiasm, spontaneity, creativity and natural talents because they are focused on everything except playing the game? The future will be complicated, but we should not lose sight of human engagement and interaction.

At an elite level of soccer, the next decade will see improved coach education, knowledge of sport science and player management. In addition, elite soccer teams will move towards high-performance environments in which the development of systematic performance models and increased accountability are commonplace. Innovations in player preparation are more challenging by the year, and expectations continue to rise. Therefore, player preparation has to be sharper and better informed. All these factors call for superior soccer science support models and deeper insights into issues relating to the management of soccer performance.

References

Chapter 1

Carter, N. 2006. *The football manager: A history.* London: Routledge.

Carter, N. 2007. Metatarsals and magic sponges: English football and the development of sports medicine. *Journal of Sport History* 34 (1): 53–74.

Carter, N. 2009. Mixing business with leisure? The football club doctor, sports medicine and the voluntary tradition. *Sport in History* 29 (1): 69–91.

Carter, N. 2010. The rise and fall of the magic sponge: Medicine and the transformation of the football trainer. *Social History of Medicine* 23 (2): 261–279.

Carter, N. 2012. *Medicine, sport and the body: A historical perspective.* London: Bloomsbury Academic.

Collins, T. 1998. *Rugby's great split: Class, culture and the origins of rugby league football.* London: Frank Cass.

Day, D. 2012. *Professionals, amateurs and performance: Sports coaching in England, 1789–1914.* Oxford: Peter Lang.

Mason, T. 1980. *Association football and English society, 1863–1915.* Brighton: Harvester Press.

Taylor, M. 2008. *The association game: A history of British football.* Harlow: Pearson.

Wilson, J. 2008. *Inverting the pyramid: A history of football tactics.* London: Orion.

Chapter 2

Bangsbo, J. 1994. *Fitness training in football: A scientific approach.* Copenhagen: August Krogh Institute, University of Copenhagen.

Bangsbo, J. 1996. *Yo-Yo test,* 31. Ancona, Italy: Kells.

Bangsbo, J. 2008. *Aerobic and anaerobic training in soccer: With special emphasis on training of youth players. Fitness training in soccer I.* Bagsvaerd, Denmark: HO+Storm.

Bangsbo, J., Krustrup, P., and Mohr, M. 2003. Physical capacity of high-level soccer players in relation to playing position. *World Congress on Science and Football–5, book of abstracts.* Gymnos Editorial Deportiva, 76.

Bangsbo, J., Mohr, M., Poulsen, A., Perez-Gomez, J., and Krustrup, P. 2006. Training and testing the elite athlete. *Journal of Exercise Science and Fitness* 4 (1): 1–14.

Bent, I., McIlroy, R., Mousley, K., and Walsh, P. 1999. *Football confidential.* BBC Worldwide Ltd.

Bourke, A. 2003. The dream of being a professional soccer player: Insight on career development options of young Irish players. *Journal of Sport and Social Issues* 27:399–419.

Iaia, F.M., and Bangsbo, J. 2010. Speed endurance training is a powerful stimulus for physiological adaptations and performance improvements of athletes. *Scandinavian Journal of Medicine and Science in Sports* 20 (Suppl. 2): 11–23.

Lever, J. 1983. *Soccer madness: Brazil's passion for the world's most popular sport.* Prospect Heights, IL: Waveland Press.

Mujika, I. 2010. Intense training: The key to optimal performance before and during the taper. *Scandinavian Journal of Medicine and Science in Sports* 20 (Suppl. 2): 24–31.

Reilly, T. 1979. *What research tells the coach about soccer.* Washington, DC: American Alliance for Health, Physical Education, Recreation and Dance.

Reilly, T. 1994. Physiological aspects of soccer. *Biology of Sport* 11:3–20.

Reilly, T., and Thomas, V. 1976. A motion analysis of work rate in different positional roles in pro football match-play. *Journal of Human Movement Studies* 2:87–97.

Schein, E. 1991. *Organisational culture and leadership.* 2nd ed. San Francisco: Jossey-Bass.

Vialli, G., and Marcotti, G. 2007. *The Italian job.* Bantam Press.

Wehbe, G.M., Hartwig, T.B., and Duncan, C.S. 2014. Movement analysis of Australian National League soccer players using global positioning system technology. *Journal of Strength and Conditioning Research* 28 (3): 834–842.

Williams, A., and Reilly, T. 2000. Talent identification and development in soccer. *Journal of Sports Sciences* 18:657–667.

Chapter 3

Buchheit, M., Simpson, B.M., and Mendez-Villanueva, A. 2013. Repeated high-speed activities during youth soccer games in relation to changes in maximal sprinting and aerobic speeds. *International Journal of Sports Medicine* 34 (1): 40–48.

Helsen, W.F., Hodges, N.J., Van Winckel, J., and Starkes, J.L. 2000. The roles of talent, physical precocity and practice in the development of soccer expertise. *Journal of Sport Sciences* 18:727–736.

Holt, N.L., and Dunn, J.G.H. 2004. Toward a grounded theory of the psychosocial competencies and environmental conditions associated with soccer success. *Journal of Applied Sport Psychology* 16:199–219.

Mendez-Villanueva, A., Buchheit, M., Simpson, B., and Bourdon, P.C. 2013. Match play intensity distribution in youth soccer. *International Journal of Sports Medicine* 34 (2): 101–110.

Mendez-Villanueva, A., Buchheit, M., Simpson, B., Peltola, E., and Bourdon, P. 2011. Does on-field sprinting performance in young soccer players depend on how fast they can run or how fast they do run? *Journal of Strength and Conditioning Research* 25:2634–2638.

Mohr, M., Mujika, I., Santisteban, J., Randers, M.B., Bischoff, R., Solano, R., Hewitt, A., Zubillaga, A., Peltola, E., and Krustrup, P. 2010. Examination of fatigue development in elite soccer in a hot environment: A multi-experimental approach. *Scandinavian Journal of Medicine and Science in Sports* 20 (Suppl. 3): 125–132.

Mujika, I. 2008. Which way to the top? *International Journal of Sports Physiology and Performance* 3:249–250.

Mujika, I., Santisteban, J., Impellizzeri, F.M., and Castagna, C. 2009a. Fitness determinants of success in men's and women's football. *Journal of Sports Sciences* 27:107–114.

Mujika, I., Spencer, M., Santisteban, J., Goiriena, J.J., and Bishop, D. 2009b. Age-related differences in repeated-sprint ability in highly trained youth football players. *Journal of Sports Sciences* 27:1581–1590.

Mujika, I., Vaeyens, R., Matthys, R., Santisteban, J., Goiriena, J.J., and Philippaerts, R.M. 2009c. The relative age effect in a professional football club setting. *Journal of Sports Sciences* 27:1153–1158.

Osgnach, C., Poser, S., Bernardini, R., Rinaldo, R., and di Prampero, P.E. 2010. Energy cost and metabolic power in elite soccer: A new match analysis approach. *Medicine and Science in Sports and Exercise* 42:170–178.

Randers, M.B., Mujika, I., Hewitt, A., Santisteban, J., Bischoff, R., Solano, R., Zubillaga, A., Peltola, E., Krustrup, P., and Mohr, M. 2010. Application of four different football match analysis systems: A comparative study. *Journal of Sports Sciences* 28:171–182.

Soligard, T., Myklebust, G., Steffen, K., Holme, I., Silvers, H., Bizzini, M., Junge, A., Dvorak, J., Bahr, R., and Andersen, T.E. 2008. Comprehensive warm-up programme to prevent injuries in young female footballers: Cluster randomised controlled trial. *British Medical Journal* 337:a2469.

Spencer, M., Pyne, D., Santisteban, J., and Mujika, I. 2011. Fitness determinants of repeated sprint ability in highly trained youth football players. *International Journal of Sports Physiology and Performance* 6:497–508.

Vaeyens, R., Malina, R.M., Janssens, M., Van Renterghem, B., Bourgois, J., Vrijens, J., and Philippaerts, R.M. 2006. A multidisciplinary selection model for youth soccer: The Ghent Youth Soccer Project. *British Journal of Sports Medicine* 40:928–934.

Chapter 4

Bayley, N., and Pinneau, S.R. 1952. Tables for predicting adult height from skeletal age: Revised for use with the Greulich-Pyle hand standards. *Journal of Paediatrics* 40:423–441.

Beunen, G., and Malina, R.M. 1988. Growth and physical performance relative to the timing of the adolescent spurt. *Exercise and Sport Sciences Reviews* 16:503–540.

Beunen, G.P., Malina, R.M., Lefevre, J., Claessens, A.L., Renson, R., and Simons, J. 1997. Prediction of adult stature and noninvasive assessment of biological maturation. *Medicine and Science in Sports and Exercise* 29:225–230.

Billows, D., Reilly, T., and George, K. 2005. Physiological demands of match-play and training in elite adolescent footballers. In *Science and football V*, ed. T. Reilly, J. Cabri, and D. Araujo, 453–461. London and New York: Routledge.

Bravo, D.F., Impellizzeri, F.M., Rampinini, E., Castagna, C., Bishop, D., and Wisloff, U. 2008. Sprint vs. interval training in football. *International Journal of Sports Medicine* 29:668–674.

Buchheit, M., Mendez-Villanueva, A., Delhomel, G., Brughelli, M., and Ahmaidi, S. 2010a. Improving repeated sprint ability in young elite soccer players: Repeated shuttle sprints vs. explosive strength training. *Journal of Strength and Conditioning Research* 24:2715–2721.

Buchheit, M., Mendez-Villanueva, A., Simpson, B.M., and Bourdon, P.C. 2010b. Match running performance and fitness in youth soccer. *International Journal of Sports Medicine* 31:818–825.

Buchheit, M., Mendez-Villanueva, A., Simpson, B.M., and Bourdon, P.C. 2010c. Repeated-sprint sequences during youth soccer matches. *International Journal of Sports Medicine* 31:709–716.

Capranica, L., Tessitore, A., Guidetti, L., and Figura, F. 2001. Heart rate and match analysis in pre-pubescent soccer players. *Journal of Sports Sciences* 19:379–384.

Castagna, C., D'Ottavio, S., and Abt, G. 2003. Activity profile of young soccer players during actual match play. *Journal of Strength and Conditioning Research* 17:775–780.

Castagna, C., Impellizzeri, F., Cecchini, E., Rampinini, E., and Barbero Alvarez, J.C. 2009. Effects of intermittent-endurance fitness on match-performance in young male soccer players. *Journal of Strength and Conditioning Research* 23:1954–1959.

Dvorak, J., George, J., Junge, A., and Hodler, J. 2007. Application of MRI of the wrist for age determination in international U-17 soccer competitions. *British Journal of Sports Medicine* 41:497–500.

Harley, J.A., Barnes, C.A., Portas, M., Lovell, R., Barrett, S., Paul, D., and Weston, M. 2010. Motion analysis of match-play in elite U12 to U16 age-group soccer players. *Journal of Sports Sciences* 28:1391–1397.

Hill-Haas, S., Coutts, A.J., Rowsell, G., and Dawson, B. 2009. Generic versus small-sided game training in soccer. *International Journal of Sports Medicine* 30:636–642.

Hill-Haas, S.V., Dawson, B., Impellizzeri, F.M., and Coutts, A.J. 2011. Physiology of small-sided games training in football: A systematic review. *Sports Medicine* 41:199–220.

Impellizzeri, F.M., Marcora, S., Castagna, C., Reilly, T., Sassi, A., Iaia, F.M., and Rampinini, E. 2006. Physiological and performance effects of generic versus specific aerobic small-sided games training physiology in football. *International Journal of Sports Medicine* 27:483–492.

Khamis, H.J., and Roche, A.F. 1994. Predicting adult stature without using skeletal age: The Khamis-Roche method. *Pediatrics* 94:504–507 (erratum in *Pediatrics* 1995, 95:457 for the corrected tables).

Largo, R.H., Fischer, J.E., and Rousson, V. 2003. Neuromotor development from kindergarten age to adolescence: Developmental course and variability. *Swiss Medical Weekly* 133:193–199.

Malina, R.M. 2011. Skeletal age and age verification in youth sport. *Sports Medicine* 41:925–947.

Malina, R.M., Bouchard, C., and Bar-Or, O. 2004. *Growth, maturation and physical activity.* 2nd ed. Champaign, IL: Human Kinetics.

Malina, R.M., Cumming, S.P., Morano, P.J., Barron, M., and Miller, S. 2005. Maturity status of youth football players: A noninvasive estimate. *Medicine and Science in Sports and Exercise* 37:1044–1052.

Malina, R.M., Pena Reyes, M.E., Figueiredo, A.J., Coelho e Silva, M., Horta, L., Miller, R., Chamorro, M., Serratosa, L., and Morate, F. 2010. Skeletal age in youth soccer players: Implication for age verification. *Clinical Journal of Sports Medicine* 20:469–474.

Marfell-Jones, M., Olds, T., Stewart, A., and Carter, J.E.L. 2006. *International standards for anthropometric assessment.* Potchesfstroom, International Society for the Advancement of Kinanthropometry.

Martinez Garcia, J.L. 2004. Ritmos de entrenamiento propuesta metodologica para el entrenamiento en el futbol. Unpublished doctoral dissertation. Facultad de Medicina, Universidad de Zaragoza, Spain.

McMillian, K., Helgerud, J., Macdonald, R., and Hoff, J. 2004. Physiological adaptation to soccer specific endurance training in professional youth soccer players. *British Journal of Sports Medicine* 39:273–277.

Meylan, C., and Malatesta, D. 2009. Effects of in-season plyometric training within soccer practice on explosive actions of young players. *Journal of Strength and Conditioning Research* 23:2605–2613.

Micheli, U. 1983. Overuse injuries in children's sports: The growth factor. *Orthopaedic Clinics of North America* 14:337–360.

Mirwald, R.L., Baxter-Jones, A.D.G., Bailey, D.A., and Beunen, G.P. 2002. An assessment of maturity from anthropometric measurements. *Medicine and Science in Sports and Exercise* 34:689–694.

Mujika, I., Santisteban, J., and Castagna, C. 2009. In-season effects of sport-term sprint and power training program on elite junior soccer players. *Journal of Strength and Conditioning Research* 23:2581–2587.

Ontell, F.K., Ivanovic, M., Ablin, D.S., and Barlow, T.W. 1996. Bone age in children of diverse ethnicity. *American Journal of Roentgenology* 167:1395–1398.

Pfeiffer, R., and Francis, R. 1986. Effects of strength training on muscle development in pre-pubescent, pubescent and post-pubescent males. *Physician and Sports Medicine* 14:134–143.

Quatman-Yates, C.C., Quatman, C.E., Meszaros, A.J., Paterno, M.V., and Hewett, T.E. 2012. A systematic review of sensorimotor function during adolescence: A developmental stage of increased awkwardness? *British Journal of Sports Medicine* 46 (9): 649–655.

Randers, M., Mujika, I., Hewitt, A., Santiseban, J., Bischoff, R., Solano, R., Zubilago, A., Peltola, E., Krustrup, P., and Mohr, M. 2010. Application of 4 different football match analysis systems: A comparative study. *Journal of Sports Sciences* 28:171–182.

Reilly, T., and Ball, D. 1984. The net physiological cost of dribbling a soccer ball. *Research Quarterly for Exercise and Sport* 55:267–271.

Reilly, T., Bangsbo, J., and Franks, A. 2000. Anthropometric and physiological predispositions for elite soccer. *Journal of Sports Sciences* 18:669–683.

Reilly, T., Williams, A.M., Nevill, A., and Franks, A. 2000. A multidisciplinary approach to talent identification in soccer. *Journal of Sports Sciences* 18:695–702.

Roche, A.F., Tyleshevski, F., and Rogers, E. 1983. Non-invasive measurement of physical maturity in children. *Research Quarterly for Exercise and Sport* 54:364–371.

Roche, A.F., Wainer, H., and Thissen, D. 1975. *Predicting adult stature for individuals.* Basel: Karger.

Rowland, T.W. 2004. *Children's exercise physiology.* 2nd ed. Champaign, IL: Human Kinetics.

Rowland, T.W. 2011. *The athlete's clock.* Champaign, IL: Human Kinetics.

Sheppard, J.M., and Young, W.B. 2006. Agility literature review: Classification, training and testing. *Journal of Sports Sciences* 24:919–932.

Sherar, L.B., Mirwald, R.L., Baxter-Jones, A.D.G., and Thomis, M. 2005. Prediction of adult height using maturity-based cumulative height-velocity curves. *Journal of Pediatrics* 147:508–514.

Simmons, C., and Paull, G.C. 2001. Season-of-birth bias in association football. *Journal of Sports Sciences* 19:677–686.

Stratton, G., Reilly, T., Williams, A.M., and Richardson, D. 2004. *Youth soccer: From science to performance.* New York: Routledge.

Stroyer, J., Hansen, L., and Klausen, K. 2004. Physiological profile and activity pattern of young soccer players during match play. *Medicine and Science in Sports and Exercise* 36:168–174.

Tanner, J.M., Healy, M.J.R., Goldstein, H., and Cameron, N. 2001. *Assessment of skeletal maturity and prediction of adult height (TW3 method).* 3rd ed. London: Saunders.

Venturelli, M., Bishop, D., and Pettene, L. 2008. Sprint training in preadolescent soccer players. *International Journal of Sports Physiology and Performance* 3:558–562.

Vrijen, J. 1978. Muscle strength development in the pre- and post-pubertal age. In *Pediatric work physiology*, ed. J. Borms and M. Hebbelinck, 152–158. Basel, Switzerland: Karger.

Chapter 5

Abernethy, B., Hanrahan, S.J., Kippers, V., Mackinnon, L.T., and Pandy, M.G. 2005. *The biophysical foundations of human movement.* Champaign, IL: Human Kinetics.

Côté, J., Baker, J., and Abernethy, B. 2007. Play and practice in the development of sport expertise. In *Handbook of sport psychology*, 3rd ed., ed. G. Tenenbaum and R.C. Eklund. 184–202. New York: Wiley.

Davids, K., Button, C., and Bennett, S. 2008. *Dynamics of skill acquisition: A constraints-led approach.* Champaign, IL: Human Kinetics.

Deci, E.L., and Ryan, R.M. 2000. The 'what' and 'why' of goal pursuits: Human needs and the self-determination of behavior. *Psychological Inquiry* 11:227–268.

Ericsson, K.A. 2003. The development of elite performance and deliberate practice: An update from the perspective of the expert-performance approach. In *Expert performance in sport: Recent advances in research on sport expertise*, ed. J. Starkes and K.A. Ericsson, 49–81. Champaign, IL: Human Kinetics.

Ericsson, K.A., and Towne, T.J. 2010. Expertise. *WIREs Cognitive Science* 1:404–416.

Fenoglio. R. 2003. The Manchester United 4 vs 4 pilot scheme for U9s. *Insight: The FA Coaches Association Journal* 6 (3): 22–23.

Ford, P.R., and Williams, A.M. 2013. The acquisition of skill and expertise: The role of practice and other activities In *Science and soccer III*, ed. A.M. Williams, 122–138. London: Routledge.

Ford, P.R., Carling, C., Garces, M., Marques, M., Miguel, C., Farrant, A., Stenling, A., Moreno, J., Le Gall, F., Holmström, S., Salmela, J.H., and Williams, A.M. 2012. The developmental activities of elite soccer players aged under-16 years from Brazil, England, France, Ghana, Mexico, Portugal and Sweden. *Journal of Sports Sciences* 30:1653–1663.

Ford, P.R., Yates, I., and Williams, A.M. 2010. An analysis of practice activities and instructional behaviours used by youth soccer coaches during practice: Exploring the link between science and application. *Journal of Sports Sciences* 28:483–495.

Guadagnoli, M.A., and Lee, T.D. 2004. Challenge point: A framework for conceptualizing the effects of various practice conditions in motor learning. *Journal of Motor Behavior* 36:212–224.

Jackson, S.A., and Csíkszentmihályi, M. 1999. *Flow in sports: The key to optimal experiences and performances.* Champaign, IL: Human Kinetics.

Kahneman, D. 2003. A perspective on judgment and choice: Mapping bounded rationality. *American Psychologist* 58:697–720.

Masters, R.S., and Poolton, J.M. 2013. Advances in implicit motor learning. In *Skill acquisition in sport: Research, theory, and practice*, 2nd ed., ed. N.J. Hodges and A.M. Williams, 59–76. London: Routledge.

McPherson, S.L., and Kernodle, M.W. 2003. Tactics, the neglected attribute of expertise: Problem representations and performance skills in tennis. In *Expert performance in sport: Recent advances in research on sport expertise*, ed. J. Starkes and K.A. Ericsson, 137–168. Champaign, IL: Human Kinetics.

Newell, A., and Rosenbloom, P.S. 1981. Mechanisms of skill acquisition and the law of practice. In *Cognitive skills and their acquisition*, ed. J.R. Anderson, 1–55. Hillsdale, NJ: Erlbaum.

Richards, P., Collins, D., and Mascarenhas, D.R.D. 2012. Developing rapid high-pressure team decision-making skills. The integration of slow deliberate reflective learning within the competitive performance environment: A case study of elite netball. *Reflective Practice* 13:407–424.

Roca, A., Ford, P.R., McRobert, A.P., and Williams, A.M. 2013. Perceptual-cognitive skills and their interaction as a function of task and skill constraints in soccer. *Journal of Sport and Exercise Psychology* 35:144–155.

Roca, A., Williams, A.M., and Ford, P.R. 2012. Developmental activities and the acquisition of superior anticipation and decision making in soccer players. *Journal of Sports Sciences* 30:1643–1652.

Schmidt, R.A., and Lee, T.D. 2011. *Motor control and learning: A behavioural emphasis*. 6th ed. Champaign, IL: Human Kinetics.

Williams, A.M., and Ford, P.R., 2013. 'Game intelligence': Anticipation and decision making In *Science and soccer III*, ed. A.M. Williams, 105–121. London: Routledge.

Wulf, G. 2007. *Attention and motor skill learning*. Champaign, IL: Human Kinetics.

Chapter 7

Asai, T., Carré, M.J., Akatsuka, T., and Haake, S.J. 2002. The curve kick of a football 1: Impact with the foot. *Sports Engineering (International Sports Engineering Association)* 5 (4): 183.

Bamaç, B., Tamer, G.S., Colak, T., Colak, E., Seyrek, E., Duman, C., Colak, S., and Özbek, A. 2011. Effects of repeatedly heading a ball on serum levels of two neurotrophic factors of brain tissue BDNF and NGF, in professional soccer players. *Biology of Sport* 28 (3): 177.

Bauer, J.A., Thomas, T.S., Cauraugh, J.H., Kaminski, T.W., and Hass, C.J. 2001. Impact forces and neck muscle activity in heading by collegiate female soccer players. *Journal of Sports Sciences* 19 (3): 171.

Besier, T.F., Lloyd, D.G., and Ackland, T.R. 2003. Muscle activation strategies at the knee during running and cutting manoeuvres. *Medicine and Science in Sports and Exercise* 35 (1): 119–127.

Brice, P., Smith, N., and Dyson, R. 2008. Curved running in soccer: Kinematic differences between the inside and outside limbs. *Proceedings of the XXVI International Conference of the Society of Biomechanics in Sports*, Seoul, Korea: Korean Society of Sports Biomechanics.

Coles, D. 2003. *Goalkeeping*. Wiltshire, UK: Crowood Press.

Dempsey, A.R., Lloyd, D.G., Elliott, B.C., Steele, J.R., Munro, B.J., and Russo, K.A. 2007. The effect of technique change on knee loads during sidestep cutting. *Medicine and Science in Sports and Exercise* 39 (10): 1765–1773.

Egan, C.D., Verheul, M.H., and Savelsbergh, G.J. 2007. Effects of experience on the coordination of internally and externally timed soccer kicks. *Journal of Motor Behavior* 39 (5): 423–432.

FIFA. 2004. *Technical report on the 2002 World Cup*.

Kellis, E., Katis, A., and Gissis, I. 2004. Knee biomechanics of the support leg in soccer kicks from three angles of approach. *Medicine and Science in Sports and Exercise* 36 (6): 1017–1028.

Khun, W. 1988. Penalty kick strategies for goalkeepers. In *Science and football: Proceedings of the First World Congress of Science and Football, Liverpool, 13–17th April 1987*, ed. T. Reilly, A. Lees, K. Davids, and W.J. Murphy, 489–492. London: Routledge.

Kollath, E., and Schwirtz, A. 1988. Biomechanical analysis of the soccer throw-in. In *Science and football: Proceedings of the First World Congress of Science and Football, Liverpool, 13–17th April 1987*, ed. T. Reilly, A. Lees, K. Davids, and W.J. Murphy, 460–467. London: Routledge.

Kristensen, L.B., Andersen, T.B., and Sørensen, H. 2004. Optimising segmental movement in the jumping header in soccer. *Sports Biomechanics* 3 (2): 195.

Lees, A., Kemp, M., and Moura, F. 2005. A biomechanical analysis of the soccer throw-in with a particular focus on the upper limb motion. In *Science and football V*, ed. T. Reilly, J. Cabri, and D. Arauj, 89–94. London: Routledge.

Lees, A., and Nolan, L. 1998. Biomechanics of soccer: A review. *Journal of Sports Sciences* 16:211–234.

Lees, A., and Nolan, L. 2002. Three dimensional kinematic analysis of the instep kick under speed and accuracy conditions. In *Science and football IV*, ed. W. Spinks, T. Reilly, and A. Murphy, 16–21. London: E & FN Spon.

Lees, A., Asai, T., Andersen, T.B., Nunome, H., and Sterzing, T. 2010. The biomechanics of kicking in soccer: A review. *Journal of Sports Sciences* 28 (8): 805.

Levendusky, T.A, Clinger, C.D., Miller, R.E., and Armstrong, C.W. 1985. Soccer throw-in kinematics. In *Biomechanics in sports II*, ed. J. Terauds and J.N. Barham, 258–268. Del Mar, CA: Academic.

McLean, S.G., Lipfert, S.W., and Van den Bogert, A.J. 2004. Effect of gender and defensive opponent on the biomechanics of sidestep cutting. *Medicine and Science in Sports and Exercise* 36:1008–1016.

Messier, S.P., and Brody, M.A. 1986. Mechanics of translation and rotation during conventional and handspring throw-ins. *International Journal of Sports Biomechanics* 2:301–315.

Nunome, H., and Ikegami, Y. 2006. Kinematics of soccer instep kicking: A comparison of two-dimensional and three-dimensional analysis. In *Proceedings of XXIV International Symposium on Biomechanics in Sports 2006*, ed. H. Schwameder, G. Strutzenberger, V. Fastenbauer, S. Lindinger, and E. Müller. Salzburg, Austria: University of Salzburg.

Plagenhoef, S. 1971. *The patterns of human motion*. Englewood Cliffs, NJ: Prentice Hall.

Putnam, C.A. 1991. A segment interaction analysis of proximal to distal sequential segmental motion patterns. *Medicine and Science in Sports and Exercise* 23 (1): 130–144.

Reilly, T., Thomas, V. 1976. The motion analysis of work-rate in different professional roles in professional football match-play. Journal of Human Movement Studies. 2 (2). p. 87-97.

Shan, G. and Westerhoff, W. 2005. Full-body kinematic characteristics of the maximal instep kick by male soccer players and parameters related to kick quality. *Sports Biomechanics*. 4, 59-72.

Shinkai, H., Nunome, H., Ikegami, Y,. and Isokawa, M. 2006. Foot movement in impact phase of instep kicking in soccer. In *Proceedings of XXIV International Symposium on Biomechanics in Sports 2006*, ed. H. Schwameder, G. Strutzenberger, V. Fastenbauer, S. Lindinger, and E. Müller. Salzburg, Austria: University of Salzburg.

Smith, N., Dyson, R., Hale, T., and Janaway, L. 2006. Contributions of the inside and outside leg to maintenance of curvilinear motion on a natural turf surface. *Gait and Posture* 24:453–458.

Smith, N., and Shay, R. 2013. Ideal dive technique in high one-handed soccer saves: Top hand versus bottom hand. In *Science and football VII: Proceedings of the Seventh World Congress on Science and Football*, ed. H. Nunome, B. Drust, and B. Dawson, 67–74. London: Routlegde.

Spratford, W., Mellifont, R., and Burkett, B. 2009. The influence of dive direction on the movement characteristics for elite football goalkeepers. *Sports Biomechanics* 8:235–244.

Sterzing, T., and Hennig, E.M. 2008. The influence of soccer shoes on kicking velocity in full-instep kicks. *Exercise and Sport Sciences Reviews* 36 (2): 91.

Suzuki, S., Togari, H., Isokawa, M., Ohashi, J., and Ohgushi, T. 1998. Analysis of the goalkeepers diving motion. In *Science and Football*, ed. T. Reilly, A. Lees, K. Davids, and W.J. Murphy, 468–475. London: E & FN Spon.

Wade, A. 1981. *The FA guide to teaching football*. London: Heinemann.

Welsh, A. 1999. *The soccer goalkeeping handbook: An authoritative guide for players and coaches*. Chicago: Masters Press.

Yang, J. 2015. The influence of motor expertise on the brain activity of motor task performance: A meta-analysis of functional magnetic resonance imaging studies. *Cognitive, Affective, & Behavioral Neuroscience* 15: 381-394.

Zetterberg, H., Jonsson, M., Rasulzada, A., Popa, C., Styrud, E., Hietala, M.A., Rosengren, L., Wallin, A., and Blennow, K. 2007. No neurochemical evidence for brain injury caused by heading in soccer. *British Journal of Sports Medicine* 41 (9): 574–577.

Chapter 8

Alentorn-Geli, E., Myer, G.D., Silvers, H.J., Samitier, G., Romero, D., Lazaro-Haro, C., and Cugat, R. 2009a. Prevention of non-contact anterior cruciate ligament injuries in soccer players. Part 1: Mechanisms of injury and underlying risk factors. *Knee Surgery, Sports Traumatology, Arthroscopy* 17 (7): 705–729.

Bahr, R., and Krosshaug, T. 2005. Understanding injury mechanisms: A key component of preventing injuries in sport. *British Journal of Sports Medicine* 39:324–329.

Barengo, N.C., Meneses-Echávez, J.F., Ramírez-Vélez, R., Cohen, D.D., Tovar, G., and Bautista,

J.E. 2014. The impact of the FIFA 11+ training program on injury prevention in football players: A systematic review. *International Journal of Environmental Research and Public Health* 11 (11): 11986–12000.

Bryant, C.X., Peterson, J.A., and Franklin, B.A. 1999. *101 frequently asked questions about 'health & fitness' and 'nutrition & weight control'.* Champaign, IL: Sagamore.

Bullock, M.P., Foster, N.E., and Wright, C.C. 2005. Shoulder impingement: The effect of sitting posture on shoulder pain and range of motion. *Manual Therapy* 10 (1): 28–37.

Cibulka, M.T., Delitto, A., and Koldehoff, R.M. 1988. Changes in innominate tilt after manipulation of the sacroiliac joint in patients with low back pain. An experimental study. *Physical Therapy* 68 (9): 1359–1363.

Cormack, S.J., Mooney, M.G., Morgan, W., and McGuigan, M.R. 2013. Influence of neuromuscular fatigue on accelerometer load in elite Australian football players. *International Journal of Sports Physiology and Performance* 8 (4): 373–378.

Croisier, J.L., Ganteaume, S., Binet, J., Genty, M., and Ferret, J.M. 2008. Strength imbalances and prevention of hamstring injury in professional soccer players: A prospective study. *American Journal of Sports Medicine* 36 (8): 1469–1475.

Dallinga, J.M., Benjaminse, A., and Lemmink, K.A. 2012. Which screening tools can predict injury to the lower extremities in team sports? A systematic review. *Sports Medicine* 42 (9): 791–815.

Dellal, A., Lago-Peñas, C., Rey, E., Chamari, K., and Orhant, E. 2015. The effects of a congested fixture period on physical performance, technical activity and injury rate during matches in a professional soccer team. *British Journal of Sports Medicine* 49 (6): 390–394.

DonTigny, R.L. 1999. Critical analysis of the sequence and extent of the result of the pathological failure of the self-bracing of the SI joint. *Journal of Manual and Manipulative Therapy* 7 (4): 173–181.

DonTigny, R.L. 2005. Critical analysis of the functional dynamics of the sacroiliac joints as they pertain to normal gait. *Journal of Orthopaedic Medicine* (UK) 27:3–10.

Ford, K.R., Myer, G.D., and Hewett, T.E. 2003. Valgus knee motion during landing in high school female and male basketball players. *Medicine and Science in Sports and Exercise* 35 (10): 1745–1750.

Gracovetsky, S. 1985. A hypothesis for the role of the spine in human locomotion: A challenge to current thinking. *Journal of Biomedical Engineering* 7 (3): 205–216.

Hägglund, M., Waldén, M., and Ekstrand, J. 2009. Injuries among male and female elite football players. *Scandinavian Journal of Medicine and Science in Sports* 19 (6): 819–827.

Hall, S.J. 1999. *Basic biomechanics.* Boston: McGraw-Hill Companies.

Hewett, T.E. 2000. Neuromuscular and hormonal factors associated with knee injuries in female athletes. Strategies for intervention. *Sports Medicine* 29 (5): 313–327.

Hewett, T.E., Myer, G.D., Ford, K.R., Heidt, R.S. Jr., Colosimo, A.J., McLean, S.G., van den Bogert, A.J., Paterno, M.V., and Succop, P. 2005. Biomechanical measures of neuromuscular control and valgus loading of the knee predict anterior cruciate ligament injury risk in female athletes: A prospective study. *American Journal of Sports Medicine* 33 (4): 492–501.

Hewett, T.E., Paterno, M.V., and Myer, G.D. 2002. Strategies for enhancing proprioception and neuromuscular control of the knee. *Clinical Orthopaedics and Related Research* Sept (402): 76–94.

Lewis, J.S.L, and Valentine, R.E. 2007. The pectoralis minor length test: A study of the intra-rater reliability and diagnostic accuracy in subjects with and without shoulder symptoms. *BMC Musculoskeletal Disorders* July 9, 8:64.

Lewit, K. 2009. *Manipulative therapy: Musculoskeletal medicine.* New York: Churchill Livingstone.

Lloyd, D.G. 2001. Rationale for training programs to reduce anterior cruciate ligament injuries in Australian football. *Journal of Orthopaedic and Sports Physical Therapy* 31 (11): 645–654.

Ludewig, P.M.L, and Reynolds, J.F. 2009. The association of scapular kinematics and glenohumeral joint pathologies. *Journal of Orthopaedic and Sports Physical Therapy* 39 (2): 90–104.

McHugh, M.P. 2009. Injury prevention in professional sports: Protecting your investments. *Scandinavian Journal of Medicine and Sciences in Sports* 19 (6): 751–752.

McHugh, M.P., Johnson, C.D., and Morrison, R.H. 2012. The role of neural tension in hamstring flexibility. *Scandinavian Journal of Medicine and Sciences in Sports* 22 (2): 164–169.

Mendiguchia, J., Alentorn-Geli, E., and Brughelli, M. 2012. Hamstring strain injuries: Are we heading in the right direction? *British Journal of Sports Medicine* 46 (2): 81–85.

Méndez-Sánchez, R., Alburquerque-Sendín, F., Fernández-de-las-Peñas, C., Barbero-Iglesias,

F.J., Sánchez-Sánchez, C., Calvo-Arenillas, J.I., and Huijbregts, P. 2010. Immediate effects of adding a sciatic nerve slider technique on lumbar and lower quadrant mobility in soccer players: A pilot study. *Journal of Alternative and Complementary Medicine* 16 (6): 669–675.

Myer, G.D., Ford, K.R., and Hewett, T.E. 2004. Rationale and clinical techniques for anterior cruciate ligament injury prevention among female athletes. *Journal of Athletic Training* 39 (4): 352–364.

Neely, F.G. 1998. Biomechanical risk factors for exercise-related lower limb injuries. *Sports Medicine* 26 (6): 395–413.

Newham, D.J. 1988. The consequences of eccentric contractions and their relationship to delayed onset muscle pain. *European Journal of Applied Physiology* 57 (3): 353–359.

Page, P., Frank, C., and Lardne, R. 2010. *Assessment and treatment of muscle imbalance: The Janda approach.* Champaign, IL: Human Kinetics.

Pappas et al. 2015. Do exercises used in injury prevention programmes modify cutting task biomechanics? A systematic review with meta-analysis. *Br J Sports Med* (10): 673-800.

Ribot-Ciscar, E., Tardy-Gervet, M.F., Vedel, J.P., and Roll, J.P. 1991. Post-contraction changes in human muscle spindle resting discharge and stretch sensitivity. *Experimental Brain Research* 86 (3): 673–678.

Schache, A.G., Crossley, K.M., Macindoe, I.G., Fahrner, B.B., and Pandy, M.G. 2011. Can a clinical test of hamstring strength identify football players at risk of hamstring strain? *Knee Surgery, Sports Traumatology, Arthroscopy* 19 (1): 38–41.

Sciascia, A., and Cromwell, R. 2012. Kinetic chain rehabilitation: A theoretical framework. *Rehabilitation Research and Practice* Epub 2012, May 14.

Sherrington, C. 1906. *The integrative action of the nervous system.* New Haven, CT: Yale University Press.

Szymanski, D. 2001. Recommendations for the avoidance of delayed-onset muscle soreness. *Strength and Conditioning Journal* 23 (4): 7–13.

Waldén, M., Hägglund, M., Magnusson, H., and Ekstrand, J. 2011. Anterior cruciate ligament injury in elite football: A prospective three-cohort study. *Knee Surgery, Sports Traumatology, Arthroscopy* 19 (1): 11–19.

Winter, D.A. 1990. *Biomechanics and motor control of human movement.* 2nd ed. New York: Wiley.

Chapter 10

Abeyaratne, R., and Horgan, C.O. 1984. The pressurized hollow sphere problem in finite elastostatics for a class of compressible materials. *International Journal of Solids and Structures* 20 (8): 715–723.

Britten, N. 2002. Jeff Astle killed by heading ball, coroner rules. *Daily Telegraph, UK*, 12 November 2002.

Cotton, R. 2007. Surface interactions of soccer balls. PhD thesis, Mechanical and Manufacturing Engineering, Loughborough University, UK.

Daish, C.B. 1972. *The physics of ball games.* London: University Press.

FIFA. 2015. *Laws of the game 2015/2016.* Zurich, Switzerland: FIFA.

Football Association. N.d. The history of the FA. www.thefa.com/thefa/whoweare/historyofthefa.

Goodyear, C. 1844. Improvement in India rubber fabrics, U.S. Patent 3633.

Hanson, H., and Harland, A. 2012. The 16th century football: 450 year old sports technology assessed by modern standards. In *Engineering of Sport Conference 2012*, ed. P. Drane and J. Sherwood, 373–378.

Lord Rayleigh. 1877. On the irregular flight of a tennis ball. *Messenger of Mathematics*, 7.

Magnus, G. 1852. *Über die Abweichung der Geschosse.* Abhandlungen der Königlichen Akademie der Wissenschaften zu Berlin, 1–23.

Mangi, F. 2014. Pakistan may surprise Maradona at World Cup in Brazil. *Bloomberg*, 20 May 2014.

Nadvi, K., Lund-Thomsen, P., Xue, H., and Khara, N. 2011. Playing against China: Global value chains and labour standards in the international sports goods industry. *Global Networks* 11 (3): 334–354.

Passmore, M., Rogers, D., Tuplin, S., Harland, A., Lucas, T., and Holmes, C. 2011. The aerodynamic performance of a range of FIFA-approved footballs. *Proceedings of the Institution of Mechanical Engineers, Part P: Journal of Sports Engineering and Technology* 226 (1): 61–70.

Price, D.S., Jones, R., and Harland, A.R. 2006. Soccer ball anisotropy modelling. *Materials Science and Engineering* 420:100–108.

Waraich, O. 2014. Where soccer gets made. *Sports Illustrated*, 11 February. www.si.com/soccer/2014/02/11/far-post-sialkot-pakistan-soccer-balls-factory

Chapter 11

Andrzejewski, M., Chmura, J., Pluta, B., Strzelczyk, R., and Kasprzak, A. 2013. Analysis of sprinting activities of professional soccer players. *Journal of Strength and Conditioning Research* 27 (8): 2134–2140.

Aroso, J., Rebelo, A., and Gomes-Pereira, J. 2004. Physiological impact of selected game-related exercises [abstract]. *Journal of Sports Sciences* 22 (6): 522.

Aziz, A.R., Chia, M., Mukherjee, S., and Teh, K.C. 2007. Relationship between measured maximal oxygen uptake and aerobic endurance performance with running repeated sprint ability in young elite soccer players. *Journal of Sports Medicine and Physical Fitness* 47 (4): 401–407.

Aziz, A.R., Chia, M., and Teh, K.C. 2000. The relationship between maximal oxygen uptake and repeated sprint performance indices in field hockey and soccer players. *Journal of Sports Medicine and Physical Fitness* 40 (3): 195–200.

Bangsbo, J., Gunnarsson, T.P., Wendell, J., Nybo, L., and Thomassen, M. 2009. Reduced volume and increased training intensity elevate muscle Na+-K+ pump alpha2-subunit expression as well as short- and long-term work capacity in humans. *Journal of Applied Physiology* 107 (6): 1171–1180.

Bangsbo, J., Mohr, M., and Krustrup, P. 2006. Physical and metabolic demands of training and match-play in the elite footballer. *Journal of Sports Sciences* 24 (7): 665–674.

Bangsbo, J., and Lindquist, F. 1992. Comparison of various exercise tests with endurance performance during soccer in professional players. *International Journal of Sports Medicine* 13 (2): 125–132.

Bell, G.J., Syrotuik, D., Martin, T.P., Burnham, R., and Quinney, H.A. 2000. Effect of concurrent strength and endurance training on skeletal muscle properties and hormone concentrations in humans. *European Journal of Applied Physiology* 81 (5): 418–427.

Bishop, D., and Spencer, M. 2004. Determinants of repeated-sprint ability in well-trained team-sport athletes and endurance trained athletes. *Journal of Sports Medicine and Physical Fitness* 44 (1): 1–7.

Bishop, D., Lawrence, S., and Spencer, M. 2003. Predictors of repeated sprint ability in elite female hockey players. *Journal of Science and Medicine in Sport* 6 (2): 199–209.

Bradley, P.S., and Noakes, T.D. 2013. Match running performance fluctuations in elite soccer: Indicative of fatigue, pacing or situational influences? *Journal of Sports Sciences* 31 (15): 1627–1638.

Bradley, P.S., Carling, C., Gomez Diaz, A., Hood, P., Barnes, C., Ade, J., Boddy, M., Krustrup, P., and Mohr, M. 2013a. Match performance and physical capacity of players in the top three competitive standards of English professional soccer. *Human Movement Science* 32 (4): 808–821.

Bradley, P.S., Lago-Penas, C., Rey, E., and Gomez Diaz, A. 2013b. The effect of high and low percentage ball possession on physical and technical profiles in English FA Premier League soccer matches. *Journal of Sports Sciences* 31 (12): 1261–1270.

Bradley, P.S., Carling, C., Archer, D., Roberts, J., Dodds A., Di Mascio, M., Paul, D., Diaz, A.G., Pearl, D., and Krustrup, P. 2011. The effect of playing formation on high intensity running and technical profiles in English FA Premier League soccer matches. *Journal of Sports Sciences* 29 (8): 821–830.

Carling, C. 2013. Interpreting physical performance in professional soccer match-play: Should we be more pragmatic in our approach? *Sports Medicine* 43 (8): 655–663.

Carling, C., Le Gall, F., and Dupont, G. 2012. Analysis of repeated high intensity running in professional soccer. *Journal of Sports Sciences* 30 (4): 325–336.

Carling, C., Bloomfield, J., Nelsen, L., and Reilly, T. 2008. The role of motion analysis in elite soccer: Contemporary performance measurement techniques and work rate data. *Sports Medicine* 38 (10): 839–862.

Castagna, C., Manzi, V., D'Ottavio, S., Annino, G., Padua, E., and Bishop, D. 2007. Relation between maximal aerobic power and the ability to repeat sprints in young basketball players. *Journal of Strength and Conditioning Research* 21 (4): 1172–1176.

Cormie, P., McGuigan, M.R., and Newton, R. 2011. Developing maximal neuromuscular power: Part 2 – training considerations for improving maximal power production. *Sports Medicine* 41 (2): 125–146.

Cronin, J.B., and Hansen, K.T. 2005. Strength and power predictors of sports speed. *Journal of Strength and Conditioning Research* 19 (2): 349–357.

Dellal, A., Chamari, K., Wong D.P., Ahmaidi, S., Keller, D., Barros, R., Bisciotti, G.N., and Carling, C. 2011. Comparison of physical and technical performance in European soccer match-play: FA Premier League and La Liga. *European Journal of Sport Science* 11 (1): 51–59.

Dellal, A., Chamari, K., Pintus, A., Girard, O., Cotte, T., and Keller, D. 2008. Heart rate responses during *small-sided games* and short intermittent running training in elite soccer players: A comparative study. *Journal of Strength and Conditioning Research* 22 (5): 1449–1457.

Demarle, A.P., Slawinski, J.J., Laffite, L.P., Bocquet, V.G., Koralsztein, J.P., and Billat, V.L. 2001. Decrease of O_2 deficit is a potential factor in increased time to exhaustion after specific endurance training. *Journal of Applied Physiology* (1985) 90 (3): 947–953.

Di Salvo, V., Baron, R., Tschan, H., Calderon Montero, F.J., Bachi, N., and Pigozzi, F. 2007. Performance characteristics according to playing position in elite soccer. *International Journal of Sports Medicine* 28 (3): 222–227.

Di Salvo, V., Gregson, W., Atkinson, G., Tordoff, P., and Drust, B. 2009. Analysis of high intensity activity in Premier League soccer. *International Journal of Sports Medicine* 30 (3): 205–212.

Di Salvo, V., Baron, R., Gonzalez-Haro, C., Gormasz, C., Pigozzi, F., and Bachi, N. 2010. Sprinting analysis of elite soccer players during European Champions League and UEFA Cup matches. *Journal of Sports Sciences* 28 (14): 1489–1494.

Di Salvo, V., Pigozzi, F., Gonzalez-Haro, C., Lauglin, M.S., and De Witt, J.K. 2013. Match performance comparison in top English soccer leagues. *International Journal of Sports Medicine* 34 (6): 526–532.

Docherty, D., and Sporer, B. 2000. A proposed model for examining the interference phenomenon between concurrent aerobic and strength training. *Sports Medicine* 30 (6): 385–394.

Dupont, G., Akakpo, K., and Berthoin, S. 2004. The effect of In-season, high intensity interval training in soccer players. *Journal of Strength and Conditioning Research* 18 (3): 584–589.

Dupont, G., Nedelec, M., McCall, A., McCormack, D., Berthoin, S., and Wisloff, U. 2010a. Effect of 2 soccer matches in a week on physical performance and injury rate. *American Journal of Sports Medicine* 38 (9): 1752–1758.

Dupont, G., McCall, A., Prieur, F., Millet, G.P., and Berthoin, S. 2010b. Faster oxygen uptake kinetics during recovery is related to better repeated sprinting ability. *European Journal of Applied Physiology* 110 (3): 627–634.

Dupont, G., Millet, G.P., Guinhouya, C., and Berthoin, S. 2005. Relationship between oxygen uptake kinetics and performance in repeated running sprints. *European Journal of Applied Physiology* 95 (1): 27–34.

Dupont, G., Blondel, N., Lensel, G., and Berthoin, S. 2002. Critical velocity and time spent at high level of $\dot{V}O_2$ for short intermittent runs at supramaximal velocities. *Canadian Journal of Applied Physiology* 27 (2): 103–115.

Fanchini, M., Azzalin, A., Castagna, C., Schena, F., McCall, A., and Impellizzeri, F.M. 2011. Effect of bout duration on exercise intensity and technical performance of small-sided games in soccer. *Journal of Strength and Conditioning Research* 25 (2): 453–458.

Gaiga, M.C., and Docherty, D. 1995. The effect of an aerobic interval training program on intermittent anaerobic performance. *Canadian Journal of Applied Physiology* 20 (4): 452–464.

Girard, O., Mendez-Villanueva, A., and Bishop, D. 2011. Repeated sprint ability – part I: Factors contributing to fatigue. *Sports Medicine* 41 (8): 673–694.

Gregson, W., Drust, B., Atkinson, G., and Salvo, V.D. 2010. Match-to-match variability of high-speed activities in premier league soccer. *International Journal of Sports Medicine* 31 (4): 237–242.

Hedrick, A. 2004. Teaching the clean. *Strength and Conditioning Journal* 26 (4): 70–72.

Helgerud, J., Engen, L.C., Wisløff, U., and Hoff, J. 2001. Aerobic endurance training improves soccer performance. *Medicine and Science in Sports and Exercise* 33 (11): 1925–1931.

Hill-Haas, S., Dawson, B., Impellizzeri, F.M., and Coutts, A. 2011. Physiology of small sided games training in football. *Sports Medicine* 41 (3): 199–220.

Hill-Haas, S., Dawson, B.T., Coutts, A.J., and Roswell, G.J. 2009. Physiological responses and time-motion characteristics of various small-sided games in youth players. *Journal of Sports Sciences* 27 (1): 1–8.

Iaia, F.M., Rampinini, E., and Bangsbo, J. 2009. High intensity training in football. *International Journal of Sports Physiology and Performance* 4 (3): 291–306.

Impellizzeri, F.M., Rampinini, E., Maffuletti, N.A., Castagna, C., Bizzini, M., and Wisloff, U. 2008. Effects of aerobic training on the exercise induced decline in short passing ability in junior soccer players. *Applied Physiology, Nutrition and Metabolism* 33 (6): 1192–1198.

Kawamori, N., Newton, R., and Nosaka, K. 2014. Effects of sled towing on ground reaction force during the acceleration phase of sprint running. *Journal of Sports Sciences* 32 (12): 1139–1145.

Krustrup, P., Mohr, M., Steensberg, A., Bencke, J., Kjær, M., and Bangsbo, J. 2006. Muscle and blood metabolites during a soccer game: Implications for sprint performance. *Medicine and Science in Sports and Exercise* 38 (6): 1–10.

Krustrup, P., Mohr, M., Ellingsgaard, H., and Bangsbo, J. 2005. Physical demands during an elite female soccer game: Importance of training status. *Medicine and Science in Sports and Exercise* 37 (7): 1242–1248.

Krustrup, P., Mohr, M., Amstrup, T., Rysgaard, T., Johansen, J., Steensberg, A., Pedersen, P.K., and Bangsbo, J. 2003. The yo-yo intermittent recovery test: Physiological response, reliability, and validity. *Medicine and Science in Sports and Exercise* 35 (4): 697–705.

Mallo, J., and Navarro, E. 2008. Physical load imposed on soccer players during small-sided training games. *Journal of Sports Medicine and Physical Fitness* 48 (2): 166–172.

McDougall, J.D., Hicks, A.L., MacDonald, J.R, McKelvie, R.S., Green, H.J., and Smith, K.M. 1998. Muscle performance and enzymatic adaptations to sprint interval training. *Journal of Applied Physiology* 84 (6): 2138–2142.

McDougall, D., and Sale, D. 1981. Continuous vs. interval training: A review for the athlete and the coach. *Canadian Journal of Applied Sport Science* 6:93–97.

McMahon, S., and Wenger, H.A. 1998. The relationship between aerobic fitness and both power output and subsequent recovery during maximal intermittent exercise. *Journal of Science and Medicine in Sport* 1 (4): 219–227.

Mohr, M., Krustrup, P., and Bangsbo, J. 2003. Match performance of high-standard soccer players with special reference to development of fatigue. *Journal of Sports Sciences* 21 (7): 519–528.

Nader, G.A. 2006. Concurrent strength and endurance training: From molecules to man. *Medicine and Science in Sports and Exercise* 38 (11): 1965–1970.

Nedelec, M., McCall, A., Carling, C., Le Gall, F., Berthoin, S., and Dupont, G. 2012. Recovery in soccer: Part I - post-match fatigue and time course of recovery. *Sports Medicine* 42 (12): 997–1015.

Nedelec, M., Wisloff, U., McCall, A., Berthoin, S., and Dupont, G. 2013. Recovery after an intermittent test. *International Journal of Sports Medicine* 34 (6): 554–558.

Phillips, S.M., Green, H.J., MacDonald, M.J., and Hughson, R.L. 1995. Progressive effect of endurance training on $\dot{V}O_2$ kinetics at the onset of submaximal exercise. *Journal of Applied Physiology* 79 (6): 1914–1920.

Rampinini, E., Bosio, A., Ferraresi, I., Petruolo, A., Morelli, A., and Sassi, A. 2011. Match-related fatigue in soccer players. *Medicine and Science in Sports and Exercise* 43 (11): 2161–2170.

Rampinini, E., Sassi, A., Morelli, A., Mazzoni, S., Fanchini, M., and Coutts, A. 2009. Repeated-sprint ability in professional and amateur soccer players. *Applied Physiology, Nutrition and Metabolism* 34 (6): 1048–1054.

Rampinini, E., Impellizzeri, F.M., Castagna, C., Azzalin, A., Ferrari-Bravo, D., and Wisloff, U. 2008. Effect of match-related fatigue on short passing ability in young soccer players. *Medicine and Science in Sports and Exercise* 40 (5): 934–942.

Rampinini, E., Coutts, A.J., Castagna, C., Sassi, R., and Impellizzeri, F.M. 2007a. Variation in top level soccer match performance. *International Journal of Sports Medicine* 28 (12): 1–7.

Rampinini, E., Impellizzeri, F.M., Castagna, C., Abt, G., Chamari, K., Sassi, A., and Marcora, S.M. 2007b. Factors influencing physiological responses to small-sided games. *Journal of Sports Sciences* 25 (6): 659–666.

Rodas, G., Ventura, J.L., Cadefau, J.A., Cusso, R., and Parra, J. 2000. A short training programme for the rapid improvement of both aerobic and anaerobic metabolism. *European Journal of Applied Physiology* 82 (5–6): 480–486.

Ronnestad, B.R., Kvamme, N.H., Sunde, A., and Raastad, T. 2008. Short-term effects of strength and plyometric training on sprint and jump performance in professional soccer players. *Journal of Strength and Conditioning Research* 22 (3): 773–780.

Silva, R.F., Cadore, E.L., Kothe, G., Guedes, M., Alberton, C.L., Pinto, S.S., Pinto, R.S., Trindade, G., and Kruel, L.F. 2012. Concurrent training with different aerobic exercises. *International Journal of Sports Medicine* 33 (8): 627–634.

Stolen, T., Chamari, K., Castagna, C., and Wisloff, U. 2005. Physiology of soccer: An update. *Sports Medicine* 35 (6): 501–536.

Tomlin, D.L., and Wenger, H.A. 2001. The relationship between aerobic fitness and recovery from high intensity exercise. *Sports Medicine* 31 (1): 1–11.

Wisloff, U., Helgerud, J., and Hoff, J. 1998. Strength and endurance of elite soccer players. *Medicine and Science in Sports and Exercise* 30 (3): 462–467.

Wisløff, U., Castagna, C., Helgerud, J., Jones, R., and Hoff, J. 2004. Strong correlation of maximal squat strength with sprint performance and vertical jump height in elite soccer players. *British Journal of Sports Medicine* 38 (3): 285–288.

Young, W. 2006. Transfer of strength and power training to sports performance. *International Journal of Sports Physiology and Performance* 1:74–83.

Zafeiridis, A., Saraslanidis, P., Manou, V., Ioakimidis, P., Dipla, K., and Kellis S. 2005. The effects of resisted sled-pulling sprint training on acceleration and maximum speed performance. *Journal of Sports Medicine and Physical Fitness* 45 (3): 284–290.

Chapter 12

Croisier, J.L., Ganteaume, S., Binet, J., Genty, M., and Ferret, J.M. 2008. Strength imbalances and prevention of hamstring injury in professional soccer players: A prospective study. *American Journal of Sports Medicine* 36:1469–1475.

Dupont, G., Akakpo, K., and Berthoin, S. 2004. The effect of in-season, high-intensity interval training in soccer players. *Journal of Strength and Conditioning Research* 18:584–589.

Ekstrand, J., Hagglund, M., and Fuller, C.W. 2011. Comparison of injuries sustained on artificial turf and grass by male and female elite football players. *Scandinavian Journal of Medicine and Science in Sports* 21 (6): 824–832.

Ericsson, K.A., Krampe, R.T., and Tesch-Römer, C. 1993. The role of deliberate practice in the acquisition of expert performance. *Psychological Review* 100 (3): 363–406.

Ferrari, B.D., Impellizzeri, F.M., Rampinini, E., Castagna, C., Bishop, D., and Wisloff, U. 2008. Sprint vs. interval training in football. *International Journal of Sports Medicine* 29:668–674.

Hill-Haas, S.V., Dawson, B.T., Coutts, A.J., and Rowsell, G.J. 2009. Physiological responses and time-motion characteristics of various small-sided soccer games in youth players. *Journal of Sports Sciences* 27:1–8.

Hill-Haas, S.V., Dawson, B.T., and Coutts, A.J. 2011. Physiology of small-sided games training in football: A systematic review. *Sports Medicine* 41 (3): 199–220.

Iaia, F.M., Rampinini, E., and Bangsbo, J. 2009. High-intensity training in football. *International Journal of Sports Physiology and Performance* 4 (3): 291–306.

Iaia, F.M., and Bangsbo, J. 2010. Speed endurance training is a powerful stimulus for physiological adaptations and performance improvements of athletes. *Scandinavian Journal of Medicine and Science in Sports* 20 (Suppl. 2): 11–23.

Junge, A., and Dvorak, J. 2007. Injuries in female football players in top-level international tournaments. *British Journal of Sports Medicine,* 41 (Suppl. 1): i3–7.

Little, T., and Williams, A.G. 2006. Suitability of soccer training drills for endurance training. *Journal of Strength and Conditioning Research* 20 (2): 316–319.

Mujika, I. 2010. Intense training: The key to optimal performance before and during the taper. *Scandinavian Journal of Medicine and Science in Sports* 20 (Suppl. 2): 24–31.

Nimmo, M.A., and Ekblom, B. 2007. Fatigue and illness in athletes. *Journal of Sports Sciences* 25:S93–S102.

Opar, D.A., Williams, M.D., Timmins, R.G., Hickey, J., Duhig, S.J., and Shield, A.J. 2015. Eccentric hamstring strength and hamstring injury risk in Australian footballers. *Medicine and Science in Sports and Exercise* 47 (4): 857–865.

Soligard, T., Nilstad, A., Steffen, K., Myklebust, G., Holme, I., Dvorak, J., Bahr, R., and Andersen, T.E. 2010. Compliance with a comprehensive warm-up programme to prevent injuries in youth football. *British Journal of Sports Medicine* 44 (11): 787–793.

Yule, S. 2014. Maintaining an in-season conditioning edge. In *High-performance training for sports*, ed. D. Joyce and D. Lewindon, 301–318. Champaign, IL: Human Kinetics.

Zebis, M.K., Skotte, J., Andersen, C.H., Mortensen, P., Petersen, H.H., Viskaer, T.C., Jensen, T.L., Bencke, J., Andersen, L.L. 2013. Kettlebell swing targets semitendinosus and supine leg curl targets biceps femoris: An EMG study with rehabilitation implications. *British Journal of Sports Medicine* 47 (18): 1192–1198.

Chapter 13

American College of Sports Medicine, Armstrong, L.E., Casa, D.J., Millard-Stafford, M., Moran, D.S., Pyne, S.W., and Roberts, W.O. 2007. American College of Sports Medicine position stand. Exertional heat illness during training and competition. *Medicine and Science in Sports and Exercise* 39 (3): 556–572.

Armstrong, L.E. 1998. Heat acclimatization. In *Encyclopedia of sports medicine and science*, ed. T.D. Fahey. Internet Society for Sports Science [Internet only].

Bartsch, P., Dvorak, J., and Saltin, B. 2008. Football at high altitude. *Scandinavian Journal of Medicine and Science in Sports* 18 (Suppl. 1): iii–iv.

Foster, C., Daines, E., Hector L., Snyder, A.C., and Welsh, R. 1996. Athletic performance in relation to training load. *Wisconsin Medical Journal* 95 (6): 370–374.

Gore, C.J., McSharry, P.E., Hewitt, A.J., and Saunders, P.U. 2008. Preparation for football competition at moderate to high altitude. *Scandinavian Journal of Medicine and Science in Sports* 18 (Suppl. 1): 85–95.

Hallagan, L.F., and Pigman, E.C. 1998. Acclimatization to intermediate altitudes. In *Encyclopedia of sports medicine and science*, ed. T.D. Fahey. Internet Society for Sports Science [Internet only].

Jehue, R., Street, D., and Huizenga, R. 1993. Effect of time zone and game time changes on team performance. National Football League. *Medicine and Science in Sports and Exercise* 25 (1): 127–131.

Kraning, K.K., 2nd, and Gonzalez, R.R. 1991. Physiological consequences of intermittent exercise during compensable and uncompensable heat stress. *Journal of Applied Physiology (1985)* 71 (6): 2138–2145.

Levine, B.D. 2002. Intermittent hypoxic training: fact and fancy. *High Altitude Medicine and Biology* 3 (2): 177–193.

Levine, B.D., and Stray-Gundersen, J. 1997. 'Living high-training low': Effect of moderate-altitude acclimatization with low-altitude training on performance. *Journal of Applied Physiology (1985)* 83 (1): 102–112.

McSharry, P.E. 2007. Effect of altitude on physiological performance: A statistical analysis using results of international football games. *British Medical Journal* 335 (7633): 1278–1281.

Nassis, G.P. 2013. Effect of altitude on football performance: Analysis of the 2010 FIFA World Cup data. *Journal of Strength and Conditioning Research* 27 (3): 703–707.

Reilly, T., Waterhouse, J., and Edwards, B. 2005. Jet lag and air travel: Implications for performance. *Clinical Sports Medicine* 24 (2): 367–380.

Reilly, T., Waterhouse, J., Burke, L.M., and Alonso, J.M. 2007. Nutrition for travel. *Journal of Sports Sciences* 25 (Suppl. 1): S125–S134.

Rundell, K.W. 2012. Effect of air pollution on athlete health and performance. *British Journal of Sports Medicine* 46 (6): 407–412.

Waterhouse, J., Reilly, T., and Atkinson, G. 1998. Melatonin and jet lag. *British Journal of Sports Medicine* 32 (2): 98–99.

Waterhouse, J., Reilly, T., Atkinson, G., and Edwards, B. 2007. Jet lag: Trends and coping strategies. *Lancet* 369 (9567): 1117–1129.

Chapter 14

Ali, A., O'Donnell, J., Von Hurst, P., Foskett, A., Holland, S., Starck, C., and Rutherfurd-Markwick, K. 2015. Caffeine ingestion enhances perceptual responses during intermittent exercise in female team-game players. *Journal of Sports Science* 5:1–12. [Epub ahead of print].

Andrade-Souza, V.A., Bertuzzi, R., de Araujo, G.G., Bishop, D., and Lima-Silva, A.E. 2015. Effects of isolated or combined carbohydrate and caffeine supplementation between 2 daily training sessions on soccer performance. *Applied Physiology, Nutrition, and Metabolism* 40 (5): 457–463.

Astorino, T.A., Matera, A.J., Basinger, J., Evans, M., Schurman, T., and Marquez, R. 2012. Effects of Red Bull energy drink on repeated sprint performance in women athletes. *Amino Acids* May 42 (5): 1803–1808.

Atherton, P.J., and Smith, K. 2012. Muscle protein synthesis in response to nutrition and exercise. *Journal of Physiology* 590 (Pt 5): 1049–1057.

Bishop, D. 2010. Dietary supplements and team-sport performance. *Sports Medicine* 40 (12): 995–1017.

Breen, L., and Phillips, S.M. 2012. Nutrient interaction for optimal protein anabolism in resistance exercise. *Current Opinion in Clinical Nutrition and Metabolic Care* 15 (3): 226–232.

Burke, L.M., Desbow, B., and Spriet, L. 2013. *Caffeine for sports performance.* Champaign, IL: Human Kinetics.

Burke, L.M., Kiens, B., and Ivy, J.L. 2004. Carbohydrates and fat for training and recovery. *Journal of Sports Sciences* 22 (1): 15–30.

Burke, L., Loucks, A., and Broad, N. 2006. Energy and carbohydrate for training and recovery. *Journal of Sports Science* 24:675–685.

Burke, L., and Kiens, B. 2006. 'Fat adaptation' for athletic performance: The nail in the coffin? *Journal of Applied Physiology* 100:7–8.

Clark, M., Reed, D., Crouse, S., and Armstrong, R. 2003. Pre- and post-season dietary intake, body composition, and performance indices of NCAA Division I female soccer players. *International Journal of Sports Nutrition and Exercise Metabolism* 13:303–319.

Cobley, J.N., McGlory, C., Morton, J.P., and Close, G.L. 2011. N-Acetylcysteine's attenuation of fatigue after repeated bouts of intermittent exercise: Practical implications for tournament situations. *International Journal of Sport Nutrition and Exercise Metabolism* 21:451–461.

Cockburn, E., Bell, P.G., and Stevenson, E. 2013. Effect of milk on team sport performance after exercise-induced muscle damage. *Medicine and Science in Sport and Exercise* 45 (8): 1585–1592.

Cox, G.R., Desbrow, B., Montgomery, P.G., Anderson, M.E., Bruce, C.R., Macrides, T.A., Martin,

D.T., Moquin, A., Roberts, A., Hawley, J.A., and Burke, L.M. 2002. Effect of different protocols of caffeine intake on metabolism and endurance performance. *Journal of Applied Physiology (1985)* 93 (3): 990–999.

Cox, G., Mujika, I., Tumilty, D., and Burke, L. 2002. Acute creatine supplementation and performance during a field test simulating match play in elite female soccer players. *International Journal of Sport Nutrition and Exercise Metabolism* 12:33–46.

Dalbo, V.J., Roberts, M.D., Stout, J.R., and Kerksick, C.M., 2008. Putting to rest the myth of creatine supplementation leading to muscle cramps and dehydration. *British Journal of Sports Medicine* 42 (7): 567–573.

de Hon, O., and Coumans, B. 2007. The continuing story of nutritional supplements and doping infractions. *British Journal of Sports Medicine* 41:800–5.

Del Coso, J., Munoz-Fernandez, V.E., Munoz, G., Fernandez-Elias, V.E., Ortega, J.F., Hamouti, N., Barbero, J.C., and Munoz-Guerra, J. 2012. Effects of a caffeine-containing energy drink on simulated soccer performance. *PLoS One* 7:e31380.

DeLuca, H.F. 2004. Overview of general physiologic features and functions of vitamin D. *American Journal of Clinical Nutrition* 80:1689S–96S.

Draeger, C.L., Naves, A., Marques, N., Baptistella, A.B., Carnauba, R.A., Paschoal, V., and Nicastro, H. 2014. Controversies of antioxidant vitamins supplementation in exercise: ergogenic or ergolytic effects in humans? *Journal of the International Society of Sports Nutrition* 11 (1): 4.

Ebine, N., Rafamantanantsoa, H.H., Nayuki, Y., Yamanaka, K., Tashima, K., Ono, T., Saitoh, S., and Jones, P.J. 2002. Measurement of total energy expenditure by the doubly labelled water method in professional soccer players. *Journal of Sports Sciences* 20 (5): 391–397.

Fallon, K. 2004. Utility of haematological and iron-related screening in elite athletes. *Clinical Journal of Sports Medicine* 14:145–152.

Foskett, A., Ali, A., and Gant, N. 2009. Caffeine enhances cognitive function and skill performance during simulated soccer activity. *International Journal of Sport Nutrition and Exercise Metabolism* 19:410–23.

Galan, F., Ribas, J., Sánchez-Martinez, P.M., Calero, T., Sánchez, A.B., and Muñoz, A. 2012. Serum 25-hydroxyvitamin D in early autumn to ensure vitamin D sufficiency in mid-winter in professional football players. *Clinical Nutrition* 31:132–6.

Gant, N., Ali, A., and Foskett, A. 2010. The influence of caffeine and carbohydrate coingestion on simulated soccer performance. *International Journal of Sport Nutrition and Exercise Metabolism* 20 (3): 191–7.

Ginde, A.A., Mansbach, J.M., and Camargo, C.A. 2009. Association between serum 25-hydroxyvitamin D level and upper respiratory tract infection in the Third National Health and Nutrition Examination Survey. *Archives of Internal Medicine* 169 (4): 384–390.

Gomez-Cabrera, M.C., Domenech, E., Romagnoli, M., Arduini, A., Borras, C., Pallardo, F.V., Sastre, J., and Vina, J. 2008. Oral administration of vitamin C decreases muscle mitochondrial biogenesis and hampers training-induced adaptations in endurance performance. *American Journal of Clinical Nutrition* 87 (1): 142–149.

Graham, T.E. 2001. Caffeine and exercise: Metabolism, endurance and performance. *Sports Medicine* 31:785–807

Gross, M., Baum, O., and Hoppeler, H. 2011. Antioxidant supplementation and endurance training: Win or loss? *European Journal of Sport Science* 11 (1): 27–32.

Hamilton, B. 2010. Vitamin D and skeletal muscle. *Scandinavian Journal of Medicine and Science in Sports* 20:182–190.

Harris, R.C., Tallon, M., Dunnett, M., Boobis, L., Coakley, J., Kim, H.J., Fallowfield, J.L., Hill, C., Sale, C., and Wise, J.A. 2006. The absorption of orally supplied β-alanine and its effect on muscle carnosine synthesis in human vastus lateralis. *Amino Acids* 30 (3): 279–289.

Harris, R.C., and Sale, C. 2012. Beta-alanine supplementation in high-intensity exercise. *Medicine and Sport Science* 59:1–17.

Heaney, R.P. 2003. Long-latency deficiency disease: Insights from calcium and vitamin D. *American Journal of Clinical Nutrition* 78:912–19.

Helms, E.R., Zinn, C., Rowlands, D.S., and Brown, S.R. 2014. A systematic review of dietary protein during caloric restriction in resistance trained lean athletes: A case for higher intakes. *International Journal of Sport Nutrition and Exercise Metabolism* 24 (2): 127–138.

Holway, F.E., and Spriet, L.L. 2011. Sport-specific nutrition: Practical strategies for team sports. *Journal of Sports Sciences* 29 (Suppl. 1): S115–S125.

Howatson, G., Bell, P.G., Tallent, J., Middleton, B., McHugh, M.P., and Ellis, J. 2012. Effect of tart cherry juice (Prunus cerasus) on melatonin levels and enhanced sleep quality. *European Journal of Nutrition* 51:909–916.

Irwin, M., Mascovich, A., Gillin, J.C., Willoughby, R., Pike, J., and Smith, T.L. 1994. Partial sleep deprivation reduces natural killer cell activity in humans. *Psychosomatic Medicine* 56 (6): 479–578.

James, L. 2012. Milk protein and the restoration of fluid balance after exercise. *Medicine and Sport Science* 59:120–126.

Jeukendrup, A.E. 2004. Carbohydrate intake during exercise and performance. *Nutrition* 20 (7): 669–677.

Josse, A.R., Atkinson, S.A., Tarnopolsky, M.A., and Phillips, S.M. 2011. Increased consumption of dairy foods and protein during diet- and exercise-induced weight loss promotes fat mass loss and lean mass gain in overweight and obese premenopausal women. *Journal of Nutrition* 141 (9): 1626–1634.

Koopman, R., Saris, W.H., Wagenmakers, A.J., and van loon, L.J. 2007. Nutritional interventions to promote post-exercise muscle protein synthesis. *Sports Medicine* 37:895–906.

Kopeć, A., Solarz, K., Majda, F., Słowińska-Lisowska, M., and Mędraś, M. 2013. An evaluation of the levels of vitamin D and bone turnover markers after the summer and winter periods in Polish professional soccer players. *Journal of Human Kinetics* 38:135–140.

Kovacs, E.M., Stegen, J.H.C.H., and Brouns, F. 1998. Effect of caffeinated drinks on substrate metabolism, caffeine excretion, and performance. *Journal of Applied Physiology (1985)* 85 (2): 709–715.

Lambert, E.V., Speechly, D.P., Dennis, S.C., and Noakes, T.D. 1994. Enhanced endurance in trained cyclists during moderate intensity exercise following 2 weeks adaptation to a high fat diet. *European Journal of Applied Physiology and Occupational Physiology* 69 (4): 287–293.

Landahl, G., Adolfsson, P., Borjesson, M., Mannheimer, C., and Rodjer, S. 2005. Iron deficiency and anemia: A common problem in female elite soccer players. *International Journal of Sports Nutrition and Exercise Metabolism* 15:689–694.

Lara, B., Gonzalez-Millan, C., Salinero, J.J., Abian-Vicen, J., Areces, F., Barbero-Alvarez, J.C., Munoz, V., Portilo, L.J., Gonzalez-Rave, J.M., and Del Coso, J. 2014. Caffeine-containing energy drink improves physical performance in female soccer players. *Amino Acids* 46:1385–92.

Larson-Meyer, D.E., and Willis, K.S. 2010. Vitamin D and athletes. *Current Sports Medicine Reports* 9:220–26.

Larson-Meyer, D., Burke, L., Stear, S., and Castell, L. 2013. A–Z of nutritional supplements: dietary supplements, sports nutrition foods and ergogenic aids for health and performance: Part 40. *British Journal of Sports Medicine* 47 (2): 118–120.

Maïmoun, L., Manetta, J., Couret, I., Dupuy, A.M., Mariano-Goulart, D., Micallef, J.P., Peruchon, E., and Rossi, M. 2006. The intensity level of physical exercise and the bone metabolism response. *International Journal of Sports Medicine* 27 (2): 105–111.

Martin, K., Smee, D., Thompson, K.G., and Rattray, B. 2014. No improvement of repeated sprint performance with dietary nitrate. *International Journal of Sports Physiology and Performance* 9:845–50.

Maughan, R. 2005. Contamination of dietary supplements and positive drug tests in sport. *Journal of Sports Sciences* 23 (9): 883–889.

Maughan, R., and Shirreffs, S. 2007. Nutrition and hydration concerns of the female football player. *British Journal of Sports Medicine* 41 (Suppl. 1): i60–63.

Maughan, R., Shirreffs, S., Merson, S., and Horswill, C. 2005. Fluid and electrolyte balance in elite male football (soccer) players training in a cool environment. *Journal of Sports Sciences* 23 (1): 73–79.

Maughan, R.J., Merson, S.J., Broad, N.P., and Shirreffs, S.M. 2004. Fluid and electrolyte intake and loss in elite soccer players during training. *International Journal of Sport Nutrition and Exercise Metabolism* 14:333–346.

Maughan, R.J., Watson, P., Evans, G.H., Broad, N., and Shirreffs, S.M. 2007. Water balance and salt losses in competitive football. *International Journal of Sport Nutrition and Exercise Metabolism* 17 (6): 583.

Moore, D.R., Robinson, M.J., Fry, J.L., Tang, J.E., Glover, E.I., Wilkinson, S.B., Prior, T., Tarnopolsky, M.A., and Phillips, S.M. 2009. Ingested protein dose response of muscle and albumin protein synthesis after resistance exercise in young men. *American Journal of Clinical Nutrition* 89 (1): 161–168.

Moran, S.M., McClung, J.P., Kohen, T., and Lieberman, H.R. 2013. Vitamin D and physical performance. *Sports Medicine* 43 (7): 601–611.

Morton, J.P., Iqbal, Z., Drust, B., Burgess, D., Close, G.L., and Brukner, P.D. 2012. Seasonal variation in vitamin D status in professional soccer players of the English Premier League. *Applied Physiology, Nutrition and Metabolism* 37:798–802.

Mujika, I., Padilla, S., Ibanez, J., Izquierdo, M., and Gorostiaga, E. 2000. Creatine supplementation and sprint performance in soccer players. *Medicine and Science in Sports and Exercise* 32 (2): 518–525.

Mullinix, M., Jonnalagadda, S., and Rosenbloom, C. 2003. Dietary intake of female US soccer players. *Nutrition Research* 23:585–593.

Muoio, D.M., Leddy, J.J., Horvath, P.J., Awad, A.B., and Pendergast, D.R. 1994. Effect of dietary fat on metabolic adjustments to maximal $\dot{V}O_2$ and endurance in runners. *Medicine and Science in Sports and Exercise* 26 (1): 81–88.

Murphy, C.H., Hector, A.J., and Phillips, S.M. 2015. Considerations for protein intake in managing weight loss in athletes. *European Journal of Sport Science* 15 (1): 21–28.

Nieman, D., and Bishop, N. 2006. Nutritional strategies to counter stress to the immune system in athletes, with special reference to football. *Journal of Sports Science* 24:763–772.

Ogan, D., and Pritchett, K. 2013. Vitamin D and the athlete: Risks, recommendations, and benefits. *Nutrients* 5:1856–68.

Osgnach, C., Poser, S., Bernardini, R., Rinaldo, R., and Di Prampero, P.E. 2010. Energy cost and metabolic power in elite soccer: A new match analysis approach. *Medicine and Science in Sports and Exercise* 42 (1): 170–178.

Ostojic, S.M. 2004. Creatine supplementation in young soccer players. *International Journal of Sport Nutrition and Exercise Metabolism* 14 (1): 95–103.

Owens, D.J., Fraser, W.D., and Close, G.L. 2015. Vitamin D and the athlete: Emerging insights. *European Journal of Sport Science* 15:73–84.

Paulsen, G., Cumming, K.T., Holden, G., Hallén, J., Rønnestad, B.R., Sveen, O., Skaug, A., Paur, I., Bastani, N.E., Østgaard, H.N., Buer, C., Midttun, M., Freuchen, F., Wiig, H., Ulseth, E.T., Garthe, I., Blomhoff, R., Benestad, H.B., and Raastad, T. 2014. Vitamin C and E supplementation hampers cellular adaptation to endurance training in humans: A double-blind, randomised, controlled trial. *Journal of Physiology* 592 (pt 8): 1887–1901.

Peternelj, T., and Coombes, J.S. 2011. Antioxidant supplementation during exercise training. *Sports Medicine* 41 (12): 1043–1069.

Pettersen, S.A., Krustrup, P., Bendiksen, M., Randers, M.B., Brito, J., Bangsbo, J., Jin, Y., and Mohr, M. 2014. Caffeine supplementation does not affect match activities and fatigue resistance during match play in young football players. *Journal of Sports Sciences* 32 (20): 1958–65.

Phillips, S.M. 2011. The science of muscle hypertrophy: Making dietary protein count. *Proceedings of the Nutrition Society* 70 (1): 100–103.

Phillips, S.M., and Van Loon, L.J. 2011. Dietary protein for athletes: From requirements to optimum adaptation. *Journal of Sports Sciences* 29 (Suppl. 1): S29–S38.

Phillips, S.M., Tang, J.E., and Moore, D.R. 2009. The role of milk- and soy-based protein in support of muscle protein synthesis and muscle protein accretion in young and elderly persons. *Journal of the American College of Nutrition* 28 (4): 343–354.

Redondo, D.R., Dowling, E.A., Graham, B.L., Almada, A.L., and Williams, M.H. 1996. The effect of oral creatine monohydrate supplementation on running velocity. *International Journal of Sport Nutrition* 6:213–221.

Reilly, T., and Thomas, V. 1979. Estimated daily energy expenditures of professional association footballers. *Ergonomics* 22 (5): 541–548.

Rico-Sanz, J., Frontera, W.R., Mole, P.A., Rivera, M.A., Rivera-Brown, A., and Meredith, C.N. 1998. Dietary and performance assessment of elite soccer players during a period of intense training. *International Journal of Sport Nutrition* 8 (3): 230–240.

Rodriguez, N.R., Dimarco, N.M., Langley, S., American Dietetic Association, Dietitians of Canada, and American College of Sports Medicine. 2009. Position of the American Dietetic Association, Dietitians of Canada, and the American College of Sports Medicine: Nutrition and athletic performance. *Journal of the American Dietetic Association* 109 (3): 509–527.

Rosenbloom, C., Loucks, A., and Ekblom, B. 2006. Special populations: The female player and the youth player. *Journal of Sports Science* 24:783–793.

Russell, M., and Pennock, A. 2011. Dietary analysis of young professional soccer players for 1 week during the competitive season. *Journal of Strength and Conditioning Research* 25 (7): 1816–1823.

Sale, C., Artioli, G.G., Gualano, B., Saunders, B., Hobson, R.M., and Harris, R.C. 2013. Carnosine: From exercise performance to health. *Amino Acids* 44 (6): 1477–1491.

Saunders, B., Sale, C., Harris, R.C., and Sunderland, C. 2012. Effect of beta-alanine supplementation on repeated sprint performance during the Loughborough Intermittent Shuttle Test. *Amino Acids* 43 (1): 39–47.

Shirreffs, S., Aragon-Vargas, L., Chamorro, M., Maughan, R., Serratosa, L., and Zachwieja, J. 2005. The sweating response of elite professional soccer players to training in the heat. *International Journal of Sports Medicine* 26 (2): 90–95.

Simopoulos, A.P. 2007. Omega-3 fatty acids and athletics. *Current Sports Medicine Reports* 6 (4): 230–236.

Singh, M., and Das, P.R. 2011. Zinc for the common cold. *Cochrane Database of Systematic Reviews* Issue 2.

Stear, S. 2006. *Fuelling fitness for sports performance.* Fisher Print.

Stegen, S., Blancquaert, L., Everaert, I., Bex, T., Taes, Y., Calders, P., Achten, E., and Derave, W. 2013. Meal and beta-alanine coingestion enhances muscle carnosine loading. *Medicine and Science in Sports and Exercise* 45 (8): 1478–1485.

Stellingwerff, T., Decombaz, J., Harris, R.C., and Boesch, C. 2012. Optimizing human in vivo dosing and delivery of β-alanine supplements for muscle carnosine synthesis. *Amino Acids* 43 (1): 57–65.

Sundgot-Borgen, J., and Tortsveit, M. 2007. The female football player, disordered eating, menstrual function and bone health. *British Journal of Sports Medicine* 41:I68–I72.

Sweeney, K.M., Wright, G.A., Glenn Brice, A., and Doberstein, S.T. 2010. The effect of beta-alanine supplementation on power performance during repeated sprint activity. *Journal of Strength and Conditioning Research* 24:79–87.

Tarnopolsky, M. 2004. Protein requirements for endurance athletes. *Nutrition* 20 (7): 662–668.

Tipton, K., and Wolfe, R. 2004. Protein and amino acids for athletes. *Journal of Sports Sciences* 22:65–79.

Volpi, E., Kobayashi, H., Sheffield-Moore, M., Mittendorfer, B., and Wolfe, R.R. 2003. Essential amino acids are primarily responsible for the amino acid stimulation of muscle protein anabolism in healthy elderly adults. *American Journal of Clinical Nutrition* 78 (2): 250–258.

Volterman, K.A., Obeid, J., Wilk, D., and Timmons, B.W. 2014. Effects of postexercise milk consumption on whole body protein balance in youth. *Journal of Applied Physiology* 117:1165–1169

Walsh, N.P., Gleeson, M., Pyne, D.B., Nieman, D.C., Dhabhar, F.S., Shephard, R.J., Oliver, S.J., Bermon, S., and Kajeniene, A. 2011. Position statement. Part two: Maintaining immune health. *Exercise Immunology Review* 17:64–103.

West, N.P., Pyne, D.B., Peake, J.M., and Cripps, A.W. 2009. Probiotics, immunity and exercise: A review. *Exercise Immunology Review* 15:107–126.

Williams, J., Abt, G., and Kilding, A.E. 2014. Effects of creatine monohydrate supplementation on simulated soccer performance. *International Journal of Sports Physiology and Performance* 9 (3): 503–510.

Wylie, L.J., Mohr, M., Krustrup, P., Jackman, S.R., Ermidis, G., Kelly, J., Black, M., Bailey, S.J., Vanhatalo, A., and Jones, A.M. 2013. Dietary nitrate supplementation improves team sport-specific intense intermittent exercise performance. *European Journal of Applied Physiology* 113:1673–1684.

Chapter 15

Alentorn-Geli, E., Myer, G.D., Silvers, H.J., Samitier, G., Romero, D., Lazaro-Haro, C., and Cugat, R. 2009a. Prevention of non-contact anterior cruciate ligament injuries in soccer players. Part 1: Mechanisms of injury and underlying risk factors. *Knee Surgery, Sports Traumatology, Arthroscopy* 17 (7): 705–729.

Alentorn-Geli, E., Myer, G.D., Silvers, H.J., Samitier, G., Romero, D., Lazaro-Haro, C., and Cugat, R. 2009b. Prevention of non-contact anterior cruciate ligament injuries in soccer players. Part 2: A review of prevention programs aimed to modify risk factors and to reduce injury rates. *Knee Surgery, Sports Traumatology, Arthroscopy* 17 (8): 859–879.

Andersen, T.E., Arnason, A., Engebretsen, L., and Bahr, R. 2004. Mechanisms of head injuries in elite football. *British Journal of Sports Medicine* 38 (6): 690–696.

Arnason, A., Andersen, T.E., Holme, I., Engebretsen, L., and Bahr, R. 2008. Prevention of hamstring strains in elite soccer: an intervention study. *Scandinavian Journal of Medical Science in Sports* 18 (1): 40–48.

Arnason, A., Sigurdsson, S.B., Gudmundsson, A., Holme, I., Engebretsen, L., and Bahr, R. 2004. Risk factors for injuries in football. *American Journal of Sports Medicine* 32 (1 Suppl.): 5S–16S.

Arnason, A., Tenga, A., Engebretsen, L., and Bahr, R. 2004. A prospective video-based analysis of injury situations in elite male football: Football incident analysis. *American Journal of Sports Medicine* 32 (6): 1459–1465.

Askling, C., Karlsson, J., and Thorstensson, A. 2003. Hamstring injury occurrence in elite soccer players after preseason strength training with eccentric overload. *Scandinavian Journal of Medical Science in Sports* 13 (4): 244–250.

Bahr, R. 2009. No injuries, but plenty of pain? On the methodology for recording overuse symptoms in sports. *British Journal of Sports Medicine* 43 (13): 966–972.

Bahr, R., and Holme, I. 2003. Risk factors for sports injuries—a methodological approach. *British Journal of Sports Medicine* 37 (5): 384–392.

Bahr, R., and T. Krosshaug. 2005. Understanding injury mechanisms: A key component of preventing injuries in sport. *British Journal of Sports Medicine* 39 (6): 324–329.

Bizzini, M., Impellizzeri, F.M., Dvorak, J., Bortolan, L., Schena, F., Modena, R., and Junge, A. 2013. Physiological and performance responses to the 'FIFA 11+' (part 1): Is it an appropriate warm-up? *Journal of Sports Sciences* 31 (13): 1481–1490.

Bizzini, M., Junge A., and Dvorak, J. 2011. *11+ manual. A complete warm-up programme to prevent injuries.* Zurich: FIFA Medical Assessment and Research Centre.

Bizzini, M., Junge A., and Dvorak J. 2013. Implementation of the FIFA 11+ football warm up program: How to approach and convince the football associations to invest in prevention. *British Journal of Sports Medicine* 47 (12): 803–806.

Bizzini, M., and Dvorak, J. 2015. FIFA 11+: An effective programme to prevent football injuries in various player groups worldwide. A narrative review. *British Journal of Sports Medicine* 49 (5): 577–579.

Borghuis, J., Hof, A.L., and Lemmink, K.A. 2008. The importance of sensory-motor control in providing core stability: Implications for measurement and training. *Sports Medicine* 38 (11): 893–916.

Brito, J., Figueiredo, P., and Fernandes, L. 2010. Isokinetic strength effects of FIFA's "The 11+" injury prevention training programme. *Isokinetics and Exercise Science* 18:211–215.

Brophy, R.H., Silvers, H.J., and Mandelbaum, B.R. 2010. Anterior cruciate ligament injuries: Etiology and prevention. *Sports Medicine and Arthroscopy Review* 18 (1): 2–11.

Caraffa, A., Cerulli, G., Projetti ,M., Aisa, G., and Rizzo, A. 1996. Prevention of anterior cruciate ligament injuries in soccer. A prospective controlled study of proprioceptive training. *Knee Surgery, Sports Traumatology, Arthroscopy* 4 (1): 19–21.

Croisier, J.L., Ganteaume, S., Binet, J., Genty, M., and Ferret, J.M. 2008. Strength imbalances and prevention of hamstring injury in professional soccer players: A prospective study. *American Journal of Sports Medicine* 36 (8): 1469–1475.

Daneshjoo, A., Mokhtar, A.H., Rahnama, N., and Yusof, A. 2012a. The effects of comprehensive warm-up programs on proprioception, static and dynamic balance on male soccer players. *PLOS ONE* 7 (12): e51568.

Daneshjoo, A., Mokhtar, A.H., Rahnama, N., and Yusof, A. 2012b. The effects of injury preventive warm-up programs on knee strength ratio in young male professional soccer players. PLOS ONE 7 (12): e50979.

Drawer, S., and Fuller, C.W. 2001. Propensity for osteoarthritis and lower limb joint pain in retired professional soccer players. *British Journal of Sports Medicine* 35 (6): 402–408.

Drawer, S., and Fuller, C.W. 2002. Evaluating the level of injury in English professional football using a risk based assessment process. *British Journal of Sports Medicine* 36 (6): 446–451.

Dvorak, J. 2009. Give Hippocrates a jersey: Promoting health through football/sport. *British Journal of Sports Medicine* 43 (5): 317–322.

Dvorak, J., Junge, A., Chomiak, J., Graf-Baumann, T., Peterson, L., Rosch, D., and Hodgson, R. 2000. Risk factor analysis for injuries in football players. Possibilities for a prevention program. *American Journal of Sports Medicine* 28 (5 Suppl.): S69–74.

Dvorak, J., Junge, A., Derman, W., and Schwellnus, M. 2011. Injuries and illnesses of football players during the 2010 FIFA World Cup. *British Journal of Sports Medicine* 45 (8): 626–630.

Dvorak, J., Junge, A., Grimm, K., and Kirkendall, D. 2007. Medical report from the 2006 FIFA World Cup Germany. *British Journal of Sports Medicine* 41 (9): 578–581; discussion 581.

Ekstrand, J., Gillquist, J., and Liljedahl, S.O. 1983. Prevention of soccer injuries. Supervision by doctor and physiotherapist. *American Journal of Sports Medicine* 11 (3): 116–120.

Ekstrand, J., Gillquist J., Moller, M., Oberg, B., and Liljedahl, S.O. 1983. Incidence of soccer injuries and their relation to training and team success. *American Journal of Sports Medicine* 11 (2): 63–67.

Ekstrand, J., Hagglund, M., and Fuller, C.W. 2011. Comparison of injuries sustained on artificial turf and grass by male and female elite football players. *Scandinavian Journal of Medical Science in Sports* 21 (6): 824–832.

Emery, C.A., and Meeuwisse, W.H. 2010. The effectiveness of a neuromuscular prevention strategy to reduce injuries in youth soccer:

A cluster-randomised controlled trial. *British Journal of Sports Medicine* 44 (8): 555–562.

Fredberg, U., Bolvig, L., and Andersen, N.T. 2008. Prophylactic training in asymptomatic soccer players with ultrasonographic abnormalities in Achilles and patellar tendons: The Danish Super League Study. *American Journal of Sports Medicine* 36 (3): 451–460.

Froholdt, A., Olsen, O.E., and Bahr, R. 2009. Low risk of injuries among children playing organized soccer: A prospective cohort study. *American Journal of Sports Medicine* 37 (6): 1155–1160.

Fuller, C.W., Dick, R.W., Corlette, J., and Schmalz, R. 2007a. Comparison of the incidence, nature and cause of injuries sustained on grass and new generation artificial turf by male and female football players. Part 1: Match injuries. *British Journal of Sports Medicine* 41 (Suppl. 1): i20–26.

Fuller, C.W., Dick, R.W., Corlette, J., and Schmalz, R. 2007b. Comparison of the incidence, nature and cause of injuries sustained on grass and new generation artificial turf by male and female football players. Part 2: Training injuries. *British Journal of Sports Medicine* 41 (Suppl. 1): i27–32.

Fuller, C.W., Ekstrand, J., Junge, A., Andersen, T.E., Bahr, R., Dvorak, J., Hagglund, M., McCrory, P., and Meeuwisse, W.H. 2006a. Consensus statement on injury definitions and data collection procedures in studies of football (soccer) injuries. *British Journal of Sports Medicine* 40 (3): 193–201.

Fuller, C.W., Ekstrand, J., Junge, A., Andersen, T.E., Bahr, R., Dvorak, J., Hagglund, M., McCrory, P., and Meeuwisse, W.H. 2006b. Consensus statement on injury definitions and data collection procedures in studies of football (soccer) injuries. *Scandinavian Journal of Medical Science in Sports* 16 (2): 83–92.

Fuller, C.W., Ekstrand, J., Junge, A., Andersen, T.E., Bahr, R., Dvorak, J., Hagglund, M., McCrory, P., and Meeuwisse, W.H. 2006c. Consensus statement on injury definitions and data collection procedures in studies of football (soccer) injuries. *Clinical Journal of Sport Medicine* 16 (2): 97–106.

Fuller, C.W., Junge, A., and Dvorak, J. 2005. A six year prospective study of the incidence and causes of head and neck injuries in international football. *British Journal of Sports Medicine* 39 (Suppl. 1): i3–9.

Fuller, C.W., Smith, G.L., Junge, A., and Dvorak, J. 2004. The influence of tackle parameters on the propensity for injury in international football. *American Journal of Sports Medicine* 32 (1 Suppl.): 43S–53S.

Gilchrist, J., Mandelbaum, B.R., Melancon, H., Ryan, G.W., Silvers, H.J., Griffin, L.Y., Watanabe, D.S., Dick, R.W., and Dvorak, J. 2008. A randomized controlled trial to prevent noncontact anterior cruciate ligament injury in female collegiate soccer players. *American Journal of Sports Medicine* 36 (8): 1476–1483.

Hagglund, M., Walden, M., and Ekstrand, J. 2006. Previous injury as a risk factor for injury in elite football: A prospective study over two consecutive seasons. *British Journal of Sports Medicine* 40 (9): 767–772.

Hagglund, M., Walden, M., and Ekstrand, J. 2007. Lower reinjury rate with a coach-controlled rehabilitation program in amateur male soccer: A randomized controlled trial. *American Journal of Sports Medicine* 35 (9): 1433–1442.

Handoll, H.H., Rowe, B.H., Quinn, K.M., and de Bie, R. 2001. Interventions for preventing ankle ligament injuries. *Cochrane Database of Systematic Reviews* 3: CD000018.

Hawkins, R.D., and Fuller, C.W. 1998. An examination of the frequency and severity of injuries and incidents at three levels of professional football. *British Journal of Sports Medicine* 32 (4): 326–332.

Hawkins, R.D., and Fuller, C.W. 1999. A prospective epidemiological study of injuries in four English professional football clubs. *British Journal of Sports Medicine* 33 (3): 196–203.

Hawkins, R.D., Hulse, M.A., Wilkinson, C., Hodson, A., and M. Gibson. 2001. The association football medical research programme: An audit of injuries in professional football. *British Journal of Sports Medicine* 35 (1): 43–47.

Heidt, R.S., Jr., Sweeterman, L.M., Carlonas, R.L., Traub, J.A., and Tekulve, F.X. 2000. Avoidance of soccer injuries with preseason conditioning. *American Journal of Sports Medicine* 28 (5): 659–662.

Hewett, T.E., Ford, K.R., Hoogenboom, B.J., and Myer, G.D. 2010. Understanding and preventing ACL injuries: Current biomechanical and epidemiologic considerations—update 2010. *North American Journal of Sports Physical Therapy* 5 (4): 234–251.

Hewett, T.E., Lindenfeld, T.N., Riccobene, J.V., and Noyes, F.R. 1999. The effect of neuromuscular training on the incidence of knee injury in female athletes. A prospective study. *American Journal of Sports Medicine* 27 (6): 699–706.

Hewett, T.E., Stroupe, A.L., Nance, T.A., and Noyes, F.R. 1996. Plyometric training in female athletes. Decreased impact forces and increased hamstring torques. *American Journal of Sports Medicine* 24 (6): 765–773.

Holmich, P., Larsen, K., Krogsgaard, K., and Gluud, C. 2010. Exercise program for prevention of groin pain in football players: A cluster-randomized trial. *Scandinavian Journal of Medical Science in Sports* 20 (6): 814–821.

Hupperets, M.D., Verhagen, E.A., and van Mechelen, W. 2009. Effect of sensorimotor training on morphological, neurophysiological and functional characteristics of the ankle: A critical review. *Sports Medicine* 39 (7): 591–605.

Impellizzeri, F.M., Bizzini, M., Dvorak, J., Pellegrini, B., Schena, F., and Junge, A. 2013. Physiological and performance responses to the FIFA 11+ (part 2): A randomised controlled trial on the training effects. *Journal of Sports Sciences* 31 (13): 1491–1502.

Inklaar, H. 1994. Soccer injuries. I: Incidence and severity. *Sports Medicine* 18 (1): 55–73.

Johnson, U., Ekengren, J., and Andersen, M. 2005. Helping soccer players at risk. *Journal of Sport and Exercise Psychology* 27:32–38.

Junge, A., Chomiak, J., and Dvorak, J. 2000. Incidence of football injuries in youth players. Comparison of players from two European regions. *American Journal of Sports Medicine* 28 (5 Suppl.): S47–50.

Junge, A., and Dvorak, J. 2004. Soccer injuries: A review on incidence and prevention. *Sports Medicine* 34 (13): 929–938.

Junge, A., and Dvorak, J. 2007. Injuries in female football players in top-level international tournaments. *British Journal of Sports Medicine* 41 (Suppl. 1): i3–7.

Junge, A., Lamprecht, M., Stamm, H., Hasler, H., Bizzini, M., Tschopp, M., Reuter, H., Wyss, H., Chilvers, C., and Dvorak, J. 2011. Countrywide campaign to prevent soccer injuries in Swiss amateur players. *American Journal of Sports Medicine* 39 (1): 57–63.

Junge, A., Rosch, D., Peterson, L., Graf-Baumann, T., and Dvorak, J. 2002. Prevention of soccer injuries: A prospective intervention study in youth amateur players. *American Journal of Sports Medicine* 30 (5): 652–659.

Kiani, A., Hellquist, E., Ahlqvist, K., Gedeborg, R., Michaelsson, K., and Byberg, L. 2010. Prevention of soccer-related knee injuries in teenaged girls. *Archives of Internal Medicine* 170 (1): 43–49.

Kuijt, M.T., Inklaar, H., Gouttebarge, V., and Frings-Dresen, M.H. 2012. Knee and ankle osteoarthritis in former elite soccer players: A systematic review of the recent literature. *Journal of Science and Medicine in Sport* 15 (6): 480–487.

Lehnhard, R., Lehnhard, H., Young, R., and Butterfield, S. 1996. Monitoring injuries in a college soccer team: The effect of strength training. *Journal of Strength and Conditioning Research* 10:115–119.

Lohmander, L.S., Ostenberg, A., Englund, M., and Roos, H. 2004. High prevalence of knee osteoarthritis, pain, and functional limitations in female soccer players twelve years after anterior cruciate ligament injury. *Arthritis and Rheumatology* 50 (10): 3145–3152.

Mandelbaum, B.R., Silvers, H.J., Watanabe, D.S., Knarr, J.F., Thomas, S.D., Griffin, L.Y., Kirkendall, D.T., and Garrett, W. Jr. 2005. Effectiveness of a neuromuscular and proprioceptive training program in preventing anterior cruciate ligament injuries in female athletes: 2-year follow-up. *American Journal of Sports Medicine* 33 (7): 1003–1010.

Meeuwisse, W.H. 1994. Assessing causation in sport injury: A multifactorial model. *Clinical Journal of Sport Medicine* 4:166–170.

Meeuwisse, W.H., Tyreman, H., Hagel, B., and Emery, C. 2007. A dynamic model of etiology in sport injury: The recursive nature of risk and causation. *Clinical Journal of Sport Medicine* 17 (3): 215–219.

Mohammadi, F. 2007. Comparison of 3 preventive methods to reduce the recurrence of ankle inversion sprains in male soccer players. *American Journal of Sports Medicine* 35 (6): 922–926.

Nielsen, A.B., and Yde, J. 1989. Epidemiology and traumatology of injuries in soccer. *American Journal of Sports Medicine* 17 (6): 803–807.

Petersen, J., Thorborg, K., Nielsen, M.B., Budtz-Jorgensen, E., and Holmich, P. 2011. Preventive effect of eccentric training on acute hamstring injuries in men's soccer: A cluster-randomized controlled trial. *American Journal of Sports Medicine* 39 (11): 2296–2303.

Peterson, L., Junge, A., Chomiak, J., Graf-Baumann, T., and Dvorak, J. 2000. Incidence of football injuries and complaints in different age groups and skill-level groups. *American Journal of Sports Medicine* 28 (5 Suppl.): S51–57.

Reis, I., Rebelo, A., Krustrup, P., and Brito, J. 2013. Performance enhancement effects of Federation Internationale de Football Association's 'The 11+' injury prevention training program in youth futsal players. *Clinical Journal of Sport Medicine* 23 (4): 318–320.

Renstrom, P., Ljungqvist, A., Arendt, E., Beynnon, B., Fukubayashi, T., Garrett, W., Georgoulis, T., Hewett, T.E., Johnson, R., Krosshaug, T., Mandelbaum, B., Micheli, L., Myklebust, G., Roos, E., Roos, H., Schamasch, P., Shultz, S., Werner, S., Wojtys, E., and Engebretsen, L. 2008. Non-contact ACL injuries in female athletes: An International Olympic Committee current concepts statement. *British Journal of Sports Medicine* 42 (6): 394–412.

Sackett, D., Strauss, S., and Richardson, W. 2000. *Evidence-based medicine: How to practice and teach EBM*. Churchill Livingstone.

Scherrington, C. 2012. Integrating evidence into clinical practice to make quality decisions. In *Brukner and Khan's clinical sports medicine*, ed. P. Brukner, S. Blair, R. Bahr et al., 11–13. Sydney: McGraw Hill.

Sharpe, S.R., Knapik, J., and Jones, B. 1997. Ankle braces effectively reduce recurrence of ankle sprains in female soccer players. *Journal of Athletic Training* 32 (1): 21–24.

Soderman, K., Werner, S., Pietila, T., Engstrom, B., and Alfredson, H. 2000. Balance board training: Prevention of traumatic injuries of the lower extremities in female soccer players? A prospective randomized intervention study. *Knee Surgery, Sports Traumatology, Arthroscopy* 8 (6): 356–363.

Soligard, T., Myklebust, G., Steffen, K., Holme, I., Silvers, H., Bizzini, M., Junge, A., Dvorak, J., Bahr, R., and Andersen, T.E. 2008. Comprehensive warm-up programme to prevent injuries in young female footballers: Cluster randomised controlled trial. *BMJ* 337:a2469.

Soligard, T., Nilstad, A., Steffen, K., Myklebust, G., Holme, I., Dvorak, J., Bahr, R., and Andersen, T.E. 2010. Compliance with a comprehensive warm-up programme to prevent injuries in youth football. *British Journal of Sports Medicine* 44 (11): 787–793.

Steffen, K., Emery, C.A., Romiti, M., Kang, J., Bizzini, M., Dvorak, J., Finch, C.F., and Meeuwisse, W.H. 2013. High adherence to a neuromuscular injury prevention programme (FIFA 11+) improves functional balance and reduces injury risk in Canadian youth female football players: A cluster randomised trial. *British Journal of Sports Medicine* 47 (12): 794–802.

Silvers-Granelli H, Mandelbaum B, Adeniji O, Insler S, Bizzini M, Pohlig R, Junge A, Snyder-Mackler L, Dvorak J.

Am J Sports Med. 2015 Nov;43(11):2628-37.

Surve, I., Schwellnus, M.P., Noakes, T., and Lombard, C. 1994. A fivefold reduction in the incidence of recurrent ankle sprains in soccer players using the Sport-Stirrup orthosis. *American Journal of Sports Medicine* 22 (5): 601–606.

Tropp, H., Askling, C., and Gillquist, J. 1985. Prevention of ankle sprains. *American Journal of Sports Medicine* 13 (4): 259–262.

van Mechelen, W., Hlobil, H., and Kemper, H.C. 1992. Incidence, severity, aetiology and prevention of sports injuries. A review of concepts. *Sports Medicine* 14 (2): 82–99.

Verhagen, E.A., and Bay, K. 2010. Optimising ankle sprain prevention: A critical review and practical appraisal of the literature. *British Journal of Sports Medicine* 44 (15): 1082–1088.

Walden, M., Atroshi, I., Magnusson, H., Wagner, P., and Hagglund, M. 2012. Prevention of acute knee injuries in adolescent female football players: Cluster randomised controlled trial. *BMJ* 344:e3042.

Williams, S., Hume, P.A., and Kara, S. 2011. A review of football injuries on third and fourth generation artificial turfs compared with natural turf. *Sports Medicine* 41 (11): 903–923.

Chapter 16

Adie, J.W., Duda, J.L., and Ntoumanis, N. 2012. Perceived coach-autonomy support, basic need satisfaction and the well- and ill-being of elite youth soccer players: A longitudinal investigation. *Psychology of Sport and Exercise* 13:51–59.

Adolph, K.E., Eppler, M.A., Marin, L., Weise, I.B., and Wechsler Clearfield, M. 2000. Exploration in the service of prospective control. *Infant Behavior and Development* 23:441–460.

Aggerholm, K., Jespersen, E., and Ronglan, L.T. 2011. Falling for the feint: An existential- investigation of a creative performance in high-level football. *Sport, Ethics and Philosophy* 5:343–358.

Amiot, C.E., Vallerand, R.J., and Blanchard, C.M. 2006. Passion and psychological adjustment: A test of the person-environment fit hypothesis. *Personality and Social Psychology Bulletin* 32:220–229.

Balague, G. 2012. *Pep Guardiola: Another way of winning: The biography*. London: Orion.

Bergkamp, D., and Winner, D. 2013. *Stillness and speed: My story*. London: Simon & Schuster.

Bishop, D., Wright, M.J., Jackson, R.C., and Abernethy, B. 2013. Neural bases for anticipation skill in soccer: An fMRI Study. *Journal of Sport and Exercise Psychology* 35:98–109.

Bornstein, G., and Goldschmidt, C. 2008. Post-scoring behaviour and team success in football. In *Myths and facts about football: The economics and psychology of the world's greatest sport*, ed. P. Andersson, P. Ayton, and C. Schmidt, 113–123. Newcastle, UK: Cambridge Scholars.

Brink, M.S., Frencken, W.G.P., Jordet, G., and Lemmink, K.A.P.M. 2014. Coaches' and players' perception of training dose: Not at perfect match. *International Journal of Sports Physiology and Performance* 9 (3): 497–502.

Brink, M.S., Visscher, C., Arends, S., Zwerver, J., Post, W.J., and Lemmink, K.A.P.M. 2010. Monitoring stress and recovery: New insights for the prevention of injuries and illnesses in elite youth soccer players. *British Journal of Sports Medicine* 44:809–815.

Brink, M.S., Visscher, C., Coutts, A.J., and Lemmink, K.A.P.M. 2012. Changes in perceived stress and recovery in overreached young elite soccer players. *Scandinavian Journal of Medicine and Science in Sports* 22:285–92.

Bronfenbrenner, U. 1979. *The ecology of human development: Experiments by nature and design*. Cambridge, MA: Harvard University Press.

Canal-Bruland, R., Lotz, S., Hagemann, N., Schorer, J., and Strauss, B. 2011. Visual span and change detection in soccer: An expertise study. *Journal of Cognitive Psychology* 23:302–310.

Carver, C.S., and Johnson, S.L. 2011. Authentic and hubristic pride: Differential relations to aspects of goal regulation, affect, and self-control. *Journal of Research in Personality* 44:698–703.

Christensen, M. 2005. The real golden balls. Interview with Andriy Shevchenko. *Four-four-two* March:49–52.

Curran, T., Appleton, P.R., Hill, A.P., and Hall, H.K. 2011. Passion and burnout in elite junior soccer players: The mediating role of self-determined motivation. *Psychology of Sport and Exercise* 12:655–661.

Curran, T., Appleton, P.R., Hill, A.P., and Hall, H.K. 2013. The mediating role of psychological need satisfaction in relationships between types of passion for sport and athlete burnout. *Journal of Sports Sciences* 31:597–606.

De Haan, F. 2008. Foppe de Haan looks back at Beijing. *World Cup blog*. http://netherlands.worldcupblog.org/olympic-and-young-oranje/foppe-de-haan-looks-back-at-bejing.html.

Deci, E.L., and Ryan, R.M. 2000. The 'what' and 'why' of goal pursuits: Human needs and the self-determination of behavior. *Psychological Inquiry* 11:227–268

Donaldson, I. 2006. The experience of cultural adjustment and its relationship with cultural Intelligence: Evidence from a diverse sample of expatriates based in the UK. Master's thesis. Manchester Business School, University of Manchester.

Drogba, D. 2009. *Didier Drogba: The autobiography*. London: Aurum Press.

Duckworth, A.L., Peterson, C., Matthews, M.D., and Kelly, D.R. 2007. Grit: Perseverance and passion for long-term goals. *Journal of Personality and Social Psychology* 92 (6): 1087–1101.

Durand-Bush, N., and Salmela, J.H. 2002. The development and maintenance of expert athletic performance: Perceptions of world and Olympic champions. *Journal of Applied Sport Psychology* 14 (3): 154–171.

Elliot, A.J. 1999. Approach and avoidance motivation and achievement goals. *Educational Psychologist* 34:169–189.

Ericsson, K.A., Krampe, R.T., and Tesch-Romer, C. 1993. The role of deliberate practice in the acquisition of expert performance. *Psychological Review* 100:363–406.

Faude, O., Kellmann, M., Ammann, T., Schnittker, R., and Meyer, T. 2011. Seasonal changes in stress indicators in high level football. *International Journal of Sports Medicine* 32 (4): 259–265.

Felton, L., and Jowett, S. 2013. The mediating role of social environmental factors in the associations between attachment styles and basic needs satisfaction, *Journal of Sports Sciences* 31 (6): 618–628.

FIFA. 2001. *FIFA big count 2000*. FIFA Communication Divisions. www.fifa.com/mm/document/fifafacts/bcoffsurv/bigcount.statspackage_7024.pdf.

FIFA. 2007. *FIFA big count 2006*. FIFA Communication Divisions. www.fifa.com/mm/document/fifafacts/bcoffsurv/bigcount.summaryreport_7022.pdf.

Ford, P.R., Ward, P., Hodges, N.J., and Williams, A.M. 2009. The role of deliberate practice and play in career progression in sport: the early engagement hypothesis. *High Ability Studies* 20:65–75.

Ford, P.R., and Williams, A.M. 2012. The developmental activities engaged in by elite youth soccer players who progressed to professional status compared to those who did not. *Psychology of Sport and Exercise* 13:349–352.

Forzoni, R.E., and Karageorghis, C.I. 2001. Participation motives in elite soccer across age groups: A test of cognitive evaluation theory. In *Proceedings of the International Society of Sport Psychology (ISSP) 10th World Congress of Sport Psychology,* ed. A. Papaioannou, M. Goudas and Y. Theodorakis, vol. 3, 318–320.

Gerrard, S. 2006. *Gerrard: My autobiography.* London: Transworld.

Gibson, J.J. 1979. *The ecological approach to visual perception.* Boston: Houghton Mifflin.

Gledhill, A., and Harwood, C. 2014. Developmental experiences of elite female youth soccer players. *International Journal of Sport and Exercise Psychology* 12 (2): 150–165.

Gray, P. 2007. *Psychology.* 5th ed. New York: Worth.

Gulbin, J., Weissensteiner, J., Oldenziel, K., and Gangé, F. 2013. Patterns of performance development in elite athletes. *European Journal of Sport Science* 13 (6): 605–614.

Haugaasen, M., and Jordet, G. 2012. Developing football expertise: A football-specific research review. *International Review of Sport and Exercise Psychology* 5 (2): 177– 201.

Haugaasen, M., Toering, T., and Jordet, G. 2014. From childhood to senior professional football: A multi-level approach to elite youth football players' engagement in football-specific activities. *Psychology of Sport and Exercise* 15:336–344.

Helsen, W.F., Starkes, J.L., and Hodges, N.J. 1998. Team sports and the theory of deliberate practice. *Journal of Sport and Exercise Psychology* 20:12–34.

Henderson, P. 2011. Man Utd in their own words: van der Sar. *GQ Magazine.* www.gq-magazine.co.uk/entertainment/articles/2011-05/31/gq-sport-manchester-united-fc-interview/page/5.

Hendry, D.T., Crocker, P.R.E., and Hodges, N.J. 2014. Practice and play as determinants of self-determined motivation in youth soccer players. *Journal of Sports Sciences* 32 (11): 1091–1099.

Hill, A.P., Hall, H.K., Appleton, P.R., and Kozub, S.A. 2008. Perfectionism and burnout in junior elite soccer players: The mediating influence of unconditional self-acceptance. *Psychology of Sport and Exercise* 9:630–645.

Holt, N.L., and Dunn, J.G.H. 2004. Toward a grounded theory of the psychosocial competencies and environmental conditions associated with soccer success. *Journal of Applied Sport Psychology* 16:199–219.

Holt, N.L., and Hogg, J.M. 2002. Perceptions of stress and coping during preparations for the 1999 women's soccer World Cup finals. *Sport Psychologist* 16:251–271.

Holt, N.L., and Mitchell, T. 2006. Talent development in English professional soccer. *International Journal of Sport Psychology* 37:77–98.

Horrocks, D. 2012. Brains in their feet? *Psychologist* 15:89–90.

Hughes, M. 2006. Crespo yearning for escape route back to Italy. *The Times*, 10 January 2006.

Ibrahimovic, Z., Lagercrantz, D., and Urbom, R. 2013. *I am Zlatan Ibrahimovic.* London: Penguin.

Ivarsson, A., and Johnson, U. 2010. Psychological factors as predictors of injuries among senior soccer players. A prospective study. *Journal of Sports Science and Medicine* 9:347–352.

Ivarsson, A., Johnson, U., and Podlog, L. 2013. Psychological predictors of injury occurrence: A prospective investigation of professional Swedish soccer players. *Journal of Sport Rehabilitation* 22:19–26.

Johnson, U., Ekengren, J., Andersen, M.B. 2005. Injury prevention in Sweden: Helping soccer players at risk. *Journal of Sport and Exercise Psychology* 27:32–38.

Jonker, L., Elferink-Gemser, M.T., Toering, T.T., Lyons, J., and Visscher, C. 2010. Academic performance and self-regulatory skills in elite youth soccer players. *Journal of Sports Sciences* 28:1605–1614.

Jordet, G. 2005a. Applied cognitive sport psychology in team ball sports: An ecological approach. In *New approaches to sport and exercise psychology,* ed. R. Stelter and K.K. Roessler, 147–174. Aachen, Germany: Meyer & Meyer Sport.

Jordet, G. 2005b. Perceptual training in soccer: An imagery intervention study with elite players. *Journal of applied sport psychology* 17:140–156.

Jordet, G. 2009a. When superstars flop: Public status and 'choking under pressure' in international soccer penalty shootouts. *Journal of Applied Sport Psychology* 21:125–130.

Jordet, G. 2009b. Why do English players fail in soccer penalty shootouts? A study of team status, self-regulation, and choking under pressure. *Journal of Sports Sciences* 27:97–106.

Jordet, G., Bloomfield, J., and Heijmerikx, J. 2013. The hidden foundation of field vision in English Premier League (EPL) soccer players. Presentation at MIT Sloan Sport Analytics Conference. www.sloansportsconference.com/wp-content/uploads/2013/02/The-hidden-foundation-of-field-vision-in-English-Premier-LeagueEPL-soccer-players.pdf.

Jordet, G., and Elferink-Gemser, M.T. 2012. Stress, coping, and emotions on the world stage: The experience of participating in a major soccer tournament penalty shootout. *Journal of Applied Sport Psychology* 24:73–91.

Jordet, G., and Hartman, E. 2008. Avoidance motivation and choking under pressure in soccer penalty shootouts. *Journal of Sport and Exercise Psychology* 30:452–459.

Jordet, G., Hartman, E., and Sigmundstad, E. 2009. Temporal links to performing under pressure in international soccer penalty shootouts. *Psychology of Sport and Exercise* 10:621–627.

Jordet, G., and Toering, T.T. 2014. Measuring performance psychology in football: A manual. Unpublished document.

Kraus, M., Huang, C., and Keltner, D. 2010. Tactile communication, cooperation, and performance: An ethological study of the NBA. *Emotion* 10:745–749.

Kristiansen, E., Roberts, G.C., and Sisjord, M.K. 2011. Coping with negative media coverage: The experiences of professional football goalkeepers. *International Journal of Sport and Exercise Psychology* 9:295–307.

Kuper, S. 2011. *Soccer men: Profiles of the rogues, geniuses, and neurotics who dominate the world's most popular sport.* New York: Nation Books.

Lazarus, R.S., and Folkman, S. 1984. *Stress, appraisal and coping.* New York: Springer.

Leite, N., Baker, J., and Sampaio, J. 2009. Paths to expertise in Portuguese national team athletes. *Journal of Sports Science and Medicine* 8:560–566.

Littlewood, M., Mullen, C., and Richardson, D. 2011. Football labour migration: An examination of the player recruitment strategies of the 'big five' European football leagues 2004–5 to 2008–9. *Soccer and Society* 12:788–805.

Littlewood, M.A., and Nesti, M. 2011. Making your way in the game: Boundary situations in England's professional football world. In *Critical essays in applied sport psychology*, ed. D. Gilbourne and M.B. Andersen, 233–249. Champaign, IL: Human Kinetics.

Lowe, S. 2011. I'm a romantic, says Xavi, heartbeat of Barcelona and Spain. *The Guardian.* February 11. www.theguardian.com/football/2011/feb/11/xavi-barcelona-spain-interview.

MacNamara, A., Button, A., and Collins, D. 2010a. The role of psychological characteristics in facilitating the pathway to elite performance. Part 1: Identifying mental skills and behaviors. *Sport Psychologist* 24:52–73.

MacNamara, Á., Button, A., and Collins, D. 2010b. The role of psychological characteristics in facilitating the pathway to elite performance. Part 2: Examining environmental and stage-related differences in skills and behaviors. *Sport Psychologist* 24:74–96.

Maradona, D.A. 2005. *El Diego: The autobiography of the world's greatest footballer.* London: Yellow Jersey Press.

Masters, R.S.W. 1992. Knowledge, knerves and know-how: The role of explicit versus implicit knowledge in the breakdown of a complex motor skill under pressure. *British Journal of Psychology* 83:343–358.

Memmert, D. 2010. Testing of tactical performance in youth elite soccer. *Journal of Sports Science and Medicine* 9:199–205.

Memmert, D. 2011. Creativity, expertise, and attention: Exploring their development and their relationships. *Journal of Sports Sciences* 29:93–102.

Memmert, D., and Roth, K. 2007. The effects of non-specific and specific concepts on tactical creativity in team ball sports. *Journal of Sports Sciences* 25:1423–1432.

Merleau-Ponty, M. 1962. *Phenomenology of perception.* New York: Humanities Press.

Mills, A., Butt, J., Maynard, I., and Harwood, C. 2012. Identifying factors perceived to influence the development of elite youth football academy players. *Journal of Sports Sciences* 30 (15): 1593–1604.

Moll, T., Jordet, G., and Pepping, G.J. 2010. Emotional contagion in soccer penalty shootouts: Celebration of individual success is associated with ultimate team success. *Journal of Sports Sciences* 28:983–992.

Naessens, G., Chandler, T.J., Kibler, W.B., and Driessens, M. 2000. Clinical usefulness of nocturnal urinary noradrenaline excretion patterns in the follow-up of training process in high-level soccer players. *Journal of Strength and Conditioning Research* 14:125–131.

Nesti, M. 2010. *Psychology in football: Working with elite and professional players.* London: Routledge.

Ntoumanis, N. 2012. A self-determination theory perspective on motivation in sport and physical education: Current trends and possible future research directions. In *Motivation in sport and exercise*, 3rd ed., ed. G.C. Roberts and D.C. Treasure, 91–128. Champaign, IL: Human Kinetics.

Orlick, T., and Partington, J. 1988. Mental links to excellence. *Sport Psychologist* 2:105–130.

Pain, M.A., Harwood, C., and Mullen, R. 2012. Improving the performance environment of a soccer team during a competitive season: An exploratory action research study. *Sport Psychologist* 26:390–411.

Pain, M.A., and Harwood, C.G. 2008. The performance environment of the England youth soccer teams: A quantitative study. *Journal of Sports Sciences* 13:1–13.

Pain, M., and Harwood, C. 2009. Team building through mutual sharing and open discussion of team functioning. *Sport Psychologist* 23:523–542.

Richardson, D., Littlewood, M., Nesti, M., and Benstead, L. 2012. An examination of the migratory transition of elite young European soccer players to the English Premier League. *Journal of Sports Sciences* 30 (15): 1605–1618.

Roberts, G.C. 2012. Motivation in sport and exercise from an achievement goal theory perspective: After 30 years, where are we? In *Advances in motivation in sport and exercise*, 3rd ed., ed. G.C. Roberts and D.C. Treasure, 5–58. Champaign, IL: Human Kinetics.

Roberts, G.C., Treasure, D.C., and Conroy, D.E. 2007. The dynamics of motivation in sport: The influence of achievement goals on motivation processes. In *Handbook of sport psychology*, 3rd ed., ed. G. Tenenbaum and R.C. Eklund, 3–30. New York: Wiley.

Roca, A., Ford, P.R., McRobert, A.P., and Williams, A.M. 2011. Identifying the processes underpinning anticipation and decision-making in a dynamic time-constrained task. *Cognitive Processes* 12:301–310.

Ronaldo. 2007. *Moments*. London: Macmillan.

Sagar, S., Busch, B.K., and Jowett, S. 2010. Success and failure, fear of failure, and coping responses of adolescent academy football players. *Journal of Applied Sport Psychology* 22 (2): 213–230.

SkySport. 2013. Premier League: Manchester City midfielder Yaya Toure says football is a science. *SkySport*. www1.skysports.com/football/news/11679/9056813/premier-league-manchester-city-midfielder-yaya-toure-says-football-is-a-science.

Snyder, C.R., Shorey, H.S., Cheavens, J., Pulvers, K.M., Adams, V.H., and Wiklund, C. 2002. Hope and academic success in college. *Journal of Educational Psychology* 4:820–826.

Southgate, G., Woodman, A., and Walsh, D. 2004. *Woody and Nord: A football friendship*. London: Penguin Books.

Sternberg, R.J., and Lubart, T.I. 1999. *Defying the crowd*. New York: Free Press.

Taylor, I.M., and Bruner, M.W. 2012. The social environment and developmental experiences in elite youth soccer. *Psychology of Sport and Exercise* 13:390–397.

Toering, T.T., Elferink-Gemser, M.T., Jordet, G., and Visscher, C. 2009. Self-regulation and performance level of elite and non-elite youth soccer players. *Journal of Sports Sciences* 27 (14): 1509–1517.

Toering, T.T., Elferink-Gemser, M.T., Jordet, G., Jorna, C., Pepping, G.J., and Visscher, C. 2011. Self-regulation of practice behavior among elite youth soccer players: An exploratory observation study. *Journal of Applied Sport Psychology* 23:110–128.

Toering, T., and Jordet, G. 2015. Self-control in professional football players. *Journal of Applied Sport Psychology* 27:335–350.

Tracy, J.L., and Robins, R.W. 2007a. The psychological structure of pride: a tale of two facets. *Journal of Personality and Social Psychology* 92:506–25.

Tracy, J.L., and Robins, R.W. 2007b. Emerging insights into the nature and function of pride. *Current Directions in Psychological Science* 16:147–150.

Vallerand, R.J. 2012. The dualistic model of passion in sport and exercise. In *Advances in motivation in sport and exercise*, 3rd ed., ed. G.C. Roberts and D.C. Treasure, 169–206. Champaign, IL: Human Kinetics.

Vallerand, R.J., Mageau, G.A., Elliot, A.J., Dumais, A., Demers, M., and Rousseau, F. 2008. Passion and performance attainment in sport. *Psychology of Sport and Exercise* 9:373–392.

Van Breukelen, H. 2011. *Winnen. Van talent naar topspeler (Winning. From talent to top player)*. Amsterdam, Netherlands: Uitgeverij L.J. Veen.

Van Yperen, N.W., and Duda, J.L. 1999. Goal orientations, beliefs about success, and performance improvement among youth elite Dutch soccer players. *Scandinavian Journal of Medicine and Science in Sports* 9:358–364.

Van Yperen, N.W. 2009. Why some make it an others do not: Identifying psychological factor that predict career success in professional adult soccer. *Sport Psychologist* 23:317–329.

Ward, P., Hodges, N.J., Starkes, J.L., and Williams, A.M. 2007. The road to excellence: Deliberate practice and the development of expertise. *High Ability Studies* 18:119–153.

Weick, K.E., and Sutcliffe, K.M. 2007. *Managing the unexpected: Resilient performance in an age of uncertainty*. San Francisco: Wiley.

Wenger, A. 2010. Panel debate at Leaders in Performance conference. *Leaders*. London, October 7.

Wilson, J. 2008. *Inverting the pyramid: The history of football tactics*. London: Orion.

Wilson, P. 2009. Sir Alex Ferguson still driven on by constant fear of failure. *The Guardian*. www.theguardian.com/football/2009/aug/16/manchester-united-birmingham-sir-alex-ferguson

Zimmerman, B.J. 2006. Development and adaptation of expertise: The role of self regulatory processes and beliefs. In *The Cambridge handbook of expertise and expert performance*, ed. K.A. Ericsson, N. Charness, P.J. Feltovich and R.R. Hoffman, 705–722. New York: Cambridge University Press.

Chapter 17

Bandura, A. 1977. Self-efficacy: Toward a unified theory of behavioral change. *Psychological Review* 84:191–215.

Brailsford, D. 2013. *Advertising Week Europe. Session from the Agenda Stage on 18/3/2013*. www.youtube.com/watch?v=ZjBd0GVyJw0.

Butland. 2012. Prepare for your biggest game. *FourFourTwo Performance*. http://performance.fourfourtwo.com/health/psychology/prepare-for-your-biggest-game.

Dante. 2014. Dante: *We weren't psychologically ready for the World Cup*. FIFA.com. www.fifa.com/world-match-centre/news/newsid/247/177/7/index.html?cid=newsletter_en_2014112 0_interview.

Deci, E.L., and Ryan, R.M. 1985. *Intrinsic motivation and self-determination in human behavior*. New York: Plenum.

Harwood, C.G. 2008. Developmental consulting in a professional soccer academy: The 5C's coaching efficacy program. *Sport Psychologist* 22:109–133.

Harwood, C.G., and Anderson, R. 2015. *Coaching psychological skills in youth soccer*. Stoke-on-Trent: Bennion-Kearny.

Horrocks, D.E, McKenna, J., Taylor, P.J., Morley, A., and Lawrence, I. Forthcoming. Preparation, structured deliberate practice and decision making in elite level football. The case study of Gary Neville (Manchester United FC and England). *International Journal of Sport Science and Coaching*.

Jordet, G., Bloomfield, J., and Heijmerikx, J. 2013. The hidden foundation of field vision in English Premier League (EPL) soccer players. Presentation at MIT Sloan Sport Analytics Conference. www.sloansportsconference.com/wp-content/uploads/2013/02/The-hidden-foundation-of-field-vision-in-English-Premier-LeagueEPL-soccer-players.pdf.

Michels, R. 2001. *Teambuilding: The road to success*. London: Reedswain.

Nideffer, R.M. 1989. *Attention control training for athletes*. New Berlin, WI: Assessment Systems International.

Pain, M.A., Harwood, C., and Anderson, R. 2011. Pre-competition imagery and music: The impact on flow and performance in competitive soccer. *Sport Psychologist* 25:212–232.

Reeves, C., Nicholls, A., and McKenna, J. 2009. Stressors and coping strategies among early and middle adolescent premier league academy soccer players: Differences according to age. *Journal of Applied Sport Psychology* 21:31–48.

Chapter 18

Andersen, M.B. 2005. 'Yeah, I work with Beckham': Issues of confidentiality privacy and privilege in sport psychology service delivery. *Sport and Exercise Psychology Review* 1:5–13.

Andersen, M.B. 2009. Performance enhancement as a bad start and a dead end: A parenthetical comment on Mellalieu and Lane. *Sport and Exercise Scientist* 20:12–14.

Balague, G. 1999. Understanding identity, value and meaning when working with elite athletes. *Sport Psychologist* 13:89–98.

Brady, A., and Maynard, I. 2010. At elite level the role of the sport psychologist is entirely about performance enhancement. *Sport and Exercise Psychology Review* 6:59–66.

Brewer, B.W., Van Raalte, J.L., and Linder, D.E. 1993. Athletic identity: Hercules' muscles or Achilles heel, *International Journal of Sport Psychology* 24:237–254.

Brown, G., and Potrac, P. 2009. You've not made the grade son: De-selection and identity disruption in elite level youth football, *Soccer and Society* 10:143–159.

Corlett, J. 1996. Sophistry, Socrates and sport psychology. *Sport Psychologist* 10:84–94.

Deci, E.L, and Ryan, R.M. 1985. *Intrinsic motivation and self-determination in human behaviour*. New York: Plenum Press.

Fletcher, D., and Wagstaff, C.R.D. 2009. Organizational psychology in elite sport: Its emergence, application and future. *Psychology of Sport and Exercise* 10:427–434.

Friesen, A., and Orlick, T. 2010. A qualitative analysis of holistic sport psychology consultants' professional philosophies. *Sport Psychologist* 24:227–244.

Gilbourne, D., and Richardson, D. 2006. Tales from the field: Personal reflections on the provision of psychological support in professional soccer. *Psychology of Sport and Exercise* 7:335–337.

Hanton, S., Neil, R., and Mellalieu, S.D. 2008. Recent developments in competitive anxiety direction and competition stress research. *International Review of Sport and Exercise Psychology* 1:45–57.

Jackson, S., and Csikzsentmihalyi, M. 1999. *Flow in sports*. Champaign, IL: Human Kinetics.

Jones, G. 1995 More than just a game: research developments and issues in competitive anxiety in sport. *British Journal of Psychology* 86:449–478.

Martens, R. 1979. About smocks and jocks. *Journal of Sport Psychology* 1:94–99.

Martens, R., Vealey, R., and Burton, D. 1990. *Competitive anxiety in sport*. Champaign, IL: Human Kinetics.

Maslow, A.H. 1968. *Toward a psychology of being*. New York: Van Nostrand Reinhold.

May, R. 1977. *The meaning of anxiety*. New York: Ronald Press.

Maynard, I.W., and Cotton, P.C. 1993. An investigation of two stress-management techniques in a field setting. *Sport Psychologist* 7:375–387.

Nesti, M. 2004. *Existential psychology and sport: theory and application*. London: Routledge.

Nesti, M. 2010. *Psychology in football: Working with elite and professional players*. London: Routledge.

Nesti, M., and Littlewood, M. 2011. Making your way in the game: Boundary situations within the world of professional football. In *Critical essays in sport psychology*, ed. D. Gilbourne and M. Andersen, 233–250. Champaign IL: Human Kinetics.

Pain, M., and Harwood, C. 2004. Knowledge and perceptions of sport psychology within English soccer. *Journal of Sports Sciences* 22:813–826.

Parker, A. 1995. Great expectations: Grimness or glamour? The football apprentice in the 1990's. *Sports Historian* 15:107–126.

Potrac, P., Jones, R.L., and Cushion, C.J. 2007. Understanding power and the coach's role in professional soccer: A preliminary investigation of coach behaviour. *Soccer and Society* 8:33–49.

Relvas, H., Littlewood, M., Nesti, M., Gilbourne, D., and Richardson, D. 2010. Organisational structures and working practices in elite European professional football clubs: Understanding the relationship between youth and professional domains. *European Sport Management Quarterly* 10:165–187.

Roderick, M. 2006. *The work of professional football: A labour of love*. London: Routledge.

Chapter 19

Bangsbo, J. 1994. The physiology of soccer—with special reference to intense intermittent exercise. *Acta Physiologica Scandinavica* 151 (Suppl. 619): 1–155.

Bangsbo, J. 2007. *Aerobic and anaerobic training in football*. Bangsbosport, www.bangsbosport.com.

Bangsbo, J., and Peitersen, B. 2000a. *Soccer systems and strategies*. Champaign, IL: Human Kinetics.

Bangsbo, J., and Peitersen, B. 2000b. *Offensive soccer tactics*. Champaign, IL: Human Kinetics.

Bangsbo, J., and Peitersen, B. 2000c. *Defensive soccer tactics*. Champaign, IL: Human Kinetics.

Bangsbo, J., and Mohr, M. 2014. *Individual training in football*. Bangsbosport, www.bangsbosport.com.

Bradley, P.S., Carling, C., Archer, D., Roberts, J., Dodds, A., Di Mascio, M., Paul, D., Diaz, A.G., Peart, D., and Krustrup, P. 2011. The effect of playing formation on high-intensity running and technical profiles in English FA Premier League soccer matches. *Journal of Sports Sciences* 29:821–830.

Bradley, P.S., Lago-Peñas, C., Rey, E., and Gomez Diaz, A. 2013. The effect of high and low percentage ball possession on physical and technical profiles in English FA Premier League soccer matches. *Journal of Sports Sciences* 31 (12): 1261–1270.

Carling, C., Bloomfield, J., Nelsen, L., and Reilly, T. 2008. The role of motion analysis in elite soccer: Contemporary performance measurement techniques and work rate data. *Sports Medicine* 38:839–862.

Carling, C. 2011. Influence of opposition team formation on physical and skill-related performance in a professional soccer team. *European Journal of Sports Sciences* 11:155–164.

Collet, C. 2013. The possession game? A comparative analysis of ball retention and team success in European and international football, 2007–2010. *Journal of Sports Sciences* 31 (2): 123–136.

Cummins, C., Orr, R., O'Connor, H., and West C. 2013. Global positioning systems (GPS) and microtechnology sensors in team sports: A systematic review. *Sports Medicine* 43:1025–1042.

Dellal, A., Chamari, K., Wong, D.P., Ahmaidi, S., Keller, D., Barros, R., Bisciotti, G.N., and Carling, C. 2011. Comparison of physical and technical performance in European soccer match-play: FA Premier League and La Liga. *European Journal of Sports Sciences* 11 (1): 51–59.

Ferguson, A. 2000. *The unique treble*. London: Hodder and Stoughton.

Hughes, C. 1990. *The winning formula*. London: William Collins Sons.

Ingebrigtsen, J., Bendiksen, M., Randers, M.B., Castagna, C., Krustrup, P., and Holtermann, A. 2012. Yo-Yo IR2 testing of elite and sub-elite soccer players: performance, heart rate response and correlations to other interval tests. *Journal of Sports Sciences* 30:1337–1345.

Lago, C. 2009. The influence of match location, quality of opposition, and match status on possession strategies in professional association football. *Journal of Sports Sciences* 27:1463–1469.

Kormelink, H., and Seeverens, T. 1997. *The coaching philosophies of Louis van Gaal and the Ajax coaches*. Royersford, PA: Reedswain.

Mascio, M., and Bradley, P.S. 2013. Evaluation of the most intense high-intensity running period in English FA premier league soccer matches. *Journal of Strength and Conditioning Research* 27 (4): 909–915.

Mohr, M., Krustrup, P., and Bangsbo, J. 2005. Fatigue in soccer: A brief review. *Journal of Sports Sciences* 23 (6): 593–599.

Roxburgh, A. 2011. The Technician interview: André Villas-Boas. *Technician* 50:2.

Tenga, A., Holme, I., Ronglan, L.T., and Bahr, R. 2010a. Effect of playing tactics on achieving score-box possessions in a random series of team possessions from Norwegian professional soccer matches. *Journal of Sports Sciences* 28 (3): 245–255.

Tenga, A., Holme, I., Ronglan, L.T., and Bahr, R. 2010b. Effect of playing tactics on goal scoring in Norwegian professional soccer. *Journal of Sports Sciences* 28 (3): 237–244.

Wilson, J. 2009. *Inverting the pyramid: The history of football tactics*. London: Orion Books.

Williams, A.M., Lee, D., and Reilly, T. 1999. *A quantitative analysis of matches played in the 1991–1992 and the 1997–1998 seasons*. London: The Football Association.

Chapter 20

Anderson, H., Ekblom, B., and Krustrup, P. 2007. Elite football on artificial turf versus natural grass: Movement patterns, technical standard and player opinion. *Journal of Sports Sciences* 8:1–10.

Bangsbo, J., and Michalsik, L. 2002. Assessment and physiological capacity of elite soccer players. In *Science and football IV*, Ed. W. Spinks, T. Reilly, and A. Murphy, 53–62. London: Routledge.

Bangsbo, J., Norregaard, L., and Thorso, F. 1991. Activity profile of competition soccer. *Canadian Journal of Sports Science* 16:110–116.

Bloomfield, J., Polman, R., and O'Donoghue, P. 2007. Physical demands of different positions in FA Premier League soccer. *Journal of Sports Science and Medicine* 6:63–70.

Bradley, P.S., Sheldon, W., Wooster, B., Olsen, P.D., Boanas, P., and Krustrup, P. 2009. High-intensity running in English FA Premier League soccer matches. *Journal of Sports Sciences* 27:159–168.

Bradley, P.S., Di Mascio, M., Bangsbo, J., and Krustrup P. 2011. Sub-maximal and maximal Yo-Yo Intermittent Endurance Test Level 2: Heart rate responses, reproducibility and application to elite soccer. *European Journal of Applied Physiology* 111:969–978.

Di Salvo, V., Baron, R., Tschan, H., Calderon Montero, F.J., Bachl, N., and Pigozzi, F. 2007. Performance characteristics according to playing position in elite soccer. *International Journal of Sports Medicine* 28:222–227.

Gregson, W., Drust, B., Atkinson, G., and Di Salvo, V. 2010. Match-to-match variability of high-speed activities in Premier League soccer. *International Journal of Sports Medicine* 31 (4): 237–242.

Krustrup, P., Mohr, M., Amstrup, T., Rysgaard, T., Johansen, J., Steensberg, A., Pedsersen, P., K., and Bangsbo, J. 2003. The Yo-Yo Intermittent Recovery Test: Physiological response, reliability and validity. *Medicine and Science in Sports and Exercise* 35:697–705.

Krustrup, P., Mohr, M., Nybo, L., Jenson, J.M., Nielson, J.J., and Bangsbo, J. 2006. The Yo-Yo IR2 Test: physiological response, reliability and application to elite soccer. *Medicine and Science in Sports and Exercise* 38:1666–1673.

Little, T., and Williams, M. 2007. Measures of exercise intensity during soccer training drills with professional soccer players. *Journal of Strength and Conditioning Research* 21 (2): 367–371.

Mohr, M., Krustrup, P., and Bangsbo, J. 2003. Match performance of high standard soccer players with special reference to development of fatigue. *Journal of Sports Science* 21:519–528.

Prozone Ltd. Leeds, UK. 2014. Personal communication.

Reilly, T., and Thomas, V. 1976. A motion analysis of work rate in different positional roles in professional football match play. *Journal of Human Movement Studies* 2:87–97.

Reilly, T. 1993. *Science and football II*. London: E & FN Spon.

Reilly, T. 1994. Physiological profile of the player. In *Football (soccer)*, ed. Ekblom, ed. London: Blackwell.

Rienzi, E., Drust, B., Reilly, T., Carter, J.E., and Martin, A. 2000. Investigation of anthropometric and work-rate profiles of elite South American international soccer players. *Journal of Sports Medicine and Physical Fitness* 40:162–169.

Smaros, G. 1980. Energy usage during football match. In *Proceedings, 1st International Congress on Sports Medicine Applied to Football*, Vol. II., ed. L. Vecchiet. Rome: Guanello.

Strudwick, T. 2006. A profile of elite soccer players with special reference to the load imposed on players during training and match-play. PhD thesis, Liverpool: John Moores University.

Chapter 21

Akenhead, R., Hayes, P.R., Thompson, K.G., and French, D. 2013. Diminutions of acceleration and deceleration output during professional football match play. *Journal of Science and Medicine in Sport* 16 (6): 556–561.

Boullosa, D.A., Abreu, L., Nakamura, F.Y., Muñoz, V.E., Domínguez, E., and Leicht, A.S. 2013. Cardiac autonomic adaptations in elite Spanish soccer players during preseason. *International Journal of Sports Physiology and Performance* 8 (4): 400–409.

Bradley, P.S., Sheldon, W., Wooster, B., Olsen, P., Boanas, P., and Krustrup, P. 2009. High-intensity running in English FA Premier League soccer matches. *Journal of Sports Sciences* 27:159–168.

Bradley, P.S., Di Mascio, M., Peart, D., Olsen, P., and Sheldon, B. 2010. High-intensity activity profiles of elite soccer players at different performance levels. *Journal of Strength and Conditioning Research* 24 (9): 2343–2351.

Bradley, P.S., Lago-Peñas, C., Rey, E., and Gomez Diaz, A. 2013. The effect of high and low percentage ball possession on physical and technical profiles in English FA Premier League soccer matches. *Journal of Sports Sciences* 31 (12): 1261–1270.

Buchheit, M., and Laursen, P. 2013. High-intensity interval training, solutions to the programming puzzle part I: Cardiopulmonary emphasis. *Sports Medicine* 43:313–338.

Buchheit, M., Mendez-Villanueva, A., Quod, M.J., Poulos, N., and Bourdon, P. 2010. Determinants of the variability of heart rate measures during a competitive period in young soccer players. *European Journal of Applied Physiology* 109:869–878.

Buchheit, M., Papelier, Y., Laursen, P.B., and Ahmaidi, S. 2007. Noninvasive assessment of cardiac parasympathetic function: Post-exercise heart rate recovery or heart rate variability? *American Journal of Physiology: Heart and Circulatory Physiology* 293:H8–H10.

Buchheit, M., Peiffer, J.J., Abbiss, C.R., and Laursen, P.B. 2009. Effect of cold water immersion on postexercise parasympathetic reactivation. *American Journal of Physiology: Heart and Circulatory Physiology* 296:421–427.

Casamichana, D., Castellano, J., and Castagna, C. 2012. Comparing the physical demands of friendly matches and small-sided games in semi-professional soccer players. *Journal of Strength and Conditioning Research* 26:837–843.

Castellano, J., and Casamichana, D. 2013. Differences in the number of accelerations between small-sided games and friendly matches in soccer. *Journal of Sports Science Medicine* 12 (1): 209–210.

Diego, M.A., and Field, T. 2009. Moderate pressure massage elicits a parasympathetic nervous system response. *International Journal of Neuroscience* 119 (5): 630–638.

Gaudino, P., Iaia, F.M., Alberti, G., Hawkins, R.D., Strudwick, A.J., and Gregson, W. 2013. Systematic bias between running speed and metabolic power data in elite soccer players: Influence of drill type. *International Journal of Sports Medicine* 34:1–5.

Gregson, W., Drust, B., Atkinson, G., and Di Salvo, V. 2010. Match-to-match variability of high-speed activities in Premier League soccer. *International Journal of Sports Medicine* 31 (4): 237–242.

Impellizzeri, F.M., Rampinini, E., Coutts, A.J., Sassi, A., and Marcora, S.M. 2004. Use of RPE-based training load in soccer. *Medicine and Science in Sports and Exercise* 36:1042–1047.

Reilly, T. 1990. Football. In *Physiology of sports*, ed. T. Reilly, N. Sher, P. Snell, and C. Williams, 371–426. London: E & FN Spon.

Rienzi, E., Drust, B., Reilly, T., Carter, J., and Martin, A. 2000. Investigation of anthropometric and work-rate profiles of elite South-American international soccer players. *Journal of Sports Medicine and Physical Fitness* 40:162–169.

Strudwick, A.J. 2006. A profile of elite soccer players with special reference to the load imposed on players during training and match-play. PhD thesis, Liverpool: John Moores University.

Varley, M.C., Fairweather, I.H., and Aughey, R.J. 2012. Validity and reliability of GPS for measuring instantaneous velocity during acceleration, deceleration, and constant motion. Journal of Sports Science 30:121–127.

Chapter 22

Bloomfield, J., Polman, R., and O'Donoghue, P. 2007. Physical demands of different positions in FA Premier League soccer. *Journal of Sports Science and Medicine* 6 (1): 63–70.

Carling, C., and Court, M. 2013. Match and motion analysis. In *Science and soccer. Developing elite performers*, ed. M. Williams, 173–198. London: Routledge.

Carling, C., Le Gall, F., and Dupont, G. 2012. Analysis of repeated high-intensity running performance in professional soccer. *Journal of Sports Sciences* 30 (4): 325–336.

Carling, C., Le Gall, F., and Reilly, T. 2010. Effects of physical efforts on injury in elite soccer. *International Journal of Sports Medicine* 31:180–185.

Coutts, A.J., and Duffield, R. 2010. Validity and reliability of GPS units for measuring movement requirements in team sports. *Journal of Science and Medicine in Sports* 113:133–135.

Di Salvo, V., Baron, R., Gonzalez-Haro, C., Gormasz, C., Pigozzi, F., and Bachl, N. 2010. Sprinting analysis of elite soccer players during European Champions League and UEFA Cup matches. *Journal of Sports Sciences* 28 (14): 1489–1494.

Di Salvo, V., Baron, R., Tschan, H., Calderon Montero, F. J., Bachl, N., and Pigozzi, F. 2007. Performance characteristics according to playing position in elite soccer. *International Journal of Sports Medicine* 28:222–227.

Gregson, W., Drust, B., Atkinson, G., and Di Salvo, V. 2010. Match-to-match variability of high-speed activities in Premier League soccer. *International Journal of Sports Medicine* 31 (4): 237–242.

Hervert, S.R., Sinclair, K., and Deakin, G.B. 2013. Does skill only conditioning help improve physiological and functional fitness in amateur soccer players? *Journal of Australian Strength and Conditioning* 21 (S2): 34–36.

Iaia, F.M., and Bangsbo, J. 2010. Speed endurance training is a powerful stimulus for physiological adaptations and performance improvements of athletes. *Scandinavian Journal of Medicine and Science in Sports* 20 (S2): 11–23.

Reilly, T. 2007. *The science of training—soccer: A scientific approach to developing strength, speed and endurance.* London: Routledge.

Chapter 23

Beauchamp, M.R., Bray, S.R., Eys, M.A., and Carron, A.V. 2002. Role ambiguity, role efficacy, and role performance: Multidimensional and mediational relationships within inter-dependent sport teams. *Group Dynamics, Theory, Research, and Practice* 6:229–242.

Dewey, J. 1933. *How we think: A restatement of the relation of reflective thinking to the educative process.* Boston: Heath.

Eys, M.A., Carron, A.V., Beauchamp, M.R., and Bray, S.R. 2003. Role ambiguity in sport teams. *Journal of Sport and Exercise Psychology* 25:534–550.

Foucault, M. 1972. *The archaeology of knowledge.* New York: Pantheon Books.

Groom, R., Cushion, C., and Nelson, L. 2011. The delivery of video-based performance analysis by England youth soccer coaches: Towards a grounded theory. *Journal of Applied Sports Psychology* 23:16–32.

Hughes, M., Cooper, S-M., and Nevill, A. 2002. Analysis procedures for non-parametric data from performance analysis. *eIJPAS* 2:6–20.

Lave, J., and Wenger, E. 1998. *Communities of practice: Learning, meaning, and identity.* New York: Cambridge University Press.

Mackenzie, R. 2014. An in-situ exploration of the reflection and experience-based learning of professional football players and coaches. Unpublished thesis, Loughborough University.

Mackenzie, R., and Cushion, C. 2013. Performance analysis in football: A critical review and implications for future research. *Journal of Sports Sciences* 31 (6): 639–676.

Moon, J.A. 2004. *A handbook of reflective and experiential learning: Theory and practice.* London: Routledge.

Potrac, P., Jones, R.L., and Cushion, C.J. 2007. Understanding power and the coach's role in professional English soccer: A preliminary investigation of coach behaviour, *Soccer and Society* 8 (1): 33–49.

Reep, C., and Benjamin, B. 1968. Skill and chance in association football. *Journal of Royal Statistical Society, Series A* 131:581–585.

Chapter 24

Akenhead, R., French, D., Thompson, K.G., and Hayes, P.R. 2014. The acceleration dependent validity and reliability of 10Hz GPS. *Journal of Science and Medicine in Sport* 17 (5): 562–6.

Andersson, H.A., Randers, M.B., Heiner-Møller, A., Krustrup, P., and Mohr, M. 2010. Elite female soccer players perform more high-intensity running when playing in international games compared with domestic league games. *Journal of Strength and Conditioning Research* 24:912–919.

Aughey, R.J. 2011. Applications of GPS technologies to field sports. *International Journal of Sports Physiology and Performance* 6:295–310.

Bangsbo, J., Nørregaard, L., and Thorsøe, F. 1991. Activity profile of competition soccer. *Canadian Journal of Sports Science* 16:110–116.

Barris, S., and Button, C. 2008. A review of vision-based motion analysis in sport. *Sports Medicine* 38:1025–1043.

Barros, R.M.L., Misuta, M.S., Menezes, R.P., Figueroa, P.J., Moura, F.A., Cunha, S.A., Anido, R., and Leite, N.J. 2007. Analysis of the distances covered by first division Brazilian soccer players obtained with an automatic tracking method. *Journal of Sports Science and Medicine* 6:233–242.

Bloomfield, J., Polman, R.C.J., and O'Donoghue, P.G. 2007. Physical demands of different positions in FA Premier League soccer. *Journal of Sports Science and Medicine* 6:63–70.

Buchheit, M., Allen, A., Poon, T.K., Modonutti, M., Gregson, W., and Di Salvo, V. 2014. Integrating different tracking systems in football: multiple camera semi-automatic system, local position measurement and GPS technologies. *Journal of Sports Sciences* 32 (20): 1844–1857.

Carling, C., Bloomfield, J., Nelsen, L., and Reilly, T. 2008. The role of motion analysis in elite soccer: Contemporary performance measurement techniques and work-rate data. *Sports Medicine* 38:839–862.

Carling, C., and Court, M. 2013. Match and motion analysis of soccer. In *Science and soccer III*, ed. M. Williams, 173–198. London: Routledge.

Carling, C., Williams, A.M., and Reilly, T. 2005. *The handbook of soccer match analysis*. London: Routledge.

Carling, C., and Williams, A.M. 2008. Match analysis and elite soccer performance: Integrating science and practice. In *Science and soccer*, ed. T. Reilly, 32–47.Maastricht, Netherlands: Shaker.

Castagna, C., Impellizzeri, F., Cecchini, E., Rampinini, E., and Alvarez, J.C. 2009. Effects of intermittent-endurance fitness on match performance in young male soccer players. *Journal of Strength and Conditioning Research* 23:1954–1959.

Castellano, J., Alvarez-Pastor, D., and Bradley, P.S. 2014. Evaluation of research using computerised tracking systems (Amisco and Prozone) to analyse physical performance in elite soccer: A systematic review. *Sports Medicine* 44:701–712.

Castellano, J., Casamichana, D., Calleja-González, J., San Román, J., and Ostojic, S.M. 2011. Reliability and accuracy of 10 Hz GPS devices for short-distance exercise. *Journal of Sports Science and Medicine* 10:233–234.

Di Salvo, V., Gregson, W., Atkinson, G., Tordoff, P., and Drust, B. 2009. Analysis of high intensity activity in Premier League soccer. *International Journal of Sports Medicine* 30:205–212.

Drust, B., Atkinson, G., and Reilly, T. 2007. Future perspectives in the evaluation of the physiological demands of soccer. *Sports Medicine* 37:783–805.

Duffield, R., Reid, M., Baker, J., and Spratford W. 2010. Accuracy and reliability of GPS devices for measurement of movement patterns in confined spaces for court-based sports. *Journal of Science and Medicine in Sport* 13:523–525.

Edgecomb, S.J., and Norton, K.I. 2006. Comparison of global positioning and computer-based tracking systems for measuring player movement distance during Australian Football. *Journal of Science and Medicine in Sport* 9:25–32.

Feito, Y., Bassett, D.R., and Thompson, D.L. 2012. Evaluation of activity monitors in controlled and free-living environments. *Medicine and Science in Sports and Exercise* 44:733–741.

Frencken, W.G., Lemmink, K.A., and Delleman, N.J. 2010. Soccer-specific accuracy and validity of the local position measurement (LPM) system. *Journal of Science and Medicine in Sport* 13:641–645.

Grigg, N., Smeathers, J., and Wearing, S. 2011. Concurrent validity of the Polar s3 Stride Sensor for measuring walking stride velocity. *Research Quarterly for Exercise and Sport* 82:424–430.

Harley, J.A., Lovell, R.J., Barnes, C.A., Portas, M.D., and Weston, M. 2011. The interchangeability of global positioning system and semiautomated video-based performance data during elite soccer match play. *Journal of Strength and Conditioning Research* 25:2334–2336.

Hughes, M.D., and Franks, I.M. 2004. *Notational Analysis of Sport: Systems for Better Coaching and performance*. London: E & FN Spon.

Intille, S.S., Lester, J., Sallis, J.F., and Duncan, G. 2012. New horizons in sensor development. *Medicine and Science in Sports and Exercise* 44 (Suppl. 1): S24–31.

James, N. 2006. The role of notational analysis in soccer coaching. *International Journal of Sports Science and Coaching* 1:185–198.

Jennings, D., Cormack, S., Coutts, A.J., Boyd, L., and Aughey, R.J. 2010. The validity and reliability of GPS units for measuring distance in team sport specific running patterns. *International Journal of Sports Physiology and Performance* 5 (3): 328–341.

Johnston, R.J., Watsford, M.L., Kelly, S.J., Pine, M.J., and Spurrs, R.W. 2014. Validity and interunit reliability of 10 Hz and 15 Hz GPS units for assessing athlete movement demands. *Journal of Strength and Conditioning Research* 28 (6): 1649–1655.

Leser, R., Baca, A., and Ogris, G. 2011. Local positioning systems in (game) sports. *Sensors (Basel)* 11:9778–9797.

Mohr, M., Krustrup P., Andersson, H., Kirkendall, D., and Bangsbo, J. 2008. Match activities of elite women soccer players at different performance levels. *Journal of Strength and Conditioning Research* 22:341–349.

Mohr, M., Krustrup, P., and Bangsbo, J. 2003. Match performance of high-standard soccer players with special reference to development of fatigue. *Journal of Sports Sciences* 21:519–528.

Orendurff, M.S., Walker, J.D., Jovanovic, M., Tulchin, K.L., Levy, M., and Hoffmann, D.K. 2010. Intensity and duration of intermittent exercise and recovery during a soccer match. *Journal of Strength and Conditioning Research* 24:2683–2692.

Pettersen, S.A., Johansen, D., Johansen, H., Berg-Johansen, V., Gaddam, V.R., Mortensen, A., Langseth, R., Griwodz, C., Stensland, H.K., and Halvorsen, P. 2014. Soccer video and player position dataset. In *Proceedings of the International Conference on Multimedia Systems (MMSys)*, Singapore, March.

Pino, P., Martinez-Santos, R., Moreno, I., and Padilla, C. 2007. Automatic analysis of football games using GPS on real time. *Journal of Sports Science and Medicine* Suppl. 10:9.

Porta, J.P., Acosta, D.J., Lehker, A.N., Miller, S.T., Tomaka, J., and King, G.A. 2012. Validating the Adidas miCoach for estimating pace, distance, and energy expenditure during outdoor overground exercise accelerometer. *International Journal of Exercise Science*, http://digitalcommons.wku.edu/ijesab/vol2/iss4/23/

Randers, M.B., Mujika, I., Hewitt, A., Santisteban, J., Bischoff, R., Solano, R., Zubillaga, A., Peltola, E., Krustrup, P., and Mohr, M. 2010. Application of four different football match analysis systems: A comparative study. *Journal of Sports Sciences* 28:171–182.

Redwood-Brown, A., Cranton, W., and Sunderland, C. 2012. Validation of a real-time analysis system for soccer. *International Journal of Sports Medicine* 33:1–16.

Reep, C., and Benjamin, B. 1968. Skill and chance in association football. *Journal of the Royal Statistical Society* 131:581–585.

Reilly, T., and Thomas, V. 1976. A motion analysis of work-rate in different positional roles in professional football match-play. *Journal of Human Movement Studies* 2:87–97.

Sarmento, H., Marcelino, R., Anguera, M.T., Campaniço, J., Matos, N., and Leitão, J.C. 2014. Match analysis in football: a systematic review. *Journal of Sports Sciences* 1:1–13.

Stevens, T.G.A., de Ruiter, C.J., van Niel, C., van de Rhee, R., Beek, P.J., and Savelsbergh, G.J. 2014. Measuring acceleration and deceleration in soccer-specific movements using a local position measurement (LPM) system. *Journal of Sports Sciences* 5:1–14.

Vickery, W.M., Dascombe, B.J., Baker, J.D., Higham, D.G., Spratford, W.A., and Duffield, R. 2014. Accuracy and reliability of GPS devices for measurement of sports-specific movement patterns related to cricket, tennis, and field-based team sports. *Journal of Strength and Conditioning Research* 28 (6): 1697–1705.

Chapter 25

Bate, R. 1988. Football chance: Tactics and strategy. In, *Science and football*, ed. T. Reilly, A. Lees, K. Davids, and W.J. Murphy, 293–301. London: E & FN Spon.

Davenport, T.H., and Harris, J.G. 2007. *Competing on Analytics: The New Science of winning.* Cambridge, MA: Harvard Business School Press.

Franks, I.M., and Miller, G. 1986. Eyewitness testimony of sport. *Journal of Sport Behaviour* 9:39–45.

Franks, I.M., and Miller, G. 1991. Training coaches to observe and remember. *Journal of Sports Sciences* 9:285–297.

McGarry, T., and Franks, I.M. 1994. A stochastic approach to predicting competition squash match-play. *Journal of Sports Sciences* 12:573–584.

Reep, C., and Benjamin, B. 1968. Skill and chance in association football. *Journal of the Royal Statistical Society Series A* 31:581–585.

Epilogue

Davenport, T.H., and Harris, J.G. 2007. *Competing on analytics: The new science of winning.* Cambridge, MA: Harvard Business School Press.

Index

Note: The italicized *f* and *t* following page numbers refer to figures and tables, respectively.

About the Editor

Tony Strudwick has experience working in national and international performance structures, providing strategic and long-term planning for management of elite athletes. He is head of performance at Manchester United Football Club, a post that involves managing a world-class department of 18 full-time and consultant performance staff members. He manages the short- and long-term strategies of the performance services, ensuring the day-to-day running of the performance department is of the highest professional standard.

Recruited by Sir Alex Ferguson, Strudwick developed a research branch of the scientific support strategy intended to further the science department at Manchester United. He helped to shape a state-of-the-art sport science laboratory at the AON Training Complex.

Since 2006, Strudwick has been part of a FIFA Club World Cup championship along with Premiership, UEFA Champions League, Carling Cup and Charity Shield winning teams. He was selected as part of the backroom team of the English F.A. to support the England national team at the 2014 FIFA World Cup. He has an extensive background in player development structures from elite youth to senior level in both England and the United States. He has completed consultancy work with Nike, Red Bull, Google, AON, and GlaxoSmithKline.

Strudwick completed his post-graduate doctoral thesis at Liverpool John Moores University in 2006. In addition, he has a comprehensive background in teaching and lecturing at the graduate level, such as being an F.A. staff teacher for the F.A. Fitness Trainer's course, while also earning a UEFA pro licence, an A licence, and a Youth Coaches Award. Strudwick has held positions with Blackburn Rovers F.C., West Ham United F.C., English F.A., Coventry City F.C., and United Soccer Academy.

About the Contributors

Jens Bangsbo is head of science in the department of nutrition, exercise and sport sciences and a member of the faculty of the science research board at the University of Copenhagen, Denmark. He is the leader of a research group focusing on cardiovascular aspects, muscle metabolism, ion transport and fatigue development in relation to physical activity and training. Dr. Bangsbo is the leader of the research group Integrative Physiology and of the Center of Team Sport and Health. Until recently he was the chairman of the Ministry of Culture Research Board for Sport in Denmark. He has published more than 300 scientific articles and more than 20 books, including some in tactical training for soccer. He is the editor of several books regarding sport and science and a member of the international steering group Football and Science.

Mario Bizzini holds a PhD and is a research associate at the Schulthess Clinic, a private orthopaedic and sports medicine center in Zürich, Switzerland, where he works for the FIFA Medical Research and Assessment Center (F-MARC) and the orthopaedic and sports medicine departments. He is a specialist in sport physiotherapy and a rehabilitation consultant for professional ice hockey and soccer teams. Dr. Bizzini has worked at three FIFA World Cups (2006, 2010, 2014), two FIFA Women's World Cups (2007, 2015) and two Olympic Games (2008, 2012). His research focuses on hip and knee rehabilitation in sports, soccer injuries and sport injury prevention. He has 57 peer-reviewed publications, 5 books and 11 book chapters on these topics and has lectured at many international congresses.

Anthony Blazevich is a professor of biomechanics at the Edith Cowan University in Western Australia. He is in the school of exercise and health sciences and is head of the Centre for Exercise and Sport Science Research. Apart from leading the way with an exhaustive research profile, Anthony is the author of Sports Biomechanics.

Chris Carling is a sport scientist at Lille Football Club (France) and senior research fellow at the University of Central Lancashire (UK). He has also worked as a consultant for the performance analysis department at Manchester Utd FC (2010-15) and as a researcher for the medical department at the Clairefontaine National Football Centre in France (2000-08). Chris has a PhD in sport science and has authored 2 books and more than 60 peer-reviewed research papers related to sport science and medicine.

Neil Carter is a senior research fellow in the International Centre for Sports History and Culture at De Montfort University, Leicester, UK. He is a social historian with expertise in the history of sport and leisure and the history of sport and medicine. He is the author of the *The Football Manager: A History* and *Medicine, Sport and the Body: A Historical Perspective.*

Carlo Castagna is head of the fitness and research department of the Italian Football Referees Association and head of the Football Training and Biomechanics Lab at the Italian Football Federation. He is one of the most active researchers in Europe in football field testing and load monitoring in young and adult players, football referee performance and futsal.

Daniel Cohen is a lecturer and researcher at the University of Santander in Bucaramanga, Colombia. He also works in research and consultancy at the High Performance Centre of Coldeportes and with several Premier League Football clubs. He is the author of articles on strength and power testing in athletes and the general population.

Gary Curneen is the head women's soccer coach at California State University at Bakersfield. He holds a UEFA A license from the Irish FA and a premier diploma from the NSCAA. He is the author of *Modern Soccer Coach* 2014 and *Modern Soccer Coach: Position-Specific Training.* Before his current role in California, he coached at Wingate University and the University of Cincinnati.

Chris Cushion completed his undergraduate degree at Brunel University and took up a PhD studentship, studying the coaching process in elite youth football in 2001. Chris has extensive experience in sport from participation to performance coaching in both the UK and United States, including 10 years of work in professional youth football for clubs such as Brentford FC, Queens Park Rangers FC and Fulham FC.

Craig Duncan is one of Australia's leading sport scientists. He is increasingly recognized by high-performance teams interested in a more holistic approach with their athletes. Dr. Duncan emphasizes to coaching and support staff the need to view their athletes as assets that need to be managed via individualized programs in order to ensure maximum performance.

Greg Dupont is head of performance science for Lille FC (LOSC, France). He has implemented a research and development department in this club. Dupont is also involved in applied research with Edinburg Napier University in Scotland. His research deals with recovery strategies, injury prevention and high-intensity training. He also worked as head of sport science for Glasgow Celtic FC from 2007 to 2009.

Sam Erith is the global lead of human performance in City Football Services. He oversees the clubs' (Manchester, New York and Melbourne City) approach and shares best practices among the clubs in the areas of medicine, sport science and psychology. Sam joined Manchester City Football Club in the summer of 2011 as head of sport science. This role involves overseeing all aspects of sport science, fitness and conditioning. Sam was head of sport science at Tottenham Hotspur Football Club for 7 years and worked for several years at the English Football Association as a sport scientist. Sam studied at Loughborough University for several years gaining a BSc (Hons) in sport science, MSc (Dist) in exercise physiology and PhD in recovery strategies after high-intensity intermittent exercise.

Dr. Paul R. Ford is a senior lecturer at the University of Brighton, UK, and honorary researcher at Liverpool John Moores University, UK. His research has been funded regularly by various sport organizations such as the English Football Association. He has published multiple peer-reviewed journal articles, book chapters, and professional articles. Paul has delivered many invited and conference presentations. His specialist areas are expert performance, skill acquisition, learning, coaching and soccer. He has worked as a consultant in his specialist areas in professional soccer with clubs and governing bodies as well as in other elite sports.

Martin Haines is an honorary lecturer at the University of Salford, Manchester, and is on the medical advisory board for the European Tour. He has consulted Premier League Football clubs and international rugby teams as well as Olympic athletes. As a director of Brytespark, he works with global organizations to refine product design for human use and develop expert systems to mitigate the risk of musculoskeletal injuries for specific populations. Martin is a former chairman of the UK Biomechanics Coaching Association, published author and international lecturer.

Henry Hanson specializes in developing an understanding of sport equipment using lab-based and advanced computer-based simulation methods. He completed his PhD on the dynamics of soccer performance at the Sports Technology Institute at Loughborough University in 2014 before joining the Adidas Futures team at the company's headquarters in Germany. Henry has undergraduate degrees in mechanical engineering and German from the University of Portland.

Andy Harland has a degree in mechanical engineering and a PhD in optical engineering from Loughborough University and has been part of the Sports Technology Research Group since 2001. Now director of the Sports Technology Institute, overseeing the largest sport engineering and technology activity in the UK, he actively researches and publishes in soccer and in areas specifically related to equipment, including balls, footwear and surfaces. He has conducted research on behalf of Adidas and FIFA and has been involved in the development of product test and analysis methods for all balls used in the FIFA World Cup since 2002.

Richard Hawkins earned his PhD from Loughborough University in 1997 investigating the epidemiology and aetiology of soccer injuries after earning BSc and MSc degrees in sport science. He went on to work for the English FA for 8 years, becoming deputy head of sport science and managing the research, coach education and national team sport science support programmes. Richard joined West Bromwich Albion in 2005 as head of sport science and conditioning before joining Manchester United as performance manager in 2008. His current role centres on the management of sport science and conditioning operations throughout the club. Specifically, strategies focus on enhancing performance, maximising readiness, and returning players to competition.

John Iga is head of sport science at the Football Association. John earned a PhD in exercise physiology both from Liverpool and John Moores University. As part of his role with the FA, John is responsible for leading the sport science programme across all national teams as well as directing the delivery of sport science–related content on all FA courses and awards.

Geir Jordet is a professor at the Norwegian School of Sport Sciences, where he conducts research on psychology and elite soccer performance. He has specialized in performing under extreme pressure, visual perception, decision making, talent development, effective learning and applied psychology in elite and professional soccer. Jordet's work is published in leading sport science and psychology journals, and it is frequently featured in major media outlets such as *New York Times*, *Wall Street Journal*, *Guardian*, BBC, *Sports Illustrated* and *Spiegel*. He is also director of psychology at the Norwegian Centre of Football Excellence, where he advises all the Norwegian professional soccer clubs, as well as the Norway national teams (senior and U21), on performance psychology.

Astrid Junge is an associate professor at the University of Zurich in the Institute of Social and Preventive Medicine. She is also the head of research at the FIFA Medical Assessment and Research Centre (F-MARC) and on the scientific board of the World Village of Women Sports.

Donald T. Kirkendall earned a PhD in exercise physiology from Ohio State University and has taught at the University of Wisconsin at Lacrosse and Illinois State University. He has also worked in sports medicine at the Cleveland Clinic Foundation and Duke University Medical Center. He has more than 80 peer-reviewed publications as lead author or co-author, more than 20 invited chapters, 9 edited reference textbooks, and 2 authored books to his credit.

Rob Mackenzie started working for Leicester City in 2009 as a first team performance analyst whilst studying for his PhD at Loughborough University. Rob was appointed head of technical scouting on Nigel Pearson's re-appointment as first team manager at the club in December 2011. Charged with introducing statistical analysis, player profiling and position-specific video analysis procedures to the scouting process, Rob supported head of recruitment and assistant manager Steve Walsh with contemporary scouting methods to complement a pre-existing traditional scouting methodology. In February 2015 Rob left Leicester City to fulfil a similar role as head of player identification at Tottenham Hotspur.

Alan McCall is a sport scientist currently working with Lille FC in France and has previously worked with Liverpool FC, Glasgow Celtic and North Queensland Fury. After studying sport and exercise science at Edinburgh's Napier University, Alan continued his studies in Australia, attaining his MSc in exercise science at Edith Cowan University. While in the southern hemisphere, he gained experience with the oval ball, completing internships with clubs in rugby union, rugby league and Aussie rules football before moving back to Scotland to take up a role with Glasgow Celtic FC.

Iñigo Mujika earned a PhD in biology of muscular exercise at the University of Saint-Etienne, France, and a PhD in physical activity and sport sciences at the University of the Basque Country. He was the senior physiologist at the Australian Institute of Sport and team selector for Triathlon Australia in 2003 and 2004. In 2005 Mujika was the physiologist and trainer for the Euskaltel Euskadi professional cycling team, and from 2006 to 2008 he was head of research and development for the Bilbao FC. From 2009 to 2013 Mujika was director of physiology and training at Araba Sport Clinic. He was physiologist of the Spanish Swimming Federation in the lead-up to the 2012 London Olympics and head of physiology and training at Euskaltel Euskadi World Tour cycling team in 2013. He is now an associate professor at the University of the Basque Country, associate researcher at Finis Terrae University in Chile, and associate editor for the *International Journal of Sports Physiology and Performance.*

Mark Nesti is a reader in sport psychology at Liverpool John Moores University, where he is also head of the MSc in sport psychology. He was the counselling sport psychologist to the first team at Bolton Wanderers football club from 2003 to 2007. Nesti has been a BASES-accredited sport psychologist since 1990 and has acted as a consultant during the past two decades with various sports at all levels of performance, from club to Olympic standard.

Sophia Nimphius is a senior lecturer in strength and conditioning at the University of Edith Cowan in Western Australia. She conducts research on neuromuscular and muscle architectural adaptations to strength and power training alongside measurement and development of strength and power.

Matt Pain is the first registered sport psychologist to be employed full-time by the Football Association, where he delivers courses and works with the England youth teams. He began working for the FA in 2002 while at Loughborough University, where he completed a PhD on the performance environment of the England youth teams. Since that time, Matt has directed the FA's range of psychology courses inputted into the FA Youth Modules and more recently developed the psychology content of the Advanced Youth Award and UEFA A licence. He has worked extensively with youth and senior athletes across a range of sports including soccer, motor sport, golf and swimming, which has helped inform practical resources for coaches and players on mental skill and talent development.

Birger Peitersen is one of Denmark's top soccer figures, having coached the Danish women's national team and the national champions of the men's league and serving as staff coach of the Danish Football Federation. In 1982, he received the highest coaching award in Denmark, the diploma in elite soccer coaching. Peitersen was the expert commentator for International European matches on Danish television in the UEFA Champions League, for Danish radio at the World Cup in 1990 and 1998 and for the European Championships in 1992 and 1996.

Mayur Ranchordas is a senior lecturer in exercise physiology and sport nutrition at Sheffield Hallam University. He has worked with top the international Premier League football players and has provided sport science support to the JLT Condor pro cycling team. Mayur also worked for the English Institute of Sport providing performance nutrition support to Olympic and world champions in various sports. Mayur is a keen triathlete and cyclist.

Darren Robinson is a UEFA pro licence coach who has worked in several roles, combining coaching at senior and academy level, sport science, performance analysis and strength and conditioning.

Sigi Schmid is the head coach of the Seattle Sounders FC after serving as head coach at UCLA for 19 years. He is a member of the National Soccer Hall of Fame and in 1999 was voted MLS head coach of the year.

Neal Smith received a PhD in sport biomechanics from Southampton University in 1999. He lectures on both the undergraduate programme and the postgraduate master's programme, in addition to supervising postgraduate research students. He is also active in providing sport science support work to athletes from a variety of sports.

Ron Smith has coached at the elite level with club and national teams in Australia and Malaysia. He contributed much to the development of many national team players in the 2006 and 2010 World Cup squads through the

Australian Institute of Sport (AIS) football program in Canberra, where he was on the inaugural coaching staff in 1982 and subsequently became head coach between 1986 and 1996. Ron recently completed his PhD at the University of Canberra and developed an educational website (www.thefootballcentre.com.au) for coaches and an app called Football Practices.

Thorsten Sterzing received his doctoral degree in sport and human movement sciences (biomechanics) at the University of Duisburg-Essen, Germany, where he also earned his undergraduate degree sport and human movement, English as a foreign language and the pedagogy of teaching. During his academic career, Dr. Sterzing lectured on the core disciplines of sport and human movement sciences, including biomechanics, sports medicine, exercise science, motor learning, and anatomy, at the University of Duisburg-Essen and at Chemnitz University of Technology, Germany. His applied research predominantly focuses on athletic footwear related to soccer, running, basketball, training, Formula 1 and tennis as well as on sport surfaces. He is an editorial board member and guest editor of the Footwear Science Journal and a reviewer for multiple scientific journals. Dr. Sterzing holds several patents related to athletic footwear. Currently, Dr. Thorsten Sterzing is senior consultant to the R&D Innovation Center's Sports Science and Engineering Laboratory of Xtep (China) Co., Ltd.

Dave Tenney is currently working in his ninth season in the Major League Soccer (MLS) as sport science and performance manager. He is currently directing the Sounders FC's high performance team, which sees him conducting performance analysis, strength and conditioning coaching and data collecting.

Viswanath B. Unnithan is a professor of paediatric exercise physiology in the Centre for Sport, Health and Exercise Research at Staffordshire University, Stoke-on-Trent, UK. His research interests have included exploring the underlying mechanisms of the high energy cost of movement seen in children with cerebral palsy and cardiorespiratory and cardiovascular issues relating to elite child athletes. His current areas of interest lie in talent identification, performance analysis and cardiovascular responses in elite youth soccer players.

Gary Walker is a first team fitness coach at Manchester United Football Club. Having joined during the 2007-2008 season, he identifies players' physical strengths and weaknesses and devises individual conditioning programmes to develop their robustness, strength and power in order to aid their on-field performance. He earned a degree in sport science at Loughborough University and completed a PhD in exercise physiology from the same institution in 2006. Gary is an accredited strength and conditioning coach with the UKSCA and NSCA and has both earned and tutored on the Football Association's Fitness Trainers Award.